# Recent Developments in Vietnamese Business and Finance

## Vietnam and the Global Economy

**Series Editors: Xuan Vinh Vo**
*(University of Economics Ho Chi Minh City, Vietnam)*
**Dong Phong Nguyen**
*(University of Economics Ho Chi Minh City, Vietnam)*

---

*Published:*

Vol. 1: *Recent Developments in Vietnamese Business and Finance*
edited by Dong Phong Nguyen, Xuan Vinh Vo, Viet Tien Ho and Mai Dong Tran

Vietnam and the Global Economy – Volume 1

# Recent Developments in Vietnamese Business and Finance


Editors

**Dong Phong Nguyen**
**Xuan Vinh Vo**
**Viet Tien Ho**
**Mai Dong Tran**

University of Economics Ho Chi Minh City (UEH), Vietnam



World Scientific

NEW JERSEY • LONDON • SINGAPORE • BEIJING • SHANGHAI • HONG KONG • TAIPEI • CHENNAI • TOKYO

*Published by*

World Scientific Publishing Co. Pte. Ltd.
5 Toh Tuck Link, Singapore 596224
*USA office:* 27 Warren Street, Suite 401-402, Hackensack, NJ 07601
*UK office:* 57 Shelton Street, Covent Garden, London WC2H 9HE

**Library of Congress Cataloging-in-Publication Data**
Names: Nguyễn, Đông Phong, editor.
Title: Recent developments in Vietnamese business and finance / editors,
Dong Phong Nguyen (University of Economics Ho Chi Minh City (UEH), Vietnam),
Xuan Vinh Vo (University of Economics Ho Chi Minh City (UEH), Vietnam),
Viet Tien Ho (University of Economics Ho Chi Minh City (UEH), Vietnam),
Mai Dong Tran (University of Economics Ho Chi Minh City (UEH), Vietnam).
Description: New Jersey : World Scientific, [2021] | Series: Vietnam and the global economy ;
Vol. 1 | Includes bibliographical references and index.
Identifiers: LCCN 2020040373 | ISBN 9789811227141 (hardcover) |
ISBN 9789811227158 (ebook) | ISBN 9789811227165 (ebook other)
Subjects: LCSH: Economic development--Vietnam. | Business enterprises--Vietnam. |
Finance--Vietnam. | Vietnam--Commerce.
Classification: LCC HC444 .R43 2021 | DDC 338.09597--dc23
LC record available at https://lccn.loc.gov/2020040373

**British Library Cataloguing-in-Publication Data**
A catalogue record for this book is available from the British Library.



For any available supplementary material, please visit
https://www.worldscientific.com/worldscibooks/10.1142/12014#t=suppl

Desk Editors: Balamurugan Rajendran/Karimah Samsudin

Typeset by Stallion Press
Email: enquiries@stallionpress.com

https://doi.org/10.1142/9789811227158_fmatter

# About the Volume Editors

**Dong Phong Nguyen** is a Professor and President of University of Economics Ho Chi Minh City (UEH), Vietnam. He has several publications in *Public Organization Review*, *Asia-Pacific Journal of Business Administration*, *Industrial Marketing Management*, *Journal of Asian Business and Economic Studies*, and *Asian-Pacific Economic Literature*.

**Xuan Vinh Vo** is a Professor of Finance and Dean of the Institute of Business Research at the University of Economics Ho Chi Minh City. He also works at CFVG Ho Chi Minh City. His research interests include accounting, finance, and international business and management. He has published his work in several high-ranked journals.

**Viet Tien Ho** is the Dean of Graduate School, University of Economics Ho Chi Minh City and Co-Director of CFVG Vietnam. He has published his work in various reputable journals.

**Mai Dong Tran** is a Lecturer at the School of International Business and Marketing, University of Economics Ho Chi Minh City, Vietnam, where he teaches Marketing Management and B2B Marketing.

https://doi.org/10.1142/9789811227158_fmatter

# About the Contributors

**Quang Hung Bui** is a Lecturer at University of Economics Ho Chi Minh City. He is also Head of Human Resources Department at University of Economics Ho Chi Minh City and Deputy Director of Innovation Institute at University of Economics Ho Chi Minh City. His major is accounting and auditing.

**Huu Man Dang** holds a PhD in Finance from La Trobe University in Australia. He is currently working at Faculty of Finance, University of Economics, The University of Danang, Vietnam. His research interests include mergers and acquisitions, corporate finance, and financial media.

**Long Dang** has a Master's degree from the CFVG center at the University of Economics Ho Chi Minh City, Vietnam. He has participated in the International Conference on Business and Finance 2019, Ho Chi Minh City, Vietnam.

**Thi Kim Thoa Dau** is currently a Lecturer at the University of Economics Ho Chi Minh City, Vietnam. She has more than 10 years of experience in teaching and researching in the accounting and auditing field and especially in public sector accounting.

**Thanh Tung Do** is a PhD Candidate at School of Business Administration, International University, Vietnam National University, Ho Chi Minh City (IU-VNU). He has a Bachelor's degree in international business at IU-VNU and a Master's of Science degree in leadership from Northeastern University (USA).

**Anh Tuan Doan** is a Senior Research Associate in Finance and Banking at the International School of Business, University of Economics Ho Chi Minh City. He holds a PhD in Finance and received the Outstanding Academic Performance Award from Feng Chia University in 2015.

**Minh Nguyet Doan** graduated from Ho Chi Minh City University of Law in 2002 before receiving his Master's degree in 2008. She is currently working as a Lecturer at Faculty of Business Management and Law, Tien Giang University.

**Tan Khoa Duong** received his Master's degree in Finance from The University of Melbourne, Australia. He has been working at University of Economics Ho Chi Minh City from 2006 where he has served as Head of Department of Monetary Trade, School of Banking, since 2014.

**Thi Anh Tien Duong** is currently a PhD Candidate at University of Economics Ho Chi Minh City, Vietnam.

**Xuan Thach Ha** is the Advance Lecturer at the University of Economics Ho Chi Minh City, and a member of Vietnam Accounting and Auditing Association.

**Duong Viet Anh Hoang** is a PhD Candidate in Economics and currently works at Faculty of Banking, University of Economics, The University of Danang, Vietnam.

**Thi Lan Huong Hoang** is a Lecturer at School of Banking and Finance, National Economics University (NEU), Vietnam. Since 2011, she has served at the university as Deputy Head of International Finance Division. She received her PhD from the National Economics University in 2013.

**Thi Kim Quy Hoang** is a Lecturer at the Faculty of Air Transport, Vietnam Aviation Academy, Ho Chi Minh, Vietnam. She is a PhD candidate in the University of Economics Ho Chi Minh City, Vietnam.

**Thu Hang Hoang** is a Full-time Teaching Staff at the School of International Business & Marketing (IBMS), University of Economics Ho Chi Minh City, and is also a PhD candidate in Commerce.

**Thi Thu Suong Huynh** is a Dean of Business Administration Faculty at University of Finance and Marketing in Ho Chi Minh City, Vietnam. She has a PhD degree in this subject from the University of Economics Ho Chi Minh City, Vietnam.

**Hoang Thi Tho Lam** is currently a senior student with a major in Business Administration at International University, Vietnam National University, Ho Chi Minh City.

**Hong My Ai Le** used to be an excellent Master's student at College of Economics at Can Tho University. She is currently a manager of her family's company.

**Quynh Hoa Le** is a Lecturer in Faculty of Economics at Thu Dau Mot University. She holds a Bachelor's of Art and a Master's of Science in Commerce from University of Economics Ho Chi Minh City, Vietnam.

**Phuong Uyen Le** is a PhD student in Finance at the University of Huddersfield in UK. She works at Faculty of Banking, University of Economics, The University of Danang, Vietnam. Her research interests include corporate finance, investments.

**Thuy Dung Le** is a PhD student in Finance. She works at Nghe An University of Economics, Vietnam. Her research interests include mergers and acquisitions, corporate finance.

**Tran Hanh Phuong Le** is a Lecturer in accounting and auditing at the Quy Nhon University, Vietnam. She has worked earlier as an assistant auditor at an audit firm, then continued to work as a general accountant for a joint stock company.

**Thi Kim Hoa Luu** is a PhD candidate in Economics. She works at University of Economics Ho Chi Minh City, Vietnam. Her research interests include policy economy, economic development.

**Ngoc Khuong Mai** is a Lecturer and Researcher at the School of Business Administration, International University, Vietnam National University, Ho Chi Minh City. He has a PhD degree in development management at School of Public Administration of the National Institute of Development Administration (NIDA), Bangkok, Thailand.

**My Tran Ngo** is an Assistant Professor at the College of Economics at Can Tho University (Vietnam). She has a Master's in Finance from the University of Groningen. She was a visiting scholar at the University of Antwerp and holds a PhD in applied economics from the University of Antwerp.

**Hoang Long Nguyen** graduated from National Economics University in May 2019, and has majored in banking and finance. He joined Vietnam Technological and Commercial Joint Stock Bank (Techcombank) in August 2019 as an Overseas Remittance Officer.

**Khanh Tung Nguyen** is a Researcher at the University of Economics Ho Chi Minh City. He conducts research in the fields of tourism. He graduated with a Master's in Marketing and International Business from Charles Sturt, Australia. He is now working for Sport Culture Tourism department in Can Tho City.

**Phong Nguyen Nguyen** is a Lecturer at the School of Accounting, University of Economics Ho Chi Minh City, Vietnam. Nguyen is also a full-member of Certified Practicing Accountants, Australia.

**Thanh Vu Nguyen** is currently working at Tien Giang Project Management Board of Civil and Industrial Construction Works, Vietnam. He has published in many prestigious international Scopus/ISSN journals, participated in international conferences and published in domestic journals. In addition, he has made many contributions to the start-up work of Vietnamese businesses.

**Tri Thanh Nguyen** is a Legal Expert, who works in the law practice industry. The theme of his Master's work included: Corporate Law, Investment Law, and Civil Law.

**Tu Nhu Nguyen** is a Lecturer at the School of Banking. She has experience in teaching Banking Management, Marketing in banking, Laws of Banking.

**Van Dat Nguyen** is currently a Lecturer in the Faculty of Economics, Tay Nguyen University, Vietnam. He has been teaching several MBA programs advanced programs, and affiliate programs. Currently, he is implementing the provincial part of a start-up project and he is also a member of the Board of Start-up of Tay Nguyen University.

**Van Phuong Nguyen** is currently an Associate Professor of Business Management at International University, Vietnam National University, Ho Chi Minh City. Before choosing to pursue an academic career, he had 11 years of working experience in the Telecom Industry in Vietnam.

**Quang Huy Pham** is a Senior Lecturer at the School of Accounting, University of Economics Ho Chi Minh City, Vietnam. He gives lectures in the following academic subjects: International Accounting, Public Sector Accounting, Accounting Principles, State Audit, Internal Control in Public Sector, etc.

**Thu Hang Pham** is a Lecturer at the Faculty of Economics. She obtained her PhD degree in Economics from National Economic University of Vietnam and MSc in Development Economics from Vietnam–Netherland's Master's program. Her fields focus on poverty, inequality, investment, taxation, market demand analysis.

**Quoc Tan Phan** graduated from the doctoral program in Management from the University of Economics Ho Chi Minh City, Vietnam. He is currently the Head of Human Resource Management Division at the School of Management, University of Economics Ho Chi Minh City, Vietnam.

**Thi Bao Quyen Phan** has graduated with a Master's of Science in Accounting and Controlling at The Hague University, Netherlands, since 2009. She is a PhD candidate at the University of Economics Ho Chi Minh City, Vietnam, at present.

**Prapon Sahapattana** acquired his Bachelor's degree from the Royal Thai Police Academy, Thailand, and served in the Royal Thai Police for more than 20 years. He received his Master's degrees from NIDA in public administration and from Syracuse University in information resources management. He received his PhD from Sam Houston State University. At present, he is an Associate Professor in Criminal Justice at GSPA — NIDA. He has been a Vice President for Administration at NIDA for three years. His research areas include policing, criminal justice system, crime survey, and computer crime.

**Nu Ngoc Han Ton** has been a PhD candidate at Graduate School of Public Administration (GSPA), National Institute of Development Administration (NIDA), Bangkok, Thailand. She has worked at the School of Business, International University, Vietnam National University, Ho Chi Minh City. Her research interests are public policy, development, and sustainable development. The real meaning of development and sustainable development in various Vietnamese provinces has become the focus of her research. Among the 17 Sustainable Development Goals (SDGs), she has been focused on salient issues related to poverty, quality of education, human development, and gender equality.

**Thi Xuan Huong Tram** is a Lecturer and Vice Dean in the School of Banking, University of Economics Ho Chi Minh City. She has vast experience in teaching, research, and as a student supervisor.

**Dang Khoa Tran** is the Head of Strategic Management Division, School of Management, University of Economics Ho Chi Minh City.

**Nhat Thien Tran** received the PhD degree in Economics from the University of Evry Val d'Essonne of the Paris, SacLay University, France (2019).

**Thi Phuong Thanh Tran** has been working as a Lecturer at University of Economics Ho Chi Minh City, Vietnam.

**Thi Thanh Huong Tran** serves as the Head of Statistics Division, Faculty of Accounting and Auditing. She graduated with a Master's and a PhD degree in Economic Statistics from Hanoi National Economics University, Vietnam.

**Tien Khoa Tran** is the Rector of International University, Vietnam National University, Ho Chi Minh City. He completed his doctorate in Marketing and International Business at Western Sydney University, Australia, in 2014.

**Trung Kien Tran** has been working as a Lecturer at the School of Public Finance, University of Economics Ho Chi Minh City. His main teaching and research areas are taxation, customs, and public finance.

**Van Long Tran** is a Lecturer of Law. He received his PhD in International and Business Law from Yokohama National University, Japan, 2016. He is currently the Head of International Law Division at the School of Law, University of Economics Ho Chi Minh City, Vietnam.

**Minh Tuan Truong** is a Lecturer and Vice Dean at School of Public Finance, University of Economics Ho Chi Minh City, Vietnam. He got his Master's in Economics from the University of Economics Ho Chi Minh City. His major is public finance.

**Kim Nhan Vo** graduated from University of Economics Ho Chi Minh City before receiving his Master's degree from Can Tho University and Institute of International Foreign Trade, New Delhi. She is currently working as a Lecturer at Faculty of Business Management and Law, Tien Giang University.

**Van Nhi Vo** is currently a Lecturer at the University of Economics Ho Chi Minh City, Vietnam. He has carried out and published a number of extensive scientific studies which are related to accounting and auditing areas.

**Kien Phuc Vu** is a Lecture at the Faculty of Accounting, Vinh Long College of Economics and Finance, Vietnam. Her research interests are mainly concentrated around accounting and management in private and public sector. She has also completed several articles as well as studies for international conferences.

https://doi.org/10.1142/9789811227158_fmatter

# Acknowledgments

This book contains selected papers submitted to and presented at the International Conference on Business and Finance 2019, organized by the University of Economics Ho Chi Minh City.

The editors would like to thank the several anonymous reviewers who provided comments and suggestions, which greatly improved the quality of the papers.

The editors would also like to thank Ms. Thi Hong Xuan Nguyen and Mr. Thanh Phuc Nguyen for their contributions and efforts as editorial assistants for this book.

https://doi.org/10.1142/9789811227158_fmatter

# Contents

*About the Volume Editors* v
*About the Contributors* vii
*Acknowledgments* xv
*Introduction* xxiii

**Part I: Corporate Finance and International Finance** 1

Chapter 1: Test of the Strategic Market-Entry Hypothesis: Evidence from Corporate Governance in Vietnam 3
by *Huu Man Dang, Duong Viet Anh Hoang, Thuy Dung Le, and Phuong Uyen Le*

Chapter 2: Base Erosion, Profit Shifting, and Tax Revenue Nexus: Empirical Evidence in Southeast Asian Countries 27
by *Trung Kien Tran*

Chapter 3: Developing the Stock Market for Economic Growth: Experiences for Vietnam in the ASEAN Regional Financial Integration 43
by *Tu Nhu Nguyen and Thi Xuan Huong Tram*

Chapter 4: Exploring the Intention to Adopt Management Accounting System in the Public Sector: An Empirical Investigation of Public Non-Income Generating Agencies 63

by *Quang Huy Pham and Kien Phuc Vu*

Chapter 5: Market Power and Risk: Evidence from ASEAN Commercial Banking System 95

by *Thi Anh Tien Duong*

**Part II: Financial Markets 115**

Chapter 6: Macroeconomics and Banks: Specific Determinants of Vietnamese Commercial Banks' Profitability from 2014 to 2018 117

by *Thi Lan Huong Hoang and Hoang Long Nguyen*

Chapter 7: Value Creation in Vietnamese Bank Mergers and Acquisitions 149

by *Tan Khoa Duong*

**Part III: Accounting 171**

Chapter 8: A Theory Extension Related to Task-Technology Fit: Considering its Impacts on ERP System Success 173

by *Thi Bao Quyen Phan and Quang Hung Bui*

Chapter 9: Factors Affecting the Adoption of the International Accounting Standards 199

by *Xuan Thach Ha and Tran Hanh Phuong Le*

Chapter 10: Value Relevance of Biological Assets Under IFRS in Asian Nations 223

by *Thi Phuong Thanh Tran*

Chapter 11: The Role of Human Resources in the Transparency of Financial Information Amidst the Increasing Trend of Financial Autonomy in Public Organizations 241

by *Thi Kim Thoa Dau and Van Nhi Vo*

**Part IV: Business Administration and Management 269**

Chapter 12: Determinants of Gender Diversity and Nationality Diversity of the Boards in Vietnamese Listed Firms 271

by *My Tran Ngo and Hong My Ai Le*

Chapter 13: The Evolution of Leadership Theories: A Literature Review 297

by *Thanh Tung Do and Ngoc Khuong Mai*

Chapter 14: How Does Authentic Leadership Influence Employee–Organization Relationship? The Mediating Role of Symmetrical Internal Communication 315

by *Mai Dong Tran, Thi Kim Quy Hoang, and Phong Nguyen Nguyen*

Chapter 15: Green Innovation, Green Entrepreneurship, and Vietnamese SME Development: The Role of Market Turbulence 337

by *Anh Tuan Doan and Tri Thanh Nguyen*

Chapter 16: The Mediating Role of Innovation Speed and Quality in the Relationship between Intellectual Capital and Firm Performance: The Case of Tien Giang Small and Medium Enterprises (SMEs) in the Early Stages 383

by *Kim Nhan Vo, Minh Nguyet Doan, Thanh Vu Nguyen, and Van Dat Nguyen*

**Part V: Marketing 409**

Chapter 17: How does CSR Influence Customer Loyalty in the Banking Sector? Evidence from Vietnam 411

by *Dang Khoa Tran*

Chapter 18: A Critical Review of Factors Affecting Tourists' Loyalty 439

by *Khanh Tung Nguyen and Dong Phong Nguyen*

Chapter 19: Supply Chain Integration: A Case Study of Vietnamese Dairy Industry 463

by *Thi Thu Suong Huynh*

Chapter 20: Research on Solutions to Improve Destination Competitiveness for Tourism Development in Can Tho City 485

by *Khanh Tung Nguyen and Dong Phong Nguyen*

Chapter 21: Buyer–Supplier Relationships, Sustainable Supplier Management, Green Design, and Firms' Performance in Vietnam 503

by *Van Phuong Nguyen, Hoang Thi Tho Lam, and Tien Khoa Tran*

Chapter 22: Exploring the Impact of Self-Construal on the Perceived Values of the Post-Purchase Product Customization: The Context of Motorcycle Customization in Vietnam 545

by *Mai Dong Tran and Long Dang*

**Part VI: Economic Development 577**

Chapter 23: How is Smartphone Advertising Important for Consumers' Purchase Intention in an Emerging Economy? Evidence from Vietnam 579

by *Dang Khoa Tran*

Chapter 24: The Impact of Public Spending for Education on Sustainable Economic Growth in Asian Countries 611

by *Minh Tuan Truong*

Chapter 25: The Role of Institutions in Economic Development: The Case of Vietnam During 2012–2015 623

by *Nu Ngoc Han Ton and Prapon Sahapattana*

Chapter 26: Science and Technology and their Applications in Enterprises in Ho Chi Minh City in the Context of the Fourth Industrial Revolution 667

by *Thi Kim Hoa Luu*

Chapter 27: Impact of the State-owned Investment and Other Factors on Economic Growth with SGMM and Bayesian Approach: The Case of Vietnam 687

by *Thi Thanh Huong Tran and Thu Hang Pham*

**Part VII: Business and Law** **705**

Chapter 28: Factors Associated with Economic Growth: An Investigation into Government Spending on R&D 707

by *Nhat Thien Tran*

Chapter 29: Factors Affecting Youth Entrepreneurial Intention and Suggestions for Policymaking: The Case of Vinh Long Province 723

by *Thu Hang Hoang and Quynh Hoa Le*

Chapter 30: E-enterprise and the Law: Realizing the Potential Risks 745

by *Van Long Tran and Quoc Tan Phan*

*Index* 759

https://doi.org/10.1142/9789811227158_fmatter

# Introduction

The first book with the title "*Recent Developments in Vietnamese Business and Finance*" in the book series published by World Scientific Group is an excellent collection of papers accepted to proceed in the International Conference on Business and Finance (ICBF) 2019, organized by the Institute of Business Research (IBR), University of Economics Ho Chi Minh City (UEH), Vietnam, on August 22–23, 2019.

The International Conference on Business and Finance (ICBF) is one of the pivotal research-related events hosted annually by the Institute of Business Research, University of Economics Ho Chi Minh City. The conference is supported and affiliated by numerous distinguished journals. We are pleased with the wide range of submissions and positive responses to the conference.

All of the papers in this book have been reviewed in a careful editorial process before being officially accepted to be presented at the conference. Each paper is reviewed by blind reviewers in addition to the appraisal of the editors' board. This book could not have been published without the support of and submissions by a large number of presenters who wished their papers to be qualified for publication by a reputable publishing company like World Scientific Group. We are very delighted by the high level of authors' investment in their papers. There were various well-qualified papers, but, unfortunately, we are only able to publish a low proportion of those submissions.

The strategic role of the Institute of Business Research (IBR), University of Economics Ho Chi Minh City, is to conduct academic research in a large number of topics, to advance fruitful international collaboration in research and in research-based conferences and to encourage international publication in business and finance fields through specialized book series and reputable journals. To date, IBR has promoted and retained an active cooperation with several scholars, academic institutions, and journals. Specifically, this book in the series could lay the foundations for the comprehensive collaboration between the IBR and the strategic partner, World Scientific Group.

We are grateful for the various constructive suggestions and meaningful comments from the distinguished guests and scholars to improve the quality of the published papers. The conference participants, with their helpful discussions in the conference, have also been invaluable for the authors.

We would like to thank Karimah Samsudin, Balamurugan Rajendran, and other cooperative staff at the World Scientific Group Company for their sincere help and supportive comments to make this first book a reality.

We highly appreciate the IBR organizing team, namely Ms. Thi Ngoc Mien Nguyen, Ms. Thi Hong Xuan Nguyen, Ms. Dang Bao Anh Phan, Mr. Thanh Phuc Nguyen, Ms. Thi Nha Truc Phan, Ms. Thi Thuc Vo, Mr. Ngoc Giau La, Mr. Xuan Duc Mai, Mr. Van Phong Vo, and Ms. Thanh Thao Tran for their important roles in organizing the conference.

Similarly, we are grateful to UEH and its affiliations including the International School of Business (ISB), CFVG, and the Institute of Business Research (IBR) for their financial and non-financial support.

# Part I

# Corporate Finance and International Finance

https://doi.org/10.1142/9789811227158_0001

Chapter 1

# Test of the Strategic Market-Entry Hypothesis: Evidence from Corporate Governance in Vietnam

**Huu Man Dang, Duong Viet Anh Hoang, Thuy Dung Le, and Phuong Uyen Le**

## Abstract

This study tests the strategic market-entry hypothesis by examining the acquisition location decisions (domestic vs. cross-border) of acquirers in the Vietnamese mergers and acquisitions market through the lens of corporate governance quality. Using a comprehensive dataset of target firms listed on Vietnamese exchanges, this study finds that cross-border firms prefer target firms with good corporate governance that enable them to quickly adapt to markets and reduce information asymmetry and differences of accounting practices, cultures, and legal frameworks. This result supports the view that cross-border acquisitions provide a method of strategic entry into foreign markets.

**Keywords:** Strategic market-entry hypothesis; Merger and acquisitions; Acquisition location; Acquirers; Target firms.

## 1. Introduction

The integration of Vietnam into the global economy is reflected in a series of important events, including Vietnam's participation in the World Trade Organization since 2007, the Association of Southeast Asian Nations Economic Communication since 2015, and a total of

15 free trade agreements (FTAs) in which comprehensive and progressive agreements for Trans-Pacific Partnerships and regional comprehensive partnership agreements are of paramount importance. Indeed, participation in and implementation of FTAs have unlocked the door to golden opportunities in conjunction with challenges for the Vietnamese business community. Furthermore, Vietnam's integration into the global economy acts as a catalyst for the burgeoning mergers and acquisitions (M&A) activities in Vietnam. This is demonstrated by the fact that M&A activities in Vietnam since 2000 have grown at a fast pace (Figure 1), becoming a key mode of foreign direct investment (FDI) (Figure 2).

According to data collected from SDC Platinum, provided by Thomson Reuters, the total value of all M&A deals in Vietnam over the 2007–2018 period surged to 48.8 billion US dollars. In the first half of 2018, foreign investors poured in roughly 4.1 billion US dollars, an increase of 82.4% over the same period in 2017, with the aim of acquiring shares in Vietnamese companies.[1] It is noticeable

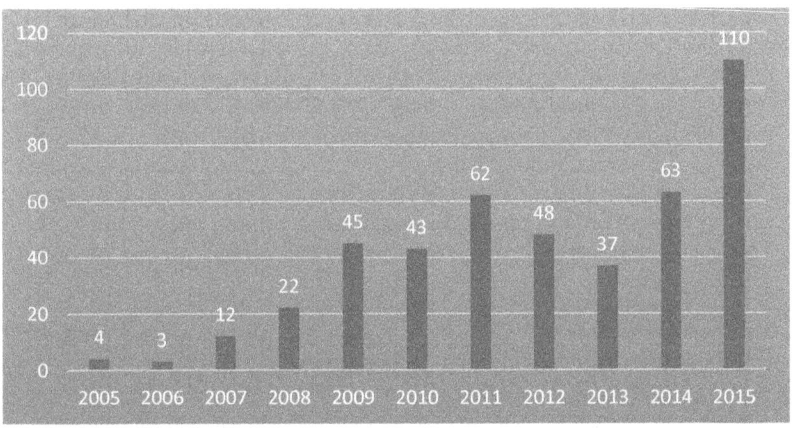


**Figure 1:** The number of completed M&A deals in Vietnam between 2005 and 2015.

*Source*: SDC Platinum database.

[1]https://baodautu.vn/dien-dan-ma-viet-nam-nam-2018-buoc-ngoat-moi-ky-nguyen-moi-d85195.html

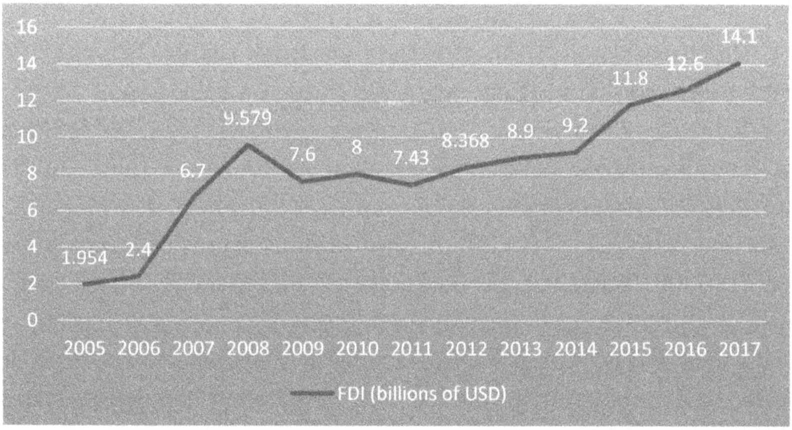


**Figure 2:** FDI inflow into Vietnam between 2005 and 2017.
*Source*: World Bank.

that, in the past, most foreign investors opted to set up projects or build new factories as an investment channel in Vietnam. Over the past 5 years, cross-border takeovers have been an increasingly popular form of FDI, as shown in the SDC Platinum database. This is because engaging in acquisitions enables foreign investors to establish strategic partnerships with local firms, thereby pursuing their market-entry strategies. Furthermore, acquiring shares in Vietnamese firms that are attractive to foreign investors is reflective of a fast-growing domestic economy, population scale, and an accelerating consumer market. Several recently successful large-valued deals offer good examples, such as the acquisition of the Saigon Beverage Company by Thai Beverage, the acquisition of Big C by Central Group, the acquisitions of Metro Cash and Carry Vietnam by TTC Holdings, the acquisition of Vinamilk by Fraser and Neave, and the acquisition of Vietcombank by Mizuho. Vietnamese M&As in the coming years are optimistically forecasted with a prevailing investment trend taking the form of equity participation and share acquisitions.

Relevant laws governing M&A activities have taken effect, promising to facilitate even more M&A activities. Accordingly, over time,

Vietnam has enacted several important laws, including the Enterprise Law, the Investment Law, the Law on Real Estate Business, and the Competition Law. Several other important laws will likely be amended and supplemented to support growth, such as the Land Law, the Securities Law, and the Anti-Corruption Law. Furthermore, Vietnam's government has issued a number of decrees (e.g., Decree No. 126/2017/ND-CP on equitization of state enterprises and Decree No. 09/2018/ND-CP on goods trading and activities) directly related to the sale and purchase of goods by foreign investors and foreign-invested economic organizations in Vietnam. These legal documents have positively impacted the Vietnamese business environment, attracting more investment in new industries. In particular, the divestment policy targeting state-owned enterprises associated with Decision No. 1232/2017/QD-TTg approved a list of 406 SOEs to be divested from 2017 to 2020. These are examples of the driving force affecting M&A trends in Vietnam.

Many problems remain, however, for the Vietnamese M&A market. First, as evidenced above, M&A activities in Vietnam are being heavily regulated, and they have yet to be consolidated and streamlined to maximize capital flow from foreign countries. Moreover, the regulations have been criticized for their lack of detail, which has caused confusion for the entities involved. Second, securities companies, financial advisors, auditors involved as intermediaries, and brokers have grown in abundance. However, they do not provide high-quality consulting or guaranteed services because of the limitations of the legal structure, human resources, databases, and information transparency. There is also the situation of vague financial statements and non-transparent disclosures that affect bid pricing and impede cross-border M&A capital flow (Pham *et al.*, 2015).

An essential problem when examining M&A activity in Vietnam is identifying the motivations for the bidder's takeover location decision. Put differently, should a bidder acquire a domestic or cross-border target firm? Apart from strategic partnership programs, Vietnamese firms (some private) have actively engaged in acquisition bidding. Therefore, gaining a deeper understanding of bidders' geographic preferences would enable Vietnamese firms to select friendly targets and avoid hostile deals. This is of paramount importance in relation to corporate governance, which helps improve corporate performance, enhances resiliency to risks, and increases sustainable value for businesses.

The corporate governance mechanism has received increasing attention in the literature and is a vital factor in the success or failure of business strategy. In the M&A context, empirical studies have shown that corporate governance is of particular interest to M&A acquirers (Zhu *et al.*, 2011; Liao, 2014; Jenter and Lewellen, 2015; Hu and Yang, 2016; Dang *et al.*, 2018). In particular, the corporate governance capacity directly influences the selection of acquisition targets, their success rates, and post-takeover integration. Thus, firms should improve their own governance mechanisms to attract investments and enhance their competitive advantages under the umbrella of economic integration.

McGee (2009) pointed out that many Vietnamese firms, especially unlisted ones, were deficient in regard to disclosure and transparency relating to financial and corporate governance reporting. This issue, in conjunction with the common practice of financial statement manipulation and earnings management, will likely continue to negatively affect bid pricing. This study aims to understand the role of corporate governance from the target firms' perspective. Accordingly, we present two research questions: "How is target corporate governance associated with bidders' takeover location decisions?" "What is the value creation resulting from the target shareholders' following these decisions?"

Employing a sample of all Vietnamese target firms publicly traded from 2005 to 2015, our results show that cross-border bidders prefer well-governed target firms, which agrees with the strategic market-entry hypothesis. Accordingly, target firms that have more board committees and higher shareholder blockholdings tend to be acquired by foreign bidders. The findings of this study provide new evidence about the importance of corporate governance in the general financial market and in the Vietnamese M&A market in particular, which is yet to be examined comprehensively.

This study makes an important contribution to the literature regarding a typical emerging market where the legal environment for M&A is volatile, unstable, and incomplete. Dang *et al.* (2018) found that cross-border acquirers were more likely to pursue local companies with fewer governance issues in advanced and stable markets. Nevertheless, the association between the target enterprise-level governance structure and the location of the bidder's position has not been fully explored in the context of Vietnam. Current research has also not indicated whether target corporate governance is significantly related to the acquirers' takeover options. Our results provide new evidence explaining the dynamics behind these decisions.

The remainder of our chapter is structured as follows. Section 2 reviews the literature and develops testable hypotheses. Section 3 describes the data and explains research methods. Section 4 discusses the results, and Section 5 concludes the chapter.

## 2. Literature Review and Hypotheses

### 2.1. *The strategic market-entry hypothesis*

Depending on the motives behind each acquisition, the acquiring company must make decisions related to the acquisition location (i.e., domestic vs. cross-border). In domestic deals, domestic acquirers often have informational and market advantages over foreign acquirers. Harris and Ravenscraft (1991) pointed out that foreign acquirers paid higher fees when acquiring target companies operating in the same sector. Cross-border acquisitions can provide quick and effective penetration of competitive international markets, where investment in new companies may be more successful in the long term.

In the current literature, the stimulus of cross-border vs. domestic has been widely examined by both finance and international business academicians (Fukao *et al.*, 2006; Zhu *et al.*, 2011; Dang *et al.*, 2018). Accordingly, domestic acquired firms perform worse than those acquired by foreign bidders at the time of takeover. Additionally, many empirical studies have shown that cross-border takeovers are used for strategic market entry into a foreign market. In particular, cross-border acquirers show stronger preference for local firms that experience good performance at the time of acquisition (Bertrand and Zitouna, 2008; Balsvik and Haller, 2010; Zhu *et al.*, 2011; Dang *et al.*, 2018). This is supported by the existence of widespread distribution networks, brand reputation, well-qualified human resources, and strong financial conditions of the well-performing local firms. This further enables foreign acquirers to adapt afterward. Additionally, information asymmetry, regarding accounting procedures and cultural and legal differences, is disadvantageous to foreign bidders. Therefore, foreign bidders tend to acquire targets that show better reporting and strong performance (Conn *et al.*, 2005; Hamberg *et al.*, 2013). More motives of cross-border acquisitions are affected by the presence of product market imperfections and information asymmetry in the capital market (Zhu *et al.*, 2011), differences in tax calculations (Weston *et al.*, 2004), and opportunities arising from market inefficiencies (Servaes and Zenner, 1994).

## 2.2. *The role of corporate governance in acquisitions*

From the perspective of country-level characteristics, Rossi and Volpin (2004) and Bris and Cabolis (2008) provided evidence that, for cross-border acquisitions, acquirers were usually from countries with stronger governance mechanisms than the target firms. Considering differences of country-level governance standards in 49 sample countries, Rossi and Volpin (2004) found that the probability of a cross-border M&A was higher when the host country's investor protections were weaker than those of the home country. Kim *et al.* (2011) also found that the decision to select foreign investment opportunities through M&A was affected by country-level quality management issues. Bae *et al.* (2013) and Starks and Wei (2013) suggested that acquirers should consider national characteristics (e.g., information transparency and corporate governance mechanisms) when making takeover location decisions. According to Bae *et al.* (2013), the possibility of cross-border M&A deals was higher when the target company was from a country that had greater information transparency.

Regarding firm-level characteristics, Chen and Su (1997) confirmed the role of target firm-level characteristics in acquisition location decision-making. Accordingly, targets acquired by foreign bidders tend to have better financial characteristics than domestic acquired firms. A study by Zhu *et al.* (2011) found evidence that cross-border bidders preferred local firms with good performance, whereas domestic bidders tended to select poor-performing firms. Nonetheless, these studies did not examine the role of corporate governance.

Several prior studies have focused on the causes of acquisition location choices from the perspective of the corporate governance quality of target firms. They found evidence supporting the strategic market-entry hypothesis. Hernando *et al.* (2009) examined acquisitions in the banking sector both within and across 25 European Union countries from 1997 to 2004, indicating that poorly managed banks were measured by high cost-to-income ratios and larger banks tended to be targeted by other banks in the same country. Kling and Weitzel (2011) investigated takeovers in China over the period of 2001–2008, finding that separate chief executive officer (CEO) and chairman of the board positions increased the likelihood of cross-border acquisitions. However, state ownership indicated fewer cross-border deals. Similarly, Dang *et al.* (2018) employed an M&A sample of eight East Asian countries, finding that cross-border acquirers tended to select targets with good corporate governance to reduce foreign investment risks. Their research also found that target firms experienced significant improvements in stock returns after official takeover announcements.

Generally, considering the quality of governance at the national level and the financial characteristics of target firms, extant studies have suggested that acquiring companies should consider corporate governance quality at the national level and the firm-level characteristics of the target firm when making decisions. The current literature also finds that the stock returns of target firms tend to increase around the event announcement date. To the best of our knowledge, existing studies have yet to consider the motives for acquisition of Vietnamese firms by foreign bidders and whether there exists a potential relationship between target firms' corporate governance quality and acquisition location decision. Given the strategic market-entry hypothesis, two further hypotheses are proposed:

**Hypothesis H1:** *Foreign bidders are likely to acquire local targets that have good corporate governance.*

**Hypothesis H2:** *Target shareholders gain positive returns in both cross-border and domestic acquisitions following the announcements.*

## 3. Data and Methodology

### 3.1. *Data*

In this study, information about bid-specific factors was obtained from the Thomson Reuters SDC Platinum database. The research sample includes all Vietnamese target firms publicly traded on the Ho Chi Minh Stock Exchange and the Hanoi Stock Exchange. The sample time frame was 2005–2015. Information regarding accounting and financial results was collected from the FiinGroup database. Formerly StoxPlus, FiinGroup is Vietnam's leading supplier of financial data, business information, and industry analyzes. To avoid weak observations, we followed the current literature on sample selection and dropped observations if bidders acquired less than 5% of the target's outstanding common shares in the transaction or if they owned less than 5% after the transaction.

After discarding observations associated with the above requirements, cross-border deals comprised 60 transactions, whereas domestic acquisitions made up 389 cases. Added together, these observations consisted of 449 acquisitions over the 2005–2015 period.

### 3.2. *Methodology*

To test the strategic market-entry hypothesis, we examined the effects of corporate governance quality on the acquisition location decision of acquirers. We employed the Probit model with cross-sectional data regression as follows:

$$\begin{aligned} \boldsymbol{CROSS\text{-}BORDER}_{i,t} = {} & \beta_0 + \beta_1 \boldsymbol{CG}_{i,j,t-1} \\ & + \beta_2 \boldsymbol{CONTROLS}_{i,t-1} \\ & + \gamma_j + \delta_t + \zeta_{i,t}, \end{aligned} \tag{1}$$

where

- **Dependent variable (*CROSS-BORDER*):** A dummy receives 1 if the nationalities of the bidder and target in the transaction, $i$, in a given announcement year, $t$, were different, and 0 otherwise.
- **Independent variable (*CG*):** *CG* represents the target firm's corporate governance quality in the transaction, $i$, in a sector, $j$. *CG* includes a set of variables that are lagged 1 year to ensure that it captures pre-acquisition characteristics of the targets, specifically the following points:
    - *Board committees* (*BCOMMITTEE*): This continuous variable indicates the number of board committees in the target firms. Board committees support boards in terms of monitoring and advisory tasks, allowing boards to achieve more efficient decision-making. Basically, the larger the number of board committees, the higher the corporate governance quality (Pathan, 2009).
    - *The power of executives* (*CEO POWER*): This CEO power index is calculated as the sum of four CEO-related dummy variables: *CEO TENURE* (a dummy variable taking 1 if the CEO tenure in year $t$ is longer than the median CEO tenure of the sample in year $t$, and 0 otherwise), *CEO INTERNAL* (a dummy variable receiving 1 if the CEO is internally hired, and 0 otherwise), *CEO DUALITY* (a dummy variable equaling 1 if the CEO also holds the position of the chairman of the board, and 0 otherwise), and *CEO OWNERSHIP* (a dummy variable taking 1 if the CEO shareholding is greater than or equal to 1%, and 0 otherwise). Following Pathan (2009), the CEO is suggested as being more powerful when he has been employed in this position for a longer time, was internally hired, also holds the position

of the chairman of the board, and holds a higher equity stake in the firm. Therefore, the maximum possible value for the CEO power index is 4, indicating more CEO power to exert greater impact on board decisions.

- *Shareholder Blockholdings* (*BLOCK*): This continuous variable indicates target blockholdings that are calculated as the percentage of ownership held by shareholders whose individual holdings are at least 5% of the target firm's stock at the year-end prior to the takeover announcement (Cronqvist and Fahlenbranch, 2009).

- **Control variables (*CONTROLS*):** This study controls the number of other factors that could potentially influence the bidders' location choices. These factors are classified into two categories as follows:

  - For deal-specific characteristics, *RELATEDNESS* is a proxy for the industry similarity between the bidder and target firms, receiving 1 if the bidder and target operate in the same line of business, and 0 otherwise (Dang and Henry, 2016); *TOEHOLD* takes 1 if the bidders have initial stake of the target prior to the acquisition, and 0 otherwise (Kim, 2012); *CASH* equals 1 if the method of payment is cash, and 0 otherwise (Chidambaran *et al.*, 2018); and *FRIENDLY* takes 1 if the deals receive the willingness of the target management, and 0 otherwise (Massa and Xu, 2013).
  - In terms of firm-level factors, *SIZE* is calculated by transforming the total assets into a natural logarithm form (Croci and Petmezas, 2015); *LEVERAGE* is the ratio of total debt over total assets (Dang and Henry, 2016); *ROA* is earnings before interest and tax divided by total assets (Kim, 2012); *MTB* is market-to-book ratio; and *SALE GROWTH* is the annual percentage increase in sales (Dang and Henry, 2016). All firm-level financial characteristics were reported in the most recent financial year ending before the takeover. Additionally, each firm-level control variable was winsorized at the 1% level to alleviate the effects of potential outliers (i.e., observations lying below 1% and above 99%).

To control for year and industry, we included year ($\delta_t$) and industry ($\gamma_j$) in the model (1). We also employed robust standard errors to tackle heteroscedasticity, clustered by industry, to solve the problem of autocorrelation.

## 4. Empirical Results

### 4.1. *Sample descriptive statistics*

Table 1 presents summary statistics in terms of deal- and firm-specific characteristics for cross-border and domestic acquisitions between 2005 and 2015. The results show that there were significant differences in deal- and firm-level characteristics between both types of acquisitions. In particular, the percentage of shares acquired by domestic bidders was 29.3% on average, which is higher than the figure for cross-border deals. Additionally, the average size of target firms acquired by foreign bidders was 394 million US dollars as opposed to 116 million US dollars for domestic targets. This means that domestic bidders tended to select small-sized firms, whereas foreign acquirers preferred large-sized firms, supporting the view that cross-border bidders expect to take advantage of economies of scale. In addition, the average *MTB* figure for cross-border targets (1.405) was higher than that of domestic targets (1.187), suggesting higher growth opportunities for target firms in cross-border deals. Both types of acquisitions appeared indifferent in terms of deal-specific characteristics

Table 2 reports summary statistics for the target firm's corporate governance characteristics according to two types of acquisition locations. The results show that the number of female board members of cross-border targets surpassed domestic targets. The assumption here is that women are more risk averse than men. Thus, the more the number of women on the boards of target firms, the more the post-acquisition profit the bidders expect to gain, which agrees with the hypothesis of strategic market entry. The results also show that the quantity of committees in cross-border targets was higher than

**Table 1:** Deal- and firm-specific characteristics of M&A deals in Vietnam, 2000–2015.

| Deal- and firm-specific characteristics | (1) Cross-border deals N | Mean | Med | SD | (2) Domestic deals N | Mean | Med | SD | Difference testing (*t*-ratio) (2) − (1) |
|---|---|---|---|---|---|---|---|---|---|
| *RELATEDNESS* | 60 | 0.117 | 0.000 | 0.32 | 389 | 0.064 | 0.000 | 0.25 | −1.46 |
| *CASH* | 60 | 0.467 | 0.000 | 0.50 | 389 | 0.401 | 0.000 | 0.49 | −0.961 |
| *FRIENDLY* | 60 | 0.600 | 1.000 | 0.49 | 389 | 0.656 | 1.000 | 0.48 | 0.83 |
| *TOEHOLD* | 60 | 0.167 | 0.000 | 0.38 | 389 | 0.293 | 0.000 | 0.46 | 2.04** |
| *SHARE SOUGHT* (%) | 60 | 0.192 | 0.150 | 0.14 | 389 | 0.198 | 0.125 | 0.18 | 0.26 |
| *SHARE ACQUIRED* (%) | 60 | 0.182 | 0.139 | 0.13 | 389 | 0.187 | 0.110 | 0.17 | 0.21 |
| *SHARE OWNED* (%) | 60 | 0.214 | 0.160 | 0.16 | 389 | 0.266 | 0.183 | 0.23 | 1.68* |
| *SIZE* (mil US$) | 58 | 394.821 | 54.017 | 1229.11 | 387 | 116.748 | 20.894 | 535.20 | −2.96*** |
| *ROA* | 57 | 0.112 | 0.075 | 0.10 | 383 | 0.089 | 0.078 | 0.10 | −1.60 |
| *LEVERAGE* | 57 | 0.384 | 0.355 | 0.25 | 381 | 0.378 | 0.326 | 0.26 | −0.15 |
| *SALES GROWTH* | 57 | 0.424 | 0.275 | 1.22 | 377 | 0.328 | 0.105 | 1.02 | 0.64 |
| *MTB* | 55 | 1.405 | 1.190 | 1.11 | 363 | 1.187 | 0.962 | 0.85 | −1.69* |

*Notes*: All continuous variables using the fiscal year ended before the acquisition, and are winsorized at the 1% level. Acquisition locations are separated into two groups (cross-border vs. domestic). Deal-specific characteristics are taken from the SDC Platinum including *RELATEDNESS, CASH, CROSS-BORDER, FRIENDLY, TOEHOLD, SHARE SOUGHT, SHARE ACQUIRED,* and *SHARE OWNED.* Firm-level variables include *SIZE, ROA, LEVERAGE, SALES GROWTH,* and *MTB.* A *t*-test is used to calculate the difference in means. Symbols ***, **, and * indicate significance at the 1%, 5%, and 10% levels, respectively.

target firms acquired by domestic bidders. Likewise, the figures for large shareholders and blockholdings of targets acquired by foreign bidders were higher.

### 4.2. *The role of target firms' corporate governance in the bidders' location decisions*

Table 3 presents the empirical analysis results of the relation between target corporate governance and bidders' location choices. The results show that the coefficient of the board committee variable

**Table 2:** Target firms' corporate governance characteristics for cross-border vs. domestic acquisitions.

| Corporate governance characteristics | Cross-border deals (1) | | | | Domestic deals (2) | | | | Difference testing ($t$-ratio) |
|---|---|---|---|---|---|---|---|---|---|
| | *N* | Mean | Med | SD | *N* | Mean | Med | SD | (2) − (1) |
| *BSIZE* (members) | 60 | 5.900 | 5.000 | 1.64 | 389 | 5.170 | 5.000 | 1.31 | −3.87*** |
| *BDIRECTORS* (%) | 60 | 0.593 | 0.600 | 0.21 | 389 | 0.592 | 0.600 | 0.18 | −0.04 |
| *BFEMALE* | 60 | 0.967 | 1.000 | 1.16 | 389 | 0.702 | 0.000 | 0.92 | −2.00** |
| *BMEETING* | 60 | 6.283 | 4.000 | 5.01 | 389 | 6.622 | 4.000 | 6.62 | 0.37 |
| *BCOMMITTEE* | 60 | 2.167 | 2.000 | 0.62 | 389 | 2.039 | 2.000 | 0.32 | −2.46** |
| *CEO TENURE* (years) | 54 | 5.426 | 3.000 | 5.29 | 334 | 4.829 | 4.000 | 3.62 | −1.04 |
| *CEO INTERNAL* | 55 | 0.836 | 1.000 | 0.37 | 335 | 0.890 | 1.000 | 0.31 | 1.13 |
| *CEO DUALITY* | 54 | 0.444 | 0.000 | 0.50 | 335 | 0.382 | 0.000 | 0.49 | −0.87 |
| *CEO OWNERSHIP* | 54 | 0.444 | 0.000 | 0.50 | 332 | 0.395 | 0.000 | 0.49 | −0.691 |
| *CEO POWER* | 54 | 2.093 | 2.000 | 1.38 | 332 | 2.111 | 2.000 | 1.22 | 0.10 |
| *LARGE SHAREHOLDERS* | 53 | 3.019 | 3.000 | 1.69 | 332 | 2.633 | 2.000 | 1.52 | −1.68* |
| *BLOCK* (%) | 53 | 0.579 | 0.607 | 0.20 | 332 | 0.500 | 0.510 | 0.22 | −2.49** |

*Notes*: All firm-level governance variables are taken from the most recent annual report that ended before acquisition, and are defined as follows: *BSIZE* is the number of directors on the board; *BDIRECTORS* is the percentage of independent directors on the board; *BFEMALE* is the number of female directors on the board; *BMEETING* is the number of board meetings in the fiscal year that ended before the announcement; *BCOMMITTEE* is the number of board committees. CEO-related characteristics and shareholder blockholdings are demonstrated in Section 3.2. A $t$-test is used to calculate difference in means. ***, **, and * indicate significance at the 1%, 5% and 10% levels, respectively.

(*BCOMMITTEE*) was positive and statistically significant. This result supports Hypothesis H1 and suggests that the bidders preferred cross-border deals when targets had more board committees. This can be explained by the fact that foreign acquirers tend to look for target firms that have monitoring tasks of high quality and fewer conflicts to minimize risks. Domestic bidders, on the contrary, are more likely to select targets that have a poorer-performing board so that they can pursue their goals of changing the executive team and the board.

We also examined the influence of the target CEO power on the bidders' geographic preferences. The results in Table 4 provide no clear-cut evidence of the correlation between CEO power and the

**Table 3:** Target firms' board committees and the bidders' location decisions.

| **Variables** | **1** | **2** | **3** |
|---|---|---|---|
| *BCOMMITTEE* | **0.570**$^{***}$ | **0.716**$^{***}$ | **0.582**$^{**}$ |
| | **(2.94)** | **(3.45)** | **(2.54)** |
| *RELATEDNESS* | | 0.884$^{***}$ | 0.948$^{***}$ |
| | | (2.87) | (2.88) |
| *CASH* | | 0.259 | 0.359 |
| | | (1.17) | (1.57) |
| *FRIENDLY* | | −0.109 | 0.004 |
| | | (−0.49) | (0.02) |
| *TOEHOLD* | | −0.598$^{***}$ | −0.565$^{**}$ |
| | | (−2.74) | (−2.46) |
| *SIZE* | | | 0.246$^{***}$ |
| | | | (3.72) |
| *LEVERAGE* | | | −0.342 |
| | | | (−1.00) |
| *ROA* | | | 1.247 |
| | | | (1.47) |
| *MTB* | | | 0.120 |
| | | | (1.21) |
| *SALES GROWTH* | | | −0.001 |
| | | | (−0.02) |
| *INTERCEPT* | −1.053 | −1.402$^{*}$ | −1.988$^{**}$ |
| | (−1.44) | (−1.84) | (−2.48) |
| Year effects | Yes | Yes | Yes |
| Industry effects | Yes | Yes | Yes |
| Obs | 429 | 429 | 388 |
| Pseudo $R^2$ | 0.178 | 0.219 | 0.261 |
| Wald $\chi^2$ | 53.33$^{***}$ | 73.74$^{***}$ | 71.21$^{***}$ |

*Notes*: This table reports the results regarding the influence of the number of board committees on the bidders' location choices, using Probit regression. $z$-ratios are shown in parentheses. $^{***}$, $^{**}$, and $^{*}$ indicate significance at the 1%, 5% and 10% levels, respectively.

acquisition location choices. Thus, CEO power is probably not a crucial determinant in acquisition location decision-making.

Table 5 demonstrates the regression results of the relation between target blockholdings and bidders' location choices. The coefficient on the *BLOCK* variable is positive and statistically significant. This implies a higher likelihood of a cross-border deal when targeted large

**Table 4:** Target firms' CEO power and the bidders' location decisions.

| Variables | 1 | 2 | 3 |
|---|---|---|---|
| *CEO POWER* | −0.022 | −0.042 | −0.048 |
| | (−0.31) | (−0.58) | (−0.62) |
| *RELATEDNESS* | | 0.686** | 0.732** |
| | | (2.17) | (2.34) |
| *CASH* | | 0.390* | 0.456** |
| | | (1.81) | (1.99) |
| *FRIENDLY* | | 0.038 | 0.120 |
| | | (0.18) | (0.51) |
| *TOEHOLD* | | −0.482** | −0.527** |
| | | (−2.11) | (−2.18) |
| *SIZE* | | | 0.261*** |
| | | | (3.78) |
| *LEVERAGE* | | | −0.322 |
| | | | (−0.91) |
| *ROA* | | | 1.312 |
| | | | (1.63) |
| *MTB* | | | 0.176* |
| | | | (1.69) |
| *SALES GROWTH* | | | 0.005 |
| | | | (0.06) |
| *INTERCEPT* | −0.402 | −0.397 | −1.769* |
| | (−0.59) | (−0.56) | (−1.94) |
| Year effects | Yes | Yes | Yes |
| Industry effects | Yes | Yes | Yes |
| Obs | 367 | 367 | 344 |
| Pseudo $R^2$ | 0.131 | 0.166 | 0.236 |
| Wald $\chi^2$ | 36.79*** | 47.59*** | 63.69*** |

*Notes*: This table reports the results regarding the influence of CEO power on the bidders' location choices, using Probit regression. $z$-ratios are shown in parentheses. ***, **, and * indicate significance at the 1%, 5%, and 10% levels, respectively.

shareholders hold a higher percentage of shares and vice versa. This result supports Hypothesis H1.

The study also incorporated three variables indicating the quality of corporate governance in one model to examine their aggregate impact on bidder location choices. Table 6 shows the overall impact of target corporate governance (i.e., board committee, CEO power, and shareholder blockholdings) on acquisition location decision-making.

**Table 5:** Target firms' blockholdings and the bidders' location decisions.

| **Variables** | **1** | **2** | **3** |
|---|---|---|---|
| *BLOCK* | **1.355**$^{***}$ | **1.352**$^{***}$ | **0.986**$^{***}$ |
| | **(3.03)** | **(2.97)** | **(1.92)** |
| *RELATEDNESS* | | 0.664$^{**}$ | 0.720$^{**}$ |
| | | (2.06) | (2.27) |
| *CASH* | | 0.465$^{**}$ | 0.445$^{*}$ |
| | | (2.06) | (1.87) |
| *FRIENDLY* | | 0.073 | 0.097 |
| | | (0.31) | (0.39) |
| *TOEHOLD* | | −0.468$^{**}$ | −0.513$^{**}$ |
| | | (−1.98) | (−2.13) |
| *SIZE* | | | 0.255$^{***}$ |
| | | | (3.72) |
| *LEVERAGE* | | | −0.433 |
| | | | (−1.25) |
| *ROA* | | | 1.219 |
| | | | (1.55) |
| *MTB* | | | 0.115 |
| | | | (1.04) |
| *SALES GROWTH* | | | 0.001 |
| | | | (0.01) |
| *INTERCEPT* | 1.355$^{*}$ | −1.203 | −2.079$^{**}$ |
| | (−1.66) | (−1.60) | (−2.28) |
| Year effects | Yes | Yes | Yes |
| Industry effects | Yes | Yes | Yes |
| Obs | 366 | 366 | 344 |
| Pseudo $R^2$ | 0.164 | 0.201 | 0.248 |
| Wald $\chi^2$ | 47.83$^{***}$ | 60.90$^{***}$ | 67.25$^{***}$ |

*Notes*: This table reports the results regarding the influence of target shareholder blockholdings on the bidders' location choices, using Probit regression. $z$-ratios are shown in parentheses. $^{***}$, $^{**}$, and $^{*}$ indicate significance at the 1%, 5%, and 10% levels, respectively.

The results in Table 6 show that the coefficient of the *BLOCK* variable was positive and statistically significant. This result once again confirms that the ownership of large shareholders was an important factor affecting bidders' geographic preferences. Accordingly, the likelihood of cross-border acquisitions is higher than that of domestic acquisitions if targeted large shareholders hold a larger percentage

**Table 6:** Target firms' corporate governance and the bidders' location decisions.

| **Variables** | **1** | **2** | **3** |
|---|---|---|---|
| *BCOMMITTEE* | **0.596***** | **0.742***** | **0.616***** |
| | **(3.15)** | **(3.61)** | **(2.76)** |
| *CEO POWER* | −0.004 | −0.028 | −0.051 |
| | (−0.05) | (−0.35) | (−0.62) |
| *BLOCK* | **1.455***** | **1.439***** | **1.122**** |
| | **(3.17)** | **(3.01)** | **(2.12)** |
| *RELATEDNESS* | | 0.926*** | 1.013*** |
| | | (2.73) | (2.98) |
| *CASH* | | 0.401* | 0.406* |
| | | (1.77) | (1.72) |
| *FRIENDLY* | | 0.001 | 0.043 |
| | | (0.00) | (0.17) |
| *TOEHOLD* | | −0.598** | −0.601** |
| | | (−2.50) | (−2.42) |
| *SIZE* | | | 0.220*** |
| | | | (3.09) |
| *LEVERAGE* | | | −0.505 |
| | | | (−1.40) |
| *ROA* | | | 0.996 |
| | | | (1.19) |
| *MTB* | | | 0.076 |
| | | | (0.68) |
| *SALES GROWTH* | | | 0.002 |
| | | | (0.03) |
| *INTERCEPT* | −2.298*** | −2.505*** | −2.884*** |
| | (−2.81) | (−2.88) | (−2.85) |
| Year effects | Yes | Yes | Yes |
| Industry effects | Yes | Yes | Yes |
| Obs | 364 | 364 | 342 |
| Pseudo $R^2$ | 0.192 | 0.239 | 0.273 |
| Wald $\chi^2$ | 53.83*** | 71.50*** | 70.43*** |

*Notes*: This table reports the results regarding the influence of target corporate governance on the bidders' location choices, using Probit regression. $z$-ratios are shown in parentheses. ***, **, and * indicate significance at the 1%, 5%, and 10% levels, respectively.

of shares. This result partially supports Hypothesis H1 and shows that foreign acquirers tended to acquire domestic firms with better governance quality.

### 4.3. *Short-term stock performance of target firms*

In this study, the event study approach was used to evaluate the impact of announcement events on the stock prices of target firms (abnormal returns) following the two types of takeover locations. Accordingly, the expected rate of return of stock $i$ on day $t$ was determined from the standard market model:

$$E(R_{it}) = \alpha_i + \beta_i \cdot R_{mt} + E(\varepsilon_{it}), \tag{2}$$

where $E(R_{it})$ is the expected returns of stock $i$ on day $t$; $R_{mt}$ is the market return on day $t$. The abnormal returns of stock $i$ on day $t$ $(AR_{it})$ are determined as follows:

$$AR_{it} = R_{it} - (a_i + b_i \cdot R_{mt}). \tag{3}$$

According to Bertrand and Zitouna (2008), the impact of each event on stock prices was felt not only on the date of the event announcement but it could also be identified for a period of time around the announcement day (*event window*). The event window starts from $T_1$ days before the event notification day to $T_2$ days after the event notification date. The event window is $(T_1, T_2)$.

The expected yield of each stock calculated above is then compared with the actual yield of each stock each day within the event window $(T_1, T_2)$. The difference between the real and expected yield of each stock during the event window is defined as cumulative abnormal return $(CAR)$:

$$CAR_{i,EW} = \sum_{t=T_1}^{T_2} AR_{it}. \tag{4}$$

In this study, we chose the approach proposed by Danbolt and Maciver (2012). Accordingly, the estimated interval, $T$, from day $t$-260 to day $t$ 41 prior to the announcement day ($T = 220$) was used to estimate market model parameters. Danbolt and Maciver (2012) indicated that this estimation period could provide all necessary historical information to estimate market parameters. Notice that $t = 0$ is the event announcement date. Table 7 reports the announcement

**Table 7:** Short-term stock performance of target firms.

| Event windows | Cross-border deals (1) $CAR_{CB}$ | Domestic deals (2) $CAR_D$ | Difference (2) − (1) | Difference (t-ratio) |
|---|---|---|---|---|
| (−40, −31) | 0.513*** | −0.075** | −0.589 | −1.51 |
| (−30, −21) | 0.564*** | −0.006* | −0.571 | −1.29 |
| (−20, −11) | 0.438*** | 0.081** | −0.357 | −0.74 |
| (−10, −1) | 0.589*** | 0.103*** | −0.486 | −0.98 |
| (−5, 0) | 0.351*** | 0.076** | −0.274 | −0.87 |
| (−1, 0) | 0.094** | 0.003* | −0.091 | −0.74 |
| 0 | 0.061** | 0.020** | −0.040 | −0.60 |
| (−1, +1) | 0.150*** | 0.034** | −0.116 | −0.66 |
| (−2, +2) | 0.333*** | 0.067** | −0.266 | −0.97 |
| (−5, +5) | 0.631*** | 0.169*** | −0.461 | −0.81 |
| (0, +1) | 0.117*** | 0.051** | −0.065 | −0.54 |
| (0, +5) | 0.341*** | 0.113** | −0.228 | −0.70 |
| (0, +10) | 0.650*** | 0.211*** | −0.439 | −0.76 |
| (0, +15) | 0.790*** | 0.254*** | −0.536 | −0.65 |
| (0, +20) | 0.928*** | 0.261*** | −0.667 | −0.61 |
| (0, +30) | 1.139*** | 0.330*** | −0.809 | −0.48 |
| (0, +40) | 1.775*** | 0.423*** | −1.351 | −0.60 |

*Notes*: This table reports the cumulative abnormal returns (*CARs*) of target firms in domestic and cross-border acquisitions for various event windows around acquisition announcement dates. *t*-test is used to test the difference in *CARs* between Cross-border and domestic acquisitions. ***, **, and * indicate significance at the 1%, 5%, and 10% levels, respectively.

returns of the target firms in cross-border and domestic acquisitions for various event windows around the takeover announcement date. The results show that target shareholders gained positive returns in both types of acquisitions surrounding the announcement date. This result is in line with Hypothesis H2. Furthermore, there is no statistically significant difference in returns between cross-border and domestic acquisitions.

## 5. Conclusion

The study evaluated the role of target corporate governance in the bidders' geographic preferences in Vietnam. The results provide evidence that cross-border bidders prefer well-governed target firms when entering a new market, which is in line with the strategic market-entry hypothesis. Accordingly, target firms with more board committees and higher shareholder blockholdings are more likely to be sought by foreign bidders in cross-border acquisitions. The findings indicate the importance of target corporate governance as drivers of the foreign bidder in acquisition decision-making.

This study is significant from both academic and practical perspectives in financial economics. Academically, this research contributes to the theoretical framework of corporate governance, acquisition location decision-making, and the impact of corporate governance on the restructuring strategies of firms in a typical emerging market.

In practical terms, this study focused on the M&A market in Vietnam to examine the potential impact of corporate governance mechanisms on bidders' acquisition location decision-making. The findings have important implications for numerous parties involved in the takeover process and for related stakeholders, such as investors on the stock market in general and regulatory and policy-setting bodies in particular. For the targets of acquisitions, it is important to focus on improving the corporate governance structure, especially when selecting board members and establishing the levels of ownership concentrations, to attract capital influx from foreign investors via cross-border acquisitions. For prospective bidding firms, the results confirm the importance of considering target firm corporate governance as a key determinant of acquisition decision-making. For investors, the findings suggest that looking toward the quality of corporate governance can minimize the risks when the deals are officially announced, which can help investors identify potential stocks involved in M&A deals. From the policy-setting bodies' perspective, it is necessary to impose regulations governing takeovers in a clear and transparent manner and to establish legal standards related to corporate governance. Regulatory and policy-setting bodies should also initiate a roadmap for developing a complete financial market in Vietnam in general and the stock market in particular to create a fair environment for all domestic and foreign investors. Put differently, to promote M&A activities, the Vietnamese legal system governing M&A activities should be improved and streamlined with detailed regulations on contract content and scope, ranging from clearly specified rights and obligations of parties involved to procedures, principles, and pricing methods. This extends to regulations on anti-acquisition to ensure a healthy competitive environment.

## Acknowledgment

We thank the participants at the 2019 UEH International Conference on Business and Finance, and the 2019 Vietnam International Conference in Finance, for very fruitful comments and suggestions. This research is granted by Funds for Science and Technology Development of the University of Danang under project number B2018-DN04-07. All remaining errors are our own.

## References

Bae, S.C., Chang, K., and Kim, D. (2013). Determinants of target selection and acquirer returns: Evidence from cross-border acquisitions. *International Review of Economics & Finance*, 27, 552–565.

Balsvik, R., and Haller, S.A. (2010). Picking "lemons" or picking "cherries"? Domestic and foreign acquisitions in Norwegian manufacturing. *Scandinavian Journal of Economics*, 112(2), 361–387.

Bertrand, O., and Zitouna, H. (2008). Domestic versus cross-border acquisitions: Which impact on the target firms' performance? *Applied Economics*, 40(7), 2221–2238.

Bris, A., and Cabolis, C. (2008). The value of investor protection: Firm evidence from cross-border mergers. *Review of Financial Studies*, 21, 605–648.

Conn, R.L., Cosh, A., Guest, P., and Hughes, A. (2005). The impact on UK acquirers of domestic, cross-border, public and private acquisitions. *Journal of Business Finance and Accounting*, 32, 815–870.

Croci, E., and Petmezas, D. (2015). Do risk-taking incentives induce CEOs to invest? Evidence from acquisitions. *Journal of Corporate Finance*, 32(C), 1–23.

Cronqvist, H., and Fahlenbrach, R. (2009). Large shareholders và corporate policies. *Review of Financial Studies*, 22, 3941–3976.

Chen, C., and Su, R. (1997). Do cross-border acquisition of U.S. targets differ from U.S. domestic takeover targets? *Global Finance Journal*, 8(1), 71–82.

Chidambaran, N., Krishnakumar, D., and Sethi, M. (2018). Cross-border vs. domestic acquisitions: Evidence from India. *Journal of Economics and Business*, 95, 3–25.

Danbolt, J., and Maciver, G. (2012). Cross-border versus domestic acquisitions and the impact on shareholder wealth. *Journal of Business Finance & Accounting*, 39, 1028–1067.

Dang, M., and Henry, D. (2016). Partial-control versus full-control acquisitions: Does target corporate governance matter? Evidence from eight East and Southeast Asian countries. *Pacific-Basin Finance Journal*, 40, 251–260.

Dang, M., Henry, D., Nguyen, M., and Hoang, V. (2018). Cross-country determinants of ownership choices in cross-border acquisitions: Evidence from emerging markets. *Journal of Multinational Financial Management*, 44, 14–35.

Fukao, K., Ito, K., Kwon, H.U., and Takizawa, M. (2006). Cross-Border Acquisitions and Target Firms' Performance: Evidence from Japanese Firm-Level Data, NBER Working Paper Series, No. 12422.

Hamberg, M., Overland, C., and Lantz, B. (2013). Board participation, toeholds and the cross-border effect. *International Business Review*, 22(5), 868–882.

Hernando, I., Nieto, M.J., and Wal, L.D. (2009). Determinants of domestic and cross-border bank acquisitions in the European Union. *Journal of Banking & Finance*, 33, 1022–1032.

Harris, R.S., and Ravenscraft, D. (1991). The role of acquisitions in foreign direct investment: Evidence from the U.S. stock market. *Journal of Finance*, 46, 825–844.

Hu, M., and Yang, J. (2016). The role of leverage in cross-border mergers and acquisitions. *International Review of Economics & Finance*, 43, 170–199.

Jenter, D., and Lewellen, K. (2015). CEO preferences and acquisitions. *Journal of Finance*, 70(6), 2813–2852.

Kim, W. (2012). Investor protection and the mode of acquisition: Implications for ownership dilution and formation of pyramids. *Financial Management*, 41(1), 55–93.

Kim, W., Sung, T., and Wei, S.-J. (2011). Does corporate governance risk at home affect investment choices abroad? *Journal of International Economics*, 85, 25–41.

Kling, G., and Weitzel, U. (2011). The internationalization of Chinese companies: Firm characteristics, industry effects and corporate governance. *Research in International Business and Finance*, 25, 357–372.

Liao, R. (2014). What drives corporate minority acquisitions around the world? The case for financial constraints. *Journal of Corporate Finance*, 26, 78–95.

Massa, M., and Xu, M. (2013). The value of (stock) liquidity in the M&A market. *Journal of Financial and Quantitative Analysis*, 48(5), 1463–1497.

McGee, R., 2009. An overview of corporate governance practices in Vietnam. *Corporate Governance in Developing Economies*, 235–238.

Pathan, S. (2009). Strong boards, CEO power and bank risk-taking. *Journal of Banking and Finance*, 33, 1340–1350.

Pham, N., Oh, K., and Pech, R. (2015). Mergers and acquisitions: CEO duality, operating performance and stock returns in Vietnam. *Pacific-Basin Finance Journal*, 35, 298–316.

Rossi, S., and Volpin, P.F. (2004). Cross-country determinants of mergers and acquisitions. *Journal of Financial Economics*, 74, 277–304.

Servaes, H., and Zenner, M. (1994). Taxes and the return to foreign acquisitions in the United States. *Financial Management*, 23(4), 42–56.

Starks, L.T., and Wei, K.D. (2013). Cross-border mergers and differences in corporate governance. *International Review of Finance*, 13, 265–297.

Weston, F., Mitchell, M., and Mulherin, H. (2004). *Takeovers, Restructuring and Corporate Governance.* New Jersey: Pearson Prentice Hall, Upple Saddle River.

Zhu, P., Jog, V., and Otchere, I. (2011). Partial acquisitions in emerging markets: A test of the strategic market entry. *Journal of Corporate Finance*, 17, 288–305.

https://doi.org/10.1142/9789811227158_0002

## Chapter 2

# Base Erosion, Profit Shifting, and Tax Revenue Nexus: Empirical Evidence in Southeast Asian Countries

**Trung Kien Tran**

### Abstract

This chapter estimates the effect of base erosion and profit shifting (BEPS) related to foreign direct investments (FDIs) on tax revenue losses in Southeast Asian countries. ASEAN members are mainly developing countries that have few experiences in aggressive tax planning of multinational enterprises (MNEs). Particularly, this chapter measures BEPS by the offshore indicator. The Offshore Investment Matrix approach shows that 3.6% of the total inward FDI stock of six Southeast Asian countries comes from offshore investment hubs. Then, this indicator is used as an input to estimate empirically the impact of the share of FDI from tax havens to the rate of return on FDI in ASEAN countries. Finally, a compatible stimulation evaluates the tax revenue losses from BEPS. The result implies the stimulated after-tax profit shifting is about $95.55 billion, which indicates tax revenue losses of $18.56 billion for Southeast Asian countries.

**Keywords:** BEPS; FDI; Tax revenue.

## 1. Introduction

In recent years, many scholars have researched on base erosion and profit shifting (BEPS), which is an emerging issue in international conferences. BEPS is a major concern, negatively affecting tax revenues in countries (Brauner, 2014; Ross and Herrington, 2013). Moreover, FDI attraction policy coupled with improper control and response of developing countries can cause more tax revenue losses (Bolwijn *et al.*, 2018; Schimanski, 2018).

The aggressive tax planning of multinational enterprises (MNEs) is continuously apparent, but the evaluation of its effect is still ignored (Bolwijn *et al.*, 2018; Janský and Šedivý, 2019). The reason for MNEs to transfer profits is easy to understand. Moreover, the public gradually acknowledges the ways that the MNEs transfer profits because of the recent leakage of private documents and thorough analytical case studies (Fuest *et al.*, 2013; Keightleý and Štupak, 2015). However, the empirical evidence of tax revenue losses from MNEs, aggressive tax planning remains scanty due to the inherent limits of measurement on transferring profits and the lack of data (Avi-Yonah and Xu, 2017; Bolwijn *et al.*, 2018; Bradbury *et al.*, 2018; Keightley and Stupak, 2015; OECD, 2015).

The effect of BEPS on tax revenues in developing countries and particularly Southeast Asian countries is still unclear. In recent years, some efforts have been implemented by fresh proposals from the European Union (EU) and the Organization for Economic Co-operation and Development (OECD) but are still restrained in developing countries (Bolwijn *et al.*, 2018; Bradbury *et al.*, 2018). Only a few studies have made significant contributions to this subject; however, none of them have focused on the case of Southeast Asian countries (Bolwijn *et al.*, 2018; Crivelli *et al.*, 2015; Janský and Palanský, 2019; Janský and Šedivý, 2019). These countries are almost all developing countries (excluding Singapore) that implement FDI attraction policies to promote economic growth. They are also more integrated into the regional and international community with significant achievements, such as the ASEAN Economic Community (AEC) establishment (Thanh *et al.*, 2014). Therefore, conducting the research about the BEPS effect in these countries is necessary.

This chapter aims to estimate the effect of BEPS on tax revenues in Southeast Asian countries. In particular, firstly, we apply the Offshore Investment Matrix (OIM) approach of UNCTAD (2015) to identify tax havens and special purpose entities (SPEs). Secondly, we measure the offshore indicator calculated from bilateral FDI stock. Based on this indicator, similar to UNCTAD (2015) and Bolwijn *et al.* (2018), we empirically explore the relationship between the offshore indicator and the rate of return on inward FDI, assuming that the more the share of investment from tax havens, the more the decreased rate of return on inward FDI. Finally, the tax revenue losses can be measured by a compatible simulation that converts the profitability gap into the actual reported FDI stock for Southeast Asian countries.

Besides this section, the remainder of this chapter is structured as follows: Section 2 presents the literature review, with a brief summary of previous similar studies; Section 3 is for research methodology and data description. Section 4 presents detailed results. Finally, Section 5 provides conclusions and some policy implications.

## 2. Literature Review

BEPS diminishes tax revenue globally (Brauner, 2014; UNCTAD, 2015). BEPS is a term that refers to *tax avoidance strategies that exploit gaps and mismatches in tax rules to artificially shift profits to low or no-tax locations.*[1] With these aggressive tax plans, the more the benefit the MNEs get, the less the tax revenue the governments collect. According to OECD (2019), BEPS practices of MNEs annually cause US$ 100–240 billion worth of losses in global tax revenue. Especially, developing countries suffer extraordinarily from BEPS as they rely on higher company tax than developed countries. Thus, many scholars have been concerned about BEPS and its effect. However, studies related to BEPS are various and difficult to classify.

In this section, we briefly review recent literature related to BEPS measurements and the relationship between BEPS and tax revenue losses. Although many studies confirm the existence of BEPS, the

[1] http://www.oecd.org/tax/beps/about/

number of studies on measuring BEPS is relatively small. Based on the data level, two main trends are recognized in the literature: *firm-specific data and country-specific data* (OECD, 2015). In terms of the country-specific data, some macroeconomic indicators such as national accounts, the balance of payments (BOP), foreign direct investment (FDI), and tax revenues are the main sources in many studies due to data availability. All these databases are publicly published by international organizations such as IMF, OECD, and UNCTAD (Bolwijn *et al.*, 2018; Bradbury *et al.*, 2018; Cobham and Janský, 2018; OECD, 2015). Regarding the firm-specific data, scholars focus on analyzing profit shifting by firm-level microeconomic data (Heckemeyer and Overesch, 2017; Janský and Kokeš, 2015; Jurušs and Kuma, 2016; Leino and Ali-Yrkkö, 2014; OECD, 2015). This trend analyzes profit-shifting behaviors in MNEs with the literature of Behavioral Finance. These papers, which are classified by country-specific data and firm-specific data, are presented in Table 1.

Measuring BEPS is still controversial. The raw indicators cannot reflect BEPS's scale; therefore, many research programs have been implemented to measure BEPS. Despite methodology debates, the approaches estimating the scale and extent of BEPS are categorized into three groups: (1) *aggregate tax rate differential*, (2) *tax haven spillover*, and (3) *offshore investment matrix*.

OECD (2015) uses Orbis data to estimate the effect of mismatches between tax systems and preferential treatment on tax revenue loss. In the paper of OECD, the tax rate differential is defined as the difference between the statutory tax rate of countries where MNEs have branches. Crivelli *et al.* (2015) use a tax haven spillover approach to measure BEPS. In particular, they estimate the effect of the unweighted average tax rate of countries classified as tax havens on the tax base. Similar to OECD (2015), Orbis database is the main source of this chapter. Meanwhile, based on the offshore investment matrix approach of UNCTAD (2015), Bolwijn *et al.* (2018) determine the list of tax havens and special purpose entities (SPEs) and then estimate the effect of BEPS related to FDI on the tax revenue by

**Table 1:** Summary of previous studies on the BEPS measurement.

| **Data level** | **Authors** | **Data source** |
|---|---|---|
| Country-level | Janský and Šedivý (2019) | Action Aid Tax Treaties Dataset |
| | Bolwijn *et al.* (2018) | IMF CDIS; *IMF BOP/IIP* |
| | Cobham and Janský (2018) | Government Revenue Database (GRD) — ICTD WIDER |
| | Janský and Palanský (2019) | IMF CDIS |
| | Crivelli *et al.* (2015) | IMF's Fiscal Affairs Department database |
| | UNCTAD (2015) | IMF CDIS; *IMF BOP/IIP* |
| Firm-specific data | Clausing (2016) | The U.S. Bureau of Economic Analysis Survey — USA |
| | Janský and Kokeš (2016) | Orbis data — Czech Republic |
| | Janský and Kokeš (2015) | Orbis data — Czech Republic |
| | Keightley and Stupak (2015) | The US Bureau of Economic Analysis Survey — USA |
| | OECD (2015) | Orbis data — All countries |
| | Cobham and Loretz (2014) | Orbis data — developing countries |
| | Leino and Ali-Yrkkö (2014) | Bank of Finland data, Finnish Tax Administration data — Finland |

the offshore calculation. In contrast with the two previous studies, Bolwijn *et al.* (2018) utilize the IMF's Coordinated Direct Investment Survey (IMF CDIS) to measure BEPS related to FDI.

The FDI-income approach is one of the compatible methods to estimate the fiscal effects of transfer profit activities (Bolwijn *et al.*, 2018; Casella, 2019; UNCTAD, 2015). As UNCTAD (2015) implies, the structure and procedure of direct investments create tax avoidance opportunities on subsequent investment income. Thereby, MNEs' tax planning influences the scale and direction of FDI. Consequently, UNCTAD (2015, p. 17) concludes *FDI can be considered as "the engine" and profit shifting "the fuel" of MNE tax avoidance schemes.*

Besides, in comparison with the firm-level data, the country-level data dominate the research on BEPS. Bradbury *et al.* (2018) indicate the country-level data are more appropriate to derive fiscal estimates of BEPS. Orbis database, the popular commercial database of firm financial statements, is collected from non-random samples of MNEs. This can affect BEPS measurement and its fiscal effect. Moreover, firm-level data are almost unavailable or unreliable in many developing countries.

Therefore, based on UNCTAD's (2015) approach and Bolwijn *et al.* (2018), this chapter empirically explores the effect of BEPS on the tax revenue in Southeast Asian countries. In terms of data used, similar to Bolwijn *et al.* (2018), IMF's Coordinated Direct Investment Survey (IMF CDIS) and IMF's Balance of Payment and International Investment Positions Statistics (IMF BOP/IIP) are the main sources for our chapter.

## 3. Methodology and Data Description

### 3.1. *Offshore investment matrix approach*

The objective of this chapter is to estimate the effect of BEPS on tax revenues in Southeast Asian countries. Firstly, we use the Offshore Investment Matrix (OIM) approach of UNCTAD (2015) to identify tax havens and special purpose entities (SPEs). Offshore Investment Matrix (OIM) is an analytical tool shaping a comprehensive map of FDI through offshore financial centers (OFCs) and offshore investment hubs.

More particularly, OIM filters investors and recipient jurisdictions in a bilateral FDI stock arrangement according to three categories: *tax havens*, *SPEs*, and *non-OFCs*. The first two categories reflect the offshore component of global FDI investment stock and the latter represents the standard FDI stock. Unlike tax havens, SPE countries are jurisdictions which not only have considerable real

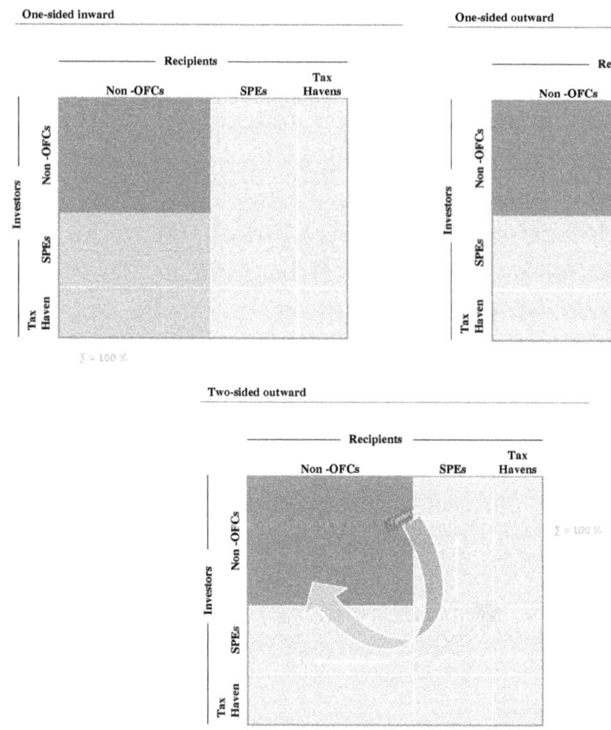


**Figure 1:** Offshore Investment Matrix approach.

*Source*: UNCTAD (2015).

economic activities but also act as financial centers for MNEs owing to the favorable tax and investment management (Bolwijn *et al.*, 2018).

As Figure 1 describes, Offshore Investment Matrix approach has two ways to analyze FDI investment through offshore hubs and conduits, called *One-sided analysis* and *Two-sided analysis*. The former considers the extent to which FDI from standard countries is routed through hubs as direct partners. The latter regards all FDI connections involved in offshore investment hubs as both investors and recipients.

The share of the investment stock is allocated to the three classifications of the OIM approach (UNCTAD, 2015). It varies according to the jurisdiction's involvement. Particularly, the classification for each investment stock is allocated as follows:

- If the investor from bilateral FDI data is a jurisdiction in the classification of the tax havens, all of the stock is allocated to the investor categorized as "tax havens".
- If the investor from bilateral FDI data is a jurisdiction in the scope of the SPE-countries, a given share of the stock is allocated to the investor categorized as "SPE countries" while the remainder is allocated to the investor categorized as "Non-OFCs". For self-declared SPE-countries, the shares are derived immediately using the share of investment stock from SPEs in total inward investment stock as reported by national Central Banks.
- If the investor from bilateral FDI data is a jurisdiction not included in the scope of the selected offshore investment hubs, all of the stock is allocated to the investor categorized as "Non-OFCs".

### 3.2. *Empirical analysis*

The main assumption of the UNCTAD methodology for the estimation of profit shifting and tax revenue losses is a negative relationship at country level between the share of inward investment stock from offshore hubs (offshore indicator, hereafter) and the rate of return on the total inward FDI stock (rate of return, hereafter). Its rationale is that FDI income from offshore investment hubs is dependent to a greater extent on profit-shifting practices with the effect of "artificially" deflating the rate of return.

In other words, this relationship is analyzed through the econometric modeling of country-level data, in which the rate of return is the dependent variable and the offshore indicator is the explanatory variable. The offshore indicator is derived as a straightforward application at the country level of the Offshore Investment Matrix illustrated in the previous section.

The relationship between the offshore indicator and the rate of return is subject to econometric estimation. The reference model is a standard empirical model (ordinary least squares with time and country effects):

$$y_{it} = \alpha + \beta x_{it} + \delta_t + \theta_k + \varepsilon_{it}, \quad (1)$$

where $i$ and $t$, respectively, refer to the country and year; $x$ denotes the offshore indicator and $y$ denotes the rate of return. Each data point $(x, y)$ is meant for a number of countries (indexed by $i$ from 1 to $N = 6$), across 6 years (indexed by $t$ from 2012 to 2017); $\delta$ represents the time effect and $\theta$ represents the country effects; $\varepsilon$ is an error term.

The size of the sample is subject to data availability on bilateral FDI inward stock, which is used to calculate the offshore indicator, and the FDI income, which calculates the rate of return. In particular, the rate of return is measured by the ratio of total FDI income (income on equity and interests on debt) over FDI inward stock. Meanwhile, the Offshore Indicator is calculated as the share of inward investment stock from offshore hubs. It can be stemmed from a straightforward application of the methodology of the Offshore Investment Matrix (one-sided inward analysis).

Once a significant relationship is established between the Offshore Indicator and the Rate of Return, the tax revenue losses can be measured by the compatible simulation with the appropriate assumptions on the profitability gap (how much FDI income is lost because of offshore hub investments) and on the average corporate tax rate.

## 4. Results and Discussion

The input data for the OIM approach is bilateral FDI inward stock collected from IMF CDIS. The total FDI inward stock of six analyzed countries is US$ 579.2 billion in 2012 (about 2.5% world FDI stock). All of them are classified as "Non-OFC countries"; therefore, we only classify the investors who invest in these countries. Following UNCTAD (2015), a specific arrangement of OFC investors' jurisdictions is implemented:

**The rule for allocation**

| Bilateral investment stock | | Offshore investment Matrix | | |
|---|---|---|---|---|
| **Investor** | **Recipient** | **Percentage of invest-ment stock** | **Investor** | **Recipient** |
| SPE-country | Other country | β %<br>(1- β) % | SPE<br>Non-OFC | Non-OFC<br>Non-OFC |
| Tax haven | Other country | 100 % | Tax Haven | Non-OFC |
| Other country | Other country | 100 % | Non-OFC | Non-OFC |
| Other country | SPE-country | α %<br>(1- α) % | Non-OFC<br>Non-OFC | SPE<br>Non-OFC |
| Other country | Tax haven | 100 % | Non-OFC | Tax Haven |
| SPE-country | SPE-country | α %<br>(1- α) % | SPE<br>Non-OFC | SPE<br>Non-OFC |
| Tax haven | SPE-country | α %<br>(1- α) % | Tax Haven<br>Tax Haven | SPE<br>Non-OFC |
| SPE-country | Tax haven | β %<br>(1- β) % | SPE<br>Non-OFC | Tax Haven<br>Tax Haven |
| Tax haven | Tax haven | 100 % | Tax Haven | Tax Haven |

| The SPE-shares *(α,β)* | | |
|---|---|---|
| **SPE-Countries** | **SPE share in inward stock (α %)** | **SPE share in outward stock (β%)** |
| Austria | 40% | 36% |
| Hungary | 58% | 81% |
| Luxembourg | 96% | 95% |
| Netherlands | 83% | 78% |

**Figure 2:** The rule for allocation of SPE countries.
*Source*: UNCTAD (2015).

(1) **Tax havens:** 38 jurisdictions originally defined by the OECD[2] (Bolwijn *et al.*, 2018; Gravelle, 2010; UNCTAD, 2015);
(2) **SPE countries:** The group includes four self-declared countries, include Austria, Hungary, Luxembourg, and the Netherlands (UNCTAD, 2015). The rule for allocation of SPE countries is to implement as Figure 2 describes.
(3) **Non-OFC countries:** Other countries excluding tax havens and SPE countries.

Based on the OIM procedure of UNCTAD (2015), we calculate the offshore indicator and the rate of return of the six Southeast Asian

[2]List of tax havens include: Anguilla, Antigua and Barbuda, Aruba, the Bahamas, Bahrain, Belize, Bermuda, British Virgin Islands, Cayman Islands, the Cook Islands, Cyprus, Dominica, Gibraltar, Grenada, Guernsey, Isle of Man, Jersey, Liberia, Liechtenstein, Malta, the Marshall Islands, Mauritius, Monaco, Montserrat, Nauru, Netherlands Antilles, Niue, Panama, Saint Kitts and Nevis, Saint Lucia, Saint Vincent and the Grenadines, Samoa, San Marino, Seychelles, Turks and Caicos Islands, United States Virgin Islands, and Vanuatu.

**Table 2:** Data sources and descriptive statistics.

| Variable | Description | Data source |
|---|---|---|
| The rate of return | The ratio of total FDI income over FDI inward stock | UNCTADSTAT, *IMF BOP/IIP* |
| The offshore indicator | The share of inward investment stock from offshore hubs (Tax havens & SPEs) | *IMF CDIS* |

| Descriptive statistics | Obs | Mean | Std. Dev. | Min | Max |
|---|---|---|---|---|---|
| The rate of return (ror) | 36 | 0.092 | 0.028 | 0.051 | 0.163 |
| The offshore indicator (offshore) | 36 | 0.036 | 0.027 | 0.001 | 0.091 |

*Source*: UNCTAD (2019), IMF (2019a, 2019b) and author's calculation.

**Table 3:** Correlation matrix.

| | The rate of return (ror) | The offshore indicator (offshore) |
|---|---|---|
| The rate of return (ror) | 1 | |
| The offshore indicator (offshore) | –0.332 | 1 |

countries. Data description and correlation matrix are presented in Tables 2 and 3, respectively.

Regarding our analysis, we use a variation of panel data techniques, including fixed effects (FEs), random effects (REs) models, and FGLS model for data features and robustness tests. In addition, Hausman test is implemented to choose between FEs and REs techniques. The empirical results are shown in Table 4.

All the three empirical techniques indicate a negative impact of the offshore indicator on the rate of return. In particular, the FGLS model is more appropriate than the others. Hausman test also

**Table 4:** The effect of the offshore indicator on the rate of return in Southeast Asian countries.

| | Fixed effects | Random effects | FGLS |
|---|---|---|---|
| The offshore indicator (offshore) | −0.2332 | −0.3091 | −0.2890* |
| Obs | 36 | 36 | 36 |
| $R^2$ | 0.1102 | 0.1102 | |
| Hausman test ($p$-value) | | 0.8581 | |

*Notes*: Dependent variable: the rate of return (ror). *is statistically significant at 1%.

indicates the compatibility of Random Effects Techniques. Meanwhile, FGLS is more suitable than Random Effects in treating autocorrelation and heteroscedasticity (Hansen, 2007). The significant coefficient (–0.289) means that 1% share of inward investment stock from havens and SPEs is correlated with a 0.289% lower reported (taxable) rate of return. The result is similar to Bolwijn *et al.* (2018). In addition, the higher significant coefficient implies that Southeast Asian countries are more vulnerable to profit shifting than other developing countries.

Due to a negative relationship between the share of inward investment from offshore investment hubs and the rate of return on inward investment, the evaluation of the tax revenue losses of Southeast Asian countries poses two concerns: (1) *Finding the "missing profits" caused by current levels of investment from offshore hubs (that are used for the estimation of the profit shifting)*; (2) *Converting this one into tax revenue losses.*

Based on the UNCTAD approach, we utilize the results of the regression analysis to simulate the differences in profitability related to the actual exposure of Southeast Asian countries to offshore investment hubs. Given an average exposure of Southeast Asian countries at 3.6% of total inward investment stock (mean of the offshore indicator), the estimated coefficient at –28.9% (Table 4, model FGLS) implies a profitability gap of 10.4 pp. As total inward investment stock in Southeast Asian countries is approximately

**Table 5:** Simulation of the profit shifting for Southeast Asian countries.

| Estimated profitability gap | Reported FDI stock (billions of dollars, 2017) | Simulated profit shifting before tax (billions of dollars) | Simulated profit shifting after tax (billions of dollars) | Simulated tax revenue loss (billions of dollars) |
|---|---|---|---|---|
| 10.4pp | 735 | 76.44 | 95.55 | 18.56 |

*Source*: UNCTAD (2019).

$735 billion, we translate the profitability gap into the actual reported FDI stock for Southeast Asian countries. Consequently, the result shows an estimate of the after-tax profit shifting of $95.55 billion and the tax revenue loss of $18.56 billion, assuming the company tax rate is 20%. Table 5 displays the steps of this simulation.

## 5. Conclusion

In conclusion, this chapter tries to achieve two main analytical points. Firstly, we apply the Offshore Investment Matrix (OIM) approach to quantify FDI through tax havens and SPEs. The results of the analysis show that 3.6% of total inward FDI stock of six Southeast Asian countries comes from offshore investment hubs in the global FDI context. This analysis is of major interest on its own. It not only measures the link between investment and taxation but also plays as an input to the next objective: Determine the fiscal impact of BEPS related to FDI. Secondly, the negative relationship between offshore FDI and investment profitability and simulation process indicates that investments through OFCs are responsible for profit shifting activities. This process causes estimated tax revenue losses worth $18.56 billion for Southeast Asian countries.

The policy implication of this chapter is also clear. To limit tax revenue losses from profit transfer of MNEs, international tax rules must be refined. At the global level, governments need to come to an agreement on international tax principles. One of the most controversial concerns is whether to establish an international tax agency that is responsible for considering rule changes that can benefit those who suffer the greatest losses. Nevertheless, the real breakthrough will only come to pass when each country strictly adheres to international tax principles.

## References

Avi-Yonah, R.S., and Xu, H. (2017). Evaluating BEPS. *Erasmus Law Review*, 10, 3.

Bolwijn, R., Casella, B., and Rigo, D. (2018). An FDI-driven approach to measuring the scale and economic impact of BEPS. *Transnational Corporations*, 25(2), 107–143.

Bradbury, D., Hanappi, T., and Moore, A. (2018). Estimating the fiscal effects of base erosion and profit shifting: data availability and analytical issues. *Transnational Corporations*, 25(2), 91–106.

Brauner, Y. (2014). What the BEPS. *Florida Tax Review*, 16, 55.

Casella, B. (2019). Looking through conduit FDI in search of ultimate investors' a probabilistic approach. *Transnational Corporations*, 26(1), 109–146.

Clausing, K. A. (2016). The effect of profit shifting on the corporate tax base in the United States and beyond. Available at SSRN 2685442.

Cobham, A., and Janský, P. (2018). Global distribution of revenue loss from corporate tax avoidance: re-estimation and country results. *Journal of International Development*, 30(2), 206–232. Retrieved from: https://onlinelibrary.wiley.com/doi/pdf/10.1002/jid.3348.

Cobham, A. and Loretz, S. (2014). International distribution of the corporate tax base: Impact of different apportionment factors under unitary taxation. *ICTD Working Paper*, 27, April. Brighton, United Kingdom: International Centre for Tax and Development. Retrieved from: https://opendocs.ids.ac.uk/opendocs/bitstream/handle/20.500.12413/11176/ICTD_WP27.pdf.

De Mooij, R. A., and Keen, M. M. (2015). *Base erosion, profit shifting and developing countries*: International Monetary Fund.

Fuest, C., Spengel, C., Finke, K., Heckemeyer, J., and Nusser, H. (2013). Profit shifting and 'aggressive' tax planning by multinational firms: Issues and options for reform. ZEW-Centre for European Economic Research Discussion Paper (13-078).

Gravelle, J. (2010). *Tax Havens: International Tax Avoidance and Evasion.* DIANE Publishing.

Hansen, C.B. (2007). Generalized least squares inference in panel and multilevel models with serial correlation and fixed effects. *Journal of Econometrics*, 140(2), 670–694.

Heckemeyer, J.H., and Overesch, M. (2017). Multinationals' profit response to tax differentials: Effect size and shifting channels. *Canadian Journal of Economics/Revue canadienne d'economique*, 50(4), 965–994.

IMF. (2019a). Balance of payment and international investment positions statistics. Retrieved from: http://data.imf.org/?sk=7A51304B-6426-40C0-83DD-CA473CA1FD52&sId=1542633711584

IMF. (2019b). Coordinated direct investment survey. Retrieved from: http://data.imf.org/?sk=40313609-F037-48C1-84B1-E1F1CE54D6D5

Janský, P., and Kokeš, O. (2015). Corporate tax base erosion and profit shifting out of the Czech Republic. *Post-Communist Economies*, 27(4), 537–546.

Janský, P., and Kokeš O. (2016). Profit-shifting from Czech multinational companies to European tax havens. *Applied Economics Letters*, 23(16), 1130–1133.

Janský, P., and Palanský, M. (2019). Estimating the scale of profit shifting and tax revenue losses related to foreign direct investment. *International Tax and Public Finance*, 26(5), 1048–1103.

Janský, P., and Šedivý, M. (2019). *Estimating the revenue costs of tax treaties in developing countries.* The World Economy.

Jurušs, M., and Kuma, E. (2016). BEPS: Impact of international tax measures on business environment in Latvia. *XVII International*, 104.

Keightley, M. P., and Stupak, J. M. (2015). *Corporate tax base erosion and profit shifting (BEPS): An examination of the data.* Congressional Research Service.

Leino, T., and Ali-Yrkkö J. (2014). How well does foreign direct investment measure real investment by foreign-owned companies?: Firm-level analysis. Firm-Level Analysis (May 15, 2014). Bank of Finland Research Discussion Paper(12).

OECD. (2015). Measuring and monitoring BEPS, Action 11. Retrieved from Paris, France: http://www.oecdilibrary.org/content/book/978926424 1343-en

OECD. (2019). OECD/G20 Inclusive Framework on BEPS: Progress Report July 2018-May 2019. Retrieved from https://www.oecd.org/tax/beps/inclusive-framework-on-beps-progress-report-july-2018-may-2019.pdf

Ross, J., and Herrington, M. (2013). A Call to Rewrite the Fundamentals of International Taxation: The OECD BEPS Action Plan. *Journal of International Tax*, 39, 15.

Schimanski, C. (2018). Do multinational companies shift profits out of developing countries? How data availability may hide the evidence

(9292564943). Retrieved from https://papers.ssrn.com/sol3/papers.cfm?abstract_id=2973490

Thanh, S. D., Bui, T. T., and Kien, T. (2014). Reforms of tax system in Vietnam: Toward international integration commitments until 2020. Available at SSRN 2486926.

UNCTAD. (2015). The fiscal role of multinational enterprises: Towards guidelines for Coherent International Tax and Investment Policies. Retrieved from https://www.tralac.org/images/docs/7262/development-unctad-working-paper-march-2015.pdf

UNCTAD. (2019). *UNCTADSTAT*. Retrieved from: https://unctadstat.unctad.org/wds/ReportFolders/reportFolders.aspx?sCS_ChosenLang=en

https://doi.org/10.1142/9789811227158_0003

# Chapter 3

# Developing the Stock Market for Economic Growth: Experiences for Vietnam in the ASEAN Regional Financial Integration

**Tu Nhu Nguyen and Thi Xuan Huong Tram**

## Abstract

This chapter assesses the impact of the stock market on the economic growth of ASEAN-5 countries and Vietnam in the period from 2006 to 2018 by using the linear regression method. The results of the study indicate that the stock market has a significant impact on economic growth in the listed countries. However, in Vietnam, there is no empirical evidence that shows the impact of Vietnam's stock index on economic growth. The last part of this chapter proposes effective policy implications for developing Vietnam's stock market and contributing to the economic growth in the future.

**Keywords:** Stock market; Economic growth; VNINDEX; Market capitalization; Stock trade.

## 1. Introduction

Over the past two decades, the stock markets of emerging economies have experienced explosive growth. The capitalization value of the global stock markets has increased from $2,000 billion (1982) to $4,700 billion (1986). After a decade, it continued to increase from $4,700 billion to $15,200 billion and be equivalent to an average annual growth rate of 15%. Emerging markets have contributed from less than 4% to 13% of the total market capitalization of the world in the same period (Levine and Zervos, 1996). The manifestation of the rapid booms in emerging markets is the speed of transactions and stock traded values increase of about $8,000 billion, from $1,600 billion (less than 3% of the transaction value of the world in 1985) to about $9,600 billion (more than 17% of the transaction value of the world in 1994).

In Asia, ASEAN countries are considered as emerging economies with outstanding growth along with the rapid development of the stock markets. It leads to many notable debates about whether the relationship between the stock market and economic development exists or not. In recent years, the development of stock market has been a common feature of financial and economic development in emerging economies. Is the stock market helping the economic growth in ASEAN countries? Some of the economists think that the stock markets in emerging countries have a little positive impact and sometimes have a negative influence on economic growth because there are not many financing investments through issuing stock (Mayer, 1988). In contrast, the studies of Levine (1991) and Bencivenga *et al.* (1996) show that the stock market can promote economic growth through creating liquidity for the capital market.

The development of the stock market has important implications for economic growth. Stock markets in ASEAN countries are still quite sensitive and vulnerable to economic shocks. Therefore, researching the impact of the stock market on economic growth brings forward many useful experiences for them, including Vietnam. Moreover, the stock market becomes an important mobilizing channel for the domestic economy. Its size has strong and solid growth steps in the context of complex fluctuations of the international financial market and the country's economy. This chapter's aim is to ascertain an overall picture of the stock market development affecting economic growth in ASEAN countries in comparison with the characteristics of Vietnam's economy. Finally, the chapter suggests many policies to develop the stock market and contribute more to the economic development in Vietnam.

## 2. Literature Review

Whether developing the stock market promotes economic growth or not is the main subject of many experimental studies. Until now, there has been no solid evidence of this relationship. Atje and Jovanovic (1993) study the relationship between the stock market and the economic growth of 39 countries. The results show that there is a statistically significant relationship between countries in the period from 1980 to 1988. This is similar to the results of Levine and Zervos's research in 1996, which uses the regression analysis with data of 41 nations from 1976 to 1993. Both these studies find a relationship between the stock market and economic growth.

The research of Boubakari and Jin (2010) gets different results of the relationship between the stock market and economic growth of five countries: Belgium, France, Portugal, the Netherlands, and England from 1995 to the first quarter of 2008. This finding indicates that there is a positive relationship between them in countries with high and liquid stock markets and the opposite of those in which the stock markets are small and less liquid.

When researching on 42 emerging markets from 1995 to 2006, Masoud and Hardaker (2012) state that developing the stock market has a good impact on economic growth. Balago (2014) concludes that bank credit, total market capitalization, and foreign direct investments have had a positive impact on economic growth in Nigeria from 1990 to 2009.

Additionally, many previous studies provide more important empirical evidence about the relationship between stock market development and economic growth in Asian countries. Typically, the research of Ahmed and Ansari (1998) in India, Pakistan, and Sri Lanka from 1973 to 1991 shows that the stock markets affect economic growth in the same way. Luintel and Khan (1999) use annual data (within 36 years and 41 years) of 10 countries: Costa Rica, Colombia, Greece, India, Korea, Malaysia, Philippines, Sri-Lanka, South Africa, and Thailand. Their experimental results show a two-way relationship between stock market development and economic growth.

However, the results of Singh (1997) and Harris (1997) from studies in developing countries from 1980 to 1990 are contradictory. Singh (1997) says that the stock market does not affect economic growth in the long term. The cause is the economic fluctuation hindering and leading to a shortage of investment capital allocated in these countries. The study of Harris (1997) in 49 countries from 1980 to 1991 shows that the value of stock transactions only affects economic growth in developed countries, while in developing countries, the stock market and economic growth are not strongly related.

From 1980 to 2004, Tang *et al.* (2007) examined the relationship between the stock market and the economic growth of 12 Asian countries. Their findings point out a long-term relationship between the two factors in 4 countries: China, Philippines, Singapore, and Taiwan. There is a two-way relationship between the stock market and economic growth in China, Hong Kong, Indonesia, Malaysia, and Thailand. Meanwhile, in the case of Japan and South Korea, this relationship exists only in the short term, there is no relationship found in other countries.

In a similar study, the findings of Azarmi *et al.* (2005) do not support developing the stock market for a positive influence on economic growth in India from 1981 to 2001. Wang and Ajit (2013) state that there is a contradictory relationship between the stock market and economic growth in China from 1996 to 2011. The results of Owusu and Odhiambo (2015) also suggest that the stock market and financial freedom development have had no impact on economic growth in Ghana in the long term.

In conclusion, an overview of the studies shows that there is a positive and a negative relationship between stock market development and economic growth. The change in this relationship relates to the economic characteristics of each country and the characteristics of the stock market in each of these countries. The study of the relationship between the stock market and economic growth in typical countries to provide empirical evidence for Vietnam is considered extremely practical and significant to develop the stock market and contribute to economic growth in Vietnam.

## 2.1. *Research methods*

This chapter uses dynamic data of ASEAN-5 countries, including: Indonesia, Malaysia, Philippines, Thailand, and Vietnam, and excluding Singapore because its booming economy does not have much similarity with other countries. The data on the stock market of the listed countries, Brunei, Laos, Cambodia, and Myanmar, are quite limited as they do not have enough research facilities. The research is conducted for the period from 2008 to 2017. The data are collected from the World Bank website (World Bank) in the form of national data.

Based on the proposal of Bilal *et al.* (2016), the research model is given to assess the impact of the stock market on the economic growth of ASEAN-5 countries as follows:

$$\begin{aligned} GDP_{it} &= \beta_0 + \beta_1 MC_{it} + \beta_2 VT_{it} + \beta_3 FDI_{it} \\ &\quad + \beta_4 TrO_{it} + \beta_5 INF_{it} + \varepsilon_{it}, \end{aligned} \tag{1}$$

Regarding the estimation method, the research uses common methods in processing panel data. First, $F$-testing between Pooled OLS and FEM models results in $p$-value, which is less than 5%. It means that FEM is selected. The study also uses the Hausman test to choose between FEM and REM, the statistical results ($p$-value) is greater than 5%, indicating that the REM model is perfectly suitable.

With the aim of evaluating and comparing the impact of the development of the stock market on economic growth for the case of Vietnam alone, the study inherits the methods of Kajurová and Rozmahel (2016), Pan and Mishra (2016), Hoque and Yakob (2017) to propose the following specific research model:

$$\begin{aligned} \ln GDP_t &= \beta_0 + \sum_{i=1}^{n} \beta_{1i} \ln GDP_{t-i} \\ &\quad + \sum_{i=1}^{n} \beta_{2i} \ln VNIDEX_{t-i} + \varepsilon_t, \end{aligned} \tag{2}$$

**Table 1:** Describing research variables.

| Variables | Empirical research | Relationship |
|---|---|---|
| GDP | Aggarwal *et al.* (2011) and Fayissa and Nsiah (2012) | |
| MC | Bekaert and Harvey (1997), Bekaert *et al.* (2001), Levine and Zervos (1998) and Bilal *et al.* (2016) | + |
| VT | Bekaert and Harvey (1997), Bekaert *et al.* (2001) Levine and Zervos (1998) | + |
| FDI | Bilal *et al.* (2016) | + |
| TrO | Bilal *et al.* (2016) | + |
| INF | Bilal *et al.* (2016) | + |
| VNINDEX | Kajurová and Rozmahel (2016), Pan and Mishra (2016), Hoque and Yakob (2017) | + |

$$\ln VNIDEX_t = \beta_0 + \sum_{i=1}^{n} \beta_{1i} \ln VNIDEX_{t-i} + \sum_{i=1}^{n} \beta_{2i} \ln GDP_{t-i} + \varepsilon_t, \quad (3)$$

where

GDP : Annual economic growth (%).
MC : The rate of market capitalization and GDP.
VT : The rate of stock trade and GDP.
FDI : The rate of foreign direct investment and GDP.
TrO : Average traded openness.
INF : Average inflation.
VNINDEX : Vietnamese stock index.

This chapter assesses the impact of the stock market on Vietnam's economic growth with a quarterly time frame from the first quarter of 2008 to the fourth quarter of 2018. It also uses the stock index to evaluate how many economic periods are there in which the stock market affects economy growth at least once (see Table 1).

## 3. Results and Discussion

### 3.1. *Overview of ASEAN-5 countries from 2008 to 2018*

Figure 1 describes the GDP growth rates of ASEAN-5 countries. Thereby, Vietnam has the smallest change in GDP per year with the rate fluctuating around 6%. While Thailand has a higher GDP fluctuation in the group, ranging from 0.691 in 2009 to the highest rate, which was 7,514 in 2010, and which fluctuated continuously in the following years. Followed by Malaysia and the Philippines, where GDP growth rate has fluctuated in many periods from 2008 to 2012. As a matter of fact, in 2009 the growth rate of Malaysia and Thailand's GDP was negative.

Besides, the inflation rate of the countries in this period also shows many notable changes (see Figure 2). While the annual GDP growth rate has been quite stable, Vietnam has the most volatile consumer price index among the five ASEAN countries, especially in the period of 2008–2012. As the figure shows, the highest rate for Vietnam is in 2008 and 2011, which is around 23% and 18%, respectively. In

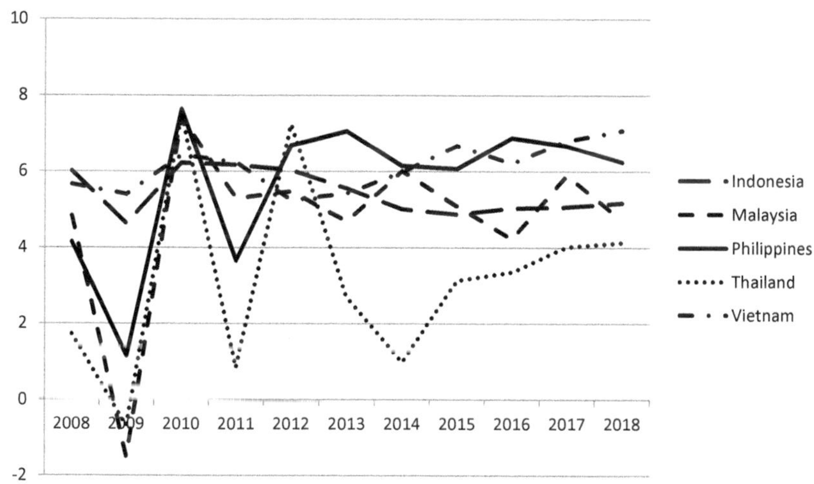


**Figure 1:** GDP of ASEAN-5 in 2008–2018 (unit: %).
*Source*: World Bank.

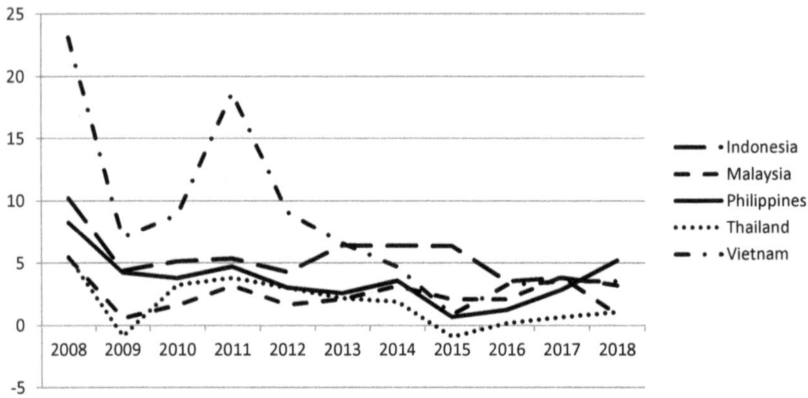


**Figure 2:** The inflation rate of ASEAN-5 in 2008–2018 (unit: %).
*Source*: World Bank.

contrast, in Thailand, although the growth rate of GDP has been uneven, the ability to control inflation in this country is quite stable and does not exceed 5% every year, which is similar to Malaysia. In the same period, Indonesia and Philippines have controlled inflation rate under 10%; however, that figure fluctuates around 5% in the following years.

As a result, post-crisis period affects the economy of ASEAN-5 because GDP growth and inflation rate fluctuate strongly and are predicted to change in the same direction from 2008 to 2012. Later, countries tried to restore and stabilize the economy with these less volatile indicators.

In addition, other indicators such as foreign direct investment and trade openness also contribute to reflect the overall picture of the economy. Figure 3 shows the rate of FDI on the GDP of the ASEAN-5 countries.

Figure 3 shows that Vietnam has the lowest rate. Moreover, Vietnam attracts a lot of foreign investment, which currently dominates GDP. The other countries account for a lower percentage, which ranges from just over 2%, to GDP. In general, in the recent period, the supply of FDI capital into ASEAN-5 countries has not changed much.

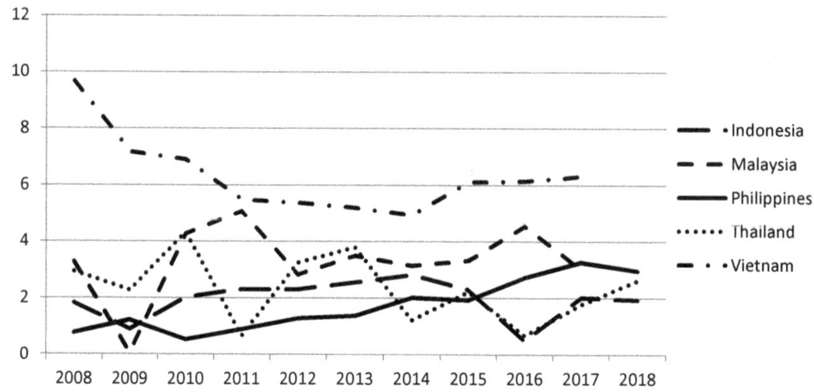


**Figure 3:** The rate FDI/GDP of ASEAN-5 in 2008–2018 (unit: % GDP).
*Source*: World Bank.

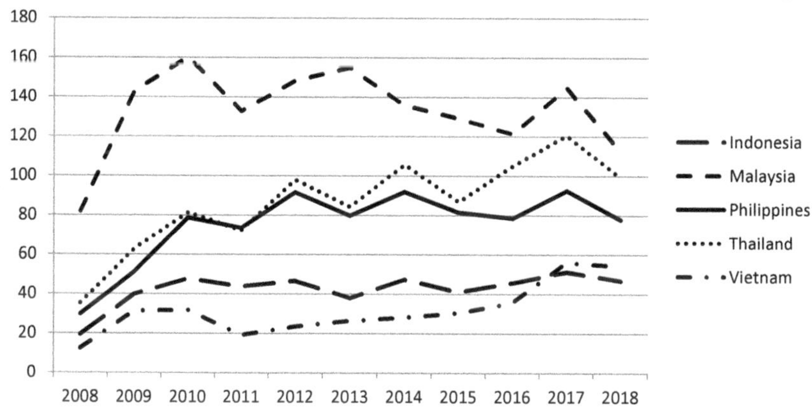


**Figure 4:** Market capitalization (%GDP) of ASEAN-5 in 2008–2018 (unit: %GDP).
*Source*: World Bank.

## 3.2. *Overview development of stock market in ASEAN-5 in 2008–2018*

Figure 4 describes the market capitalization of ASEAN-5 countries. It can be seen that Vietnam has the lowest market capitalization. In 2017, Vietnam's increased to 51.6% of GDP, like Indonesia. Malaysia and Thailand are the first and the second leading countries with a ratio of over 100% of GDP.

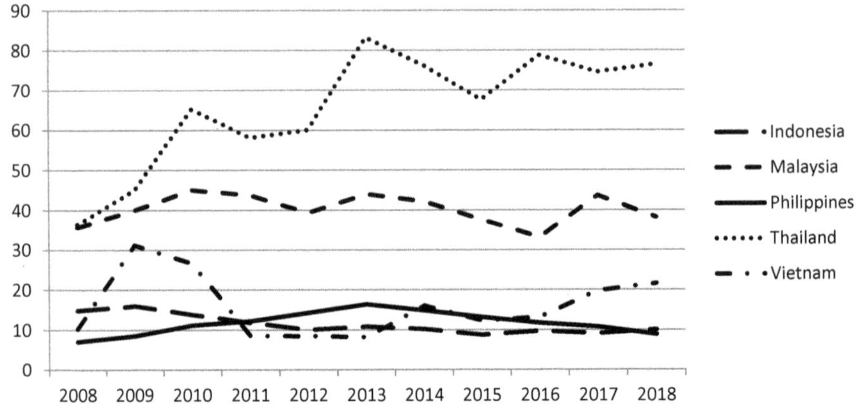


**Figure 5:** Stock trade of ASEAN-5 (unit: % GDP).
*Source*: World Bank.

With the value of stock trade, the leading countries are still Thailand and Malaysia (accounting for 50–85% of GDP). Vietnam is on par with the Philippines and Indonesia (approximately 10–20% of GDP). The details are shown in Figure 5.

### 3.3. *The relationship between economic growth and stock market in Vietnam in the period of 2008–2018*

In comparison with ASEAN-5 countries, although Vietnam has a fairly stable economy because the economic indicators do not fluctuate strongly and abnormally, the market capitalization and stock trade are still average and lower than in Thailand and Malaysia. However, when assessing the development of the domestic stock market from 2008 up to now, Vietnam's stock market has made outstanding achievements that reflect in the significant increase in the number of listed companies (Figure 6).

In 2011, there was an outstanding development of the Vietnam stock market when the number of listed stocks increased up to 744 companies, while there were only about 338 listed companies in 2008.

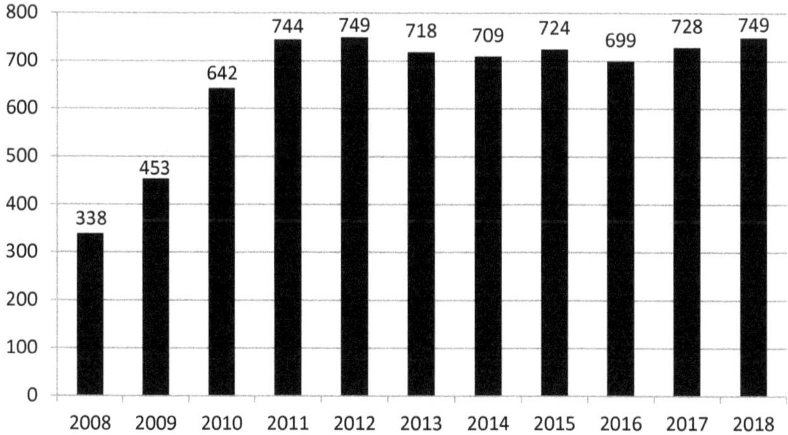


**Figure 6:** The number of listed companies in 2008–2018.
*Source*: State Securities Commission of Vietnam.

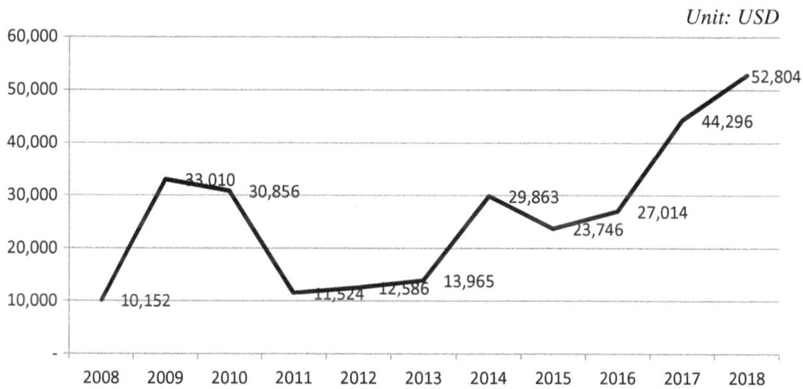


**Figure 7:** Total of stock trade in 2008–2018 (unit: USD).
*Source*: World Bank.

Since 2011, the number of listings has been relatively stable. In addition, the total value of transactions has increased significantly (see Figures 7 and 8).

*Unit: % GDP*

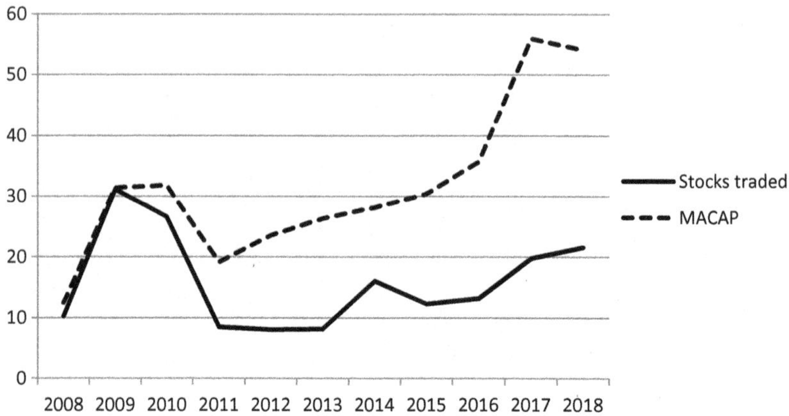


**Figure 8:** Market capitalization and stock trade in 2008–2018 (unit: % GDP). *Source*: World Bank.

## 3.4. *The research results*

### 3.4.1. *The impact of stock market on economic growth in ASEAN-5 countries*

In Table 2, the value of the variables is around the average value of the sample, except for observations, but not significant. The growth rate of Vietnam has been close to the average value in the larger dimension, reflecting that Vietnam has a fairly stable economy and good growth compared to the research group. However, the value of market capitalization and the value of stock trade of Vietnam are below the average of the group in the period of 2008–2017, proving that the Vietnam stock market does not really promote economic growth.

The value of the foreign investment in Vietnam is the highest in the observed group in the research period. It can be seen that Vietnam attracts a large amount of foreign direct investments. Trade openness is quite high and close to the average rate, reflecting that Vietnam has a trade deficit due to the remaining countries. Vietnam's inflation rate is also relatively stable and does not fluctuate as much as that of other countries, including Thailand and Malaysia.

**Table 2:** Descriptive statistics of variables.

| Variables | Mean | Max. | Min. | Std. Dev. |
|---|---|---|---|---|
| GDP | 4,9791 | 7,6320 | −1,5140 | 2,0785 |
| MC | 259,3591 | 548,7950 | 9,4810 | 163,1323 |
| VT | 28,3783 | 83,2460 | 5,5270 | 22,8621 |
| FDI | 3,1024 | 9,6630 | 0,0570 | 2,0510 |
| TrO | 1,0382 | 1,2893 | 0,7513 | 0,1309 |
| INF | 4,4245 | 23,1160 | −0,9000 | 4,2163 |

**Table 3:** VIF variance results.

| Variables | VIF | 1/VIF |
|---|---|---|
| MC | 1.69 | 0.5901 |
| VT | 1.88 | 0.5306 |
| FDI | 1.41 | 0.7083 |
| TrO | 1.75 | 0.5704 |
| INF | 1.64 | 0.6108 |
| Mean VIF | 1.68 | |

Table 3 shows the results of multicollinearity testing between variables. The factor VIF variance is less than 2.5, indicating that the multicollinearity phenomenon between variables is negligible.

Table 4 presents the reliable estimation of the effect of the stock market on economic growth of ASEAN-5 countries.

#### 3.4.1.1. Assessing the impact of the stock market on economic growth

The reliable results (1% significance level) indicate that the MC variable has a positive impact on GDP. The implication of an increase in MC helps higher economic growth. In contrast, the value of stock trade, variable VT, has a negative correlation with GDP. As this variable increases, the impact on the economic growth of the research group increases.

**Table 4:** Dynamic panel regression analysis.

| **Variable** | **GDP** |
|---|---|
| MC | $0.0053^{***}$ |
| | (2.70) |
| VT | $-0.0376^{**}$ |
| | (−2.53) |
| FDI | $0.492^{***}$ |
| | (3.42) |
| TrO | $-4.641^{*}$ |
| | (−1.87) |
| INF | −0.0564 |
| | (−0.75) |
| _cons | $8.174^{***}$ |
| | (3.39) |

*Notes*: $t$ statistics in parentheses $^{*}p < 0.1$, $^{**}p < 0.05$, $^{***}p < 0.01$.

#### 3.4.1.2. Assessing the impact of other variables on economic growth

The FDI variable has a positive correlation with GDP, indicating that the country attracting more and more foreign direct investments fosters economic growth. TrO variables have a negative impact on GDP, reflecting that ASEAN countries' expanding trade does not improve economic growth. The INF variable is not statistically significant, indicating that there is no clear empirical evidence of the significant impact of inflation on economic growth in the ASEAN-5 countries.

### 3.4.2. *Research results on effects of the stock market on Vietnam's economic growth*

With a series of data from the first quarter of 2008 to the fourth quarter of 2018, the study uses the ADF testing method to determine stopability, co-integration testing through Johansen method to investigate whether there exists a long-term relationship between variable GDP and VNINDEX. Granger inspection is to determine the degree of influence of variables in the short term, and the error correction

**Table 5:** ADF test results of GRGDP.

| | **Test statistic** | **1% Critical value** | **5% Critical value** | **10% Critical value** |
|---|---|---|---|---|
| $Z(t)$ | –3.317 | –2.405 | –1.677 | –1.299 |

*Note*: $p$-value for $Z(t) = 0.0009$.

**Table 6:** ADF test results of VNINDEX at level 3.

| | **Test statistic** | **1% Critical value** | **5% Critical value** | **10% Critical value** |
|---|---|---|---|---|
| $Z(t)$ | –4.001 | –3.594 | –2.936 | –2.602 |

*Note*: $p$ value for $Z(t) = 0.0014$.

model is to monitor the adjustment process of the Vietnam stock market from the short-term state towards long-term equilibrium. The test results show that the GDP and the VNINDEX stop at level 3.

Tables 5 and 6 show that the absolute value of the statistical test is greater than the critical value at 10%, 5%, or 1% significance level. The ADF test results show that GDP is a stop chain.

The selection of the optimal delay for the model is made by applying the VAR model to the initial data series of the variables with a lag of 5. The model automatically selects the optimal delay according to the criteria LR, FPE, AIC, SC, HQ.

According to test results, the selected delay is 1 according to FPE, AIC, SC, and HQ criteria. Next, the research conducts the VAR model according to the latency of 1 (Table 7). The study uses Granger test to test the causal relationship between economic growth and stock index. The test results show that there exists an impact relationship of VNINDEX on GDP, but it is not meaningful to the equation of GDP impact on VNINDEX. This proves that the stock index has a significant impact on Vietnam's economic growth. However, GDP has a very weak relationship with VNINDEX (Table 8).

**Table 7:** Latency results of Var model.

| Lag | LogL | LR | FPE | AIC | SC | HQ |
|---|---|---|---|---|---|---|
| 0 | 19.2304 | | 0.001647 | −0.73321 | −0.65448 | −0.703583 |
| 1 | 60.8679 | 83.279 | 0.000332* | −2.33488** | −2.09869* | −2.246** |
| 2 | 64.8592 | 7.9789 | 0.000333 | −2.33443 | −1.94078 | −2.1863 |
| 3 | 67.9821 | 6.2458 | 0.000346 | −2.29711 | −1.746 | −2.08972 |
| 4 | 80.9788 | 25.993 | 0.000237 | −2.67995 | −1.97138 | −2.41331 |
| 5 | 89.1612 | 16.365* | 0.002 | −2.85792 | −1.9919 | −2.53203 |

*Notes*: $^{*}p < 0.1$, $^{**}p < 0.05$, $^{***}p < 0.01$.

**Table 8:** Granger test of GDP and VNINDEX.

| Equation | Excluded | $\chi^2$ | df | Prob > $\chi^2$ |
|---|---|---|---|---|
| GRGDP | VNINDEX | 17.59 | 3 | 0.001 |
| GRGDP | ALL | 17.59 | 3 | 0.001 |
| VNINDEX | GRGDP | 2.2174 | 3 | 0.529 |
| VNINDEX | ALL | 2.2174 | 3 | 0.529 |

With regard to the relationship between economic growth and VNINDEX, although the stock market is a significant capital mobilization channel that contributes to building investment capital for growth, the economy does not affect the securities activities as expected. As a result, investors are interested in other information affecting the investment behavior on the stock market rather than the GDP.

## 4. Conclusion and Experiences for Vietnam

### 4.1. *Conclusion*

This chapter confirms with reliable results the important role of the stock market in the economic development of Asian countries, including Vietnam.

### 4.2. *Experiences for Vietnam*

(1) There can be a two-way relationship between stock market development and economic growth. It means that in a stable economic country, the development of the stock market has a positive impact on economic growth. This is a valuable experience for Vietnam to facilitate economic growth through the stock market channel. The country must prepare necessary prerequisites to stabilize the economy through construction and development institutions and legal systems.
(2) Deriving from FDI research a positive correlation to GDP, Vietnam needs to continue implementing policies to attract FDI. So, for the transparency of the financial market and a stable political economy, it is important to avoid capital withdrawal from the market that causes complicated consequences.
(3) The average market capitalization value of the stock market has a positive impact on GDP. It means that increasing capitalization in the market contributes positively to GDP growth. Therefore, finding out solutions to develop the stock market is necessary.
(4) Stock trading value is negatively correlated with GDP. The increase in the value of transactions in the market restrains economic growth. In Vietnam, increases in the stock price affect GDP. Therefore, the policies must aim at stable economic development because any economic shock pushes the stock price resulting in loss of control.
(5) The results of the research in ASEAN-5 countries show that inflation has no impact on GDP, but the level of inflation growth of the countries has been quite stable. In recent years, significant inflation in Vietnam has influenced economic growth.

In conclusion, it is necessary to set up a synchronous policy to ensure the development of the Vietnamese stock market, which is a basis to promote economic growth.

## References


Aggarwal, R., Demirgüç-Kunt, A., and Peía, M.S.M. (2011). Do remittances promote financial development? *Journal of Development Economics*, 96(2), 255–264.

Ahmed, S.N., and Ansari, M.I. (1998). Financial sector development and economic growth: The South-Asian experience. *Journal of Asian Economics*, 9(3), 503–517.

Atje, R., and Jovanovic, B. (1993). Stock markets and development. *European Economic Review*, 37, 632–640.

Azarmi, T., Lazar, D., and Jeyapaul, J. (2005). Is the Indian stock market a casino? *Journal of Business and Economics Research*, 3(4), 63–72.

Balago, G.S. (2014). Financial sector development and economic growth in Nigeria: An empirical investigation. *International Journal of Finance and Accounting*, 3(4), 253–265.

Bekaert, G., and Harvey, C.R. (1997). Emerging equity market volatility. *Journal of financial Economics*, 43(1), 29–77.

Bekaert, G., Harvey, C. R., and Lundblad, C. (2001). Emerging equity markets and economic development. *Journal of Development Economics*, 66(2), 465–504.

Bencivenga, V.R., Bruce D.S., and Ross, M.S. (1996). Equity markets, transactions costs, and capital accumulation: An illustration. *The World Bank Economic Review*, 10(2), 241–265.

Bilal, Chen, S., and Kormal, B. (2016). Impact of stock market development on economic growth: Evidence from income countries. *Management and Administrative Science Review*, 5(2), 86–97.

Boubakari, A., and Jin, D. (2010). The role of stock market development in economic growth: Evidence from lower middle incomes Euronext countries. *International Journal of Financial Research*, 1(1), 14–20.

Fayissa, B., and Nsiah, C. (2012). Financial Development and Remittances in Africa and the Americas: A Panel Unit-Root Tests and Panel Cointegration Analysis.

Harris, R. (1997). Stock market and development: A re-assessment. *European Economic Review*, 41, 139–146.

Hoque, M. E. and Yakob, N. A. (2017). Revisiting stock market development and economic growth nexus: The moderating role of foreign capital inflows and exchange rates. *Cogent Economics & Finance*, 5(1), 1329975.

Kajurová, V., and Rozmahel, P. (2016). Stock market development and economic growth: Evidence from the European Union. *Acta Universitatis Agriculturae et Silviculturae Mendelianae Brunensis*, 64(6), 1927–1936.

Levine, R. (1991). Stock market, growth and tax policy. *Journal of Finance*, 46, 1445–1465.

Levine, R., and Zervos, S. (1996). Stock market development and long run growth. *World Bank Economic Review*, 10(2), 323–339.

Levine, R., and Zervos, S. (1998). Stock markets, banks, and economic growth. *American Economic Review*, 537–558.

Masoud, N., and Hardaker, G. (2012). The impact of financial development on economic growth. *Studies in Economics and Finance*, 29(3), 148–173.

Mayer, C. (1988). New issues in corporate finance. *European Economic Review*, 32, 1167–1188.

Owusu, E.L., and Odhiambo, N.M. (2014). Stock market development and economic growth in Ghana: An ARDL-bounds testing approach. *Applied Economics Letters*, 21(4), 229–234.

Pan, L., and Mishra, V. (2018). Stock market development and economic growth: Empirical evidence from China. *Economic Modelling*, 68, 661–673.

Singh, A. (1997). Financial liberalization, Stock markets and economic development. *The Economic Journal*, 107, 771–782.

Tang, H.P., Habibullah, M.S., and Chin-Hong, P. (2007). Stock market and economic growth in selected Asian countries. RePEc:PRA:MPRAPA: 37649.

Wang, B., and Ajit, D. (2013). Stock market and economic growth in China. *Economics Bulletin*, 33(1), 95–103.

https://doi.org/10.1142/9789811227158_0004

# Chapter 4

# Exploring the Intention to Adopt Management Accounting System in the Public Sector: An Empirical Investigation of Public Non-Income Generating Agencies

**Quang Huy Pham and Kien Phuc Vu**

## Abstract

This research is to explore and validate the components and factors that affect the intention to adopt (ITA) management accounting systems (MAS) among public non-income generating agencies (PNGAs) in one of the provinces in Vietnam. This study employs primary data from a survey of 436 accountants working in these entities. Quantitative analysis methods applied to test the hypothesis in the research included Cronbach's Alpha reliability analysis, exploratory factor analysis (EFA), confirmatory factor analysis (CFA), and structural equation models (SEMs). The results show that perceived usefulness (PU), perceived ease of use (PEOU), perceived financial cost (PFC) play important roles in affecting ITA of MAS. In addition, many group analyzes (MGA) of SEM are conducted to test the moderation effect of leadership on the relationship between PU, PEOU, PFC, and ITA. Despite some limitations, the findings of this study not only serve as a reference for PNGAs regarding application of MAS through better understanding the motivations and barriers in MAS implementation but also for the providers in seeking an effective way to approach the basic needs of potential customers.

**Keywords:** Management accounting system; Public non-income generating agency; Technology acceptance model.

## 1. Introduction

Management accounting system (MAS) can be the best method to help all organizations cope with their organizational and environmental conditions (Etemadi *et al.*, 2009; Hoque, 2011) through providing helpful information for planning, controlling, monitoring, and decision-making (Soobaroyen and Poorundersing, 2008; Ismail and Isa, 2011). Meanwhile, well-designed and sophisticated MAS provides managers with suitable information for setting performance objectives, performance assessment standards, and feedback to enhance managerial performance (MP).

With regard to the benefits of MAS adoption and the differences in implementing modern management accounting methods and techniques between developed and developing countries due to different national and organizational conditions (Etemadi *et al.*, 2009; Van Helden and Uddin, 2016), research on MAS has come a long way in accounting for determinants of applying MAS among the entities (Chenhall and Langfield-Smith, 1998; Al-Omiri and Drury, 2007; Halbouni and Nour, 2014; Leite *et al.*, 2015; Anh, 2016). Upon each empirical examination, there is a diversity of critical factors concluded to have a significant influence on the adoption depending on the context and the method of research applied. Surprisingly, most of the studies on MAS mainly focus on private sector organizations, hence they do not provide enough useful insights for the public sector, especially PNGAs, although MAS is supposed to be a suitable tool to adapt and to apply autonomy effectively in PNGAs. In addition, on October 25, 2017, the Vietnam Party Central Committee released the 19 resolution-NQ/TW on renovating the organization and administration system and improving the performance of the PNGAs, which asserted the role and importance of the PNGAs among other economic entities of the national economy; therefore, renovation of their operation mechanism becomes essential in the context of reducing state budget constraints (Nguyen, 2018).

In response to the need for more studies on MAS among PNGAs, this research provides some insights into the construct of the intention of MAS adoption. With the view that adoption can be regarded as the initial step for continued use to take place, the researchers expect the contribution of the study can serve in several aspects. First, the introduction of MAS enhances better understanding of the benefits of adopting MAS, especially in the midst of rapid technological changes and the request for autonomy among the PNGAs. Moreover, an increase in knowledge can lead to changes in behavior (Fabrigar *et al.*, 2006). In other words, the more the intentions are based on full knowledge, the better the outcomes can be predicted. Following this logic, knowledge about MAS is important in explaining the choices of adoption among PNGAs. Secondly, with the aim to introduce a model based on new determinants to predict intention of MAS adoption, the research not only focuses on the attitudes of PNGAs when they adopt a new system but also examines whether the relationships between the attitudes of PNGAs and their adoption intention of MAS change under different levels of leadership or not. Thirdly, apart from implications shedding light for future research, the implications of MAS adoption are presented based on users' behaviors, values, and costing, and can serve as a reference for PNGAs and for the providers in finding effective methods to catch the attention of the potential customers.

The rest of this study is organized as follows. Section 2 presents a theoretical background, hypotheses, and research model. Section 3 proposes a methodology and experimental setup. The result is highlighted in Section 4. Based on these results, the researchers draw conclusions and present implications to develop future research in the last section.

## 2. Theoretical Background, Hypotheses, and Research Model

### 2.1. *Extended TAM*

TAM, proposed by Davis (1989) and Davis *et al.* (1989), is adapted from the theory of reasoned action, and is widely applied by many scholars and practitioners to determine users' intentions towards the adoption of new technology. This model is originally conceived to model the implementation of information systems (IS) in the workplace (Bhattacherjee, 2001a, 2001b; Bhattacherjee and Premkumar, 2004; Yang *et al.*, 2012; Gao and Bai, 2014). The purpose of TAM is to confirm the impact of external variables on internal variables such as attitudes and intentions (Legris *et al.*, 2003; Kwon and Wen, 2010). The two particular beliefs proposed in this model, PU and PEOU (Davis *et al.*, 1989), have direct positive effects on measured usage (Wallace and Sheetz, 2014).

### 2.1.1. *Perceived ease of use*

PEOU is considered as one of the main beliefs in the framework of TAM and conceptualized as the degree to which a person believes that using a particular system would be effortless (Davis, 1989). Thus, the PNGAs are more likely to adopt MAS if they perceive it to be easy to use and does not involve too much hassle to operate. In other words, the easier the MAS is to learn and use, the more the likelihood of it being adopted by the organizations. Meanwhile, many studies over the past decade prove the evidence regarding the critical effect of PEOU on intention, either directly or indirectly with its effect on PU (Davis *et al.*, 1989; Agarwal and Prasad, 1999; Venkatesh and Morris, 2000; Yang, 2005; Yang *et al.*, 2012). Therefore, we postulate the following:

**Hypothesis H1:** *PEOU has a significant positive impact on PU of adoption.*

**Hypothesis H2:** *PEOU has a significant positive impact on PNGAs' intentions to adopt MAS.*

### 2.1.2. *Perceived usefulness*

Within the framework of TAM, users' ITA information technology is predicated largely on their PU of the system (Davis, 1989; Davis *et al.*, 1989). In the context of MAS, the users adopt the system if they keep in view that the system brings benefits such as using MAS enables them to accomplish tasks more effectively; improves the organizations' performance; and gives the organization greater control over the work. On the contrary, users would refuse to use a system in case they believe their job performance can be decreased by using it (Buabeng-Andoh, 2018). Hence, in accordance with TAM, the following hypothesis is suggested:

**Hypothesis H3:** *PU has a significant positive impact on PNGAs' intentions to adopt MAS.*

### 2.1.3. *Perceived financial cost*

According to previous empirical research, PU and PEOU are not the only beliefs that mediate the impact of the external environment on attitude and intentions (Alsajjan and Dennis, 2010). In response to this limitation, many scholars have focused on the extension of TAM by including additional variables to enhance its specificity, predictability, and explanatory power (Davis *et al.*, 1989; Chin and Gopal, 1995; Karahanna and Limayem, 2000; Legris *et al.*, 2003; Venkatesh *et al.*, 2003; Çelik, 2008; Lee, 2009; Chong *et al.*, 2010; Chiou and Shen, 2012). Considering this, with aims to ascertain what factors considerably affect the organization to adopt MAS, the additional construct that is taken into the research structure is PFC. PFC is the extent to which the users believe that applying MAS would be costlier than other options. In other words, if MAS fails to deliver at a suitable cost, then it has a negative effect on the TAM. Therefore, this study hypothesizes the following:

**Hypothesis H4:** *PFC has a significant negative impact on PNGAs' intentions to adopt MAS.*

## 2.2. *Management accounting systems*

In uncertain environments, the achievement of useful information leads to enhance resource allocation and raises the possibility of an improved positive outcome (Hammad *et al.*, 2010). In other words, a conditional association presumes that useful information assists managers to make effective decisions and improves MP (Baines and Langfield-Smith, 2003; Chenhall, 2003; Hammad *et al.*, 2010). Well-designed and sophisticated MAS is likely to supply managers with information suitable for setting performance objectives, performance assessment standards, and feedback on performance leading to enhanced MP. MAS is considered sophisticated when it produces information that is broad in scope, has high timeliness, high aggregation, and integration (Moores and Yuen, 2001; Rasid *et al.*, 2011).

As mentioned above, the characteristics of MAS applied in the research are based on the findings of Chenhall and Morris (1986) which include scope, timeliness, aggregation, and integration. According to Chenhall and Morris (1986), scope, which is relevant to the focus, quantification, and time horizon of the information, could limit or enlarge depending on whether the information coming in is internal or external to the organization, financial or non-financial, and past- or future-oriented. Timeliness refers to how immediately the information can be supplied upon request. While the categorization of information by time period or functional area is defined as aggregation, functional boundaries that help coordinate various segments within a sub-unit are referred to as integration characteristics of MAS.

The rapid technological innovations largely change the external environment of organizations and consecutively affect the internal processes like MAS (Mat *et al.*, 2010; Urquidi and Ripoll, 2013). Information technology comprises information and communication technology equipment systems as well as accounting software (Ismail and King, 2007). The application of accounting software in accounting releases many advantages as accountants are just responsible for checking the legality and validity of accounting documents and analyzing the output information (Nguyen, 2010). Therefore, such advances in technologies like information technology (IT) and computerization also lead the flows of management accounting information (MAI) in organizations to be more integrated, timely, accurate, and relevant (Granlund, 2011).

**Hypothesis H5:** *MAS positively affects PEOU of adoption.*

Viewed as an integral part of a business's information and control systems, a sophisticated MAS (broad in scope, timely, integrated, and aggregated) is able to provide essential information for managers to make decisions that enhance performance of management (Mia and Patiar, 2001; Hoque, 2011; Santos *et al.*, 2012; McManus, 2013).

Furthermore, technology is supposed to have significant influences on scope and aggregation of MAS through providing aggregated financial or non-financial information from different parts of the entities, information from inside or outside, and related to historical or current events in a timely manner (Mia and Winata, 2008; Zawawi and Hoque, 2010; Granlund, 2011). Moreover, MAI in organizations is more valuable, timely, accurate, and relevant with the support of advances in technologies like information technology and computerization (Granlund, 2011). For that reason, this system is always considered as an effective tool for the staff undertaking accounting work.

**Hypothesis H6:** *MAS positively affects PU of adoption.*

Although the adoption of new systems can bring so many advantages to the entities, it still raises costs. The organizations have to organize equipment, technical facilities to provide a training program for accountants so that they can use the equipment proficiently, effectively, and conduct the right to access and update the information to ensure the confidentiality of accounting information. Moreover, security concerns, lack of standards, regulations, and the very complexity of the industry's network structure (Zhu *et al.*, 2004) also increase the cost if the adoption is approved.

**Hypothesis H7:** *MAS negatively affects PFC of adoption.*

### 2.3. *Moderating effects of leadership*

With the highly regarded attribution in various organizations, the aspect of leadership is an indispensable aspect for almost all employers in both the public and private sectors, especially in the era of globalization (Lee, 2000). Besides, the PNGAs' leaders are stipulated to be responsible for organizing and guiding the implementation of accounting work following the law on accounting (Law No 88. 2015). PNGAs' leaders are increasingly viewed as key in the mechanism's widespread efforts to promote autonomy for improvement. This releases leaders out of boundary spanners, operating between the organizations and the larger policy environment, and transmitting their aligned (or misaligned) values, ideas, and rules. Considering these, PNGAs' leaders should take into account aspects including strategic capabilities (SCs) and dynamic capabilities (DCs).

### 2.3.1. *Strategic capabilities*

SCs of the organization can lie in its resource dimensions, operating functions, or its "networks of interdependence within the firm, between the firm and in its environment" (Lenz, 1980, p. 226). According to Simon *et al.* (2015), a capability must consist of three distinctive characteristics to possess strategic import despite an organization's possession of many basic skills or capabilities to function efficiently, including the value to the customer, the organization's capability to do better than its competitors, and the SCs being difficult to imitate or replicate (Hubbard and Beamish, 2011). The costs incurred when applying the new system consist of the initial purchase price, equipment cost, repair or updating charges. In general, the leaders with higher SCs are more apt to be the early adopters. They also manage to find financial resources to apply the new system and put up with technologically inconvenient factors to do with technological complexity, the financial cost of adoption, and finding out new experiences because the long-term benefits are their top concern. Therefore, this study hypothesizes as follows:

**Hypothesis H8a:** *SCs positively moderate the effect of PEOU on the ITA MAS.*

**Hypothesis H8b:** *SCs positively moderate the effect of PU on the ITA MAS.*

**Hypothesis H8c:** *SCs negatively moderate the effect of PFC on the ITA MAS.*

### 2.3.2. *Dynamic capabilities*

DCs are a set of specific and identifiable processes such as product development, strategic decision-making, and alliancing (Eisenhardt and Martin, 2000). In this respect, leaders tend to identify DCs through seeking appropriate ways of improving performance or just enabling these identified capabilities and managing any on-going tensions arising as part of the reconfiguration process instead. DCs can moderate the effects of the organizations' perceptions of their adoption intention. The leaders with higher DCs are more likely to have a stronger ITA MAS for the same level of perceptions about the MAS. They are more likely to be involved in the new MAS and tend to put up with the financial cost of applying the new system, perceive the relative advantages of the new system, and further adopt the new system in comparison to those with low DCs. Hence, this study hypothesizes as follows:

**Hypothesis H9a:** *DCs positively moderate the effect of PEOU on the ITA MAS.*

**Hypothesis H9b:** *DCs positively moderate the effect of PU on the ITA MAS.*

**Hypothesis H9c:** *DCs negatively moderate the effect of PFC on the ITA MAS.*

## 2.4. *Research model*

The research model based on the extended TAM with MAS, which presents one leadership moderator leading to the intention of adopting MAS in Vinh Long PNCAs, is depicted in Figure 1.

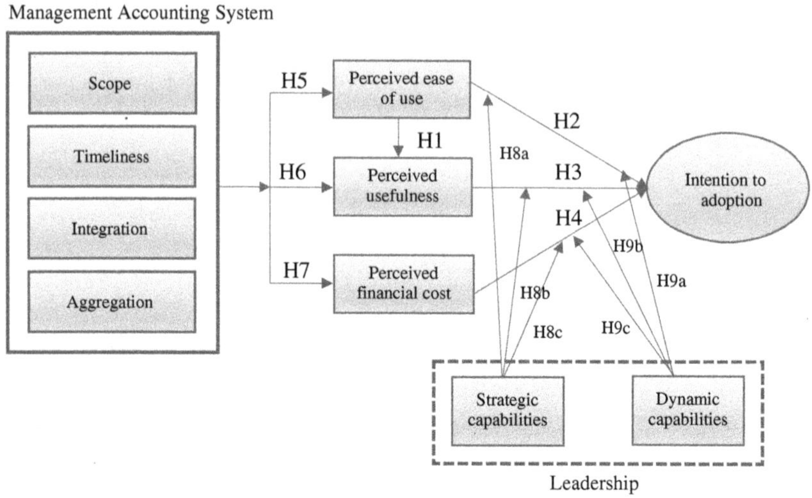


**Figure 1:** Proposed research model.

## 3. Proposed Methodology and Experimental Setup

### 3.1. *Procedure*

The translation and back-translation process is used to develop a Vietnamese version of the scale. Besides, to ensure the validity and contribute to the improvement in the structure and layout of the questionnaire, two experts with experience of applying MAS among Vinh Long PNGAs conducted the pilot test. They were requested not only to review the descriptive and the objective questions and provide their feedback but also to check any ambiguity or misleading information. As a result, the items and questions in the proposed questionnaire were adjusted, and a structured questionnaire was developed for the collection of primary data. These questionnaires were provided from December in 2018 to March in 2019 and were personally collected by the researchers.

### 3.2. *Data collection*

Quota sampling procedure followed in the survey was based on the numbers of areas among Vinh Long PNGAs. Once the SEM technique is applied for analytical procedures, it can concern various overall fit indices and the selection of the appropriate approach (Lei and Wu, 2007). In this respect, a "critical sample size" of 200 is proposed by Sivo *et al.* (2006) and Hoelter (1983) to provide sufficient statistical power for data analysis. While according to Bollen (1989) it is sufficient to have a minimum of five samples, there is an agreement among many scholars that the sample size must be 10–20 times the number of observed variables (Hair *et al.*, 2010; Kline, 2011; Harrell, 2015). Therefore, the minimum sample size needed for this study was 410 for the estimation of the theoretical model containing 41 parameters. Finally, 436 complete responses were obtained because some of them were erroneous and incomplete. There were some regions that could not reach the target number, but not significantly (i.e., Binhminh; Binhtan; Mangthit); therefore, the survey sample was considered as a representative of the whole and the results of this sample are also the results focusing on the ITA the MAS among Vinh Long PNGAs.

### 3.3. *Measurements of variables*

In this research, constructs were measured using multiple items validated in prior literature and modified to fit the context of MAS adoption. The 5-point Likert scale was employed in this research as a psychometric scale that is used to capture the responses from the respondents and produce a reliable and valid outcome (Zikmund *et al.*, 2010). Table 1 describes a sample questionnaire comprising all 41 attributes.

- **Independent variable:** Six items on Scope (Chenhall and Morris, 1986; Cheng, 2012; Etemadi *et al.*, 2009; Susanto, 2010; Chung *et al.*, 2012); four items on Timeliness (Chenhall and Morris, 1986; Agbejule, 2005; Etemadi *et al.*, 2009; Susanto, 2010); four items on Integration (Chenhall and Morris, 1986; Agbejule, 2005; Bouwens and Abernethy, 2000); six items on Aggregation (Chenhall and Morris, 1986; Bouwens and Abernethy, 2000; Agbejule, 2005).

**Table 1:** Measures and items.

| Construct | Measurement items |
|---|---|
| **Scope** | |
| SCOP1 | Information corresponds to possible future events |
| SCOP2 | Qualification of the likelihood of future events appears |
| SCOP3 | Non-economic information including customer preferences, employee attitudes are focused |
| SCOP4 | Information associates with broad factors external to the organization |
| SCOP5 | Non-financial information refers to the productivity |
| SCOP6 | Non-financial information relates to market information |
| **Timeliness** | |
| TIME1 | Information that is provided immediately as requested |
| TIME2 | Information that is purveyed automatically immediately |
| TIME3 | Reports that are supplied regularly on a systematic, regular basis |
| TIME4 | Relevant information is reported without delay right after the appearance of the event |
| **Integration** | |
| INTE1 | Information on the precise goal of the activities of all departments within the organization |
| INTE2 | Information relates to the influence on different departments' decisions on the performance of the organization |
| INTE3 | Cost and price information of the departments are provided suitably |
| INTE4 | Information on the impact of decisions on the organization, and the influence of other departments' decisions on responsible areas |
| **Aggregation** | |
| AGGR1 | Information supplied in the different sections or functional areas in the organization |
| AGGR2 | Information has affected events on particular time periods |
| AGGR3 | Information has been processed to show the effect of events on different functions |
| AGGR4 | Information on the effect of different departments' activities on summary reports |

*(Continued)*

**Table 1:** (*Continued*)

| Construct | Measurement items |
|---|---|
| AGGR5 | Information has been formatted suitably for input into decision models |
| AGGR6 | Information in forms enable managers to conduct "what-if" analysis |
| **Perceived ease of use** | |
| PEOU1 | Interacting with MAS does not request a lot of organization mental effort |
| PEOU2 | It would be easy for the organization to become skillful at using MAS |
| PEOU3 | MAS is considered to be easy to use |
| **Perceived usefulness** | |
| PU1 | Using MAS enables the responsible department to accomplish tasks more effectively |
| PU2 | Using MAS improves the organizations' performance |
| PU3 | Using MAS gives the organization greater control over the work |
| **Perceived financial cost** | |
| PFC1 | Using MAS is a cost burden to the organization |
| PFC2 | The device setup to using MAS in the organization costs lots of money |
| PFC3 | The fee to update the software is expensive for the organization |
| **Intention to adopt** | |
| ITU1 | Our organization intends to adopt MAS in the future |
| ITU2 | Our organization aims to adopt MAS in the future |
| ITU3 | Our organization plans to adopt MAS in the future |
| **Strategic capabilities** | |
| STR1 | Good leadership and vision |
| STR2 | Selection and retention of good staff |
| STR3 | Adaptability/flexibility |
| STR4 | Innovation and creativity |
| **Dynamic capabilities** | |
| DYN1 | Strategic thinking |
| DYN2 | Flexible leadership |
| DYN3 | Networks and alliances |
| DYN4 | Knowledge management |
| DYN5 | Technology flexibility |

- **Dependent variable:** Three items on PEOU (Davis, 1989; Davis *et al.*, 1989); three items on PU (Davis *et al.*, 1989; Wu *et al.*, 2007); three items on PFC (Luarn and Lin, 2005; Sripalawat *et al.*, 2011); three items on ITA (Davis *et al.*, 1989; Davis, 1993).
- **Moderating variable:** Three items on SCs (Moffat and Simon, 2011; Sarasvathy and Dew, 2013); five items on DCs (von Krogh *et al.*, 2001; Simon, 2010).

### 3.4. *Statistical data analysis*

An initial screening of each scale was conducted using item-total correlations (Cronbach's Alpha) and EFA through using SPSS 25.0. CFA was applied to assess the psychometric properties of the scales and test the discriminant validity of the measures, and SEM was conducted through AMOS 22.0. Maximum likelihood (ML) estimation procedures were used because these afford more security in samples which cannot present multivariate normality (Muthen and Kaplan, 1985). Besides, the MGA is performed in this research for the examination of the existence of the moderating effects on the research model.

## 4. Result

### 4.1. *Descriptive characteristics of the usable respondents*

Among the 436 usable respondents, 105 respondents (24.08%) are males, and 331 respondents (75.92%) are females. The distribution of age is as follows: From 20 to under 30 (9.63%), from 30 to under 40 (33.03%), from 40 to under 50 (44.72%), 50–60 (12.29%). Educational levels are generally high. Respondents who completed junior college numbered 15.60%, while respondents who completed university numbered 84.40% of the survey sample. Additionally, the distribution of duration of the experience (the respondents' experience in working as an accountant) is as follows: under 3 years (11.47%), 3 to under 6 years (19.27%), 6 to under 9 years (23.85%), and over 9 years (45.41%).

### 4.2. *Results of structural modeling analysis*

#### 4.2.1. *Analysis of measurement model*

The construct validity is the extent to which a set of measured variables actually represents the theoretical latent constructs those are designed to measure (Hair *et al.*, 2010, p. 631). Thus, CFA was applied to purify the measurement model and to assess the convergent and discriminant validity. Cronbach's Alpha was calculated to analyze the internal consistency of the construct and its reliability. There were six observed variables of the scales with Corrected Item — Total Correlation under 0.30 deleted, provided this does not affect the meaning of the construct. Apart from factor loadings (standardized estimates), Average Variance Extracted (AVE) and Composite Reliability (CR) for each construct were used in this study to test the reliability of all constructs (Nunnally, 1978; Hair *et al.*, 1998; Byrne, 2001; Holmes-Smith, 2001). The results presented in Table 2 demonstrate an acceptable level of reliability for all constructs.

The procedure described by Fornell and Larcker (1981) is used to test for discriminant validity in this study. The AVE for all variables exceeds the suggested value of 0.50, implying that the variance captured by the construct is significantly greater than that attributable to error. Additionally, AVE measures for all constructs are much larger than the square of the correlation between them providing overall evidence of discriminant validity (Fornell and Larcker, 1981). These values are reported on the diagonal of Table 3.

Third, the overall fit indices of measurement model are $df = 584$, $\chi^2/df = 1.275$, $p < 0.001$, GFI $= 0.919$, TLI $= 0.975$, CFI $= 0.978$, and RMSEA $= 0.025$. Thus, the results of CFA show that the indices are over their respective common acceptance levels as stated by Bagozzi and Yi (1988), Hair *et al.* (1998), and Byrne (2001).

#### 4.2.2. *Analysis of structural model*

##### 4.2.2.1. Structural model

The following step is to test the structural model for the research, the overall fit indices for the structural model are $df = 339$,

**Table 2:** Reliability and convergent validity assessment.

| Variables | Item | Indicator reliability (factor loadings) | Convergent validity average variance extracted, (AVE) | Construct reliability | | Discriminant validity |
|---|---|---|---|---|---|---|
| | | | | Cronbach's Alpha (CA) | Composite reliability (CR) | |
| Scope | SCOP1 | 0.755 | 0.511 | 0.839 | 0.839 | Yes |
| | SCOP2 | 0.712 | | | | |
| | SCOP3 | 0.732 | | | | |
| | SCOP4 | 0.622 | | | | |
| | SCOP5 | 0.748 | | | | |
| Timeliness | TIME1 | 0.786 | 0.620 | 0.862 | 0.867 | Yes |
| | TIME2 | 0.706 | | | | |
| | TIME3 | 0.848 | | | | |
| | TIME4 | 0.808 | | | | |
| Integration | INTE1 | 0.807 | 0.669 | 0.858 | 0.858 | Yes |
| | INTE2 | 0.791 | | | | |
| | INTE4 | 0.859 | | | | |
| Aggregation | AGGR1 | 0.714 | 0.607 | 0.858 | 0.860 | Yes |
| | AGGR2 | 0.727 | | | | |
| | AGGR3 | 0.839 | | | | |
| | AGGR5 | 0.830 | | | | |
| Perceived ease of use | PEOU1 | 0.770 | 0.619 | 0.829 | 0.830 | Yes |
| | PEOU2 | 0.777 | | | | |
| | PEOU3 | 0.821 | | | | |

| | | | | | | |
|---|---|---|---|---|---|---|
| Perceived usefulness | PU1 | 0.813 | 0.690 | 0.869 | 0.870 | Yes |
| | PU2 | 0.815 | | | | |
| | PU3 | 0.854 | | | | |
| Perceived financial cost | PFC1 | 0.732 | 0.570 | 0.798 | 0.799 | Yes |
| | PFC2 | 0.773 | | | | |
| | PFC3 | 0.749 | | | | |
| Intention to adoption | ITA1 | 0.851 | 0.580 | 0.803 | 0.805 | Yes |
| | ITA2 | 0.740 | | | | |
| | ITA3 | 0.684 | | | | |
| Strategic capabilities | STR1 | 3.53 | 0.603 | 0.858 | 0.858 | Yes |
| | STR2 | 3.55 | | | | |
| | STR3 | 3.58 | | | | |
| | STR4 | 3.68 | | | | |
| Dynamic capabilities | DYN1 | 3.65 | 0.619 | 0.889 | 0.890 | Yes |
| | DYN2 | 3.52 | | | | |
| | DYN3 | 3.63 | | | | |
| | DYN4 | 3.55 | | | | |
| | DYN5 | 3.65 | | | | |

*Source*: Researchers' Computation (2019).

**Table 3:** Discriminant validity based on Fornell–Larcker criterion analysis.

| | DYN | SCOP | TIME | AGGR | STR | PU | INTE | PEOU | ITA | PFC |
|---|---|---|---|---|---|---|---|---|---|---|
| DYN | 1 | | | | | | | | | |
| SCOP | 0.075 | 1 | | | | | | | | |
| TIME | −0.043 | 0.041 | 1 | | | | | | | |
| AGGR | 0.045 | 0.210 | 0.166 | 1 | | | | | | |
| STR | 0.118 | 0.120 | 0.081 | 0.047 | 1 | | | | | |
| PU | 0.043 | 0.171 | 0.174 | 0.159 | 0.114 | 1 | | | | |
| INTE | −0.035 | 0.165 | 0.071 | 0.067 | 0.107 | 0.175 | 1 | | | |
| PEOU | −0.057 | 0.254 | −0.004 | 0.153 | 0.254 | 0.324 | 0.173 | 1 | | |
| ITA | −0.046 | 0.285 | 0.168 | 0.083 | 0.247 | 0.307 | 0.281 | 0.326 | 1 | |
| PFC | −0.164 | 0.038 | 0.222 | 0.352 | −0.080 | −0.107 | 0.064 | −0.047 | −0.169 | 1 |

*Source*: Researchers' Computation (2019).

**Table 4:** Hypothesis testing results.

| Relevant hypothesis | Relevant path | Estimate | S.E. | C.R. | *p*-Value | Inference |
|---|---|---|---|---|---|---|
| H1 | PEOU ⇒ PU | 0.068 | 0.026 | 2.657 | 0.008 | Supported |
| H2 | PEOU ⇒ ITA | 0.048 | 0.022 | 2.145 | 0.032 | Supported |
| H3 | PU ⇒ ITA | 0.123 | 0.036 | 3.410 | 0.000 | Supported |
| H4 | PFC ⇒ ITA | 0.269 | 0.057 | 4.740 | 0.000 | Supported |
| H5 | MAS ⇒ PEOU | 0.248 | 0.058 | 4.266 | 0.000 | Supported |
| H6 | MAS ⇒ PU | 0.217 | 0.059 | 3.713 | 0.000 | Supported |
| H7 | MAS ⇒ PFC | −0.116 | 0.050 | −2.305 | 0.021 | Supported |

*Source*: Researchers' Computation (2019).

$\chi^2/df = 1.489$, $p < 0.001$, GFI = 0.926, TLI = 0.964, CFI = 0.968, and RMSEA = 0.034. Based on the rules of prior studies (Bagozzi and Yi, 1988; Hair *et al.*, 1998; Byrne, 2001), the results show that the fit indices for this structural model are quite acceptable.

4.2.2.2. Hypothesis testing

Properties of the causal paths, including standardized path coefficients ($\beta$) and $p$-values, are shown in Table 4. The result proves that PEOU has a respective influence on PU ($\beta = 0.269$; $p < 0.05$), thus, H1 is supported. The effects of PU, PEOU, PFC on ITA are significant ($\beta = 0.248, 0.217, -0.116$; $p < 0.05$); hence, H2–H4 are supported. As for the relationships between MAS and PEOU, PU, PFC, the effects of MAS on PFC are more significant than that of MAS on PEOU and PU with $\beta = 0.123$ in comparison with $\beta = 0.068$ and $\beta = 0.048$ ($p < 0.05$), respectively hence, H5–H7 are supported.

To assess the indirect effects, the bootstrapping bias-corrected confidence interval procedure was applied to the mediation model (Preacher and Hayes, 2008). The bootstrapping technique was applied in this research with a total of 1,500 random observations generated from the original sample and 95% confidence intervals in the estimation of the proposed model. The estimation results show that bias and the standard deviation of the bias (SE-Bias) between bootstrapping estimation and the ML used in the verification appeared, but standard deviations of the bias are not statistically significant, proving that the estimated results in this study are reliable.

### 4.2.3. *Moderating effects of leadership*

#### 4.2.3.1. Multiple group analysis

MGA can be used to examine the existence of the moderating effects on the structural model by analyzing the significance of the differences between parameters considered by the structural model between the groups proposed (Singh, 1995; Byrne, 2001; Arbuckle, 2003).

#### 4.2.3.2. Strategic capabilities

For the formation of the groups, the researchers divided the sample of SCs into two different groups (high SCs vs. low SCs) in line with the sample median. The results of the test of the difference between the compatibility criteria between the Variance Measurement model (VMm) and Partial Invariance Measurement model (PIMm) show that the difference between the two models is statistically significant ($p = 0.000 < 0.05$). Therefore, the VMm is selected to conclude the difference of factors in the research model between the two median groups. Table 5 shows that there are significant differences in the unstandardized coefficients of PEOU ($\beta = 0.286$; $p < 0.05$), PU ($\beta = 0.261$, $p < 0.05$), and PFC ($\beta = -0.107$, $p < 0.05$) affecting ITA, which can be observed via the moderating effect of SCs, thus H8a, H8b, and H8c are supported. Therefore, the relationship between PEOU and ITA and the relationship between PU and ITA are stronger among respondents with a high level of SCs than among respondents with a low level of SCs. However, the relationship between PFC and ITA is weaker among respondents with a high level of SCs than among respondents with a low level of SCs.

4.2.3.3. Dynamic capabilities

The researchers divide the sample of DCs into two different groups (high DCs vs. low DCs) in accordance with the sample median. The results of the test of the difference between the compatibility criteria between the VMm and PIMm show that the difference between the two models is statistically significant ($p = 0.000 < 0.05$). Therefore, the VMm is selected to conclude the difference of factors in the research model between the two median groups. As can be seen in Table 6, significant differences in the unstandardized coefficients of PEOU ($\beta = 0.374$, $p < 0.05$), PU ($\beta = 0.167$, $p < 0.05$), and PFC ($\beta = 0.122$, $p < 0.05$) affecting ITA can be observed via the moderating effect of DCs, thus H9a, H9b, and H9c are supported. Hence, the relationship between PEOU and ITA and the relationship between PU and ITA are stronger among respondents with a high level of DCs than among respondents with a low level of DCs. However, the relationship between PFC and ITA is weaker among respondents with a high level of DCs than among respondents with a low level of DCs.

## 5. Discussion and Conclusion

The results of the study, which are based on the extended TAM model, enhance the understanding of the antecedents of MAS

**Table 5:** Research findings on the whole sample and the moderating role of the degree of strategic capabilities.

| Causal relationship | Low strategic capabilities ($n = 233$) Estimate | Low strategic capabilities ($n = 233$) $P$ | High strategic capabilities ($n = 203$) Estimate | High strategic capabilities ($n = 203$) $P$ | Difference between (high strategic capabilities parameters − low strategic capabilities) Estimate | Difference between (high strategic capabilities parameters − low strategic capabilities) $P$ | Hypothesis testing results |
|---|---|---|---|---|---|---|---|
| ITA ⇐ PEOU | 0.111 | 0.172 | 0.397 | 0.000 | 0.286 | −0.172 | H8a is supported |
| ITA ⇐ PU | 0.069 | 0.412 | 0.330 | 0.000 | 0.261 | −0.412 | H8b is supported |
| ITA ⇐ PFC | −0.171 | 0.025 | −0.064 | 0.256 | 0.107 | 0.231 | H8c is supported |
| **Model** | $\chi^2$ | *df* | $P$ | **TLI** | **CFI** | **RMSEA** | |
| Variance measurement | 826.680 | 678 | 0.000 | 0.968 | 0.971 | 0.022 | |
| Partial measurement invariance | 851.316 | 685 | 0.000 | 0.964 | 0.968 | 0.024 | |
| Differences | 24.636 | 7 | 0.000 | −0.004 | −0.003 | 0.002 | |

*Source*: Researchers' Computation (2019).

**Table 6:** Research findings on the whole sample and the moderating role of degree of dynamic capabilities.

| | **Low dynamic capabilities ($n = 249$)** | | **High dynamic capabilities ($n = 187$)** | | **Difference between parameters (high dynamic dynamic capabilities)** | | |
|---|---|---|---|---|---|---|---|
| **Causal relationship** | **Estimate** | ***P*** | **Estimate** | ***P*** | **Estimate** | ***P*** | **Hypothesis testing results** |
| ITA ⇐ PEOU | 0.077 | 0.295 | 0.451 | 0.000 | 0.374 | −0.295 | H9a is supported |
| ITA ⇐ PU | 0.137 | 0.090 | 0.304 | 0.000 | 0.167 | −0.090 | H9b is supported |
| ITA ⇐ PFC | −0.170 | 0.014 | −0.048 | 0.467 | 0.122 | 0.453 | H9c is supported |
| **Model** | $\chi^2$ | ***df*** | ***P*** | **TLI** | **CFI** | **RMSEA** | |
| Variance measurement | 800.499 | 678 | 0.000 | 0.974 | 0.976 | 0.020 | |
| Partial measurement invariance | 832.422 | 685 | 0.000 | 0.969 | 0.971 | 0.022 | |
| Differences | 31.923 | 7 | 0.000 | −0.005 | −0.005 | 0.002 | |

*Source*: Researchers' Computation (2019).

acceptance to be adopted and how the leadership moderates the relationships between PNGAs' beliefs and their intention of MAS adoption, and offers some relevant implications and suggestions for future research. Through empirically investigating via responses to a survey of 419 PNGAs in Vinh Long province, the results reveal three major theoretical implications present in turn.

(1) This study confirms the findings of previous research in relation to the characteristics of MAS and provides extensive theoretical explanations for the argument that PNGAs can base their decision to adopt MAS on their beliefs of the benefits and costs that can be gathered from this system. The results of the present study suggest that PU, PEOU should be factors influencing and creating the impetus for future intentions of MAS adoption.
(2) In contrast with previous research, we add to the literature by exploring the effect of PFC as the factor influencing the intention of MAS adoption. With the view that autonomy is an essential trend and preliminary condition for the development of the economy and reducing the constraint of budgets, all the PNGAs in the process of autonomy have to find a solution to enhance the management and control all the activities, especially the operating cost. For this reason, the PNGAs tend to invest in the new system with caution in regard to the cost.
(3) With regard to the moderating effects of leadership, the SCs and DCs particularly, the relationship between PEOU, PE, and ITA is more sensitive among the PNGAs which own leadership with high strategic and dynamic capabilities than among the PNGAs which own lower ones. In contrast, the moderating effects of strategic and dynamic capabilities can have a negative influence on the relationship between PFC and ITA. In other words, in comparison with high strategic and dynamic capabilities, the leader with lower strategic and dynamic capabilities tends to refuse to apply MAS in case the cost is expected to be high.

This study also offers some important managerial implications for how to increase the ITA MAS among PNGAs, particularly for PNGAs in Vinh Long. First, the leader should take a lead in exploring new approaches to closing the skills gap among the employees through eliminating barriers for learning to apply the new system and improve the speed of searching for new knowledge by training and education. Secondly, managers must identify the change speed of technology and pay attention to increasing management knowledge and practices.

Concretely speaking, MAS providers can use leadership as the criterion for segmenting the market to satisfy the needs of various groups of consumers, they can provide high leadership (high strategic and dynamic capabilities) with more useful and more tailored services for MAS to give assistance and find solutions to making effective decisions and enhancing the management performance, and to facilitating more low leadership (high strategic and dynamic capabilities) to get access to suitable and economic costs (Suoranta and Mattila, 2004). This study also suggests that MAS providers should endeavor to minimize the price of MAS and offer a straightforward way to deliver benefits and improve ease of use to boost PNGAs' adoption intention of MAS.

Apart from contributing to such knowledge, this study still suffers from several limitations that provide opportunities for further research. First, because the data of this research are collected from accountants working in the public education sectors and public hospitals only, given this study's limited scope, further research can generalize this study's sample to the respondents of other positions of organizations. Secondly, there are some regions in the sample failing to meet the standard of quantity; hence, future researchers should address this problem. Thirdly, there is still claim for replicated research to gain a better understanding of the patterns of the existence of the moderating effects through another procedure, because although MGA can be used in this research model, methods cannot allow for the plotting of the moderation relationships. Fourthly, based on the cross-sectional research method, the relation between intention and actual use is still questionable, therefore, future researchers should apply the longitudinal analysis by taking into consideration the evolution of MAS acceptance.

## References

Agarwal, R., and Prasad, J. (1999). Are individual differences germane to the acceptance of new information technologies? *Decision Sciences*, 30(2), 361–391. doi:10.1111/j.1540-5915.1999.tb01614.x

Agbejule, A. (2005). The relationship between management accounting systems and perceived environmental uncertainty on managerial performance: A research note. *Accounting and Business Research*, 35(4), 295–305. doi:10.1080/00014788.2005.9729996

Al-Omiri, M., and Drury, C. (2007). A survey of factors influencing the choice of product costing systems in UK organizations. *Management Accounting Research*, 18(4), 399–424. doi:10.1016/j.mar.2007.02.002

Alsajjan, B., and Dennis, C. (2010). Internet banking acceptance model: Cross-market examination. *Journal of Business Research*, 63(9–10), 957–963. doi:10.1016/j.jbusres.2008.12.014

Anderson, J.C., and Gerbing, D.W. (1988). Structural equation modeling in practice: A review and recommended two-step approach. *Psychological Bulletin*, 103(3), 411–423. doi:10.1037/0033-2909.103.3.411

Anh, D.N.P. (2016). Factors affecting the use and consequences of management accounting practices in a transitional economy: The case of Vietnam. *Journal of Economics and Development*, 18(1), 54–73.

Arbuckle, J.L. (2003). AMOS 5.0: Update to the AMOS User's Guide. Smallwaters Corporation, Chicago, IL.

Bagozzi, R.P., and Yi, Y. (1988). On the evaluation of structural equation models. *Journal of the Academy of Marketing Science*, 16(1), 74–94. doi:10.1007/bf02723327

Baines, A., and Langfield-Smith, K. (2003). Antecedents to management accounting change: A structural equation approach. *Accounting, Organizations and Society*, 28(1), 675–698.

Bhattacherjee, A. (2001a). Understanding information systems continuance: An expectation-confirmation model. *MIS Quarterly*, 25(3), 351. doi:10.2307/3250921

Bhattacherjee, A. (2001b). An empirical analysis of the antecedents of electronic commerce service continuance. *Decision Support Systems*, 32(2), 201–214. doi:10.1016/s0167-9236(01)00111-7

Bhattacherjee, A., and Premkumar, G. (2004). Understanding changes in belief and attitude toward information technology usage: A theoretical model and longitudinal test. *MIS Quarterly*, 28(2), 351–370.

Bollen, K.A. (1989). A new incremental fit index for general structural equation models. *Sociological Methods and Research*, 17, 303–316. https://doi.org/10.1177%2F0049124189017003004

Bouwens, J., and Abernethy, M.A. (2000). The consequences of customization on management accounting system design. *Accounting, Organizations and Society*, 25(3), 221–241. doi:10.1016/s0361-3682(99)00043-4

Buabeng-Andoh, C. (2018). Predicting students' intention to adopt mobile learning. *Journal of Research in Innovative Teaching and Learning*. doi:10.1108/jrit-03-2017-0004

Byrne, B.M. (2001). *Structural Equation Modeling with AMOS: Basic Concepts, Applications, and Programming*. Mahwah, NJ: Lawrence Erlbaum Associates.

Çelik, H. (2008). What determines Turkish customers' acceptance of internet banking? *International Journal of Bank Marketing*, 26(5), 353–370. doi:10.1108/02652320810894406

Cheng, M. (2012). The joint effect of budgetary participation and broad-scope management accounting systems on management performance. *Asian Review of Accounting*, 20(3), 184–197. doi: 10.1108/13217341211263256

Chenhall, R.H. (2003). Management control systems design within its organizational context: Findings from contingency-based research and directions for the future. *Accounting, Organizations and Society*, 28(2–3), 127–168. doi:10.1016/s0361-3682(01)00027-7

Chenhall, R., and Langfield-Smith, K. (1998). The relationship between strategic priorities, management techniques and management accounting: An empirical investigation using a systems approach. *Accounting, Organizations and Society*, 23(3), 243–264. doi:10.1016/s0361-3682(97)00024-x

Chenhall, R.H., and Morris, D. (1986). The impact of structure, environment, and interdependence on the perceived usefulness of management accounting system. *The Accounting Review*, 61(1), 16–35.

Chin, W.W., and Gopal, A. (1995). Adoption intention in GSS: Relative importance of beliefs. *ACM SigMIS Database*, 26(2–3), 42–64.

Chiou, J.-S., and Shen, C.-C. (2012). The antecedents of online financial service adoption: The impact of physical banking services on Internet banking acceptance. *Behaviour & Information Technology*, 31(9), 859–871. doi:10.1080/0144929x.2010.549509

Chung, S.-H., Su, Y.-F., and Yu-Ju, S. (2012). Broad scope management accounting system and managerial performance: The impact of role ambiguity and functional difference. *African Journal of Business Management*, 6(30), 8873–8878. https://doi.org/10.5897/AJBM11.2181

Congress. (2015). Law No. 88/2015/QH13. Accounting Law. Hanoi: National Assembly. Accessed from: https://luatvietnam.vn/ke-toan/luat-88-2015-qh13-quoc-hoi-101336-d1.html

Davis, F.D. (1989). Perceived *Usefulness, Perceived Ease of Use, and User Acceptance of Information Technology. MIS Quarterly*, 13(3), 319. doi:10.2307/249008

Davis, F.D. (1993). User acceptance of information technology: System characteristics, user perceptions and behavioral impacts. *International Journal of Man-Machine Studies*, 38(3), 475–487. doi:10.1006/imms.1993.1022

Davis, F.D., Bagozzi, R.P., and Warshaw, P.R. (1989). User acceptance of computer technology: A Comparison of two theoretical models. *Management Science*, 35(8), 982–1003. doi:10.1287/mnsc.35.8.982

Eisenhardt, K.M., and Martin, J.A. (2000). Dynamic capabilities: What are they? *Strategic Management Journal*, 21(10–11), 1105–1121. doi:10.1002/1097-0266(200010/11)21:10/11<1105:aid-smj133>3.0.co;2-e

Etemadi, H., Dilami, Z.D., Bazaz, M.S., and Parameswaran, R. (2009). Culture, management accounting and managerial performance: Focus Iran. *Advances in Accounting*, 25(2), 216–225.

Fabrigar, L.R., Petty, R.E., Smith, S.M., and Crites, S.L., Jr. (2006). Understanding knowledge effects on attitude-behavior consistency: The role of relevance, complexity, and amount of knowledge. *Journal of Personality and Social Psychology*, 90(4), 556–577.

Fornell, C., and Larcker, D.F. (1981). Evaluating structural equation models with unobservable variables and measurement error. *Journal of Marketing Research*, 18(1), 39. doi:10.2307/3151312

Gao, L., and Bai, X. (2014). A unified perspective on the factors influencing consumer acceptance of internet of things technology. *Asia Pacific Journal of Marketing and Logistics*, 26(2), 211–231. doi:10.1108/apjml-06-2013-0061

Granlund, M. (2011). Extending AIS research to management accounting and control issues: A research note. *International Journal of Accounting Information Systems*, 12(1), 3–19. doi:10.1016/j.accinf.2010.11.001

Hair, J.F., Anderson, R.E., Tatham, R.L., and Black, W.C. (1998). *Multivariate Data Analysis with Readings*, 5th edition. Englewood Cliffs, NJ: Prentice-Hall.

Hair, J.F., Black, W.C., Babin, B.J., and Anderson, R.E. (2010). *Multivariate Data Analysis: A Global Perspective*, 7th edition. Upper Saddle River, NJ: Pearson.

Zawawi, H.M.N., and Hoque, Z. (2010). Research in management accounting innovations. *Qualitative Research in Accounting and Management,* 7(4), 505–568. doi:10.1108/11766091011094554

Halbouni, S.S., and Nour, M.A. (2014). An empirical study of the drivers of management accounting innovation: A UAE perspective. *International Journal of Managerial and Financial Accounting*, 6(1), 60. doi:10.1504/ijmfa.2014.060512

Hammad, S.A., Jusoh, R., and Ghozali, I. (2010). Decentralization, perceived environmental uncertainty, managerial performance and management accounting system information in Egyptian hospitals. *International Journal of Accounting and Information Management*, 21(4), 314–330.

Harrell, J.F. (2015). *Regression Modeling Strategies: With Applications to Linear Models, Logistic and Ordinal Regression, and Survival Analysis*, 2nd edition. Berlin, Germany: Springer International Publishing.

Hoelter, J.W. (1983). The analysis of covariance structures. *Sociological Methods & Research,* 11(3), 325–344. doi:10.1177/00491241 83011003003

Holmes-Smith, P. (2001). *Introduction to Structural Equation Modelling using LISREL*. Perth: ACSPRI-Winter training program.

Hoque, Z. (2011). The relations among competition, delegation, management accounting systems change and performance: A path model. *Advances in Accounting*, 27(2), 266–277.

Hubbard, G., and Beamish, P. (2011). *Strategic Management: Thinking Analysis and Action*, 4th edition. Sydney: Pearson Prentice Hall.

Ismail, K., and Isa, C.R. (2011). The role of management accounting systems in advanced manufacturing environment. *Australian Journal of Basic and Applied Sciences*, 5(9), 2196–2209.

Ismail, N.A., and King, M. (2007). Factors influencing the alignment of accounting information systems in small and medium sized Malaysian manufacturing firms. *Journal of Information Systems and Small Business*, 1(1–2), 1–20.

Karahanna, E., and Limayem, M. (2000). E-mail and V-mail usage: Generalizing across technologies. *Journal of Organizational Computing and Electronic Commerce*, 10(1), 49–66. doi:10.1207/s15327744joce100103

Kline, R.B. (2011). *Principles and Practice of Structural Equation Modeling*, 3rd edition. New York, USA: The Guilford Press.

Kwon, O., and Wen, Y. (2010). An empirical study of the factors affecting social network service use. *Computers in Human Behavior*, 26(2), 254–263.

Lee, S.J. (2009). Online communication and adolescent social ties: Who benefits more from Internet use? *Journal of Computer-Mediated Communication*, 14(3), 509–531. doi:10.1111/j.1083-6101.2009.01451.x

Lee, S.K.V. (2000). *The Demand for Business and Management Education in Hong Kong Beyond 1997*. In Rowley, C., and Fitzgerald, R. (eds.), *Managed in Hong Kong: Adaptive Systems, Entrepreneurship and Human Resource*. London: Frank Cass.

Legris, P., Ingham, J., and Collerette, P. (2003). Why do people use information technology? A critical review of the technology acceptance model. *Information and Management*, 40(3), 191–204. doi:10.1016/s0378-7206(01)00143-4

Lei, P.-W., and Wu, Q. (2007). Introduction to structural equation modeling: Issues and practical considerations. *Educational Measurement: Issues and Practice*, 26(3), 33–43. doi:10.1111/j.1745-3992.2007.00099.x

Leite, A.A., Fernandes, P.O., and Leite, J.M. (2015). Contingent factors that influence the use of management accounting practices in the Portuguese textile and clothing sector. In *The International Journal of Management Science and Information Technology, Special Issue: 2015 Spanish-Portuguese Scientific Management Conference*, pp. 59–78.

Lenz, R.T. (1980). Strategic capability: A concept and framework for analysis. *Academy of Management Review*, 5(2), 225–334. doi: 10.5465/amr.1980.4288736

Luarn, P., and Lin, H.-H. (2005). Toward an understanding of the behavioral intention to use mobile banking. *Computers in Human Behavior*, 21(6), 873–891. doi:10.1016/j.chb.2004.03.003

Mat, T.Z.T., Smith, M., and Djajadikerta, H. (2010). Management accounting and organizational change: an exploratory study in Malaysian manufacturing firms. *Journal of Applied Management Accounting Research*, 8(2), 51–82.

McManus, L. (2013). Customer accounting and marketing performance measures in the hotel industry: Evidence from Australia. *International Journal of Hospitality Management*, 33(1), 140–152. https://doi.org/10.1016/j.ijhm.2012.07.007

Mia, L., and Patiar, A. (2001). The use of management accounting systems in hotels: An exploratory study. *International Journal of Hospitality Management*, 20(2), 111–128. doi:10.1016/s0278-4319(00)00033-5.

Mia, L., and Winata, L. (2008). Manufacturing strategy, broad scope MAS information and information and communication technology. *The British Accounting Review*, 40(2), 182–192. doi: 10.1016/j.bar.2008.02.003

Moffat, P., and Simon, A. (2011). Strategic management capabilities that drive West Australian law firm success. *Academy of Taiwan Business Management Review*, 7(1), 1–12.

Moores, K., and Yuen, S. (2001). Management accounting systems and organizational configuration: A life-cycle perspective. *Accounting, Organizations and Society*, 26(4–5), 351–389. doi:10.1016/s0361-3682(00)00040-4

Muthen, B., and Kaplan, D. (1985). A comparison of some methodologies for the factor analysis of non-normal Likert variables: A note on the size of the model. *The British Journal of Mathematical and Statistical Psychology*, 45, 19–30.

Nguyen, D.H. (2010). Organizing accounting work in the context of information technology application. *Accounting Review*, 85, 24–27.

Nguyen, T.G. (2018). Renovating the financial mechanism of public non-business units in the spirit of central resolution 6 (course XII). *Review of Finance*, 1(1+2), 60–64.

Nunnally, J.C. (1978). *Psychometric Theory*, 2nd edition. New York: McGraw-Hill.

Preacher, K.J., and Hayes, A.F. (2008). Asymptotic and resampling strategies for assessing and comparing indirect effects in multiple mediator models. *Behavior Research Methods*, 40(3), 879–891. doi:10.3758/brm.40.3.879

Santos, L.L, Gome, C., Arroteia, N., and Almeida, P. (2012). The perception of management accounting in the Portuguese lodging industry. In *Global Business and Technology Association, GBATA 16th Annual International Conference,* Baku, Azerbaijan. doi: 10.13140/2.1.2631.3282

Sarasvathy, S.D., and Dew, N. (2013). Without judgement: An empirically based entrepreneurial theory of the firm. *Review of Austrian Economics*, 26(3), 277–296.

Simon, A. (2010). Resources, dynamic capabilities and Australian business success. *Journal of Global Business and Technology*, 6(2), 12–31.

Simon, A., Bartle, C., Stockport, G., Smith, B., Klobas, J.E., and Sohal, A. (2015). Business leaders' views on the importance of strategic and dynamic capabilities for successful financial and non-financial business performance. *International Journal of Productivity and Performance Management*, 64(7), 908–931. doi:10.1108/ijppm-05-2014-0078

Singh, J. (1995). Measurement issues in cross-national research. *Journal of International Business Studies*, 26(3), 597–619. doi: 10.1057/palgrave.jibs.8490188

Sivo, S.A., Fan, X.T., Witta, E.L., and Willse, J.T. (2006). The search for "optimal" cutoff properties: Fit index criteria in structural equation modeling. *The Journal of Experimental Education*, 74(3), 267–288. https://psycnet.apa.org/doi/10.3200/JEXE.74.3.267-288

Soobaroyen, T., and Poorundersing, B. (2008). The effectiveness of management accounting systems. *Managerial Auditing Journal*, 23(2), 187–219. doi:10.1108/02686900810839866

Sripalawat, J., Thongmak, A., and Ngramyarn A. (2011). M-banking in Metropolitan Bangkok and a Comparison with Other Countries. *Journal of Computer Information Systems*, 51(3), 67–76. doi: 10.1080/08874417.2011.11645487

Suoranta, M., and Mattila, M. (2004). Mobile Banking and Consumer Behaviour: New Insights into the Diffusion Pattern. *Journal of Financial Services Marketing*, 8(4), 354–366. doi: 10.1057/palgrave.fsm.4770132

Urquidi, A.C., and Ripoll, V.M. (2013). The choice of management accounting techniques in the hotel sector: the role of contextual factors. *Journal of Management Research*, 5(2), 65–82.

Van Helden, J., and Uddin, S. (2016). Public sector management accounting in emerging economies: A literature review. *Critical Perspectives on Accounting*, 41, 34–62. doi:10.1016/j.cpa.2016.01.001

Venkatesh, V., Morris, M. G., Davis, G. B. and Davis, F. D. (2003). User acceptance of information technology: Toward a unified view. *MIS Quarterly*, 27(3), 425. doi:10.2307/30036540

Venkatesh, V., and Morris, M.G. (2000). Why don't men ever stop to ask for directions? Gender, Social influence, and their role in technology acceptance and usage behavior. *MIS Quarterly*, 24(1), 115–139. doi:10.2307/3250981

von Krogh, G., Nonaka, I., and Aben, M. (2001). Making the most of your company's knowledge: a strategic framework. *Long Range Planning*, 34(4), 421–439.

Wallace, L.G., and Sheetz, S.D. (2014). The adoption of software measures: A technology acceptance model (TAM) perspective. *Information & Management*, 51(2), 249–259. doi:10.1016/j.im.2013.12.003

Wu, J.-H., Wang, S.-C., and Lin, L.-M. (2007). Mobile computing acceptance factors in the healthcare industry: A structural equation model. *International Journal of Medical Informatics*, 76(1), 66–77. doi:10.1016/j.ijmedinf.2006.06.006

Yang, H., Liu, H., and Zhou, L. (2012). Predicting young Chinese consumers' mobile viral attitudes, intents and behavior. *Asia Pacific*

*Journal of Marketing and Logistics*, 24(1), 59–77. doi:10.1108/13555851211192704

Yang, K.C.C. (2005). Exploring factors affecting the adoption of mobile commerce in Singapore. *Telematics and Informatics*, 22(3), 257–277. doi:10.1016/j.tele.2004.11.003

Rasid, Z.A.S., Abdul Rahman, A.R., and Ismail, K.W. (2011). Management accounting and risk management in Malaysian financial institutions. *Managerial Auditing Journal*, 26(7), 566–585. doi:10.1108/02686901111151314

Zhu, K., Kraemer, K.L., and Dedrick, J. (2004). Information technology payoff in e-business environments: An international perspective on value creation of e-business in the financial services industry. *Journal of Management Information Systems*, 21(1), 17–54. doi:10.1080/07421222.2004.11045797

Zikmund, W.G., Babin, B.J., Carr, J.C., and Griffin, M. (2010). *Business Research Methods*, 8th edition. Mason, HO: Cengage Learning.

https://doi.org/10.1142/9789811227158_0005

# Chapter 5

# Market Power and Risk: Evidence from ASEAN Commercial Banking System

**Thi Anh Tien Duong**

## Abstract

The purpose of this chapter is to assess the causal relationship between the market power and risks of ASEAN commercial banks. Using the data of 118 ASEAN commercial banks between 2002 and 2017, we measure the market power using the Lerner index and risk using measures, including the $Z$-score and the Loan Loss Provision ratio. We establish a panel vector auto-regression to estimate this relationship. Our results indicate that there is a causal relationship between the market power and risks of ASEAN banks, supporting both the competition-stability and the competition-fragility theories. The results of this study are the basis for policy suggestions for investors and executive managers to improve banking performance through risk reduction.

**Keywords:** Bank market power; Bank risk; PVAR; ASEAN.

## 1. Introduction

In recent decades, market power and risk have been particularly attractive topics for researchers across the world, especially after the 2008–2009 financial crisis. Most of the relationship between market power and risk has been evaluated by one-dimensional studies on market power and banking risk, supporting the theory of competition-fragility (Keeley, 1990; Beck *et al.*, 2013; Fu *et al.*,

2014; Jiang *et al.*, 2017). Other studies support the hypothesis of competition-stability (Berger and Hannan, 1998; Laeven, 2004; Berger *et al.*, 2009; Liu and Wilson, 2013; Anginer *et al.*, 2014).

In contrast, several studies have assessed a one-way impact of risks on bank market power (De Guevara *et al.*, 2005; Fungáčová *et al.*, 2010; Simpasa, 2010). However, few studies are analyzing the Granger Causality between market power and risk in the emerging financial market in Southeast Asia, though much research has been done on the African (Kouki and Al-Nasser, 2017), European (Fiordelisi and Mare, 2014; Jayakumar *et al.*, 2018; Pradhan *et al.*, 2019), American (Koetter *et al.*, 2012; Kasman and Carvallo, 2014) or Chinese financial markets (Tan, 2018).

Therefore, this study was conducted to provide reliable empirical evidence of the Granger Causality relationship between market power and risks of commercial banks in Southeast Asian countries from 2003 to 2017 and help commercial banks, investors, macro managers, policymakers have a greater reference basis.

## 2. Related Literature and Hypotheses

Competition and stability in the banking system have an interwoven relationship, which is both a driving force for banks to improve productivity and operational efficiency as well as the factor affecting the stability of the banking system. Therefore, this issue has been vigorously debated academically among researchers. There are two conflicting theories about the relationship between competition and stability, competition-fragility and competition-stability.

The theory of unstable competition shows that there is a trade-off between market power and the financial stability of banks. In other words, increasing market power will lead to risks, causing disruption. Originating this view, Keeley (1990) points out that increasing competition reduces the Charter value, which in turn led to a collapse in US banks in the 1970s and 1980s. Because commercial banks accept high risks to increase profits, ready to lend at a higher value than the guaranteed value, despite the deterioration in the loan portfolio.

Moreover, the reckless behavior of interest rate control of banks also reduces the effectiveness of operations, brand value is also eroded, and this is the cause for risks for US commercial banks (Hellmann *et al.*, 2000). Besides, market power can adversely affect financial stability and destabilize the banking system (Boyd and De Nicolo, 2005).

Similar to this view, Saurina Salas *et al.* (2007) confirmed that market power is the cause of the disruption of banks. Most recently, Kabir and Worthington's (2017) study supports the hypothesis of unstable competition when using data of Islamic banks and conventional banks from 16 developing countries between 2000 and 2012. Research shows that the Charter value and branding erosion has been reduced by a highly competitive market that has caused more risks for banks.

Many recent empirical studies (Beck *et al.*, 2013; Fu *et al.*, 2014; Jiang *et al.*, 2017) also support the competition-fragility hypothesis. Therefore, the author hypothesizes as follows:

**Hypothesis H1:** *Increasing bank market power is the cause of increased bank risk.*

The theory of stable competition states that there is no trade-off between market power and the financial stability of banks. In other words, market power will not be the cause of the risk, not causing the risk of disruption, instead it brings financial stability to banks.

Supporting this view, Berger *et al.* (2009) use the data of commercial banks in 23 developed countries from 1999 to 2005, and provide evidence that the greater the bank's market power, the more the bank's overall risk tends to decline, resulting in more stability. On the other hand, when increasing the market power, a bank will face risks in the loan portfolio, but this can be partially offset by increasing the bank's equity.

By taking a capitalization perspective, Schaeck and Čihák (2007) show that there is a positive and significant relationship between market power and the financial stability of banks when using data of European banks in the period 1999–2004. In other words, competition between banks is intensifying; capitalization is still the primary factor of the bank to increase its market power, contributing to repel the consequences of instability in the market currency and bringing financial stability to the bank.

Liu and Wilson (2013), using data of Japanese banks from 2000 to 2009, show that market power has the opposite impact of bank risk. In other words, the greater the market power, the more the risk will be repelled, leading to increased stability in banks.

Research by Goetz (2017) shows that the increasing market power in the finance market significantly improves the stability of banks using data of US banks from 1976 to 2006. Besides, many other empirical studies (Berger and Hannan, 1998; Laeven, 2004; Anginer *et al.*, 2014) support the competition-stability theory. Therefore, the study hypothesizes as follows:

**Hypothesis H2:** *Increasing bank market power is the cause of bank risk reduction.*

Empirical studies have examined the impact of risks on the market in the banking industry (De Guevara *et al.*, 2005; Kasman and Carvallo, 2014; Tan and Floros, 2014). Most studies consider credit risk, liquidity risk, and insolvency risk of the bank. Because these types of risks are always highly dangerous for commercial banks, they are reduced to increase the bank market power:

**Hypothesis H3:** *Reduced bank risk is the cause of increased bank market power.*

## 3. Methodology

### 3.1. *Data*

Data of studies are taken from Bankscope's source. To avoid frequency, we consider the consolidated financial report. We filter the data from commercial banks, including listed and unlisted banks, and eliminate banks with less than five reporting years and those with the latest reporting years no later than 2016. After cleaning the data, our final sample included 118 commercial banks in eight countries: Cambodia, Indonesia, Laos, Malaysia, Philippines, Singapore, Thailand, and Vietnam, between 2002–2017. It is uniformly converted to USD currency at the local currency/USD exchange rate from the IMF source.

### 3.2. *Calculating market power: The Lerner index*

Following more recent research (De Guevara and Maudos, 2007; Ariss, 2010; Fu *et al.*, 2014), we calculate competitiveness directly through the Lerner index, which is determined by calculating the difference between price and marginal cost as a percentage of the price (Berger *et al.*, 2009; Fu *et al.*, 2014) and defined as follows:

$$Lerner_{it} = \frac{\mathrm{P}_{TA,it} - \mathrm{MC}_{TA,it}}{\mathrm{P}_{TA,it}}, \tag{1}$$

where

- $\mathrm{P}_{TA,it}$ is the price of total assets calculated by the ratio of total revenues (interest and non-interest income) to total assets for the bank $i$ at time $t$; $\mathrm{MC}_{TA,it}$ is the marginal cost of total assets for bank $i$ at time $t$.
- The Lerner index is estimated at the bank level; therefore, the evolution of market power is analyzed to study the development of competition over time, and the higher values of the index mean the greater market power (Ariss, 2010; Fiordelisi and Mare, 2014; Fu *et al.*, 2014). This paper considers the analysis of the natural logarithm of Lerner to ensure that the variables among $[-\infty, +\infty]$ are distributed symmetrically.
- Similarly to other studies (Berger *et al.*, 2009; Fiordelisi and Mare, 2014; Fu *et al.*, 2014), we estimate the marginal cost using the translog cost function with three inputs, one single output, and a trend over time. As the author uses bank random effects, the final

specification is as follows:

$$
\begin{aligned}
LnTC_{it} = {} & \alpha_0 + \alpha_1 lnTA_{it} + \frac{1}{2}\alpha_2(lnTA_{it})^2 + \alpha_3 lnw_{1it} + \alpha_4 lnw_{2it} \\
& + \alpha_5 lnw_{3it} + \alpha_6 lnTA_{it}lnw_{1it} + \alpha_7 lnTA_{it}lnw_{2it} \\
& + \alpha_8 lnTA_{it}lnw_{3it} + \alpha_9 lnw_{1it}lnw_{2it} + \alpha_{10} lnw_{1it}lnw_{3it} \\
& + \alpha_{11} lnw_{2it}lnw_{3it} + \frac{1}{2}\alpha_{12}(lnw_{1it})^2 + \frac{1}{2}\alpha_{13}(lnw_{2it})^2 \\
& + \frac{1}{2}\alpha_{14}(lnw_{3it})^2 + \alpha_{15} Trend + \frac{1}{2}\alpha_{16}(Trend)^2 \\
& + \alpha_{17} TrendlnTA_{it} + \alpha_{18} Trendlnw_{1it} \\
& + \alpha_{19} Trendlnw_{2it} + \alpha_{20} Trendlnw_{3it} + \varepsilon_{it}, \qquad (2)
\end{aligned}
$$

$$
\begin{aligned}
MC_{it} = {} & \frac{\partial TC_{it}}{\partial TA_{it}} = (\alpha_1 + \alpha_2 lnTA_{it} + \alpha_6 lnw_{1it} + \alpha_7 lnw_{2it} \\
& + \alpha_8 lnw_{3it} + \alpha_{17} Trend) * \frac{TC_{it}}{TA_{it}}, \qquad (3)
\end{aligned}
$$

where $TC_i$ is the total costs; $TA_i$ is the total assets; $w_i$ is the price of the factors of production, defined as follows: $w_1$ is the price of purchased funds; interest expense/total deposit and short-term funding, $w_2$ is the price of physical capital: non-interest expenses/fixed assets, and $w_3$ is the price of labor: labor expenses/total assets; *Trend* is the influence of technological changes that lead to shifts in the cost function over time; $a_0, \ldots, a_{20}$ is regression coefficient to be estimated; $\varepsilon_{it}$ is the random error, and a two-component error term measured as follows: $\varepsilon_{it} = u_{it} + \nu_{it}$.

### 3.3. *Calculation-based risk*

Based on financial statement data, bank risks are measured by the $Z$-score index and loan loss provision ratio — LLP (Tan and Floros, 2013; Fu *et al.*, 2014).

- The $Z$-score is used to measure the solvency risk of commercial banks. It is a reverse proxy of the firm's probability of failure, and it combines profits, leverage, and volatility back in a single measure. For each bank $i$ and time $t$, it is determined as follows:

$$\text{Zscore}_{it} = \frac{\text{ROA}_{it} + \text{E}_{it}/\text{TA}_{it}}{\delta\text{ROA}_{it}}, \tag{4}$$

where ROA is the return on assets; E/TA is the ratio of equity to total assets; ROA is the standard deviation of return on assets. The higher the $Z$-score, the greater the stability, and the lower the risk (Fiordelisi and Mare, 2014; Fu *et al.*, 2014). We consider the analysis of the natural logarithm of $Z$-score to ensure that the variables among $[-\infty, +\infty]$ are distributed symmetrically.

- The loan loss provision ratio ($LLPTA$) is calculated by loan loss provision to total assets, which is used to measure the output quality of banks, management capacity of bank managers, and how managers invest in high-risk assets (Tan and Floros, 2013; Fu *et al.*, 2014).

### 3.4. *Panel VAR model*

We consider the causal relationship between power and risk through a system of $PVAR$ models. The two variables included in the model are market power and risk, and lags of the two variables, in which the short-term dynamic relationship is defined (Lütkepohl, 2006; Fiordelisi *et al.*, 2011; Delis *et al.*, 2017).

Following Berger and DeYoung (1997), Love and Zicchino (2006), and Saeed and Izzeldin (2016), the dynamic relationship between endogenous variables is shown in the $PVAR$ equation as follows:

$$w_{i,t} = \mu_i + \mu_{i,t} + \varphi(l)w_{it-1} + \varepsilon_{it}, \tag{5}$$

where $w_{it}$ consists of two random variables, market power and risk, $\mu_i$ is a $(k \times 1)$ vector of the blocking coefficient vector constant over time given for each specific bank, $\varphi(\ell)$ is the matrix $(k \times k)$ of the coefficient of the lag variable (the parameter to estimated), $\varphi(\ell) \equiv \sum_{j=1}^{p} \varphi_j \ell^{j-1}$, to collect the unique and cross effects of those lag variables depends on observation. And $\varepsilon_{it}$ is a $(1 \times k)$ vector of errors measurement with characteristics, $E(\varepsilon_{it}) = 0$, $(E, \varepsilon_{it}\varepsilon'_{it}) = \sum \varepsilon, E(\varepsilon_{it}\varepsilon'_{it}) = 0$ for all $t > s$.

The coefficient of $\mu_i$ in equation (5) is correlated with the error part, and through least square regression OLS will lead to bias coefficients as in Love and Zicchino (2006), and Saeed and Izzeldin (2016).

For solving the above issue, especially in highly observable table data with few timelines, we are advised to transform the model to eliminate the fixed effects individually and then use the system *GMM* estimation method to use the delay of observations as instruments' variable (Arellano and Bover, 1995).

After performing the regression system *PVAR* equation, we estimate the impulse response functions (IRF) and variance decomposition (VDC) to identify the orthogonal shocks between market power variables and risk variables. We use the IFRS to assess the current and future response of market power to the shock of risk and the opposite. Variance decompositions calculate the percentage of shift on market power explained by the shock of risk over time and the opposite.

In particular, we determine the causal relationship between market power and risk according to the two *PVAR* equations with the following structure:

$$\begin{aligned} Lerner_{it} &= f(\beta, Lerner_{i,lag}, Risk_{i,lag}, \varepsilon_i, \eta_{it}). \\ Risk_{it} &= f(\gamma, Risk_{i,lag} Lerner_{i,lag}, \varepsilon_i, \eta_{it}), \end{aligned} \tag{6}$$

where $i$ is the bank; $t$ is the time; *Risk* is measured by the $Z$-score index and loan loss provision ratio for the bank $i$ in time $t$; Lerner is the market power for bank $i$ in time $t$; $lag = (1 \ldots j)$.

## 4. Empirical Results and Discussion

### 4.1. *Market power and risk results*

Table 1 statistics describe the variables for the number of observations (Obs), average (Mean), standard deviation (Std. Dev), minimum (Min), and maximum (Max) for banks.

**Table 1:** Statistics describe the variables for ASEAN banks.

| Variable | Obs | Mean | Std. Dev. | Min | Max |
|---|---|---|---|---|---|
| Lerner | 1.694 | 0.1083 | 1.5940 | −42.5827 | 1.6212 |
| *Z*-score | 1.694 | 1.7870 | 1.4037 | −0.2934 | 30.3965 |
| *LLPTA* | 1.694 | 0.0365 | 0.4984 | 0.0000 | 20.3972 |
| lLerner | 1.490 | −1.3263 | 0.7157 | −6.3760 | 0.4832 |
| *lZ*-score | 1.688 | 0.4645 | 0.4638 | −2.1529 | 3.4143 |

*Notes*: Lerner is market power, *Z*-score and *LLPTA* are risks; The probability of Lerner and the *Z*-score are skewed so lLerner calculated the logarithm of Lerner, *lZ*-score calculated the logarithm of *Z*-score.

Table 1 shows the average Lerner index is 0.1083, which is similar to that of Fu *et al.*'s (2014) 0.38 for Asia Pacific commercial banks, Chan *et al.*'s (2015) 0.244 for the ASEAN-5 banks, and Khan *et al.*'s (2016) 0.19 also for ASEAN banks.

Next, the average *Z*-score of 1.787 and a loan loss provision ratio (*LLPTA*) of 0.036 are similar to the average *Z*-score of 30.59 and the average loan loss provision ratio of 0.02 for the Asia Pacific commercial banks (Fu *et al.*, 2014).

### 4.2. *Panel VAR result*

For performing the regression *PVAR* model, the optimal lag length $j$ of the independent variable needs to be selected in the system of Eq. (6). We select the lag length so that the minimum values of *MBIC*, *MAIC*, *MQIC*, and *CD* are maximum. The result in Table 2 shows that the optimal lag length is one, which is similar to Saeed and Izzeldin's (2016) and Kabir and Worthington's (2017) results.

For the *PVAR* estimation, the condition necessary to perform the analysis of values obtained from the model was that it needed to test the stationarity of the variables in the model. Because this study uses unbalanced table data, Fisher Phillips–Perron (PP) panel unit root test is consistent with the null hypothesis Ho that all table data are not non-stationary. The results of the ADF test are usually very

**Table 2:** Optimal lag length selection for *PVAR* model on estimation sample.

| Lag | CD | J | J p-value | MBIC | MAIC | MQIC |
|---|---|---|---|---|---|---|
| 1 | 0.9195 | . | . | . | . | . |
| 2 | 0.8932 | . | . | . | . | . |
| 3 | 0.8383 | . | . | . | . | . |
| 4 | 0.6943 | . | . | . | . | . |

*Notes*: The values of *MBIC*, *MAIC*, *MQIC* are minimum; CD is maximum.

**Table 3:** Fisher-type unit-root test for lLerner, *lZ*-score, and *LLPTA*.

| | *Statistic* | *p-value* |
|---|---|---|
| ***lLerner*** | | |
| *P* (Inverse chi-squared) | 762.7853 | 0.0000 |
| *Z* (Inverse normal) | −9.8397 | 0.0000 |
| *L**(Inverse logit *t*) | −16.6170 | 0.0000 |
| Pm(Modified inv.chi-squared) | 25.6645 | 0.0000 |
| ***lZ-score*** | | |
| *P* (Inverse chi-squared) | 762.2646 | 0.0000 |
| *Z* (Inverse normal) | −13.7916 | 0.0000 |
| *L**(Inverse logit *t*) | −17.1253 | 0.0000 |
| Pm(Modified inv.chi-squared) | 24.2233 | 0.0000 |
| ***LLPTA*** | | |
| *P* (Inverse chi-squared) | 764.1429 | 0.0000 |
| *Z* (Inverse normal) | −11.2353 | 0.0000 |
| *L**(Inverse logit *t*) | −15.9924 | 0.0000 |
| Pm(Modified inv.chi-squared) | 24.3097 | 0.0000 |

*Notes*: Lag length is one; based on Dickey–Fuller test.

sensitive to the choice of lag length, so the optimal lag length standard is taken from the result of Table 2. The results of the Fisher Phillips–Perron Panel unit root test in Table 3 show that all four tests obtained p-value with significance level below 5%, so the null hypothesis Ho that all panel series are non-stationary for market power and risk in banks can be rejected, meaning lLerner, *lZ*-score,

**Table 4:** Eigenvalue stability condition in PVAR.

| **Eigenvalue** <br> **Real** | **Imaginary** | **Modulus** |
|---|---|---|
| *Model: lLerner and Z-score* | | |
| 0.9240 | 0 | 0.9240 |
| −0.2679 | 0 | 0.2679 |
| *Model: lLerner and LLPTA* | | |
| 0.8652 | 0 | 0.8652 |
| 0.1515 | 0 | 0.1515 |

*Note*: The stability condition of PVAR when all the eigenvalues lie inside the unit circle (see Figures 1 and 2).

and *LLPTA* in unbalanced data panel show *PVAR* satisfies stop condition. Table 4 shows all the eigenvalues lie inside the unit circle so *PVAR* satisfies stability condition (see Figures 1 and 2).

Table 5 shows both panel VAR estimates (model (1) Granger causality between lLerner and *lZ*-score, and model (2) between lLerner and *LLPTA*) for all sample banks.

The impact of bank risk (*lZ*-score) on bank market power is positive and is significant at 5% (column 2, model (1) of Table 5). On the other hand, the impact of bank market power (lLerrner) on bank risk (*lZ*-score) is positive and significant at 1%. Thus, the change in bank risk ratio (*lZ*-score) is the cause of the change in bank market power (lLerner). This result supports Hypothesis H3 and the shift in bank market also is the cause of the difference in the bank risk ratio (*lZ*-score) — the results support Hypothesis H2 and competition-stability theory.

Table 5 presents the causal relationship between the market power and the risk ratio determined by the loan loss provisions ratio (*LLPTA*). Results (model (2), column 3) show that the impact of bank risk (*LLPTA*) on bank market power (lLerner) is positive and significant at 1% (column 3, model (2) of Table 5). The impact of bank market power on bank risk (*LLPTA*) is positive and significant at 5%. Thus, the change in the risk ratio is

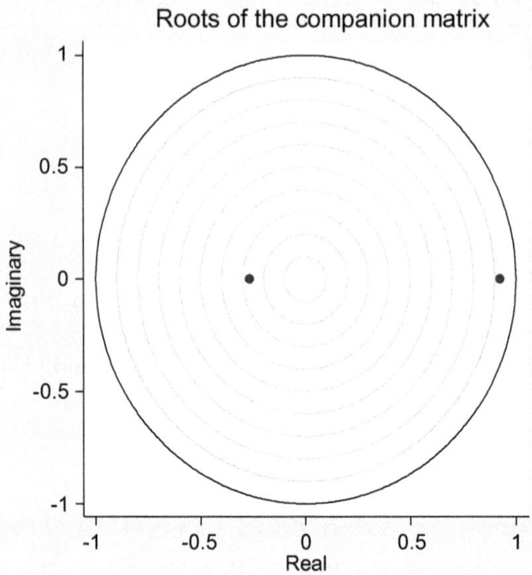


**Figure 1:** Stability condition of *PVAR*: Lerner and *Z*-score.

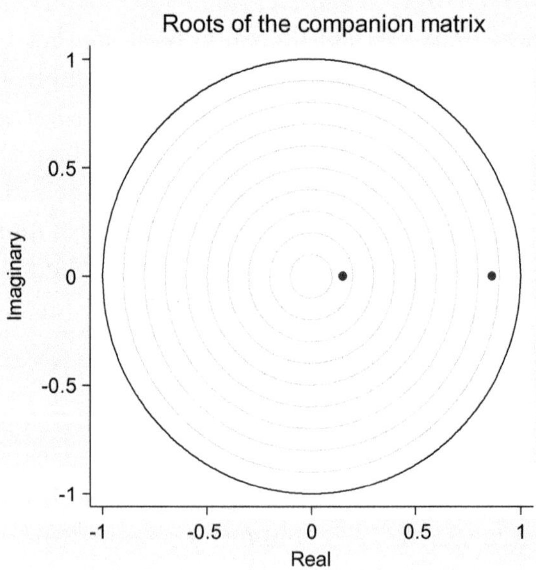


**Figure 2:** Stability condition of *PVAR*: Lerner and *LLPTA*.

**Table 5:** Granger causality analysis results: lLerrner $lZ$-score (1) and lLerner $LLPTA$ (2).

| | *lLerner* | *lLerner* |
|---|---|---|
| **Variable** | **(1)** | **(2)** |
| $lLernert - 1$ | $0.647^{***}$ | $0.320^{**}$ |
| | [3.09] | [2.22] |
| $lZ\text{-score}_{t-1}$ | $1.088^{**}$ | |
| | [1.96] | |
| $LLPTA_{t-1}$ | | $28.54^{***}$ |
| | | [3.53] |
| | ***lZ-score*** | |
| $lLerner_{t-1}$ | $0.233^{***}$ | |
| | [2.99] | |
| $lZ\text{-score}_{t-1}$ | 0.00952 | |
| | [0.05] | |
| | | *LLPTA* |
| $lLerner_{t-1}$ | | $0.00322^{**}$ |
| | | [2.22] |
| $LLPTA_{t-1}$ | | $0.697^{***}$ |
| | | [3.70] |
| $N$ | 1167 | 1173 |
| Hansen's J chi2(12) | $p = 0.359$ | $p = 0.869$ |

*Notes*: This table presents the coefficient estimation for the three baseline variables in the $PVAR$ model. $T$ statistics in brackets, $^{***}p < 0.01$, $^{**}p < 0.05$, $^{*}p < 0.1$. PVAR-Granger causality Wald test: $H_0$ does not exclude Granger-cause equation variable, $H_a$ excludes Granger-caused equation variable.

the cause of the change of bank market power. The difference of bank market power is also the cause of the change in the bank loan loss provisions ratio — the results support Hypothesis H1, the competition-fragility theory, and correspond with the findings of Ariss (2010), Dima *et al.* (2014), and Kabir and Worthington (2017).

## 4.3. *Impulse response functions and variance decompositions*

Figures 3(a) and 3(b) present the Impulse-response functions to shocks, for $PVAR$ model with three variables including lLerner,

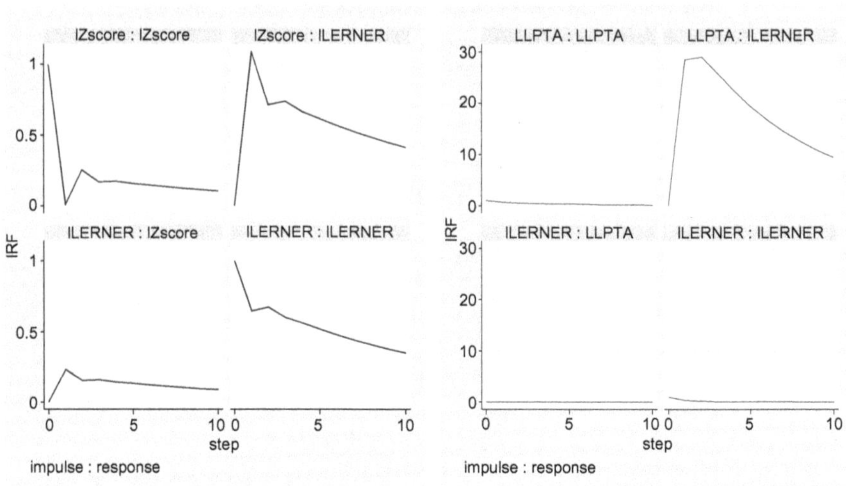


(a) (b)

**Figure 3:** (a) Impulse-response functions for one lag *VAR* of lLerner and *lZ*-score, and (b) Impulse-response functions for one lag *VAR* of lLerner and *LLPTA*.

*lZ*-score, and *LLPTA* for *ASEAN* banks. The dashed lines are 5% standard error confidences around the estimate.

The result in (Figure 3) shows a shock to the *lZ*-score, which results in a strong increase in the lLerner for the first stage, but this immediately declines and continues to hold this pattern for the next stage (in the upper right corner of (Figure 3(a))). While a shock to the lLerner results in a slight increase in the *lZ*-score for the first stage, it slightly reduces and lasts for the next stages until the 5th stage is no longer affected (in the corner of (Figure 3(a))).

Figure 3(b) shows that a shock to the *LLPTA* results in a strong increase in the lLerner for the first stage but does not affect the second and third stages, following which it strongly reduces throughout the next stages (in the upper right corner of (Figure 3(b))). While a shock to the lLerner no longer affects the first stage, it lasts for the next stages (in the under left corner of (Figure 3(b)).

The results of Table 6a's analysis of variance decomposition between market power (lLerner) and risk ratio (*lZ*-score) are shown as follows:

**Table 6a:** Forecast variance decomposition for impulse variable: lLerner and *lZ*-score.

| Response variable | Impulse variable | |
|---|---|---|
| | **lLerner** | ***lZ*-score** |
| **lLerner** | | |
| 0 | 0 | 0 |
| 1 | 1 | 0 |
| 2 | 0.8465 | 0.1535 |
| 3 | 0.8376 | 0.1624 |
| 4 | 0.8248 | 0.1752 |
| 5 | 0.8189 | 0.1811 |
| 6 | 0.8145 | 0.1855 |
| 7 | 0.8116 | 0.1884 |
| 8 | 0.8094 | 0.1906 |
| 9 | 0.8078 | 0.1922 |
| 10 | 0.8065 | 0.1935 |
| ***lZ*-score** | | |
| 0 | 0 | 0 |
| 1 | 0.0143 | 0.9857 |
| 2 | 0.2011 | 0.7989 |
| 3 | 0.2599 | 0.7401 |
| 4 | 0.3122 | 0.6878 |
| 5 | 0.3467 | 0.6533 |
| 6 | 0.3729 | 0.6271 |
| 7 | 0.3928 | 0.6072 |
| 8 | 0.4083 | 0.5917 |
| 9 | 0.4205 | 0.5795 |
| 10 | 0.4304 | 0.5696 |

**Table 6b:** Forecast variance decomposition for impulse variable: lLerner and *LLPTA*.

| Response variable | Impulse variable | |
|---|---|---|
| | **lLerner** | ***LLPTA*** |
| **lLerner** | | |
| 0 | 0 | 0 |
| 1 | 1 | 0 |
| 2 | 0.6641 | 0.3359 |
| 3 | 0.5491 | 0.4509 |
| 4 | 0.4998 | 0.5002 |
| 5 | 0.4741 | 0.5259 |
| 6 | 0.4590 | 0.5410 |
| 7 | 0.4493 | 0.5507 |
| 8 | 0.4429 | 0.5571 |
| 9 | 0.4384 | 0.5616 |
| 10 | 0.4353 | 0.5647 |
| ***LLPTA*** | | |
| 0 | 0 | 0 |
| 1 | 0.1871 | 0.8129 |
| 2 | 0.2212 | 0.7788 |
| 3 | 0.2379 | 0.7621 |
| 4 | 0.2471 | 0.7529 |
| 5 | 0.2526 | 0.7474 |
| 6 | 0.2561 | 0.7439 |
| 7 | 0.2585 | 0.7415 |
| 8 | 0.2601 | 0.7399 |
| 9 | 0.2613 | 0.7387 |
| 10 | 0.2621 | 0.7379 |

The change in market power is explained by the risk ratio (*lZ*-score) of nearly 16% for the first stages and more than 19% for the next stages. Thus, the influence of risk on market power has a relatively large explanation in the subsequent stages. On the other hand, the change in risk ratio (*lZ*-score) is explained by the market power of just over 4%.

Table 6b shows that the *LLPTA* of nearly 34% demonstrates the change in market power for the first stages, and this figure is more than 56% for the next stages. On the other hand, the shift in risk ratio (*LLPTA*) is explained by the market power of just over 2%.

## 5. Conclusion

A *PVAR* approach has been used to model and to quantify the interaction between market power and risk. Our findings measure market power and risk, besides analyzing the causal relationship between market power and risk throughout the *PVAR* model.

An interesting result of the *PVAR* model is that both the impact (i) of risk (*lZ*-score and *LLPTA*) on market power and (ii) of market power on risk, are significant for the sample of ASEAN banks.

Except for the impact of market power on risk and vice versa, *IRF* and *VDC* indicate that the causal relationship between market power and risk is rigid for *ASEAN* banks. There is a change in risk that shows close causality: (1) The increase in risk (*LLPTA*) leads to an increase in market power; (2) a decrease in risk, increases stability (*lZ*-score) and also leads to a rise in market power; on which the important role of management is focused.

On the contrary, causality from market power to risk is positive for *ASEAN* banks. An increase in market power leads to an increase in the loan loss provisions ratio (*LLPTA*) so that there is a trade-off between market power and risk for these banks. On the other hand, an increase in market power leads to bank risk reduction, increases stability (*lZ*-score), thus supporting the competition-stability theory.

Our results have some policy implications. First, commercial banks need to consider maintaining a high ratio of loans to total assets to maintain a high level of financial stability for banks, thereby contributing to improving bank market power. Second, bank executives in business operations need to improve the management of the bank's expense and income, which requires considerations between traditional activities and diversification strategies. Diversification strategies face high levels of risk; however, investors tend to be more biased in diversifying large banks (Batten and Vo, 2016). This helps banks improve their competitiveness, thus contributing to increased bank stability. Third, our findings provide evidence that a causal relationship exists between market power and stability, besides supporting both competition-stability and competition-fragility theories, suggesting managers should focus on solving this issue by developing appropriate policies for banks.

## References

Anginer, D., Demirguc-Kunt, A., and Zhu, M. (2014). How does competition affect bank systemic risk? *Journal of Financial Intermediation*, 23(1), 1–26.

Arellano, M., and Bover, O. (1995). Another look at the instrumental variable estimation of error-components models. *Journal of Econometrics*, 68(1), 29–51.

Ariss, R.T. (2010). On the implications of market power in banking: Evidence from developing countries. *Journal of Banking & Finance*, 34(4), 765–775.

Batten, J.A., and Vo, X.V. (2016). Bank risk shifting and diversification in an emerging market. *Risk Management*, 18(4), 217–235.

Beck, T., De Jonghe, O., and Schepens, G. (2013) Bank competition and stability: Cross-country heterogeneity. *Journal of Financial Intermediation*, 22(2), 218–244.

Berger, A.N., and DeYoung, R. (1997). Problem loans and cost efficiency in commercial banks. *Journal of Banking & Finance*, 21(6), 849–870.

Berger, A.N., and Hannan, T.H. (1998). The efficiency cost of market power in the banking industry: A test of the "quiet life" and related hypotheses. *Review of Economics and Statistics*, 80(3), 454–465.

Berger, A.N., Klapper, L.F., and Turk-Ariss, R. (2009). Bank competition and financial stability. *Journal of Financial Services Research*, 35(2), 99–118.

Boyd, J.H., and De Nicolo, G. (2005). The theory of bank risk taking and competition revisited. *The Journal of Finance*, 60(3), 1329–1343.

Chan, S.-G., Koh, E.H., Zainir, F., and Yong, C.-C. (2015). Market structure, institutional framework and bank efficiency in ASEAN 5. *Journal of Economics and Business*, 82, 84–112.

De Guevara, J.F., and Maudos, J. (2007). Explanatory factors of market power in the banking system. *The Manchester School*, 75(3), 275–296.

De Guevara, J.F., Maudos, J., and Pérez, F. (2005). Market power in European banking sectors. *Journal of Financial Services Research*, 27(2), 109–137.

Delis, M., Iosifidi, M., and Tsionas, M.G. (2017). Endogenous bank risk and efficiency. *European Journal of Operational Research*, 260(1), 376–387.

Dima, B., Dincă, M.S., and Spulbăr, C. (2014). Financial nexus: Efficiency and soundness in banking and capital markets. *Journal of International Money and Finance*, 47, 100–124.

Fiordelisi, F., and Mare, D.S. (2014). Competition and financial stability in European cooperative banks. *Journal of International Money and Finance*, 45, 1–16.

Fiordelisi, F., Marques-Ibanez, D., and Molyneux, P. (2011). Efficiency and risk in European banking. *Journal of Banking & Finance*, 35(2), 1315–1326.

Fu, X.M., Lin, Y.R., and Molyneux, P. (2014). Bank competition and financial stability in Asia Pacific. *Journal of Banking & Finance*, 38, 64–77.

Fungáčová, Z., Solanko, L., and Weill, L. (2010). Market power in the Russian banking industry. *Economic Internationale*, (4), 127–145.

Goetz, M.R. (2017). Competition and bank stability. *Journal of Financial Intermediation*, 35, 57–69.

Hellmann, T.F., Murdock, K.C., and Stiglitz, J.E. (2000). Liberalization, moral hazard in banking, and prudential regulation: Are capital requirements enough? *American Economic Review*, 147–165.

Jayakumar, M., Pradhan, R.P., Dash, S., Maradana, R.P., and Gaurav, K. (2018). Banking competition, banking stability, and economic growth: Are feedback effects at work? *Journal of Economics and Business*, 96, 15–41.

Jiang, L., Levine, R., and Lin, C. (2017). *Does Competition Affect Bank Risk?* 0898-2937, National Bureau of Economic Research.

Kabir, M.N., and Worthington, A.C. (2017). The 'competition–stability/fragility' nexus: A comparative analysis of Islamic and conventional banks. *International Review of Financial Analysis*, 50, 111–128.

Kasman, A., and Carvallo, O. (2014). Financial stability, competition and efficiency in Latin American and Caribbean banking. *Journal of Applied Economics*, 17(2), 301–324.

Keeley, M.C. (1990). Deposit insurance, risk, and market power in banking. *The American Economic Review*, 80, 1183–1200.

Koetter, M., Kolari, J.W., and Spierdijk, L. (2012). Enjoying the quiet life under deregulation? Evidence from adjusted Lerner indices for US banks. *Review of Economics and Statistics*, 94(2), 462–480.

Kouki, I., and Al-Nasser, A. (2017). The implication of banking competition: Evidence from African countries. *Research in International Business and Finance*, 39, 878–895.

Khan, H.H., Ahmad, R.B., and Gee, C.S. (2016). Bank competition and monetary policy transmission through the bank lending channel: Evidence from ASEAN. *International Review of Economics & Finance*, 44, 19–39.

Laeven, L. (2004). The political economy of deposit insurance. *Journal of Financial Services Research*, 26(3), 201–224.

Liu, H., and Wilson, J.O. (2013). Competition and risk in Japanese banking. *The European Journal of Finance*, 19(1), 1–18.

Love, I., and Zicchino, L. (2006). Financial development and dynamic investment behavior: Evidence from panel VAR. *The Quarterly Review of Economics and Finance*, 46(2), 190–210.

Lütkepohl, H. (2006). Structural vector autoregressive analysis for cointegrated variables. *Advances in Statistical Analysis*, 90(1), 75–88.

Pradhan, R.P., Arvin, M.B., Nair, M., and Bennett, S.E. (2019). Inter-linkages between competition and stabilisation policies in the banking sector and stock market development in Europe. *Applied Economics*, 51(39), 4313–4324.

Saeed, M., and Izzeldin, M. (2016). Examining the relationship between default risk and efficiency in Islamic and conventional banks. *Journal of Economic Behavior & Organization*, 132, 127–154.

Saurina Salas, J., Jimenez, G., and Lopez, J.A. (2007). How Does Competition Impact Bank Risk Taking? *EFA 2007 Ljubljana Meetings Paper.*

Schaeck, K., and Čihák, M. (2007). Banking competition and capital ratios. *IMF Working Papers*, 1–40.

Simpasa, A. (2010). Characterising market power and its determinants in the Zambian banking industry. *MPRA Paper*, No. 27232.

Tan, Y. (2018). The impacts of competition and risk on profitability in Chinese banking: Evidence from Boone indicator and stability inefficiency. *Annals of Economics & Finance*, 19(2), 523–554.

Tan, Y., and Floros, C. (2013). Market power, stability and performance in the Chinese banking industry. *Economic Issues*, 18(2), 65–89.

Tan, Y., and Floros, C. (2014). Risk, profitability, and competition: Evidence from the Chinese banking industry. *The Journal of Developing Areas*, 48(3), 303–319.

# Part II

# Financial Markets

https://doi.org/10.1142/9789811227158_0006

# Chapter 6

# Macroeconomics and Banks: Specific Determinants of Vietnamese Commercial Banks' Profitability from 2014 to 2018

**Thi Lan Huong Hoang and Hoang Long Nguyen**


## Abstract

This chapter aims at determining factors that affect the profitability of commercial banks in Vietnam when an additional indicator, i.e., net interest margin (NIM), is added to the research model besides return on equity (ROE) and return on asset (ROA). The yearly data of GDP growth rate, inflation rate, cost to income ratio, non-interest income over total operating income ratio, loan to total assets ratio, equity to total assets ratio, customer deposits to total assets ratio, loan loss provisions over total loans ratio, operating income over total assets, and total assets from 2014 to 2018 of 24 Vietnamese commercial banks were employed in this research. Under the generalized least square regression method, the empirical results show that when the bank profitability is measured by NIM, non-interest income over total operating income ratio has a negative effect on bank profitability while the ratios of customer deposits to total assets, loan loss provisions over total loans, and operating income over total assets have positive effects on bank profitability, and these effects are statistically significant. The cost to income ratio, total assets, equity to total assets, and GDP growth rate also have negative impacts on bank profitability. Meanwhile, the rate of the loan outstanding to total assets and inflation rate show positive influences on bank profitability, and these effects are statistically insignificant. Implications and suggestions for further studies are provided at the end.


**Keywords:** Bank-specific determinants; NIM; Profitability; ROE; ROA; Vietnam commercial banks.

## 1. Introduction

### 1.1. *Rationale*

Commercial banks play an important role in the financial system of a country, whether developed or developing, since they act as financial intermediaries between those who are in surplus of capital and those who are in need of capital. An efficient banking system contributes positively to economic development — when it converts deposits into productive investments and provides better service quality to consumers, then it promotes economic activities. In other words, the effectiveness of the banking system is closely related to the health of an economy (Nguyen and Nguyen, 2016). One of the important factors demonstrating the effectiveness of the banking system is its profitability. Recognition of determinants of the banking system's profitability, therefore, is essential for policymakers and bank leaders. There are many studies on the determinants of bank profitability in Vietnam and around the world. Most studies focus on the impact of macroeconomic and bank-specific factors on commercial banks' profitability. However, these studies produce different empirical results. Regarding the relationship between Vietnam's GDP growth rate and bank profitability, for example, Ha and Nguyen (2017) report a positive effect while Le and Bui (2016) realize a negative influence. These controversial results can come from inconsistency in selecting determinants and indicators.

In most research around the world, return on equity (ROE) or return on asset (ROA) is selected as the major indicator of bank profitability. Vietnam researchers share the same case except for Le and Bui (2016) and Tran (2014). According to Tue (2018), from 2015 to 2017, despite the fact that the 4.0 technological revolution helps increase Vietnamese commercial banks' non-interest income, their interest income still occupies the majority of the profits, ranging from 70% to 80% of total income on average. This chapter is, therefore, conducted with an additional indicator of bank profitability, i.e., net interest margin (NIM), aiming at identifying factors that affect the profitability of Vietnamese commercial banks based on a new measurement. Then, implications are provided to contribute to increasing the profitability of the Vietnamese banking system. To achieve the above objectives, the question of *What are macroeconomic and bank-specific factors that affect the profitability of Vietnamese commercial banks?* is expected to be persuasively answered through this research.

## 1.2. *Literature review*

AL-Omar and AL-Mutairi (2008) relate bank-specific factors to the profitability of the Kuwaiti banking sector during 1993–2005. To achieve this goal, the authors use panel data of 7 national commercial banks. Using ordinary least square (OLS) and seemingly unrelated regression (SUR) methods, estimation outputs show that equity to assets ratio and bank size (measured by log of total assets) are positively related to the profitability (measured by ROA) while non-interest assets to total assets ratio has a negative effect on banks' profitability. The coefficients of loan to assets ratio and operating cost to total assets ratio are statistically insignificant.

Athanasoglou *et al.* (2008) examine the impact of bank-specific and macroeconomic factors on Greek commercial banks' profitability. This study uses unbalanced panel data of Greek banks during 1985–2001 and employs generalized method of moments (GMMs) method. The estimation outputs show that capital variable (equity/assets), productivity growth (rate of change in inflation-adjusted gross total revenue/personnel), and expected inflation positively affected banks' profitability (measured by ROA); credit risk (measured by loan loss provision/loans) and operating expenses management (measured by operating expenses/assets) are negatively related to banks' profitability.

Gul *et al.* (2011) research the correlation between bank-specific, macroeconomic factors in Pakistani commercial banks. Using panel data of 15 top banks of Pakistan for the 2005–2009 period, this research employs pooled ordinary least square (POLS) method for regression. The regression outputs indicate that GDP growth, inflation (measured by consumer price index, CPI), bank size (measured by natural logarithm of total assets), ratio of total loans to total assets, and ratio of total deposits to total assets have a positive effect on banks' profitability (measured by ROA). In contrast, ratio of equity to total assets and market capitalization negatively affect banks' profitability, but the coefficients of these indicators are statistically insignificant. Ali *et al.* (2011) also study bank-specific and macroeconomic determinants of commercial banks' profitability in Pakistan. Their study used panel data of 22 public and private sector commercial banks of Pakistan during 2006–2009 and employed POLS method. Their results show that banks' profitability measured by ROA, GDP growth, and ratio of operating income to total assets positively affect banks' profitability, while ratio of loan loss provision to total loans, capital adequacy ratio (CAR), and CPI negatively affect banks' profitability. The coefficients of natural logarithm of total assets, ratio of total operating expenses to net-interest income, and ratio of total deposits to total assets are statistically insignificant. Bank profitability measured by ROE, GDP growth, and ratio of operating income to total assets has a positive effect on banks' profitability, while ratio of total operating expenses to net-interest income has a negative effect. The coefficients of natural logarithm of total assets, CAR, ratio of loan loss provision to total loans, ratio of total deposits to total assets, and CPI are statistically insignificant.

Sufian and Habibullah (2009) discuss the bank-specific, macroeconomic determinants of the banking system's profitability in China from 2000 to 2005. Their findings suggest that bank size (measured by natural logarithm of total assets), overhead costs (measured by net-interest expenses to total assets), and the growth of money supply are statistically significant and negatively related to Chinese banks' profitability (measured by ROA) while ratio of non-interest income to total assets, level of capitalization (equity/total assets), and GDP growth are statistically significant and positively related to Chinese banks' profitability. The coefficients of liquidity (total loans/total assets) and inflation and credit risk (loan loss provisions/total loans) are statistically insignificant. This research explores further by developing two models that illustrate the impact of these factors on the profitability of two types of banks: state-owned banks and joint-stock banks. For joint-stock commercial banks, credit risk has a positive effect on bank profitability, while overhead costs have a negative effect. The coefficients of liquidity, bank size, ratio of non-interest income to total assets, level of capitalization, GDP growth, inflation, and the money supply growth are statistically insignificant. For state-owned banks, liquidity, credit risk, GDP growth, and level of capitalization positively affect the profitability, while overhead costs and the money supply growth negatively affect the profitability. The coefficients of bank size, ratio of non-interest income to total assets, and inflation are statistically insignificant.

Căpraru and Ihnatov (2015) estimate the effect of bank-specific and macroeconomic factors on bank profitability of the EU15 banking system. They use panel data of 386 banks of 15 countries in the EU from the period of 2001–2011 and the fixed-effect model (FEM) method. In research models, the authors use return on average assets (ROAA), NIM, and return on average equity (ROAE) as dependent variables. Bank profitability measured by NIM, bank size (measured by logarithm of total assets), management efficiency (cost to income ratio), credit risk (measured by non-performing loans/gross loans), liquidity risk (loans to customer deposits ratio), and business mix indicator (measured by other operating income/average assets) have a negative influence on banks' profitability, while the coefficients of capital adequacy (equity/total assets), inflation, and GDP per capita growth are statistically insignificant. Bank profitability measured by ROAA, management efficiency, and credit risk has a negative influence on bank profitability, while bank size, business mix indicator, inflation, and GDP per capita growth positively influence bank profitability. The coefficients of liquidity risk and capital adequacy are statistically insignificant. When bank profitability is measured by ROAE, inflation, GDP per capita growth, and business mix indicator positively influence the profitability. Management efficiency, credit risk, and liquidity risk negatively influence the profitability of banks in EU 15 countries. The coefficients of bank size and capital adequacy are statistically insignificant.

Several studies on the profitability of the commercial banking system have been conducted in Vietnam. Pham (2013) investigates the relationship between NPL and banks' profitability by measuring the effect of NPL ratio on ROE ratio. This research used the unbalanced panel data of 34 commercial banks from 2005 to 2012 and employed estimation methods of POLS, FEM, and random-effect model (REM). Results show that NPL ratio has negative effect on banks' profitability. This relationship is attributed to the fact that the main business of Vietnamese commercial banks is lending. When borrowers cannot repay principal and interest, banks must liquidate borrowers' collateral. However, the liquidity of these assets is normally not high, so the banks have to increase loan loss provisions, leading to a reduction in banks' profits.

Ha and Nguyen (2017) explore the impact of non-interest income on banks' profitability (measured by ROE and ROA). Using panel data of 34 banks from the period 2005–2014, this research applied regression methods such as POLS, FEM, REM, and PCSE. The authors found that non-interest income positively affects banks' profitability. This proves that an increase in non-interest income leads to an increase in bank total income. In addition, the authors also discuss the relationship of GDP growth and bank size with banks' profitability. They suggest that GDP growth positively influences banks' profitability. As the economy grows, efficient firms lead to surplus funds in the market for banks to mobilize as well as more companies expand their production and business, resulting in increased demand for loans. This leads to increased profitability of banks. Similarly, bank size positively influences banks' ROA and ROE. The authors explain that large banks are easier to access and mobilize funds than smaller banks. As banks expand their businesses, large banks have more profitable business opportunities than small banks.

Nguyen and Nguyen (2016) determine factors affecting banks' profitability in Vietnam. Based on panel data of 28 commercial banks from the period 2002–2013, the authors employ POLS method on ROE and ROA ratios as dependent variables. The research outputs show that bank size and operating costs positively affect ROE and

**Table 1:** Summary of previous research in Vietnam.

| Author | Data and estimation method | Dependent variable | Independent variable |
|---|---|---|---|
| Pham (2013) | 34 Vietnamese banks during 2005–2012. Estimated by POLS, FEM and REM methods. | ROE | lnAsset, non-performing loans to total loans, loan loss provisions to total loans, operating income to total assets, operating expenses to total assets |
| Ha and Nguyen (2017) | 34 Vietnamese banks during 2005–2014. Estimated by POLS, FEM, REM and PCSE methods. | ROE, ROA | Non-interest income to total income, equity to total assets, loan to total assets, cost to income ratio, lnAsset, GDP growth rate, NIM |
| Nguyen and Nguyen (2016) | 28 Vietnamese banks during 2002–2013. | ROE, ROA | lnAsset, equity to total assets, loan to total assets, operating expenses to total assets |
| Le and Bui (2016) | 20 Vietnamese banks during 2007–2015. Estimated by POLS, FEM and REM methods. | NIM | Loan to total asset, equity to total assets, GDP growth rate, inflation rate |
| Tran (2014) | 22 Vietnamese banks during 2006–2012. Estimated by GMM method. | ROE, ROA, NIM | lnAsset, non-performing loans to total loans, equity to total assets, deposit to total assets, loan to total assets, GDP growth rate, inflation rate |

ROA. Capital ratio has a positive effect on ROA, while it has a negative impact on ROE. Inflation rate, GDP growth, and stock market growth (measured by ratio of the average transaction value on the Vietnamese stock market to the annual GDP) have positive impacts on profitability of banks. There is no statistically significant relationship between ratio of loan to assets and banks' profitability. State-owned commercial banks' profitability is higher than joint-stock commercial banks' profitability. With a similar research question, the research of Le and Bui (2016) measured the impact of CPI, GDP growth, ratio of loan to total assets, and ratio of equity to total assets on NIM ratio of banks. Using panel data of 20 commercial banks from the period 2007–2015, this study employed POLS, FEM and REM methods. The authors realize that GDP growth negatively affects NIM ratio of banks. In contrast, CPI, ratio of loan to total assets, and ratio of equity to total assets have a positive effect on banks' NIM ratio, but the correlation between CPI and NIM ratio is statistically insignificant.

Table 1 shows that in previous studies conducted in Vietnam, banks' profitability is typically measured by two main indicators: ROA and ROE, except for Le and Bui (2016) and Tran (2014) who used NIM as another measurement. Different dependent variables lead to differences in regression results. Previous studies do not examine the correlation between NIM and two ratios, i.e., non-interest income to total income and operating income to total assets. This research, instead, examines the relationship between these variables, with more updated data from the period 2014–2018.

## 2. Methodology

### 2.1. *Data collection procedure*

In respect to bank-specific variables, similar to previous research papers, financial ratios are also used as explanatory variables. They are calculated from the items on banks' yearly financial statements that are published on the banks' websites. Nine ratios as bank-specific variables are selected. In terms of macroeconomic variables, GDP growth rate and inflation rate are selected from websites of Vietnam's General Statistics Office (GSO) and the World Bank. Balanced panel data of 24 commercial banks in Vietnam from the period 2014–2018 create the size of 120 observations.

## 2.2. *Research model*

Following Le and Bui (2016), six additional bank-specific variables are added in this research. Since banks' total assets are measured in million VND, the total assets are transformed into natural logarithms of total assets to be appropriate with the units of other variables. Hence, the econometric model in this project is as follows:

$$\begin{aligned} NIM_{i,t} = {} & \beta_1 + \beta_2 ETA_{i,t} + \beta_3 LTA_{i,t} + \beta_4 GDP_t + \beta_5 INFL_t \\ & + \beta_6 lnAsset_{i,t} + \beta_7 DETA_{i,t} + \beta_8 CTI_{i,t} + \beta_9 LPTL_{i,t} \\ & + \beta_{10} NII_{i,t} + \beta_{11} OITA_{i,t} + u_{i,t}, \end{aligned}$$

where $i$ is bank and $t$ is year, the description of the variables is listed in Table 2. $\beta_2, \beta_3, \beta_4, \beta_5, \beta_6, \beta_7, \beta_8, \beta_9, \beta_{10}$ and $\beta_{11}$ are coefficients of explanatory variables. The residuals are denoted by $u$. $\beta_1$ is intercept. The additional variables are similar to those in Tran (2014), Ha and Nguyen (2017), and Pham (2013).

## 2.3. *Variables*

### 2.3.1. *Dependent variable*

In the literature, banks' profitability is typically measured by ROA, ROE, and NIM. ROA shows how a bank's management generates profits from the bank's assets, but ROA can be biased because of off-balance-sheet activities (Athanasoglou *et al.*, 2008). Off-balance-sheet profits are added to banks' total profit, but the denominator of ROA does not include off-balance-sheet assets.

ROE implies the return to shareholders on their equity and equals ROA divided by equity to total assets ratio (financial leverage multiplier). The relationship between ROE and ROA implies the tradeoff

**Table 2:** Variables' description.

| Symbol | Variable | Unit | Data source |
|---|---|---|---|
| | **Dependent variable** | | |
| NIM | Net-interest margin | % | Financial statements |
| | **Explanatory variable** | | |
| | **Macroeconomic variables** | | |
| GDP | GDP growth rate | % | World Bank, GSO |
| INFL | Inflation rate | % | World Bank, GSO |
| | **Bank-specific variables** | | |
| LTA | Loan to total assets ratio | % | Financial statements |
| ETA | Equity to total assets ratio | % | Financial statements |
| lnAsset | Natural logarithm of total assets | % | Financial statements |
| DETA | Customer deposits to total assets ratio | % | Financial statements |
| CTI | Cost to income ratio | % | Financial statements |
| LPTL | Loan loss provision to total loans ratio | % | Financial statements |
| OITA | Operating income to total assets | % | Financial statements |
| NII | Non-interest income to total operating income | % | Financial statements |

between risks and profits. In other words, this relationship clearly reflects the level of risk tolerance in bank operations when equity-to-total assets ratio measures financial leverage. But only ROE does not reflect the risks associated with high leverage as financial leverage is affected by regulations (Athanasoglou *et al.*, 2008).

So NIM appears as the key ratio to measure bank profitability. NIM measures the revenue earned from interest activities, so the ratio of NIM represents the bank's efficiency and how successful the loans and investments made by the bank are. Moreover, Vietnamese banks have the largest share of total income from net interest income because the main business activities of banks are traditional activities (taking deposits and making loans). Therefore, a bank with high net interest income is usually profitable and ROA and ROE ratios are higher than for other banks (Tran, 2014). NIM is used as a dependent variable in studies of Tran (2014) and Ho and Nguyen (2014).

### 2.3.2. *Independent variables*

#### 2.3.2.1. Bank capitalization

Equity to total assets ratio measures capital adequacy and it represents how well the bank is capitalized. This ratio is employed in the research of Obamuyi (2013). Abreu and Mendes (2002) find that well-capitalized banks face low predicted bankruptcy and funding costs and higher interest margins on profitable assets, thus showing a positive relationship between the ratio and bank profitability. Furthermore, larger equity decreases the demand and costs for external funding, leading to an increase in banks' profitability. In contrast, smaller equity implies higher funding costs, leading to a decline in banks' profitability.

**Hypothesis H01:** *The relationship between Vietnamese banks' profitability and equity to assets ratio is statistically insignificant.*

**Hypothesis H11:** *The relationship between Vietnamese banks' profitability and equity to assets ratio is statistically significant.*

#### 2.3.2.2. Loans

Total loans to total assets ratio measures banks' loans. This ratio is employed in the research of Tran (2014). The main source of banks' income is making loans, so loans are expected to have a positive effect on banks' profitability. More customer deposits are transformed into banks' loans leading to an increase in banks' profitability.

However, some other papers find a negative correlation between loans and the profitability of banks. When a bank extends its loan portfolio size, it has to pay additional costs for provisions (Menicucci and Paolucci, 2016). Consequently, a too high share of the loan to total assets can imply that banks rapidly grow their loan portfolio, paying a higher cost for provisions, and this circumstance causes a negative influence on banks' profitability.

**Hypothesis H02:** *The relationship between Vietnamese banks' profitability and loan to assets ratio is statistically insignificant.*

**Hypothesis H12:** *The relationship between Vietnamese banks' profitability and loan to assets ratio is statistically significant.*

2.3.2.3. Customer deposits

Banks are dependent substantially on customer deposits to make loans to borrowers. The more the customer deposits, the more the available funds that a bank uses to make loans to borrowers and the more the interest revenue that banks earn. Customer deposits over the total assets ratio are used to measure customer deposits and this ratio is used in the study of Tran (2014).

Lee and Hsieh (2013) report that a higher amount of deposits gives opportunities to banks to generate more interest income, while a lower amount of deposits negatively influences banks' profitability. Therefore, customer deposits positively correlate with banks' profitability. It can be said that a higher amount of deposits would allow a bank to extend the lending activities and consequently generate more profits.

Naceur and Goaied (2001) find that banks with high profitability are those that have a high share of customer deposits in their total assets. An increase in customer deposits leads to an increase in funds for lending activities and investments, leading to banks' higher profitability.

**Hypothesis H03:** *The relationship between Vietnamese banks' profitability and customer deposits to total assets ratio is statistically insignificant.*

**Hypothesis H13:** *The relationship between Vietnamese banks' profitability and customer deposits to total assets ratio is statistically significant.*

2.3.2.4. Loan loss provisions

The ratio of loan loss provisions over the total loan ratio is employed to measure banks' loan loss provisions. This ratio appears in the research of Pham (2013). The level of loan loss provisions can be a signal for a bank's asset quality. A higher amount of loan loss provisions, therefore, indicates a lower credit quality in the bank's loan portfolio. Low credit quality of loans increases the provisioning costs and lowers total income from the loans. As a result, a high ratio of loan loss provisions to total loans can imply poor credit quality and higher risk in a bank's loan portfolio, leading to a decrease in the bank's profitability. For this reason, loan loss provisions to total loans ratio is predicted to have a negative impact on banks' profitability.

**Hypothesis H04:** *The relationship between Vietnamese banks' profitability and loan loss provisions to total loans ratio is statistically insignificant.*

**Hypothesis H14:** *The relationship between Vietnamese banks' profitability and loan loss provisions to total loans ratio is statistically significant.*

2.3.2.5. Expenses management

Expenses management refers to managing the costs of operating a bank such as administrative costs and staff salaries. It is measured by the cost to income ratio. This ratio appears in the research of Ha and Nguyen (2017).

The relationship between the expenses and profits simply implies that higher expenses lower banks' profits and vice versa. However, this is not always true. The reason is that a higher share of expenses to total income can be related to a higher volume of banking activities, leading to higher banks' earnings (Kosmidou, 2008).

**Hypothesis H05:** *The relationship between Vietnamese banks' profitability and cost to income ratio is statistically insignificant.*

**Hypothesis H15:** *The relationship between Vietnamese banks' profitability and cost to income ratio is statistically significant.*

2.3.2.6. GDP growth rate

During the period, GDP growth rate increases as well as the demand of people for lending (Dietrich and Wanzenried, 2011). Hence, thanks to the demand, banks can extend lending activities, leading to higher interest income (Garcia and Guerreiro, 2016). Dietrich and Wanzenried (2014) conclude that yearly GDP growth rate positively correlates with banks' profitability.

**Hypothesis H06:** *The relationship between Vietnamese banks' profitability and GDP growth rate is statistically insignificant.*

**Hypothesis H16:** *The relationship between Vietnamese banks' profitability and GDP growth rate is statistically significant.*

2.3.2.7. Inflation rate

Al-Jafari and Alchami (2014) write that the influence of the inflation rate on banks' profitability depends on the expectations of banks' managers about the inflation rate. Perry (1992) suggests that if banks fully forecast inflation rate, they can properly adjust interest rates to increase their earnings faster than their operating costs, leading to an increase in banks' profits. Molyneux and Thornton (1992) report a positive influence of the inflation rate on banks' profitability. In contrast, if banks cannot fully forecast inflation rate, they cannot adjust interest rates appropriately to ensure that banks' expenditure increases faster than their earnings (Perry, 1992), leading to lower profits.

**Hypothesis H07:** *The relationship between Vietnamese banks' profitability and inflation rate is statistically insignificant.*

**Hypothesis H17:** *The relationship between Vietnamese banks' profitability and inflation rate is statistically significant.*

2.3.2.8. Bank size

Bank size appears in the research of Obamuyi (2013) as an explanatory variable and it is represented by the natural log of total assets. The influence of size on banks' profitability in related papers is examined with the assumption that large banks can get higher profits thanks to economies of scale. Bank size can result in economies of scale whereby banks can provide services at a lower cost (Kosmidou, 2008). In addition, larger banks are assumed to be more efficient and more profitable than smaller banks when larger banks normally have more products than smaller ones. Hence, larger banks can enter into markets that smaller banks cannot access (Menicucci and Paolucci, 2016). In contrast, some research suppose that larger banks can suffer scale of inefficiencies (Berger and Humphrey, 1997) because increasing the bank size can only save little costs (Boyd and Runkle, 1993). Thus, smaller banks can have higher profitability than larger ones. The empirical evidence is not the same. Berger and Humphrey (1997) find economies of scale for large banks. Scholtens (2000) confirms that small banks' profits grew faster than larger banks'. Naceur (2003) realizes that size significantly and negatively correlates with the bank profitability.

**Hypothesis H08:** *The relationship between Vietnamese banks' profitability and the bank size is statistically insignificant.*

**Hypothesis H18:** *The relationship between Vietnamese banks' profitability and the bank size is statistically significant.*

2.3.2.9. Revenue diversification

Revenue diversification is measured by the ratio of non-interest income to total income. This ratio is utilized in the research of Ha and Nguyen (2017).

Elsas *et al.* (2010) find that commercial banks typically increase revenue diversification by doing fee-based business. Banks also broaden their activities to trading activities or underwriting insurance contracts.

Revenue diversification can enhance bank profitability through higher income from non-interest businesses (Elsas *et al.*, 2010). Nevertheless, DeYoung and Rice (2004) realize that a greater level of revenue diversification does not mean bank profitability is improved. However, a bank has a higher level of profitability when it has a higher level of revenue diversification.

**Hypothesis H09:** *The relationship between Vietnamese banks' profitability and non-interest income to total income ratio is statistically insignificant.*

**Hypothesis H19:** *The relationship between Vietnamese banks' profitability and non-interest income to total income ratio is statistically significant.*

2.3.2.10. Asset management

Efficiency in banks' asset management for generating profits is measured by the ratio of operating income over total assets. This ratio appears in the research of Ali, Akhtar, and Ahmed (2011). This ratio shows banks' efficiency in asset exploitation and it typically has a positive effect on bank profitability (Ali *et al.*, 2011). Ali *et al.* (2011) report that the ratio positively correlated with bank profitability.

**Hypothesis H010:** *The relationship between Vietnamese banks' profitability and operating income to total assets ratio is statistically insignificant.*

**Hypothesis H110:** *The relationship between Vietnamese banks' profitability and operating income to total assets ratio is statistically significant.*

Explanatory variables in previous researches and their expected signs are summarized in Table 3.

## 2.4. *Estimation methods*

STATA software is employed in this research. The correlation matrix is employed to examine the existence of multicollinearity problems between explanatory variables. A number of estimation techniques, including POLS, FEM, and REM, are utilized in this study. Breusch and Pagan Lagrangian test is used to determine the better model between POLS and REM. After that, Hausman test results are used to select the more appropriate model between FEM and REM. The results of Hausman test suggest that FEM is the more appropriate model than REM. Nevertheless, when Modified Wald test for

**Table 3:** Expected sign for explanatory variables.

| Variable | Author (year) | Previous research sign | Expected sign |
|---|---|---|---|
| GDP growth rate (GDP) | Tran (2014), Le and Bui (2016) | +/− | + |
| Inflation rate (INFL) | Tran (2014), Le and Bui (2016) | +/− | |
| Loan to total assets (LTA) | Le and Bui (2016) | + | + |
| Equity to total assets (ETA) | Le and Bui (2016) | + | + |
| Bank size (lnAsset) | Ha and Nguyen (2017) | + | + |
| Customer deposits over total assets (DETA) | Tran (2014) | + | + |
| Loan loss provisions to total loans (LPTL) | Pham (2013) | − | − |
| Cost to income (CIR) | Ha and Nguyen (2017) | − | − |
| Non-interest income to total operating income (NII) | Ha and Nguyen (2017) | + | + |
| Operating income to total assets (OITA) | Ali, Akhtar, and Ahmed, (2011) | + | + |

heteroskedasticity is conducted, it suggests that FEM encounters heteroskedasticity. On the other hand, Woolridge test confirms that the dataset also encounters autocorrelation problems. These reasons make the regression results estimated by POLS, FEM, and REM methods inefficient and unreliable. Therefore, GLS method is applied to estimate the research model. This method can address problems of autocorrelation and heteroskedasticity. Thus, the estimation results are efficient and reliable.

## 3. Results

### 3.1. *Data description*

Table 4 demonstrates the descriptive statistics of the 24 banks' data during the period from 2014 to 2018. Based on the dispersion

**Table 4:** Descriptive statistics.

| Variable | Observations | Mean | Std. Dev. | Min | Max |
|---|---|---|---|---|---|
| NIM | 120 | 2.816312 | 1.131666 | 0.9807728 | 8.198646 |
| CIR | 120 | 54.68371 | 12.15225 | 28.74657 | 88.0593 |
| NII | 120 | 17.67143 | 12.55158 | −25.93977 | 50.66965 |
| lnAsset | 120 | 18.7075 | 1.043927 | 16.577 | 20.99561 |
| LTA | 120 | 58.3908 | 10.25595 | 22.52535 | 75.30163 |
| ETA | 120 | 8.394822 | 3.118843 | 4.06177 | 22.02968 |
| DETA | 120 | 68.29291 | 11.36444 | 7.484621 | 89.37174 |
| LPTL | 120 | 1.240728 | 0.3651869 | 0.7752018 | 2.448807 |
| OITA | 120 | 3.200112 | 1.33611 | 1.180517 | 9.615378 |
| GDP | 120 | 6.5532 | 0.4020312 | 5.984 | 7.08 |
| INFL | 120 | 3.1786 | 1.261035 | 0.879 | 4.71 |

levels reported from the standard deviation above, *CIR*, *NII*, *LTA*, and *DETA* are substantially more volatile compared with the other variables.

Based on the correlation matrix above (Table 5), no pair of explanatory variables has the correlation coefficient greater than 0.8. This implies that there are no multicollinearity problems in the research model or among chosen explanatory variables.

### 3.2. *Regression results*

The regression results for three models: POLS, FEM, and REM are shown in Tables 6–10.

Breusch and Pagan Lagrangian multiplier test is conducted to choose a better model between POLS and REM with a pair of hypotheses:

**Hypothesis H0:** *Pool ordinary least square model is correct*

**Hypothesis H1:** *Random effect model is correct*

Where $\alpha$ equals 5%, $p$-value equals 0.0001, and $p$-value is less than $\alpha$. Therefore, the null hypothesis is rejected so the random effect model is appropriate. To choose the best model between FEM and REM, Hausman test is conducted with a pair of hypotheses:

**Table 5:** Correlation matrix.

| | **NIM** | **CIR** | **NII** | **lnAss** | **LTA** | **ETA** | **DETA** | **LPTL** | **OITA** | **GDP** | **INF** |
|---|---|---|---|---|---|---|---|---|---|---|---|
| NIM | 1.00 | | | | | | | | | | |
| CIR | −0.44 | 1.00 | | | | | | | | | |
| NII | −0.06 | −0.11 | 1.00 | | | | | | | | |
| lnAss | 0.06 | −0.48 | 0.29 | 1.000 | | | | | | | |
| LTA | 0.23 | −0.21 | −0.16 | 0.270 | 1.00 | | | | | | |
| ETA | 0.31 | 0.06 | 0.13 | −0.57 | −0.12 | 1.00 | | | | | |
| DETA | −0.14 | 0.12 | −0.01 | 0.245 | 0.36 | −0.27 | 1.00 | | | | |
| LPTL | 0.07 | −0.22 | 0.38 | 0.318 | −0.31 | −0.12 | 0.01 | 1.00 | | | |
| OITA | 0.93 | −0.53 | 0.25 | 0.195 | 0.18 | 0.31 | −0.15 | 0.19 | 1.00 | | |
| GDP | 0.09 | −0.13 | 0.05 | 0.165 | 0.29 | −0.10 | 0.02 | −0.10 | 0.15 | 1.00 | |
| INF | −0.05 | −0.03 | 0.212 | 0.019 | −0.075 | −0.027 | −0.165 | 0.130 | 0.021 | −0.359 | 1.000 |

**Table 6:** Estimation results for POLS, FEM, and REM.

| **Variables** | **(1) POLS** | **(2) FEM** | **(3) REM** |
|---|---|---|---|
| CIR | 0.00693*** | −0.00161 | 0.00330 |
| | (0.00172) | (0.00262) | (0.00204) |
| NII | −0.0292*** | −0.0312*** | −0.0296*** |
| | (0.00157) | (0.00185) | (0.00167) |
| lnAsset | 0.00876 | −0.157 | −0.0277 |
| | (0.0256) | (0.0992) | (0.0332) |
| LTA | 0.00141 | 0.00320 | 0.00155 |
| | (0.00200) | (0.00343) | (0.00237) |
| ETA | 0.00722 | −0.0147 | −0.00333 |
| | (0.00762) | (0.0137) | (0.00943) |
| DETA | 0.000670 | −0.000954 | 0.000395 |
| | (0.00161) | (0.00189) | (0.00169) |
| LPTL | 0.0354 | 0.0556 | 0.0415 |
| | (0.0512) | (0.0518) | (0.0501) |
| OITA | 0.894*** | 0.824*** | 0.874*** |
| | (0.0155) | (0.0379) | (0.0221) |
| GDP | −0.132*** | −0.0772 | −0.130*** |
| | (0.0441) | (0.0569) | (0.0394) |
| INFL | −0.0176 | −0.00941 | −0.0180 |
| | (0.0138) | (0.0135) | (0.0118) |
| Constant | 0.618 | 4.223** | 1.652** |
| | (0.634) | (1.648) | (0.727) |
| Obs | 120 | 120 | 120 |
| $R^2$ | 0.981 | 0.959 | |
| Number of Bank1 | | 24 | 24 |

*Notes*: Standard errors in parentheses. $^{***}p < 0.01$, $^{**}p < 0.05$, $^{*}p < 0.1$.

**Table 7:** Breusch and Pagan Lagrangian test result.

| $\chi^2$ **statistic** | **Prob.** |
|---|---|
| 14.32 | 0.0001 |

**H0:** *Random effect model is correct*

**H1:** *Fixed effect model is correct*

**Table 8:** Hausman test result.

| $\chi^2$ **statistic** | **Prob.** |
|---|---|
| 19.97 | 0.0296 |

**Table 9:** Woolridge test result.

| $F$**(1,23)** | **Prob.** |
|---|---|
| 7.856 | 0.0101 |

**Table 10:** Modified Wald test result.

| $\chi^2$ **statistic** | **Prob.** |
|---|---|
| 10338.53 | 0.0000 |

Where $\alpha$ equals 5%, $p$-value equals 0.0296, and the *p-value* is less than 0.05. Therefore, the null hypothesis is rejected so the fixed effect model is appropriate. Consequently, FEM is the best model between POLS, REM, and FEM.

To ensure that the regression results of FEM are efficient and reliable, it is necessary to conduct tests for autocorrelation and heteroskedasticity problems.

Woolridge test for autocorrelation in panel data is conducted to examine whether there is autocorrelation with a pair of hypotheses:

**H0:** *No autocorrelation in the panel data*

**H1:** *Autocorrelation in the panel data*

Where $\alpha$ equals 5%, the $p$-value of the test is 0.0101, so $p$-value is less than 0.05. The null hypothesis is rejected. Therefore, there is autocorrelation in the panel dataset.

Modified Wald test is conducted to test heteroskedasticity problems in FEM with a pair of hypotheses:

**H0:** *Homoskedasticity*

**H1:** *Heteroskedasticity*

Where $\alpha$ equals 5%, the $p$-value of the test is 0.0000. The null hypothesis is rejected. Consequently, heteroskedasticity problems exist in FEM.

Based on the test results mentioned above, heteroskedasticity and autocorrelation problems make the estimation results of FEM inefficient and unreliable. To address these problems in the research model, GLS estimation method is employed to ensure that regression results for the model are efficient and reliable. The estimation results by using GLS method are as follows.

Overall, at $\alpha$ equal to 0.05, the null hypotheses including H01, H02, H05, H06, H07, H08 cannot be rejected and the alternative hypotheses including H13, H14, H19, H110 are accepted.

According to Table 11, the relationship between cost to income ratio and *NIM* is statistically insignificant and the coefficient of the ratio implies that the ratio has a negative impact on bank profitability. A one percent increase in cost to income ratio decreases *NIM* by 0.0018278%, ceteris paribus. This result is consistent with the paper of Ha and Nguyen (2017). The ratio indicates the efficiency in expenses management of banks, the sign of the coefficient shows that higher efficiency in expenditure management leads to higher profitability for banks. Nguyen *et al.* (2018) also suggest that only banks managing their operating costs efficiently can keep their income increase faster than their expenses, ensuring higher profitability.

The relationship between loan to total assets ratio and *NIM* is statistically insignificant and the coefficient of the ratio implies that the ratio has a positive impact on bank profitability. If the ratio increases by one percent, ceteris paribus, *NIM* increases by 0.0107114%. This result is consistent with the research of Nguyen and Nguyen (2016). The sign of the coefficient shows that the more loans banks provide to

**Table 11:** Estimation results by using GLS.

| **Variables** | **GLS** |
|---|---|
| CIR | −0.00183 |
| | (0.00502) |
| NII | −0.0317*** |
| | (0.00521) |
| lnAsset | −0.239 |
| | (0.215) |
| LTA | 0.0107 |
| | (0.0106) |
| ETA | −0.0430 |
| | (0.0293) |
| DETA | 0.0182** |
| | (0.00810) |
| LPTL | 0.880*** |
| | (0.313) |
| OITA | 0.890*** |
| | (0.0548) |
| GDP | −0.103 |
| | (0.109) |
| INFL | 0.0171 |
| | (0.0318) |
| Constant | 3.222 |
| | (3.182) |
| Observations | 120 |
| Number of Bank1 | 24 |

*Notes*: Standard errors in parentheses.
$^{***}p < 0.01$, $^{**}p < 0.05$, $^{*}p < 0.1$.

their customers, the more interest income they can earn. In addition, Nguyen *et al.* (2018) also state that commercial banks in Vietnam emphasize on developing new customer loans, leading to an increase in banks' profitability.

The relationship between deposits to total assets ratio is statistically significant and the coefficient of the ratio shows that the ratio positively affects banks' profitability. Ceteris paribus, a one percent increase in the ratio results in an increase in *NIM* by 0.0181814%. This result is consistent with the research of Menicucci and Paolucci (2016). As mentioned above, customer deposits are the main source of funds that banks employ to make loans to borrowers. On the other hand, commercial banks in Vietnam have a high share of income from interest income and they emphasize developing new loans. Therefore, customer deposits play a pivotal role in the lending activities of banks. The more the loans delivered to borrowers, the more the profits the bank generates.

Equity to total assets ratio negatively correlates with *NIM* and this relationship is statistically insignificant. Ceteris paribus, a one percent increase in the ratio leads to a decrease in *NIM* by 0.0429909%. This result is consistent with a study of Ho and Nguyen (2014). The relationship can be explained such that commercial banks do not take full advantage of equity in doing their business for generating income. When banks increase the ratio of equity over total assets, they get additional funds for lending activities without paying interest on these funds. Moreover, the banks also save a sum of money from not paying interests on these funds. This theoretically increases banks' profitability. However, the growth rate of profits does not keep pace with the growth of equity, leading to a decline in the bank's profit. This explanation is similar to the conclusion of Ho and Nguyen (2014) on the relationship. On the other hand, Ha and Nguyen (2017) suggest another reason that investors who invest in banks want to make their capital more profitable, so they put more pressure on generating higher income on the banks. The number of assets for lending activities increases, leading to an increase in risks of banks. Hence, profitability decreases.

The inflation rate positively correlates with *NIM* and this relationship is statistically insignificant. If the inflation rate increases by one percent, ceteris paribus, *NIM* increases by 0.0171234%. This result is consistent with the research of Tran (2014). This relationship can be explained such that banks adjust interest rates appropriately so that banks' expenditure increases slower than their earnings, leading to banks' higher profitability. Another possible explanation is suggested by Batten and Vo (2019) that banks do not bear any costs related to inflation or that banks pass the costs to their customers, leading to an increase in banks' profitability.

*GDP growth rate* negatively correlates with *NIM* and this relationship is statistically insignificant. If *GDP growth rate* increases by one percent, ceteris paribus, *NIM* will decrease by 0.1027458%. This result is consistent with the research of Le and Bui (2016). An increase in *GDP growth rate* is the signal of economic growth. During the period of economic growth, lending demand increases. This facilitates banks' mobilizing fund activities. At the same time, when the economy grows well, households and firms can expand business and production activities and investment, leading to an increase in demand for loans. However, banks employ a lot of assets for lending leading to increased risks and if the loan portfolio quality is not high, it leads to an increase in risk provision that reduces the profitability of the bank. This explanation is consistent with a study of Ha and Nguyen (2017).

*Bank size* negatively affects *profitability* when the coefficients of *lnAsset* are negative, and this influence is statistically insignificant. If *lnAsset* increases by one percent, ceteris paribus, *NIM* decreases by 0.00239373%. This result is consistent with the research of Batten and Vo (2019). In Vietnam, small banks tend to grow rapidly in scale, focusing on expanding market share but not focusing on credit quality, negatively affecting *profitability* (Nguyen *et al.*, 2018). While larger banks can encounter difficulties in the management of business activities, they are often under pressure to lend to state-owned enterprises, resulting in bad debts. This weakens the profitability of large banks. This opinion is also found in the research of Tran (2014).

Operating income to total assets ratio is reported to have a positive effect on *NIM* and this relationship is statistically significant. Ceteris paribus, a one percent increase in the ratio leads to an increase in *NIM* by 0.8899748%. This result is consistent with the research of Ali *et al.* (2011). Banks' efficient management and exploitation of their assets bring about high efficiency for the banks' business activities. Thus, banks' profits increase, making their profitability increase as well. The opinion above is also found in a study by Pham (2013).

Non-interest income over the total operating income ratio is reported to have a negative impact on bank profitability and this relationship is statistically significant. A 1% increase in non-interest income ratio decreases *NIM* by 0.0316633%, ceteris paribus. This result is inconsistent with the research of Ha and Nguyen (2017). The reason is that Ha and Nguyen (2017) use ROA and ROE to measure bank profitability. This relationship can be explained based on the research results of Le (2017) that when banks engage in different non-lending activities, these activities can affect banks' lending activities. Banks can decrease the lending interest rates to borrowers who also use other services provided by the banks which generate fees and commissions such as underwriting insurance contracts. It can be said that there is a tradeoff between non-lending business and lending activities in the Vietnamese banking system.

Loan loss provision to total loan ratio positively correlates with *NIM* and this relationship is statistically significant. Ceteris paribus, a one percent increase in the ratio leads to an increase in *NIM* by 0.8796238%. This result is consistent with the research results of Tran (2014). The positive effect of loan loss provisions on bank profitability can be explained such that high-risk loans generate higher interest income for banks. This result is in contrast to many other studies, but this result is consistent with the situation of Vietnam where the banking system in recent years has focused on credit growth, although the quality of loans has not improved (Tran, 2014).

## 4. Discussion and Conclusion

In general, this research shows some different results as compared with initial expectations. However, these results are consistent with other studies in Vietnam and the world.

The impact of non-interest income on bank profitability is needed to be considered carefully. This result is different from many other studies in Vietnam, but this also stems from measuring banks' profitability by different ratios. In fact, most banks are shifting their business models from focusing on lending activities with net interest income accounting for 73–75% of the total income of banks to being less dependent on lending businesses, therefore increasing non-interest income. Therefore, the negative effect of non-interest income on *NIM* is quite consistent with the fact in Vietnam.

The negative effect of non-interest income on banks' profitability is statistically significant. This result is in contrast to most other studies' results in Vietnam, but this difference can stem from usage of different indicators as measurement (ROE, ROA). Surprisingly, expenses management negatively correlates with bank profitability, but this relationship is statistically insignificant. Besides, contrary to the initial expectations, bank size, GDP growth rate, and bank capitalization have negative effects on bank profitability, but these effects are statistically insignificant.

In short, non-interest income, customer deposits, asset management, and inflation rate are the factors affecting the profitability of commercial banks in Vietnam. This answer is consistent with Ho and Nguyen (2014) and Ali *et al.* (2011).

Among 24 commercial banks considered in this chapter, there are nine banks that are still not listed on Vietnam's stock market. Besides, three to four banks were listed on the stock market after 2017. Therefore, they do not suffer regulations of information disclosure, so they do not fully clarify quarterly financial reports from 2014 to 2018. For this reason, the data on the quarterly period are limited, while the data of macroeconomic variables are published quarterly. Hence, it influences the accuracy of empirical results. On the other hand, since they do not suffer information disclosure regulations, they also do not provide information on non-performing loans. Therefore, the empirical results cannot reflect fully the impact of the credit quality of loans on banks' profitability. Moreover, many banks sell a large amount of non-performing loans to Vietnam Asset

Management Company (VAMC); this decreases the amount of non-performing loans on the balance sheets of the banks, but they do not earn money from these deals to finance their business activities. It means the information on non-performing loans is not published fully on banks' financial statements. So the research results are not consistent with the fact in Vietnam.

The current banking system in Vietnam includes not only Vietnamese banks but also foreign banks such as HSBC, ANZ, and joint venture banks. Furthermore, foreign investors have been inclined to invest in Vietnamese banks recently. Therefore, it will be interesting to examine the relationship between foreign ownership and bank profitability in future research.

## References

Abreu, M., and Mendes, V. (2002). Commercial bank interest margin and profitability: Evidence for some EU countries. In *Pan-European Conference Jointly Organised by the IEFS-UK & University of Macedonia Economic & Social Sciences, Thessaloniki, Greece, May*, 34(2), 17–20.

Ali, K., Akhtar, M.F., and Ahmed, H.Z. (2011). Bank-specific and macroeconomic indicators of profitability — Empirical evidence from the commercial banks of Pakistan. *International Journal of Business and Social Science*, 2(6), 235–242.

Al-Jafari, M.K., and Alchami, M. (2014). Determinants of bank profitability: Evidence from Syria. *Journal of Applied Finance & Banking*, 4(1), 29.

AL-Omar, H., and AL-Mutairi, A. (2008). Bank-specific determinants of profitability: The case of Kuwait. *Journal of Economic and Administrative Sciences*, 24(2), 20–34. doi:10.1108/10264116200800006

Athanasoglou, P.P., Brissimis, S.N., and Delis, M.D. (2008). Bank-specific, industry-specific and macroeconomic determinants of bank profitability. *Journal of International Financial Markets, Institutions and Money*, 18(2), 121–136. doi:10.1016/j.intfin.2006.07.001

Batten, J. and Vo, X.V. (2019). Determinants of bank profitability — Evidence from Vietnam. *Emerging Markets Finance and Trade*, 55(6), 1417–1428. doi:10.1080/1540496X.2018.1524326

Berger, A.N., and Humphrey, D.B. (1997). Efficiency of financial institutions: International survey and directions for future research. *European Journal of Operational Research*, 98(2), 175–212.

Boyd, J.H., and Runkle, D.E. (1993). Size and performance of banking firms: Testing the predictions of theory. *Journal of Monetary Economics*, 31(1), 47–67.

Căpraru, B., and Ihnatov, I. (2015) Determinants of bank's profitability in EU15. *Annals of the Alexandru Ioan Cuza University — Economics*, 62(1), 93–101. doi:10.1515/aicue-2015-0007

DeYoung, R., and Rice, T. (2004). Noninterest income and financial performance at U.S. commercial banks. *Financial Review*, 39(1), 101–127. doi:10.1111/j.0732-8516.2004.00069.x

Dietrich, A., and Wanzenried, G. (2011). Determinants of bank profitability before and during the crisis: Evidence from Switzerland. *Journal of International Financial Markets, Institutions and Money*, 21(3), 307–327. doi:10.1016/j.intfin.2010.11.002

Dietrich, A., and Wanzenried, G. (2014). The determinants of commercial banking profitability in low-, middle-, and high-income countries. *The Quarterly Review of Economics and Finance*, 54(3), 337–354. doi:10.1016/j.qref.2014.03.001

Elsas, R., Hackethal, A., and Holzhäuser, M. (2010). The anatomy of bank diversification. *Journal of Banking and Finance*, 34(6), 1274–1287.

Garcia, M.T.M., and Guerreiro, J.P.S.M. (2016). Internal and external determinants of banks' profitability: The Portuguese case. *Journal of Economic Studies*, 43(1), 90–107. doi:10.1108/JES-09-2014-0166

Gul, S., Irshad, F., and Zaman, K. (2011). Factors affecting bank profitability in Pakistan. *Romanian Economic Journal*, 14(39), pp. 61–87.

Ha, V.D., and Nguyen, D.H.A. (2017). Impacts of non-traditional income on profitability and risk of Vietnamese Commercial Banks. *Hochiminh City Open University Journal of Science*, 54(3), 3–12.

Ho, T.H.M., and Nguyen, T.C. (2014). Income diversification and determinants of profitability of Vietnamese commercial banks. *Journal of Banking Technology*, No. 106+107, 13–23.

Kosmidou, K. (2008). The determinants of banks' profits in Greece during the period of EU financial integration. *Managerial Finance*, 34(3), 146–159. doi:10.1108/03074350810848036

Le, T.D. (2017). The interrelationship between net interest margin and non-interest income: evidence from Vietnam. *International Journal of Managerial Finance*, 13(5), 23.

Le, T.P., and Bui, X.D. (2016). Some Factors Affecting Profit Rate at The Commercial Banks in Vietnam, 2, 28–41.

Lee, C.-C., and Hsieh, M.-F. (2013). The impact of bank capital on profitability and risk in Asian banking. *Journal of International Money and Finance*, 32, 251–281. doi:10.1016/j.jimonfin.2012.04.013

Menicucci, E., and Paolucci, G. (2016). The determinants of bank profitability: Empirical evidence from European banking sector. *Journal of Financial Reporting and Accounting*, 14(1), 86–115. doi:10.1108/JFRA-05-2015-0060

Molyneux, P., and Thornton, J. (1992). Determinants of European bank profitability: A note. *Journal of Banking & Finance*, 16(6), 1173–1178. doi:10.1016/0378-4266(92)90065-8

Naceur, S.B. (2003). The Determinants of the Tunisian Banking Industry Profitability: Panel Evidence. *ERF Research Fellow.*

Naceur, S.B., and Goaied, M. (2001). The determinants of the Tunisian deposit banks' performance. *Applied Financial Economics*, 11(3), 317–319. doi:10.1080/096031001300138717

Nguyen, D.T., Ta, H.T., and Nguyen, H.T.D. (2018a). What determines the profitability of Vietnam commercial banks? *International Business Research*, 11(2), 231. doi:10.5539/ibr.v11n2p231

Nguyen, P.N.T., and Nguyen, P.T.T. (2016). Factors affecting profitability of the commercial bank system in Vietnam. *Journal of Economics and Development*, 228(6), 52–59.

Nguyen, T.D.C., Luong, T.T.H., and Nguyen, T.T.T. (2018). Analysis of Internal Factors Affecting Bank Profitability: Evidence from Listed Banks on Vietnam Stock Market. *The 5th IBSM International Conference on Business, Management and Accounting, Hanoi Industry University of Vietnam Proceeding*, pp. 461–472.

Obamuyi, T.M. (2013). Determinants of banks' profitability in a developing economy: Evidence from Nigeria. *Organizations and Markets in Emerging Economies*, 4(2), 97–111.

Perry, P. (1992). Do banks gain or lose from inflation. *Journal of Retail Banking*, 14(2), 25–30.

Pham, H.H.T. (2013). Impacts of bad debts on commercial banks' profitability. *Banking Science and Training Review*, 142(3), 34–38.

Scholtens, B. (2000). Competition, Growth, and Performance in the Banking Industry. *Center for Financial Institutions Working Papers*, pp. 00–18, Wharton School Center for Financial Institutions, University of Pennsylvania.

Sufian, F., and Habibullah, M.S. (2009). Bank specific and macroeconomic determinants of bank profitability: Empirical evidence from the China banking sector. *Frontiers of Economics in China*, 4(2), 274–291. doi:10.1007/s11459-009-0016-1

Tue, A. (2018). The bank income structure is gradually shifting away from the traditional model. Retrieved from https://vietnambiz.vn/co-cau-thu-nhap-ngan-hang-dang-dan-chuyen-minh-khoi-mo-hinh-truyen-thong-48080.htm

Tran, V.D. (2014). Determinants of profitability of commercial banks in Vietnam. *Banking Review*, 16, 2–11.

https://doi.org/10.1142/9789811227158_0007

# Chapter 7

# Value Creation in Vietnamese Bank Mergers and Acquisitions

**Tan Khoa Duong**

## Abstract

This chapter seeks evidence of the value creation associated with bank mergers and acquisitions in Vietnam. Accounting-based approach is used to test the value-maximizing hypothesis. 1-year pre-merger performance indicators of acquiring banks are directly compared to 3-year post-merger performance indicators of the consolidated banks to find out sources of value creation. This study finds that Vietnamese acquiring banks, 3 years after the mergers, can increase their deposit market share and credit market share but cannot increase their market power in the setting price. In terms of efficiency gains, this study finds strong evidence to show that the consolidated banks can improve their profitability measured by three measures: return on asset (ROA), return on equity (ROE), and net margin on assets. Except for the improvement in operating efficiency ratio, other efficiency measures are not statistically different from zero.

**Keywords:** Bank M&As; Bank consolidations; Bank efficiency.

## 1. Introduction

The financial service industry is now consolidating around the world. Mergers and acquisitions (M&As) among financial institutions occur at a quick pace in the United States and Europe and will possibly do so at a rapid pace in Vietnam in the future to solve the problem of financial distress. A large number of bank merger studies such as Pilloff and Santomero (1997), Berger *et al.* (1999), and Cornett *et al.* (1992, 2006) were conducted to investigate the motivations and the value gains associated with bank mergers and acquisitions. The bank merger literature indicates several motivations that can explain the bank merger wave. They are the value-maximizing hypothesis, which includes the increasing market power and increasing operational efficiency motivations, and non-value-maximizing hypothesis, which includes the managerial influences hypothesis and regulator's influences hypothesis. The empirical results from this literature for different regions suggest that consolidation in banking in Europe leads to both efficiency improvement and shareholder value creation. On the other hand, there is little evidence of efficiency gains as well as shareholder value gains for bank deals in the United States. The contrary empirical results from Europe and the American market, together with the fact that few papers study bank merger gains in other markets, especially in Vietnam, raise a question: "Can bank mergers and acquisitions in other markets such as the case of Vietnamese banking system create value?" This chapter is designed to test the value-maximizing hypothesis by using the Vietnamese bank mergers' data.

In general, there are two main approaches used by researchers to measure the total gains from bank mergers: the accounting-based approach and the market-based approach. The accounting-based approach assumes that the accounting data can capture potential value gains from bank mergers. It involves comparing pre- and post-merger performance of the combined bank to address whether the M&As can lead to an improvement in bank efficiency. The market-based approach involves examining the stock price performance of bidder and target banks around the merger announcement by employing an event study framework. This approach assumes that the merger creates value if the shareholders' value increases on the announcement of the deal. Since acquiring banks absorb all Vietnamese target banks, this study only compares pre-merger performance of acquiring banks to post-merger performance of the combined banks.

In this chapter, a benchmark of banks that are the same size and have similar characteristics with acquiring banks is formed to capture the bank's specific characteristics' effects. Therefore, 1-year pre- and 3-year post-merger benchmark-adjusted performance is directly compared. This study finds that there is strong evidence suggesting that the acquiring banks in Vietnam cannot increase their market power to set deposit and loan rates; however, they can significantly increase the market share in two most important markets–deposit market and credit market–more rapidly than their peers in the benchmark group. In addition, the consolidated banks can statistically improve their profitability 3 years after the mergers. By the end of year +3 (year 0 is the year when the merger finished), the ROA, ROE, and net interest margin on assets of consolidated banks are 0.78%, 9.49%, and 1.75%, respectively, which are above their peers of the same size and have similar characteristics (all differences are statistically significant at 5% level). Moreover, this study finds evidence which suggests that the improvement in the consolidated banks' profitability does not come at the expense of a deterioration in the regulatory capital requirement. In fact, the combined banks can significantly increase the equity to assets ratio to the level of 1.34% above their peers, and the improvement is also significant at 5%. In terms of credit quality and other operational efficiency indicators, this study finds little evidence supporting the hypothesis that there are improvements in post-merger operations of the consolidated banks. Most of the variables that measured post-merger operational efficiency and credit quality are not significantly different from zero, except for the operating income to total assets ratio, which is significant at 10%.

## 2. Literature Review

According to bank M&A literature, there are two main motivations explaining the bank merger wave around the world. They are value-maximizing motivation and non-value maximizing motivation.

### 2.1. *The value-maximizing motivation*

The first motivation of a bank merger is value-maximizing motivation. This can be done through increasing bidder banks' market power in setting prices or through increasing bidder banks' operational efficiency.

The increasing of market power: this can be done if the acquiring bank succeeds in reducing some of its main competitors by acquiring those competitors. Researchers usually find that mergers and acquisitions among banks that have significant local market overlap can increase local market concentration and allow the consolidated bank to increase profits by setting prices less favorable to customers. For example, Berger and Hannan (1989) find that banks in more concentrated markets charge higher rates on small business loans and pay lower rates on retail deposits. Moreover, the finding of Hannan and Berger (1991) that bank deposit rates slowly respond to changes in open market interest rates, especially more slowly when rates increase than when they decrease, also supports the increasing market power motivation of bank mergers.

The increasing of operational efficiency: that is likely due to the cost synergies and revenue synergies explaining why many banks expand geographically through M&A activity. For cost synergies, the consolidation can enable the cost to be reduced if scale or scope economies can be achieved. These very cost synergies can be created by eliminating overlapped facilities such as branches, business units, and redundant costs such as employee cost, administrative costs, and marketing costs. Everything else being equal, lower aggregated costs would let profits increase and hence maximize shareholders' values. Revenue synergies can be achieved in the same manner as cost synergies. Scale and scope economies can enable larger banks to offer more and multiple products to increase the market share through transferring the excess skill from the bidder to the targeted bank. In other words, the consolidated banks can generate greater revenue by cross-selling various products to the target's customers without increasing the cost significantly and hence increase profitability.

## 2.2. *Non-value-maximizing motivation*

### 2.2.1. *The managerial influences*

In many cases, the bank manager can pursue his or her own interest in conducting the merger, especially in the bank where agency problem exists. One of the managerial private interest is the empire-building hypothesis. It is possible that the bank manager wants to engage in bank mergers and acquisitions in order that he or she can receive personal gains because the executive compensation tends to positively correlate to the bank size. For example, Kaoru *et al.* (2007) use advertisement expenses as a percentage of total assets as a variable to test the empire-building hypothesis. They find that the consolidated banks in Japan do not significantly increase advertisement expenses and conclude that there is no evidence supporting this hypothesis. Another reason explaining the bank CEO's behavior to conduct a bank merger without value-maximizing is to exploit the "too big to fail" policy. It is likely that the failure of some major financial institutions, including one which is formed from several mergers, threatens the stability of the whole banking system or even the whole economy. Therefore, this kind of "too big to fail" bank is certainly protected by taxpayers from failure. When a bank is considered "too big to fail", it has an incentive to take unnecessary risk with the hope of higher return for shareholders. Nevertheless, this higher return comes at the expense of the government which has a liability to protect the bank against bankruptcy. This feature can be an attractive feature of "too big to fail" banks' category and a good justification for such a bank's CEO to engage in large bank M&As. However, one problem with the "too big to fail" argument is to determine when the bank is "too big to fail". For example, Citicorp was already the biggest bank holding company in the USA before it conducted the merger with Travelers. Hence, the benefit of "too big to fail" can be small for a bank to conduct M&A when this bank is already covered by the "too big to fail" policy.

### 2.2.2. *The government's influences*

In some cases, the government can encourage consolidation within the banking system, especially in a financial crisis period. During the financial crisis, the government should provide financial assistance for healthy banks to acquire unhealthy banks because it can be cheaper to do so than to let such unhealthy banks fail.

## 2.3. *The research methodologies*

Most academic studies in the bank merger literature follow one of two approaches to estimate the merger-related gains from bank mergers. The first one is accounting-based approach that uses accounting data to investigate post-merger performance changes in the merged bank. The second one is market-based approach that uses the movement in market stock prices of the acquirer and target banks around the merger announcement to determine the value gains from bank mergers. This section discusses both approaches.

### 2.3.1. *The accounting-based approach*

This approach assumes that the accounting data can capture the potential value gains from bank mergers. It involves comparing profitability ratios such as return on assets (ROAs), return on equity (ROE), and cost ratios such as interest expense on assets, total expenses to total revenue ratio, and so on before and after the bank mergers and acquisitions to determine whether the M&As can lead to improvement in bank efficiency. The advantages of this approach are that accounting performance can be directly measured and that the used data are both easily obtained and well-understood. Furthermore, accounting data measures actual performance, not the investors' expectations, therefore it is more reliable than equity returns. One of the drawbacks of this approach is that it is hard to distinguish between the effect of increasing market power and the effect of increasing efficiency on the post-merger performance of consolidated banks. The results of studies that used accounting-based approach are mixed. Some researchers find improvement in post-merger performance, some do not. For example, Cornett and Tehranian (1992), Rhoades (1998), Cornet *et al.* (2006) find profitability ratios associated with bank M&As improved, while Berger and Humphrey (1992) find no improvement in these ratios.

### 2.3.2. *The market-based approach*

The market-based approach involves examining the stock price performance of bidder and target banks around the bank mergers' announcement by employing an event study framework. This approach assumes that the merger creates value if the shareholders' value increases on the announcement of the deal. Most studies using this approach analyze the abnormal returns of the bidder and target separately, but some research also examine the total change in shareholders' value. Proponents of the market-based approach argue that market data not accounting data are better indicators of real economic changes associated with bank M&As. However, this approach, like any other approach, has its own problems. The first drawback of this approach is that the information of the deal can be leaked prior to the announcement day, which raises a crucial question about the analyzed window that should be used by researchers to capture the merger-related value gains. The second drawback is that, as Malatesta (1983) suggests, measurements of the wealth effects of mergers are sensitive to model specification. The third drawback of this approach is that it fails to distinguish between the effect of the merger's announcement information and the effect of information about how the deal is financed on shareholders' value gains. For example, a stock payment is usually interpreted as a signal of "overvaluation" by investors. Therefore, it is possible that the negative announcement returns to bidder banks are attributed either to negative signaling or to the value-destroying of the deal. Consistent with this argument, Houston and Ryngaert (1994) find that returns to bidders are significantly greater in bank mergers financed by cash than mergers financed by stock. The fourth drawback of this approach is that bank M&As are largely anticipated and that abnormal returns may not appear in the analyzed window, hence raising the difficulty for researchers to draw conclusions on value created. The fifth shortcoming is that, like accounting-based approach, market-based approach fails to determine whether changes in shareholders' value based on the movement of stock prices are from changes in market power or from changes in operational efficiency.

### 2.4. *Empirical result of bank mergers*

The literature on value gains from bank mergers and acquisitions in the US using the accounting-based approach seems to yield mixed results. Some researchers find improvement in post-merger performance, while some do not. For example, Hannan and Rhoades (1987) examine the impact of bank mergers on the ratios of net income before extraordinary items to assets and non-interest expenses to assets and find that bank mergers and acquisitions affect neither income nor non-interest expenses. A later study by Rhoades in 1990 still confirms his earlier work that there is no performance effect due to mergers. Moreover, Linder and Crane (1992) investigate the post-merger performance by aggregating acquirer and target data 1 year before the deal and comparing this to the data 1 and 2 years after the merger. Their results are consistent with that of Rhoades that bank mergers do not lead to improvement in operating income. On the other hand, Cornett and Tehranian (1992) present one of the most notable studies that show improvement in post-merger performance. In this study, Cornett and Terhanian find that post-merger ROE of the merged banks is 3.9% above the industry and is statistically significant. Furthermore, they also find that the consolidated banks attract more deposits and loans and that employee productivity is increased. These results still hold in an extended study of Cornett *et al.* (2006). Using the same methodology as in 1992, Cornett *et al.* (2006) show that combined banks 2 years after the merger have ROA, ROE, and net interest margins that are statistically improved.

Results of studies that use event study framework to examine the stock price movement often suggest that there is little evidence of total gains from bank consolidation in the US. Instead, researchers usually document what is called "the wealth redistribution". It means that the value of the target bank increases, while the value of the bidder bank decreases around the announcement day and that the combination of these two effects roughly cancels each other because the bidder banks are usually bigger in size than the target banks. For example, Houston and Ryngaert (1994) use a sample of 153 mergers from 1985 to 1991 to investigate abnormal returns around the merger announcement of the bidder, target, and the combined entity in which the combined abnormal return is calculated as weighted average abnormal return using relative size. Their results suggest that, for the window [–5,0] in which 0 denotes the announcement day, bidder banks suffer a negative abnormal return of –2.3%, while targeted banks enjoy a positive abnormal return of 14.4%, both are highly statistically significant at 1%. However, the total gain is only 0.04% and is insignificant. In one other paper that investigates the long run stock performance, Madura and Wiant (1994) use a sample of 152 mergers from 1983 to 1987 to examine the abnormal return and cumulative abnormal return of bidder banks 36 months following the merger. They find that monthly abnormal returns of bidder banks are all negative, except only for 4 months, over 36 months post-merger. More importantly, cumulative abnormal returns of bidders are all negative in the 36 months and become significant from month +3 (month 0 is defined as the month in which the announcement occurred). At the end of month +36, bidder banks suffer a loss of −27.06% and this negative abnormal return is significant at 5%.

In Europe, where the bank merger wave happens after that of the US, research on bank mergers seem to yield conclusive results. Bank mergers in Europe tend to result in both efficiency gains and enhanced shareholder value. For example, Huizinga *et al.* (2001) examine 53 European bank M&As between 1994 and 1998 and find evidence of cost efficiency improvements. Ismail *et al.* (2009) use a sample of 35 bank mergers in Europe from 1992 to 1997 to measure performance changes. They find that industry-adjusted cash flow return, loan quality, and cost-efficiency of the merging banks improve after the merger, but there is no change in profitability. A number of other studies that use the event study framework present a general result of positive value creation. Beitel *et al.* (2004) use a sample of 98 large bank mergers in Europe between 1985 and 2000 and indicate positive cumulative abnormal returns for the combined target and bidder shareholders.

Kaoru *et al.* (2007), who use a sample of consolidations of banks in Japan from 1990 to 2004, find that ROA for consolidated banks increases about 5 years after the mergers are completed, but this change is not significant. In addition, they also find that there is a decrease in the capital to assets but not in the non-performance loans and that there is no evidence consistent with the managerial empire-building hypothesis. In another study, Kimie (2005) examines the mergers that occurred among Japanese city banks from 2000 and finds that the consolidation of a healthy bank with an unhealthy bank does not create a healthy bank and that consolidations between weak banks do not help create a strong bank.

## 3. Hypothesis Testing

The main aim of this chapter is to test the value-maximizing hypothesis of the bank mergers in Vietnam, including both the increasing market power hypothesis and the increasing operational efficiency hypothesis.

### 3.1. *Increasing market power hypothesis*

The consensus results from bank merger literature suggest that when a bank can increase its market power, it would charge more on loans, pay less on deposits, and thus the spread between them would increase. For this reason, this study uses three variables: return on loan, expense paid on deposit, and the spread between return on loan and expense paid on deposit to test for the increasing market power hypothesis. In addition, since the deposit market and credit market are considered the two most important markets in Vietnamese banking industry, it is likely that the acquiring banks are trying to expand these two markets more rapidly than their peers to achieve future benefits. Therefore, this study uses two more market variables: deposit share market and credit share market. If the bank M&As are conducted from this motivation, the consolidated banks following M&A activities should have a low cost paid for deposits, higher returns on loans, higher spread between the loan rate and deposit rate, and be able to expand deposit and credit market share more rapidly than their peers. Therefore, the null and alternative hypotheses are as follows:

**Hypothesis H0:** *There is no increase in market power for acquiring banks.*

**Hypothesis H1:** *The merged bank increases market power. It is the benchmark-adjusted spread between return on loan and expense on deposit increase 3 years after the merger, and their market shares increase more rapidly than those of their peers.*

### 3.2. *Increasing operational efficiency hypothesis*

If a bank merger is conducted for increasing operational efficiency motivations, the consolidated bank after M&A should increase its operational efficiency. In other words, there should be improvements in financial ratios that capture the banks' efficiency performance. For this reason, this study uses a set of financial ratios to investigate the post-merger performance to find out the source of value creation. Hence, the null and alternative hypotheses are as follows:

**Hypothesis H0:** *There is no increase in efficiency for acquiring banks.*

**Hypothesis H1:** *The merged bank increases efficiency. In other words, there are improvements in the benchmark-adjusted financial ratios that capture acquiring banks' post-merger performance.*

## 4. Data Description and Methodology

### 4.1. *Data description*

The main objective of this chapter is to focus only on mergers and acquisitions within banks. Hence, there are nine bank mergers in Vietnam from 2008 to 2015 in the author's initial sample that satisfy the criteria. The total assets, deposits, and credits of all nine acquiring banks, by the end of 1 year before the merger, account for 36.2%, 35.54%, and 24.27% of the Vietnamese banking industry, respectively. Therefore, the size of these bank mergers is big compared to Vietnamese economic conditions.

Data for announcements of bank mergers and acquisitions in Vietnam are collected from Thompson Reuters database. In addition, all target banks in Vietnam are consolidated into the acquiring banks, therefore financial data of all banks are obtained from the financial reports of the acquiring banks before the M&A deals and consolidated banks after the M&A deals. Table 1 describes the

**Table 1:** Descriptive statistics.

| | Mean | | |
|---|---|---|---|
| **Million USD** | **Bidder** | **Target** | **Differences** |
| Total assets | 8.086 | 1.196 | 6.890** |
| Deposit | 6.088 | 934 | 5.154** |
| Total loan | 4.628 | 666 | 3.962* |
| Shareholders' equity | 583 | 132 | 451** |
| Return on assets (ROA) (%) | 0.63 | 1.26 | −0.63 |
| Return on equity (ROE) (%) | 9.88 | 4.82 | 5.06 |
| Equity to assets (%) | 8.38 | 25.96 | −17.58** |
| Loan to equity (%) | 625.75 | 404.90 | 220.85** |
| Deposit to equity (%) | 843.50 | 481.65 | 361.85** |

*Notes*: $N = 8$ since this study excludes one merger in which target's financial reports are not disclosed to the market. Assume that USD/VND = 23,000. $^{**}$, $^{*}$ denote significant at 5%, and 10%, respectively.
*Source*: Acquiring and target banks' financial report.

data descriptive statistics of acquiring banks and target banks in the sample.

The first two columns of Table 1 describe the mean of bidder and target banks' financial status before the M&A deals. The last column describes the mean differences between bidders and targets. The $t$-statistics test is then conducted to test for significance of differences.

#### 4.1.1. *Size*

Table 1 shows that acquirer banks tend to be larger than the target ones in terms of both total assets and shareholder's equity. The mean of the acquirers' assets is US$ 8,086 million, while the mean of the targets' total assets is US$ 1,196 million. The difference in mean total assets between bidder and target banks is US$ 6,890 million and statistically significant at 5%. In terms of equity, the mean of bidder and target shareholders' equity are US$ 583 and US$ 132 million, respectively. The US$ 451 million difference in shareholder's equity between bidder and target is also significant at 5%.

#### 4.1.2. *Deposits and loans*

Bidder banks on average attract more deposits and make more loans compared to target banks. The differences in deposits and loans between bidder banks and target banks are US$ 5,154 and US$ 3,962 million and are significant at 5% and 10%, respectively.

#### 4.1.3. *Profitability*

It seems that bidder banks are not more profitable than target banks because differences in ROA and ROE between bidder and target banks are all insignificant. In terms of capital adequacy ratio, it seems that bidder banks attract more deposits and make more loans per unit of equity than target banks do (the differences in deposit to equity and loan to equity are all significant at 5%). Therefore, acquiring banks' equity to asset ratio is statistically much lower than that of target banks.

## 4.2. *Research methodology*

Given the several shortcomings of the market-based approach and the lack of stock price data, because most of the acquiring banks in Vietnam are not listed on the announcement day, the accounting-based approach will be more suitable to measure the post-performance changes following bank mergers and acquisitions in Vietnam. Therefore, this chapter compares directly pre- and post-merger performance to investigate the value created from bank M&As (Table 2). This method was first used by Cornett *et al.* (2002, 2006).

One year pre- and 3-year post-merger ratios are calculated to test using the $t$-statistic. Let us denote as $X$ the value of ratios (defined

**Table 2:** Indicators used to identify sources of value creation in Vietnamese bank M&A.

| Indicator | Objectives of indicators |
|---|---|
| (1) Market power indicator | To measure the market power in setting price and market share of bidder banks. |
| (2) Profitability indicator | Measure the ability of banks to generate profits after the merger. Three main ratios ROA, ROE, and net interest margin on assets are examined. |
| (3) Capital adequacy indicator | Measure the bank's ability to meet the regulated capital requirements and still attract loans and deposits. To do so, this study creates three main ratios: equity to assets, loan to equity, and deposit to equity. |
| (4) Credit quality indicator | Measure the changes in the credit quality of the bank. To do so, this study uses two main ratios: Reserve for possible loan loss to total loan and non-performing loan rate. |
| (5) Efficiency indicator | Measure the bank's ability to operate more efficiently after the mergers. To do so, this study uses five ratios. They are operating efficiency; total expenses to revenues; total cost to assets; cost-efficiency in using fund; and deposit utilization. |

**Table 3:** Measures definition used to measure post-merger performance.

| Ratio | Definition |
|---|---|
| **Market power indicators** | |
| 1. Average loan rate charge | Interest income on loan divided by total loan. |
| 2. Expense paid on deposit | Interest expense paid on deposit divided by total deposit. |
| 3. Net interest margin (NIM) | Difference between average loan rate charge and interest paid on deposit. |
| 4. Credit market share | Total loan divided by the banking industry's total loan. |
| 5. Deposit Market share | Deposit divided by the banking industry's total deposit. |
| **Profitability indicators** | |
| 6. Return on assets (ROA) | Net income after tax divided by total assets. |
| 7. Return on equity (ROE) | Net income after tax divided by total equity. |
| 8. Net interest margin on assets | Interest income minus interest expense divided by total assets. |
| **Capital adequacy indicators** | |
| 9. Equity to assets | Shareholders' equity divided by total assets. |
| 10. Loan to equity | Total loan divided by total shareholders' equity. |
| 11. Deposit to equity | Deposit divided by shareholders' equity. |
| **Credit quality indicators** | |
| 12. Reserve for possible loan loss | Reserve for possible loan loss divided by total loan. |
| 13. Non-performing loan rate | Non-performing loan divided by total loan. |
| **Efficiency indicators** | |
| 14. Operating efficiency | Operating income divided by total asset. |
| 15. Total expenses to revenues | Operating expenses divided by operating revenues. |
| 16. Total cost to assets | Total expenses to assets. |
| 17. Cost-efficiency in using fund | Interest expense paid on total liability. |
| 18. Deposit utilization | Total loan divided by deposit. |

in Table 3), the $t$-statistic is calculated using the formula as follows:

$$t = \frac{\left(\sum_{i=1}^{N} (X^i_{\text{post}} - X^i_{\text{pre}})/N\right)}{(\sigma/\sqrt{N})}, \tag{1}$$

where year 0 is the year when the merger finished, $X^i_{\text{post}}$, $X^i_{\text{pre}}$ denote post-merger performance of the consolidated bank $i$ at the end of year 3 and pre-merger performance of the acquiring bank $i$ at the end of year −1, respectively, $\sigma$ is the standard deviation of the distribution of changes in the acquiring banks' performance, $N$ is the number of bank mergers and acquisitions.

The market power indicators and the other operational efficiency indicators to test the increasing market power hypothesis and the increasing operational efficiency hypothesis in this study are explained in Tables 2 and 3 in the previous section.

## 5. Empirical Results

Table 4 reports empirical results for acquiring banks' post-merger performance in Vietnam from 2008 to 2015. The first column shows the performance indicators as well as performance measures. The next three columns describe acquirers' benchmark-adjusted performance for year −1, year +3, and the differences between year +3 and year −1, respectively. The last column shows the $p$-value for the difference in benchmark-adjusted performance between year +3 and year −1.

### 5.1. *The increasing market power hypothesis*

There is little evidence to suggest that the consolidated banks following the mergers significantly increase their market power when compared to their peers which have the same characteristics. However, the consolidated banks 3 years after the merger can increase both deposit market share and credit market share.

In terms of the ability to set prices, 3 years after the merger, the consolidated banks in Vietnam can pay less 0.92% on deposits, charge 1.35% more on loans, and can increase 2.27% in their net interest margin when compared to their main competitors. However, these differences are not statistically at the conventional level of confidence, which implies that the acquiring banks cannot increase their

**Table 4:** Empirical results for Vietnamese consolidated banks' performance.

| | **Benchmark-adjusted performance** | | | |
|---|---|---|---|---|
| | **1 year pre-merger (%)** | **3 years post-merger (%)** | **Differences in mean (%)** | ***p*-value (%)** |
| **Market power indicators** | | | | |
| 1. Average loan rate charge | 0.57 | 1.92 | 1.35 | 66 |
| 2. Expense paid on deposit | 1.08 | 0.16 | −0.92 | 29 |
| 3. Net interest margin | −0.51 | 1.76 | 2.27 | 45 |
| 4. Credit market share | −0.17 | 0.76 | 0.93** | 2 |
| 5. Deposit market share | −0.32 | 0.65 | 0.97** | 4 |
| **Profitability indicators** | | | | |
| 6. Return on average asset (ROA) | 0.03 | 0.78 | 0.75** | 2 |
| 7. Return on average equity (ROE) | 3.12 | 9.49 | 6.37** | 3 |
| 8. Net interest margin on assets | 0.51 | 1.75 | 1.24** | 5 |
| **Capital adequacy indicators** | | | | |
| 9. Equity to asset | −0.60 | 0.74 | 1.34** | 4 |
| 10. Loan to equity | 46.59 | −84.62 | −131.21 | 28 |
| 11. Deposit to equity | 95.14 | −211.15 | −306.29 | 11 |
| **Credit quality indicators** | | | | |
| 12. Loan loss reserve to total loan | 0.53 | 0.09 | −0.44 | 12 |
| 13. Non-performing loan rate | 1.96 | 0.35 | −1.61 | 14 |
| **Efficiency indicators** | | | | |
| 14. Operating income to total assets | 1.06 | 2.10 | 1.04* | 7 |
| 15. Total expenses to revenues | 2.02 | 2.93 | 0.92 | 75 |
| 16. Total cost to asset | 0.45 | 0.70 | 0.25 | 27 |
| 17. Expense paid on total liabilities | 0.63 | −0.16 | −0.79 | 26 |
| 18. Deposit utilization | −6.67 | 11.67 | 18.34 | 17 |

*Notes*: **, * denote significant at 5% and 10%, respectively.

market power. Despite this fact, there is strong evidence suggesting that the consolidated banks can increase their market share more rapidly than their competitors. One year pre-merger the acquiring bank's credit market share and deposit market share are −0.17% and −0.32%, respectively, below those of competitors, but these numbers increase to 0.76% and 0.65% above their competitors by the end of year +3. The increased 0.93% and 0.97% in credit and deposit market share, respectively, are all significant at 5%.

## 5.2. *The increasing operational efficiency hypothesis*

### 5.2.1. *Profitability indicators*

The main picture of acquiring banks' profitability indicators is that there is strong evidence of improvement in profitability 3 years after the bank merger deals. All three ratios measuring the consolidated banks' profitability are statistically significant at 5%.

#### 5.2.1.1. Return on assets (ROA) and return on equity (ROE)

This study finds strong evidence of improvement in ROA and ROE ratios of Vietnamese acquiring banks. For example, ROA of acquiring banks by the end of year −1 is 0.03% higher than that of banks in the benchmark, but at the end of year +3, consolidated banks improve the ROA ratio to 0.78% above the benchmark. Similarly, the benchmark-adjusted ROE of consolidated banks also increases from 3.12% above, in year −1, to 9.49% above the benchmark in year +3. More importantly, the differences in benchmark-adjusted ROA and ROE, 0.75% in ROA and 6.37% in ROE, are all statistically significant at 5%. The evidence in this chapter is consistent with findings in the profitability of the consolidated banks in Cornett and Tehranian (1992) and Cornett *et al.* (2006). It seems that the increasing market share in both deposit and credit markets, the two most important markets in the Vietnamese banking industry, in the post-merger period can help the consolidated banks sell more financial products, serve more customers by starting to implement cross-selling strategies, and therefore increase their profitability.

5.2.1.2. Net margin on assets
This ratio is used to measure how well the banks can manage their assets to generate the interest income after subtracting for the interest paid for depositors. Compared to the benchmark, on average, 3 years after the merger, Vietnamese acquiring banks improve this ratio by 1.24%. The ratio of net interest margin on assets increases from 0.51% above to 1.75% above that of their peers and the 1.24% difference is also significant at 5%. The possible reason for this increase in the NIM on assets can be the successful transferring of management skills from the acquiring banks, which possess better management skills, to the target banks, which are not able to exploit their assets portfolios.

### 5.2.2. *Capital adequacy indicators*

This study finds evidence suggesting that the consolidated banks cannot attract more deposits and cannot make more loans than banks in the benchmark. Using the benchmark-adjusted number for comparison, the ratio of loan to equity and deposit to equity both decreased from the level of 46.59% and 95.14% above the benchmark to the level of –84.62% and –211.15% below the benchmark, respectively, but the differences are not significant for both ratios. Regarding the equity to assets ratio, there is evidence indicating that the decrease in both ratios, loan to equity and deposit to equity, leads to an improvement in acquiring banks' regulated capital adequacy. On average, by the end of year +3, the consolidated banks' equity to assets ratio statistically increases to 1.34% (from –0.6% below to 0.74% above the benchmark, significant at 5%).

### 5.2.3. *Credit quality indicators*

Overall, there is no evidence to suggest that the combined banks can improve the credit quality 3 years after the merger. Although both ratios measure the credit quality, loan loss reserve to total loan and non-performing loan rate of consolidated banks show a decrease of −0.44% and −1.61%, respectively, compared with the benchmark (and the $p$-values are 12% and 14%), those differences are not significant at the conventional level of confidence. The reason for this result can be that acquiring banks, after the deal, start to apply a stricter procedure to recognize bad loans, hence more non-performing loans at target banks are disclosed when targets' loan portfolios are consolidated into those of the bidders. Therefore, it is possible that it takes more time for the acquiring banks to deal with non-performing loans to improve the credit quality of the consolidated banks.

### 5.2.4. *Efficiency indicators*

The operating income to assets ratio shows how well the acquiring banks manage their assets to generate profits. In the 4-year period from year −1 to year +3, acquiring banks are able to increase this ratio by 1.04%, from 1.06% above to 2.10% above the benchmark. In addition, the difference (1.04%) is significant at the conventional level of confidence of 10%. The other four efficiency ratios: total expense to revenues, total cost to asset, expense paid on total liabilities, and deposit utilization show no improvement or deterioration in the acquiring banks' efficiency because the changes in those ratios are all insignificant. One of the possible reasons for this result is that the expected saving costs of bank mergers are not always realized in the future because it is usually the case that bidder banks reported unexpected costs associated with the mergers.

## 6. Conclusion

This chapter uses a sample of bank mergers in Vietnam to test the value-maximizing hypothesis, including the increasing market power hypothesis and increasing operational efficiency hypothesis. To test for these hypotheses, this study uses the accounting-based approach because of the several well-known shortcomings of the market-based approach and the lack of stock prices of many Vietnamese acquiring banks. One year pre-merger benchmark-adjusted performances of acquiring banks are directly compared to the 3-year benchmark-adjusted post-merger performances of consolidated banks to find out sources of value creation.

It appears that there are three main sources of value creation associated with bank mergers in Vietnam. First, the consolidated banks 3 years after the merger can increase their deposit market share and credit market share, but not the market power, more rapidly than their peers which are not involved in a bank M&A deal. Second, there is strong evidence to suggest that the consolidated banks can improve their post-merger profitability. All three important profitability measures ROA, ROE, and NIM on assets are all statistically significant above their peers in the benchmark. In addition, it seems that the increase in the profitability of consolidated banks does not come with a deterioration in the level of the combined banks' capital adequacy. The ratio equity to assets of the consolidated banks, in fact, statistically significantly improves and is 0.74% higher than that of their competitors. Finally, despite the fact that there is little evidence of changes in most of the efficiency performance measures, the consolidated banks still can improve the overall operating efficiency by significantly increasing the operating income to total assets ratio.

## References


Beitel, P., Schiereck, D., and Wahrenburg, M. (2004). Explaining M&A success in European banks. *European Financial Management*, 10(1), 109–139.

Berger, A.N., Demetz, R.S., and Strahan, P.E. (1999). The consolidation of the financial services industry: causes, consequences, and implications for the future. *Journal of Banking and Finance*, 23, 135–194.

Berger, A.N., and Hannan, T.H. (1989). The price-concentration relationship in banking. *Review of Economics and Statistics*, 71(2), 291–299.

Berger, A.N., and Hannan, T.H. (1998). The efficiency cost of market power in the banking industry: A test of the "quiet life" and related hypotheses. *Review of Economics and Statistics*, 80(3), 454–465.

Berger, A.N., and Humphrey, D.B. (1992). Megamergers in banking and the use of cost efficiency as an antitrust defense. *Antitrust Bulletin*, 37(3), 541–600.

Cornett, M.M., and Tehranian, H. (1992). Changes in corporate performance associated with bank acquisitions. *Journal of Financial Economics*, 31, 211–234.

Cornett, M.M., McNutt, J.J., and Tehranian, H. (2006). Performance changes around bank mergers: Revenue enhancements versus cost reductions. *Journal of Money, Credit, and Banking*, 38(4), 1013–1050.

Hannan, T.H., and Berger, A.N. (1991). The rigidity of prices: Evidence from the banking industry. *American Economic Review*, 81(4), 938–945.

Hannan, T.H., and Rhoades, S.A. (1987). Acquisition targets and motives: The case of the banking industry. *The Review of Economics and Statistics*, 69(1), 67–74.

Houston, J.F., James, C.M., and Ryngaert, M.D. (2001). Where do merger gains come from? Bank mergers from the perspective of insiders and outsiders. *Journal of Financial Economics*, 60, 285–331.

Houston, J.F., and Ryngaert, M.D. (1994). The overall gaining from large bank mergers. *Journal of Banking and Finance*, 18(6), 1155–1176.

Huizinga, H., Nelissen, J., and Vennet, R.V. (2001). Efficiency Effects of Bank Mergers and Acquisitions, No 01-088/3, Tinbergen Institute Discussion Papers, Tinbergen Institute.

Ismail, A., Davidson, I., and Frank, R. (2009). Operating performance of European bank merger. *The Service Industries Journal*, 29(3), 345–366.

Kaoru, H., Sakai, K., and Tsuru, K. (2007). Consolidation of banks in Japan: Cause and consequences. RIETI Discussion paper series 07-E-059.

Kimie, H. (2005). Did efficiency improve? Megamergers in the Japanese banking sector. CNAEC Research Series 05-02, Korea Institute for International Economic Policy.

Linder, J., and Crane, D. (1992). What it takes to make bank mergers pay. *American Banker*, 22 July, p. 4 and p. 9.

Malatesta, P.H. (1983). The wealth effect of merger activity and the objective functions of merging firms. *Journal of Financial Economics*, 11, 155–181.

Pilloff, S.J., and Santomero, A.M. (1997). "The value effects of bank mergers and acquisitions". Working Papers — Financial Institutions Center at The Wharton School.

Rhoades, S.A. (1998). The efficiency effects of bank mergers: An overview of case studies of nine mergers. *Journal of Banking and Finance*, 22, 273–291.

The state bank of Vietnam www.sbv.gov.vn.

# Part III
# Accounting

https://doi.org/10.1142/9789811227158_0008

# Chapter 8

# A Theory Extension Related to Task-Technology Fit: Considering its Impacts on ERP System Success

**Thi Bao Quyen Phan and Quang Hung Bui**

## Abstract

Previous research has consistently shown the relationship between task-technology fit (TTF) and information system (IS) success for individuals, but little work has shown interest in this relationship at an organizational level of analysis. This study investigates the role of TTF in enterprise resource planning (ERP) system success at the firm level. The survey data are collected from 84 ERP-adopted enterprises working in Vietnam. PLS-SEM analyzes support the expected direct and indirect relationships between TTF and ERP system success. Implications of the findings are discussed.

**Keywords:** Task-technology fit; Effective use; ERP system success; TTF theory.

## 1. Introduction

In the last few decades, business organizations have relied more on information and communication technologies to handle their day-to-day operations efficiently. Enterprise resource planning (ERP) is one of the most popular forms of information technology (IT) among new IT for businesses. ERP is a packaged complex business software designed to integrate business processes and functions through using a single database to permit the sharing of common data and information in real time (Nah *et al.*, 2001). According to Callaway (1999), the ERP can provide an array of benefits that are both tangible (e.g., reduced personnel, inventory, IT and procurement, transportation, and logistics costs; improved cash flow management, revenue, and profits) and intangible (e.g., increased visibility of corporate data, speed of decision-making, and control over global business operations; improved customer responsiveness and business processes). Even Nicolaou and Bhattacharya (2008) point out that "firms which implement an ERP system must be conscious of and circumspect enough to realize that ERPs are different from other IT systems". They make firms' business processes and operational efficiencies change positively (Matolcsy *et al.*, 2005; Nicolaou & Bhattacharya, 2008).

Because of the advantages ERPs bring as mentioned above, even though they are expensive and complex systems, the market for the ERPs has been tremendously expanded in the fiercely competitive environment since its introduction in 1988 (Muscatello, 2003). For example, its revenue (including license, maintenance, and subscription), about $38 billion in 2008 (Ifinedo *et al.*, 2010), has grown to more than twice to approach nearly $82.2 billion in 2016 and is expected to continuously increase and reach $84.7 billion by 2021.[1]

However, regardless of the fact that a majority of business organizations have achieved expected performance outcomes, a considerable number of enterprises still have not gained success from the implemented ERPs. Therefore, to help avoid ERP project failures, researchers, practitioners, and academics are increasingly interested in analyzing factors determining ERP success. Ngai *et al.* (2008), Ram and Corkindale (2014), Finney and Corbett (2007), and

[1]These figures are quoted from Allert Pang's report (December 1, 2017) that is posted on the website Apps Run The World. Retrieved September 18, 2018 from https://www.appsruntheworld.com/top-10-erp-software-vendors-and-market-forecast/.

Al-Mashari *et al.* (2003) conclude systematic reviews and propose a list of identified critical success factors (CSFs) in an ERP context. Among identified technology-related CSFs, it seems that the fit between technology and the tasks it supports is missing. Previous studies in the literature critically concern task–technology fit (TTF) and individual performance (Goodhue and Thompson, 1995; Kositanurit *et al.*, 2006), however, there are virtually no academic studies which examine the linkage between TTF and ERP system success.

Moreover, there are many studies which attempt to assess perceptions of CSFs and ERP system success between different stakeholder groups (Ram and Corkindale, 2014). However, there are no studies examining perceptions regarding TTF and ERP success from the point of view of accountants. This study attempts to fill this gap. Accountants and accounting professions are chosen in the present study because previous research show that they are dramatically affected by ERP implementation (Newman and Westrup, 2005; Rom and Rohde, 2006; Scapens and Jazayeri, 2003).

The principal purpose of this study is to test the relationship (both direct and indirect effects) between TTF and ERP success from accounting professions' perceptions. The results of this study are of value to any company whether or not they implement ERP systems. Especially, the research highlights the importance of the fit between technologies and users' tasks in explaining how technology leads to expected information system (IS) success in ERP context. Furthermore, the findings of the study provide empirical evidence to expand the list of technology-related CSFs in the ERP context.

The rest of this chapter is organized as follows: Section 2 starts with a review of previous research concerning the phenomenon being studied and proposes a research hypothesis. Section 3 presents and describes the research methodology. Section 4 reports and analyzes the results of this study. Finally, the chapter concludes with theoretical and managerial implications, several particular limitations, and directions for future research.

## 2. Literature Review and Hypotheses

### 2.1. *Task-technology fit*

Goodhue and Thompson (1995) propose and empirically test a comprehensive TTF in the theoretical model. Their framework is to assert positive impacts of information technology on individual performance, namely: technology (1) must be utilized and (2) must be a good fit with the tasks it supports (see Figure 1). TTF construct in their model refers to *the degree to which a technology assists an individual in performing his or her portfolio of tasks* (Goodhue and Thompson, 1995, p. 216).

However, the original TTF theory explaining the fit between technology and tasks is supported in terms of individual attitude and intention, but a little research addressing the phenomenon is studied at the organizational level. The present research adopts the concepts of TTF applied in the organizational context. This approach is similar to the one Nguyen (2007) conducts in his study. Accordingly, TTF in this context is defined as the degree of matching or alignment between the capabilities of an ERP system and the demand

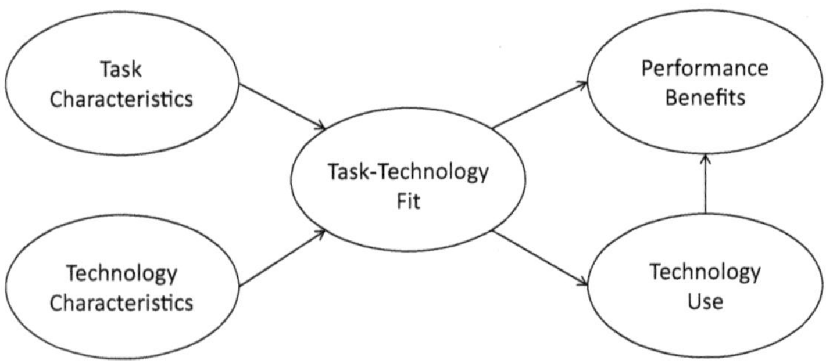


**Figure 1:** Task-technology fit theory.
*Source*: Goodhue and Thompson (1995).

for tasks that must be performed to achieve desired organizational goals.

## 2.2. *Effective use*

Utilization is often referred to as "the behavior of employing the technology in completing tasks" (Goodhue and Thompson, 1995, p. 218), which is measured as the frequency of use or the diversity of applications employed (Davis, 1989; Thompson *et al.*, 1994). In the original TTF theory, use is a "proportion of times the individual decided to use the system" to complete the whole set of tasks (Goodhue and Thompson, 1995, p. 218). However, the IS is constantly changing. Enterprise systems adopted in business organizations nowadays are more mandatory than voluntary, thus, conceptualizations of the system use mentioned seem likely inappropriate.

In this study, the authors focus on ERP system used in the adoption and ongoing context. During these periods, as noted by Shang and Seddon (2002), once users become accustomed to the new enterprise system, they gingerly begin to explore its functions, then feel sufficiently comfortable with these functions and features, and finally master their system. At that time, they begin to get creative with it. Moreover, as Musaji (2015) concludes, users in the post-implementation stage probably apply their understanding of how the system operates and attempt to push it a step further than it is designed to go. It means that it takes less time for ongoing users to complete their tasks. Therefore, use in the adoption and ongoing context measured by hours/frequency of use/proportion of times the individual decided to use the system is unreasonable.

Given system-use-related literature and firm-level-related analysis unit, the authors decided to choose effective system use (Doll and Torkzadeh, 1998) as ERP adoption and on-going use in this study. When users become more sophisticated, these experienced users can be expected to accomplish their tasks more efficiently and effectively. In brief, according to Doll and Torkzadeh (1998), Deng *et al.* (2004), use in this study refers to how effectively an ERP system is used for the fundamental organizational functions such as problem-solving/decision-making, work integration, and work planning.

### 2.3. *Success of ERP system*

There is limited research that concentrates on measuring the success of an ERP system (Mukti and Rawani, 2016). Therefore, on the ground that the ERP system is a kind of IS, this chapter attempts to review all popular measurements of IS and ERP system success available in the literature.

A review of IS success shows the variety of definitions of IS success.[2] Some of them are summarized in Table 1. Accordingly, there does not exist a particular formal definition of the phenomena of IS success. Each kind of stakeholder has a different definition about the IS success in an organization (Grover *et al.*, 1996; Ifinedo, 2011). For instance, from the point of the system developers, the IS success is achieved when IS project is completed on time, under budget, and functions correctly. For customers/users, an IS is successful if it improves user satisfaction or performance (Guimaraes and Igbaria, 1997). From the organizational perspective, IS success contributes to the company's profits or creates competitive advantages. In addition, it should be noted that IS success also depends on the type of system to be evaluated (Seddon *et al.*, 1999).

However, this current study focuses on the IS success measurement conceptualizations that draw from DeLone and McLean (1992). As the DeLone and McLean IS success model provides a schema for categorizing, the various IS success measures (Ifinedo, 2011) and their framework are widely used to assess the effectiveness or success of

---

[2]Most of the following sections in relation to IS success are quoted from the study of Nguyen *et al.* (2015).

**Table 1:** Some definitions of IS success.

| Authors | Definition |
|---|---|
| Lucas Jr. (1978, p. 29) | "Because of the extreme difficulty of measuring implementation success through cost/benefit studies, some other indicator of success is needed. The most appealing indicator for this purpose from a measurement standpoint is system use". |
| Gatian (1994, p. 119) | "If an effective system is defined as one that adds value to the firm, any measure of system effectiveness should reflect some positive change in user behavior, e.g., improved productivity, fewer errors or better decision-making". |
| Rainer Jr. and Watson (1995, p. 84) | "An EIS[a] should be developed in response to a specific business need, such as a need to be more responsive to changing customer desires, to improve product quality, or to improve organizational communications. Systems that do not support business objectives are unlikely to succeed". |
| Bailey and Pearson (1983, p. 530) | "Measuring and analyzing computer user satisfaction is motivated by management's desire to improve". |
| Byrd *et al.* (2006, p. 448) | "... the effects of IS along a path can lead to better organizational performance, in this case, lower overall costs". |
| Goodhue and Thompson (1995, p. 213) | "... MIS[b] success ultimately corresponds to what DeLone & McLean label individual impact...". |

*Notes*: [a]EIS: Executive information system; [b]MIS: management information system.

IS at the organizational level (Petter *et al.*, 2008). Accordingly, ERP system success constitutes net benefits/performance impacts, including individual impacts and organizational impacts that such a system directs towards.

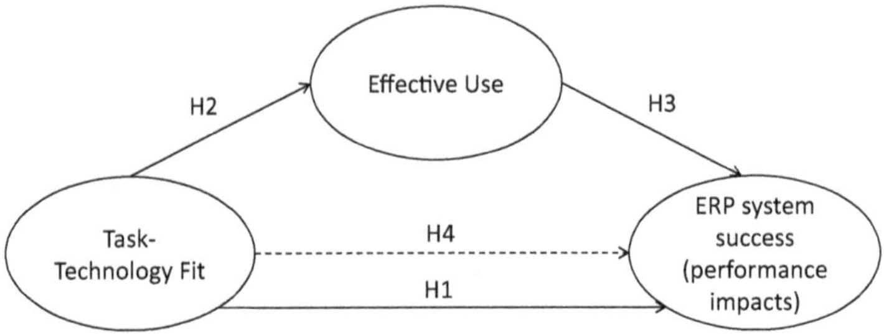


**Figure 2:** A proposed research model.

### 2.4. *TTF, effective use, and enterprise system success*

Drawing on a basis of the highly significant paths in TTF theory (Goodhue and Thompson, 1995), this study proposes four hypotheses (see Figure 2):

**Hypothesis H1:** *TTF influences directly ERP system success.*

**Hypothesis H2:** *TTF influences directly effective use.*

**Hypothesis H3:** *Effective use influences directly ERP system success.*

**Hypothesis H4:** *TTF influences indirectly ERP system success via effective use.*

## 3. Research Methodology

### 3.1. *Sample frame*

Our target population is current business organizations adopting the ERP systems in Vietnam for at least 1 year as this research focuses on the implementation and post-implementation stage. This study is analyzed at the firm level. Therefore, a key point in terms of measuring organizational impacts is that it must ensure that the person evaluating the organizational impacts is in a position to make such an assessment. Asking the assessment from individual accountants (because this study aims to only investigate a particular stakeholder's perspective) will not be effective as they cannot be in a position to make this judgment. In such cases, asking chief financial officers and accounting-related senior managers is possibly a more appropriate way to measure the phenomenon of interest. In addition, according to Shang and Seddon (2002), it takes 2–3 years for users to become familiar with a new enterprise system and extract the maximum benefits from it.

In conclusion, informants in this study are defined as CFOs as well as accounting-related senior managers who take part in organizations' implementing of ERP systems for at least 1 year and have at least 2-year working experience at the current position.

### 3.2. *Measures*

All research constructs included in this study have reflective multi-item scales derived from the relevant literature. Each item in the survey employs a 7-point Likert scale (1 = strongly disagree, 7 = strongly agree). TTF is measured by using a 6-item scale adapted from Jarupathirun (2007). The scale for effective use includes 11 items in the work of Deng *et al.* (2004), being adapted from Doll and Torkzadeh (1998). ERP system success is measured with four items in relation to individual impacts and eight items concerning organizational impacts (Sedera, 2006; Sedera and Gable, 2004).

### 3.3. *Data collection*

To test this hypothesis, a questionnaire is designed to collect data. Each of the items in the questionnaire, in relation to the three variables mentioned in the hypothesis, is reviewed for content validity by an expert panel that has a high level of knowledge and skill relating to ERP systems. The initial questionnaire is piloted on 10 respondents randomly selected from the sample frame and then revised on the basis of the feedback from their responses.

Given that our data are collected from a single source, we took a number of steps suggested by Podsakoff *et al.* (2003) to minimize the possibility of bias. These steps relate to instrument design as well as data collection procedures. First, the authors used multiple items for each construct and ensured the neutral wording of items. For example, in terms of each item, the authors do not ask the respondents to agree or disagree with the item-related statement as it can give the impression that the authors are expecting a certain response. Instead, the authors rephrased the question to include the response dimension: *How important is* ... Then the authors supplied appropriate response categories such as *extremely rejected, considerably rejected, a little rejected, neutral, a little agreed, considerably agreed*, and *extremely agreed*. Second, following the "protecting respondent anonymity and reducing evaluation apprehension" strategy proposed by Podsakoff *et al.* (2003), the authors assured respondents of the anonymity of their responses and emphasized that there are no right or wrong answers. This enabled them to answer questions as honestly as possible. Third, the authors adopted Podsakoff *et al.*'s (2003) "separation of measurement" strategy and as a result, separated the measurement of predictors and criterion variables in the questionnaire. In doing so, this study eliminated cases in which respondents relied on their prior response to answer subsequent questions.

This study utilized an email survey to collect data. However, there was no data available on the contact details of the chief financial officers or managers in relation to accounting-related departments working in all ERP-implemented business organizations in Vietnam. As it is extremely difficult to obtain this type of data, a convenience-sampling method was used. A list of email addresses consisting of 3853 potential informants was built up from public sources such as Vietnamese Business Directory, Vietnam Panpages, and personnel relationships of authors such as Master's students and alumni of the university where the authors are employed. By emailing all potential respondents with several follow-ups managed via SurveyMonkey program, after three months, 198 responses were received. The response rate was low, approximately 5.2%, since the number of enterprises adopting the ERP systems in Vietnam are few as this has

**Table 2:** Demographic characteristics.

| | Frequency | % | Min | Max | Mean |
|---|---|---|---|---|---|
| A. Informants | | | | | |
| Position in the firm | | | | | |
| CFO | 11 | 13.1 | | | |
| Senior controller | 32 | 38.1 | | | |
| Chief accountant | 27 | 32.1 | | | |
| Others | 14 | 16.7 | | | |
| Total | 84 | 100.0 | | | |
| **Gender** | | | | | |
| Male | 41 | 48.8 | | | |
| Female | 43 | 51.2 | | | |
| Total | 84 | 100.0 | | | |
| **Age** | | | | | |
| <25 | 6 | 7.1 | | | |
| 25–34 | 67 | 79.8 | | | |
| 35–44 | 6 | 7.1 | | | |
| >44 | 5 | 6.0 | | | |
| Total | 84 | 100.0 | | | |
| **Years at current position (years)** | | | 1 | 20 | 6.5 |
| **Work experience adopting the ERP systems (years)** | | | 1 | 5 | 2.7 |
| B. Companies | | | | | |
| Type of industry | | | | | |
| Manufacture | 49 | 58.3 | | | |
| Service | 16 | 19.0 | | | |
| Commerce | 19 | 22.7 | | | |
| Total | 84 | 100.0 | | | |
| **Type of company** | | | | | |
| 100% foreign-owned enterprises | 23 | 27.4 | | | |
| State-owned enterprises (≥ 51% government capital) | 15 | 17.9 | | | |
| Private enterprises/ limited enterprises | 30 | 35.7 | | | |
| Joint venture with foreign partners | 13 | 15.5 | | | |
| Joint venture with domestic partners | 3 | 3.5 | | | |
| Total | 84 | 100.0 | | | |

*(Continued)*

**Table 2:** (*Continued*)

| | Frequency | % | Min | Max | Mean |
|---|---|---|---|---|---|
| **Company size** | | | | | |
| <10 | 5 | 5.9 | | | |
| 10–50 | 9 | 10.7 | | | |
| >50–100 | 18 | 21.4 | | | |
| >100–200 | 24 | 28.6 | | | |
| >200–500 | 17 | 20.2 | | | |
| >500–1000 | 7 | 8.4 | | | |
| >1000 | 4 | 4.8 | | | |
| Total | 84 | 100.0 | | | |
| C. ERP | | | | | |
| **Type of ERP** | | | | | |
| SAP | 30 | 35.5 | | | |
| Oracle | 14 | 16.7 | | | |
| Others | 40 | 47.8 | | | |
| Total | 84 | 100.0 | | | |
| **Time since ERP adoption (years)** | | | 1 | 5 | 3.1 |

still not become popular.[3] Among these responses, 45 organizations did not adopt ERP systems, 12 responses showed an irrelevant respondent position, 31 responses were from people without enough work experience, nine were found incomplete, 12 responses had too short response duration (less than five minutes), five were outliers, and thus only 84 were considered valid. All official respondents were enterprises adopting the ERP systems for at least 1 year. Detailed descriptive statistics relating to the informants' characteristics are in Table 2.

## 4. Data Analysis, Results and Discussions

In this study, we used the PLS approach (Hair Jr *et al.*, 2014) because of the limitation of a valid sample size. Accordingly, data

[3]This information is quoted from Vietnamese e-commerce index report proposed by Vietnam E-commerce Association. Retrieved March 17, 2018, from http://ebi.vecom.vn/Upload/Document/Bao-Cao/Bao-cao-EBI-2017-Final.pdf.

were analyzed in two stages, via operation of the SmartPLS 3.8 application module (Ringle *et al.*, 2015). This two-stage analytical approach comprising a measurement model and a structural model evaluation is better than a one-step evaluation (Hair Jr *et al.*, 2010). The measurement models describe the measurements of constructs and structural models define the relationships among constructs in structural models (Hair Jr *et al.*, 2017).

### 4.1. *Assessment of the measurement model*

To assess the measurement model, reliability, convergent validity, and discriminant validity of each measurement scale are estimated.

*Construct reliability* measures the stability and consistency of the scale. It is evaluated through internal consistency reliability and indicator reliability (Hair Jr *et al.*, 2014). Composite reliability (CR) is considered as a measure of internal consistency reliability. In Table 3, it can be seen that all constructs having CR over the cutoff value of 0.7 (Hair Jr *et al.*, 2014) are regarded as satisfactory (Bernstein and Nunnally, 1994). However, TTF's CR is 1, an exceptionally high value. It can be explained that six items measuring TTF tap into different aspects, which are TTF's outcomes and are still highly correlated. Thus, these items of TTF should not be redundant (Hair Jr *et al.*, 2017, p. 112).

Indicator reliability is assessed through outer loadings. Table 3 shows that the outer loadings of most observed items range from 0.7 to 1.0, while the cutoff value is 0.7 (Hair Jr *et al.*, 2014). Nevertheless, the loading of indicator OI3 is too low, just achieving 0.2. Therefore, such an item is eliminated from OI scale.

The average variance extracted (AVE) values of all constructs are acceptable as they are higher than 0.5 (Fornell and Larcker, 1981).

The authors evaluate the discriminant validity of the measurements following the procedure proposed by Fornell and Larcker (1981). Table 4 shows that the square roots of AVE of all first-order factors range between 0.8 and 0.9, which are well above the corresponding correlations between these variables, thus indicating the discriminant validity of the measurements.

**Table 3:** Internal consistency, indicator reliability, and convergent validity analyzes.

| **First-order factor** | **Indicator** | **Loading**[a] | **Composite reliability**[b] | **AVE**[c] |
|---|---|---|---|---|
| TTF | TTF1 | 0.9 | 1 | 0.9 |
| | TTF2 | 1.0 | | |
| | TTF3 | 1.0 | | |
| | TTF4 | 0.9 | | |
| | TTF5 | 0.9 | | |
| | TTF6 | 1.0 | | |
| Effective use | USE1 | 0.7 | 0.9 | 0.6 |
| | USE2 | 0.9 | | |
| | USE3 | 0.8 | | |
| | USE4 | 0.7 | | |
| | USE5 | 0.8 | | |
| | USE6 | 0.8 | | |
| | USE7 | 0.8 | | |
| | USE8 | 0.8 | | |
| | USE9 | 0.7 | | |
| | USE10 | 0.8 | | |
| | USE11 | 0.7 | | |
| ERP system success (performance impacts) | II1 | 0.8 | 0.9 | 0.6 |
| | II2 | 0.8 | | |
| | II3 | 0.8 | | |
| | II4 | 0.8 | | |
| | OI1 | 0.8 | | |
| | OI2 | 0.9 | | |
| | OI3 | *0.2* | | |
| | OI4 | 0.7 | | |
| | OI5 | 0.8 | | |
| | OI6 | 0.9 | | |
| | OI7 | 0.8 | | |
| | OI8 | 0.7 | | |

*Notes*: [a]All item loadings $>0.7$ indicate indicator reliability (Hair Jr *et al.*, 2014).
[b]All AVE $>0.5$ indicate convergent reliability (Fornell and Larcker, 1981; Hair Jr *et al.*, 2014).
[c]All CR $>0.708$ indicates internal consistency (Hair Jr *et al.*, 2014).

**Table 4:** Discriminant validity (Fornell and Lacker criterion).

| | ERP system success | TTF | Use |
|---|---|---|---|
| ERP system success | **0.8** | | |
| TTF | 0.7 | **0.9** | |
| Use | 0.6 | 0.6 | **0.8** |

*Note*: Bold values are the square root of AVE.

**Table 5:** Discriminant validity (Heterotrait-Montrait).

| | ERP system success | TTF | Use |
|---|---|---|---|
| ERP system success | | | |
| TTF | 0.7 | | |
| Use | 0.7 | 0.7 | |

*Note*: The values are in HTMT ratios.

This study also employs the Heterotrait-Montrait (HTMT) test (Henseler *et al.*, 2015), which is more stringent than Fornell and Larcker (1981), to evaluate the discriminant validity. Table 5 indicates that all HTMT values are maintained at 0.7 (significantly below 1.0), providing clear evidence for discriminant validity.

To address any possible common method effect, we conduct Harman's single-factor test to determine the extent of method variance in the data. The results show that this study is not affected by common method bias issue.

## 4.2. *Assessment of the structural model*

Structural models are tested through computations of beta $\beta$, $R^2$, and respective $t$-values with use of a bootstrapping technique, according to resampling of 5,000 (Hair Jr *et al.*, 2017).

### 4.2.1. *Hypotheses testing*

The results of the structural model are shown in Table 6. Our hypothesis offers adequate explanatory power, with $R^2$ value of effective use

**Table 6:** Results of hypotheses testing.

| H | Relationship | Std $\beta$ | Std error | $t$-Value | Decision | 95% CI LL | 95% CI UL |
|---|---|---|---|---|---|---|---|
| H1 | TTF → ERP system success | 0.5 | 0.1 | $5.8^{***}$ | Supported | 0.3 | 0.7 |
| H2 | TTF → Effective use | 0.6 | 0.1 | $8.5^{***}$ | Supported | 0.5 | 0.7 |
| H3 | Effective use → ERP system success | 0.3 | 0.1 | $3.1^{***}$ | Supported | 0.2 | 0.5 |
| H4 | TTF → Effective use → ERP system success | 0.2 | 0.1 | $2.7^{***}$ | Supported | 0.1 | 0.4 |

*Notes*: $^{***}p < 0.001$, $R^2$ (effective use = 0.405, ERP system success = 0.569).

being 40.5% and of ERP system success, 56.9%. We find that TTF significantly influences ERP system success ($\beta = 0.5$, $p < 0.001$). It means that the match or congruence between system capabilities and the requirements of the tasks helps to achieve performance goals as well as allows enterprises to operate smoothly and efficiently by ERP systems support; as a result, desired organizational outcomes can be considerably enhanced. Thus, H1 is supported.

Moreover, H2 and H3 are also acceptable at significant levels ($p < 0.001$ with $\beta = 0.6$ and 0.3, respectively). The findings of these hypotheses confirm that TTF predicts effective use, which in turn enhances performance impacts. The better the "fit" of technology to tasks becomes, the more effectively the ERP systems are utilized, and the more the organizations gain expected success.

Finally, tests for the indirect influence of TTF on ERP system success via effective use are conducted following the detailed instruction proposed by Nitzl (2016), Carrión *et al.* (2017). Their method employs Consistent PLS Bootstrapping. The results are also shown in Table 6, implying that the indirect influence (with $\beta = 0.2$) is meaningful with its $t$-value equal to 2.7. Furthermore, the methods of Nitzl (2016) and Carrión *et al.* (2017) indicate the type of mediation by calculating the variance accounted for (VAF) that determines the extent to which the variance of the dependent variable is directly explained by the independent variable and how much of the target construct's variance is explained by the indirect relationship via the mediator variable.

$$\begin{aligned}\text{VAF} &= \frac{indirect\_effect}{total\_indirect\_effects + direct\_effect} \\ &= \frac{0.2}{0.2 + 0.5} = 28.6\% \end{aligned} \tag{1}$$

Based on the above calculation, the authors conclude that the mediation relationship between TTF and ERP system success is partial (Hair Jr *et al.*, 2014).

#### 4.2.2. *Alternative model*

To further understand how our proposed research model can increase explanatory power in an ERP context, this study extensively tested the original paths of TTF theory in relation to the impacts among TTF, effective use, and individual performance with the same dataset. To put it differently, we replaced ERP system success with individual performance, which is defined as the extent to which the IS has influenced users' capabilities and effectiveness (Gable *et al.*, 2003; Sederaand Gable, 2004). Table 7 confirms that TTF and effective use are also positively associated with individual performance with the explanatory power on it being only 49.9%, however, in the hypotheses of the current study, 56.9% of the variance in ERP system success is explained.

The results obtained from the above two models demonstrate the importance of TTF for an implemented ERP system. The matching between features of an ERP system's technology and the tasks required not only leads to an increase in user capabilities and effectiveness but also plays an extremely significant role in explaining its success. It can be said that TTF is considered a critical success factor in ensuring an ERP system that achieves desired organizational goals. Given the expectation that advanced technologies should provide adequate support for successful outcomes and based on findings of this study, business organizations should be increasingly interested

**Table 7:** Results of alternative model.

| H | Relationship | Std $\beta$ | Std error | $t$-Value | Decision | 95% CI LL | 95% CI UL |
|---|---|---|---|---|---|---|---|
| H1 | TTF → Individual performance | 0.4 | 0.1 | 3.9*** | Supported | 0.2 | 0.6 |
| H2 | TTF → Effective use | 0.6 | 0.1 | 8.6*** | Supported | 0.5 | 0.8 |
| H3 | Effective use → Individual performance | 0.4 | 0.1 | 3.2*** | Supported | 0.2 | 0.5 |
| H4 | TTF → Effective use → Individual performance | 0.3 | 0.1 | 2.9*** | Supported | 0.1 | 0.4 |

*Notes*: $^{***}p < 0.001$, $R^2$ (effective use = 0.406, individual performance = 0.499).

in selecting ERP software meeting a requirement that its technology must be a good fit with the tasks it supports.

### 4.2.3. *PLS multiple-group analysis*

To explore whether there exists a significant difference in the proposed relationships between implementation organizations and post-implementation organizations, our approach is to divide the group by length of ERP duration. The literature review provides empirical evidence, which is the basis for deciding how long the implementation period can last. Specifically, Shang and Seddon (2002) reveal that it takes 1–2 years for enterprises to recognize the organizational benefits, while 2–3 years is an essential time for users to become familiar with a new enterprise system and extract the maximum benefits from it. O'Leary (2000) and McAfee (1999) report that the whole installation process of ERP takes between 1 and 3 years, with an average of 21 months. Meanwhile, Stratman (2001) concludes that the weighted average ERP implementation time from the 43 respondents is about 17.1 months. Likewise, Mabert *et al.* (2000) collect detailed ERP timeline information from the survey of 479 US manufacturing firms and estimate that the average time from the start of installation to going live is 17.5 months. More comprehensively, Hawking *et al.* (2004) divide ES maturity into three stages: the beginning period within the first 12 months, the consolidation period within 1–3 years after implementation, and the mature period, which begins 3 years after ES implementation. Given these proofs, the authors chose to utilize a 2-year implementation period, and thus, after a 2-year period, ERP-implemented organizations begin the post-implementation phase.

In accordance with Hair Jr *et al.* (2014), Parametric Test and the Welch-Satterthwaite Test for PLS-MGA are adopted to compare the difference in impact between organizations that are in ERP implementation duration with those that are in ERP post-implementation duration. Therefore, the data file is split into two groups: the first including 20 cases with lower than two ERP-adopted years, the second including the remaining cases. This study ran bootstrapping with sample size set to 1,000 in accordance with the commonly suggested rule of thumb (Hair Jr *et al.*, 2014). The results of PLS-MGA presented in Table 8 indicate that length of ERP duration moderates the relationships between use and ERP system success, between TTF and ERP system success at a significant level of 0.00. Specifically, effective use just has significantly strong impact on ERP system success in organizations being in post-implementation duration, however, this relationship is not supported in organizations being in the implementation stage. In addition, TTF

**Table 8:** Results of PLS-MGA for ERP implementation and post-implementation organizations.

| H | Relationship | Path coefficients-diff (implementation-post-implementation) | Parametric test's $p$-value (implementation vs. post-implementation) | Welch-Satterthwaite test's $p$-value (implementation vs. post-implementation) |
|---|---|---|---|---|
| H1 | TTF → ERP system success | 0.6 | 0 | 0 |
| H2 | TTF → Use | 0.2 | 0.2 | 0.1 |
| H3 | Use → ERP system success | 0.6 | 0 | 0 |

has a significantly higher impact on ERP system success in organizations that are in ERP implementation duration at a significant level of 0.00.

The findings of PLS-MGA reconfirm that TTF and effective use significantly influence ERP system success, however, to different extents. In the implementation stage, TTF is the most important antecedent leading to enhance ERP system success, while in the post-implementation period, expected performance impacts are affected by both TTF and effective use.

## 5. Conclusions and Implications for Research

### 5.1. *Implications for research*

Building on the TTF theory, this study proposed and tested the relationship between TTF and performance impacts, however, in an extensive way. In simpler terms, this study contributes to the literature by filling existing gaps in relation to TTF research. Specifically, original TTF theory adopts individual impacts as surrogates of IS success, while the current study directly investigates the impact of TTF on ERP system success. In addition, we assess the phenomenon from the point of view of accounting managers. This can lead to a better explanation of the importance of TTF because accountants are considered as multi-role persons who directly enter input as well as who directly utilize system output to make decisions in a timely manner. Therefore, their perspectives about the fit between technology and task are more appropriate, complete, and accurate. Finally, also of most importance, we analyze the current phenomenon at the organizational level, which has not been conducted before.

### 5.2. *Implications for practice*

This study provides valuable experience in relation to system success in the ERP environment for managers. They realize that operational and strategic effectiveness can be achieved and enhanced if an ERP system's technology matches with the tasks it supports. Hence, adopting an appropriate ERP system at the beginning when such a system is implemented makes an important contribution to the successful deployment of ERP applications later. In other words, in terms of enterprises without ERP systems, managers must pay more attention to selecting an ERP system that meets such "fit" when having the intention to adopt an ERP system. For ERP-implemented organizations, they should be mindful of reaching an agreement with ERP vendors on maintaining ERP systems to retain such a "fit" as much as possible.

Second, this research not only focuses on the importance of "fit" between technology and tasks but also assures the role of effective use on ERP system success. TTF's impacts on organizational benefits are more improved when ERP system is utilized effectively. Thus, managers need to find out how to maximize the effective utilization of ERP systems in their firms.

Finally, ERP system success is affected by TTF in the implementation stage, but more complicatedly, by both TTFs and effective use in the post-implementation period. This means that managers must always pay attention to maintain and increase the extent of TTF during the duration that ERP is adopted regardless of the implementation or post-implementation period. Nevertheless, an ERP system can be appropriate for business operations at an early stage, though it often has the tendency of being less relevant at later stages because of new business requirements and characteristics that increasingly emerge. Therefore, selecting a packaged standardized ERP system that (1) is adopted popularly to enable to maintain the system relevance and (2) is highly flexible to enable it to be customized to the business operations' new requirements and characteristics is critical.

## 5.3. *Limitations*

Due to time and budget constraints, the measurement scales adopted in this study are originally developed in the context of Western countries. This cannot truly reflect the nature of the study's construct in the context of Vietnam. As a result, the findings of the current study can be affected because of potential measurement bias. This problem could have been mitigated if the scales had been more extensively augmented by additional explored items and tested qualitatively prior to the field survey.

## 5.4. *Conclusions*

The present study provides empirical evidence about the positive impact of TTF on ERP system success. Understanding this relationship is crucial because ERPs are increasingly being widely adopted in Vietnam and because most firms have gone beyond the pre-implementation stage. Thus, firms should shift their focus to choosing an ERP system meeting a good "fit" between technology and the tasks it supports to receive the desired outcomes from their huge investments.

## References

Al-Mashari, M., Al-Mudimigh, A., and Zairi, M. (2003). Enterprise resource planning: A taxonomy of critical factors. *European Journal of Operational Research*, 146(2), 352–364.

Bailey, J.E., and Pearson, S.W. (1983). Development of a tool for measuring and analyzing computer user satisfaction. *Management Science*, 29(5), 530–545.

Bernstein, I.H., and Nunnally, J. (1994). *Psychometric Theory*. New York: Mc-Graw-Hill.

Byrd, T.A., Thrasher, E.H., Lang, T., and Davidson, N.W. (2006). A process-oriented perspective of IS success: Examining the impact of IS on operational cost. *Omega*, 34(5), 448–460. doi:http://dx.doi.org/10.1016/j.omega.2005.01.012

Callaway, E. (1999). *Enterprise Resource Planning: Integrating Applications and Business Processes Across the Enterprise*. Computer Technology Research Corporation, Charleston, United States.

Carrón, G.C., Nitzl, C., and Roldán, J.L. (2017). Mediation analyses in partial least squares structural equation modelling: Guidelines and empirical examples. *Partial Least Squares Path Modeling* (pp. 173–195): Springer International Publishing, Cham, Switzerland.

Davis, F.D. (1989). Perceived Usefulness, Perceived ease of use, and user acceptance of information technology. *MIS Quarterly*, 13(3), 319–340.

DeLone, W.H., and McLean, E.R. (1992). Information systems success: The quest for the dependent variable. *Information Systems Research*, 3, 60–95.

Deng, X., Doll, W., and Truong, D. (2004). Computer self-efficacy in an ongoing use context. *Behaviour & Information Technology*, 23(6), 395–412.

Doll, W.J., and Torkzadeh, G. (1998). Developing a multidimensional measure of system-use in an organizational context. *Information & Management*, 33(4), 171–185.

Finney, S., and Corbett, M. (2007). ERP implementation: a compilation and analysis of critical success factors. *Business Process Management Journal*, 13(3), 329–347. doi:10.1108/14637150710752272

Fornell, C., and Larcker, D.F. (1981). Structural equation models with unobservable variables and measurement error: Algebra and statistics. *Journal of Marketing Research*, 18(3), 382–388.

Gable, G., Sedera, D., and Chan, T. (2003). Enterprise systems success: A measurement model. *ICIS 2003 Proceedings*, 48.

Gatian, A.W. (1994). Is user satisfaction a valid measure of system effectiveness? *Information & Management*, 26(3), 119–131. doi: http://dx.doi.org/10.1016/0378-7206(94)90036-1

Goodhue, D.L., and Thompson, R.L. (1995). Task-technology fit and individual performance. *MIS Quarterly*, 19(2), 213–236.

Grover, V., Seung Ryul, J., and Segars, A.H. (1996). Information systems effectiveness: The construct space and patterns of application. *Information & Management*, 31(4), 177–191. doi: http://dx.doi.org/10.1016/S0378-7206(96)01079-8

Guimaraes, T., and Igbaria, M. (1997). Client/server system success: Exploring the human side. *Decision Sciences*, 28(4), 851–876.

Hair Jr, J.F., Sarstedt, M., Hopkins, L., and G. Kuppelwieser, V. (2014). Partial least squares structural equation modeling (PLS-SEM). *European Business Review*, 26(2), 106–121. doi:10.1108/ebr-10-2013-0128

Hair Jr, J.F., Sarstedt, M., Ringle, C.M., and Gudergan, S.P. (2017). *Advanced Issues in Partial Least Squares Structural Equation Modeling.* Sage Publications Inc., Thousand Oaks, United States.

Hair Jr., J.F., Black, W.C., Babib, B.J., and Anderson, R.E. (2010). *Multivariate Data Analysis*, 7th edition. New York Pearson.

Hawking, P., Stein, A., and Foster, S. (2004). Revisiting ERP systems: Benefit realization. Paper presented at the *Proceedings of the 37th Annual Hawaii International Conference on System Sciences.*

Henseler, J., Ringle, C.M., and Sarstedt, M. (2015). A new criterion for assessing discriminant validity in variance-based structural equation modeling. *Journal of the Academy of Marketing Science*, 43(1), 115–135.

Ifinedo, P. (2011). Examining the influences of external expertise and in-house computer/IT knowledge on ERP system success. *Journal of Systems and Software*, 84(12), 2065–2078. doi: http://dx.doi.org/10.1016/j.jss.2011.05.017

Ifinedo, P., Rapp, B., Ifinedo, A., and Sundberg, K. (2010). Relationships among ERP post-implementation success constructs: An analysis at the organizational level. *Computers in Human Behavior*, 26(5), 1136–1148. doi:http://dx.doi.org/10.1016/j.chb.2010.03.020

Jarupathirun, S. (2007). Exploring the influence of perceptual factors in the success of web-based spatial DSS. *Decision Support Systems*, 43(3), 933–951.

Kositanurit, B., Ngwenyama, O., and Osei-Bryson, K.-M. (2006). An exploration of factors that impact individual performance in an ERP environment: An analysis using multiple analytical techniques. *European Journal of Information Systems*, 15(6), 556–568. doi:10.1057/palgrave.ejis.3000654

Lucas Jr, H.C. (1978). Empirical evidence for a descriptive model of implementation. *MIS Quarterly*, 2(2), 27–42.

Mabert, V.A., Soni, A., and Venkataramanan, M. (2000). Enterprise resource planning survey of US manufacturing firms. *Production and Inventory Management Journal*, 41(2), 52.

Matolcsy, Z.P., Booth, P., and Wieder, B. (2005). Economic benefits of enterprise resource planning systems: some empirical evidence. *Accounting & Finance*, 45(3), 439–456.

McAfee, A. (1999). The impact of enterprise resource planning systems on company performance. Paper presented at the *Wharton Electronic Supply Chain Conference*, Philadelphia.

Mukti, S.K., and Rawani, A.M. (2016). ERP system success models: A literature review. *ARPN Journal Of Engineering And Applied Sciences*, 11(3), 1861–1875.

Musaji, Y. (2015). ERP post implementation issues. Retrieved from

Muscatello, J.R. (2003). *An Exploratory Study of the Implementation of Enterprise Resource Planning (ERP)*. Cleveland State University.

Nah, F.F.H., Lau, J.L.S., and Kuang, J. (2001). Critical factors for successful implementation of enterprise systems. *Business Process Management Journal*, 7(3), 285–296. doi:10.1108/14637150110392782

Newman, M., and Westrup, C. (2005). Making ERPs work: accountants and the introduction of ERP systems. *European Journal of Information Systems*, 14(3), 258–272. doi:10.1057/palgrave.ejis.3000539

Ngai, E.W., Law, C.C., and Wat, F.K. (2008). Examining the critical success factors in the adoption of enterprise resource planning. *Computers in Industry*, 59(6), 548–564.

Nguyen, T.D. (2007). Factors affecting the utilization of the internet by internationalizing firms in transition markets: Evidence from Vietnam. *Marketing Intelligence & Planning*, 25(4), 360–376. doi:10.1108/02634500710754592

Nguyen, T. T., Nguyen, T.M., and Cao, T. H. (2015). Information systems success: a literature review. In *International Conference on Future Data and Security Engineering* (pp. 242–256). Springer, Cham.

Nicolaou, A., and Bhattacharya, S. (2008). Sustainability of ERPS performance outcomes: The role of post-implementation review quality. *International Journal of Accounting Information Systems*, 9(1), 43–60.

Nitzl, C. (2016). The use of partial least squares structural equation modelling (PLS-SEM) in management accounting research: Directions for future theory development. *Journal of Accounting Literature*, 37, 19–35.

O'Leary, D. E. (2000). *Enterprise Resource Planning Systems: Systems, Life Cycle, Electronic Commerce, and Risk.* Cambridge University Press, Cambridge, United Kingdom.

Petter, S., DeLone, W., and McLean, E. (2008). Measuring information systems success: models, dimensions, measures, and interrelationships. *European Journal of Information Systems*, 17(3), 236–263. doi:10.1057/ejis.2008.15

Podsakoff, P.M., MacKenzie, S.B., Lee, J.-Y., and Podsakoff, N.P. (2003). Common method biases in behavioral research: A critical review of the literature and recommended remedies. *Journal of Applied Psychology*, 88(5), 879.

Rainer Jr, R.K., and Watson, H.J. (1995). The keys to executive information system success. *Journal of Management Information Systems*, 12(2), 83–98.

Ram, J., and Corkindale, D. (2014). How "critical" are the critical success factors (CSFs)? *Business Process Management Journal*, 20(1), 151–174. doi:10.1108/bpmj-11-2012-0127

Ringle, C.M., Wende, S., and Becker, J.-M. (2015). SmartPLS 3: SmartPLS GmbH. Retrieved from http://www.smartpls.com

Rom, A., and Rohde, C. (2006). Enterprise resource planning systems, strategic enterprise management systems and management accounting. *Journal of Enterprise Information Management*, 19(1), 50–66. doi:10.1108/17410390610636878

Scapens, R.W., and Jazayeri, M. (2003). ERP systems and management accounting change: Opportunities or impacts? A research note. *European Accounting Review*, 12(1), 201–233. doi:10.1080/0963818031000087907

Seddon, P., Staples, S., Patnayakuni, R., and Bowtell, M. (1999). Dimensions of information systems success. *Communications of the AIS*, 2(3es), 5.

Sedera, D. (2006). *Enterprise Systems Success: A Measurement Model.* Doctor of Philosophy, Queensland University of Technology, Faculty of Information Technology.

Sedera, D., and Gable, G. (2004). A factor and structural equation analysis of the enterprise systems success measurement model. *ICIS 2004 Proceedings*, 36.

Shang, S., and Seddon, P.B. (2002). Assessing and managing the benefits of enterprise systems: The business manager's perspective. *Information Systems Journal*, 12(4), 271–299.

Stratman, J.K. (2001). *Information Integration for Supply Chain Management: An Empirical Investigation of ERP Systems in Manufacturing.* Ph.D. Dissertation, University of North Carolina.

Thompson, R.L., Higgins, C.A., and Howell, J.M. (1994). Influence of experience on personal computer utilization: Testing a conceptual model. *Journal of Management Information Systems*, 11(1), 167–187.

https://doi.org/10.1142/9789811227158_0009

Chapter 9

# Factors Affecting the Adoption of the International Accounting Standards

**Xuan Thach Ha and Tran Hanh Phuong Le**

## Abstract

With the trend of integrating the world and regional economy, financial markets have expanded strongly, especially capital markets. Moreover, the International Accounting Standards (IAS/IFRS) have become a global language in the preparing and presenting of financial statements. The objective of this chapter is to examine the macro factors affecting the adoption of IAS/IFR in Vietnam. The authors use mixed methods based on logarithm models with secondary data of 147 countries to examine the following factors: culture, economic growth, capital markets, education, foreign operation, law, and politics. The authors propose implications of promoting the process of IAS/IFRS adoption in the country.

**Keywords:** IAS/IFRS; Adoption; Macro factors; Accounting; Auditing.

## 1. Introduction

In the context of market globalization, international accounting and securities organizations want the harmonization of accounting standards to promote investments and increase economic integration between nations and regions. Thus, a "common accounting language" is necessary to ensure transparency, clarity, comparability across the world, providing greater utility for the analysts, managers, and investors to make decisions. Most countries adopt the International

Accounting Standards (IAS/IFRS). Vietnam is building a roadmap for accounting and auditing into 2025 in harmony with international standards.

International studies about the IAS/IFRS adoption from various perspectives provide a comprehensive picture of the level of harmonization between national accounting standards and the International Accounting Standards. Most of the previous studies refer to costs and problems associated with the adoption of IAS/IFRS in the developed countries (Delvaille *et al.*, 2005; Larson and Street, 2004; Nobes and Parker, 2004). However, the studies focus mainly on developed countries, while studies on developing countries are still relatively limited.The empirical studies on the factors that affect the IAS/IFRS adoption in developing countries are necessary; however, they are not properly addressed. The question posed is: Is a developing country eligible to adopt IAS/IFRS? The subject has great scientific and practical significance to provide a proper solution that is appropriate to the characteristics of developing countries.

## 2. Literature Review

### 2.1. *Research on the benefits of adopting IAS/IFRS in countries*

The development of global accounting and taxonomy helps improve the quality of information on financial statements such as comparability, transparency, timeliness, and relevance. Therefore, many countries intend to adopt IAS/IFRS or converge with IAS/IFRS (Daske and Gebhardt, 2008; Vera, 2014).

First, the business can attract capital, enhance its opportunities, become more competitive, and integrate into the world market easily. Typically, the company significantly reduces the cost of issuing bonds and raising capital because of higher credit index (Saudagaran and Diga, 2003). Second, IAS/IFRS improve not only business efficiency but also the quality of management and information, increase the accuracy of forecasts (Ashbaugh and Pincus, 2001), facilitate the comparison between the companies operating in the same market (Whittington, 2005), and improve the quality of accounting and internal control system of the enterprise (Christopher and Christian, 2014).

Third, many pieces of research prove that one of the benefits is how IAS/IFRS reflects the value of the enterprise. Horton and Serafeim (2010) show that the adoption of IAS/IFRS increases the values of companies in the UK, France, and Italy. Aubert and Grudnitski (2011) identify differences in return on assets (ROA) of the companies by using IAS/IFRS and GAAP in Belgium, Finland, France, Italy, Netherlands, Sweden, Switzerland, and the UK. In particular, the German and Norwegian companies show great differences.

Finally, a quick integration with IAS/IFRS helps countries save money on drafting, promulgate technical documents (Leuz, 2003; Daske and Gebhardt, 2008), and improve the quality of human resources in accounting, auditing, and finance (De George *et al.*, 2016).

## 2.2. *Studies do not support the IAS/IFRS adoption*

Each nation's environmental difference is a barrier to the adoption of IAS/IFRS: lack of political will, local culture, and strong national will (Callao *et al.*, 2007). Difficulties that the enterprises face when adopting IAS/IFRS are due to the complex nature of the standards, lack of guidance when adapting reality, a close link between financial statement and tax, frequent changes of IAS/IFRS, or lack of knowledge of employees (Ihab and Nedal, 2013). Environmental factors control cost–benefit analysis for changing reporting regimes. Conversion costs are a concern (Hail *et al.*, 2010).

Developing countries also cope with many difficulties in resources for IAS/IFRS adoption. According to the study of Lasmin (2011), human resources and accounting systems in developing countries are not strong enough to adopt IAS/IFRS. Cătălina (2016) states that the ability to adopt and judge IAS/IFRS professionally is difficult.

The process of adoption is not synchronized and lack of current legal guidance and regulators to help decipher the uncontrolled accounting information is a cause for concern rather than the protection of investors (Ehoff and Dahli, 2014). Moreover, the adoption of IAS/IFRS needs a lot of time, effort, and cost to be built (Bae *et al.*, 2008), which is similar to the previous study. Besides, the companies need to build IT systems when adopting IAS/IFRS to support the processing, collection, and presentation of financial information from the enterprise department and outside.

### 2.3. *The factors affecting the adoption of IAS/IFRS*

The adoption of IAS/IFRS in different countries is not the same because of some factors: culture, economy, capital markets, education, foreign operations, law, politics, etc.

In the process of formation and development, countries and regions establish and shape their characteristics. These traits originate from the business, legal, and cultural environment. The environment, which influences the accounting system of countries and creates certain differences, offers diversity and richness in international accounting (Irvine and Lucas, 2006; Tymothy and Hector, 2007; Alia and Branson, 2011; Nguyen, 2014). Diversity in national accounting comes from the economy (Larson, 1993; Tran, 2016), politics (Baker *et al.*, 2007), law (Kantor *et al.*,1995), taxes, business, and occupation. Environmental factors are always intertwined (Choi and Meek, 2011; Kim and Yang, 2012).

The research focuses on understanding the status of developed countries when adopting IAS/IFRS such as the EU, Australia, Japan, etc. These countries have financial markets and regulatory systems that are developed. Recently, some authors have investigated in depth the factors that affect the adoption of IAS/IFRS in transition economies (Vinícius *et al.*, 2018). Few studies investigate IAS/IFRS adoption in countries with similar economic, cultural, and social characteristics. Therefore, the process of adopting IAS/IFRS in such countries should be considered. Most of the studies focus on factors affecting the adoption of IAS/IFRS in countries, focusing particularly on developed countries. For the past five years, the authors have begun to look at the impact of factors on the adoption of IAS/IFRS in emerging countries. However, the research is still limited, especially about developing countries in the ASEAN region, which have similar characteristics.

Research in developing countries up to now has not fully addressed the adoption of IAS/IFRS. The authors mainly use qualitative methods from the literature review, situational assessment, and local accounting standards convergence. The papers focus on the difficulty in adopting IAS/IFRS in different countries, the importance of adoption of IAS/IFRS, and the proposed approach and road map for each country. However, the authors do not explain specifically how the factors affect the adoption of IAS/IFRS in these countries. This complex issue should be considered with caution. Finally, the research on macro factors affecting IAS/IFRS in countries has not been implemented, which is noticeable.

## 2.4. *The proposed model and research hypotheses*

**Hypothesis H1:** *Countries with Anglo–Saxon culture show more potential to adopt IAS/IFRS than other countries.*

Nobes (1998) points out that countries influenced by similar cultural values tend to adopt the same standards. So, the same cultural values affect IAS/IFRS adoption. Chamisa (2000) argue that IAS/IFRS adoption is easier for countries with an Anglo–Saxon culture through the effects of the IASB and the development of IAS/IFRS.

**Hypothesis H2:** *The higher the country's economic growth, the more likely the country is to apply IAS/IFRS.*

The countries' economic problems are considered when the manipulation of accounting data occurs. The lower the level of economic development of countries, the lower the accounting system (Doupnik and Salter, 1995). Mueller (1968) assumes that the level of economic development has a certain impact on accounting practice in a country. In particular, Adkari and Tondkar (1992) show that the level of economic growth has a positive effect on the development of the accounting system.

**Hypothesis H3:** *Countries that have capital markets are more likely to adopt IAS/IFRS.*

When analyzing the role of IAS/IFRS in improving the quality of disclosed financial information to capital markets in developing countries, Chamisa (2000) confirms the significant impact of these standards on emerging financial markets in these countries. Jemakowicz (2006) states that countries with open financial markets have more opportunities to adopt IAS/IFRS.

**Hypothesis H4:** *The higher the level of the educational system of a country, the more likely the country is to adopt IAS/IFRS.*

The educational system affects the scientific, technological, and economic environment and the sustainable development of each country. The educational system affects the accounting principles of each country. Doupnik and Salter (1995) argue that the IAS/IFRS adoption is a strategic decision because the country must understand and apply these standards that require a high educational system combined with professional competence.

**Hypothesis H5:** *Countries that have a higher level of open foreign listings are more likely to adopt IAS/IFRS.*

Cook and Wallace (1990) conclude that countries that have open economies would have more international pressure. These pressures are the complexity of international economic integration. The emerging countries in Asia have a narrow market (not consumed) but cheap labor. They have a comparative advantage in labor costs. These benefits are likely to attract foreign investors to expand their economic activities to the world. Therefore, countries can have the advantages of adopting IAS/IFRS to facilitate international transactions.

**Hypothesis H6:** *Countries having a "common law" legal system are more likely to adopt IAS/IFRS than the other countries.*

Nobes (1998) points out the importance of the legal system as a major factor in accounting for countries. Common law countries (also known as Anglo–Saxon countries) with the major administration of the regime provide predominant financial markets and accounting systems for the benefit of investors and creditors. Hence, the state is not a privileged user of accounting information. Also, the role of the state is to build a legal framework for the proper functioning of the capital markets.

**Hypothesis H7:** *Countries with higher democratic political systems tend to adopt IAS/IFRS.*

Hassab *et al.* (2003) state that the higher the political system a country has, the more the accounting system develops. Hence, according to Sami and Welsh (1992), the institutional political system has a great influence on the decision of whether or not to adopt the new accounting standards.

Based on the background theory combined with expert surveys, the authors propose the research model in Figure 1.

## 3. The Research Method

The research uses the mixed research method, as follows:

- **Step 1:** Document overview, defining theoretical foundations and background theories for research.
- **Step 2:** Qualitative research methods. The research uses GT (Grounded Theory) by a survey of 20 experts.
- **Step 3:** Quantitative research methods: The research examines and quantifies the relationship between factors through the verification tool and the logit regression model.
- **Step 4:** Research results, discussion, and policy implications.

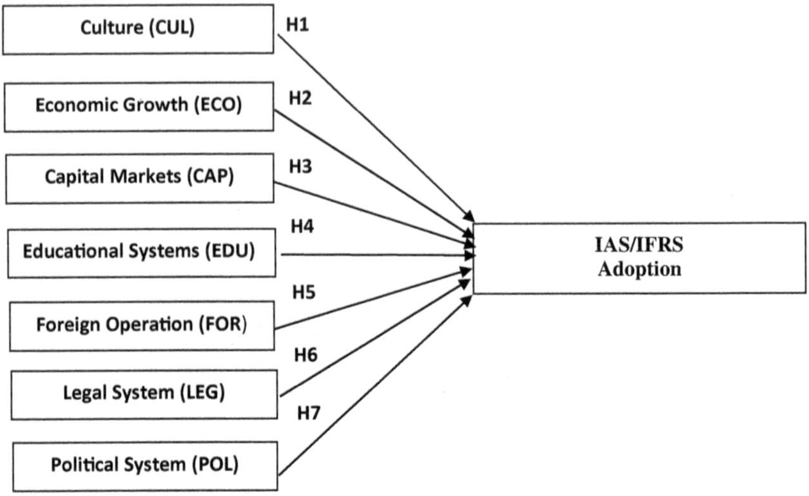


**Figure 1:** The research model.

### 3.1. *The qualitative research*

The Expert Interview Questions identify factors as the basis for a formal survey of 20 experts. The experts are divided into four groups:

- **Group 1:** Representatives of agencies issuing national standards, policies and regulations, and professional associations: two persons.
- **Group 2:** Accountants in companies: eight people.
- **Group 3:** Representatives from the Securities and Exchange Commission or Auditor: about two persons.
- **Group 4:** Researchers, lecturers, directors of companies: eight persons (four directors in firms and four researchers, lecturers who know IAS/IFRS).

### 3.2. *Quantitative research*

$$\begin{aligned} LOGIT[IAS/IFRS = 1] = \alpha 0 &+ \alpha 1^{*} CUL + \alpha 2^{*} ECO \\ &+ \alpha 3^{*} CAP + \alpha 4^{*} EDU + \alpha 5^{*} FOR \\ &+ \alpha 6^{*} LEG + \alpha 7 * POL + \varepsilon. \end{aligned} \tag{1}$$

**Table 1:** Data collection resources.

| Content | Variables | Scale | Data resources | Expected effect |
|---|---|---|---|---|
| ***Dependent variable*** | | | | |
| IAS/IFRS: IAS/IFRS adoption in countries at 31/12/2017 (1: If countries have adopted IAS/IFRS; 0: If countries have not adopted IAS/IFRS) | | | | |
| ***Independent variables*** | | | | |
| Macro variables | Culture (CUL) | = 1 if the country has Anglo–Saxon culture = 0 if the country does not have Anglo–Saxon culture | World Bank — World Development Indicators (WDI) | + |
| | Economic growth (ECO) | Logarithm of Gross domestic products (GDP) | | + |
| | Capital markets (CAP) | = 1 if country has capital market = 0 if country does not have capital market | | + |
| | Educational system (EDU) | Literacy rate in the education system (from Wikipedia) | | + |
| | Foreign operation (FOR) | FDI/GDP(FDI, Foreign direct investment) | | + |
| | Legal system (LEG) | = 1 if country has common law<br>= 0 if country does not have common law | | + |
| | Political system (POL) | Gastil index 1978 (from 1 to 7) | Freedom House | + |

The dependent variable is a dummy variable, assuming a value of 1 if the country adopts IAS/IFRS and a value of 0 if the country does not adopt IAS/IFRS until 2017.

Independent variables: Culture (CUL), Economic growth (ECO), Capital markets (CAP), Educational system (EDU), Foreign operation (FOR), Legal system (LEG), Political system (POL).

Parameters: $\alpha 0$, $\alpha 1$, $\alpha 2$, ... , $\alpha_n$

Error: $\varepsilon$

#### 3.2.1. *Select sample size*

The sample size of $n = 147$ is consistent. The authors select non-probable samples because the constraint in the secondary data collection process for information concerning the country is not favorable. Samples are conveniently selected because of the convenience of data collection and objective assurance in the data collection of non-probability sampling.

#### 3.2.2. *Data collection*

The data are collected from the website www.iasplus.com/country/country.htm (Table 1). The 147 countries are divided into two groups: countries that adopt IAS/IFRS (with or without modification) and a group of countries by the end of 2017, not adopting IAS/IFRS. Relevant information is collected primarily from the World Bank — World Development Indicators (WDI).

## 4. Research Results and Discussion

### 4.1. *Research results*

#### 4.1.1. *Results of qualitative research from the expert survey*

The result is that 100% of experts agree on the macro factors and scale in the survey. They do not add a new factor or scale. By the end of qualitative research, the authors identify seven factors that influence the adoption of IAS/IFRS: Culture, Economic Growth,

**Table 2:** Results of qualitative research from an expert survey.

| Variables | Scale | Number of experts interviewed | Number of experts agree | Rate of agree (%) |
|---|---|---|---|---|
| Culture (CUL) | = 1 if the country has Anglo–Saxon culture = 0 if the country does not have Anglo–Saxon culture | 20 | 20 | 100 |
| Economic growth (ECO) | Logarithm of GDP in 2017 (million USD) | 20 | 20 | 100 |
| Capital markets (CAP) | = 1 if the country has capital market = 0 if the country does not have capital market | 20 | 20 | 100 |
| Educational system (EDU) | Literacy rate in the education system | 20 | 20 | 100 |
| Foreign operation (FOR) | = FDI/GDP | 20 | 20 | 100 |
| Legal system (LEG) | = 1 if the country has common law = 0 if the country does not have common law | 20 | 20 | 100 |
| Political system (POL) | Gastil Index 1978 (from 1 to 7) | 20 | 20 | 100 |

Education, Politics, Law, Foreign operations, and Capital markets (Table 2).

#### 4.1.2. *Results of quantitative research*

##### 4.1.2.1. Descriptive statistics of the macro variables

Table 3 shows that there has been Economic growth (ECO) on an average of 577,129.541 million USD. The educational system (EDU)

**Table 3:** Descriptive statistics of the variables: ECO, EDU, FOR, POL.

| Variable | $N$ | Minimum | Maximum | Mean | Std. Deviation |
|---|---|---|---|---|---|
| ECO | 147 | 592.48 | 20,654,745 | 577,129.541 | 2,345,385.96937 |
| EDU | 147 | 27 | 100 | 86.51 | 18.42 |
| FOR | 147 | −61 | 54 | 1.848 | 9.20476 |
| POL | 147 | 1 | 7 | 3.47 | 2.143 |
| Valid N | 147 | 1 | 2 | 3 | 4 |

**Table 4:** Descriptive statistics of the variables: CUL, CAP, LEG.

| | CUL | | CAP | | LEG | |
|---|---|---|---|---|---|---|
| **Variables** | **Countries that don't have Anglo–Saxon culture** | **Countries that have Anglo–Saxon culture** | **Countries that don't have capital markets** | **Countries that have capital markets** | **Countries that don't have the common law** | **Countries that have the common law** |
| **Frequency** | 102 | 45 | 30 | 117 | 130 | 17 |
| **Percentage** | 69.4% | 30.6% | 20.4% | 79.6% | 88.4% | 11.6% |

is presented by literacy rate. Countries have a literacy rate of 86.51% on average. The average Gastel index of the Political system variable (POL) is 3.47, which means that the countries in the samples are characterized by a medium level of political freedom. Foreign listing variable (FOR) is determined by the FDI/GDP ratio of 147 countries in 2017 that shows the average of this ratio in the sample, 1.848%.

Table 4 shows that: 45 countries have Anglo–Saxon culture (30.6%), 117 countries have capital markets (79.6%), and 17 countries have a common law (11.6%).

4.1.2.2. Univariate analysis

The aim of the univariate analysis is to examine the difference between the group of countries that adopt the IAS/IFRS and those that do not adopt these standards. Hence, the study applies two types of statistical tests: the Kolmogorov–Smirnov test to compare

**Table 5:** Kolmogorov–Simirnov test.

| Macro variables | Kolmogorov–Smirnov $Z$ | $N$ | Sig. |
|---|---|---|---|
| CUL | 0.440 | 147 | 0.000 |
| ECO | 0.403 | 147 | 0.000 |
| CAP | 0.489 | 147 | 0.000 |
| EDU | 0.219 | 147 | 0.000 |
| FOR | 0.341 | 147 | 0.000 |
| LEG | 0.525 | 147 | 0.000 |
| POL | 0.168 | 147 | 0.000 |

**Table 6:** Mann–Whitney test.

| Macro variables | Mean Rank IAS/IFRS = 0 | Mean Rank IAS/IFRS = 1 | $Z$ | Asymp. Sig. (2-tailed) |
|---|---|---|---|---|
| CUL | 63.11 | 75.62 | –1.497 | 0.134 |
| ECO | 64.84 | 74.33 | –1.005 | 0.315 |
| CAP | 69.66 | 74.64 | –0.682 | 0.495 |
| EDU | 46.97 | 78.01 | –2.966 | 0.003 |
| FOR | 58.03 | 76.37 | –1.763 | 0.078 |
| LEG | 77.11 | 73.54 | –0.615 | 0.539 |
| POL | 99.24 | 70.25 | –2.817 | 0.005 |

some variables' mean averages (Table 5) and the Mann–Whitney test for other variables in respect of the outcome of the Kolmogorov test result (see Table 6).

**Kolmogorov–Smirnov test:** Table 5 shows that the data are not normal (Sig. $< 0.05$).

- **Mann–Whitney test:** Table 6 shows that EDU and POL have the least differences between the two groups (Sig. $< 0.05$). The average indicates that the countries which adopt IAS/IFRS are characterized by a high level of education and a democratic political system than those of non-IAS/IFRS countries. These factors such as CUL, ECO, CAP, FOR, and POL do not significantly differ between the two groups.

- **Correlation matrix:** Table 7 shows that CUL, CAP, FOR, and LEG variables are excluded from the model (Sig. > 0.05). CAP – EDU variables are correlated (Sig. value < 0.05). Similarly, the Sig value of LEG, CUL, and ECO is less than 0.05. Therefore, it is suitable to eliminate CUL, CAP, FOR, and LEG variables. In conclusion, based on the Univariate analysis, it can be concluded that countries which adopt IAS/IFRS are characterized by an environment that is highly democratic, high economic growth, and higher numbers of the educated.

4.1.2.3. Multivariate analysis

The remaining independent variables match the model after performing correlation testing: ECO, EDU, and POL.

Logistic regression of the model is estimated as follows:

$$Ln(p/(1-p)) = 0.868 + 0.001^{*}ECO + 0.031^{*}EDU - 0.315^{*}POL$$

- **Test of regression coefficients (Wald Test):** The Wald test shows that the relationship between IAS/IFRS and the dependent variable in the model is statistically significant with a confidence level of over 95% (Sig. value < 0.05). Therefore, the ECO, EDU, POL variables are relevant (see Table 8).
- **The influence of the variables:** The EDU variable has the strongest influence, and the variables POL and ECO reflect the lowest effect.
- **The level of accurate forecasting of the model:**
  - Classification Table

Table 9 shows the correct forecasting rate for the entire model of 87.8%. This ratio is high indicating that the model's prediction level is quite accurate.

- The suitability of the model

Table 10 has a Sig. value < 0.05. So, the correlation between IAS/IFRS variable and independent variables is statistically significant, with a confidence interval greater than 95%.

**Table 7:** Correlation matrix.

| | | IAS/IFRS | CUL | ECO | CAP | EDU | FOR | LEG | POL |
|---|---|---|---|---|---|---|---|---|---|
| IAS/IFRS | Pearson Correlation | 1 | 0.124* | −0.268** | 0.056 | 0.255** | 0.060 | −0.051 | −0.238* |
| | Sig. (2-tailed) | 5 | 0.135 | 0.001 | 0.497 | 0.002 | 0.471 | 0.540 | 0.004 |
| CUL | Pearson Correlation | 0.124* | 1 | 0.052 | 0.043 | −0.036 | −0.053 | 0.452** | −0.084 |
| | Sig. (2-tailed) | 0.135 | 6 | 0.533 | 0.602 | 0.667 | 0.522 | 000 | 0.313 |
| ECO | Pearson Correlation | −0.268** | 0.052 | 1 | 0.117 | 0.130 | 0.015 | 0.334** | −0.058 |
| | Sig. (2-tailed) | 0.001 | 0.533 | 7 | 0.158 | 0.116 | 0.860 | 000 | 0.483 |
| CAP | Pearson Correlation | 0.056 | 0.043 | 0.117 | 1 | 0.180* | 0.05 | 0.13 | −0.173 |
| | Sig. (2-tailed) | 0.497 | 0.602 | 0.158 | 8 | 0.029 | 0.547 | 0.116 | 0.036 |
| EDU | Pearson Correlation | 0.255** | −0.036 | 0.130 | 0.180* | 1 | 0.125 | 0,126 | −0.380** |
| | Sig. (2-tailed) | 0.002 | 0.750 | 0.116 | 0.029 | 9 | 0.136 | 0.128 | 0.00 |
| FOR | Pearson Correlation | 0.060 | −0.053 | 0.015 | 0.005 | 0.125 | 1 | 0.163* | −0.081 |
| | Sig. (2-tailed) | 0.471 | 0.522 | 0.86 | 0.547 | 0.136 | 10 | 0.049 | 0.331 |
| LEG | Pearson Correlation | −0.051 | 0.452** | 0.334** | 0.130 | 0.126 | 0.163* | 1 | −0.149* |
| | Sig. (2-tailed) | 0.540 | 0.000 | 0.000 | 0.116 | 0.128 | 0.049 | 11 | 0.071 |
| POL | Pearson Correlation | −0.238* | −0.084 | −0.058 | −0.173 | −0.380** | −0.081 | −0.149* | 1 |
| | Sig. (2-tailed) | 0.004 | 0.313 | 0.483 | 0.036 | 0.00 | 0.331 | 0.071 | 12 |

*Notes*: **Correlation is significant at the 0.01 level (2-tailed). *Correlation is significant at the 0.05 level (2-tailed).

**Table 8:** Variables in the model.

| Variables in the Equation | | | | | | | | | |
|---|---|---|---|---|---|---|---|---|---|
| | | | | | | | Exp(B) | 95% C.I. for EXP(B) | |
| | | **B** | **S.E.** | **Wald** | ***df*** | **Sig.** | **OR** | **Lower** | **Upper** |
| Step 1 | ECO | 0.001 | 0.004 | 2.74 | 1 | 0.008 | 1.00 | 1.000 | 1.011 |
| | EDU | 0.031 | 0.013 | 5.746 | 1 | 0.017 | 1.032 | 1.013 | 1.064 |
| | POL | −0.315 | 0.147 | 4.585 | 1 | 0.032 | 0.730 | 0.582 | 0.983 |
| | Constant | 0.868 | 1.35 | 0.413 | 1 | 0.520 | 2.383 | 13 | 14 |

**Table 9:** The level of accurate forecasting of the model.

| | | | Predicted | | |
|---|---|---|---|---|---|
| | | | IAS/IFRS adoption | | |
| **Observed** | | | **Not adopt IAS/IFRS** | **Adopt IAS/IFRS** | **Percentage Correct** |
| Step 1 | IAS/IFRS adoption | Not adopt IAS/IFRS | 3 | 19 | 15.8 |
| | | Adopt IAS/IFRS | 2 | 128 | 98.4 |
| Overall Percentage | | | 14.1 | 14.2 | **87.1** |

*Note*: The cut value is 0.5.

**Table 10:** Omnibus tests of model coefficients.

| | | $\chi^2$ | *df* | **Sig.** |
|---|---|---|---|---|
| Step 1 | Step | 21.699 | 3 | 0.00 |
| | Block | 21.699 | 3 | 0.00 |
| | Model | 21.699 | 3 | 0.00 |

**Table 11:** 2-Log likelihood.

| Step | 2-Log likelihood | Cox & Snell $R^2$ | Nagelkerke $R^2$ |
|---|---|---|---|
| 1 | 91.680[a] | 0.137 | 0.256 |

[a]Estimation terminated at iteration number 7 because parameter estimates changed by less than .001.

∘ The level of interpretation of the model

Table 11 shows that the level of explanation of the model is 189.791. The 2-log-likelihood value has good explanations with the overall model.

### 4.2. *Discussion*

The results show that CUL, CAP, FOR, and LEG variables have no significant impact on IAS/IFRS adoption. IAS/IFRS adoption in countries does not rely on the existence of capital markets, foreign operations, and law. The EDU, ECO, and POL variables have a significant impact on the decision to adopt IAS/IFRS. Meaning that countries adopt IAS/IFRS based on economic growth, development education, and democratic political system.

We apply the data of Vietnam at the end of the fiscal year on December 31, 2017. The results show that Vietnam can fully adopt IAS/IFRS in the future (72.41%).

## 5. Conclusion and Recommendation

### 5.1. *Conclusion*

The research is built on a model of empirical research on factors influencing IAS/IFRS adoption in various countries: Economic Growth, Education, and Politics. The accuracy of the model is high (over 85%). Therefore, the research achieves the research purposes. A country with a high level of education, economic growth, and a democratic political system is more likely to adopt IAS/IFRS than others.

In particular, culture is the most influential factor in the IAS/IFRS adoption process. This shows that countries can learn from those early adopting countries that have a similar culture.

## 5.2. *Recommendation for macro factors affecting the adoption of IAS/IFRS*

### 5.2.1. *Educational system factor*

The Ministry of Finance should attach importance to the development of an IAS/IFRS qualified human resource training and development strategy by coordinating with the Ministry of Education and Training to develop accounting towards integration. The collaboration with universities, professional organizations, and supporting agencies is to organize training and foster and update accounting knowledge in the spirit of the issued accounting standards and towards Access to IAS/IFRS. The Ministry of Finance should give the Professional Association the right to translate, draft, and update the IAS/IFRS. Moreover, they should continue to promote cooperation with training institutions (universities, the country Association of Certified Public Accountants) and international professional organizations such as CPA Australia, ACCA, and ICAEW.

Moreover, accountancy training institutions actively improve the quality of accounting training. The need to innovate curriculum and improve teaching methods is one of the important issues contributing to the improvement of the accounting infrastructure, in which education institutions including universities, colleges, the institutes need to innovate their accounting training program in a way that enhances the teaching of VAS, IAS/IFRS-related content, rather than teaching skills, processing accounts for the training of people. Highly qualified accounting practitioners are able to adopt IAS/IFRS effectively. Finally, expanding links with international universities, enlisting the co-operation of large corporations and professional organizations, and enabling students to gain access to the workplace and receive scholarships and job opportunities in the process of learning and after graduation are necessary.

### 5.2.2. *Economic growth factor*

The state should have clear strategies to maintain economic growth at the rate recorded in 2017 to support the economic growth factor, which helps enterprises be more favorable to adopting IAS/IFRS. The level of inflation in the economy should be strictly controlled, stable, and must not affect the fluctuation of the economy. The state should gradually improve the economic and legal environment in line with the requirements of IAS/IFRS. Further, the state should issue the enterprise management mechanism by way of obtaining accounting information, which is one of the important bases for testing the quality and effectiveness of business management.

### 5.2.3. *Political system factor*

To fully apply IAS/IFRS, the executive, legislative, and judicial sectors should coordinate with each other based on ensuring their independence by their respective functions of assignment, support, and control as required by the law. Besides, promoting initiative and creativity of subordinates, stepping up the decentralization, and ensuring the uniform management of the system can help in the adoption of IAS/IFRS. The government must enact policies to mobilize investment in the construction of socioeconomic infrastructure and to train high-quality human resources to meet the development process. Taking initiative and creating favorable conditions for the country's construction and development help the country integrate with the rest of the world actively. The state apparatus needs to be streamlined, the contingent of cadres and civil servants need to have the qualities, capabilities, and the qualifications of professionals. The state should intensify the dialog with the people and the enterprises through various information channels so that the guidelines, policies, and laws are closer to reality.

## 5.3. *Limitations of the research*

The estimation model is missing data and some macro and microenvironment variables can affect the adoption of IAS/IFRS. The difficulties are data collection and restrictions on selection.

## References

Adhikari, A. and Tondkar, R.H. (1992). Environmental factors influencing accounting disclosure requirements of global stock exchanges. *Journal of International Financial Management and Accounting*, 4(2), 75–105. doi: https://doi.org/10.1111/j.1467-646X.1992.tb00024.x

Alia, M., and Branson, J. (2011). The illusion of comparable European IFRS financial statements — The view of auditors, analysts, and other users. *Accounting and Management Information Systems*, 10(2), 106–134.

Ashbaugh, H., and Pincus, M. (2001). Domestic accounting standards, international accounting standards, and the predictability of earnings. *Journal of Accounting Research*, 39(3), 417–434. doi: https://doi.org/10.1111/1475-679X.00020

Aubert, F., and Grudnitski, G. (2011). The impact and importance of mandatory adoption of international financial reporting standards in Europe. *Journal of International Financial Management and Accounting*, 22(1), 132–157. doi: https://doi.org/10.1111/j.1467-646X.2010.01043.x

Bae, K.-H., Tan, H., and Welker, M. (2008). International GAAP differences: The impact on foreign analysts. *Accounting Review*, 83(3), 593–628. doi: https://doi.org/10.2308/accr.2008.83.3.593

Baker, M., Stefan, N., and Jeffrey, W. (2007). The effect of dividends on consumption. *Brookings Paper on Economic Activity*, 277–291. Retrieved from_SSRN: https://ssrn.com/abstract=983433

Callao, S., Jarne, J., and Laínez, A. (2007). Adoption of IFRS in Spain: Effect on the comparability and relevance of financial reporting. *Journal of International Accounting, Auditing, and Taxation*, 16, 148–178. doi: 10.1016/j.intaccaudtax.2007.06.002

Cătălina, F.P. (2016).The role of institutional pressures in developing countries implication for IFRS. *Theoretical and Applied Economics*, 2(607), 27–40.

Chamisa, E.E. (2000). The relevance and observance of the IASC standards in developing countries and the particular case of Zimbabwe. *The International Journal of Accounting*, 35(2), 267–286.

Choi, F.D., and Meek, G.K. (2011). *International Accounting*, 7th edition. Prentice-Hall, NewYork.

Christopher, W.N., and Christian, S. (2014). The qualitative characteristics of financial information and managers' accounting decisions: Evidence from IFRS policy changes. *IASB Research Forum*, 1, 1–46. Retrieved from http://archive.ifrs.org/Meetings/MeetingDocs/Other%20Meeting/2014/October/ABR-2014-0103-Qualitative-characteristics.pdf

Daske, H., and Gebhardt, G. (2008). International financial reporting standards and experts' perceptions of disclosure quality. *Abacus,* 42, 33–45. doi: https://doi.org/10.1111/j.1467-6281.2006.00211.x

De George, E., Xi Li, and Lakshmanan, S. (2016). *A review of the IFRS adoption literative.* Forthcoming. Review of Accounting Studies, 21, 898–1004. Online publication date: 3-Jun-2016.

Delvaille, P., Gabi, E., and Chiara, S. (2005). International financial reporting convergence: Evidence from three continental european countries. *Accounting in Europe*, 2, 137–164. doi:https://doi.org/10.1080/09638180500379103

Doupnik, T.S., and Salter, S.B. (1995). External environment, accounting practices, and culture: A preliminary test of a general model of international accounting development. *The International Journal of Accounting*, 30, 189–207.

Ehoff, C., and Dahli, G. (2014). Lower of cost or market inventory valuation: IFRS versus US GAAP. *Journal of Business & Economics Research*, 12(1), 19–21. doi: 10.19030/jber.v12i1.8372

Hail, L., Leuz, C., and Wysocki, P. (2010). Global accounting convergence and the potential adoption of IFRS by the U.S., (Part I): Conceptual underpinnings and economics analysis. *Accounting Horizons*, 24(3), 355–394. doi: https://doi.org/10.2308/acch.2010.24.3.355

Hail, L., Leuz, C., and Wysocki, P. (2010). Global accounting convergence and the potential adoption of IFRS by the U.S. (Part II): Political factors and future scenarios for U.S. accounting standards. *Accounting Horizons*, 24(4), 567–588. doi: https://doi.org/10.2308/acch.2010.24.4.567

Hassab, E.H.R., Epps, R.W., and Saíd, A.A. (2003). The impact of environmental factors on accounting development: An Egyptian longitudinal study. *Critical Perspectives on Accounting*, 14(3), 273–292.

Horton, J., and Serafeim, G. (2010). Market reaction to and valuation of IFRS reconciliation adjustments: First evidence from the UK. *Review of Accounting Studies*, 15(4), 725–751. doi: https://doi.org/10.1007/s11142-009-9108-5

Ihab, A., and Nedal, S. (2013). The advantages and the challenges of adopting IFRS into UAE stock market. *International Journal of Business and Management*, 8(19), 1–23. doi:10.5539/ijbm.v8n19p1

Irvine, H.J., and Lucas, N. (2006). The globalization of accounting standards: the case of the United Arab Emirates. In *The 3rd International Conference on Contemporary Business 2006*, University of Wollongong, Australia, pp. 2–24.

Kantor, J., Clare, B.R., and Stephen, B.S. (1995). Financial reporting practices in selected Arab countries: An empirical study of

Egypt, Saudi Arabia, and the United Arab Emirates. *International Study of Management Organization*, 25(3), 31–45. https://doi.org/10.1080/00208825.1995.11656658

Kim, M.S., and David, C.Y. (2012). Factors affecting IFRS adoption. *International Journal of Business,* 17(3), 276–298. ISSN: 1083–4346.

Larson, R.K. (1993). International accounting standards and economic growth: An empirical investigation of their relationship in Africa. *Research in Third World Accounting,* 2, 27–43. https://doi.org/10.1111/j.1467-646X.1995.tb00054.x

Larson, R.K., and Street, D.L. (2004). Convergence with IFRS in an expanding Europe: Progress and obstacles identified by large accounting firms 'survey.*Journal of International Accounting, Auditing, and Taxation,* 13, 89–119.

Lasmin, R. (2011). An institutional perspective on IFRS adoption in developing countries. *Academy of Accounting and Financial Studies Journal,* 15(2), 61–71. Retrieved from https://www.researchgate.net/publication/228301545

Leuz, C. (2003). IAS versus US GAAP: Information asymmetry-based evidence from Germany's New Market. *Journal of Accounting Research*, 41, 445–472. Retrieved from SSRN: https://ssrn.com/abstract=275348 or http://dx.doi.org/10.2139/ssrn.275348

Mueller, G. (1968). Accounting principles generally accepted in United States Vs. those accepted elsewhere. *International Journal of Accounting Education and Research*, 1, 91–103.

Nguyen, T.T.P. (2014). *Factors affecting the application of international accounting standards in the country.* Master's Thesis on Economics, University of Economics Ho Chi Minh city.

Nobes, C. (1998). Towards a general model of the reasons for international differences in financial reporting.*Abacus,* 34, 162–187. doi: https://doi.org/10.1111/1467-6281.00028

Nobes, C., and Parker, R. (2006). *Comparative international accounting*, 9th Edition, Edinburgh: Pearson Education, Ltd.

Saudagaran, M.S., and Diga, G.J. (2003). Economic integration and accounting harmonization options in emerging markets: Adopting the IASC/IASB model in ASEAN. *Research in Accounting in Emerging Economies*, 5, 239–266.

Tran, Q.T. (2016). Factors affecting the application of the international accounting standards. In *Proceedings of the Workshop "IFRS — Opportunities and Challenges When Applied in the Country*, pp. 79–84.

Tymothy, S.D., and Hector, P. (2007). *International Accounting.* McGraw-Hill: Irwin, 2007, ISBN-13: 978-0-07-250775-1, ISBN-10: 0-07-259775-6.

Vera, P. (2014). Fair value accounting and its usefulness to financial statement users. *Journal of Financial Reporting and Accounting*, 12(2), 102–116. Retrieved from SSRN: https://ssrn.com/abstract=2365712 or http://dx.doi.org/10.2139/ssrn.2365712

Vinícius, S.D.L., Gerlando, A.S., Franco de Lima, L.N.G.C., and Iran, S.L. (2018). Effects of the adoption of IFRS on the credit market: Evidence from Brazil. *The International Journal of Accounting*, 53(2), 77–101. doi:10.2308/jiar-52192

Whittington, G. (2005). The adoption of international accounting standards in the European Union. *European Accounting Review*, 14(1), 127–153. doi: https://doi.org/10.1080/0963818042000338022

https://doi.org/10.1142/9789811227158_0010

# Chapter 10

# Value Relevance of Biological Assets Under IFRS in Asian Nations

**Thi Phuong Thanh Tran**

## Abstract

This chapter examines the value relevance of fair value (fv) accounting for biological assets under IAS 41 *Agriculture*, using a panel dataset extracted from listed firms in 10 Asian countries from 2014 to 2018. The model of Ohlson (1995) is adjusted to operationalize value relevance as the ability of book value to explain the market value. This chapter also compares countries valuing biological assets at historical cost (HC) and FV. The results of the study prove that recognized biological assets are value-relevant at FV, and more relevant than using the cost model. Therefore, the regulators, preparers of financial statements, and users can have better understanding of the valuation methods of biological assets and the market valuation implications of IAS 41.

**Keywords:** Biological assets; Fair value accounting; Historical cost; Accounting regulations.

## 1. Introduction

The vital change of the accounting standards, especially in international financial reporting standards (IFRSs), towards fair value (FV) accounting causes controversy among practitioners. Researchers who criticize FV accounting argue that FV inherits more manipulation and induces less efficient investment decisions (Liang and Wen, 2007; Ronen, 2008; Watts, 2003), or that FV does not necessarily make investors better off and that its usefulness has not been demonstrated

(Ball, 2006). On the contrary, supporters (e.g., Gigler *et al.*, 2007) conclude that FV provides stronger signals of financial distress, or (Choy, 2006) that information in the financial statement measured by FV is more relevant than historical cost (HC).

Almost all academic studies related to FV focus mainly on the context of financial instruments. Consideration of FV issues in other contexts (e.g., agricultural sector) is much less common. To help redress this circumstance, this chapter focuses on the method in the context of agriculture, particularly in biological assets. This method is regulated in International Accounting Standard (IAS) 41 “Agriculture”.

IAS 41 was issued in 2000 and first applied to annual periods beginning on or after January 1, 2003, introducing FV to all biological assets in agricultural activities. Therefore, this standard brings the debate into the agricultural accounting domain. Some authors claim that applying FV for biological assets could lead to irrelevant information because of the absence of active markets for some biological assets or due to the fact that each biological asset has its own attributes and life cycle (Martins *et al.*, 2012).

The vital change of the accounting standards, especially in IFRS, towards FV accounting causes controversy among practitioners.

This study focuses on the following research objectives:

- Examine biological asset value are relevant at FV under IAS 41;
- Investigate whether the value relevance of biological assets is impacted by the measurement methods of FV and HC.

The analysis of the panel dataset is extracted from non-financial listed firms in 10 Asian countries in the agricultural sector during the period from 2014 to 2018.

Overall, the results show that the value of biological assets under the FV model is value relevant. Additionally, comparing data from two samples of nations, one applying the local standards based on HC and the other FV for biological assets, there are different influences on market value.

The remainder of the chapter is structured as follows. Section 2 reviews relevant literature, Section 3 describes research methodology, and empirical results and discussion are provided in the fourth section. Finally, the last section presents the conclusion.

## 2. Theoretical Framework and Literature Review

### 2.1. *Theoretical framework*

According to IAS 41 "Agriculture", the value of biological assets is measured on initial recognition, and at subsequent reporting dates at FV fewer costs to sell. FV measurement is guided in IFRS 13 "Measurement of FV". There is an immediate recognition of the distinction between the initial measurement and the subsequent measurement in the profit or loss account, with an influence on the result. As a consequence, the depreciation and the impairment of the assets mentioned by IAS 41 are not necessary. The change in FV of biological assets can be a part of physical changes (e.g., growth of biological assets: from calves to adult cows) and changes in price (e.g., The FV of cows of the same age can change over time). IAS 41 encourages (optional) disclosure of the two components when explaining the increase in the FV of the current and future period.

In the particular context when a market-determined price is not available and the entity cannot assure a reliable estimate of FV, an entity is permitted to use the "unreliability clause" and recognize the biological assets concerned at cost less depreciation and impairment [IAS 41.30].

For bearer biological assets, IASB recently amended IAS 41 in relation to bearer plants that are used in the production or supply of agricultural produce and expect to bear produce for more than one period, with amendments effective for annual periods beginning on or after January 1, 2016. In these amendments, bearer plants that are yet to reach maturity are measured at accumulated cost. Entities can choose either the cost model or the revaluation model for mature bearer plants under IAS 16.

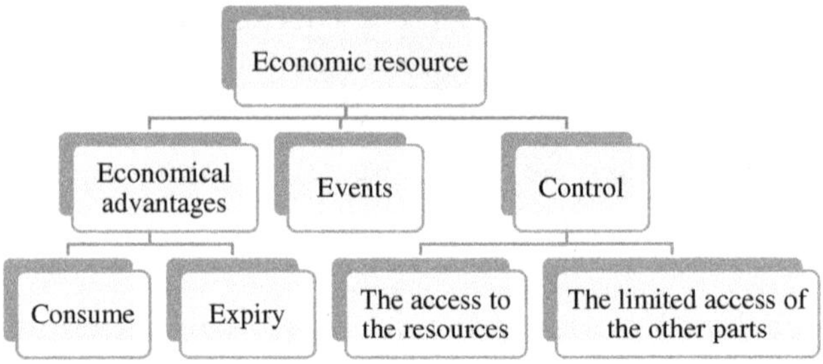


**Figure 1:** Asset's features.
*Source*: Stere (2001, p.18).

## 2.2. *Literature review*

### 2.2.1. *Concepts of asset and biological asset*

According to the International Accounting Standard Board (IASB), the definition of an asset is given as a present economic resource controlled by the entity based on past events. POP (2008) present that certain assets have their own features (see Figure 1).

"Economic resource" is a right that has the potential to produce economic benefits. (Conceptual framework 2018, 4.4)

The term "consume" in the above figure refers to the delimitation and separation of the economic benefits over the resources that they come from. The "expiry" refers to the fact that the potential of the resource decreases in time. Thus, the fact that the resources are limited is proved.

"Control" means that the entity has access to the resources from its own patrimony, but at the same time, the access of the other entities to the resources is restricted (POP, 2008).

In this paragraph, I also identify the biological asset concept. According to Kurniawan *et al.* (2014), the biological asset is a plant or livestock controlled by an entity that can bring economic benefits or not. Livestock is organized, single, or multicellular creatures, having the capacity to move and feel (Kurniawan *et al.*, 2014). Plant is the name of the vegetal organism with an organization that is simpler than of the animals, and derives substances from the roots, containing chlorophyll, and cellulose-derived cells (Kurniawan *et al.*, 2014).

According to Kurniawan *et al.* (2014), a biological asset is controlled or held by agribusinesses, so that farmers or businesses can take advantage of it. The benefits that can be derived from the biological asset are the benefits of beliefs, social benefits, and economic benefits. Religious and social benefits can be viewed as spiritual benefits. For farmers, the biological asset is a tool not only to earn money but also to connect people with the gods or in their social relationships.

However, the definition of the biological asset in IAS 41 has a number of differences. According to IASB, the biological asset is a living animal or plant, based on past events, and is controlled by the business. The biological asset is different from other types of assets because it can undergo biological transformation that comprises the process of growth, genetic transformation, production, and procreation, both from a qualitative perspective and from a quantitative point of view (IAS 41.5).

The definition of the biological asset in IAS 41 has some limitations. The first limitation is that IAS 41 allows the recognition of the economic benefits of biological assets even when economic benefits are unrealized. This will reduce the credibility of financial information because the life of biological assets is unknown as they can die anytime from diseases.

The second limitation is ambiguity and no specific guidance when classifying biological assets (Aryanto, 2011). According to economic benefits, IAS 41 divides biological assets into bearer biological assets and consumable biological assets. Bearer biological assets are self-regenerating (e.g., livestock from which milk is produced, grapevines, fruit trees, and trees from which firewood is harvested but the tree remains). In contrast, consumable biological assets are harvested as agricultural produce or are sold as biological assets (e.g., livestock intended for meat production, livestock held for sale, fish in farms, crops such as maize and wheat, and trees grown for lumber) (IAS 41.44).

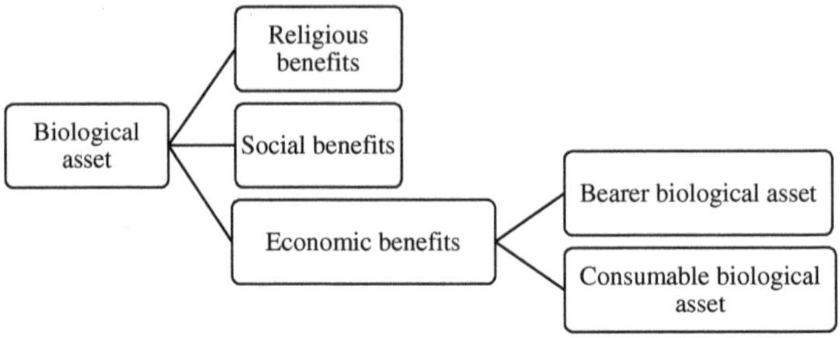


**Figure 2:** Biological asset's features.

The third limitation is that IAS 41 only refers to economic benefits, not the spiritual benefits of the biological asset because these benefits cannot be measured in monetary units.

From the above analysis, Figure 2 summarizes the characteristics of biological assets.

Thus, according to the discussion above, the concept of "biological assets" is summarized as follows:

> *A biological asset is an asset (including a plant or a living animal) that is controlled by the entity and has the potential to produce benefits (including spiritual and economic benefits). It can be categorized into two types: bearer biological asset and consumable biological asset. Furthermore, biological assets can be divided into mature or immature assets depending on the level or conditions they achieve at a time.*

### 2.2.2. *Asset revaluations and value relevance of non-current assets*

According to IASB, most of the non-current assets are allowed the revaluation method at an FV such as tangible and intangible assets [IAS 16, IAS 38[1]], biological assets [IAS 41], and investment properties [IAS 40]. When a company applies a revaluation method for its assets, the value relevance of information in financial statements can be questionable for users. Some studies investigate asset revaluations

[1]International Accounting Standard (IAS) 16 — Property, Plant, and Equipment. International Accounting Standard (IAS) 38 — Intangible asset.

by firms to find the answers to this issue. Aboody *et al.* (1999) conduct their study on UK firms and conclude that PPE revaluations have predictive power regarding future profitability. Another paper from Easton *et al.* (1993) (henceforth EEH), which investigates the value relevance of Australian industrial firms from 1981 to 1990, finds that the significant explanatory power of aggregate revaluation reserve increments for returns over earnings and earnings changes, even for price-to-book ratios. To extend EEH, Barth and Clinch (2006) partition assets into major asset classes, which are financial and non-financial assets, and estimate the relation between revalued amounts and an estimate of firm value based on analysts' earnings forecasts. Their findings suggest revalued financial, tangible, and intangible assets are value-relevant. Similarly, Oliveira *et al.* (2010) find that net earnings, reported goodwill, and other intangible assets are significantly associated with the stock price in Portugal.

This study extends previous studies by focusing on the revaluation of biological assets at FV. Instead of a specific country, we conduct the research for some Asian countries that both adopt IFRS and do not consider the difference of information relevance between these groups.

### 2.2.3. *Challenges of accounting of biological assets*

There is an increasing trend in controversial debates about FV accounting. On the one hand, many studies focus on the use of information on financial statements when comparing between HC and FV of assets with different results; however, most of them are the advantages of FV accounting. Argilés Bosch *et al.* (2012) compare the accounting difficulties that arise from the use of the two valuation methods and conclude that FV is more useful than the HC in the decision-making processes of agents in the agricultural sector and in the preparation of financial statements. Furthermore, the FV provides more information than HC whenever there is an observable market price that managers cannot adjust or an independently observable and reliable estimate of the market price (Ball, 2006). On the other hand, FV accounting also suffers some disadvantages such as the higher volatility of reported results or management manipulation (e.g., Ball, 2006; Hitz, 2007; Muller *et al.*, 2011; Mala and Chand, 2012).

Although previous studies suggest that FV is relevant for users of financial statements, the reliability of FVs can be questionable if this method's inputs have been unobservable. So, the disclosure of significant information applied could reduce asymmetry problems between the company and its users (Gonçalves *et al.*, 2017; Sundgren *et al.*, 2018). In particular, Gonçalves *et al.* (2017) use 389 firm-year observations from 2011 to 2013 of listed firms in 27 countries. This study also concludes that the FV model is more value-relevant for firms exhibiting higher disclosure levels. According to Sundgren *et al.* (2018), disclosure quality is significantly associated with analysts following bid–ask spreads.

In brief, despite some drawbacks of FV, guidance in IAS 41 is accepted worldwide as recommendations for many countries. In comparison to previous studies related to biological assets, this chapter aims to test the value relevance of biological assets at FV and also examines whether there is a difference between FV and HC by using Ohlson (1995) model.

### 2.2.4. *Development of hypotheses*

The first research objective seeks to examine whether biological assets explain market values. Previous studies on this issue are mixed. While some studies find that value of biological assets influences decision-making of investors (Argiles *et al.*, 2012; de Silva *et al.*, 2015) or that the recognized amount of biological assets under the FV model is value-relevant (Gonçalves *et al.*, 2017), other studies do not support the value relevance of biological assets (Martins *et al.*, 2012; de Silva *et al.*, 2015). Thus, the first hypothesis does not have strong evidence from previous studies:

**Hypothesis H1:** *Biological assets are value-relevant at FV under IAS 41.*

The second research objective is to investigate whether the value relevance of biological assets is impacted by the measurement methods of FV and HC. Some previous studies suggest that no significant differences exist between the two valuation methods to assess future cash flows (Argilés Bosch *et al.*, 2011). However, there is more predictive power of future earnings under fair valuation of biological assets or possibly users have more difficulties, make larger miscalculations, and make poorer judgments with HC than with FV accounting (Argilés Bosch *et al.*, 2011 2012). Thus, a positive signal is expected for the second hypothesis:

**Hypothesis H2:** *The value relevance of biological assets under FV is higher than the HC.*

## 3. Methodology

### 3.1. *Sample*

We focus on all non-financial companies that are listed on the Stock Exchange of 10 Asian countries[2] during 2014–2018. We exclude financial institutions (including insurance firms, diversified financial firms, banks) and utility firms, respectively, from the sample because of the difference in the capital structure (Fama and French, 1992) as well as in presenting financial statements (Basil and Khaled, 2011). We focus on the agricultural sector as well as manufacturing, forestry, fishing, and mining.

Adopting IFRS 13[3] is effective from 2013; however, analyzing and inferring about information pertaining to the year of adoption can be constrained because of some exceptions and exemptions based on IFRS 1[4] (Gastón *et al.*, 2010). As a result, countries (and firms) that adopt recording based on FV (IAS and/or IFRS) before 2013 are selected because of considering 2013 as the

[2]The countries are: Japan, Korea, Malaysia, Sri Lanka, Taiwan (IFRS adoption) and China, Indonesia, Philippines, Thailand, Vietnam (local accounting regulations).

[3]International Financial Reporting Standard (IFRS) 13 — Fair Value Measurement.

[4]International Financial Reporting Standard (IFRS) 1 — First-time Adoption of International Financial Reporting Standards.

limit year and thus the sample in this study comprises observations after 2014 (see Gonçalves *et al.*, 2017). Selecting countries adopting IFRS is based on the website of IFRS[5] and data in this study are collected from Thomson Reuters. In this study, we consider both nations where IFRS are fully applied and nations that have not adopted IFRS yet.

### 3.2. *Empirical model*

Following the accounting-based valuation model of Ohlson (1995), previous studies related to value relevance consider the linear relation between accounting amount (e.g., the book value of equity, earnings per share, etc.) and market value of the firm (or equity) (see Gonçalves *et al.*, 2017). This approach is also employed for non-financial assets, for example, intangible assets (Oliveira *et al.*, 2010), goodwill (Baboukardos and Rimmel, 2014), and tangible and intangible assets (Barth and Clinch, 2006). The scope of this chapter is the value relevance of biological assets.

Value relevance of biological assets is tested in a regression where a firm's market value is a function of the book value of equity and earnings. This relation is tested in the first model test with the market value per share (*MV*) as the dependent variable, and book value per share (*BV*) and earnings per share (*E*) as the independent variables. Additionally, this first model includes one control variable that is the firm size (*SIZE*)

$$MV_{i,t} = \beta_0 + \beta_1 BV_{i,t} + \beta_2 E_{i,t} + \beta_3 SIZE_{i,t} + \mu_{it} \qquad (1)$$

For the second regression to test H1, the BV variable is divided into two variables including (i) book value of assets excluding biological asset (BV-Bio.asset), and (ii) biological asset (Bio.asset), see

[5]See https://www.ifrs.org/use-around-the-world/use-of-ifrs-standards-by-jurisdiction/#profiles.

Equation (2).

$$MV_{i,t} = \beta_0 + \beta_1 BV - Bio.asset_{i,t} + \beta_2 Bio.asset_{i,t} + \beta_3 E_{i,t} + \beta_4 SIZE_{i,t} + \mu_{it} \qquad (2)$$

To test H2, we use model 2 for two groups of nations, those that have fully adopted IFRS and those following local standards.

## 4. Results

### 4.1. *Descriptive analysis*

Table 1 presents descriptive statistics for the independent and control variables.

The Spearman rank correlation coefficients reported in Table 2 show that all independent variables are correlated with the stock price. BV and BV_BIO.ASSET are positively correlated with market value. The correlation coefficient of BIO.ASSET is not high. In multivariate analysis, according to Gujarati (2995), correlations between independent variables are frequently accepted to be not risky if they are less than 0.8 or 0.9. In the Spearman test, the correlation coefficients are higher than 0.8 for the BV and BIO.ASSET variables, but this has no effect on the analysis because both variables are not used together in the same model.

**Table 1:** Descriptive statistics.

| | *N* | Minimum | Maximum | Mean | Std. Deviation |
|---|---|---|---|---|---|
| MV | 178 | .00 | 4.95E+12 | 1.4205E+11 | 6.89957E+11 |
| BV | 178 | .00 | 84456.00 | 2836.6742 | 14015.05670 |
| BV_BIO.ASSET | 178 | .00 | 83066.80 | 2717.8828 | 13612.87306 |
| BIO.ASSET | 178 | .00 | 3586.67 | 124.7733 | 461.19556 |
| E | 170 | .00 | 1117.30 | 19.6348 | 106.11727 |
| SIZE1 | 178 | 1.00 | 3.00 | 1.9888 | .26013 |
| Valid *N* (list wise) | 170 | | | | |

**Table 2:** Correlations (Spearman).

| | | | MV | BV | BV_BIO. ASSET | BIO. ASSET | E | SIZE1 |
|---|---|---|---|---|---|---|---|---|
| Spearman's ρ | MV | Correlation Coefficient | 1.000 | .476** | .567** | .456** | .459** | .384** |
| | | Sig. (2-tailed) | — | .000 | .000 | .000 | .000 | .000 |
| | | *N* | 178 | 178 | 178 | 178 | 170 | 178 |
| | BV | Correlation Coefficient | .476** | 1.000 | .612** | .852** | .027 | .325** |
| | | Sig. (2-tailed) | .000 | — | .000 | .000 | .728 | .000 |
| | | *N* | 178 | 178 | 178 | 178 | 170 | 178 |
| | BV_BIO. ASSET | Correlation Coefficient | .567** | .612** | 1.000 | .269** | .209** | .237** |
| | | Sig. (2-tailed) | .000 | .000 | — | .000 | .006 | .001 |
| | | *N* | 178 | 178 | 178 | 178 | 170 | 178 |
| | BIO. ASSET | Correlation Coefficient | .456** | .852** | .269** | 1.000 | .099 | .260** |
| | | Sig. (2-tailed) | .000 | .000 | .000 | — | .199 | .000 |
| | | *N* | 178 | 178 | 178 | 178 | 170 | 178 |
| | E | Correlation Coefficient | .459** | .027 | .209** | .099 | 1.000 | .268** |
| | | Sig. (2-tailed) | .000 | .728 | .006 | .199 | — | .000 |
| | | *N* | 170 | 170 | 170 | 170 | 170 | 170 |
| | SIZE1 | Correlation Coefficient | .384** | .325** | .237** | .260** | .268** | 1.000 |
| | | Sig. (2-tailed) | .000 | .000 | .001 | .000 | .000 | — |
| | | *N* | 178 | 178 | 178 | 178 | 170 | 178 |

*Note*: **Correlation is significant at the 0.01 level (2-tailed).

**Table 3:** Regression results.

| | Unstandardized coefficients | | Standardized coefficients |
|---|---|---|---|
| **Model** | **B** | **Std. Error** | **β** |
| 1 (Constant) | −2.817E+12 | 2.969E+11 | — |
| BV | 2358471.061 | 5716368.800 | .022 |
| E | 2153322698 | 377511637.1 | .324 |
| SIZE1 | 1.464E+12 | 1.492E+11 | .552 |
| 2 (Constant) | −2.804E+12 | 2.969E+11 | — |
| BV | 11790772.39 | 10279141.22 | .111 |
| E | 2106907267 | 379600096.1 | .317 |
| SIZE1 | 1.463E+12 | 1.492E+11 | .552 |
| BIO.ASSET | −229186770.3 | 207640934.5 | −.106 |

**Model Summary**[c].

| Model | $R$ | $R^2$ | Adjusted $R^2$ | Std. Error of the estimate | Durbin-Watson |
|---|---|---|---|---|---|
| 1 | .725[a] | .526 | .518 | 4.90220E+11 | — |
| 2 | .728[b] | .530 | .518 | 4.89898E+11 | 1.007 |

*Notes*: [a]Predictors: (Constant), SIZE1, BV, E. [b]Predictors: (Constant), SIZE1, BV, E, BIO.ASSET. [c]Dependent Variable: MV.

### 4.2. *Research model*

In Table 3, the adjusted $R^2$ statistic in each of models 1 and 2 is greater than 0.5 and confirms that when biological assets are extracted separately, the explanatory power of the model improves.

In model 1, BV and E are statistically and positively significant. Thus, both variables are associated with the listed companies' market value. To test H1, model 2 excludes biological assets per share (BIO.ASSET) from book value per share (BV). The results show that while book value excluding biological assets per share (BV_BIO.ASSET) and earnings per share (E) are statistically and positively significant, BIO.ASSET is negative. Thus, these results do not confirm H1.

**Table 4:** Regression results of nations do not use FV.

| | Coefficients[a] | | |
|---|---|---|---|
| | Unstandardized Coefficients | | Standardized Coefficients |
| **Model** | **B** | **Std. Error** | **β** |
| 1 (Constant) | −3.882E+12 | 2.444E+12 | — |
| BV | −35140284.11 | 130606401.8 | −.025 |
| E | 10040563155 | 5260271103 | .198 |
| SIZE1 | 2.617E+12 | 1.159E+12 | .229 |
| 2 (Constant) | −6.780E+12 | 2.626E+12 | — |
| BV | 4320759704 | 1724816413 | 3.096 |
| E | 21500443279 | 8332411444 | .423 |
| SIZE1 | 4.218E+12 | 1.280E+12 | .369 |
| BV_BIO.ASSET | −6070054773 | 2019960379 | −1.415 |
| BIO.ASSET | −4029602279 | 1696726432 | −2.401 |

*Note*: [a]Dependent Variable: MV.

With regard to H2, there is a test to examine whether there is a difference in the influence on the market value between two groups of nations that use FV and cost model. Results from Table 4 show that BV in model 1 and BV_BIO.ASSET or BIO.ASSET in model 2 of the second group are negatively significant, confirming H2.

## 5. Conclusions

Overall, in contrast to some previous studies, the results of this study do not support value relevance of biological assets when using an FV method according to IAS 41. However, excluding the number of biological assets, there is a positive influence of book value and earnings per share on entities' market value. Moreover, when comparing the two groups of countries, countries that adopt IFRS have a better impact on market value than other countries that use the cost model.

Results are robust and not influenced by bias in criterion evaluation, subjective assessment. This research focuses on the total amount of biological assets and collects data from Asian countries where capital markets have less development than EU's or US's.

However, more research requires a classification of biological assets into bearer and consumable biological assets because the FV of consumable biological assets is captured by the market faster than for bearer biological assets. Moreover, bearer biological assets are held for a long time for use in the operating activities, so it is more difficult to assess their FV.

This chapter provides other empirical evidence available in the current literature. First, it is one of the first studies to focus on the adoption of IAS 41 in Asian countries. The analysis uses a sample of listed companies from several Asian nations adopting IAS 41 during the period of five years, while previous studies focused on other countries or other continents with a shorter surveyed period. Secondly, compared with prior studies, the valuation model of Ohlson (1995) is adjusted to measure the sensitivity, cause, and effect between the book and market value of a given firm and assess the effects of disclosure levels for non-financial assets (biological assets).

This research also contributes to the current debate on FV showing the advantages of FV method compared to other methods such as cost model, so that users of financial statements can rely on this understanding to make decisions. Furthermore, there are implications provided to regulatory agencies and standard setters for considering before the issue of the new regulation.

Nowadays, the application of FV has become increasingly popular not only as a finance term but also in other fields of economics. As a result, the educational system needs to improve in order to meet the practices. The findings of this study contribute to educational materials in the accounting and valuation field. Therefore, lecturers, accountants, valuers, and students can use it as a real case study to practice.

## References

Aboody, D., Barth, M.E., and Kasznik, R. (1999). Revaluations of fixed assets and future firm performance: Evidence from the UK. *Journal of Accounting and Economics*, 26, 149–178. https://doi.org/10.1016/S0165-4101(98)00040-8

Argilés Bosch, J.M., Sabata Aliberch, A., and García Blandón, J. (2012). A comparative study of difficulties in accounting preparation and judgement in agriculture using fair value and historical cost accounting for biological assets valuation. *Accounting Preparation and Judgement in Agriculture* 5, 109–142.

Aryanto, Y.H.J.A.a.S. (2011). Theoretical failure of IAS 41. doi:http://dx.doi.org/10.2139/ssrn.1808413

Aliberch, A.S., and Blandón, J.G. (2012). A comparative study of difficulties in accounting preparation and judgment in agriculture using fair value and historical cost for biological assets valuation. *Revista de Contabilidad*, 15(1), 109–142.

Baboukardos, D., and Rimmel, G. (2014). Goodwill under IFRS: Relevance and disclosures in an unfavorable environment. *Accounting Forum*, 38, 1–17. https://doi.org/10.1016/j.accfor.2013.11.001

Ball, R. (2006). International financial reporting standards (IFRS): Pros and cons for investors. *Accounting and Business Research*, 36, 5–27. https://doi.org/10.1080/00014788.2006.9730040

Barth, M.E., and Clinch, G. (2006). Discussion of revalued financial, tangible, and intangible assets: association with share prices and non-market-based value estimates. *Journal of Accounting Research*, 36, 235. https://doi.org/10.2307/2491315

Basil, A., and Khaled, H. (2011). Revisiting the capital–structure puzzle: UK evidence. *The Journal of Risk Finance*, 12, 329–338. https://doi.org/10.1108/15265941111158505

Choy, A.K. 2006. Fair value as a relevant metric: A theoretical investigation. *SSRN Electronic Journal*. https://doi.org/10.2139/ssrn.878119

da Silva, R.L.M., Nardi, P.C.C., and de Souza Ribeiro, M. (2015). Results Management and Valuation of Biological Assets. *Brazilian Business Review*, 12(4), 1.

Easton, P.D., Eddey, P.H., and Harris, T.S. (1993). An investigation of revaluations of tangible long-lived assets. *Journal of Accounting Research*, 31, 1. https://doi.org/10.2307/2491161

Fama, E.F., and French, K.R. (1992). The cross-section of expected stock returns. *The Journal of Finance*, 47, 427–465. https://doi.org/10.1111/j.1540-6261.1992.tb04398.x

Gastón, S.C., García, C.F., Jarne, J.I.J., and Laínez Gadea, J.A. (2010). IFRS adoption in Spain and the United Kingdom: Effects on accounting numbers and relevance. *Advances in Accounting*, 26, 304–313. https://doi.org/10.1016/j.adiac.2010.08.003

Gigler, F., Kanodia, C., Venugopalan, R. (2007). Assessing the information content of mark-to-market accounting with mixed attributes: The case of cash flow hedges. *Journal of Accounting Research*, 45, 257–276. https://doi.org/10.1111/j.1475-679X.2007.00232.x

Gonçalves, R., Lopes, P., and Craig, R. (2017). Value relevance of biological assets under IFRS. *Journal of International Accounting, Auditing and Taxation*, 29, 118–126. https://doi.org/10.1016/j.intaccaudtax.2017.10.001

Hitz, J.-M. (2007). The decision usefulness of fair value accounting – A theoretical perspective. *European Accounting Review*, 16, 323–362. https://doi.org/10.1080/09638180701390974

IAS 1 (n.d.). IAS 1 — Presentation of Financial Statements.

IAS 16 (n.d.). IAS 16 — Property, Plant and Equipment.

IAS 38 (n.d.). IAS 38 — Intangible Assets.

IAS 41 (n.d.). IAS 41 — Agriculture.

IFRS 1 (n.d.). IFRS 1 — First-time Adoption of International Financial Reporting Standards.

IFRS 13 (n.d.). IFRS 13 — Fair Value Measurement.

Kurniawan, R., Mulawarman, A.D., and Kamayanti, A. (2014). Biological assets valuation reconstruction: A critical study of IAS 41 on agricultural accounting in Indonesian farmers. *Procedia-Social and Behavioral Sciences*, 164, 68–75.

Leuz, C., and Verrecchia, R.E. (2000). The economic consequences of increased disclosure. *Journal of Accounting Research*, 38, 91. https://doi.org/10.2307/2672910

Liang, P.J., and Wen, X. (2007). Accounting measurement basis, market mispricing, and firm investment efficiency. *Journal of Accounting Research*, 45, 155–197. https://doi.org/10.1111/j.1475-679X.2007.00227.x

Mala, R., and Chand, P. (2012). Effect of the global financial crisis on accounting convergence. *Accounting & Finance*, 52, 21–46. https://doi.org/10.1111/j.1467-629X.2011.00418.x

Martins, A., Almeida, R., and Jesus, T. (2012). The Impact of IAS 41 and its relevant value in listed agricultural companies. *Portuguese Accounting Journal*, 2, 577–616.

Muller, K.A., Riedl, E.J., and Sellhorn, T. (2011). Mandatory fair value accounting and information asymmetry: Evidence from the European real estate industry. *Management Science*, 57, 1138–1153. https://doi.org/10.1287/mnsc.1110.1339

Ohlson, J.A. (1995). Earnings, book values, and dividends in equity valuation. *Contemporary Accounting Research*, 11, 661–687.

Oliveira, L., Rodrigues, L.L., and Craig, R. (2010). Intangible assets and value relevance: Evidence from the Portuguese stock exchange. *British Accounting Review*, 42, 241–252. https://doi.org/10.1016/j.bar.2010.08.001

Pop, A., and Deaconu, S.C. (2008). Assets — Biological assets. The seasonal model in agriculture. *Theoretical and Applied Economics*, 7(7), 3.

Ronen, J. 2008. To fair value or not to fair value: A broader perspective. *Abacus* 44, 181–208. https://doi.org/10.1111/j.1467-6281.2008.00257.x

Sundgren, S., Mäki, J., and Somoza-Lóez, A. (2018). Analyst coverage, market liquidity and disclosure quality: A study of fair-value disclosures by European real estate companies under IAS 40 and IFRS 13. *International Journal of Accounting*, 53, 54–75. https://doi.org/10.1016/j.intacc.2018.02.003

Watts, R.L. (2003). Conservatism in accounting part I: Explanations and implications. *Accounting Horizons*, 17, 207–221. https://doi.org/10.2308/acch.2003.17.3.207

https://doi.org/10.1142/9789811227158_0011

## Chapter 11

# The Role of Human Resources in the Transparency of Financial Information Amidst the Increasing Trend of Financial Autonomy in Public Organizations

Thi Kim Thoa Dau and Van Nhi Vo

### Abstract

The purpose of this research is to determine criteria evaluating the transparency level of financial information and the role of human resources in improving the transparency level of financial information amidst the increasing trend of financial autonomy of Vietnamese public organizations. Hypotheses derived from this research are evaluated using PLS-SEM methodology with the support of Smart PLS 3.2.7 software. The results from the sample of 164 public organizations in Vietnam determine four factors including leaderships' support, chief accountant expertise, accountant expertise, and level of financial autonomy that have a significant impact on the transparency of financial information. Additionally, this research also explores the role of the intermediary variable among these four factors in the research model.

**Keywords:** Financial information transparency; Public sector accounting; Quality of accounting information; Support from leadership; Chief accountant expertise; Accountant expertise.

## 1. Introduction

Public organizations use government budgets to manage and provide public services to the society. Hence, transparency in financial information would help the government to assess and evaluate the effectiveness of budget usage and also create a foundation to establish policies for monitoring and delegating government budgets wisely and effectively (Chan, 2011; Bolivar *et al.*, 2007). Additionally, transparency of financial information is also considered a critical factor in eliminating corruption and activating the accountability mechanism of public organizations (Joshi, 2010). Especially, in today's globalization, transparency of financial information is a strategy to entice investments and support domestically and internationally (Coronel, 2001).

Meanwhile, the Vietnamese economy is developing based on the industrialization trend, but it faces many problems, specifically corruption. Vietnam KPIs in terms of budget transparency and corruption in the public sector are always at a very low level compared with the world at moderate levels and continues to be one of the countries with significant corruption (Cam Tu, 2018). This impacts the effectiveness of using government budgets, so trust from people, from investors is significantly reduced. Moreover, the government is pushing socialization in the public sector through incentivizing public organizations to move to the financial autonomy model to reduce the burden on government budgets and improve the quality of public services. Following this trend, the operational model and audiences using information from these public organizations become more complex and diversified. Because of these requirements, public organizations have to provide transparency in financial information to mitigate corruption and cope with external requirements to survive and develop.

Research focusing on the transparency of financial information in the public sector attracts lots of attention from world researchers. The majority of the different pieces of research focus on determining factors affecting transparency in financial information. From these factors, it helps to define implications for improving the transparency in financial information. Among determined factors, human resources are considered one of the key factors that significantly affect the transparency of financial information. This conclusion is derived from many pieces of world research, such as Rodríguez Bolívar *et al.* (2013), Xu *et al.* (2003), Xu (2003), Komala (2012), and Rapina (2014).

These human resources include people who are directly involved in organizing and implementing financial information systems to establish and provide transparency of financial information. These audiences are leaders, chief accountants, and accountants (Ahmad *et al.*, 2013). However, up to now, the research direction in the public sector in Vietnam has not yet received a lot of attention. As the structure in terms of organizing and operating of Vietnamese public sector has more characteristics compared with the public sector and private sector in other parts of the world determining the impact of human resources on the transparency of financial information has a huge meaning in pushing the transparency of financial information in Vietnamese public sector following the increasing trend of financial autonomy.

The following Section 2 describes the literature review on the basis of which the hypotheses and research model are built. Then, Section 3 introduces the research methodology. Section 4 presents the outcomes of this research. And finally, Section 5 presents the conclusions from this research's results.

## 2. Literature Review

### 2.1. *Transparency of financial information*

Transparency of financial information significantly impacts the development of the society and organizations' operations (Strong *et al.*, 1997). It is also considered as a solution for asymmetric information in the public sector (Alt *et al.*, 2001). However, the term "transparency" is not defined consistently or clearly

(Dapko, 2012). Transparency is a desired characteristic of financial information, but is not defined clearly in the case of financial information, even during financial crises periods calling for the improvement of transparency in financial information (Barth and Schipper, 2007). Most of the definitions are proposed by studies that approach transparency based on the direction toward transparency (i.e., what and how to do it in order to achieve transparency).

Public organizations use government budget for providing public services to society, so they are required to disclose information with transparency about their activities' financial and operational effectiveness (Bakar *et al.*, 2015). Perspective about approaching transparency following the direction of information establishment emphasizes the requirement of the availability of information and users' capabilities in approaching information (Williams, 2015). According to Barth and Schipper (2007), disclosed information has to be arranged in a useful structure and be communicated with ease of understanding to the users. However, besides the disclosure of information, what is of equal significance is that the information be of unquestionable quality (Lourenço, 2015). Reputation and public trust in the public organization can be lost forever if the quality of disclosed information is low (Lee and Kwak, 2011). Following the accounting conceptual framework of IPSASB (2014), when the organization publishes quality financial information, then the transparency of the financial information is increased. Quality of financial information established by IPSASB (2014) includes the following criteria: relevance, faithful representation (completeness, substance, neutrality), comparability, understandability, timeliness, and verifiability. According to Xu *et al.* (2003), and McLeod and Schell (2007), criteria to evaluate the quality of financial information consist of accuracy, sufficiency, consistency, and timeliness. In the public sector, transparency in financial information also relates to the accountability mechanism (Solberg, 2010). It mentions the obligation of organizations in responding to people through an informational report about using the public budget, and this helps people to evaluate the effectiveness (Wong and Welch, 2004). Information related to the accountability mechanism creates information availability (Lindstedt and Naurin, 2010).

Therefore, a theoretical overview defines three standardized criteria for creating transparency of financial information, and they are published information, quality of information, and the accountability mechanism (Williams, 2015; Lindstedt and Naurin, 2010). However, these criteria are evaluated following different perspectives such as research area, researchers' points of view, and also users' points of view after completion of evaluation.

### 2.2. *Role of human resources in the transparency of financial information*

Based on the theoretical foundation, many researchers came to the conclusion that an organization can only fulfill the expectations and required values both internal and external, as well as the social standards about providing transparency of financial information, if it has to create certain changes in terms of organizing and implementing the accounting information system (Nogueira and Jorge, 2016). In order to create quality financial information, there is a requirement for the quality of the accounting information system (Sacer and Oluic', 2006). According to contingency theory, there is no one accounting information system that can be applied to all organizations, all situations, and globally. Every organization has its own accounting information system depending on its characteristics (Otley, 1980). Based on that, many pieces of research focus on both internal and external factors impacting the structure of the accounting information system. Among these factors, human factor is determined as one of the most important factors deciding the structure and successful implementation of the accounting information system (like Ahmad *et al.*, 2013; Romney and Steinbart, 2006; Azhar, 2007; Wisna, 2015). Ahmad *et al.* (2013) affirm the quality of the accounting information system is positively impacted by factors of human resources and management commitment. In which, management commitment is a general commitment consisting of commitment from top management, functional members, and among functions for common organizational goals. Specifically, people directly involved in the accounting information system are top management, chief accountants, and accountants (Ahmad *et al.*, 2013).

Most researchers apply agency theory, asymmetric theory to explain the role of leadership in deciding the level of transparency of financial information (Zimmerman, 1977; Harrison and Freeman, 1999; Rodríguez Bolívar *et al.*, 2013). The role of management in the transparency of financial information is demonstrated through committing, supporting in building strategies, and implementing the accounting information system (Komala, 2012); supporting necessary financial resources (Komala, 2012); and participating in managing policies related to the internal control system within the accounting information system (Dau Thi Kim Thoa *et al.*, 2015). Especially, when the government is pushing for financial autonomy in public organizations, the leadership plays a pivotal role in deciding things with regard to structure, resources, planning, and finances of the organization (Decree 16/2015/DecreeGovernment).

Professional accounting is also a critical requirement to achieve transparency and accountability mechanism in developing countries (Okpala, 2012). Since chief accountants and accountants are directly involved in operating the accounting information system to create financial information, if they are not good enough, then the quality of financial information remains low (Okpala, 2012). Furthermore, in today's economy, the role of accounting is not only about filling journal entries and creating accounting reports but also focusing on analyzing data to support management in make decisions (Nguyen Bich Lien, 2012).

## 3. Research Methodology

### 3.1. *Research hypotheses*

#### 3.1.1. *Level of financial autonomy in organizations*

When the organization has a high level of financial autonomy, it implies an expanded operating scope for the organization and also better financial capability. Financial capability is considered as one of the key factors deciding the content of published information in the public sector, and this is proven by many pieces of research (such as Baber, 1983; Ingram, 1984; Giroux and Deis, 1993; Evans and Patton, 1987; Robbins and Austin, 1986; Cheng, 1992; Laswad *et al.*, 2005). Several reasons explain the impact of this factor on the transparency of financial information in the public sector. Firstly, organizations receive government budgets and support for managing or providing public services to society; hence, they are under the controlling pressure and also need to create trust in governmental organizations, individual support, and citizens about using public resources appropriately for the jobs assigned. Moreover, they also have to voluntarily and transparently publish information (Ingram, 1984; Robbins and Austin, 1986; Ingram and DeJong, 1987; Copley, 1991). Secondly, organizations with a big operating scale are under pressure to publish to ensure the transparency of financial information for the end-users more than organizations with a smaller scale (Rodríguez Bolívar *et al.*, 2013). Thirdly, organizations with good financial capability have better conditions and are more active in hiring human resources in both quantity and quality and develop appropriate infrastructure to organize a better accounting information system (García and Garcí-García, 2010). Additionally, effective organizations, with good financial capability and management are ready to provide quality financial information to build trust and the reputation of the organization (Michaelowa and Borrmann, 2006), or to attract more investments and support (Cheung *et al.*, 2007).

Based on these above analyzes, the first hypothesis is proposed as follows:

**Hypothesis H1:** *Level of financial autonomy positively impacts the transparency of financial information.*

### 3.1.2. *Leaderships' support*

Management has the right to decide the usage of government budget in providing public services to society, but it does not have the same benefits compared with people who receive public services. In order to reduce the conflict of interest, management has to have results to prove their doings in line with their responsibilities (Jensen and Meckling, 1976; Fama, 1980) and let related audiences monitor their actions (Rodríguez Bolívar *et al.*, 2013). Besides deciding which financial information is provided to external people, it is management that knows better than anyone else about which financial information is needed for decision-making (Ismail, 2009). Based on that, management decides the level of participation and support resources and necessary finances for organizing the accounting information system (Komala, 2012).

However, the level of proactive support from management in implementing the accounting information system significantly relies on the capability of financial autonomy (García and García-García, 2010). Resources and appropriate infrastructure are required to provide transparency of financial information. These conditions are usually available at organizations with high financial capability (Guillamón *et al.*, 2011). Additionally, Zimmerman (1973) and Baber (1983) realize that public organizations serving large populations are also organizations with strong financial capability. As a result of this, managements have to face higher pressure in explaining about managing and using public resources (Guillamón *et al.*, 2011).

Based on the above analyzes, two hypotheses are built as follows:

**Hypothesis H2:** *Leaderships' support positively impacts the transparency of financial information.*

**Hypothesis H3:** *Level of financial autonomy positively impacts leaderships' support.*

### 3.1.3. *Chief accountant expertise*

In order to successfully implement the accounting information system, the role of the chief accountant is critical (Ismail, 2007, 2009). The chief accountant is considered as part of the leadership team, responsible for planning and monitoring organization financial activities (Komala, 2012). In order to fulfill this role, the chief accountant expertise factor is normally researched through the understanding in terms of accounting, accounting information system, and leadership capability expertise and experiences (Ang *et al.*, 2001; Ismail, 2009; Komala, 2012). From the above analyzes, the next hypothesis is proposed:

**Hypothesis H4:** *The chief accountant's expertise positively impacts the transparency of the financial information.*

### 3.1.4. *Accountant expertise*

An accountant also plays a critical role in implementing the accounting information system. Similar to the chief accountant, the definition of an accountant is also demonstrated through the understanding of the accountant about accounting (Anderson *et al.*, 1995; Ahire *et al.*, 1996). Since they are responsible for collecting, archiving, and processing data, and providing financial information, their understanding of accounting is very important and much required (Nguyen Bich Lien, 2012). Mistakes during the implementation of the accounting information system are significantly reduced if accountants have high accounting expertise, especially when filling estimated accounting entries depending on accountants' estimations (Dau Thi Kim Thoa *et al.*, 2015).

However, management hugely affects employees' positive attitude for the job. When management demonstrates moral values, provides a clear road map, and has a positive attitude toward the transparency of financial information, then it impacts employees' behaviors and attitude in the public sector (Aziz *et al.*, 2015). Furthermore, when the organization has a high level of financial autonomy, management has more power in terms of hiring appropriate accountants matching with the organization's needs. Organizations with good talent development policy improve the collaboration, loyalty, and satisfaction of employees (Dau Thi Kim Thoa *et al.*, 2015). From the results of the above research, the hypotheses about the relationships between the role of leadership and employees are arrived at. Firstly, organization leaders impact the chief accountant, and then the chief accountant affects accountants because the chief is also considered as part of the leadership team managing the accounting function of the organization (Komala, 2012).

From the above analyzes, we arrive at the following hypotheses:

**Hypothesis H5:** *Accountants' expertise positively impacts the transparency of financial information.*

**Hypothesis H6:** *Leaderships' support positively impacts the chief accountant's expertise.*

**Hypothesis H7:** *The chief accountant's expertise positively impacts the accountants' expertise.*

From the above analyzes, the research model is proposed as shown in Figure 1.

### 3.2. *Research measurement*

The research methodology consists of five potential research definitions and measurements of these definitions being built and tested from research all over the world. In which, transparency in financial information measurement (TRANS) applies measurement from Lee *et al.* (2002) with cube multidimensional measurement consisting of 15 components with 65 total observed variables. Components measuring transparency in financial information include: Appropriate Amount (AA), Accessibility (ACC), Believability (BEL), Completeness (COM), Relevancy (REL), Concise Representation

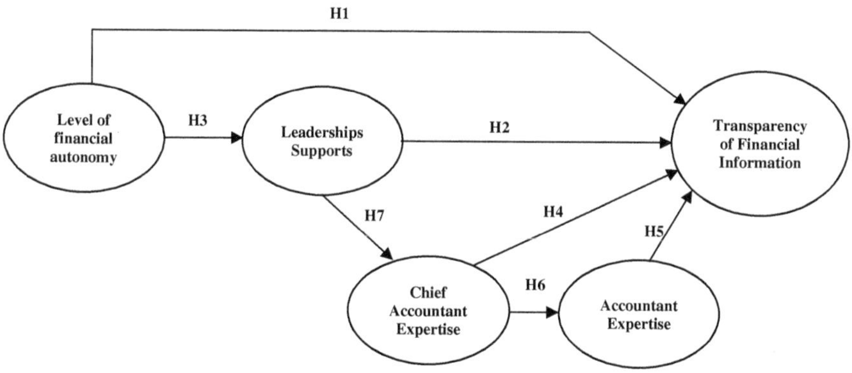


**Figure 1:** The research model.

(CR), Consistent Representation (COR), Ease of Operation (EO), Free of Error (FFE), Interpretability (INP), Objectivity (OB), Reputation (REP), Security (SEC), Timeliness (TIM), and Understandability (UND).

The definition of leaderships' support inherits measurement from Komala (2012) with single dimension measurement consisting of seven observed variables focusing on three areas: authority, participation, commitment.

Similarly, the measurement for the definition of chief accountant's expertise (AM) also inherits measurement from Komala (2012) consisting of six observed variables, and this is a single dimension measurement. This measurement relatively reflects all characteristics needed in a chief accountant, and they are accounting expertise, experiences, and leadership capability.

Definition of accountant expertise (AC) is also based on the measurement for chief accountant expertise from the research of Komala (2012). However, experiences and leadership capability are excluded because accountants only execute as per direction from the leadership and the chief accountant, so they do not need to have experiences and leadership capability. Reducing these two criteria reduces two observed variables in this definition measurement.

Measurements of transparency in financial information, leaderships' support, chief accountant expertise, and accountant expertise follow the 7-point Likert scale, with 1 indicating "completely disagree" and increasing to 7, indicating "completely agree".

For the definition of financial autonomy (FA), measurement is a nominal scale with one choice following the level of financial autonomy. Level of financial autonomy of public organizations in Vietnam is classified as per Decree 16/2015/Decree-Government consisting of 4 levels and coded the same with 4 nominal scales: 1 — Autonomy with complete spending and investing; 2 — Autonomy with complete spending; 3 — Autonomy with partial spending; 4 — Government always supporting with spending.

### 3.3. *Research sample*

The research samples of this study are all public organizations operating in Vietnam. Observed samples are people who have deep understanding about accounting in the public sector and currently work at public organizations with at least 2 years of experience to ensure observed samples have sufficient understanding about the research area and also about the reality at the organization to appropriately answer the questionnaire (Bavik, 2016). Observed samples in this research consist of: top management (Head, Vice Head of the function), chief accountant, accountants working at public organizations (see Table 1).

The number of necessary observed samples needed for PLS-SEM is tenfold that of the structural model (Hair *et al.*, 2016). This research proposes seven paths, so the number of samples required is 70. The result has been determined after sanitizing 164 questionnaires and tables collected from 17 provinces and cities and from public organizations in different areas with different financial levels of autonomy. With large and diversified research samples, this represents a bigger picture and enhances the value of the research outcomes. The statistical results of the sample size are the following.

**Table 1:** Statistics of the sample size.

| **Sample size ($n = 164$)** | **Quantity** | **(%)** | **Sample size ($n = 164$)** | **Quantity** | **(%)** |
|---|---|---|---|---|---|
| **Research Area** | | | | | |
| Ho Chi Minh | 83 | 50.6 | Journalism | 2 | 1.2 |
| Binh Duong | 9 | 5.5 | Science and Technology | 3 | 1.8 |
| Vinh Long | 17 | 10.4 | | | |
| Soc Trang | 14 | 8.5 | Agriculture | 5 | 3.0 |
| Ben Tre | 15 | 9.1 | Construction | 7 | 4.4 |
| Ha Noi | 6 | 3.7 | *Environment and Resource* | 2 | 1.2 |
| Vung Tau | 1 | 0.60 | | | |
| Thanh Hoa | 1 | 0.6 | Transportation | 3 | 1.8 |
| Thai Nguyen | 3 | 1.8 | Trading | 1 | 0.6 |
| Son La | 1 | 0.6 | | | |
| Hue | 1 | 0.6 | **Level of Ownership** | | |
| Hung Yen | 1 | 0.6 | Often self-financing and investing | 8 | 4.9 |
| Phu Tho | 1 | 0.6 | | | |
| Nha Trang | 2 | 1.2 | | | |
| Da Nang | 6 | 3.7 | Often self-financing | 43 | 26.2 |
| Da Lat | 1 | 0.6 | | | |
| Binh Phuoc | 2 | 1.3 | Often partial self-financing | 46 | 28.0 |
| **Year of Experience** | | | Often government-financing | 67 | 40.9 |
| >10 year | 75 | 45.7 | | | |
| 5–10 year | 56 | 34.2 | | | |
| 2–5 year | 33 | 20.1 | | | |
| | | | **Position** | | |
| **Industry** | | | Head of | 13 | 7.9 |
| Training and Education | 96 | 58.5 | Organization | 13 | 7.9 |
| | | | Vice Head of | 28 | 17.1 |
| Medical | 28 | 17.1 | Organization | 28 | 17.1 |
| Culture, Sport, and Tourism | 17 | 10.4 | Chief Accountant | 48 | 29.3 |
| Transportation | 3 | 1.8 | | | |

## 4. Research Results and Discussion

### 4.1. *Testing measurement model*

Measurements of definitions in the research model are result-oriented, so the measurement model is also result oriented measurement.

Evaluating the measurement model is to evaluate measurement scale through three criteria, including reliability, convergent validity, and discriminant validity with the support from software Smart PLS_SEM 3.2.7. The result of this evaluation is presented in Table 2. Specifically, the scale reliability is at a high value, while Cronbach Alpha is at (0.731; 1) and composite reliability is at (0.880; 1) satisfying the acceptable threshold of ($\geq$0.7).

Factor loadings of all observed variables are in the range (0.747; 1) satisfying the acceptable threshold of (>0.7). AVE index is reasonably good when all values are greater than 0.674 (greater than eliminating threshold of 0.5). Though the AVE index of TRANS definition is 0.421, this does not impact the research outcome because TRANS is a cube multidimensional measurement so duplication of variables is inevitable when running on Smart PLS. Through two indexes, it demonstrates a high level of convergent validity for all definitions. The discriminant validity of potential definitions is also at an acceptable level when the HTMT index (heterotrait-monotrait ratio) is lower than 0.9. From these results, we come to the conclusion that measurements of all definitions in this research are of high values.

After evaluating the measurement model twice, measurements of definitions determined are found to be of high values. The number of observed variables of transparency definition is reduced from 65 to 43. Measurement of leaderships' support definition has reduced 1 observed variable. Measurements of chief accountant expertise (AM) and accountant expertise (AC) remain unchanged.

## 4.2. *Testing structural model*

The structural model in this research is presented in Figure 1, and this is a complex structural model consisting of 4 latent variables (TRANS, CM, AM, AC) and one observed variable (FA). These variables are classified through 4 endogenous variables (TRANS, CM, AM, AC) and 4 exogenous variables (CM, FA, AM, AC).

Table 2: Measurement of the definitions.

| | Observing variables | Loading factor |
|---|---|---|
| **AA** | **Appropriate amount (Cronbach Alpha: 0.866; CR = 0.937; AVE = 0.882)** | |
| AA1 | This information is of sufficient volume for our needs | 0.941 |
| AA2 | The amount of information is neither too much nor too little | 0.937 |
| **ACC** | **Accessibility (Cronbach Alpha: 0.925; CR = 0.974; AVE = 0.817)** | |
| ACC1 | This information is easily accessible | 0.873 |
| ACC2 | This information is quickly accessible when needed | 0.919 |
| ACC3 | This information is easily obtainable | 0.920 |
| ACC4 | This information is easily retrievable | 0.901 |
| **BEL** | **Believability (Cronbach Alpha: 1.000; CR = 1.000; AVE = 1.000)** | |
| BEL3 | This information is trustworthy | 1.000 |
| **COM** | **Completeness (Cronbach Alpha: 0.868; CR = 0.910; AVE = 0.718)** | |
| COM2 | This information is sufficiently complete for our needs | 0.873 |
| COM3 | This information has sufficient breadth and depth for our task | 0.888 |
| COM4 | This information includes all necessary values | 0.857 |
| COM5 | This information is complete | 0.766 |
| **CR** | **Concise representation (Cronbach Alpha: 0.866; CR = 0.909; AVE = 0.714)** | |
| CR1 | This information is presented in a compact form | 0.829 |
| CR2 | This information is formatted compactly | 0.810 |
| CR3 | This information is presented concisely | 0.876 |
| CR4 | The representation of this information is compact and concise | 0.864 |
| **COR** | **Consistent representation (Cronbach Alpha: 0.903; CR = 0.939; AVE = 0.838)** | |
| COR1 | This information is consistently presented in the same format | 0.922 |
| COR2 | This information is represented in a consistent format | 0.924 |
| COR3 | This information is presented consistently | 0.901 |

(Continued)

**Table 2:** (*Continued*)

| | Observing variables | Loading factor |
|---|---|---|
| **EO** | **Ease of operation (Cronbach Alpha: 0.860; CR = 0.915; AVE = 0.782)** | |
| EO1 | This information is easy to manipulate to meet our needs | 0.880 |
| EO2 | This information is easy to aggregate | 0.914 |
| EO3 | This information is easy to combine with other information | 0.859 |
| **FFE** | **Free of error (Cronbach Alpha: 1.000; CR = 1.000; AVE = 1.000)** | |
| FFE3 | This information is accurate | 1.000 |
| **INP** | **Interpretability (Cronbach Alpha: 0.829; CR = 0.898; AVE = 0.745)** | |
| INP1 | It is easy to interpret what this information means | 0.872 |
| INP2 | This information is interpretable easily | 0.905 |
| INP3 | The measurement units of this information are clear | 0.810 |
| **OB** | **Objectivity (Cronbach Alpha: 0.879; CR = 0.918; AVE = 0.738)** | |
| OB1 | This information was objectively collected | 0.747 |
| OB2 | This information is based on facts | 0.898 |
| OB3 | This information presents an impartial view | 0.918 |
| OB4 | This information is objective | 0.864 |
| **REL** | **Relevancy (Cronbach Alpha: 0.885; CR = 0.921; AVE = 0.744)** | |
| REL1 | This information is appropriate for our work | 0.826 |
| REL2 | This information is relevant to our work | 0.874 |
| REL3 | This information is applicable to our work | 0.903 |
| REL4 | This information is useful to our work | 0.844 |
| **REP** | **Reputation (Cronbach Alpha: 0.917; CR = 0.948; AVE = 0.858)** | |
| REP1 | This information has a reputation for quality | 0.931 |
| REP2 | This information comes from good sources | 0.931 |
| REP3 | This information has a good reputation' | 0.917 |
| **SEC** | **Security (Cronbach Alpha: 0.731; CR = 0.881; AVE = 0.787)** | |
| SEC1 | This information is protected against unauthorized access | 0.907 |
| SEC2 | This information can only be accessed by people who should see it | 0.866 |

**Table 2:** (*Continued*)

| | Observing variables | Loading factor |
|---|---|---|
| **TIM** | **Timeliness (Cronbach Alpha: 0.795; CR = 0.880; AVE = 0.710)** | |
| TIM1 | This information is sufficiently up-to-date for our work | 0.847 |
| TIM2 | This information is sufficiently timely | 0.884 |
| TIM3 | This information is sufficiently current for our work | 0.795 |
| **UND** | **Understandability (Cronbach Alpha: 0.829; CR = 0.841; AVE = 0.853)** | |
| UND1 | The meaning of this information is easy to understand | 0.912 |
| UND3 | This information is easy to comprehend | 0.935 |
| **AM** | **Chief Accountant expertise (Cronbach Alpha: 0.903; CR = 0.925; AVE = 0.674)** | |
| AM1 | Knowledge of accounting | 0.831 |
| AM2 | Knowledge of accounting information system | 0.833 |
| AM3 | Knowledge of managerial | 0.782 |
| AM4 | Experience on accounting | 0.847 |
| AM5 | Experience on accounting information system | 0.836 |
| AM6 | Experience on managerial | 0.796 |
| **CM** | **Support of leadership (Cronbach Alpha: 0.950; CR = 0.961; AVE = 0.833)** | |
| CM2 | Participating in choosing of hardware | 0.890 |
| CM3 | Participating in choosing of software | 0.883 |
| CM4 | Participating in implementing of system | 0.953 |
| CM5 | Participating in system maintenance and problems solving | 0.953 |
| CM6 | Committing in planning of further developments | 0.879 |
| **AC** | **Accountant expertise (Cronbach Alpha: 0.909; CR = 0.936; AVE = 0.786)** | |
| AM1 | Knowledge of accounting | 0.886 |
| AM2 | Knowledge of accounting information system | 0.914 |
| AM4 | Experience on accounting | 0.862 |
| AM5 | Experience on accounting information system | 0.883 |
| **FA** | **Financial Autonomy (Cronbach Alpha: 1.000; CR = 1.000; AVE = 1.000)** | |
| **FA** | Level of financial autonomy | 1.000 |

Evaluating the structural model is to test the relationships among endogenous variables and exogenous variables in this research model through proposed hypotheses (Hair *et al.*, 2016). The structural model is evaluated through the proposed process by Hair *et al.* (2016:191), including the following steps: (i) test multicollinearity; (ii) test the appropriateness and meaning level of the research model; (iii) test $R^2$ level; (iv) test the impact of $f^2$; (v) test the appropriateness of model forecasting capability $Q^2$; (vi) test the impact of $q^2$; and (vii) analyze intermediary variables.

Results assessing the direct relationships among structurals are presented in Table 3 and Figure 2.

According to $p$ values, coefficients ($\beta$ and $R^2$) assess the relationships between endogenous variables and exogenous variables. Firstly, the model with endogenous TRANS is explained up to 42.6% ($R^2 = 0.426$) by factors in the proposed research model. All 4 exogenous variables affect TRANS with decreasing impact, respectively: AM (chief accountant expertise) ($\beta = 0.477$); FA (level of financial autonomy) ($\beta = 0.209$); AC (accountant's expertise) ($\beta = 0.133$); and CM (leadership support) ($\beta = 0.124$).

**Table 3:** Result from PLS evaluation.

| **Hypothesis** | **Correlation** | $R^2$ | $\beta$ | **Standard deviation** | $p$**-values** |
|---|---|---|---|---|---|
| | **TRANS** | **0.426** | | | |
| **H1** | CM → TRANS | | 0.124 | 0.052 | 0.020*** |
| **H2** | AM → TRANS | | 0.477 | 0.073 | 0.000* |
| **H4** | AC → TRANS | | 0.133 | 0.066 | 0.050*** |
| | FA → TRANS | | 0.209 | 0.068 | 0.003** |
| | **AM** | **0.065** | | | |
| **H3** | CM → AM | | 0.256 | 0.073 | 0.001** |
| | **AC** | **0.428** | | | |
| **H6** | AM → AC | | 0.654 | 0.055 | 0.000* |
| | **CM** | **0.028** | | | |
| **H6** | FA → CM | | 0.168 | 0.073 | 0.025*** |

*Notes*: *, **, *** significance, respectively, 0.001%, 0.1%, and 5%.

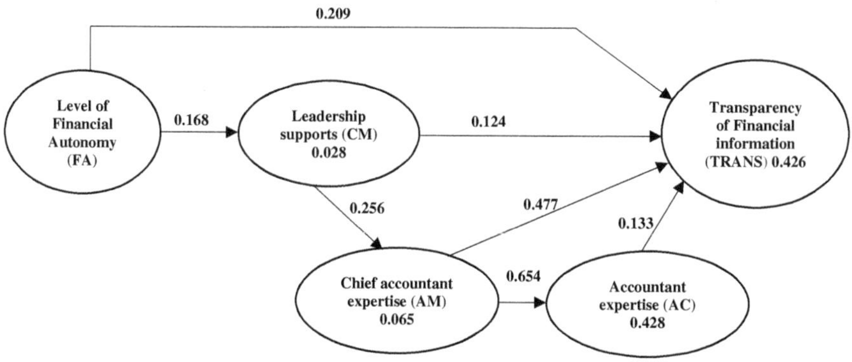


**Figure 2:** Result from the research model evaluation.

For the model with endogenous variable (AM) being insignificantly affected by CM ($\beta = 0.256$), CM helps to explain the discriminant validity of AM at 0.065. AC is being significantly impacted by AM ($\beta - 0.654$) with a high level of discriminant validity of AC ($R^2 = 0.428$). CM is also being insignificantly affected by FA ($\beta = 0.168$).

The value of $f^2$ presented in Table 4 once again acknowledges that TRANS is significantly impacted by AM ($f^2 = 0.208$) and less impacted by CM, FA, and AC. AM is affected by SF at low level ($f^2 = 0.029$), while AC is significantly affected by AM ($f^2 = 0.749$). This outcome proves that there are no missing exogenous variables in this research model that significantly affect the endogenous variables.

Evaluating the result of $Q^2$ presented in Table 4 shows that all $Q^2$ values are greater than 0. This proves the high forecasting capability of exogenous variables for endogenous variables in the model. $Q^2$ values presented in Table 4 also show the appropriateness of the forecasting capability of the research model. Exogenous variables affect the appropriateness of TRANS forecasting capability, and they are AM, FA, CM, AC with decreasing $q^2$, respectively (0.055, 0.019, 0.006, and 0.005).

This research expands the indirect relationships by evaluating the role of the mediate variables. According to the analytical result of the mediate variables in Table 5, there are three mediate variables

**Table 4:** Evaluated result of $f^2$, $Q^2$, and $q^2$.

| **Endogenous** | **TRANS** | | **AM** | | **AC** | | **CM** | |
|---|---|---|---|---|---|---|---|---|
| $Q^2$ | **0.163** | | **0.043** | | **0.307** | | **0.020** | |
| **Exogenous** | $f^2$ | $q^2$ | $f^2$ | $q^2$ | $f^2$ | $q^2$ | $f^2$ | $q^2$ |
| AM | 0.208 | 0.055 | | | 0.749 | 0.442 | | |
| AC | 0.017 | 0.005 | | | | | | |
| CM | 0.024 | 0.006 | 0.070 | 0.045 | | | | |
| SF | 0.071 | 0.019 | | | | | 0.029 | 0.021 |

in this research model. Specifically, (1) CM acts as an intermediary variable in the affected relationship between FA and TRANS; (2) AM acts as an intermediary variable in the affected relationship between CM and TRANS; and (3) AC acts as an intermediary variable in the affected relationship between AM and TRANS. All 3 variables (CM, AM, and AC) are in complementary mediation.

In order to increase the research outcome values, this study implements several solutions to mitigate the deviation from the Common method variance. Specifically, the research applies Marker variable following a suggestion by Lindell and Whitney (2001), and it shows no deviation in measurement when the coefficient of the Marker variable compared with latent variables in the research model is within the range (−0,004; 0,190). which has a very low compared tolerance threshold of $\beta > 1$. VIF index of each independent variable in this model is within the range of (1.000; 1.905), which is very small compared with the eliminating threshold of 5. This result shows no multicollinearity phenomenon in this research model.

## 4.3. *Discussion*

The research results prove factors in this research model significantly explained up to 42.6% of the discriminant validity scale of transparency in financial information of Vietnamese public organizations. Among which, the factor having the strongest impact on the transparency of financial information is the chief accountant

**Table 5:** Analytical results of mediation variable.

| | Direct effect | | | Indirect effect | | | |
|---|---|---|---|---|---|---|---|
| **Models** | **95% confidence interval of the direct effect** | $p$ **Values** | **Significance ($p < 0.05$)** | **95% confidence interval of the direct effect** | $p$ **Values** | **Significance ($p < 0.05$)** | **Conclusion** |
| **SF → CM → TRANS** | [−0.453, −0.184] | 0.001 | Yes | [0.008, 0.085] | 0.050 | Yes | Complementary mediation |
| **CM → AM → TRANS** | [−0.075, 0.169] | 0.002 | Yes | [0.093, 0.213] | 0.000 | Yes | Complementary mediation |
| **AM → AC → TRANS** | [0.359, 0.065] | 0.000 | Yes | [0.034, 0.187] | 0.051 | Yes | Complementary mediation |

expertise, with impact level at 47.7%. Next is the level of financial autonomy (20.9%), followed by the accountant expertise (13.3%), and leaderships' support (12.4%). Besides direct impact relationships, the research also explores a few indirect impact relationships. Specifically, leaderships' support acts as a mediate variable in the impacted relationship between the level of financial autonomy and transparency in financial information. Leaderships' support also indirectly impacts the transparency of financial information through the chief accountant's expertise. Similarly, chief accountant's expertise indirectly impacts the transparency of the financial information through the mediate variable of accountant expertise.

These outcomes also coincide with similar outcomes from research of Komala (2012), Harrison and Sayogo (2014), Rapina (2014), Fitrios (2016), Ahmad *et al.* (2013), O'Brien (2005), Romney and Steinbart (2006), Azhar (2007), Piccoli (2008), Marshall and Paul (2012), and Wisna (2015). These studies all came to acknowledge the critical role of human factor in managing and organizing the implementation of the accounting information system to provide transparency of the financial information.

This research outcome also acknowledges that during the period in which the financial autonomy in the public sector is strongly encouraged, financial autonomy not only contributes to reducing burden on government budget but also contributes to the improvement of the transparency of the financial information. The higher the financial autonomy, the higher the focus required to develop resources, especially for positions such as management, chief accountant, and accountants. The organization has to improve transparency of financial information.

## 5. Conclusions

This research acts complementary to the theoretical foundation system regarding criteria in evaluating the transparency of financial information in Vietnamese public organizations. Additionally, the research explores 4 factors having a direct impact on the transparency of financial information, and they are: level of financial autonomy, leaderships' support, chief accountant's expertise, and accountants' expertise. The research also proves the role of the intermediary variable, that is, human factor (leaderships' support, chief accountant's expertise, and accountants' expertise) during the period in which the financial autonomy in the public sector is strongly encouraged.

Analytical data are very reliable due to lack of multicollinearity and deviation regarding measurement methodologies. The research result is similar to prior research worldwide, and also in line with the reality of pushing toward the financial autonomy in Vietnamese public organizations nowadays.

From the research results of identifying direct and indirect factors impacting the transparency of financial information, it is implied that in order to improve the transparency of financial information, organizations need to focus on improving the level of financial autonomy and having hiring policies in place to develop human resources appropriately.

## References


Ahire, S.L., Golhar, D.Y., and Waller, M.A. (1996). Development and validation of TQM implementation constructs. *Decision Sciences*, 27(1), 23–56.

Ang, C.L., Davies, M.A., and Finlay, P.N. (2001). An empirical model of it usage in the Malaysian public sector. *Journal of Strategic Information Systems*, 10, 159–174.

Anderson, J.C., Rungtusanatham, M., Schroeder, R.G., and Devaraj, S. (1995). A path analytic model of a theory of quality management underlying the Deming management method: Preliminary empirical findings. *Decision Sciences*, 26(5), 637–658.

Al-Hiyari, Ahmad, *et al.* (2013). Factors that affect accounting information system implementation and accounting information quality: A survey in University Utara Malaysia. *American Journal of Economics*, 3(1), 27–31.

Alt, J.E., Lassen, D.D., and Skilling, D. (2001). Fiscal transparency, gubernatorial popularity, and the scale of government: Evidence from the states. EPRU Working Paper, University of Copenhagen, p. 16.

Azhar, S. (2007). *Sistem Informasi Akuntansi Konsep Dan Pengembangan Berbasis Komputer*. Bandung: Lingga Jaya.

Baber, W.R. (1983). Towards Understanding the Role of Auditing in The Public Sector. *Journal of Accounting and Economics*, 5(3), 213–227.

Bakar, N. B. A., and Saleh, Z. (2015). Review of literature on factors influencing public sector disclosure: The way forward. *Asian Journal of Business and Accounting*, 8(2), 155–184.

Barth, M.E., and Schipper, K. (2007). Financial reporting transparency. *Journal of Accounting, Auditing and Finance*, 173–190.

Barth, M. E., and Schipper, K. (2008). Financial reporting transparency. *Journal of Accounting, Auditing & Finance*, 23(2), 173–190.

Bavik, A. (2016). Developing a new hospitality industry organizational culture scale. *International Journal of Hospitality Management*, 58, 44–55.

Bolivar, M.P.R., Caba Perez, C., and Lopez Hernandez, A.M. (2007). E-government and public financial reporting: The case of Spanish regional governments. *American Review of Public Administration*, 37(2), 142–177.

Cam Tu (2018). Vietnam is in the top of the least public budget countries in the world. *Radio the Voice of Vietnam*. Retrieved from https://vov.vn/kinh-te/viet-nam-o-top-cac-quoc-gia-it-cong-khai-ngan-sach-nhat-the-gioi-744862.vov

Chan, J.L. (2011). IPSAS and government accounting reform in developing countries. [Online] Available at: ⟨Http://Blog-Pfm.Imf.Org/Files/Chan2006ipsasgafdc.pdf⟩. [Accessed 7 May 2017].

Cheng, R.H. (1992). An empirical analysis of theories on factors influencing state government accounting disclosure. *Journal of Accounting and Public Policy*, 11, 1–42.

Copley, P.A. (1991). The association between municipal disclosure practices and audit quality. *Journal of Accounting and Public Policy*, 10(4), 245–266.

Coronel, S.S. (2001). Fighting for the right to know. In S.S. Coronel (ed.), *The Right to Know: Access-To-Information in Southeast Asia*. Bangkok, Thailand: Raintree Publishing, Inc, pp. 1–20.

Dapko, J.L. (2012). *Perceived Firm Transparency: Scale and Model Development*. PhD Thesis. University of South Florida.

Dau Thi Kim Thoa and Phan Thi Thuy Quynh (2015). *The factors affect accounting financial information quality of non-business organizations at Ho Chi Minh City*. University of Economics Ho Chi Minh City.

Evans, J.H., Patton, J.M., (1987). Signalling and monitoring in public-sector accounting. *Journal of Accounting Research*, 25(Suppl.), 130–158.

Fitrios, R. (2016). Factors that influence accounting information system implementation and accounting information quality. *International Journal of Scientific and Technology Research*, 5(5), 192–198.

García, A.C., and García-García, J. (2010). Determinants of online reporting of accounting information by Spanish local government authorities. *Local Government Studies*, 36(5), 679–695.

Giroux, G., and Deis, D. (1993). Investor interests and government accounting disclosure. *Accounting, Auditing & Accountability Journal*, 6(1), 63–78.

Government. (2015). *Decree 16/2015/ND-CP dated Feb 14, 2015 on mechanism-exercising-the-autonomy-of-Public-Administrative-Units.* Retrieved from: https://thukyluat.vn/45112/nghi-dinh-16-2015-nd-cp/tag.html

Guillamón, M.D., Bastida, F., and Benito, B. (2011). The determinants of local government's financial transparency. *Local Government Studies*, 37(4), 391–406.

Hair Jr, J.F., Hult, G.T.M., Ringle, C., and Sarstedt, M. (2016). *A primer on partial least squares structural equation modeling (PLS-SEM).* Sage publications.

Harrison, J., and Freeman. R.E. (1999). Stakeholders, social responsibility, and performance: Empirical evidence and theoretical perspectives. *Academy of Management Journal*, 42(5), 479–485.

Harrison, T.M., and Sayogo, D.S. (2014). Transparency, participation, and accountability practices in open government: A comparative study. *Government Information Quarterly*, 31(4), 513–525.

Ingram, R.W. (1984). Economic incentives and the choice of state government accounting practice. *Journal of Accounting Research*, 22(1), 126–134.

Ingram, R.W., and DeJong, D.V. (1987). The effect of regulation on local government disclosure practices. *Journal of Accounting and Public Policy*, 6(4), 245–270.

Ismail, N.A. (2009). Factors influencing AIS effectiveness among manufacturing SMEs: Evidence from Malaysia. *The Electronic Journal of Information Systems in Developing Countries*, 38(1), 1–19.

Joshi, A. (2010). Review of Impact and Effectiveness of Transparency and Accountability Initiatives: Annex 1 Service Delivery. Paper prepared for the Transparency and Accountability Initiative Workshop, October 2010. 14–15 Available at: https://www.ids.ac.uk/files/dmfile/IETAAnnex1ServicedeliveryJoshiFinal28Oct2010,pdf. [Accessed 22 July 2017].

Komala, A.R. (2012). The influence of the accounting managers knowledge and the top managements support on the accounting information system and its impact on the quality of accounting information: A case of Zakat Institutions in Bandung. *Journal of Global Management*, 1, 53–73.

Lee, G. and Kwak, Y. (2010). Open Government Implementation Model: Moving to Increased Public Engagement. *IBM Center for The Business of Government.* http://www.businessofgovernment.org/report/opengovernment-implementation-model-moving-increasedpublic-engagement. [Accessed: 10-3-2018].

Lee, G., and Kwak, Y. (2011). Open Government Implementation Model: Moving to Increased Public Engagement. IBM Center for The Business of Government.

Lee, Y.W., Strong, D.M., Kahn, B.K., and Wang, R.Y. (2002). AIMQ: A methodology for information quality assessment. *Information and Management*, 40(2), 133–146.

Lindell, M.K., and Whitney, D.J. (2001). Accounting for common method variance in cross-sectional research designs. *Journal of Applied Psychology*, 86(1), 114–121.

Lindstedt, C., and Naurin, D. (2010). Transparency is not enough: Making transparency effective in reducing corruption. *International political science review*, 31(3), 301–322.

Lourenço, R.P. (2015). An analysis of open government portals: A perspective of transparency for accountability. *Government Information Quarterly*, 32(3), 323–332.

Marshall, B.R., and Paul, J.S. (2012). *Accounting Information Systems*, 12th edition. Pearson Prentice Hall.

McLeod, R., and Schell, G.P. (2007). *Management information systems.* USA: Pearson/Prentice Hall.

Nguyen Bich Lien. (2012). Identify and control the factors that affect the quality of accounting information in the environment of applying enterprise resource planning (ERP). PhD thesis. University of Economics Ho Chi Minh City.

Nogueira, S.P.S., and Jorge, S.M.F. (2016). Explanatory factors for the use of the financial report in decision-making: Evidence from local government in Portugal. *Spanish Accounting Review*, 19(2), 216–226.

O'brien, J.A., and Marakas, G.M. (2005). *Management Information System*, 7th edition. New York: Mcgraw- Hill/Irwin Companies.

Okpala, K.E. (2012). Fiscal accountability dilemma in Nigeria public sector: A warning model for economic retrogression. *Research Journal of Finance and Accounting*, 3(6), 113–132.

Otley, D.T. (1980). The contingency theory of management accounting: Achievement and prognosis. *Accounting, Organizations and Society*, 5(4), 413–428.

Piccoli, G. (2008). *Information Systems for Managers: Text and Cases.* USA: John Wiley and Sons.
Rapina (2014). Factors influencing the quality of accounting information. *Research Journal of Finance and Accounting,* 5(2), 148–152.
Robbins, W.A., and Austin, K.R. (1986). Disclosure quality in governmental financial reports: An assessment of the appropriateness of a compound measure. *Journal of Accounting Research,* 24(2), 412–421.
Rodríguez Bolívar, M.P., Alcaide Muñoz, L., and Lόpez Hernández, A.M. (2013). Determinants of financial transparency in government. *International Public Management Journal,* 16(4), 557–602.
Rommey, M.B., and Steinbart, P.J. (2006). *Accounting Information System,* 10th edition. USA: Pearson Education, Inc.
Rommey, M. B., and Steinbart, P. J. (2006). *Accounting Information System.* New Jersey: Prentice-Hall.
Sacer, I.M., *et al.* (2006). Accounting information system's quality as the ground for quality business reporting. In *IADIS International conference, e-commerce 2006,* p. 59.
Solberg, M. (2010). *A Survey Analysis of Transparency in Three Asian Regulatory Agencies Responsible for Medical Products.* PhD Thesis. University of Southern California.
Strong, D.M., Lee, Y.W., and Wang, R.Y. (1997). Data quality in context. *Communications of the ACM,* 40(5), 103–110.
Wong, W., and Welch, E. (2004). Does e-government promote accountability? A comparative analysis of website openness and government accountability. *Governance: An International Journal of Policy, Administration, and Institutions,* 17(2), 275–297.
Williams, A. (2015). A global index of information transparency and accountability. *Journal of Comparative Economics,* 43(3), 804–824.
Wisna, N. (2015). Organizational culture and its impact on the quality of accounting information systems. *Journal of Theoretical and Applied Information Technology,* 82(2), 1–7.
Xu, H. (2003). *Critical Success Factors for Accounting Information System Data Quality.* PhD Thesis. The University of Southern Queenland, Australia.
Xu, H., Nord, J.H., Nord, G.D., and Lin, B. (2003). Key issues accounting information quality management: Australian case studies. *Industrial Management and Data Systems,* 103, 461–470.

# Part IV

# Business Administration and Management

https://doi.org/10.1142/9789811227158_0012

# Chapter 12

# Determinants of Gender Diversity and Nationality Diversity of the Boards in Vietnamese Listed Firms

**My Tran Ngo and Hong My Ai Le**

## Abstract

This study aims at identifying the determinants of gender diversity and nationality diversity in the boards of Vietnamese listed firms. The data are hand-collected from 257 companies listed on the Ho Chi Minh stock exchange (HOSE) and 214 companies listed on the Ha Noi stock exchange (HNX) in the period 2015–2017. The main analyzing methods include Pooled OLS, REM, FEM, and GMM. The research results show that gender diversity is determined by three factors, *industry, family firm, and board size.* Concerning the determinants of nationality diversity of the board, there is evidence that firm size, foreign ownership, state ownership, and proportion of foreign sales predict the nationality diversity. Based on these results, some administrative implications are proposed to improve the structure of the board, including expanding business scale, promoting exports, limiting the increase in the number of members on the board of directors, reducing state ownership, and increasing foreign ownership.

**Keywords:** Board of directors; Gender diversity; Nationality diversity.

## 1. Problem Statement

Studies on corporate governance and human resource management, especially for high-level human resources, have made significant con tributions to business performance (Ali and Konrad, 2017). In other words, there is a positive relationship between the human resource management system and the financial performance of businesses in general. It is believed that human resources is an important factor that positively affects business performance (Huselid, 1995). Indeed, high-level human resources on the board of directors plays an extremely important role, regarding the organization's survival in general. The board of directors decides the strategies and builds plans as well as is responsible for monitoring the board of management, which is supposed to have great impact on the entire business.

Previously, a number of articles have explored and discovered important factors related to the relationship between the board and firm performance. Many of these studies appreciate the diversity of the board of directors. They argue that it is a contributing factor to business performance, as board diversity can be a supportive tool for implementing development strategies (Ali and Konrad, 2017). Factors such as *age, gender, nationality, academic and professional qualifications of members, life experiences, attitudes, and personalities* are used as proxies for board diversity (Milliken and Martins, 1996).

Two kinds of diversity received the interests of scholars: gender diversity and nationality diversity (Carter *et al.*, 2010; Darmadi, 2011; Erhardt *et al.*, 2003; Oxelheim and Randøy, 2003). Gender diversity is measured through the percentage of female members in the board. Some previous studies find evidence of the positive influence of female participation on the board of directors. Nationality diversity is measured through the proportion of foreigners on the board. Richard (2000) argues that nationality diversity is related to the success of businesses in pursuing growth strategies because multinational members on the board can offer many connections to more diverse customers as well as more diverse resources. Hence, the question of what are the determinants of board diversity remains to be explored by many researchers. Especially, this research topic in Vietnam is relatively new and rare. As a result, this study is conducted to find out which are the determinants of a board's diversity in the firms listed on the Vietnamese stock exchange. This study is one of the first studies on the topic in Vietnam.

## 2. Methodology

### 2.1. *Hypotheses*

There are two types of board diversity examined in this study, gender diversity and nationality diversity. Each type of diversity is affected by some different factors. Hence, we employ two research models, separately for each kind of diversity. The hypotheses are mainly grounded on resource-dependent theory.

#### 2.1.1. *Hypotheses on the determinants of gender diversity*

2.1.1.1. Firm size

Some previous studies have found evidence of the impact of firm size on gender diversity. The results of de Jonge (2014) show that the larger the company, the more the female members on the board. The larger the company size, the more diverse and complex the operations. Hence, larger firms need different experiences, perspectives, and ideas coming from a board with diversity, especially gender diversity. The evidence of the effect of firm size on gender diversity is also consistent with the study of Hillman *et al.* (2007).

Besides, McCormick Hyland and Marcellino (2002) also state that the appearance of female members on the board will increase the ability to appoint women to important management positions. Moreover, the larger the size of the company, the more the pressure on the board members to conform to social expectations (Hillman *et al.*, 2007; Meyer and Rowan, 1977; Saeed *et al.*, 2016). Large-scale companies are able to understand and respond to diverse stakeholders, and thus are more likely to engage more diverse leaders on the board (Zahra and Pearce II, 1990).

According to Boston Consulting Group, about 25% of CEOs or board members in Vietnamese businesses are women.[1] In recent years, there have been more and more famous female leaders in large

[1]Vietnam has the highest female CEO rate in Southeast Asia. https://theleader.vn/viet-nam-co-ty-le-nu-ceo-cao-nhat-dong-nam-a20171215003825749.htm [Accessed on October 9, 2018].

enterprises in Vietnam. For example, Ms. Nguyen Thi Nga is the chairman of the board of directors of BRG Group; Ms. Le Thu Thuy is the president of SeABank; Ms. Mai Kieu Lien is the general director of Vietnam Dairy Corporation; Ms. Cao Thi Ngoc Dung is the chairman of the board and CEO of Phu Nhuan Jewelry Company; Ms. Nguyen Thi Mai Thanh is the chairman of Refrigeration Electrical Engineering Corporation (REE); Ms. Nguyen Thi Phuong Thao is the co-founder and chairman of Sovico Holdings, found and holds the position of CEO of Vietjet Air; Ms. Thai Huong is the chairman of TH True Milk Company, chairman of Bac A bank. As a result, on the Vietnamese stock exchange, it is expected that there is a positive association between firm size and gender diversity.

**Hypothesis H1:** *Firm size has a positive relationship with the percentage of female members on the board.*

2.1.1.2. Industry

The nature of the industry is likely to affect the representation value of women in management. According to Hillman *et al.* (2007), there is a tendency to increase the interests of female representatives on the company's management in a large female employment-based industry. Some previous studies show that the financial and service sectors are promising sectors for women who want to advance their careers. And of course, there will be a higher tendency for the appearance of women on the board (McCormick Hyland and Marcellino, 2002). Hence, we expect the following hypothesis:

**Hypothesis H2:** *Companies operating in the customer services sector will have a higher percentage of female members on the board than other sectors.*

2.1.1.3. Company's risk

The author supports the view of Martín-Ugedo and Minguez-Vera (2014) that because of the influence of gender, women tend to be more cautious in investment decisions as they dislike risks. Regarding gender characteristics, most women prefer safety, certainty, assurance, and stability. They dislike risk and elusive situations (Martín-Ugedo and Minguez-Vera, 2014). Therefore, companies with high risks in business are less likely to have more female members on the board.

Similarly, Saeed *et al.* (2016) argue that in an uncertain business environment, there is a reduction of the presence of women on the board. The research results show that the company's risk impacts the percentage of female members on the board of directors, in both developed countries and emerging economies. Some other studies have shown similar results, i.e., companies that face higher uncertainties tend to have fewer female members on the board (Adams and Ferreira, 2004). Therefore, it is expected that the company's risk has a negative impact on the percentage of female members on the board.

**Hypothesis H3:** *The company's risk has a negative relationship with the percentage of female members on the board.*

2.1.1.4. Family firm

Abdullah (2014) concludes that women are often appointed to the board based on the connection between their families and the owners. In other words, women appear more on the board of family companies compared to other types of businesses. Similarly, Ruigrok *et al.* (2007) give the evidence that women seem to have more opportunities to become directors in family companies than other types of businesses. Indeed, women have played an important role in family companies for a long time. Under the impact of globalization, the presence of women in the family company board tends to be increasing. And to adjust to changes in institutional and economic liberalization, family companies increasingly strengthen women's presence in response to social expectations (Saeed *et al.*, 2016). In Vietnam, there are many large family companies. Hence, it is expected that with the advantage of getting support from family members, female leaders have more opportunities to participate on the boards.

**Hypothesis H4:** *Family companies will have a higher percentage of female members on the board than other types of companies.*

2.1.1.5. State ownership

Enterprises, especially state-owned enterprises, are under pressure to meet social expectations. Maintaining a gender balance committee in a state company signals that the government appreciates the diversity and prospects of women's career advancement. Therefore, the higher the state-owned enterprise, the more likely it is that a female member joins the board (Saeed, *et al.*, 2016). The study of Tran and Nguyen (2015) in the Vietnam market also concludes that state agencies are considered to be at the forefront of creating opportunities for women.

In 2012, the Prime Minister approved the National Strategy on Gender Equality for the period 2011–2020. One of the goals of this strategy was that the percentage of female entrepreneurs reaches 35% by 2020. With this goal, it is clear that state-owned companies are interested in balancing gender at the management level. Therefore, there is the probability that the more the company has state ownership, the more women are appointed to the boards of directors.

**Hypothesis H5:** *State ownership has a positive relationship with the proportion of female members on the board of directors.*

2.1.1.6. Board size

One of the important roles of the board of directors is monitoring (Tricker and Tricker, 2015). According to Raheja (2005), the supervisory role can only be completed with a diverse and sufficient size of directors. Since management is often dominated by male members, it is not easy to appoint a woman to the board unless the size of the board is large enough (Abdullah, 2014). In other words, the larger the size of the council, the more the opportunities for women to participate in leadership. According to Burke (1999) and De Cabo *et al.* (2011), to increase women's representation in management, the company needs to consider increasing the size of the board. Therefore, it is expected that the size of the council has a positive impact on the percentage of female members on the board.

**Hypothesis H6:** *Board size has a positive relationship with the percentage of female members on the board.*

### 2.1.2. *Hypotheses on the determinants of nationality diversity*

#### 2.1.2.1. Firm size

The size of the company is found to be an important determinant that significantly affects the presence of foreign directors (Oxelheim and Randøy 2003). The larger the size of the company, the more diverse and complex its operations. And the larger the size of the company, the more the decisions and strategies that are taken and considered carefully. Therefore, large companies need more experience, different views, and different ideas from a diverse board. In addition, the larger the company size, the more likely it is to expand business, increase exports, and develop a subsidiary network in foreign markets. As a result, they need foreign members who are knowledgeable and experienced in the international market to map out appropriate strategies for the company. Hence, the following hypothesis is proposed:

**Hypothesis H7:** *Firm size has a positive relationship with the proportion of foreign members on the board.*

#### 2.1.2.2. State ownership

In contrast to gender diversity, previous studies show that the higher the percentage of shares owned by the state, the lower the percentage of foreigners on the board. High levels of state-owned shares are often associated with important industries or companies with a strong strategic direction for the country. In fact, companies with the majority of government holdings often prefer the safe investment market, despite the low growth potential. Therefore, companies with large shareholders are not particularly attractive to foreign investors (Greve and Ruigrok, 2003). For example, in the Vietnamese market, state corporations such as Vietnam Oil and Gas Group, Vietnam

Electricity Corporation, and the Vietnam Post and Telecommunications Corporation have no foreign members on the boards. Therefore, it is expected that the percentage of shares owned by the state has a negative impact on the proportion of foreigners on the board.

**Hypothesis H8:** *State ownership has a negative relationship with the proportion of foreign members on the board.*

2.1.2.3. Foreign ownership

According to Greve and Ruigrok (2003), the proportion of shares owned by foreign investors triggers the appointment of foreign members to the board. Besides, the presence of foreign members attracts more foreign investors. The higher the percentage of shares held by foreign investors, the greater the likelihood of the presence of foreign members on the board. As a result, a higher proportion of international members is observed in companies with higher foreign ownership (Estélyi and Nisar, 2016, Oxelheim and Randøy, 2003).

In Vietnam, when foreign investors pour capital into companies, they tend to recommend more foreign members to be a part of the board to represent their interests. For example, Tung Kuang Industrial Joint Stock Company has 9/9 members who are foreigners. Vietnam Taya Wire and Cable Joint Stock Company have 7/7 members who are all foreigners. These companies are all listed on the Vietnamese stock exchange. Therefore, the next hypothesis is suggested as follows:

**Hypothesis H9:** *The proportion of shares owned by foreign investors has a positive relationship with the proportion of foreign members on the board.*

2.1.2.4. Subsidiaries in foreign countries

A director's international background can be an important factor in deciding to expand the business beyond national boundaries. Boards with foreign nationality can be a driving force in decisions to scale up when a foreign subsidiary is established (Estélyi and Nisar, 2016). According to Zhao and Riber (2013), the board of directors becomes internationalized over time. Corporations need to focus on how to fit into the global environment when complexity is constantly increasing. Large-scale companies tend to expand their business, increase export volume, and develop a subsidiary network in foreign markets. Therefore, they need foreign leaders who are knowledgeable and experienced in the international market to map out appropriate strategies for the company. Typically, FPT Telecom Group has a network of subsidiaries present in 33 countries around the world. In FPT's board of directors, the proportion of foreigners accounts for 43% of the total members. As a result, the following hypothesis is presented:

**Hypothesis H10:** *The number of subsidiaries operating abroad has a positive relationship with the proportion of foreigners on the board.*

2.1.2.5. Proportion of foreign sales

Research by Ruigrok *et al.* (2007) concludes that the complexity of internationalization activities increases the presence of foreigners on the board. To sell products abroad, a company needs to understand the international market, including preferences, culture, habits, customer needs, as well as laws and economic barriers. Therefore, the company needs to add foreign members to the board because of their knowledge and experience in the international arena. Oxelheim and Randøy (2003) also conclude that higher levels of internationalization are associated with higher numbers of international directors (Oxelheim and Randøy, 2003).

Besides, when companies increase their presence in foreign markets, they attract more foreign investors. Increasing the level of internationalization allows the company to better understand its market and foreign customers, thereby gaining information and knowledge about overseas markets. The need to expand international business networks can facilitate the appointment of foreigners into the board (Greve and Ruigrok, 2003). Therefore, it is expected that the higher the rate of foreign sales, the higher the probability of a foreigner appearing on the board.

**Hypothesis H11:** *The proportion of foreign sales of the company has a positive relationship with the proportion of foreigners on the board.*

## 2.2. *Research model*

Based on the development of the above-mentioned hypotheses, the research model on diversity is presented as two models. The first model represents the determinants of gender diversity (Figure 1) and the second model represents the determinants of nationality diversity (Figure 2).

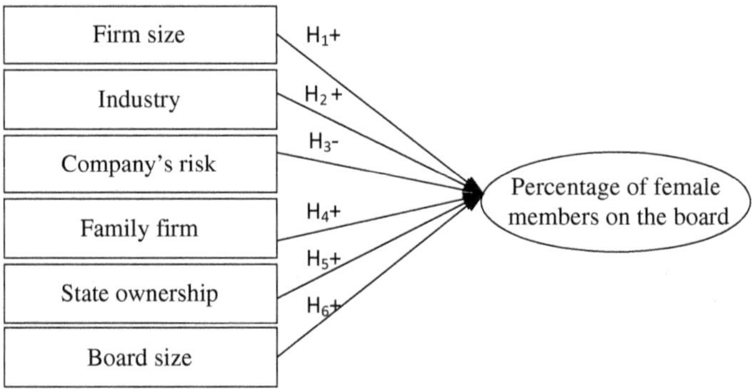


**Figure 1:** Research model on the determinants of gender diversity.

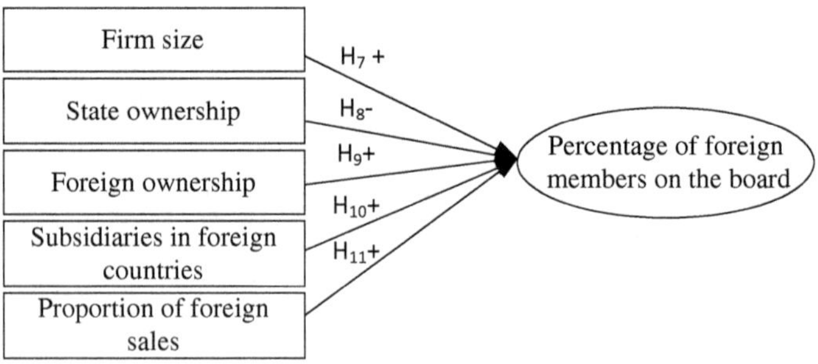


**Figure 2:** Research model on the determinants of nationality diversity.

## 2.3. *Data and analysis method*

### 2.3.1. *Data*

This study uses panel data which are hand-collected from the annual report from 257 companies listed on Ho Chi Minh stock exchange (HOSE) and 214 listed on the Ha Noi stock exchange (HNX) in the period 2015–2017. These reports are downloaded from stock websites such as www.vietstock.vn, www.cafef.vn, as well as the main websites of companies.

The sampling criterion for firms to be included in the sample is that there must be sufficient information about the board of directors and important business data for the period 2015–2017. After eliminating inappropriate companies, the number of firms included is 471. With reference to the dummy variable of industry, companies in the sample are classified based on the Global Industry Classification Standards (GICS) including 10 groups: Energy, Materials, Industry, Consumer goods, Essential consumer goods, Healthcare, Information technology, Real estate, Utility services, and Finance.

### 2.3.2. *Analysis method*

First, the research model is estimated by Pooled OLS regression to identify the most basic issues of the relationship between independent variables and dependent variables. The regression equation for the determinants of gender diversity is estimated as follows:

$$\begin{aligned} BGD = \alpha &+ \beta_1 FS + \beta_2 INS + \beta_3 FR + \beta_4 FF \\ &+ \beta_5 SO + \beta_6 BS + \varepsilon, \end{aligned} \tag{1}$$

where $BGD$ represents the percentage of female members on the board. Independent variables include *firm size* ($FS$), *industry* ($INS$), *company's risk* ($FR$), *family firm* ($FF$), *state ownership* ($SO$), *and board size* ($BS$). Variable descriptions are presented in Table 1. The regression equation for the determinants of gender diversity is

**Table 1:** Measurement of variables used in the research model.

| Variable name | Variable code | Measurement | Citation | Expected sign |
|---|---|---|---|---|
| **Dependent variables** | | | | |
| Percentage of female members on the board | *BGD* | Total female members on the board/ Total board members | Hyland and Marcellino (2002); Saeed and associates (2016); Ugedo and Vera (2014); Cabo *et al.* (2012); Hillman *et al.* (2007); Abdullah (2014); Jonge (2014); Bohdanowicz (2015) | |
| Percentage of foreign members on the board | *ND* | Total foreign members on the board/ Total board members | Estélyi and Nisar (2016); Ruigrok *et al.* (2015); Oxelheim *et al.* (2013); Riber and Annie (2013); Greve and Ruigrok (2003) | |
| **Independent variables** | | | | |
| Firm size | *FS* | Total sales | Hyland and Marcellino (2002); Saeed and associates (2016); Hillman *et al.* (2007); Jonge (2014); Oxelheim *et al.* (2013) | + |
| Industry | *INS* | Dummy variables, getting value 1 if the company operates in the customer services sector, getting value of 0, vice versa | Hyland and Marcellino (2002); Hillman *et al.* (2007); Jonge (2014) | + |
| Company's risk | *FR* | Total debt/Total asset | Saeed *et al.* (2016); Ugedo and Vera (2014); Cabo *et al.* (2012) | − |

| | | | | |
|---|---|---|---|---|
| Family firm | *FF* | Dummy variables, getting value 1 if the company is family-controlled, getting value of 0, vice versa.Family companies are defined as holding more seats in the board than other individuals and organizations. | Saeed *et al.* (2016); Ugedo and Vera (2014); Abdullah (2014); Jonge (2014) | + |
| State ownership | *SO* | Total number of shares owned by the state/Total shares of the company | Saeed *et al.* (2016); Bohdanowicz (2015); Greve and Ruigrok (2003) | + |
| Board size | *BS* | Total board members | Cabo *et al.* (2012); Abdullah (2014); Burke (1999) | + |
| Foreign ownership | *FI* | Total number of shares owned by the foreign investors/Total shares of the company | Estélyi and Nisar (2016); Oxelheim *et al.* (2013); Greve and Ruigrok (2003) | + |
| Subsidiaries in foreign countries | *SUB* | Number of subsidiaries, representative offices and branches of the company operating abroad | Estélyi and Nisar (2016); Riber and Arnie (2013) | + |
| Proportion of foreign sales | *CI* | Percentage of overseas sales on total sales | Ruigrok *et al.* (2015); Oxelheim *et al.* (2013); Greve and Ruigrok (2003) | + |

estimated as follows:

$$ND = \alpha + \beta_1 FS + \beta_2 SO + \beta_3 FI + \beta_4 SUB + \beta_5 CI + \varepsilon, \qquad (2)$$

where *ND* represents the percentage of foreign members on the board. Independent variables include *firm size* (*FS*), *state ownership* (*SO*), *foreign ownership* (*FI*), *subsidiaries in foreign countries* (*SUB*), *and proportion of foreign sales* (*CI*).

However, Pooled OLS ignores the time and space elements of panel data, which can result in the appearance of autocorrelation or causing the model to be wrong because the assumption is too strict. Besides, this method does not take into account the factors that cannot be obtained or the individual effects of each company, while the phenomenon often occurs in empirical research (Baltagi, 2008). To solve this problem, Models 1 and 2 are regressed by a more efficient method, which is the fixed effect model (FEM) and random effect model (REM). The test is carried out to determine which estimation method is best suited.

In addition, another problem can exist when estimating Models 1 and 2. According to some previous studies, these two models are likely to encounter the problem of endogeneity. Companies with higher overseas sales can appoint more foreign members to the board. However, the causal relationship can also function reasonably well as the presence of foreign members can promote the company's international experience, thereby contributing positively to foreign sales (Oxelheim and Randøy, 2003). The size of the company can affect gender diversity of the board, but on the contrary, it is also possible that women prefer to work in a large-scale company (Saeed *et al.*, 2016). This causal relationship can cause the regression methods presented in the previous section to be misleading. To solve this problem, GMM estimation method is used. This is also a method used by some previous studies such as the study by Oxelheim and Randøy (2003), Saeed, *et al.* (2016), and Martín-Ugedo and Minguez-Vera (2014).

## 3. Results

### 3.1. *Descriptive statistics*

The descriptive statistics of variables are presented in Table 2. The average female members on the boards of companies listed on the Vietnamese stock exchange is 15.4%; the highest presence rate is 80% and the lowest presence rate is 0%. As we can see, male members almost overwhelm the number of women on the board of directors of these companies. Overall, the percentage of female members on the board of directors is still modest, which indicates that gender diversity is not popular in listed companies in the period 2015–2017.

The presence of foreign members in the council is at 4.60% on average. The highest presence rate is 100% and the lowest presence rate is 0%. Compared to gender diversity, nationality diversity is more modest. The size of the company is captured in the company's sales revenue. According to the results from Table 2, the average sales revenue of the listed companies in the sample is VND 2,881,262 billion.

The number of companies operating in the customer services sector accounts for 42% of the sample. In this group, the real estate industry dominates with 57 companies, accounting for 12% of the research sample. Approximately 14.70% of companies in the research sample are family companies. This result shows that family firms only account for a modest part of the total number of listed companies in the Vietnamese stock market. Table 3 also shows that the average rate of total debt over the total asset is 49.20% and the average state ownership is 16.60%.

The size of the board is calculated based on the number of members participating on the board. The average board size of listed companies on the Vietnamese stock market is about five to six people. The minimum value is 3 and the maximum value is 13 members. The companies with number of board members above 10 or more only account for a very small part of the research sample, with seven

**Table 2:** Descriptive statistics.

| Variables | Unit | Observation | Mean | Standard error | Min | Max |
|---|---|---|---|---|---|---|
| **Dependent variables** | | | | | | |
| Percentage of female members in the board | % | 1,413 | 0.154 | 0.170 | 0.000 | 0.800 |
| Percentage of foreign members in the board | % | 1,413 | 0.046 | 0.134 | 0.000 | 1.000 |
| **Independent variables** | | | | | | |
| Firm size | Billion VND | 1,413 | 2,881.262 | 9,916.396 | −20.166 | 153,697.100 |
| Industry | | 1,413 | 0.416 | 0.493 | 0 | 1 |
| Company's risk | % | 1,413 | 0.492 | 0.269 | 0.000 | 4.668 |
| Family firm | | 1,413 | 0.147 | 0.355 | 0 | 1 |
| State ownership | % | 1,413 | 0.166 | 0.246 | 0.000 | 1.000 |
| Board size | | 1,413 | 5.612 | 1.286 | 3 | 13 |
| Foreign ownership | % | 1,413 | 0.112 | 0.151 | 0.000 | 0.873 |
| Subsidiaries in foreign countries | | 1,413 | 0.101 | 0.600 | 0 | 7 |
| Proportion of foreign sales | % | 1,413 | 0.055 | 0.183 | 0.000 | 0.993 |

**Table 3:** Estimated results on the determinants of gender diversity.

| Variable name | Variable code | OLS | REM | GMM |
|---|---|---|---|---|
| Firm size | *FS* | 1.12e-07 | −1.16e-07 | 2.50e-06 |
| Industry | *INS* | 0.085*** | 0.082*** | 0.083*** |
| Company's risk | *FR* | −0.021 | −0.011 | −0.028 |
| Family firm | *FF* | 0.084*** | 0.056*** | 0.082*** |
| State ownership | *SO* | −0.012 | −0.020 | −0.029 |
| Board size | *BS* | −0.008** | 0.002 | −0.012*** |
| Observations | | 1.413 | 1.413 | 1.413 |
| Sig-value | | 0.000 | 0.000 | 0.000 |

*Notes*: ***, ** represent the significance levels of 1% and 5%, respectively.

companies. The percentage of foreign investors is measured by taking the number of shares owned by foreigners divided by the total number of shares of the company. The average rate is 11.20%, which is rather low. The minimum value of 0% implies that some companies have no foreign investment. The highest value is 87%, indicating that there are cases in which foreign investors almost completely control capital at the company.

Subsidiaries operating abroad are calculated by counting the number of subsidiaries, branches, or representative offices in foreign countries. This variable has an average value of only 0.10, suggesting that the expansion of business scale and foreign market penetration of companies in the research sample is very weak. There are cases in which the company owns up to seven subsidiaries (including branches and representative offices). There are also cases in which there are no overseas companies even though the company still participates in export markets. In fact, the establishment of overseas subsidiaries, branches, or representative offices is an issue that needs to be considered carefully. Therefore, the expansion of business scale to foreign markets of Vietnamese companies still faces many limitations. The average proportion of foreign sales is only 5.50%. This is very modest, which indicates that the main revenue source of listed companies on Vietnam's stock market is almost entirely from the domestic market.

## 3.2. Results on the determinants of gender diversity and nationality diversity on the board of firms listed in the Vietnamese stock market

### 3.2.1. Results on the determinants of gender diversity

Before estimating Model 1, the correlation among variables has been checked.[2] The correlation coefficients are rather low. Hence, it is possible that the problem of heteroskedasticity does not exist.

According to Table 3, regression results estimated by OLS, REM, and GMM are nearly the same. The result of the Hausman test indicates the appropriateness of REM over FEM. There is evidence of the impact of industry, family firm, and board size on gender diversity. The industry has a positive relationship with the percentage of female members on the board. This result implies that if the company operates in the customer services sector (including Consumer goods, essential consumer goods, Cham Healthcare, Real Estate, and Finance) it will have a higher percentage of female members than the rest. This result is consistent with the results of McCormick Hyland and Marcellino (2002), Hillman *et al.* (2007), de Jonge (2014), and Tran and Nguyen (2015).

Family companies have a positive relationship with the percentage of female members on the board, implying that if the company is a family company, there is a higher percentage. This result is similar to results from studies by Abdullah (2014) in Malaysia and de Jonge (2014) in China and India. The board size also has a strong correlation to the percentage of female members, but the sign of the coefficient is opposite as expected. Hence, the evidence shows that in the Vietnamese market, the larger the size of the board, the smaller the percentage of female members. This result can be due to the regulation of board size in the Vietnamese stock market. According to Clause 5, Article 13, Decree 71/2017/ND-CP guiding public administration (effective from August 1, 2017), the listed company

[2]Due to the limitation of space, the correlation matrix is not presented. It will be supplied upon request.

**Table 4:** Estimated results on the determinants of nationality diversity.

| Variable name | Variable code | OLS | FEM | GMM |
|---|---|---|---|---|
| Firm size | *FS* | 1.18e-06*** | −5.44e-08 | 1.18e-06*** |
| State ownership | *SO* | −0.045*** | −0.053*** | −0.044*** |
| Foreign ownership | *FI* | 0.463*** | 0.038** | 0.461*** |
| Subsidiaries in foreign countries | *SUB* | −0.002 | −0.001 | −0.002 |
| Proportion of foreign sales | *CI* | 0.110*** | 0.118*** | 0.143*** |
| Observations | — | 1.413 | 1.413 | 1.413 |
| Sig-value | — | 0.000 | 0.000 | 0.000 |

*Note*: ***, ** represent the significance levels of 1% and 5%, respectively.

must ensure that at least 1/3 of the total members of the board of directors are independent members. Accordingly, independent board members act as supervisors, reducing the risk of abuse of the powers of managers and executives, contributing to protecting the legitimate interests of shareholders, especially small shareholders. According to the results from Table 4, in the Vietnamese market, women tend to be supported by their families to participate on the boards rather than including independent female members from outside. Therefore, in case the size of the board increases, as the number of independent members is greater, the likelihood of female representation shrinks since it is very hard to appoint an independent female member to the board in Vietnamese companies.

There is no statistical evidence that the size of the company has an impact on the percentage of female members on the board. This means that the fluctuations in scale (through revenue targets) do not affect the possibility of women to be present on the board. This can be explained through the report of Le and Nguyen (2016) in a study on Vietnam, which states that women mainly own small and medium enterprises, especially super small enterprises. Up to 98.8% of women-owned enterprises are micro and small, of which small-scale enterprises account for 72% and small businesses account for 27%.

There is no statistical evidence that the company's risk has an impact on the percentage of female members on the board. This means that the volatility of risk does not affect the possibility of women to be present on the board. State ownership is found to have no effect on the percentage of female members on the board of directors. Although the Prime Minister approves the National Strategy on Gender Equality for the period 2011–2020, and one of the goals is the percentage of women entrepreneurs reaching 35% by 2020, according to IFC's report, the owner enterprises with women on the board are mostly small and super small companies. In other words, the strategy of gender equality mainly focuses on small and medium enterprises, especially micro-enterprises rather than joint-stock companies. Abdullah (2014) and de Jonge (2014) do not find the impact of share ownership on gender diversity in the board of Vietnamese companies.

### 3.2.2. *Results on the determinants of nationality diversity*

The correlation among variables is checked before estimating Model 2.[3] The correlation matrix shows that a few independent variables strongly correlate with each other. However, when checking the phenomenon of multicollinearity by VIF, the VIF value of each independent variable and the average VIF value are less than 2, indicating that the model does not show multicollinearity.

The regression results of OLS and GMM in Table 4 are quite similar. The Hausman test indicates the choice of FEM to estimate Model 2. At the 1% significance level, there are four factors that affect the percentage of foreign members on the board, including *firm size, state ownership, foreign ownership, and proportion of foreign sales.*

Firm size has a positive relationship with the proportion of foreigners on the board, which implies that the larger the size of the company, the higher the proportion of foreigners on the board. This result is completely consistent with those found by Oxelheim and

[3]Due to the limitation of space, the correlation matrix is not presented. It will be supplied upon request.

Randøy (2003). Accordingly, the larger the company size, the more the complexity of the operations, especially as they tend to expand their business, increase exports, and penetrate foreign markets. And this is very relevant to Vietnam's growing export situation every year. In short, the larger the size of the company, the more the foreign members appearing on the board.

State ownership has a negative relationship with the proportion of foreigners on the board, which supports the expectations posed by $H_8$. This result implies that the higher the state ownership, the lower the proportion of foreigners on the board. This result is quite similar to Greve *et al.* (2015). In addition, the proportion of shares owned by foreign investors is found to have a positive relationship with the proportion of foreigners on the board. This result is the opposite of that on state ownership. This result indicates that when foreign investors increase their ownership, their control of the company is stronger and their presence on the board is also higher. Estélyi and Nisar (2016), Oxelheim and Randøy (2003), and Greve and Ruigrok (2003) also find similar results.

The proportion of sales abroad has a positive relationship with the proportion of foreign members on the board. This shows that the higher the overseas sales, the more the company can expand; they need additional foreign members on the board because those members can understand the market and foreign customers better. This result is quite similar to studies by Ruigrok *et al.* (2007), Oxelheim and Randøy (2003), and Greve and Ruigrok (2003).

There is no statistical evidence that the existence of a subsidiary operating abroad has an impact on the proportion of foreign members on the board. This means that the increase in the number of subsidiaries abroad has no effect on the presence of foreigners on the board. According to the data, only 16 companies have subsidiaries, representative offices, or branches in foreign countries. These cases can be due to the fact that they are just established or under construction during the period recorded in the annual report but have no activity so there is no revenue.

## 4. Conclusion and Policy Implications

This study aims at identifying the determinants of gender diversity and nationality diversity in the board of directors of listed companies in the Vietnam stock market in the period 2015–2017. Data are hand-collected from 471 listed firms in the Vietnamese stock exchanges. The equation for the two models is estimated by Pooled OLS, FEM, REM, and GMM.

With respect to the determinants of gender diversity, three factors are found to have an impact, *industry, family firm, and board size*. Particularly, companies operating in consumer goods, essential consumer goods, healthcare, real estate, and finance sectors have a higher percentage of female members on the board than other sectors. The family-controlled companies have a higher percentage of female members on the board than other types of companies. Finally, the larger the board of directors, the lower the rate of female members on the board. There is no statistical evidence on the impact of the remaining independent variables consisting of the size of the company, the percentage of shares owned by the state, and the risk of the company on the gender diversity of listed firms in the Vietnamese stock market.

Similarly for the determinants of nationality diversity, the results show that the size of the company, the percentage of shares owned by the state, the percentage of shares owned by foreign investors, and the proportion of sales to foreign countries have a significant impact on nationality diversity. Accordingly, the larger the size of the company, the higher the proportion of foreigners on the board. The more the shares owned by the state, the lower the number of foreign members on the board. Conversely, the percentage of foreign members on the board increases with the share owned by foreign investors. Finally, the higher the company's overseas sales, the more the foreign members appointed to the board. The remaining independent variable, a subsidiary operating in a foreign country, has no statistical impact on nationality diversity of listed firms in the Vietnamese stock market.

Based on these results, various implications to improve the diversity in the board of directors are proposed. First, companies should focus on using appropriate solutions and strategies to enhance sales revenue, percentage of sales abroad, and the ownership of foreign investors. Besides, it is recommended to limit the expansion of the board of directors and the percentage of shares owned by the state. On the other hand, if the company belongs to the customer services or family-owned industry, the company has a lot of advantages to enhance gender diversity. They need to maximize their strengths to improve the structure of the board. There is a need to consider the potential of greater board diversity, and the optimal solutions to encourage and facilitate women to participate in the remaining sectors or other types of companies.

## References

Abdullah, S.N. (2014). The causes of gender diversity in Malaysian large firms. *Journal of Management & Governance*, 18(4), 1137–1159.

Adams, R.B., and Ferreira, D. (2004). Gender diversity in the boardroom. *European Corporate Governance Institute, Finance Working Paper*, 57, 30.

Ali, M., and Konrad, A.M. (2017). Antecedents and consequences of diversity and equality management systems: The importance of gender diversity in the TMT and lower to middle management. *European Management Journal*, 35(4), 440–453.

Baltagi, B. (2008). *Econometric Analysis of Panel Data.* John Wiley & Sons.

Burke, R. (1999). Women on Canadian corporate boards of directors: getting the numbers right! *Corporate Governance: An International Review*, 7(4), 374–378.

Carter, D.A., D'Souza, F., Simkins, B.J., and Simpson, W.G. (2010). The gender and ethnic diversity of US boards and board committees and firm financial performance. *Corporate Governance: An International Review*, 18, 396–414.

Darmadi, S. (2011). Board diversity and firm performance: The Indonesian evidence. *Corporate Ownership and Control Journal*, 8(2–4), 450–466.

De Cabo, R.M.,Gimeno, R., and Escot, L. (2011). Disentangling discrimination on Spanish boards of directors. *Corporate Governance: An International Review*, 19(1), 77–95.

de Jonge, A. (2014). The glass ceiling that refuses to break: Women directors on the boards of listed firms in China and India. In *Women's Studies International Forum*. Elsevier, pp. 326–338.

Erhardt, N.L., Werbel, J., and Shrader, C.B. (2003). Board of director diversity and firm financial performance. *Corporate Governance: An International Review*, 11, 102–111.

Estélyi, K.S., and Nisar, T.M. (2016). Diverse boards: Why do firms get foreign nationals on their boards? *Journal of Corporate Finance*, 39, 174–192.

Greve, P., Biemann, T., and Ruigrok, W. (2015). Foreign executive appointments: A multilevel examination. *Journal of World Business*, 50(4), 674–686.

Greve, P., and Ruigrok, W. (2003). *The internationalisation of top management teams and boards in Nordic countries.* 29th European International Business Academy (EIBA) conference, Copenhagen.

Hausman, J.A. (1978). Specification tests in econometrics. *Econometrica: Journal of the Econometric Society*, 46(6), 1251–1271.

Hillman, A.J., Shropshire, C., and Cannella Jr, A.A. (2007). Organizational predictors of women on corporate boards. *Academy of Management Journal*, 50(4), 941–952.

Huselid, M.A. (1995). The impact of human resource management practices on turnover, productivity, and corporate financial performance. *Academy of Management Journal*, 38(3), 635–672.

Le, Q.C., and Nguyen, V.H. (2016). *Small and Medium Enterprises Owned by Women in Vietnam: Current Status and Policy Recommendations.* Ha Noi: National Economics University.

Martín-Ugedo, J.F., and Minguez-Vera, A. (2014). Firm performance and women on the board: Evidence from Spanish small and medium-sized enterprises. *Feminist Economics*, 20(3), 136–162.

McCormick Hyland, M., and Marcellino, P.A. (2002). Examining gender on corporate boards: A regional study. *Corporate Governance: The International Journal of Business in Society*, 2(4), 24–31.

Meyer, J.W., and Rowan, B. (1977). Institutionalized organizations: Formal structure as myth and ceremony. *American Journal of Sociology*, 83(2), 340–363.

Milliken, F.J., and Martins, L.L. (1996). Searching for common threads: Understanding the multiple effects of diversity in organizational groups. *Academy of Management Review*, 21(2), 402–433.

Oxelheim, L., and Randøy, T. (2003). The impact of foreign board membership on firm value. *Journal of Banking & Finance*, 27(12), 2369–2392.

Raheja, C.G. (2005). Determinants of board size and composition: A theory of corporate boards. *Journal of Financial and Quantitative Analysis*, 40(2), 283–306.

Richard, O.C. (2000). Racial diversity, business strategy, and firm performance: A resource-based view. *Academy of Management Journal*, 43(2), 164–177.

Ruigrok, W., Peck, S., and Tacheva, S. (2007). Nationality and gender diversity on Swiss corporate boards. *Corporate Governance: An International Review*, 15(4), 546–557.

Saeed, A., Belghitar, Y., and Yousaf, A. (2016). Firm-level determinants of gender diversity in the boardrooms: Evidence from some emerging markets. *International Business Review*, 25(5), 1076–1088.

Tran, T.M.D., and Nguyen, T.V.T. (2015). Intellectual women with management leadership. *VNU Journal of Science: Social Sciences and Humanities*, 3(1–12).

Tricker, R.B., and Tricker, R.I. (2015). *Corporate Governance: Principles, Policies, and Practices*. Oxford University Press, USA.

Zahra, S.A., and Pearce II, J.A. (1990). Determinants of board directors' strategic involvement. *European Management Journal*, 8(2), 164–173.

Zhao, A., and Riber, C. (2013). *The Effects of Internationalization on the Composition of Board of Directors: A Quantitative Study of Swedish Multinational Corporations*. Bachelor Thesis. Uppsala University.

https://doi.org/10.1142/9789811227158_0013

# Chapter 13

# The Evolution of Leadership Theories: A Literature Review

**Thanh Tung Do and Ngoc Khuong Mai**

## Abstract

Leadership theories have evolved over the decades, reflecting its complex and multifaceted nature. This narrative literature review aims to analyze significant leadership literature in popular leadership course books and published peer-reviewed English articles, from which future research directions can be extrapolated.Various development stages of leadership, which hold different research values, are examined and discussed. Since some emerging theories appear to be understudied (shared/distributive leadership, complexity theory of leadership, etc.), there are arguably much scope and opportunities for these to be developed in the future.

**Keywords:** Leadership; Leadership theories; Complexity; Literature review.

## 1. Introduction

Leadership has a relatively long history, moving from a set of personality traits to a complex, multifaceted, and ever-changing process. Various studies on leadership propose theories suitable for different contexts and catalyze varying outcomes. Leadership is recognized as a key factor affecting business performance, corporate culture, and employees' attitudes (Wang *et al.*, 2011; Elenkov, 2002; Koene *et al.*, 2002; Ogbonna and Harris, 2000). Scholars also examine and point out that different leadership approaches result in different outcomes. For example, ethical leadership tends to improve organizational citizenship behavior (Ruiz-Palomino *et al.*, 2011); leader–member exchange leadership enhances creative work involvement (Volmer *et al.*, 2012), and transformational leadership facilitates innovation (Jia *et al.*, 2018).

The abundance of leadership theories and approaches in the literature require scholars to conduct comprehensive evaluation and categorization. There also exist few comprehensive literature reviews on this field. Stogdill (1975) attempts to review earliest leadership theories such as traits theories, exchange theories, expectancy-reinforcement theories, path–goal theory, and contingency theory. The author concludes that these available theories are ideologically biased and should be comprehensively combined. Van Seters and Field (1990) review nine different eras of leadership, namely Personality, Influence, Behavior, Situation, Contingency, Transactional, Anti-Leadership, Culture, and Transformational Era. The two scholars also call for a conceptual integrative framework that connects different leadership approaches. Recently, Asrar-ul-Haq and Anwar (2018) have conducted a literature review on classical perspectives of leadership and its linkage with different outcomes. The two authors also propose a research agenda on studying leadership from a multiperspective in developing countries, especially in Southern Asia. Clark and Harrison (2018) use 11 interrelated eras of leadership framework adapted from Alimo-Metcalfe (2013) and King (1990) to review significant leadership literature and conclude that future research opportunities involve servant leadership as well as skill and entrepreneurial approach to leadership. However, as this field of study involves a variety of theories that evolve over time, those literature reviews are conceived to be insufficient. It is therefore vital to review prominent leadership theories that contemporary research attempts to address.

This narrative literature review chapter aims to answer the following questions:

- **Q1:** What does extant literature currently contribute to the understanding of leadership and its evolution?
- **Q2:** What are some of the leadership theories and concepts that future research should focus on?

First, the authors searched for publications on leadership theories from respected online academic databases such as Web of Science, Google Scholar, Emerald Insight, Science Direct, and Pro Quest. Only notable articles that cover leadership theories and literature reviews on leadership are included. *Leadership*, *leadership theory*, and *leadership literature review* are keywords used for the search. Selected articles are subjected to a qualitative review that is carried out independently by the two authors. After comparing separate assessments and reaching consensus, the authors analyze the remaining papers, then discuss and propose areas for future research on leadership. Besides, some sections related to leadership theories in popular leadership handbooks and textbooks such as *Leadership: Theory and Practice* by Northouse (2018) and *Leadership in Organizations* by Yukl (2013) are used in the review.

This literature review starts with the definitions of leadership, prevailing approaches to leadership, then continues with emerging conceptions of leadership. Later, these leadership theories are discussed and some directions for further leadership research are proposed.

## 2. Definition of Leadership

There is a variety of leadership definitions and approaches in the literature. Most of them assume that leadership is a process whereby intended influences are exerted over colleagues or subordinates to guide, structure, and support activities and relationships at a group or firm level (Yukl, 2013). Northouse (2018) defines leadership as a process whereby a single person influences his or her followers to achieve a shared goal. Leadership, according to this definition, deals with influence, interaction, and relationships between leaders and subordinates. Yukl (2013) comes up with a broader definition of leadership, which considers various attributes that not only facilitate the success of a group or an organization but also make sure it is ready to handle future challenges. Leadership, as defined by Yukl, is the process in which, through influences and facilitation, leaders and followers understand and reach consensus on future objectives and how to achieve mutual goals.

There is an evolution of various leadership theories, ranging from trait, behavior, contingency, transformation to a newly-introduced one called complexity theory of leadership (Uhl-Bien *et al.*, 2007; Yukl, 2013; Northouse, 2018). The next sections briefly review different leadership concepts from past to present and discuss how they inform future empirical research and practices of this phenomenon.

## 3. Prevailing Approaches to Leadership

### 3.1. *Trait theory and competence theory of leadership*

The classical root of leadership theories begins with the work of Stogdill (1948), which was then known as the trait theory of leadership. According to Northouse (2018), the trait approach is developed based on theoretical assumptions of the Great Man theory of Thomas Carlyle, which assumes that powerful leaders are made of numerous innate or learned characteristics. This approach emphasizes numerous leadership characteristics, varying from personality and skills, to values and attributes (Yukl, 2013). Brandstätter (2011) defines personality traits as abilities, behaviors, and attributes of temperament as an overarching approach of an individual.

According to Çpğaltay (2015) and Stogdill (1948), the most referenced traits and abilities are intelligence, self-confidence, decisiveness, consistency, and sociability. Northouse (2018), on the other hand, states that the Five-Factor Personality Model is the most mutually agreed and supported model among scholars. As defined in Northouse (2018), this model includes *Neuroticism* (characteristics of leaders who are miserable, fearful, insecure, vulnerable, and unfriendly), *Extraversion* (characteristics of leaders who are sociable, assertive, and have positive energy), *Openness* (characteristics of leaders who are informed, innovative, insightful, and eager to learn), *Agreeableness* (characteristics of leaders who are conforming, believing, and cultivating), and *Conscientiousness* (characteristics of leaders who are detailed, organized, controlled, reliable, and decisive).

The trait theory of leadership is expanded to leadership skills and competences, in which leadership competencies can be learned and leadership skills involve technical, human, and conceptual skills (Katz and Kahn, 1978; Zaccaro *et al.*, 2000). Other leadership concepts developed later are leadership motive profile theory (McClelland and Boyatzis, 1982) and emotional intelligence in leadership (Goleman, 2006; Walter *et al.*, 2011).

### 3.2. *Behavioral leadership*

Based on the outcomes of the work of Blake and Mounton (1964), the behavioral leadership approach develops a new way to define and conceptualize a leadership model that highlights the actions and behaviors of leaders rather than their inherent characteristics (Yukl, 2013). Most findings in behavioral leadership are converted into Blake and Mouton's managerial leadership grid of 1964. This grid is beneficial for leaders to understand and develop relevant leadership behaviors (Çğaltay, 2015).

In addition, the research carried out at Ohio State and Michigan Universities assume that leaders exhibit dual behavior types: considerate (people-oriented) and imitating structure (task-oriented) (Northouse, 2018). According to Yukl (2013), while task-oriented leaders provide their subordinates with direct and detailed instructions on their assigned tasks, relationship-oriented leaders focus on developing mutual relationships, fostering collaboration, and improving commitments. Although many scholars refer to this two-factor model to find a comprehensive theory of leadership, this dual behavior fails to take situations into account and identify which behaviors are effective in such contexts (Yukl, 2013). Yukl *et al.* (2002) mention about change-oriented leadership and combine it with the foregoing two-factor leadership behaviors to conceptualize a hierarchical taxonomy of leadership behavior. Over the years, many other leadership theories related to behaviors have been put forth, for example, leadership reward and punishment (Podsakoff *et al.*, 1984), participative leadership (Huang *et al.*, 2010), or ethical leadership, servant leadership, spiritual leadership, authentic leadership, and so on (Çğaltay, 2015).

### 3.3. *Situational leadership*

On account of Reddin (1967)'s 3-D administrative style theory, another approach emerged in the late 1960s called situational or contingency leadership (Aronson, 2009). Hersey and Blanckhard (1969) develop the Situational Leadership Theory based on Reddin's theory, aiming to illustrate varying leadership behaviors required in different contexts: directing, coaching, supporting, and delegating (Graeff, 1983). Besides, there are major works under the umbrella of the situational approach with varying results (Butler Jr and Reese, 1991; Thompson and Glasø, 2015; Silverthorne, 2000).

Fiedler's Contingency Theory (1964, 1967) implies that effective leadership stems from harmonious linkages between leadership behaviors, time, and settings. This model includes three variables (leader–member relations, task structure, and position power) and two leadership styles (task-motivated and relationship-motivated) (Campbell and Fiedler, 1968).

Path–Goal Theory, developed by House (1971), contains two leadership behaviors: instructing-supportive and success oriented-participatory. This theory refers to how leaders clearly determine the path to achieve the goals, remove possible hindrances on the way, and motivate their subordinates to accomplish the allocated goals (House and Mitchell, 1974).

Kerr and Jermier (1978) introduce the substitute theory of leadership, meaning that leadership can be replaced with processes and task structures. Murphy *et al.* (1992) develop cognitive resource theory and state that leaders have to take advantage of followers' intellectual abilities and experiential capabilities to improve organizational capabilities.

It can be argued that situational leadership approaches contribute to leadership effectiveness and organizational outcomes. However, some criticisms remain in terms of the over-dependence of employees on their leaders to fulfill goals, poor quality of measurements (Northouse, 2018), or the complex nature and doubtful validity of this approach (Yukl, 2013).

### 3.4. *Transformational leadership*

A new leadership era in literature is marked by the introduction of Charismatic leadership by House in 1976, followed by Transformational and Transactional leadership by Burns in 1978.

Charismatic leadership discusses various personality characteristics (e.g., dominant and desire to influence), behaviors (e.g., shows competence and articulates goals), and impact on subordinates (e.g., affection toward leader and obedience) (Northouse, 2018).

With regard to the transformational approach, leaders develop their leadership styles after identifying personal values that guide the actions and values of other people at the workplace (Burns, 1978). In 1985, Bass extended Burns's (1978) research findings by adding *Laissez–Faire Leadership* to the models of transformational and transactional leaderships. Bass calls the new model a *Full Range of Leadership Model.*

In the full range model, transformational leadership factors involve idealized influence, inspirational motivation, intellectual stimulation, and individualized consideration. Idealized influence deals with how leaders act as role models for followers. Inspirational motivation is how leaders set goals for followers and motivate them toward a shared vision. Intellectual stimulation deliberates on how leaders help followers to be more creative, innovative, and careful when dealing with problems. Individualized consideration describes how considerate and supportive leaders are towards their followers' demands. Contingent reward and Management-by-exception are two factors of transactional leadership. The former is how leaders reward their followers and in turn expect them to be active. The latter is how leaders use feedback, criticism, and reinforcement in either an active or passive way. Laissez-faire or non-transaction factor means that leaders rule out responsibility, provide no feedback, and express no concerns for the needs of their followers (Çğaltay, 2015; Northouse, 2018).

One limitation of transformational leadership, according to Lord (2008), lies in not only the conceptualization of leaders as individuals but also its failure to consider the organizational context and the advent of unpredictable leadership. The author argues that the ignorance of organizational context can result in limited understanding of the creation of organizational change. In addition, Yukl (2013) states that transformational leaders may lack the cognitive skills required for facing increasingly complex and tough difficulties due to changed environmental situations. Similarly, according to Northouse (2018), there is no definite conclusion about a causal relation between transformational leadership and organizational change. Hence, a gap exists in the conceptualization of leadership when dealing with organizational context and the emergence of change and innovation.

## 4. Emerging Conceptions of Leadership

According to Bennis (2007), although scholars view leadership as a leading concept in organizational research, they have not yet agreed upon a unified theoretical perspective of this phenomenon. Some research practitioners rely on traditional approaches to conceptualize leadership that appears to be comprehensive. By contrast, other scholars exhibit a critical view towards prevailing leadership approaches and therefore prefer to employ newly emerging conceptions of relational leadership, shared and distributed leadership, or complexity theory of leadership in their studies (Drath *et al.*, 2008).

### 4.1. *Shared/distributed and relational leadership*

Under the shared/distributed approach, leadership is viewed as reciprocal, recursive influence processes among multiple leaders with different but inter-related responsibilities (Yukl, 2013). According to Van Ameijde *et al.* (2009, p. 776), distributed leadership is defined as *a shared influence process to which several individuals contribute*. The group of authors also mention that this leadership approach *arises from the interactions of diverse individuals which together form a group or network in which essential expertise is a dispersed quality.* Bolden (2011) says that most research interest in shared/distributed leadership is on education fields. In contrast, the author highlights that only one-fifth of published papers on distributed leadership and one-quarter of published papers on shared leadership can be accessed in business and management journals. This is indicative that this leadership approach is still not familiar in the business and management fields.

According to Yukl (2013, p. 295), relational leadership considers leadership as *part of an evolving social order that results from interactions, exchanges, and influence processes among many people in an organization.* Researchers of relational leadership aim to explore the social process and recurrent connections that describe the ways collective efforts can fulfill shared goals. Uhl-Bien (2006) defines this approach as a relational and ethical process of individuals who are making collective efforts to foster positive change. Most research on relational leadership is found in the education or healthcare industry, while little notice is paid to exploring this theory and its effects on organizational functions, especially in other sectors (Akram *et al.*, 2016).

Shared/distributed and relational theories seem inadequate to describe the impact of leadership, especially of the chief executive officer (CEO) or the top management, on the organizations (Yukl, 2013). Marion and Uhl-Bien (2001) mention the complexity theory of leadership is more relevant to the upper echelons. Moreover, this theory is also used to illustrate emergent processes and help organizations adapt to the current chaotic environment.

### 4.2. *Complexity theory of leadership*

Complexity theory of leadership looks at leadership theory from a relational standpoint and draws upon the complexity science to categorize leadership as an asset of a social system (Clarke, 2013). Hence, leadership within complexity theory can be defined in a more comprehensive way, involving structures, activities, and processes that facilitate the organizations to face challenges like uncertainty, ambiguity in the working environment (Clarke, 2013).

Similarly, Uhl-Bien *et al.* (2007) propose that complexity leadership theory is relevant in today's challenging, complex, and knowledge-driven era, which demands the creation of knowledge, learning processes, and innovative solutions. These authors identify three types of processes in this leadership theory. Administrative leadership refers to actions and conclusions made by the formal hierarchy of the firm (CEO, directors, managers, and other formal leaders). These people oversee action planning and coordination at work (Yukl, 2013; Uhl-Bien *et al.*, 2007). Although administrative leadership bears resemblance to traditional leadership behaviors, it is merely a part of the whole leadership process in complexity leadership theory. Adaptive leadership is *an emergent, interactive dynamic that produces adaptive outcomes in a social system* (Uhl-Bien *et al.*, 2007, p. 306). This leadership behavior represents a process arising from collective interactions of those with diverse knowledge and opinions aiming to handle problems and conflicts (Yukl, 2013). Yukl also states that the process within adaptive leadership catalyzes innovative ideas and insights that are vital for conflict resolution and responsive adaptation to turbulence and prospective changes. Enabling leadership is how an individual or a team fosters interactions among different agents, enhances self-organization, enables others to access necessary resources, and provides a spark for creative ideas to be implemented (Yukl, 2013; Uhl-Bien *et al.*, 2007). Yukl (2013) also highlights another role of enabling leadership: keeping administrative leadership and adaptive leadership stable and mutually well-matched.

### 4.3. *Complexity leadership and transformational leadership*

According to Marion and Uhl-Bien (2002), Complexity Leadership differs from traditional leadership approaches in a number of ways. Specifically, leadership in complexity theory does not directly affect organizational dynamics but through a process of collective interaction and emergence, embedded in managerial roles yet diffused through the complex system (Uhl-Bien *et al.*, 2007; Marion and Uhl-Bien, 2002). In a paper presented at a conference, Marion and Uhl-Bien (2002) pointed out some differences between Complexity Leadership with the commonly used leadership theory, transformational leadership. The comparison of the two authors is summarized in Table 1.

In addition, Transformational Leadership Theory (leader-oriented) cannot fully explain organizational creativity and the process that facilitates the adaptation of organizations to the environments. On the other hand, the complexity theory of leadership (process-oriented) addresses this issue and further explains the responsibilities of leaders in the adaptation process (Yukl, 2013; Marion and Uhl-Bien, 2002). From this perspective, Complexity Leadership is considered to remediate the restriction of Transformational Leadership, especially in the study of organizational change and innovation in the current complex and ambiguous working environment.

### 4.4. *Previous studies on complexity theory of leadership*

Research on complexity theory of leadership is scarce. Much of the published work on this concept is literature reviews based on theoretical and conceptual discussion/analysis (Nienaber and Svensson, 2013; Hogue and Lord, 2007; Schneider and Somers, 2006; Halbesleben *et al.*, 2003). For example, Schneider and Somers (2006) review literature in general systems theory and complex adaptive system to present a rudimentary leadership model and introduce nonlinear methodologies called dynamic systems simulation and artificial

**Table 1:** Complexity leadership and transformational leadership.

| Transformational leadership | Complexity leadership |
|---|---|
| Sees control as top-down, according to the leaders' decisions | Sees control as bottom-up, related to the dynamics of the system |
| Focuses on top-down, leader-centric activity | Focuses on bottom-up, collective interactions within the whole social network |
| Sees leaders as central to organizational functions and outcome | Sees leaders as an important part of a larger dynamic |
| Describes leaders as "managers of meaning" | Describes leaders as "managers of emergence" |
| Outlines transformation as inducing subordinates to go beyond their self-interests for collective achievements and success | Outlines transformation as an emergent dedication to innovation and productivity from different objectives at the bottom of the hierarchy |
| Transforms the followers' behaviors around a mutual vision | Transforms a social system into a neural network of varied and flexible agents |
| Converts individuals into their own replicas | Converts individuals into varied but interrelated complex adaptive agents |
| Defines social action as stable relationships or numerous linear events | Defines social action as a collection of events involving nonlinear activities |

*Source*: Adapted from Marion & Uhl-Bien (2002).

neural networks for scholars to refer to in developing and analyzing leadership models under complexity theory. In a piece of research on two case studies in the Netherlands, Nooteboom and Termeer (2013) utilize complexity leadership theory and participatory observation techniques to identify adaptive and enabling leadership strategies that can spur innovation in a complex environment. Recently, Mendes *et al.* (2016) reviewed the literature on complexity leadership theory, learning and innovation in turbulent environments, and reflected on how adaptive, administrative, and enabling leadership behaviors in the theory simultaneously affect organizational outcomes. Specifically, they proposed that complexity leadership theory can be employed to better explain the emergence of organizational learning and innovation that consequently affect performance. The group of authors also called attention to the further development and examination of this conceptual framework.

## 5. Conclusion and Areas for Future Research

Leadership is undeniably an interesting theme for researchers to explore over many years. A variety of leadership concepts and theories are postulated by many authors and scholars (Çğaltay, 2015; Northouse, 2018; Yukl, 2013; Burns, 1978; House, 1971; Campbell and Fiedler, 1968). Early studies are conducted to investigate the outcomes of mainly well-known leadership styles such as transformational leadership, ethical leadership, leader–member exchange leadership (Wang *et al.*, 2011; Ogbonna and Harris, 2000; Ruiz-Palomino *et al.*, 2011; Volmer *et al.*, 2012; Jia *et al.*, 2018). These prevailing approaches facilitate a moderate but insufficient understanding of leadership and its impact.

Nevertheless, this field has evolved over the decades. Emerging conceptions of this field of study, such as shared leadership, distributed leadership, relational leadership, and complexity theory of leadership, appeared and have contributed to the wealth of leadership literature. These new leadership concepts are understudied in the literature and empirical research; thus yielding potential research opportunities for the future. More studies that examine the effects of other emerging leadership concepts on workplace dynamics are encouraged to advance the field.

In addition, it is believed that adopting a leader-centered standpoint can result in a narrowed understanding of leadership phenomenon in organizations (Mendes *et al.*, 2016; Yukl, 2013; Uhl-Bien *et al.*, 2007). According to Yukl (2013) and Rosing *et al.* (2011), individual and dyadic theories are insufficient to address the complexities that organizations face in the present day. Considering this research gap, Complexity Leadership Theory, which is considered to remediate the restriction of other theories, especially the widely used approach, i.e., Transformational Leadership (Marion and Uhl-Bien, 2002), should receive the attention it deserves.

Further empirical research is also needed to advance the complexity theory of leadership as an approach. Empirical studies on this leadership theory are scarce. Some studies theoretically discuss complexity leadership and its influences on some phenomena such as performance, organizational learning, and innovation (Nienaber and Svensson, 2013; Hogue and Lord, 2007; Schneider and Somers, 2006; Halbesleben *et al.*, 2003, Mendes *et al.*, 2016). Since the results from these studies potentially allow for bias, future empirical and even longitudinal studies conducted within different contexts are encouraged to both further explore this leadership approach and validate its association with other outcomes. Notably, Mendes *et al.* (2016) call for research to validate the relationships among complexity leadership theory, organizational learning, and innovation. To the best of the authors' knowledge, there are little or even no empirical studies examining such associations. Hence, this is also a research gap that future studies could consider.

## References

Akram, T., Lei, S., Hussain, S.T., Haider, M.J., and Akram, M.W. (2016). Does relational leadership generate organizational social capital? A case of exploring the effect of relational leadership on organizational social capital in China. *Future Business Journal*, 2(2), 116–126.

Alimo-Metcalfe, B. (2013). A critical review of leadership theory. In Leonard, H.S., Lewis, R., Freedman, A.M., and Passmore, J. (eds.), *The Wiley-Blackwell Handbook of the Psychology of Leadership, Change and Organizational Development*. San Francisco: John Wiley and Sons, pp. 15–47.

Aronson, E. (2009). Integrating leadership styles and ethical perspectives. *Canadian Journal of Administrative Sciences/Revue Canadienne Des Sciences de l'Administration*, 18(4), 244–256.

Asrar-ul-Haq, M., and Anwar, S. (2018). The many faces of leadership: Proposing research agenda through a review of literature. *Future Business Journal*, 4(2), 179–188.

Bennis, W. (2007). The challenges of leadership in the modern world: Introduction to the special issue. *American Psychologist*, 62(1), 2–5.

Bhattacharyya, S.S., and Jha, S. (2018). Literature review of leadership theories. *Strategic Leadership Models and Theories: Indian Perspectives*, Emerald Publishing Limited, pp. 7–18.

Blake, R.R., and Mouton, J.S. (1964), *The Managerial Grid: Key Orientations for Achieving Production Through People*. Houston, Tex: Gulf Pub. Co.

Bolden, R. (2011). Distributed leadership in organizations: A review of theory and research. *International Journal of Management Reviews*, 13(3), 251–269.

Brandstätter, H. (2011). Personality aspects of entrepreneurship: A look at five meta-analyses. *Personality and individual differences*, 51(3), 222–230.

Burns, J.M. (1978). *Leadership*. New York: Harper and Row.

Butler Jr., J.-K., and Reese, R.M. (1991). Leadership style and sales performance: A test of the situational leadership® model. *Journal of Personal Selling and Sales Management*, 11(3), 37–46.

Campbell, R.N., and Fiedler, F.E. (1968). A theory of leadership effectiveness. *Administrative Science Quarterly*, 13(2), 344.

Clark, C.M., and Harrison, C. (2018). Leadership: The complexities and state of the field. *European Business Review*, 30(5), 514–528.

Clarke, N. (2013). Model of complexity leadership development. *Human Resource Development International*, 16(2), 135–150.

Çoğaltay, N. (2015). Conceptual perspectives on leadership. In Karadağ, E. (ed.), *Leadership and Organizational Outcomes Meta-Analysis of Empirical Studies*. Switzerland: Springer International Publishing.

Drath, W.H., McCauley, C.D., Palus, C.J., Van Velsor, E., O'Connor, P.M.G., and McGuire, J.B. (2008). Direction, alignment, commitment: Toward a more integrative ontology of leadership. *The Leadership Quarterly*, 19(6), 635–653.

Elenkov, D.S. (2002). Effects of leadership on organizational performance in Russian companies. *Journal of Business Research*, 55(6), 467–480.

Goleman, D. (2006). *Emotional Intelligence*. New York: Bantam.

Graeff, C.L. (1983). The situational leadership theory: A critical view. *Academy of Management Review*, 8(2), 285–291.

Halbesleben, J.R.B., Novicevic, M.M., Harvey, M.G., and Buckley, M.R. (2003). Awareness of temporal complexity in leadership of creativity and innovation: A competency-based model. *The Leadership Quarterly*, 14(4–5), 433–454.

Hersey, P., and Blanchard, K. (1969). Life cycle theory of leadership. *Training and Development Journal*, 23(2), 26–34.

Hogue, M., and Lord, R.G. (2007). A multilevel, complexity theory approach to understanding gender bias in leadership. *The Leadership Quarterly*, 18(4), 370–390.

House, R.J. (1971). A path goal theory of leader effectiveness. *Administrative Science Quarterly*, 16(3), 321.

House, R.J. (1976). A 1976 theory of charismatic leadership. Working Paper Series 76-06, Southern Illinois University Fourth Biennial Leadership Symposium.

House, R.J., and Mitchell, T.R. (1974). Path-goal theory and leadership. *Journal of Contemporary Business*, 3, 81–97.

Huang, X., Iun, J., Liu, A., and Gong, Y. (2010). Does participative leadership enhance work performance by inducing empowerment or trust? The differential effects on managerial and non-managerial subordinates. *Journal of Organizational Behavior*, 31(1), 122–143.

Jia, X., Chen, J., Mei, L., and Wu, Q. (2018). How leadership matters in organizational innovation: A perspective of openness. *Management Decision*, 56(1), 6–25.

Katz, D., and Kahn, R.L. (1978). *The Social Psychology of Organizations*. New York: Wiley.

Kerr, S., and Jermier, J.M. (1978). Substitutes for leadership: Their meaning and measurement. *Organizational Behavior and Human Performance*, 22(3), 375–403.

Koene, B.A., Vogelaar, A.L., and Soeters, J.L. (2002). Leadership effects on organizational climate and financial performance. *The Leadership Quarterly*, 13(3), 193–215.

Lord, R. (2008). Beyond transactional and transformational leadership: Can leaders still lead when they don't know what to do? In M. Uhl-Bien and R. Marion (eds.), *Complexity Leadership Part 1: Conceptual Foundations*. Charlotte, NC: Information Age, pp. 155–184.

Marion, R., and Uhl-Bien, M. (2001). Leadership in complex organizations. *The Leadership Quarterly*, 12(4), 389–418.

Marion, R., and Uhl-Bien, M. (2002). Complexity v. transformation: The new leadership revisited. In Presented at *Managing the Complex IV — Conference on Complex Systems and the Management of Organizations*, Ft. Meyers, FL.

McClelland, D.C., and Boyatzis, R.E. (1982). Leadership motive pattern and long-term success in management. *Journal of Applied Psychology*, 67(6), 737.

Mendes, M., Gomes, C., Marques-Quinteiro, P., Lind, P., and Curral, L. (2016). Promoting learning and innovation in organizations through complexity leadership theory. *Team Performance Management: An International Journal*, 22(5/6), 301–309.

Murphy, S.E., Blyth, D., and Fiedler, F.E. (1992). Cognitive resource theory and the utilization of the leader's and group members' technical competence. *The Leadership Quarterly*, 3(3), 237–255.

Nienaber, H., and Svensson, G. (2013). An analysis of the contribution of leadership to organizational performance using complexity science. *Journal of Management Development*, 32(8), 836–851.

Nooteboom, S.G., and Termeer, C.J.A.M. (2013). Strategies of complexity leadership in governance systems. *International Review of Public Administration*, 18(1), 25–40.

Northouse, P.G. (2018). *Leadership: Theory and Practice*, 8th edition. Thousand Oaks, CA: Sage Publications, Inc.

Ogbonna, E., and Harris, L.C. (2000). Leadership style, organizational culture and performance: Empirical evidence from UK companies. *The International Journal of Human Resource Management*, 11(4), 766–788.

Podsakoff, P.M., Todor, W.D., Grover, R.A., and Huber, V.L. (1984). Situational moderators of leader reward and punishment behaviors: Fact or fiction?. *Organizational Behavior and Human Performance*, 34(1), 21–63.

Reddin, W.J. (1967). 3-D Management style theory-typology based on task and relationships orientations. *Training and Development Journal*, 21(4), 8–17.

Rosing, K., Frese, M., and Bausch, A. (2011). Explaining the heterogeneity of the leadership-innovation relationship: Ambidextrous leadership. *The Leadership Quarterly*, 22(5), 956–974.

Ruiz-Palomino, P., Ruiz-Amaya, C., and Knörr, H. (2011). Employee organizational citizenship behavior: The direct and indirect impact of ethical leadership. *Canadian Journal of Administrative Sciences/ Revue Canadienne Des Sciences de l'Administration*, 28(3), 244–258.

Schneider, M., and Somers, M. (2006). Organizations as complex adaptive systems: Implications of Complexity Theory for leadership research. *The Leadership Quarterly*, 17(4), 351–365.

Silverthorne, C. (2000). Situational leadership theory in Taiwan: A different culture perspective. *Leadership and Organization Development Journal*, 21(2), 68–74.

Stogdill, R.M. (1948). Personal factors associated with leadership: A survey of the literature. *The Journal of Psychology: Interdisciplinary and Applied*, 25, 35–71.

Stogdill, R.M. (1975). The evaluation of leadership theory. *Academy of Management Proceedings*, 1975(1), 4–6.

Thompson, G., and Glasø, L. (2015). Situational leadership theory: A test from three perspectives. *Leadership and Organization Development Journal*, 36(5), 527–544.

Uhl-Bien, M. (2006). Relational leadership theory: Exploring the social processes of leadership and organizing. *The Leadership Quarterly*, 17(6), 654–676.

Uhl-Bien, M., Marion, R., and McKelvey, B. (2007). Complexity leadership theory: Shifting leadership from the industrial age to the knowledge era. *The Leadership Quarterly*, 18(4), 298–318.

Van Ameijde, J.D.J., Nelson, P.C., Billsberry, J., and van Meurs, N. (2009). Improving leadership in Higher Education institutions: A distributed perspective. *Higher Education*, 58(6), 763–779.

Van Seters, D.A., and Field, R.H.G. (1990). The evolution of leadership theory. *Journal of Organizational Change Management*, 3(3), 29–45.

Volmer, J., Spurk, D., and Niessen, C. (2012). Leader–member exchange (LMX), job autonomy, and creative work involvement. *The Leadership Quarterly*, 23(3), 456–465.

Walter, F., Cole, M.S., and Humphrey, R.H. (2011). Emotional intelligence: Sine qua non of leadership or folderol?. *Academy of Management Perspectives*, 25(1), 45–59.

Wang, H., Tsui, A.S., and Xin, K.R. (2011). CEO leadership behaviors, organizational performance, and employees' attitudes. *The Leadership Quarterly*, 22(1), 92–105.

Yukl, G.A. (2013). *Leadership in Organizations*, 8th edition. New Delhi: Pearson Prentice Hall.

Yukl, G., Gordon, A., and Taber, T. (2002). A hierarchical taxonomy of leadership behavior: Integrating a half century of behavior research. *Journal of Leadership and Organizational Studies*, 9(1), 15–32.

Zaccaro, S., Mumford, M., Connelly, M., Marks, M., and Gilbert, J. (2000). Assessment of leader problem-solving capabilities. *The Leadership Quarterly*, 11(1), 37–64.

https://doi.org/10.1142/9789811227158_0014

# Chapter 14

# How Does Authentic Leadership Influence Employee–Organization Relationship? The Mediating Role of Symmetrical Internal Communication

**Mai Dong Tran, Thi Kim Quy Hoang, and Phong Nguyen Nguyen**

## Abstract

This current study examines the impacts of authentic leadership (AL) on symmetrical internal communication (SIC) and employee–organization relationships (EORs) in the context of the aviation industry in Vietnam. The proposed model and hypotheses are tested using survey data from 175 employees working in aviation organizations in Ho Chi Minh City. The structural equation modeling (SEM) results indicate that AL positively affects EORs both directly and indirectly, through SIC. The results mean SIC acts as a device connecting AL to enhanced EORs. Also, the study provides theoretical and practical implications as well as suggested directions for future research.

**Keywords:** Authentic leadership; Employee–organization relationships; Symmetrical internal communication.

## 1. Research Background

Internal communication is always a vital process by which employees share information, targets, and relationships, make meaning and establish an organizational culture as well as an organizational value

(Berger, 2008). Internal communication is considered a fundamental factor of modern organizations. Numerous scholars have suggested that effective internal communication plays a critical role in developing positive follower attitudes such as trust, organizational commitment (Jo and Shim, 2005), job satisfaction (Gray and Laidlaw, 2004), identification with an organization (Smidts *et al.*, 2001), and positive employee–organization relationships (EORs)(Men and Stacks, 2014). These attitudes and behaviors, in turn, increase productivity, improve performance, and build greater relationships with other stakeholders (Men and Stacks, 2014).

Recognizing the importance of employees in achieving an organization's successes, researchers have broadly conducted studies exploring the drivers of internal communication effectiveness. Grunig *et al.* (2003) suggested that a participative organizational culture, an organic structure, gender equality, and power symmetry are the key factors that facilitate the organization's internal communication. However, in recent years, researchers have noticed the influences of leadership on internal communication. Leaders' communication styles are one of the main contextual factors in the internal communication system in the organization (Men, 2014) that affect followers' attitudes and behaviors (Berger, 2008; Kim and Rhee, 2011; Men and Stacks, 2014). Furthermore, leaders enable context and determine the degree to which internal communication takes place.

Leadership at different organizational levels directly or indirectly determines structural forms, organizational culture and climate, power distribution, and communication. Different types of leaderships advocate different communication styles to influence followers and thus constitute a major component of the internal communication system (Men, 2014). In addition, the leader's communication competencies and behaviors, as well as leadership styles, are closely connected to work outcomes and the quality of EORs.

Most previous studies investigated the relationships between internal communication and general leadership style (Kim and Rhee, 2011; Shen, 2011; Waters *et al.*, 2013; Men, 2014; Men and Stacks, 2014). Similarly, a prominent role of a specific leadership style in that relationship has not yet been proven broadly in various contexts in research, i.e., authentic leadership (AL). AL embraces considerable effects on the internal communication system in an organization (Men and Stacks, 2014). According to George *et al.* (2007), authentic leaders demonstrate a passion for their purpose, lead with their hearts as well as their heads, and their values are practiced consistently. Previous scholars suggested that authentic leaders establish long-term, meaningful relationships and have the self-discipline to get results. They know who they are and become true to themselves. Thus, they proactively foster positive environments where their employees can efficiently conduct two-way communication, including feedback about their managers, whether it is good or not.

Furthermore, authentic leaders openly share information and expressions of their true thoughts and feelings while trying to minimize displays of inappropriate emotions (Kernis, 2003). They do not hesitate to disclose information related to making decisions or any issues happening within the organization which employees have the right to know and respond to. Besides, authentic leaders recognize that leadership is not about their success or about getting loyal subordinates to follow them (George *et al.*, 2007). Thanks to their characters, authentic leaders are noted to foster long-term relationships with their subordinates. Moreover, they act in harmony with their words as well as deep personal values and convictions to build credibility and win the respect and trust of followers (Walumbwa *et al.*, 2008). These things make a significant contribution to employee engagement and improve the quality of EORs. Although AL generates numerous positive outcomes, most studies are conducted in western countries, which are characterized by individualism value and low-power distance (Gardner *et al.*, 2011).

Recently, a few empirical studies have directly examined the effects of internal communication with EORs (Kim, 2007; Kim and Rhee, 2011; Men, 2014; Men and Stacks, 2014; Shen, 2011; Waters *et al.*, 2013). In contrast, some researchers have tested the linkages between internal communication and organization performance (Dozier, 1990; Grunig *et al.*, 2003; Meng and Berger, 2012;

Michaelson and Stacks, 2014; Yates, 2006) as well as the influences of leadership styles, particularly AL, on top manager's communication forms of effective internal communication, employee engagement, and positive EOR (Kang and Sung, 2017; Men, 2015; Men and Stacks, 2014). Leadership styles and excellent communication have significantly proven to nurture better relationships between employees and their organizations (Kang and Sung, 2017; Kernis, 2003; Lockwood, 2007; Michaelson and Stacks, 2014).

However, the studies on the relationship among leadership styles, internal communication, and the quality of EOR have limitations in Vietnam's current business context. Vietnamese enterprises' perceptions of these strategic problems have been misunderstood (Luu, 2019). They have not determined the importance of effective internal communication in enhancing company performance, specifically, top manager's roles in applying leadership perspectives to increase employee commitment through effective internal communication systems in the organization (Luu, 2019). Thus, this study develops a leadership–communication–relation (LCR) framework that explains how AL affects EORs in the context of the aviation industry in Vietnam. This study also tests the direct effect of AL style on EORs, and the mediating role of symmetrical internal communication on the relationship between AL and EORs. The findings provide significant implications for communication professionals and organizational leaders on how to develop the best practices of internal communication and positive employee attitudes and behavior that contribute to organizational effectiveness in a transition market.

## 2. Theoretical Background and Hypothesis Development

### 2.1. *Authentic leadership and symmetrical internal communication*

Authentic leaders are generally highly aware of their values and are more likely to act following these values. Through their consistent actions, they become role models for their followers. Based on their openness and truthfulness, an openly sharing environment is created in their organization. In this respect, Walumbwa *et al.* (2008, 2010) argue that authenticity is often accompanied by open communication, disclosure, and the expressions of one's true and genuine thoughts and feelings. Likewise, authentic leaders recognized that, once they are true to themselves and their followers, accurate flow of information will come to them. Further, the importance of two-way internal communication is always embraced in organizations in which authentic leaders lead. To maintain sustainable relationships with subordinates, authentic leaders genuinely care about the employees' well-being. Notably, they highly emphasize the symmetrical notion of non-manipulations of followers (Walumbwa *et al.*, 2010). Moreover, in the AL construct suggested by Walumbwa *et al.* (2008), one of the core dimensions is balanced processing of information, which refers to critical responsibilities of AL in processing information to make decisions. In other words, authentic leaders do not hesitate to reckon with any issues; even if these matters bring negative impacts for them. Interestingly, authentic leaders are willing to support an open and fair working environment with transparent information for their employees (Men and Stacks, 2014). Particularly, to the extent possible, authentic leaders disclose work-related information in a transparent and open fashion, as long as doing so does not violate the privacy or safety of others.

Additionally, when undesirable situations occur and full disclosure would be inappropriate, such leaders release as much information as possible while communicating the reasons for withholding certain facts. As a result, followers catch up with the reasons behind a leader's decision, which limits the fear of the unknown and fosters feelings of trust (Gardner *et al.*, 2011). Similarly, due to their high self-awareness and internalized moral perspective, authentic leaders are open to feedback, whether it is good or not about themselves. Thus, AL communication is characterized by openness, consistency, transparency, truthfulness, and accountability (Men and Stacks, 2014). Moreover, Men (2014) reports a positive correlation between

AL and SIC. The study also demonstrates the role of leadership's communication with followers in an internal communication setting. In addition, when employees are supervised by authentic leaders, they are more likely to perceive the organization's communication as symmetrical. Based on the discussion, this study hypothesizes as follows:

**Hypothesis H1:** *Authentic leadership has a positive effect on symmetrical communication.*

### 2.2. *Authentic leadership and employee–organization relationships*

AL has been linked to diverse antecedents and outcomes, both theoretically and empirically (Gardner *et al.*, 2011). Many researchers provide evidence that AL can be great for any organization or team. Overall, Gardner *et al.* (2011) propose that AL is connected to the positive leader (psychological well-being), positive follower's behaviors and attitudes such as empowerment, job outcomes, job satisfaction, organizational citizenship behaviors, employee engagement, trust in leadership, motivation, innovation to work, and organizational outcomes (openness of organizational climate and firm financial performance). Scholars also present the negative relationship between AL and undesirable outcomes such as follower burnout (Gardner *et al.*, 2011). Together, these results provide evidence of the predictive validity of the AL construct. AL receives great attention due to increasing changes in the business environment and crisis periods. People believe that authenticity is a crucial element that leaders need to have to lead their organization to succeed in a dynamic environment like today's. Therefore, there is a variety of research, noting a positive linkage between AL and various outcomes such as perceived leader effectiveness, followers' extra efforts, satisfaction with the leader (Moriano *et al.*, 2011; Neider and Schriesheim, 2011), followers' essential need satisfaction, followers' organizational commitment (Neider and Schriesheim, 2011), and followers' affective commitment (Leroy *et al.*, 2012). Likewise, Walumbwa *et al.* (2008) and Wong and

Cummings (2009) find that AL contributes to employees' job performance and trust. A study by Jensen and Luthans (2006) reveals that authentic leaders have positive impacts on employees' work happiness and organizational commitment. Authentic leaders are identified with consistent actions based on their values. What they say and do is associated with their fundamental and deeply rooted shared values with the organization and high moral standards. Thus, authentic leaders increase their followers' trust and commitment (Berger, 2008). Men (2011) suggests that employees' favorable identification of the organization and employee engagement is cultivated by the perceived credibility of an organization's senior leadership. Next, when the organization's leadership is considered as trustworthy and credible, employees tend to engage with the organization more. Identical notions may also be applied to the employees' immediate leaders. Additionally, authentic leaders can easily become role models for their subordinates because they never ignore their followers' perspectives and utilize such inputs in making decisions. They are oriented toward building a quality relationship with their followers. A positive environment, including higher levels of disclosure, transparency, two-way communication, and relationship orientation characterized by AL, establishes a context where employees feel trusted and empowered. Based on these specific contributions, employee trust, control mutuality, satisfaction, and commitment to the organization are boosted. Therefore, this study hypothesizes as follows:

**Hypothesis H2:** *Authentic leadership has a positive effect on employee–organization relationships.*

### 2.3. *Symmetrical communication and employee–organization relationships*

Previous studies have provided significant evidence on the effectiveness of SIC in fostering EORs. Kim and Rhee (2011) argue that SIC and EORs are antecedents influencing communication behaviors of the leaders. The study also reports a significant positive correlation between SIC and EORs. In line with this, Vu (2013) investigates

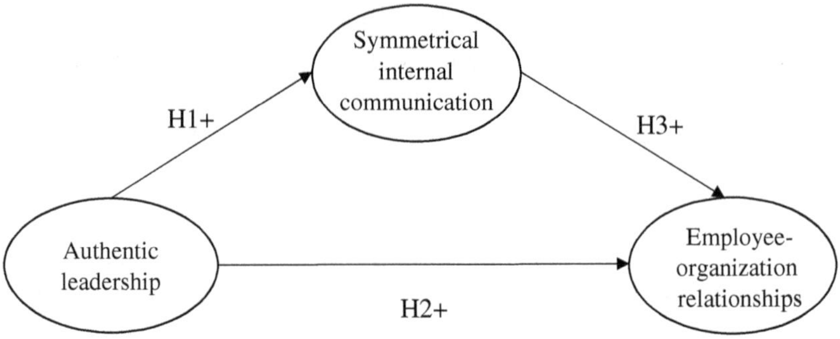


**Figure 1:** The proposed model.

the effects of the four-dimensional internal communication construct on employee engagement with a sample of employees working in Ho Chi Minh's large companies and finds that effective internal communication enhances employee engagement and makes a significant contribution to the company's development. Besides, Kang and Sung (2017), Men (2014), and Men and Stacks (2014) suggest that SIC has a strong connection to EORs. Furthermore, Grunig *et al.* (2003) note that excellent employee communications could ultimately nurture quality employee relationships and supportive employee behaviors toward the organizations. Based on the above-mentioned discussion, this study hypothesizes as follows:

**Hypothesis H3:** *Symmetrical internal communication has a positive effect on employee–organization relationships.*

The proposed research model is shown in Figure 1.

## 3. Research Methods

### 3.1. *Measurement scale*

The measures of key constructs in this study are adapted from previous studies (Grunig and Huang, 2000; Kang and Sung, 2017; Neider and Schriesheim, 2011). AL is assessed using the 14-item scale of Neider and Schriesheim (2011) which comprises four dimensions: self-awareness, relational transparency, internalized morals, and balanced processing. The SIC scale with five items is adapted from Kang and Sung (2017) and Dozier *et al.* (2010) with some modifications based on reviewing literature as well as capturing the Vietnamese context. EORs are assessed along the dimensions of trust, satisfaction, commitment, and control mutuality in Grunig and Huang (2000)'s 12 item-scale. The combined English questionnaire is translated into Vietnamese and then back-translated into English to ensure instrument equivalence following the procedure suggested by Brislin (1970). The Vietnamese self-administrated survey is printed and sent to respondents for data collection. All items are measured by a 5-point Likert scale, including "totally disagree" (=1), "disagree" (=2), "neutral" (=3), "agree" (=4), "totally agree" (=5). SPSS and AMOS 24.0 are used to test the measurements and structural models.

## 4. Sampling and Demographics

The model and hypotheses are examined using datasets collected from respondents who are employees in aviation organizations in Ho Chi Minh City. These companies operate and provide a wide range of services and products for the aviation industry in Vietnam, such as flight operations, ground services, maintenance services, duty-free products, air cargo, and air traffic control. These organizations are selected because the aviation industry has grown and contributed significantly to Vietnam's economy (Tyler, 2016). It also attracts a large number of employees. Besides, internal communication within these companies plays an integral role as this function decides the degree of flexibility and consistency that employees demonstrate in carrying out activities related to their duties. Moreover, the aviation industry in Vietnam is characterized by highly competitive intensity, particularly high-quality labor pressure, among many domestic airlines as well as foreign airlines in Asia (Tyler, 2016). Thus, the interaction between the leaders and their followers in these organizations through an SIC setting helps ensure a long term relationship. The

**Table 1:** Demographic profile ($n = 175$).

| Demographic profile | Category | Frequency | Percent |
|---|---|---|---|
| Gender | Female | 98 | 56.0 |
| | Male | 77 | 44.0 |
| Age | <3 | 100 | 57.1 |
| | 30–40 | 72 | 41.1 |
| | >40 | 3 | 1.7 |
| Education background | High school | 18 | 10.3 |
| | Vocational school | 5 | 2.9 |
| | Bachelor's degree | 126 | 72.0 |
| | Master's degree | 26 | 14.9 |
| Working experiences | <2 | 39 | 22.3 |
| | 2–5 | 26 | 14.9 |
| | 5–10 | 72 | 41.1 |
| | >= 10 | 36 | 20.6 |
| | 5 | 2 | 1.1 |
| | Total | 175 | 100.0 |

convenience sampling approach to self-administrated questionnaires is conducted to collect data. The researchers delivered questionnaires to 200 participants, of which 183 were collected after two weeks. However, eight questionnaires were eliminated because they were invalid (the questionnaires had missing values). Hence, 175 questionnaires were valid for the current research, which resulted in a response rate of 87.5%. In comparison with the minimum sample size, this rate is satisfactory.

The demographic characteristics of 175 respondents are illustrated in Table 1. There are more female respondents (56%) than male respondents (44%) in this sample. In terms of age, more than half of the respondents are under 30, and a minimal rate of participants is over 40. Table 1 also shows that the majority of respondents have a Bachelor's degree (72%). Likewise, the results demonstrated that more than a third of the respondents have 5–10 years of work experience. In contrast, only 1.1% of respondents have been working for their organization for over 5 years.

## 5. Data Analysis and Hypothesis Testing

### 5.1. *Reliability and validity test*

The AL measurement contained four dimensions with 14 items: Self-awareness (ALS, three items), Rational Transparency (ALR, three items), Internalized Moral Perspective (ALI, four items), and Balanced Processing (ALB, four items). The CFA result for AL showed quite fit data. However, the factor loading of ALI4 is not significant ($0.44 < 0.5$) and caused the averaged variance extracted (AVE) to be under 0.5. Thus, the researcher removed ALI4 to attain a CFA model with acceptable fit data. All of the criteria are appropriate (TLI = 0.979, CFI = 0.984, and RMSEA = 0.043). The result presented that the AL measurement has a suitable degree of fit with the data collected. Table 2 presents the reliability and validity of the AL measurement scale. It can be seen that the AL measurement is reliable since Cronbach Alpha and the composite reliability value (CR) of four sub-components are high (>0.70). Regarding the convergent validity, AVE values of AL's sub-components are significant (>0.5). Besides, from Table 3, it can be seen that correlations of the

**Table 2:** Summarized data of CR, AVE, and Cronbach's $\alpha$ (AL).

| Dimension | Item | Factor loadings | Reliability |
|---|---|---|---|
| Balanced processing | ALB2 | 0.90 | Cronbach's $\alpha = 0.909$ |
| | ALB4 | 0.85 | AVE = 0.718 |
| | ALB3 | 0.83 | CR = 0.910 |
| | ALB1 | 0.81 | |
| Self-awareness | ALS2 | 0.99 | Cronbach's $\alpha = 0.852$ |
| | ALS1 | 0.87 | AVE = 0.699 |
| | ALS3 | 0.60 | CR = 0.870 |
| Internalized moral standard | ALI2 | 0.81 | Cronbach's $\alpha = 0.723$ |
| | ALI1 | 0.70 | AVE = 0.5 |
| | ALI3 | 0.60 | CR = 0.732 |
| Rational transparency | ALR1 | 0.76 | Cronbach's $\alpha = 0.827$ |
| | ALR2 | 0.80 | AVE = 0.608 |
| | ALR3 | 0.80 | CR = 0.829 |

**Table 3:** Correlation of AL.

| Correlation | Estimate |
|---|---|
| ALB $\leftrightarrow$ ALS | 0.761 |
| ALB $\leftrightarrow$ ALI | 0.682 |
| ALB $\leftrightarrow$ ALR | 0.617 |
| ALS $\leftrightarrow$ ALI | 0.669 |
| ALS $\leftrightarrow$ ALR | 0.645 |
| ALI $\leftrightarrow$ ALR | 0.558 |

**Table 4:** Summarized data of CR, AVE, and Cronbach's $\alpha$ (SIC).

| | Factor loadings | Reliability |
|---|---|---|
| S3 $\leftarrow$ SIC | 0.69 | Cronbach's $\alpha = 0.796$ |
| S5 $\leftarrow$ SIC | 0.75 | AVE = 0.501 |
| S4 $\leftarrow$ SIC | 0.66 | CR = 0.798 |
| S1 $\leftarrow$ SIC | 0.72 | |

pairs of sub-components are less than 0.8 and significant at 0.001. Thus, these findings supported reliability, convergent validity, and within-construct discriminant validity for the AL construct.

The SIC scale is measured by four items. Based on the CFA result, the model is suitable for the collected data with all the loading factors that are more than 0.50. The appropriate indices from the measurement model are: CFI = 1.000, TLI = 1.024, and RMSEA = 0.000, which represented a very good fit of the model. Moreover, from Table 4 it can be seen that both CR and AVE are above the thresholds (0.798 and 0.501, respectively). Therefore, this measurement has a proper standard for reliability and convergent validity.

The EOR scale consisted of four dimensions: Trust (ET, two items), Satisfaction (ES, three items), Commitment (EC, three items), and Control Mutuality (EM, three items). The CFA result indicated proper fit of the data: CFI = 0.967, TLI = 0.951, and RMSEA = 0.072. The reliability and validity tests results are shown

**Table 5:** Summarized data of CR, AVE, and Cronbach's $\alpha$ (EORs).

| Dimension | Item | Factor loadings | Reliability |
|---|---|---|---|
| Control mutuality | EM3 | 0.81 | Cronbach's $\alpha = 0.874$ |
| | EM1 | 0.85 | AVE $= 0.700$<br>CR $= 0.875$ |
| | EM2 | 0.85 | |
| Satisfaction | ES1 | 0.93 | Cronbach's $\alpha = 0.826$ |
| | ES2 | 0.88 | AVE $= 0.646$<br>CR $= 0.841$ |
| | ES3 | 0.59 | |
| Trust | ET3 | 0.91 | Cronbach's $\alpha = 0.888$ |
| | ET1 | 0.88 | AVE $= 0.809$<br>CR $= 0.894$ |
| Commitment | EC3 | 0.84 | Cronbach's $\alpha = 0.792$<br>AVE $= 0.657$<br>CR $= 0.793$ |

**Table 6:** Correlation of EORs.

| Correlation | Estimate |
|---|---|
| EM $\leftrightarrow$ ES | 0.637 |
| EM $\leftrightarrow$ ET | 0.687 |
| EM $\leftrightarrow$ EC | 0.679 |
| ES $\leftrightarrow$ ET | 0.590 |
| ES $\leftrightarrow$ EC | 0.728 |
| ET $\leftrightarrow$ EC | 0.292 |

in Table 5, where it can be seen that Cronbach $\alpha$ and the CR values of all sub-components are significant (>0.80). In terms of convergent validity, the AVE values of EORs' sub-components are acceptable (>0.5). Furthermore, correlations of the pairs of sub-components are less than 0.8 and significant at 0.001 (Table 6). Therefore, the reliability, convergent validity, and within-construct discriminant validity of EOR construct are achieved.

The saturated model is also analyzed using AMOS 24.0 for checking the discriminant validity between all constructs. The results

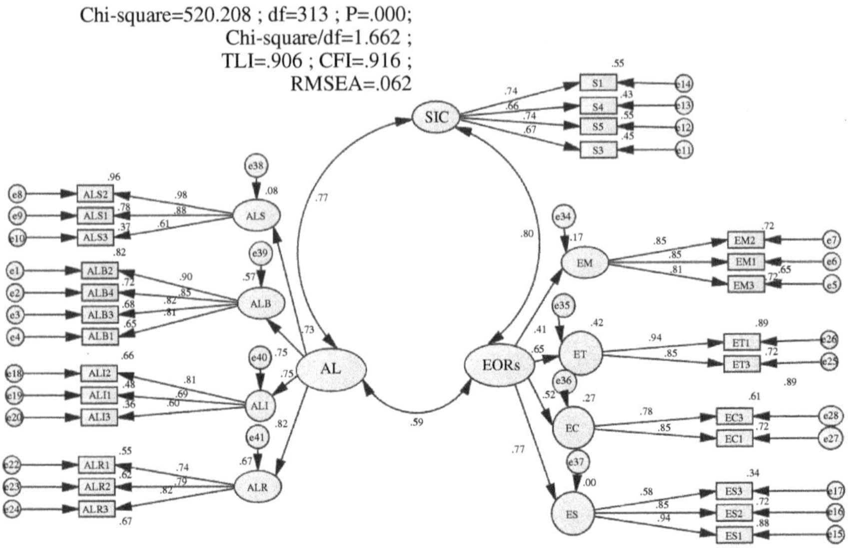


**Figure 2:** SEM analysis results for the saturated model.

**Table 7:** Constructs' correlation.

| **Correlation** | **Estimate** |
|---|---|
| SIC ↔ AL | 0.770 |
| SIC ↔ EORs | 0.801 |
| AL ↔ EORs | 0.586 |

(TLI = 0.906, CFI = 0.916, and RMSEA = 0.062) are appropriate. Therefore, the saturated model is relevant to the data (Figure 2). Table 7 presents the discriminant validity of all scales, which is also achieved for the correlations between the three pairs of constructs ranging from 0.586 to 0.801, which are well under 0.85 (Kline, 2011).

## 5.2. *Hypothesis testing results*

The theoretical model has been used to test the three causal paths through the three hypotheses. The significant parameter estimates results showed that the standardized estimates for three hypotheses

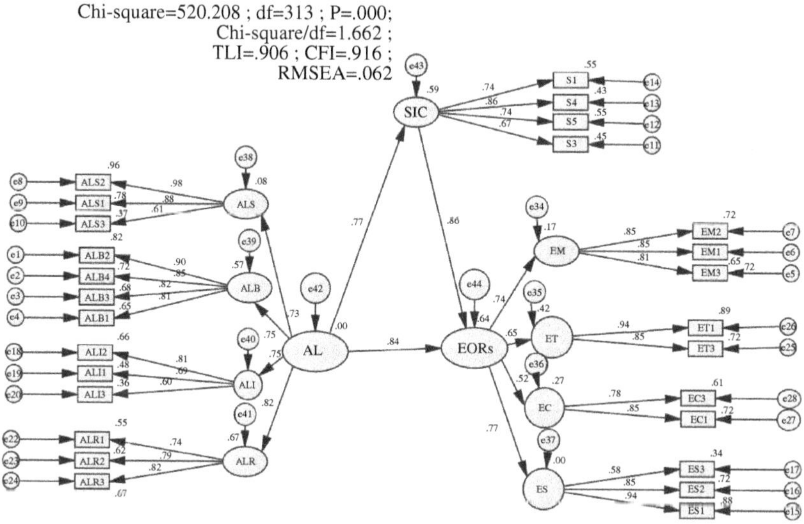


**Figure 3:** The hypothesized structural model.

**Table 8:** Hypothesis testing results.

| **Hypothesis** | | **Standard estimate** | ***p*-value** | **Result** |
|---|---|---|---|---|
| H1: AL has a positive effect on SIC. | SIC ← AL | 0.770 | *** | Supported |
| H2: AL has a positive effect on EORs. | EORs ← AL | 0.840 | *** | Supported |
| H3: SIC has a positive effect on the EORs. | EORs ← SIC | 0.860 | *** | Supported |

*Note*: $^{***}p < 0.001$.

are statistically significant and in the hypothesized direction. Therefore, these three hypotheses are supported. Further details about the hypotheses of the present thesis are discussed in the next section. Model estimation yielded a good fit: $\chi^2 = 520.208$; $df = 218$;

$p$-value = 0.000; $\chi^2/df$ = 1.662; RMSEA = 0.062; CFI = 0.906; TLI = 0.916 (Figure 3).

Moreover, the model indicated that all factor loadings on the latent constructs are significant and substantial ($\geq 0.50$). Likewise, the model presented that all three paths are statistically significant ($p < 0.05$). Table 8 shows that the standardized estimates for these hypotheses are all significant ($\beta = 0.77, 0.84$, and 0.86, respectively). Thus, these three hypotheses are supported.

## 6. Discussion and Implications

### 6.1. *Discussion*

Leadership as a research topic has always attracted attention of many scholars in the world in various fields. It plays a vital role in positive organizational outcomes. Dinh *et al.* (2014) posted that effective leadership is one of the core factors to bring about success of any organization. Furthermore, the importance of leadership is proven in many research studies, including qualitative, quantitative, and mixed methods (Dinh *et al.*, 2014; Gardner *et al.*, 2011). Similarly, the contribution of effective leadership to organizational outcomes, such as job satisfaction, employee commitment, job creativity, etc., is revealed in previous studies. AL, one of the emerging leadership theories, has a positive impact on the behaviors of employees (Men and Stacks, 2014). However, AL has not been explored widely in both theoretical and empirical studies. Moreover, the importance of such a leadership style has not yet gained awareness among Vietnamese organizations. The current study aims to explore the effects of AL on SIC and EORs. Honestly, these three lineages have not been given sufficient attention by Vietnamese scholars. The current study provided support for all three hypotheses in the proposed model. AL is found to have a positive impact on both the SIC and the EORs, while the SIC also positively impacted the EORs.

With respect to the path coefficient among variables, previous studies suggested that AL contributes to enhancing the relationship between employees and their organizations. Gardner *et al.* (2011) revealed that AL is connected to followers' positive behaviors. Likewise, Walumbwa *et al.* (2010) found an authentic leader has a positive effect on employee commitment. Next, Men and Stacks (2014) reported a positive correlation between AL and EORs. This finding is consistent with previous research and supports the significant connection between AL and EORs in the Vietnamese context. The notion that AL affects the SIC is supported in this study ($\beta = 0.77$, $p < 0.001$). The finding is also supported by previous studies of Men and Stacks (2014), which might be the first empirical evidence of the positive influence of AL in SIC. Therefore, the current study provides more empirical evidence in the Vietnamese context to support their studies. The research result also revealed that SIC has a strong influence on EORs ($\beta = 0.86$, $p < 0.001$). This positive relationship was also proven in the studies of Kang and Sung (2017), Men (2014), and Men and Stacks (2014). Moreover, this study provides more empirical evidence for the linkage between SIC and the EORs in the Vietnamese context.

## 6.2. *Implications*

The study revealed the direct and indirect impact of AL on EORs and its relationship with SIC. Results showed that organizational leadership and its influences play an integral role in an organization's internal communication's effectiveness. In terms of AL, the positive influences of AL in organizations continue to be indicated. Moreover, this study applied AL in the context of Vietnam, a transition market. These things make a significant contribution to AL theory and its outcomes in terms of examining this leadership cross-culturally. In regards to SIC, this study result demonstrates that SIC is one of the critical factors that contribute to the success of organizations. SIC, characterized by trust, open sharing, and two-way communication, builds an open and comfortable environment where employees can easily access the flow of information to make decisions. Further, such an environment helps tie up the relationship between employees and their organization.

Some practical implications emerge from the findings of this study, useful for managers who want to lead their companies efficiently with a high degree of employee commitment and nurture a better relationship with their followers in the aviation sector and other fields. First, a two-way, employee-centered, responsive SIC should be maintained and developed to attain effectiveness in organizational communication. Notably, internal communication is a crucial strategic factor in the aviation system in Vietnam because of its role in ensuring the safety of the whole aviation mechanism. Also, based on this internal communication, the employees confidently express their ideas to improve the company's performance. The aviation field belongs to service industries, so employee performance significantly affects customer's behaviors and loyalty. Positive employee performance contributes to nurturing better customer perception of organizations.

Furthermore, in a working environment with an SIC, employees also get sufficient information to make decisions independently and efficiently. So, fostering effective internal communication is a crucial responsibility of leaders. Likewise, when leading organizations, leaders should act consistently with their values and their words to get support from their followers. Also, they should be accountable for what they say and do to create rational transparency, cultivate quality relationship between organizations and their employees, and support positive employees' behaviors. Next, by openly sharing information, SIC should be developed encompassing all leaders, managers, and employees. Lastly, the study indicates that positive employee behaviors are generated strongly from the leadership style. Therefore, based on the research findings, to nurture positive behaviors of subordinates, leaders should advocate ethical, rationally transparent, and balanced leadership styles. Besides, their actions should be consistent with their morals and values in leading organizations.

### 6.3. *Limitations and further research directions*

The study has certain limitations which should be addressed in future research. First, data are collected for the quantitative research from a single source using a single survey, which may cause the inflation of the estimate of the correlation between variables due to common method variance. Moreover, as the convenient sampling technique is used to collect data, some respondents may not be knowledgeable about the research issues. Finally, this study only focused on the aviation sector in Ho Chi Minh City. Further studies should be conducted in various sectors across more cities in Vietnam.

Some directions for further research are as follows: First, besides exploring the effect of AL on SIC and EORs, the impact of dimensions of Vietnamese culture, such as Confucianism, Collectivism, etc., on organizational outcomes should be investigated. Moreover, a variety of samples including more organizations, more and different fields, and more cities should be applied in further research to achieve generalizability. Additionally, AL outcomes like EORs should be examined with the organization level and team level instead of at the individual level in future research. As suggested by Gardner *et al.* (2011), future research needs to consider the antecedents of AL such as positive ethical climate as well as psychological capacities and the effect of these antecedents on SIC and EORs in the research model above. Moreover, AL is a four-dimensional construct, so further research should examine separately the impact of each dimension on EORs or SIC to get a wider view of this concept. Finally, the forms of organizations such as state-owned enterprises, foreign-invested enterprises, and privately owned enterprises should be examined in future studies.

## Acknowledgments

The authors are most grateful to two reviewers for very helpful comments and suggestions.

## References

Berger, B.K. (2008). Employee/organizational communications. *Institute for Public Relations*, 1–23. Online at: http://www.instituteforpr.org/topics/employee-organizational-communications.

Brislin, R.W. (1970). Back-translation for cross-cultural research. *Journal of Cross-Cultural Psychology*, 1(3), 185–216. https://doi.org/10.1177/135910457000100301

Dinh, J.E., Lord, R.G., Gardner, W.L., Meuser, J.D., Liden, R.C., and Hu, J. (2014). Leadership theory and research in the new millennium: Current theoretical trends and changing perspectives. *Leadership Quarterly*, 25(1), 36–62. https://doi.org/10.1016/j.leaqua.2013.11.005

Dozier, D.M. (1990). The innovation of research in public relations practice: Review of a program of studies. *Public Relations Research Annual.* https://doi.org/10.1207/s1532754xjprr0201-4_1

Gardner, W.L., Cogliser, C.C., Davis, K.M., and Dickens, M.P. (2011). Authentic leadership: A review of the literature and research agenda. *Leadership Quarterly.* https://doi.org/10.1016/j.leaqua.2011.09.007

George, B., Sims, P., McLean, A.N., and Mayer, D. (2007). Discovering your authentic leadership. *Harvard Business Review*, 85(2), 129–138.

Gray, J., and Laidlaw, H. (2004). Improving the measurement of communication satisfaction. *Management Communication Quarterly.* https://doi.org/10.1177/0893318903257980

Grunig, J.E., and Huang, Y.-H. (2000). From organization effectiveness to relationship indicators: Antecedents of relationships, public relations strategies, and relationship outcomes. In *Public Relations As Relationship Management: A Relational Approach to the Study and Practice of Public Relations*, pp. 23–53.

Grunig, L.A.,Grunig, J.E., and Dozier, D.M. (2003). Excellent public relations and effective organizations: A study of communication management in three countries. https://doi.org/10.4324/9781410606617

Jensen, S.M., and Luthans, F. (2006). Relationship between entrepreneurs' psychological capital and their authentic leadership. *Journal of Managerial Issues*, 18(2), 254–273.

Jo, S., and Shim, S.W. (2005). Paradigm shift of employee communication: The effect of management communication on trusting relationships. *Public Relations Review.* https://doi.org/10.1016/j.pubrev.2005.02.012

Kang, M., and Sung, M. (2017). How symmetrical employee communication leads to employee engagement and positive employee communication behaviors. *Journal of Communication Management.* https://doi.org/10.1108/jcom-04-2016-0026

Kernis, M.H. (2003). Toward a conceptualization of optimal self-esteem. *Psychological Inquiry.* https://doi.org/10.1207/S15327965PLI1401_01

Kim, H.S. (2007). A multilevel study of antecedents and a mediator of employee–Organization relationships. *Journal of Public Relations Research.* https://doi.org/10.1080/10627260701290695

Kim, J.N., and Rhee, Y. (2011). Strategic thinking about employee communication behavior (ECB) in public relations: Testing the models of megaphoning scouting effects in Korea. *Journal of Public Relations Research.* https://doi.org/10.1080/1062726X.2011.582204

Kline, R.B. (2011). *Principles and Practice of Structural Equation Modeling: Third Edition. Structural Equation Modeling.* https://doi.org/10.1038/156278a0

Leroy, H., Palanski, M.E., and Simons, T. (2012). Authentic leadership and behavioral integrity as drivers of follower commitment and performance. *Journal of Business Ethics.* https://doi.org/10.1007/s10551-011-1036-1

Lockwood, N.R. (2007). Leveraging employee engagement for competitive advantage. *SHRM Research Quarterly*, 52(3), 1–11.

Luu, T.T. (2019). Linking authentic leadership to salespeople's service performance: The roles of job crafting and human resource flexibility. *Industrial Marketing Management*, May, 1–16. https://doi.org/10.1016/j.indmarman.2019.06.002

M. Dozier, D., Grunig, L.A., and Grunig, J.E. (2010). *Manager's guide to excellence in PR and communication management.* Public Relations and Communication Management.

Men, L. (2014). Why leadership matters to internal communication: Linking transformational. *Journal of Public Relations Research.* https://doi.org/10.1080/1062726X.2014.908719

Men, L.R. (2011). How employee empowerment influences organization-employee relationship in China. *Public Relations Review.* https://doi.org/10.1016/j.pubrev.2011.08.008

Men, L.R. (2014). Why leadership matters to internal communication: Linking transformational leadership, symmetrical communication, and employee outcomes. *Journal of Public Relations Research* 26(3), 256–279. https://doi.org/10.1080/1062726X.2014.908719

Men, L.R. (2015). The internal communication role of the chief executive officer: Communication channels, style, and effectiveness. *Public Relations Review*, 41(4), 461–471. https://doi.org/10.1016/j.pubrev.2015.06.021

Men, L.R., and Stacks, D. (2014). The effects of authentic leadership on strategic internal communication and employee-organization relationships. *Journal of Public Relations Research* 26(4), 301–324. https://doi.org/10.1080/1062726X.2014.908720

Meng, J., and Berger, B.K. (2012). Measuring return on investment (ROI) of organizations' internal communication efforts. *Journal of Communication Management.* https://doi.org/10.1108/13632541211278987

Michaelson, D., and Stacks, C.W. (2014). *A Professional and Practitioner's Guide to Public Relations Research, Measurement, and Evaluation: Second Edition.* Business Expert Press, LLC.

Moriano, J.A., Molero, F., and Lévy Mangin, J.-P. (2011). Authentic leadership concept and validation of the ALQ in Spain. *Psicothema*, 23(2), 336–341.

Neider, L.L., and Schriesheim, C.A. (2011). The authentic leadership inventory (ALI): Development and empirical tests. *Leadership Quarterly.* https://doi.org/10.1016/j.leaqua.2011.09.008

Shen, H. (2011). Organization-employee relationship maintenance strategies: A new measuring instrument. *Journalism and Mass Communication Quarterly.* https://doi.org/10.1177/107769901108800210

Smidts, A., Pruyn, Ad Th.H., and Van Riel, C.B.M. (2001). The impact of employee communication and perceived external prestige on organizational identification. *Academy of Management Journal.* https://doi.org/10.2307/3069448

Tyler, T. (2016). Meeting airline needs. *IATA Annual Review 2016*, 72(1), 6–8.

Vu, X.T.T. (2013). *The Effect of Internal Communication on Employee's Engagement.* Master thesis, University of Economic Ho Chi Minh City.

Walumbwa, F.O., Avolio, B.J., Gardner, W.L., Wernsing, T.S., and Peterson, S.J. (2008). Authentic leadership: Development and validation of a theory-based measure. *Journal of Management* 34 (1): 89–126. https://doi.org/10.1177/0149206307308913

Walumbwa, F.O., Wang, P., Wang, H., Schaubroeck, J., and Avolio, B.J. (2010). Retracted: Psychological processes linking authentic leadership to follower behaviors. *Leadership Quarterly.*, 25, 1071. https://doi.org/1.1016/j.leaqua.2010.07.015

Waters, R.D., Bortree, D.S., and Tindall, N.T.J. (2013). Can public relations improve the workplace? Measuring the impact of stewardship on the employer-employee relationship. *Employee Relations.* https://doi.org/10.1108/ER-12-2012-0095

Wong, C., and Cummings, G. (2009). Authentic leadership: A new theory for nursing or back to basics? *Journal of Health, Organisation and Management.* https://doi.org/10.1108/14777260910984014

Yates, K. (2006). Internal communication effectiveness enhances bottom-line results. *Journal of Organizational Excellence.* https://doi.org/10.1002/joe.20102

https://doi.org/10.1142/9789811227158_0015

# Chapter 15

# Green Innovation, Green Entrepreneurship, and Vietnamese SME Development: The Role of Market Turbulence

**Anh Tuan Doan and Tri Thanh Nguyen**

## Abstract

Micro, small, and medium enterprises (MSMEs) are a significant part of Vietnam's national economy, contributing up to 40% of GDP. However, in today's globalized world, competition in the marketplace is increasingly complex. Besides, the state is more concerned with environmental sustainability. Thus, Vietnamese enterprises, especially MSMEs or small-medium enterprises (SMEs) that want to stand up and develop, should pay attention to innovation by not only considering business opportunities but also the benefits of being environmentally friendly businesses. The goals of this study are to investigate the impact of green innovation (GI) on SME development (SMED) in turbulent market conditions with the mediation effect of green entrepreneurship (GE). Based on the research results, the study provides useful solutions to help SMEs develop and policymakers adjust their policies. The activating of SMEs' activities in Ho Chi Minh City business corresponds to the demographic census of this study. A sample comprising 280 senior managers of SMEs is surveyed for the study. The questionnaire tool is used to measure the research variables. A 5-point Likert scale is used to measure the questionnaire. To test the hypotheses, the study uses the SEM method with the support of Amos software.

**Keywords:** Green innovation; Green entrepreneurship; SMEs development, Market turbulence.

## 1. Introduction

Nowadays, the role of innovation for environmental sustainability is growing significantly. This is evidenced by relevant studies that focus on what is important to decision makers in organizations. Numerous studies stress the increasing significance of sustainability as a criterion of innovation (Adams *et al.*, 2012; Nidumolu *et al.*, 2009; Varadarajan, 2017). There are many terms such as eco-innovation, eco-friendly innovations, environmentally sustainable innovations, sustainable innovation, green innovations (GIs), and so forth. In the academic literature on the issues, these terms are used to denote innovations with the focus on durable environment sustainability. This study uses the term "Green Innovation (GI)" with a stipulation, which is that the innovations diminish the impact of organizational activities on the natural environment.

Two years ago, the natural environment in central Vietnam was severely impacted by a disaster, which involved a foreign direct investment (FDI) company discharging untreated wastewater into the environment. After this disaster, policymakers developed numerous activities and increasingly strict regulations for punishing environmentally harmful behaviors. These policies encourage producers to control the impacts of their activities on the natural environment to mitigate negative reputation and additional cost. Thus, responding to the incremental environment pressure, manufacturers use GI, which is considered an important tool to obtain sustainable development. Despite the significance and benefits of GI, in many cases, the contribution of producers in GI has been below expectation (Abdullah *et al.*, 2016). Some manufacturers are prevented from participating in innovations because of the difficulties involved and still lock into the established routines. Achieving the adoption of GI involves certain important factors, including *stakeholder compression, environmental protection act, firm size, and characteristics of manager, staff, and business field* (Gonzàlez-Benito and Gonzàlez-Benito, 2006; Etzion, 2007).

Although GI and GE literature is plentiful, little research attention is focused on the Vietnamese industries. The economic, social, community, market conditions of Vietnam are different from other areas. The composition of customers and their preferences change swiftly, thus forming market turbulence. Moreover, Vietnam's industries are mostly involved in SMEs, which play important roles in the national market, and contribute to over 40% of GDP (Hoang, 2016). According to the report by the General Statistics Office, in 2017 there were nearly 517,900 SMEs operating in the country, up 51.6% compared to 2012, when SMEs accounted for 98.1%. They are mostly located in Ho Chi Minh City, in which 172,979 SMEs operate. In the global market, SMEs contribute to economic growth and competition (Mesquita and Lazzarini, 2008). SME activities allow SMEs to remain competitive, meeting the requirements of customers, and promoting innovation. The important role of SMEs is in wealth and job production, thus generating consequences and producing a set of services and products. However, their limited resources and capabilities around human and financial resources, and research and marketing, indicate they will fall without globalizing their activities. In turbulent market conditions, the globalization of environmental pressures makes the role of SMEs more eminent. However, the question is whether confirming the development of SMEs forms the GE approach, which stems from GI in turbulent market conditions. In this study, the development of SMEs comprises incremental employment, the performance of finance, and the newborn industries (Mangematin *et al.*, 2003). Confidently, it can be concluded that SMEs' development and turbulent market conditions have not received attention in previous studies. Based on the massive literature review, a clear gap in evidence on the growth of SMEs from GI and GE amidst market turbulence is confirmed. Based on the advances mentioned above, the activating of SMEs' activities in Ho Chi Minh Business City corresponds to the demographic census of this study.

At the firm level, GI is researched in two specific aspects. According to the study of Caputo (2014), one aspect concerns factors related to enabling GI, namely stakeholder pressures, environmental protection acts, redundant resources, expected economic benefits, employees, and environmental awareness of managers. The other aspect focuses on the outcome of GI. Many studies debate on how policies had driven GIs influence on innovation and firm performance. Porter hypothesis (Porter and Van der Linde, 1995) provides an appropriate conclusion, which indicates the relationship or mechanism between GI and corporate performance. In general, his hypothesis discloses an innovation-offset term. Thus, a company's increasing resource efficiency leads to higher economic efficiency. The impact of corporate GI on firm performance is an undisputed conclusion, some empirical studies indicate the positive effect of corporate GI on business performance (Amores-Salvadó *et al.*, 2014; Rennings and Rammer, 2011). In some cases, this effect is costly in the short term but becomes positive in the long term (Horváthová, 2012). However, identifying and classifying GI activities of firms should consider the significant barriers. Besides, some companies have inadequate capacities, which reduce their proper understanding of GI measures.

Previously, factors that influence the implementation of GI of firms have been examined in some studies (Lin *et al.*, 2011; Tseng, 2013). GI can be classified into four main categories, including technological innovation, process innovation, the performance of management, and product design. Klassen and Whybark (1999) present an array of green measures that help manufacturers adjust processes in the design of products so that negative environmental consequences are diminished. Moreover, well-designed environmental standards can act as an incentive for producers to introduce green products with lower cost and differentiations (Chen *et al.*, 2006). Thus, GI improves products or processes that work towards sustainability and the reduction of environmental pressures. Rennings and Rammer (2011) and Kemp and Pearson's (2007) studies indicate that GI can significantly decrease environmental pollution and thus can create sustainable development. In Vietnam, compared to other developing countries, environmental pollution is not handled efficiently, due to the fact that serious measures are not adopted promptly, especially in the making and consumption of green products (Lin *et al.*, 2013). This study presents the original topic deliberating on the theme of GI and green manufacturing.

In this context, this study accesses an emerging phenomenon, called green entrepreneurship (GE). The GE approach is the outcome of innovation that has the potential to solve environmental problems by creating new products and technology (York and Venkataraman, 2010). GE considers sustainability as the strategic foundation, which is related to a sustainable economy. Since the global economic crisis in 2009, national plans and reports of international meetings have been utilizing the concept of green economy. According to UNEP, these reports see green economy or sustainable economy as an economic activities system which aims to develop the value of people's lives. This system embraces the manufacture, consumption, and allocation of goods and services. In the green economy model, there is a priority focus on environmental issues and sustainable businesses (UNEP, 2011). Thus, prevention of imminent generation of primary environmental risk and natural scarcity is considered an essential aspect of GE. Uslu *et al.* (2015) present that GE encourages manufacturers to use regenerable energy resources, recycle wastes, and pay more attention to animal and organic farming. Kirkwood and Walton (2010) present that the motivation of ecopreneurs or green entrepreneurs is to create sustainable businesses with strong underlying green values. It is what makes green entrepreneurs extraordinary in the world of business. The original credence of such an entrepreneur focuses on the primariness of the environmental and social consciousness more than rigorous economic achievement. Thus green entrepreneurs are of tremendous significance to the economy as job creation is their crucial contribution (Farinelli *et al.*, 2011). Based on this review, Silajdžić *et al.* (2015) investigate the private sector to find that green entrepreneurs bring positive influences on society and gain desired business profitability as well. Activities of green entrepreneurs consequently develop sustainability for industries and enhance green growth (Sarkar, 2013). The above-mentioned studies indicate the important role of GI and GE in the modern world.

Based on the benefits of GI, GE, on the development of Vietnam's SMEs, which are mentioned above, this study aims to offer a comprehensive approach assessing GI. Moreover, this study's conclusion evaluates the impact of GE on the development of SMEs in turbulent market conditions. The remainder of this study is established as follows: A discussion of the literature related to GI, GE, SMEs development, and turbulent market conditions is presented in Section 2. Section 3 presents the research methodology, empirical models, and variables, and Section 4 displays results. The conclusion is available in Section 5.

## 2. Literature Review and Hypothesis Development

### 2.1. *Definition of SMEs in Vietnam*

Initially, this study focuses on the literature review of SMEs, which are a specific type of organization with a different set of primaries than the other organizations. Based on previous studies, SMEs form a varied group in terms of size, sector variety, and so forth. The definition of SME is inconclusive because every country adopts different criteria, which are employment, sales, total net asset, and investment level, for their definition purposes. However, the most common basis for definition is the number of employees, which has a threshold from the majority micro-enterprises and startups with nearly no employees to medium-sized enterprises with more than 200 employees (Ayyagari *et al.*, 2007).

In Vietnam, SMEs play a significant role, accounting for 98% of all enterprises, 50% of employment, and 40% of GDP (Vietnam-briefing, 2017). SME's definition in Vietnam depends on the 04/2017/QH14 Law on Support for Small- and Medium-sized Enterprises (SME Law), which was introduced by the government and took effect from January 1, 2018. Based on the definition of SME Law, MSMEs or SMEs are manufacturer and service units that have less than 200 employees, who register with the state social insurance scheme in a year, and satisfy either of the subsequent two criteria: (1) the total capital is no more than VND100 billion, and (2) the entire revenue of the previous year does not surpass VND 300 billion. At a global level, there are many reasons that make significant literature on GI and GE of SMEs imminent. According to OECD (Murphy, 2002), SMEs' form a large group internationally, which contributes between 96% and 99% of the total number of enterprises. On the other hand, SMEs also contribute to a large share of the pollution. According to ECEI (2010), SMEs are responsible for approximately half of the total pollution in the EU. Each of the SMEs is characterized by variety and distinctiveness, thus their innovation for sustainability is different (Bos-Brouwers, 2010).

Moreover, the inadequate capability of SMEs results from financial limitation and resource constraints, which inhibit their proactive innovation process. SMEs cannot manage to pay for the investment necessary to compare with larger organizations or approve comparable strategies (Abor and Biekpe, 2007). From this point of view, numerous previous studies indicate that SMEs focus on environmental and social issues and thus exploit niches that are more suited to their capabilities. The interest of each company is not the same, so each company with different size should follow different strategies for its business. Previous studies indicate that SMEs have advantages, in that they are characterized by dominant control of owner–managers, so SMEs' behavior is often implied in terms of the psychological representation of the owner–manager (Jenkins, 2009). Thus, SMEs are able to innovate fundamentally and participate effectively in niche markets with GI to a greater extent than larger companies. This controversy is based on the distinction of organizational structures and capabilities whereby SMEs will innovate dissimilarly than larger companies for GI (Aragón *et al.*, 2008). This is further supported by numerous works of literature presented where SMEs originated based on business sustainability showed growth and successfully spread GI in niche markets (Klewitz and Hansen, 2014). SMEs are also termed green entrepreneurs, sustainable entrepreneurs, and ecopreneurs, and are thus also covered by this study definition of SMEs.

### 2.2. *The effect of green innovation on green entrepreneurship*

Previous studies indicate that green product innovation and green process innovation are components of GI (Chang, 2011;

Chen *et al.*, 2006; Lin *et al.*, 2014). GI is the development of products or processes that enhance green product design, quality, safety, and sustainable power, and avoid negative environmental effects, non-reusable materials, so forth (Chen *et al.*, 2006). Green product innovation relates to the development of green product design, standardization, and reduces the negative collision of the product on the original nature. Typically, the use phase and the discard phase of products significantly impact the environment. Contrarily, green product innovation takes the role of addressing the negative influence of producing, using, and discarding products on the environment. GI also can develop the implementation of environmental management that meets their obligation of environmental protection. The dedication of the firm to the development of GI can meet the environmental legislation as well as build up the barriers to other competitors (Dangelico and Pontrandolfo, 2010). Recently, there have been significant associations between GI, GE, and green businesses. Companies involve high sustainability of businesses, thus can facilitate the generation of GE. GE fosters firms to alter their strategies and maneuvers, then they can offset the cost of improving environmental impact. In general, GI comprises the diminution of destructive environmental effects, development of resources productivity, and is extensively studied (Porter and Linde, 1995; Wong, 2013).

According to Farinelli *et al.* (2011), GE or ecopreneur-ship can be defined as the implementation of innovations involved in sustainability. In this definition, the main goals of GE are implementing sustainability and promoting green economy. Miller's (1983) studies indicate entrepreneurship at the individual and organization levels is an important concept. Obviously, entrepreneurship relates to the creation of fresh business models and different products in established firms. In this way, previous studies indicate that the owner-managers' effort constantly develops their economic position and inventive behavior (Croitoru, 2012). Consistently, the way a green entrepreneur views and assesses the potential of resources and opportunities is based on their lenses of environmental commitment (Gibbs, 2008). Thus, a potential definition of entrepreneurship is *an innovation process that relates utilizing opportunities with enormous exertion and persistence, besides receiving financial, rational, social risks.* These risks are offset by the inspiration of attaining financial benefit, accomplishment, self-satisfaction, and autonomy (Hisrich *et al.*, 2002). These arguments lead to the following hypothesis.

**Hypothesis H1:** *GI has a significant effect on GE.*

### 2.3. *Green entrepreneurship and SME development*

Many previous studies indicate that entrepreneurship is positively involved in the strategic decision-making of a company and its administration form (Farinelli *et al.*, 2011; Kraus *et al.*, 2012). Meanwhile, entrepreneurship also significantly depends on vigorous capability, evolution incentive, and business implementation (Lee *et al.*, 2001). The measurements of innovative behavior comprise *innovativeness, pro-activeness* (*PA*), and *risk-taking* (*RT*), which are popularly employed (Covin and Wales, 2012).

PA relates to the capability of firms to seize new opportunities. Proactive organizations help to monitor trends of the market. Proactiveness increases its ability for identifying the imminent demands of current customers and foresees shifts in need or rising problems. Thus, proactiveness can start novel venture opportunities and eliminate the operations and products with expired life cycles (Dess and Lumpkin, 2005). Proactive companies prefer to recognize changes and act on those comprehensions ahead of their business rivals. Owner-managers who exercise proactiveness have their eye on the future. Thus, they always look for new possibilities for growth and development. The next dimension is innovativeness. Innovativeness refers to the efforts of companies to create and look for new opportunities and fresh solutions. Innovation involves creativity and experimentation that result in the elimination of existing solutions and methods to make way for new products, services, and technological processes (Hong *et al.*, 2013). Finally, the last dimension that is presented in this chapter is RT. According to the study of Dess and Lumpkin (2005), RT refers to the inclination of a company to take possession of a venture opportunity even though it has a probability of failure in it. Thus, though the company is unable to understand whether the opportunities will be successful or fail, it performs fearlessly without comprehending the result. To be successful via entrepreneurship, companies normally must embark upon riskier alternatives. This means staying away from the processes or products that existed in the past. Previous research indicates that there is a strong correlation between increased risk and pioneering designs and projects (Tan, 2001). According to the financial field, companies that prefer risk-taking will obtain high financial returns. Though high risk should raise the probability of scheme failure, it is an appropriate example for another project (Anderson *et al.*, 2009).

Usually, bringing new products successfully to the market is the essential lifeblood for most businesses. However, new product development is also a complex and difficult task, which involves generating non-existent and pioneering things by way of manufacturing fresh outcomes. As these elements are related to the circumstances of achievement in deriving benefit, the absence of support of firms' form innovation is a significant obstacle, which can be altered and increased by effort within the company. Numerous studies indicate a positive relationship between entrepreneurship and incremental innovation (Bouncken *et al.*, 2016), thus the tendency towards entrepreneurship causes innovation to develop. Based on this point, many studies present a background for the elements influencing the development of SMEs.

Sidik (2012)'s study indicates that the traits of an entrepreneur and the performance of the SME relate to the development of the SME. Thus, it offers a proposition framework of valuable dimensions to assess entrepreneurship and SME development (SMED). These arguments lead to the following hypothesis:

**Hypothesis H2:** *GE has a significant effect on SMED.*

### 2.4. *The moderating impact of market turbulence*

According to the study of Tsai and Yang (2013), MT is regarded more in the strategic choices of firms and is one of the most essential environmental factors in the market. MT is associated with the rate of change in the structure of customers and their preferences in an industry. These changes are caused by several factors, however, the primary cause for these variations is the uncertainty and changeable nature of exterior dimensions (Theodosiou *et al.*, 2012).

In an industry, the rate of change in customer preferences for products and services is reflected by MT (Olson *et al.*, 2005; Jaworski and Kohli, 1993). So, MT is the core foundation of environmental turbulence. The rate of variation in the market and/or the rate of changes in the technology is indicated by the environmental turbulence in an industry (Kim and Atuahene-Gima, 2010). In this study, MT distinguishes between the market and technologies that stem from turbulence. The reasons considered are that dissimilar foundation of turbulence could affect opportunities and hazards of companies (Danneels and Sethi, 2011). Another reason is related to managerial practices, in which a sheet conceptualization of environmental turbulence is considered essential for determining comprehensions (Buganza *et al.*, 2009). To make a profit, companies create competitive advantages by the creation of value for customers. In this case, they need a clear understanding of their customer, which companies gain by checking and scrutinizing the industry environment (Grant, 2016).

Numerous previous studies present that there are several theoretical perspectives of market turbulence. These theories indicate that MT can adjust the influence of company innovativeness on implementation. With the intense changes in the market environment, companies that change to sufficiently reply to environmental changes will succeed. Thus, companies act on creativity to unceasingly adjust their products, services, and processes to meet changes in customer demands (Cui *et al.*, 2005). Innovative companies are characterized by the will to build initiative plans to arrest fresh products of market niches and to meet the unpredictable demands of customers (Lumpkin and Dess, 2001). In particular situations, at the intensities of MT conditions, the innovation of companies can be of significant value in satisfying customers' rapidly changing needs and wants (Santos-Vijande and Álvarez-González, 2007). Thus,

Rhee *et al.* (2010) suggest that to successfully address alterations in the market properly and continue to involve in that ecosystem, a firm's innovation can be a strategic instrument. Once encountered with a high level of MT, the firms' effort to take more initiatives and perform the implementation of their pioneering strategies well increases (Hult *et al.*, 2004). Generally, firms which value above-average innovativeness can gain extra advantage from the customer's unpredictable demands, invent fresh ways to address customers' difficult issues, and reconfigure their assets to support their prosperous deal with market changes. This reasonable ratiocination indicates that when MT is rare, the firm innovativeness effects business performance positively (Tsai and Yang, 2013).

Some previous studies indicate the existence of the association between entrepreneurship, the SME's performance, and environmental turbulence. Thus, the reviewing and analyzing of this relationship is essential. According to Lumpkin *et al.* (2009), it is on the basis of entrepreneurship that companies become conscious of the changes in the market preference. Thus, the executive groups attend to the alteration in the industry and to the customer's needs. It is based on the organization of MT and appropriate drivers that the decision makers make significant efforts to bridge the cognitive gap between market precedences and comparatively homogeneous resources. Firms that have strong entrepreneurship can rapidly meet the changes of customer preferences. The study of Devezer *et al.* (2014) indicates that diverse levels of revenue or increased cognizance of coming generations determine these preferences. Especially for SMEs, such performance can have negative influence on the environmental turbulence.

During this intense condition, firms should dedicate additional resources and should approve new plans that are related as elements to prevent poor performance hazard (Li *et al.*, 2008). The uncertainty of estimating customer needs is caused when the intense environmental turbulence significantly influences the entrepreneurial companies. In a changeable environment, firms favor correspondence activities rather than considering superior entrepreneurial situations. The study of Iyer (2011) indicates that by analyzing customer preferences, one of the considerations of companies is marginal improvements. In summary, the study of Wales *et al.* (2013) indicates that the positive association between the entrepreneurship and performance of SMEs may not be an expectation.

Drawing from previous studies, we can confidently confirm that there are limited studies on the influence of GI and GE in MT conditions on development of SMEs. Despite the rich literature on each variable, most authors find irrelevant studies, which deliberate on the MT conditions as a moderator in the correlation of variables for the development of SMEs. Thus, these arguments lead to the following hypothesis:

**Hypothesis H3:** *Market turbulence adequately moderates the relationship between GI and SME development.*

## 3. Methodology

This section presents and elaborates on the data and methods used for the empirical analysis of this study. First, a description of the research design and process is presented followed by a measure of the constructs and operationalization of the survey dataset. Subsequently, the methods used to assess the data will be elaborated. To create a research design, the authors consider the kind of model and measure which is suitable for the subject of the study. The focus of this research is examining the three factors affecting the performance of SMEs, including GI and GE. Besides, this study also tests market turbulence conditions, which moderate the relationship between GI and GE. An operation model is presented in Figure 1. This study uses primary data, which was collected from SMEs in Ho Chi Minh City. Thus, a questionnaire survey design is used as the data collecting method. The research includes two phases, a pilot study and the main survey. The pilot study is carried out by the qualitative method and the main survey by quantitative method.

### 3.1. *Qualitative research*

Based on relevant previous studies, this study proposes three hypotheses, which are presented in Section 2. Then, the model is

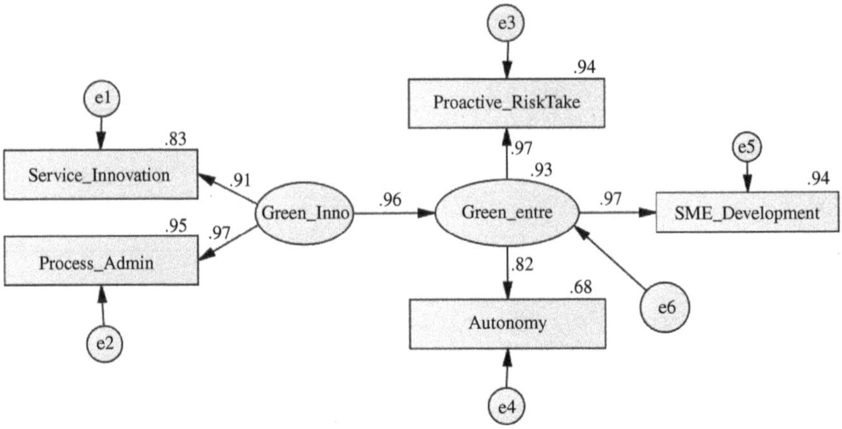


**Figure 1:** The conceptual model.

modified and the preliminary scale is selected for the questionnaire of the study. After finishing the preliminary questionnaire, the authors conduct the focus group with 10 owner–managers of SMEs, including a manager of a Logistics firm, two owner–managers of law firms, three managers of retailers, two owners of IT firms, and two owners of food field startups. These owner–managers have an interest in sustainable business, indeed some of them have tried out options and some have even made some achievements. This is the reason that they have been selected in this study. Besides the focus group instrument, the authors also conduct an in-depth interview with an expert, Mr. Pham Ngoc Hung who is a lawyer and vice-chairman of the Ho Chi Minh City Union of Business Associations (HUBA). He has significant experiences in supporting SMEs and has deep knowledge of the market of Vietnam. The focus group and the in-depth interview help to obtain the appropriate items in the context of Vietnamese business. It also helps to ensure that the content and meaning of words used in the initial measurement scales are suitable and understandable. Then, the authors are able to modify their conclusions appropriately.

Although most of the measurements of the constructs are mentioned in the previous literature, this pilot study is necessary to make appropriate analysis and is easy to understand in the context of studying. During the interview and focus group, some significant feedback is received and suggested by the participants to improve the official questionnaire (see Appendix A). After finishing the pilot study, these adjustments lead to the following final questionnaire, which was reviewed carefully for the measurement of each construct.

### 3.2. *Quantitative research*

After the qualitative research, the questionnaire becomes more appropriate and understandable. Thus, the main survey is conducted by using convenience samples, which are mostly collected in District 6 of Ho Chi Minh City. Besides, the online survey is also considered a potential instrument. The process of the quantitative research follows these phases.

Firstly, the questionnaire is composed for the research. The questionnaire is designed in English, and then it is translated into Vietnamese for delivering to respondents. Secondly, the definition of sample size is provided. Based on enormous previous studies, the method of estimating the sample designs the size of the sample. In general, the sample size is equal to or more than 100 and is minimum of five observations for each scale. The model in this study comprises four factors with 25 scales, so that the minimum sample size is: $25 \times 5 = 125$ observations.

For standard multiple regression analysis, the required sample is recommended to be $n > 50+8m$ (where $m$ = number of independent variables). There are two independent variables, which are the component of the second-order structure (GI) in this research. Thus, the minimum sample required to run multiple regression in this study is $n > 50+8\times 2 = 66$ observations. Therefore, this study uses the sample size of 216 observations. This sample size is appropriate for EFA and CFA. After that, sampling is conducted based on convenience sampling.

The questionnaire is issued to the participants via both direct and indirect methods. In the direct method, participants of this research, which are the owner–managers of SMEs in District 6 of Ho Chi Minh City, receive the questionnaire and are required to fulfill the questionnaire on the guidance of the authors. In the indirect method, the questionnaire is deployed via the Internet by Google docs. In this way, the survey link is sent to participants via Gmail and Facebook. The participants can answer the survey by clicking on the link and keying their answer and submitting the link to the researcher. Data collection is conducted over a month. The number of expected receivable questionnaires is about 280, which comprises 230 questionnaires by the direct method, and 50 questionnaires by the indirect method.

After that, the authors receive the questionnaires and gleen through to ensure suitable results. In this stage, the authors collect answers, and filter the erroneous questionnaires. Then, the usable data of this study is narrowed down to 216 observations. It is suitable as per the requirement of the minimum sample size: 125 observations.

## 3.3. *Measures of the constructs*

In the following part, the operationalization of the survey dataset for the statistical analysis is discussed. First, the independent variables are discussed, followed by the dependent variables and subsequently the moderator variables.

### 3.3.1. *Independent variables*

To measure GI in the individual SMEs, the independent variables *Service Innovation*, *Administrative Innovation*, and *Process Innovation* are constructed per type of GI. Additionally, the combined independent variable *GI* is created.

#### 3.3.1.1. Green innovation

The independent variables *Service Innovation, Adminstrative Innovation*, and *Process Innovation* measure the presence of two forms of GI within the SMEs. According to studies of Ndubisi and Iftikhar (2012), the variable GI with 15 items is used in previous studies. Every dimension involves *Service Innovation*, *Administrative Innovation*, and *Process Innovation*, which are assessed by five items. Based on the pilot study, the combination of *Administrative Innovation* and *Process Innovation* is conducted. Thus *Admin Process Innovation* is the consequential variable measured by seven questions that are adopted from Ndubisi and Iftikhar (2012). Plausible reason is based on the study of Chang (2011), which only uses Green Process and Green Product to measure GI.

### 3.3.2. *Dependent variables*

To measure the development of SMEs in individual firms, the dependent variable *SMED* is constructed.

#### 3.3.2.1. SMEs development

The dependent variable assessed by nine items is *SMED*, which is created and recommended by researchers to comprise three items for each dimension (Ebrahimi and Mirbargkar, 2017). However, the pilot study indicates that there are different conditions in Vietnam, thus the respondent of the pilot study receives indifferently in three dimensions. They recommend that *SMED* should be a variable. In general, six scales are selected, and the relevant items in these variables range from 1 (strongly agree) to 5 (strongly disagree) with the 5-point Likert scale. Based on the pilot study, the *SMED* increase is measured by six questions that are adopted from Ebrahimi and Mirbargkar (2017).

### 3.3.3. *Mediator variables*

*Proactive Risk-taking* and *Autonomy* are used to measure GE in the individual firms.

#### 3.3.3.1. Green entrepreneurship

The mediator variable with 13 items used in the previous studies (Ndubisi and Iftikhar, 2012) is assessed. GE is offered by authors to include five items of *Risk-taking* and *Proactiveness*, and three items of *Autonomy* dimensions. After the pilot study, there is a lot of feedback, which influences the decision of selecting dimensions. Finally, there are two dimensions, *Proactive Risk-Taking* and *Autonomy*. The relevant items in these variables use a range from 1 (strongly agree) to 5 (strongly disagree) with the 5-point Likert scale. *Proactive Risk-Taking* is measured by five questions from Ndubisi and Iftikhar (2012). The combination also is based on the studies of Lee (2001) and Kraus (2011), which ask pilot respondents before considering the appropriate scale used. The items of *Autonomy* consist of three questions adopted from Ndubisi and Iftikhar (2012).

#### 3.3.4. *Moderator variables*

Based on the study of Wang *et al.* (2015), there are three questionnaires, which are used to measure *Market turbulence*. The relevant items in these variables use a range from 1 (strongly agree) to 5 (strongly disagree) with the 5-point Likert scale.

### 3.4. *Data collection*

In this study, the collected data are used once and participants are ensured that data are collected anonymously. The online survey is designed by using the web-based tool Google Form, which is one of the famous tools for online surveys. Afterward, the link to reach the survey is put online and executives from SMEs are invited to participate by email and on social media platforms like Facebook. Data information of participants is based on Saigon Bizhub Company, which supports SMEs to share experiences and connects businesses. Besides, an offline survey is also conducted in District 6 of Ho Chi Minh City by the enthusiastic support of the local officers. Over a period of 45 days, a total of 280 respondents participated in the online and face-to-face survey, while 260 of those finalized the questionnaire, which means a response rate of 92.28%. Additionally, 44 out of the 260 complete responses had to be deleted for the adjusted dataset. Among others, companies with non-engagement responses were deleted.

## 4. Data

This section reports the result of the research. Firstly, the collection and description of data are presented. Then, the reliability and validity of the scale measurement are tested by Cronbach's Alpha and EFA. Finally, SEM is used to assess the hypothesis and concept model.

### 4.1. *Descriptive statistics*

The outcome of respondents is presented in Table 1, which includes 95 females (occupied 44%) and 121 males (56%). In terms of age, respondents' ages mostly range from 25 to 35 (41.2%); the youngest and oldest respondents, who are under 25 and over 55, make up about 7.9% (17 respondents) and 6% (13 respondents), respectively. Those are lower than respondents of two groups aged 35–45 and 45–55, which have 70 respondents (32.4%) and 27 respondents (12.5%), respectively.

Regarding educational backgrounds of respondents, 131 (60.6%) respondents have university education. Then, the highest education of this research has 35 respondents (16.2%). There are six respondents (2.8%) and 44 respondents (20.4%) who finished their primary and secondary education, respectively. The outcome of the survey also indicates that the majority of SMEs are businesses in the service field with 139 respondents (64.4%). The rest with 77 respondents (35.6%) have businesses in manufacturing. After that, normal distribution of the data collection is investigated, thus Skewness and Kurtosis tests are used. The result indicates that there are no items above absolute of two. It means normality assumption for all variables.

### 4.2. *Exploratory factor analysis*

Initially, exploratory factor analysis (EFA) is conducted to estimate the measurement scales. EFA helps to define which set of items load together as a group or are answered similarly by respondents (Leech *et al.*, 2005). To support CFE in AMOS, EFA process of this study is conducted through Maximum Likelihood Estimation with Promax rotation method. In EFA, KMO indicator, and Bartlett's test are conducted. In the conceptual model, there are four latent factors: *Green Innovation, Green Entrepreneurship, SMEs Development, and Market Turbulence.* GI and GE both are second-order factors, which

Table 1: Descriptive statistics.

| | Descriptive | Frequency | Percentage |
|---|---|---|---|
| Gender | Female | 95 | 44 |
| | Male | 121 | 56 |
| Age | Under 25 | 17 | 7.9 |
| | 25–35 | 89 | 41.2 |
| | 35–45 | 70 | 32.4 |
| | 45–55 | 27 | 12.5 |
| | Over 55 | 13 | 6 |
| Education | Primary education | 6 | 2.8 |
| | Secondary education | 44 | 20.4 |
| | University | 131 | 60.6 |
| | Postgraduate | 35 | 16.2 |
| Position | Entrepreneur | 65 | 30.1 |
| | Manager | 114 | 52.8 |
| | Staff | 37 | 16.8 |
| Field | Manufacturer | 77 | 35.6 |
| | Service | 139 | 64.4 |
| Revenue (VND) | Under 10 billion | 160 | 74.1 |
| | 10–50 billion | 34 | 15.7 |
| | 50–100 billion | 3 | 1.4 |
| | 100–300 billion | 16 | 7.4 |
| | Over 300 billion | 3 | 1.4 |
| Side (Employee) | 10 | 113 | 52.3 |
| | 10–49 | 74 | 35.3 |
| | 50–100 | 12 | 5.6 |
| | 101–200 | 7 | 3.2 |
| | Over 200 | 10 | 4.6 |
| Firm size | Micro | 105 | 48.6 |
| | Small | 84 | 38.9 |
| | Medium | 27 | 12.5 |

comprise *SI, API for GI, and PRT, A for GE.* Based on this, EFA of this study is conducted separately with each factor. The results on GI and GE both present that the two factors can explain variance (Table 2). EFA is conducted four times to examine the structure or relationship between variables before we run CFA to test model fit (Appendix B).

**Table 2:** Result of EFA.

| Variable | Dimensions | Item | Deleted | KMO | Cumulative |
|---|---|---|---|---|---|
| GI | SI | SI1_SI5 | SI3 | 0.945*** | 56.407 |
| | API | API1-API7 | API1, API6 | | 5.737 |
| GE | PRT | PRT1-PRT5 | | 0.888*** | 51.444 |
| | A | A1-A3 | | | 8.686 |
| SMED | | SMED1-SMED6 | SMED1, SMED5 | 0.907*** | 56.477 |
| MT | | MT1-MT3 | | 0.731*** | 70.224 |

*Note*: ***Significant at the 0.01 level.

**Table 3:** The results of Cronbach's Alpha.

| | Cronbach's Alpha |
|---|---|
| Service innovation (SI) | 0.886 |
| Admin process innovation (API) | 0.918 |
| SME development (SMED) | 0.853 |
| Proactive risk-taking (PRT) | 0.857 |
| Autonomy (A) | 0.859 |
| Market turbulence (MT) | 0.874 |

### 4.3. *Reliability master*

To ensure reliable measurement of the research concept, Cronbach's Alpha is conducted for each construct. As previously mentioned, Cronbach's Alpha should be above 0.7, however some exclusive studies accept Cronbach's Alpha in a range from 0.6 to 0.69 (Leech *et al.*, 2005). Besides, correlation of each specific item with the total of the other items in the scale (Corrected Item — Total correlation) is moderately high and should be above 0.4 (Leech *et al.*, 2005). Another point to note, series of actions should be conducted if the value of total correlation is negative or less than 0.3, thus the mean score of the questionnaires should be reviewed. The horrific situation that the item should be deleted for conceptual fit purpose is likely. In this study, Cronbach's Alpha ranges between 0.85 and 0.92, and is presented in Table 3.

### 4.4. *Confirmatory factor analysis*

Following EFA, the indicators are used to conduct confirmatory factor analysis (CFA) that loads on each derived factor across groups to verify that the measurement model derived in EFA fits the data in an independent validation sample. The independent validation samples are used to conduct CFA, which is conducted separately in each group. Numerous CFAs are conducted, including a CFA of the measurement model derived using EFA, and a CFA testing the hypothesized factor structure based on the structure of both groups, with high and low turbulent market conditions. The model goodness of this study is of excellent range, which is below the preference threshold of 0.08, suggesting that it is appropriate and the specified model reproduces the observed covariance matrix among all indicators.

In terms of these combinations of measures in the work of Hu and Bentler (1999), preference in a combination of CFI is larger than 0.95 and SRMR is less than 0.08. To further solidify evidence, we add that the RMSEA is less than 0.06. Results confirm the factor structure derived in EFA as the best fitting measurement model (RMSEA = 0.057, SRMR = 0.043, CFI = 0.958, P-Close = 0.147) when compared with the group measurement model, which has mediocre fit in both the high and low turbulent market conditions (RMSEA = 0.030, SRMR = 0.043, CFI = 0.934, P-Close = 1.000). The aim of CFA group conduction is to guarantee model fit when evaluating H3. After analyzing the fit of the full CFA model, model specification and fit are considered for each latent variable sub-cluster of the hypothesized model in an individual group to assure the measurement model for all latent variables individually. By using EFA procedures of the latent variables, CFA results confirm the measurement model (Table 4).

Besides Cronbach's Alpha, CFA reliability and validity also consider the values of the composite reliability (CR), the average variance extracted (AVE), and maximum share variance (MSV). Construct reliability and validity of measurement models are confirmed, which is indicated by all values in Table 5.

**Table 4:** CFA results.

| Non-Group CFA | | | Group CFA | | |
|---|---|---|---|---|---|
| **Measure** | **Estimate** | **Threshold** | **Measure** | **Estimate** | **Threshold** |
| CMIN | 300.680 | — | CMIN | 1410.012 | — |
| DF | 177.000 | — | DF | 885.000 | — |
| CMIN/DF | 1.699 | Between 1 and 3 | CMIN/DF | 1.593 | Between 1 and 3 |
| CFI | 0.958 | >0.95 | CFI | 0.934 | >0.95 |
| SRMR | 0.043 | <0.08 | SRMR | 0.043 | <0.08 |
| RMSEA | 0.057 | <0.06 | RMSEA | 0.030 | <0.06 |
| PClose | 0.147 | >0.05 | PClose | 1.000 | >0.05 |

**Table 5:** The values of the composite reliability.

| | **CR** | **AVE** | **MSV** | **MaxR(H)** | **SMED** | **GI** | **GE** |
|---|---|---|---|---|---|---|---|
| SMED | 0.852 | 0.590 | 0.891 | 0.856 | 0.768*** | | |
| GI | 0.901 | 0.820 | 0.937 | 0.923 | 0.890*** | 0.906*** | |
| GE | 0.841 | 0.728 | 0.937 | 0.884 | 0.944*** | 0.968*** | 0.853*** |

*Note*: ***Significant at the 0.001 level.

Table 5 shows that estimative correlations of the latent variables between pairs of constructs lie from 0.768 to 0.906. The correlations are significant at 95% with a range from 0.841 to 0.901, which is primarily less than 1.0, with the confidence intervals presenting discriminant validity (Steenkamp and Van Trijp, 1991). However, the high correlation of 0.968 between GI and GE, of 0.944 between GE and SMED, and of 0.890 between value to GI and value to SMED require additional examination.

Three separate additional empirical tests for the discriminant validity of scales measuring GI, GE, and SMED are done by employing chi-square alternative exams for the constrained and unconstrained models (Ngoc Thuy and Nguyen Hau, 2010). The result indicates that the unconstrained model with two separate constructs (i.e., GI and GE, GI and SMED, GE and SMED) is a better fit than the constrained model with one construct (i.e., the correlations between GI and GE, GI and SMED, GE and SMED are constrained

**Table 6:** Discriminant examination.

| Correlation | Unconstraine Chi-square/DF | Constrained Chi-square/DF | Difference Chi-square/DF | $p$-Value |
|---|---|---|---|---|
| GI and GE | 177.035/109 | 194.302/110 | 17.267/1 | 0.000 |
| GI and SMED | 95.916/59 | 106.900/60 | 10.984/1 | 0.000 |
| GE and SMED | 80.774/49 | 89.187/50 | 8.423/1 | 0.004 |

to 1.00). According to the testing discriminant validity between GI and GE, statistics present that when constraining the correlation to 1.0, degree of freedom ($df$) decreases from 110 to 109, chi-square decreases form 194.302 (for constrained model) to 177.035 (for unconstrained model), which is a significant decrease ($p < 0.001$). The related empirical result is obtained for the scales measuring between GI and SMED; GE and SMED. The achievement of discriminant validity is presented in Table 6.

## 5. Empirical Results

### 5.1. *Structural equation modeling*

The hypothesized structural model encompasses the following variables: (1) *observed endogenous variables* (*GI, GE, SMED, MT*), (2) *the latent exogenous variable GI, and MT,* (3) *the latent endogenous variables SMED,* and (4) *the unobserved exogenous variables comprising error terms and latent factor residual terms.* Latent variables are deployed by ellipses in the model, while observed variables are deployed by rectangles and work for indicators of their respective underlying latent variable construct. According to Byrne (2010), endogenous variable characterizes dependent variables, which are envisaged by other variables in the model, whereas exogenous variables are equivalent to independent variables.

Table 7 depicts the theoretically driven structural model and its parameter estimated individually. To represent the independent contributions of each observed variable, thus standardized regression

**Table 7:** Regression coefficient of research hypotheses test.

| Variables relationship | Std $\beta$ | Hypothesis | Impact |
|---|---|---|---|
| Hypothesis 1 | | | |
| GI-GE | 0.953*** | Confirmed | Positive |
| Hypothesis 2 | | | |
| GE-SMED | 0.969*** | Confirmed | Positive |

*Note*: Significance of correlations: $^{***}p < 0.001$.

coefficients (SRC) are used, and they also predict the respective latent variable.

Goodness of fit statistics: $p > 0.05$; CMIN/DF 1.691; GFI 0.882; TLI 0.950; CFI 0.958; RMSEA 0.57.

The starting point for the evaluation of an SEM path model is R2 of the two endogenous latent variables in the reflective measurement model that can be interpreted as a normal linear regression coefficient (Byrne, 2010). For the latent endogenous variable, GE accounts for 92.6%. That number indicates that GI explains 92.6% of the variation in GE. Furthermore, for SMED, R2 accounts for 94%. That number indicates that 94% of the variation in SMED is due to GE. For this model, GI has a significant relationship to GE and GE also has a significant relationship to SMED. These things are in the supposed tendency, in that in SMEs with greater levels of GI, greater levels of GE, and greater levels of SMED. Also, the two path coefficients can be interpreted as standardized regression coefficients that result from an ordinary linear regression analysis. On GI and GE relationship, for a one-unit increase in the independent variable, the model predicts that GE, a dependent variable, will increase by 0.953 units. And on the other hand, for a one-unit increase in GE, the model predicts that SMED increases by 0.969.

### 5.2. *SEM of moderator analysis and hypothesis overview*

After successfully conducting all two-hypothesis analyzes, all relevant data are given to test the influence of market turbulence as a

**Table 8:** Test statistics for moderating effect.

| Model | DF | CMIN | *P* | Hypothesis |
|---|---|---|---|---|
| Structural weights | 4 | 3.854 | 0.426 | Unconfirmed |

**Table 9:** Overview of accepted and rejected hypotheses.

| **Hypothesis** | **Description** | **Accepted/rejected** |
|---|---|---|
| H1 | GI has a significant effect on GE | Accepted |
| H2 | GE has a significant effect on SMED | Accepted |
| H3 | Market turbulence adequately moderates the relationship between GI and SMED | Rejected |

moderator variable. In general, moderating effects are not considered within structural equation model, but in the literature, the importance of moderators to understand complex relationships is repeatedly highlighted (Chin *et al.*, 2003). Such analysis examines whether an MT variable influences the relationship between the independent variable and the dependent variable.

To test the effect of the moderator variable, the variable is computed into two dichotomous variables. The first includes all respondents who answer that the mean of MT variable has a low degree of market turbulence ($<2.5$). The second variable includes all respondents with high MT ($>2.51$). This step is necessary to calculate the effect with both dichotomous variables separately. To check the difference between insignificant groups and multi-group methods, the calculation of Nested model comparison CMIN/DF is conducted with a confidence interval of 95%. Table 8 shows the results for the dependent variables. With a confidence interval of 95% and $p$-value larger than 0.05, it can be said that the moderator variable has no moderating effect on the direct relationship between GI and SMED.

Nested model comparisons, assuming unconstrained model to be correct, are shown in Table 8.

Table 9 represents an overview of the tested hypotheses and shows whether the hypotheses can be accepted or rejected.

## 6. Conclusion, Discussion, and Limitations

### 6.1. *Conclusion*

The thesis provides several implications for theory and practice. These findings contribute to the importance of GI, Entrepreneurship during the development of SMEs, and especially to the theoretical effect of market turbulence.

The first theoretical result refers to the studies of Lin *et al.* (2011), Tseng (2013), and Ebrahimi and Mirbargkar (2017). The studies conclude that the performance of SMEs is significantly dependent on Innovation and Entrepreneurship, which even implies at Green approach. Ebrahimi and Mirbargkar (2017) indicate that to meet customer needs and creates business value, SMEs must invest significantly in processes and innovative technological products. Therefore, decision makers can be hopeful towards business development in SMEs if GI and GE are used properly. Majority of the approaches underline the point that SMEs play a greater role than larger firms in good job creation opportunities and in creating employment. To do so, they may follow new approaches and consent to logical risks, which could further enterprise development and employment.

Another contribution of this thesis to the theory is that it can be stated that MT/dynamism is not relevant for the development of SMEs and their choice for one type of Green innovative strategy. This finding contradicts the argumentation of several researchers that the environment affects SMEs' development and the way organizational innovation takes place (Ebrahimi and Mirbargkar, 2017). The explanation can be that the environment is fast-changing but GI and GE are often long-term relationships, which means it makes no sense for SMED to look at the actual environmental situation when it can be frequently changed during the relationship. To lessen the impact of MT requires essential support of the government, comprising the following: Firstly, adequate legal motivations to fortify markets for GE, in which long-term effects are considered; Secondly, a consolidated legal system with appropriate applications to engage private sector investment in GI; Finally, the original market economy should be considered in future.

In summary, the outcome of this study provides several contributions to the existing literature concerning GI and GE with a focus on the Development of SMEs across all industries. Furthermore, it is intended that the findings inspire more SMEs to form green approaches to acquire and absorb necessary competencies for their long-term competition.

### 6.2. *Discussion*

The discoveries of this study have primary implications at the statistical, theoretical, and empirical levels regarding the innovation, entrepreneurship, and development of the industry for SMEs with the green approach as well as the relationships among these latent variables and associated turbulent market conditions. Due to the evident role of innovation and entrepreneurship in all industries, the current academic literature and amount of empirical studies are extensive. However, the motivation for performing this study is the lack of quantitative empirical evidence on the green approach, which exactly is the influence of GI and GE, with varying degrees of turbulent market conditions, on the development of SMEs. A lot of niches in this wide field still need to be discovered. Research is rarely conducted on the Vietnamese market concerning the primary position of innovation and entrepreneurship in a turbulent market environment, and the results of this research thus contain important points. This thesis contributes to empirical implication by focusing on organizational learning in SMEs and the choice for GI and GE strategy. The literature review narrows organizational learning down into GI and GE as part of SMED. The results of the Amos analysis in Tables 7–9 show a significant positive correlation between GI and GE. Therefore, it is possible to accept the first hypothesis. Due to the empirical findings, it can be argued (with a 95% CI, and $p$-value $< 0.001$) that GI leads to the choice of GE relationship. Current academic literature from

Lin *et al.* (2011), Tseng (2013), and Ebrahimi and Mirbargkar (2017) support the hypothesis that a high GI is a perfect condition for GE, which prefers proactive risk-taking and high autonomy. Compared to the study of Ebrahimi and Mirbargkar (2017), the scope of the relationship between GI and GE in this study almost doubles with 0.95. Furthermore, the results of SMED as an outcome are expected in which both $t$-statistics with $p$-value less than 0.001 show that GE affects the development of SMEs. This represents an expected finding according to literature from Ebrahimi and Mirbargkar (2017) who also support the hypothesis that the scope of the relationship between GI, GE, and SME is approximately double, thus the greater the level of GE, the greater the level of SMED. Therefore, it seems to be the case that organizations must increase their GI to strengthen their competitiveness, and this should be a suitable strategy for firms (Tseng, 2013).

Nevertheless, this study rejects Hypothesis H3. With $p$-value larger than 0.05 it can be said that MT does not affect the relationship between GI and SMED. This represents an unexpected finding according to literature from Ebrahimi and Mirbargkar (2017) who argue that MT conditions do not influence GI and SMED. But within current literature, different scholars argue that environmental turbulences can affect GI and SMED relationship and that green firms have opportunities to handle turbulent markets or a turbulent business environment (Ebrahimi and Mirbargkar, 2017). Those are important results, which demonstrate that the actual situation of the external environment is not considered in SMEs during the decision-making process for a type of green strategic approach. For SMED, it seems to be more relevant to choose the ideal type of GE for GI than handling turbulent market conditions. GI and GE can be the cause that SMEs are often long-term oriented, because any environmental situation mostly exists in the short-term. In general, the unsupported result of H3 is plausible for several reasons. Regarding the moderating effects of the environment, other research has also presented a blended pattern of findings (Gatignon and Xuereb, 1997; Li and Calantone, 1998). Such a pattern can probably be proven by industry alternations in the flow of innovativeness and in terms of thoughtfulness to environmental conditions. A meta-analytic study of Kirca *et al.* (2005) and the study of Augusto and Coelho (2009) also cannot find the evidence for the moderation of numerous environmental moderators on the relationship between market orientation, innovativeness, and firm performance. Especially, Kirca *et al.*'s (2005) study indicates that the non-parametric sign test with the estimate of $\pi$ is $p = 0.5$ (or 7/14) and finds insignificant moderation in the relationship between antecedent variables and performance. Thus, there is enough empirical evidence to conclude that MT also is an insignificant moderator in the relationship between GI and SMED.

According to the results of the SEM, H1 and H2 can be accepted but H3 must be rejected. In relation to the main research hypothesis, it can be stated that GI and GE cause the development of SMEs with the green approach. However, the given data of the structural equation modeling are clear and strongly disagree with a paper of Ebrahimi and Mirbargkar (2017) that MT has a moderating effect on the development of SMEs with a choice for GI and GE relationship.

### 6.3. *Limitations*

When interpreting research findings, several limitations appear and must be kept in mind. This section reflects upon these restrictions and ends with a recommendation for future research within this area. Firstly, only Vietnamese SMEs are contacted to participate in this study. Thus, the findings must be interpreted in that cultural context. In further research, the sampling strategy can be improved and a probability sampling can enhance the representativeness of the research. Furthermore, the given dataset is gathered in a cross-sectional online survey, which means that the results represent the situation of the participants at a specific point of time and therefore lack generalizability.

A future study with longitudinal data can be used instead of a cross-sectional approach in SMEs and the chosen type of relationship. Moreover, the study also includes an offline survey with respondents who had businesses in District 6 of Ho Chi Minh City at the time of researching. Although that is one of the big districts of Ho Chi

Minh City, the biggest city of Vietnam, it still does not represent all SMEs in Vietnam. Similarly, the amount of 216 participants represents a limitation of the research, there being nearly a million SMEs in Vietnam. In future research, the sample size should be increased to improve the generalizability of findings. It is essentially difficult to convince more SMEs to participate in either an online or offline survey within a period of a month. Therefore, a longer inquiry period can automatically increase the number of completed surveys. For the present research, only completed surveys are considered and a screening of the uncompleted surveys reveals that many participants lost interest at the same stage of the online and offline survey. A reduction or restructuring of items or gift incentives can enhance the motivation to complete the survey.

Finally, certain improvements for further research topics in this area need to be addressed. A possible next step is the performance of qualitative research (in-depth interview) to gain a deeper understanding of SMEs' development and their types of strategic green approaches. An investigation, in the form of qualitative research, can validate the outcome regarding the moderating effect of the turbulent market environments as well as the positive linear relationship between the independent variables and dependent variables. In addition, future research could concentrate on possible differences between industries through the focus on one or two industries. As already mentioned in the previous section, only Vietnamese SMEs participate in this study. Thus, it is advisable for further research to gather data from different countries to increase the generalizability and reliability of the findings.

## Appendix A

### A.1. *Green Innovation*

#### A.1.1. *Service innovation*

- Our company has introduced new green services to the market.
- Our company has introduced many modifications to the existing services.

- Our company constantly seeks new and green services.
- Our company has introduced more green services than our competitors.
- The green services that we have introduced have caused significant changes in the industry.

#### A.1.2. *Admin process innovations*

- Our company is constantly benchmarking our operating systems to world-class standards.
- Work practices are constantly updated to enhance efficiency.
- Our company uses technology constantly to enhance the quality of green services.
- Our company invests heavily in the development of new green operating systems.
- Management constantly seeks new ways to improve the administration systems with green attitudes.
- Our competitors use our operating systems as a benchmark.

### **A.2. *Green entrepreneurship***

#### A.2.1. *Proactive risk-taking*

- Our company constantly seeks new opportunities related to our present operations.
- Our company is usually the first to introduce new green services in our industry.
- Management accepts that certain suggestions in the field of green attitudes may fail when implemented.
- Our company constantly seeks green investment opportunities to improve our business performance.
- In this company, the new (green-based approach) venture failure is viewed as learning experience.

#### A.2.2. *Autonomy*

- Our employees are encouraged to take responsibility for their work.
- Our employees are supposed to get the job done with minimal supervision.
- Our employees are encouraged to prioritize their work.

### A.3. *SMEs development*

- Revenue growth is desirable, considering green products.
- Green products have reduced production costs.
- The profits from the sales are good.
- Formation of industries is done exclusively to produce goods and new green products.
- Creation of new freight transport systems is compatible with green products.
- This organization invested to increase the expertise to produce green products.

### A.4. *Market turbulence*

- Consumer preferences change unpredictably in the market.
- Competition in our product market is relentless.
- Technology in our industry changes rapidly.

## Appendix B

### B.1. *Factor 1 KMO and Bartlett's*

| | |
|---|---|
| Kaiser–Meyer–Olkin measure of sampling adequacy. | 0.945 |
| Bartlett's test of sphericity | 1716.795 |
| *df* | 66 |
| Sig. | 0.000 |

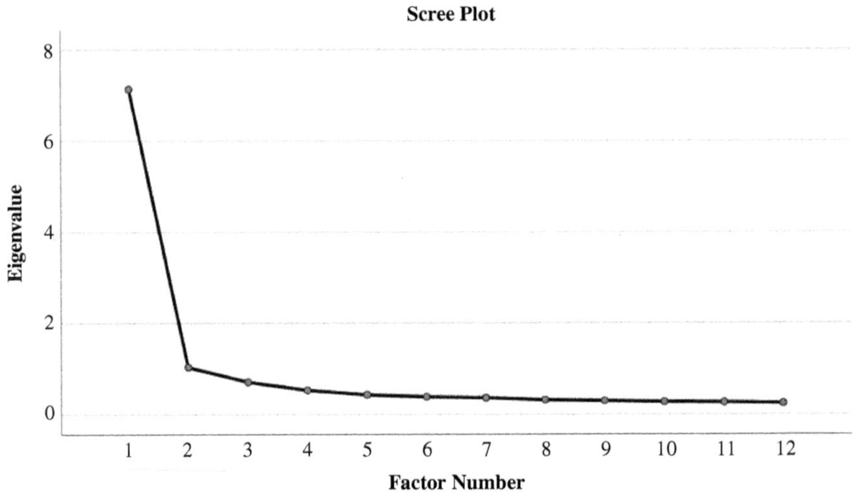

## B.2. *Factor 2 KMO and Bartlett's*

| | |
|---|---|
| Kaiser–Meyer–Olkin measure of sampling adequacy | 0.888 |
| Bartlett's test of sphericity | 858.631 |
| *df* | 28 |
| Sig. | 0.000 |

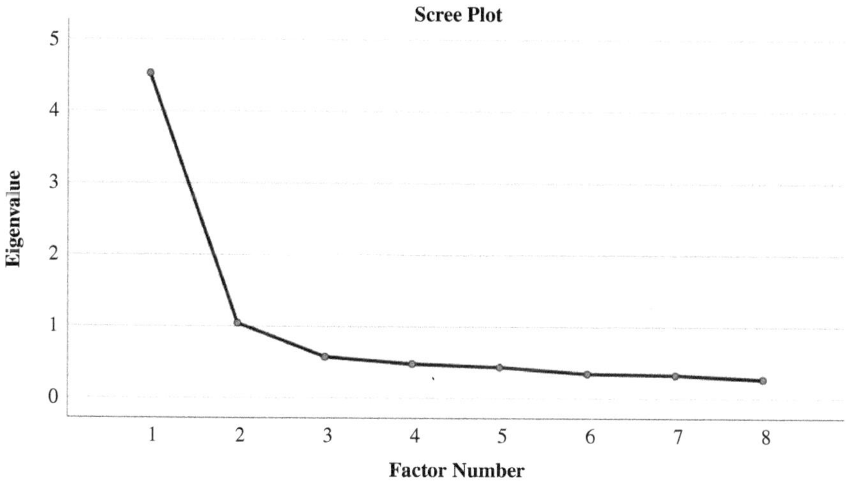

## B.3. *Factor 3 KMO and Bartlett's*

| | |
|---|---|
| Kaiser–Meyer–Olkin measure of sampling adequacy | 0.907 |
| Bartlett's test of sphericity | 1219.055 |
| *df* | 36 |
| Sig. | 0.000 |

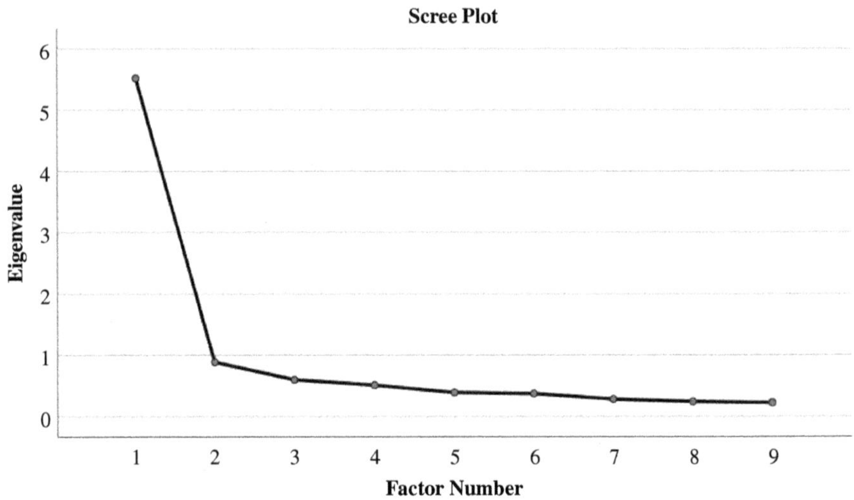

## B.4. *Factor 4 KMO and Bartlett's*

| | |
|---|---|
| Kaiser–Meyer–Olkin measure of sampling adequacy | 0.731 |
| Bartlett's test of sphericity | 332.788 |
| *df* | 3 |
| Sig. | 0.000 |

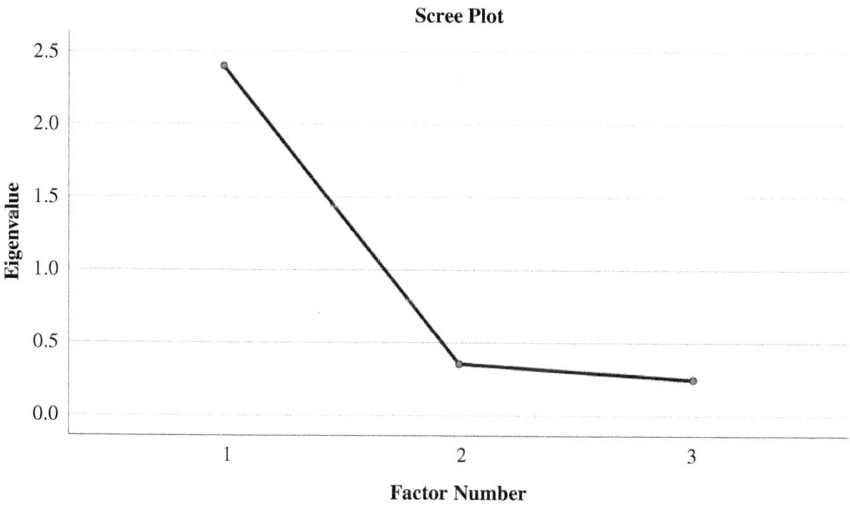

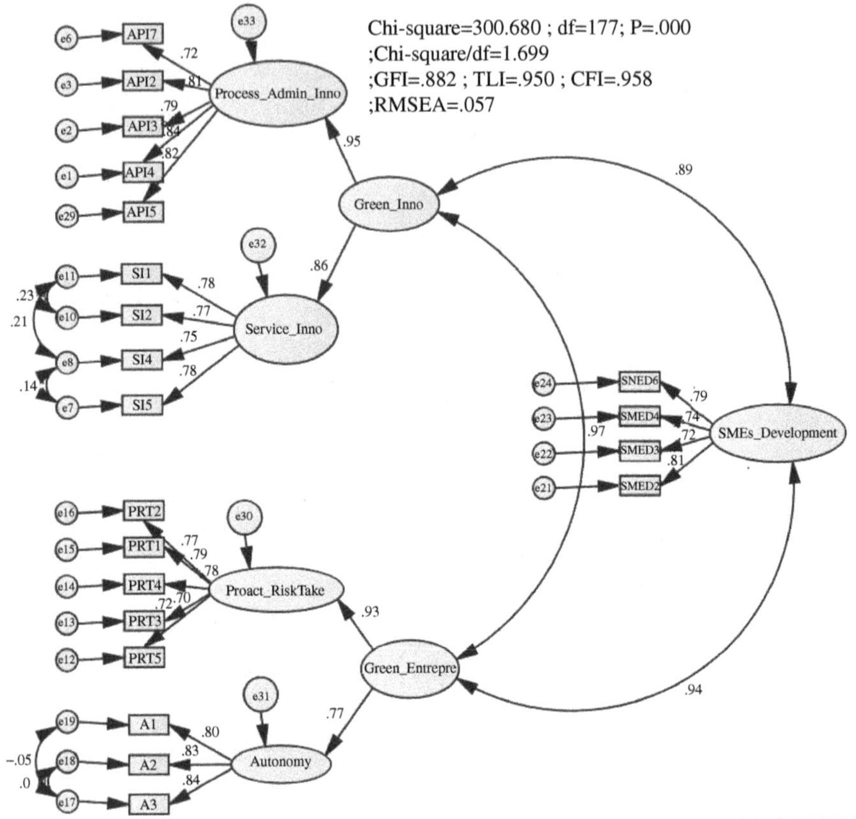


## References


Abdullah, M., Zailani, S., Iranmanesh, M., and Jayaraman, K. (2016). Barriers to green innovation initiatives among manufacturers: The Malaysian case. *Review of Managerial Science*, 10(4), 683–709.

Abor, J., and Biekpe, N. (2007). Corporate governance, ownership structure and performance of SMEs in Ghana: implications for financing opportunities. Corporate Governance: *The International Journal of Business in Society*, 7(3), 288–300.

Adams, R., Bessant, J., Jeanrenaud, S., Overy, P., and Denyer, D. (2012). *Innovating for sustainability: A systematic review of the body of knowledge*. Network for Business Sustainability. Retrieved from: nbs.net/knowledge

Amores-Salvadó, J., Martin-de Castro, G., and Navas-López, J.E. (2014). Green corporate image: moderating the connection between environmental product innovation and firm performance. *Journal of Cleaner Production*, 83, 356–365.

Anderson, B.S., Covin, J.G., and Slevin, D.P. (2009). Understanding the relationship between entrepreneurial orientation and strategic learning capability: An empirical investigation. *Strategic Entrepreneurship Journal*, 3(3), 218–240.

Aragón-Correa, J.A., Hurtado-Torres, N., Sharma, S., and García-Morales, V.J. (2008). Environmental strategy and performance in small firms: A resource-based perspective. *Journal of Environmental Management*, 86(1), 88–103.

Augusto, M., and Coelho, F. (2009). Market orientation and new-to-the-world products: Exploring the moderating effects of innovativeness, competitive strength, and environmental forces. *Industrial Marketing Management*, 38(1), 94–108.

Ayyagari, M., Beck, T., and Demirguc-Kunt, A. (2007). Small and medium enterprises across the globe. *Small Business Economics*, 29(4), 415–434.

Bos-Brouwers, H.E.J. (2010). Corporate sustainability and innovation in SMEs: Evidence of themes and activities in practice. *Business Strategy and the Environment*, 19(7), 417–435.

Bouncken, R.B., Plüschke, B.D., Pesch, R., and Kraus, S. (2016). Entrepreneurial orientation in vertical alliances: Joint product innovation and learning from allies. *Review of Managerial Science*, 10(2), 381–409.

Buganza, T., Dell'Era, C., and Verganti, R. (2009). Exploring the relationships between product development and environmental turbulence: The case of mobile TLC services. *Journal of Product Innovation Management*, 26(3), 308–321.

Byrne, B.M. (2016). *Structural Equation Modeling with AMOS: Basic Concepts, Applications, and Programming*, 3rd Edition. New York, NK: Routledge.

Caputo, M.R. (2014). Comparative statics of a monopolistic firm facing price-cap and command-and-control environmental regulations. *Energy Economics*, 46, 464–471.

Chang, C.-H. (2011). The influence of corporate environmental ethics on competitive advantage: The mediation role of green innovation. *Journal of Business Ethics*, 104(3), 361–370.

Chen, Y.-S., Lai, S.-B., and Wen, C.-T. (2006). The influence of green innovation performance on corporate advantage in Taiwan. *Journal of Business Ethics*, 67(4), 331–339.

Chin, W.W., Marcolin, B.L., and Newsted, P.R. (2003). A partial least squares latent variable modeling approach for measuring interaction effects: Results from a Monte Carlo simulation study and an electronic-mail emotion/adoption study. *Information Systems Research*, 14(2), 189–217.

Croitoru, A. (2012). The theory of economic development: An inquiry into profits, capital, credit, interest and the business cycle (translated from the German by Redvers Opie, New Brunswick (USA) and London (UK): Transaction Publishers). *Journal of Comparative Research in Anthropology and Sociology*, 3(2), 1–13.

Covin, J.G., and Wales, W.J. (2012). The measurement of entrepreneurial orientation. *Entrepreneurship Theory and Practice*, 36(4), 677–702.

Cui, A.S., Griffith, D.A., and Cavusgil, S.T. (2005). The influence of competitive intensity and market dynamism on knowledge management capabilities of multinational corporation subsidiaries. *Journal of International Marketing*, 13(3), 32–53.

Dangelico, R.M., and Pontrandolfo, P. (2010). From green product definitions and classifications to the Green Option Matrix. *Journal of Cleaner Production*, 18(16–17), 1608–1628.

Danneels, E., and Sethi, R. (2011). New product exploration under environmental turbulence. *Organization Science*, 22(4), 1026–1039.

Dess, G.G., and Lumpkin, G.T. (2005). The role of entrepreneurial orientation in stimulating effective corporate entrepreneurship. *The Academy of Management Executive*, 19(1), 147–156.

Devezer, B., Sprott, D.E., Spangenberg, E.R., and Czellar, S. (2014). Consumer well-being: Effects of subgoal failures and goal importance. *Journal of Marketing*, 78(2), 118–134.

Ebrahimi, P., and Mirbargkar, S. M. (2017). Green entrepreneurship and green innovation for SME development in market turbulence. *Eurasian Business Review*, 7(2), 203–228.

Etzion, D. (2007). Research on organizations and the natural environment, 1992–present: A review. *Journal of Management*, 33(4), 637–664.

Farinelli, F., Bottini, M., Akkoyunlu, S., and Aerni, P. (2011). Green entrepreneurship: the missing link towards a greener economy. *Atdf Journal*, 8(3/4), 42–48.

Gatignon, H., and Xuereb, J.-M. (1997). Strategic orientation of the firm and new product performance. *Journal of Marketing Research*, 77–90.

Gibbs, D. (2008). Sustainability entrepreneurs, ecopreneurs and the development of a sustainable economy. *Greener Management International*, 55, 63–78.

González-Benito, J., and González-Benito, Ó. (2006). A review of determinant factors of environmental proactivity. Business Strategy and the environment, 15(2), 87–102.

Grant, R.M. (2016). *Contemporary Strategy Analysis: Text and Cases Edition*, 9th Edition. John Wiley & Sons.

Hair, J., Money, A., Samouel, P., and Page, M. (2007). *Research Methods for Business*. New Jersey: John Wiley & Sons.

Hair, J.F., Black, W.C., Babin, B.J., Anderson, R.E., and Tatham, R.L. (2006). *Multivariate Data Analysis*, 6th edition. Upper Saddle River, NJ: Pearson/Prentice Hall.

Henseler, J., Hubona, G., and Ray, P.A. (2016). Using PLS path modeling in new technology research: updated guidelines. *Industrial Management & Data Systems*, 116(1), 2–20.

Hisrich, R., Peters, M., and Shepherd, D. (2002). *Entrepreneurship*. McGraw-Hill.

Hoang, Q.N. (2016). Legislative policy in support of Vietnam SMEs: Analysis and propositions. *International Journal of Economics and Finance*, 8(2), 226.

Hoang, T., and Chu, N.M.N. (2005). *Data Analysis in SPSS*. Statistics Publisher (in Vietnamese).

Hong, J., Song, T.H., and Yoo, S. (2013). Paths to success: how do market orientation and entrepreneurship orientation produce new product success? *Journal of Product Innovation Management*, 30(1), 44–55.

Horbach, J. (2008). Determinants of environmental innovation — New evidence from German panel data sources. *Research Policy*, 37(1), 163–173.

Horváthová, E. (2012). The impact of environmental performance on firm performance: Short-term costs and long-term benefits? *Ecological Economics*, 84, 91–97.

Hu, L.t., and Bentler, P.M. (1999). Cutoff criteria for fit indexes in covariance structure analysis: Conventional criteria versus new alternatives. *Structural Equation Modeling: A Multidisciplinary Journal*, 6(1), 1–55.

Hult, G.T.M., Hurley, R.F., and Knight, G.A. (2004). Innovativeness: Its antecedents and impact on business performance. *Industrial Marketing Management*, 33(5), 429–438.

Iyer, K.N. (2011). Demand chain collaboration and operational performance: Role of IT analytic capability and environmental uncertainty. *Journal of Business & Industrial Marketing*, 26(2), 81–91.

Jaworski, B.J., and Kohli, A.K. (1993). Market orientation: Antecedents and consequences. *The Journal of Marketing*, 57(3), 53–70.

Jenkins, H. (2009). A "business opportunity" model of corporate social responsibility for small- and medium-sized enterprises. *Business Ethics: A European Review*, 18(1), 21–36.

Kemp, R., and Pearson, P. (2007). Final report MEI project about measuring eco-innovation. UM Merit, Maastricht, 10.

Kim, N., and Atuahene-Gima, K. (2010). Using exploratory and exploitative market learning for new product development. *Journal of Product Innovation Management*, 27(4), 519–536.

Kirca, A.H., Jayachandran, S., and Bearden, W.O. (2005). Market orientation: A meta-analytic review and assessment of its antecedents and impact on performance. *Journal of Marketing*, 69(2), 24–41.

Kirkwood, J., and Walton, S. (2010). What motivates ecopreneurs to start businesses? *International Journal of Entrepreneurial Behavior & Research*, 16(3), 204–228.

Klassen, R.D., and Whybark, D.C. (1999). Environmental management in operations: The selection of environmental technologies. *Decision Sciences*, 30(3), 601–631.

Klewitz, J., and Hansen, E.G. (2014). Sustainability-oriented innovation of SMEs: A systematic review. *Journal of Cleaner Production*, 65, 57–75.

Kraus, S., Rigtering, J.C., Hughes, M., and Hosman, V. (2012). Entrepreneurial orientation and the business performance of SMEs: A quantitative study from the Netherlands. *Review of Managerial Science*, 6(2), 161–182.

Lee, C., Lee, K., and Pennings, J.M. (2001). Internal capabilities, external networks, and performance: A study on technology-based ventures. *Strategic Management Journal*, 22(6–7), 615–640.

Leech, N.L., Barrett, K.C., and Morgan, G.A. (2005). *SPSS for Intermediate Statistics*, 2nd edition. New Jersey: Lawrence Erlbaum Associates, Inc.

Li, T., and Calantone, R.J. (1998). The impact of market knowledge competence on new product advantage: Conceptualization and empirical examination. *The Journal of Marketing*, 62, 13–29.

Li, Y., Guo, H., Liu, Y., and Li, M. (2008). Incentive mechanisms, entrepreneurial orientation, and technology commercialization: Evidence from China's transitional economy. *Journal of Product Innovation Management*, 25(1), 63–78.

Lin, H., Zeng, S., Ma, H., Qi, G., and Tam, V.W. (2014). Can political capital drive corporate green innovation? Lessons from China. *Journal of Cleaner Production*, 64, 63–72.

Lin, R.-J., Tan, K.-H., and Geng, Y. (2013). Market demand, green product innovation, and firm performance: Evidence from Vietnam motorcycle industry. *Journal of Cleaner Production*, 40, 101–107.

Lin, Y., Tseng, M.-L., Chen, C.-C., and Chiu, A.S. (2011). Positioning strategic competitiveness of green business innovation capabilities using hybrid method. *Expert Systems with Applications*, 38(3), 1839–1849.

Lumpkin, G.T., Cogliser, C.C., and Schneider, D.R. (2009). Understanding and measuring autonomy: An entrepreneurial orientation perspective. *Entrepreneurship Theory and Practice*, 33(1), 47–69.

Lumpkin, G.T., and Dess, G.G. (2001). Linking two dimensions of entrepreneurial orientation to firm performance: The moderating role of environment and industry life cycle. *Journal of Business Venturing*, 16(5), 429–451.

Mangematin, V., Lemarié, S., Boissin, J.-P., Catherine, D., Corolleur, F., Coronini, R., and Trommetter, M. (2003). Development of SMEs and heterogeneity of trajectories: The case of biotechnology in France. *Research Policy*, 32(4), 621–638.

Mesquita, L.F., and Lazzarini, S.G. (2008). Horizontal and vertical relationships in developing economies: Implications for SMEs' access to global markets. *Academy of Management Journal*, 51(2), 359–380.

Miller, D. (1983). The correlates of entrepreneurship in three types of firms. *Management Science*, 29(7), 770–791.

Murphy, M. (2002). *The OECD Small and Medium Enterprise Outlook*. OECD Publishing, Paris. https://doi.org/10.1787/sme_outlook-2002-en.

Ngoc Thuy, P., and Nguyen Hau, L. (2010). Service personal values and customer loyalty: A study of banking services in a transitional economy. International *Journal of Bank Marketing*, 28(6), 465–478.

Nguyen, D.T., and Nguyen, T.M.T. (2011). *Marketing Research – Structural Equation Modeling (SEM) Application*. Ho Chi Minh City, Vietnam: Labor Publisher (in Vietnamese).

Nidumolu, R., Prahalad, C.K., and Rangaswami, M.R. (2009). Why sustainability is now the key driver of innovation. *Harvard Business Review*, 87(9), 56–64.

Olson, E.M., Slater, S.F., and Hult, G.T.M. (2005). The performance implications of fit among business strategy, marketing organization structure, and strategic behavior. *Journal of Marketing*, 69(3), 49–65.

Oly Ndubisi, N., and Iftikhar, K. (2012). Relationship between entrepreneurship, innovation and performance: Comparing small and medium-size enterprises. *Journal of Research in Marketing and Entrepreneurship*, 14(2), 214–236.

Porter, M., and Linde, C. (1995). Green and competitive: Ending the stalemate. In *The Dynamics of the eco-efficient economy: Environmental Regulation and Competitive Advantage*. Cheltenham: Edward Elgar Publishing, p. 33.

Porter, M.E., and Van der Linde, C. (1995). Toward a new conception of the environment-competitiveness relationship. *Journal of Economic Perspectives*, 9(4), 97–118.

Rennings, K., and Rammer, C. (2011). The impact of regulation-driven environmental innovation on innovation success and firm performance. *Industry and Innovation*, 18(03), 255–283.

Rhee, J., Park, T., and Lee, D.H. (2010). Drivers of innovativeness and performance for innovative SMEs in South Korea: Mediation of learning orientation. *Technovation*, 30(1), 65–75.

Santos-Vijande, M.L., and Álvarez-González, L.I. (2007). Innovativeness and organizational innovation in total quality-oriented firms: The moderating role of market turbulence. *Technovation*, 27(9), 514–532.

Sarkar, A. (2013). Promoting eco-innovations to leverage sustainable development of eco-industry and green growth. *European Journal of Sustainable Development*, 2(1), 171.

Schonlau, M., Ronald Jr, D., and Elliott, M.N. (2002). *Conducting Research Surveys via e-Mail and the Web*. Rand Corporation. https://www.rand.org/pubs/monograph_reports/MR1480.html. Also available in print form.

Sidik, I.G. (2012). Conceptual framework of factors affecting SME development: Mediating factors on the relationship of entrepreneur traits and SME performance. *Procedia Economics and Finance*, 4, 373–383.

Silajdžić, I., Kurtagić, S.M., and Vučijak, B. (2015). Green entrepreneurship in transition economies: A case study of Bosnia and Herzegovina. *Journal of Cleaner Production*, 88, 376–384.

Steenkamp, J.-B.E., and Van Trijp, H.C. (1991). The use of LISREL in validating marketing constructs. *International Journal of Research in Marketing*, 8(4), 283–299.

Tan, J. (2001). Innovation and risk-taking in a transitional economy: A comparative study of Chinese managers and entrepreneurs. *Journal of Business Venturing*, 16(4), 359–376.

Theodosiou, M., Kehagias, J., and Katsikea, E. (2012). Strategic orientations, marketing capabilities and firm performance: An empirical investigation in the context of frontline managers in service organizations. *Industrial Marketing Management*, 41(7), 1058–1070.

Tsai, K.-H., and Yang, S.-Y. (2013). Firm innovativeness and business performance: The joint moderating effects of market turbulence and competition. *Industrial Marketing Management*, 42(8), 1279–1294.

Tseng, M.-L. (2013). Modeling sustainable production indicators with linguistic preferences. *Journal of Cleaner Production*, 40, 46–56.

Uslu, Y.D., Hancıoğlu, Y., and Demir, E. (2015). Applicability to green entrepreneurship in Turkey: A situation analysis. *Procedia-Social and Behavioral Sciences*, 195, 1238–1245.

Varadarajan, R. (2017). Innovating for sustainability: A framework for sustainable innovations and a model of sustainable innovations orientation. *Journal of the Academy of Marketing Science*, 45(1), 14–36.

Vietnam-briefing (2017, October 27). Facilitating SME Growth in Vietnam (Koushan Das, Ed.). Retrieved May 19, 2018, from http://www.vietnam-briefing.com/news/facilitating-sme-growth-vietnam.html/

Wales, W.J., Gupta, V.K., and Mousa, F.-T. (2013). Empirical research on entrepreneurial orientation: An assessment and suggestions for future research. *International Small Business Journal*, 31(4), 357–383.

Wang, G., Dou, W., Zhu, W., and Zhou, N. (2015). The effects of firm capabilities on external collaboration and performance: The moderating role of market turbulence. *Journal of Business Research*, 68(9), 1928–1936.

Wong, S.K.S. (2013). Environmental requirements, knowledge sharing and green innovation: Empirical evidence from the electronics industry in China. *Business Strategy and the Environment*, 22(5), 321–338.

York, J.G., and Venkataraman, S. (2010). The entrepreneur–environment nexus: Uncertainty, innovation, and allocation. *Journal of Business Venturing*, 25(5), 449–463.

https://doi.org/10.1142/9789811227158_0016

Chapter 16

# The Mediating Role of Innovation Speed and Quality in the Relationship between Intellectual Capital and Firm Performance: The Case of Tien Giang Small and Medium Enterprises (SMEs) in the Early Stages

**Kim Nhan Vo, Minh Nguyet Doan, Thanh Vu Nguyen, and Van Dat Nguyen**

## Abstract

The purpose of this chapter is to test the model by using structural equation modeling using partial least squares (PLS-SEM) to analyze data collected from 395 small and medium enterprises (SMEs) in Tien Giang province, Vietnam. The results show that the three components of intellectual capital (IC), namely human capital, structural capital (SC), and relational capital, are positively related to firms' performance, considering the mediating role of innovation speed and quality of a firm in the early stages. The findings indicate that an effective way to improve SMEs' performance is by enhancing their intangible capitals and innovation by using PLS-SEM software. The collected samples are limited in the cultural province of the delta region, thus this limits generalization to other contexts. Guidelines for practical solutions to help SMEs enhance their competitive advantage and gain the best firm performance in their business are included.

**Keywords:** Intellectual capital; Innovation; SMEs' performance.

## 1. Introduction

In resource-based theory (RBT), firms have limited resources, thus they need to integrate with their capabilities to contribute to competitive advantage (Barney *et al.*, 2001). In the context of RBT, there are two types of resources, including tangible and intangible resources (such as financial and physical assets, human capital, and patents) that the firm can use to perform its business strategy (Barney *et al.*, 2001). The outcome is gained through unique resources and the combination of knowledge to create innovation and product development (Danneels, 2002). RBT emphasizes different characteristics of the firm, reflecting that different firms own different resources and capabilities (Eisenhardt and Martin, 2000; Monteiro *et al.*, 2008; Tho, 2018). It can help firms create competitive advantage. RBT argues that to gain a competitive advantage, "a firm resource must have four VRIN attributes (valuable, rare, imitable, and non-substitutable) compared with firms' competitors".

To gain competitive advantage, firms need to enhance their capabilities in using their resources, which include various capitals. Among capitals mentioned above, the extant research on intellectual capital (IC) mostly focuses on the developed countries from an accounting and financial perspective (Bontis, 2001). Stewart and Capital (1997) define IC as the intellectual material that is formalized and captured to create wealth by creating a higher-valued asset. Following the study of Curado and Bontis (2007), IC is defined as including human capital, structural capital (SC), and relational capital. Furthermore, IC research is necessary for learning and improvement (Curado and Bontis, 2007). This capital is difficult not only to measure but also to evaluate, however, the IC of an organization shows the wealth of ideas and ability for innovation which can create high value for firms (Curado and Bontis, 2007).

According to the knowledge-based view (KBV) of the firm (Grant, 1996), knowledge-based resources are considered as one of the most important resources. KBV theory shows that organizational capabilities are basic factors for competitive advantage and capabilities are a firm's abilities to use resources to achieve their goals. Moreover, these knowledge-based resources significantly contribute to firm performance and competitive advantage (Donate and Guadamillas, 2015; Obeidat *et al.*, 2016). Particularly, Grant (1991) states that SMEs cannot be presumed to be well-endowed with tangible assets. Especially, SMEs performance in service is largely dependent on the successful management of organizational knowledge (Bisharat *et al.*, 2016). Therefore, the authors suggest that SMEs should utilize intangible assets such as IC and organizational capital to enhance their performance to gain competitive advantage.

It is easily recognized that the private sector plays an important role in enhancing a nation's competitive advantage. To a large extent, private enterprises often contribute employment opportunities and income to labor and create and distribute goods and services that offer people a greater choice in their purchasing. In developing countries, they contribute to economic development as well. In Vietnam, the private sector with small and medium enterprises (SMEs) has emerged and contributed to socioeconomic development, and SMEs' role has been crucial. From 2012 to 2017, the number of SMEs has ballooned, accounting for 98.1%, while large enterprises only account for 1.9% (*General Statistics Office, 2017*), thus SMEs are a significant factor in the Vietnamese economy (Table 1).

It is difficult to define SMEs because of the changes over time, variations from country to country, and the different size ranges (Peres and Stumpo, 2000). SMEs are firms that are small in terms of capital, labor, or revenue. According to the criteria of World Bank (WB), micro-enterprises are enterprises with less than ten employees, small enterprises with the number of employees from ten to less than 200 people and capital of less than US$ 20 billion, and medium enterprises have 200–300 employees and the capital is from US$20 to US$100 billion. In each country, people have set criteria to identify SMEs. In Vietnam, Article 6, Decree No. 39/2018/ND-CP dated March 11, 2018 also regulates SMEs according to the size of capital and number of employees in each economic sector. Thus, firms with over 100 employees are removed from this study and survey

**Table 1:** Types of SMEs in Vietnam.

| | | **SME types under Decree 39/2018** | | | **SME types under Decree 56/2009** | | |
|---|---|---|---|---|---|---|---|
| **Areas** | **Criteria** | **Micro** | **Small** | **Medium** | **Micro** | **Small** | **Medium** |
| Agriculture, forestry, aquaculture, industry and construction | No. of employees ($e$)* | ≤10 | ≤100 | ≤200 | ≤10 | ≤200 | ≤300 |
| | Total capital ($BV$)** | ≤3 | ≤20 | ≤100 | | ≤20 | ≤100 |
| | Annual revenue ($BV$)** | ≤3 | ≤50 | ≤200 | | | |
| Trading and Services | No. of employees ($e$)* | ≤10 | ≤50 | ≤100 | ≤10 | ≤50 | ≤100 |
| | Total capital ($BV$)** | ≤3 | ≤50 | ≤100 | | ≤10 | ≤50 |
| | Annual revenue ($BV$)** | ≤10 | ≤100 | ≤300 | | | |

*Notes*: *employees; **Billion Vietnam Dong.
*Source*: Nguyen (2019).

samples are only from firms established and in the early stages (under 5 years). Moreover, it is necessary to study SMEs in rural regions because their resources are more limited than big companies'. Our research only focuses on SMEs, and excludes larger companies. This focus allows us to draw detailed conclusions for this specific context of Tien Giang province of Vietnam because of specific characteristics of this region, which contains the Mekong Delta. Moreover, Tien Giang is a short distance from Ho Chi Minh City, the largest city of Vietnam. Especially, this study also focuses on owners of SMEs in the early stages to understand their expectations related to some concepts in this study.

The rest of this chapter is organized and outlined as follows. The next section shows the theoretical background of key concepts related to IC, innovation, and firm performance in the early stages, which is followed by the development of proposed hypotheses. The research method is then analyzed and reported, which features figures for data collection. Data analysis, result discussions, and implications are figured out in the final sections of the chapter.

## 2. Literature Review

### 2.1. *Firm performance*

The performance of SMEs attracts interest among academic researchers. Firm performance is defined as the level of success of a firm (Chelliah *et al.*, 2010). Moreover, Chatterjee and Lim (2000) study the relationship between the external factors and internal factors of SMEs in Singapore and their performance. Besides that, Parnell (2002) reviews the current challenges and new directions in competitive research. He outlines the major conceptual and empirical challenges facing competitive strategy researchers and presents recommendations for future research. According to Sebhatu (2008), firm performance refers to the extent to which an organization succeeds or achieves its objectives and strategies. Venkatraman and Ramanujam (1986) focus on using both financial and non-financial dimensions to measure firm performance. According to Venkatraman and Ramanujam (1986), to measure the performance of SME firms, both growth and financial aspects are needed to be considered, in which non-financial aspect is also important to capture all the dimensions of firm performance. Gomes *et al.* (2006) suggest that both financial and non-financial measures can evaluate firm performance, and non-financial measures are more important and useful for firm performance measurement of small organizations. Therefore, this study utilizes perceptual measures to evaluate SMEs' performance. According to Wang *et al.* (2018), firm performance has two main outcomes, including operational performance and financial performance. Operational performance involves analyzing a company's performance against its objectives and goals. In other words, operational performance comprises real results or outputs compared with intended outputs. Financial performance refers to measuring a company's operations and policies in monetary terms. Moreover, human capital is an indispensable factor for producing new products, improving managerial caliber, and enhancing quality and productivity (Cabello-Medina *et al.*, 2011). Moreover, human capital improves financial outcomes because staff talent can help increase sales revenues and reduce cost (Cabello-Medina *et al.*, 2011; Soo *et al.*, 2017).

### 2.2. *Intellectual capital*

Previous studies have developed several IC concepts at the firm level. Bontis (1998) shows that there are three categories of IC, namely, human, customer, and SCs. Based on recent studies, it is suggested that IC consists of three major components, i.e., human capital, SC, and relational capital (Sharabati *et al.*, 2010). Essentially, based on a knowledge management perspective, this model illustrates that there is a direct and positive relation between IC and firm performance (Stewart and Capital, 1997). In the early stages, SMEs are often limited within their resources. To enhance their capabilities so as to gain competitive advantage, SMEs choose the best way by focusing on their intangible resources such as human capital, relational capital, and SC. Among the three IC components, human capital is employees' knowledge, skills, attitudes, innovativeness, loyalty, wisdom, and experiences, which other firms cannot easily imitate and apply (Seleim *et al.*, 2007; Campbell *et al.*, 2012). Therefore, the authors only study some essential IC for SMEs, including human capital, relational capital, and SC in this chapter. Phusavat *et al.* (2011) show that IC is one of the antecedents of innovation.

### 2.3. *Structural capital*

SC is an intangible organizational resource that cannot be taken away by employees when they are off work or leave their jobs (Edvinsson and Malone, 1997). It includes procedures, routines, capabilities, databases, software, information systems, company trademarks, images, copyrights, and patents (Aramburu and Saenz, 2011). SC represents unique approaches to performing tasks and activities, which can hardly be imitated by competitors. By focusing on SC, firms can improve their work processes by enhancing service quality, improving communication, and solving problems effectively. This results in higher quality and lower cost, which can lead to business success (Aramburu and Saenz, 2011). Furthermore, SC can also provide guidelines to avoid unnecessary efforts in the value creation process, which helps to attain desired employee productivity and revenue growth (Phusavat *et al.*, 2011), thus the authors suggest that SC relates to innovation. In line with the analysis above, the authors put forward the following hypotheses:

**Hypothesis H1a:** *SC has a positive effect on innovation speed (IS).*

**Hypothesis H1b:** *SC has a positive and significant influence on innovation quality (IQ).*

### 2.4. *Human capital*

For many years, there have been several studies in relation to the factors affecting the startup performance (Elfring and Hulsink, 2007; Gilbert *et al.*, 2006). The most prominent of these studies is the important role of human capital in the development of enterprises, in particular of SMEs (Kyereboah-Coleman, 2007). In addition, Ahmad and Hoffmann (2008), based on RBT, argue that human resources can create a competitive advantage for startups. While Samad (2013) defines human capital as the ability to manage a business and argues that a business with effective management skills stays in business as well as explores business opportunities. In short, human capital contributes significantly to improving firm performance. Similarly, recent research by Hisrich and Drnovsek (2002) show that management capacity, expressed by education level, management experience, entrepreneurial experience, and knowledge of business, has a positive impact on the performance of newly established SMEs. In contrast, some studies do not provide evidence of a positive relationship between human capital and performance (Appuhami, 2007). In addition, the studies by Subramaniam and Youndt (2005) and Newman *et al.* (2017) agree that human capital is a direct factor affecting the business performance of enterprises. Human capital is defined as the accumulated value of investing in the employees' training and competence (Edvinsson and Malone, 1997). It also includes the competence, skills of employees (Roos and Roos, 1997). In addition, Zambon (2002) states that human capital includes the collective knowledge, creativity, and innovativeness of all members within an organization. Ucbasaran *et al.* (2002) argue that a firm's human capital and other knowledge-related resources are resources that have the potential to be rare, inimitable, and non-substitutable, and hence be the source of competitive advantage. According to Sharabati *et al.* (2010), human capital is one pillar of IC.

Moreover, previous studies were done by some authors in different countries and industries (Cabrita and Bontis, 2008; Chen *et al.*, 2014; Costa *et al.*, 2014). Kianto *et al.* (2017) present that human capital is a key antecedent of both structural and relational capital. In other words, human capital (i.e., employees' knowledge, skills, and motivation) contributes to the development of relational and structural capital. Moreover, Marr and Chatzkel (2004) summarize that SC includes customer capital and organizational capital. Our study suggests that knowledge-based resources can affect IC components both directly and indirectly. Thus, human capital is one of the pillars of structural and relational capital and IC. Therefore, the authors put forward the following hypotheses:

**Hypothesis H2a:** *HC has positive relations to IS.*

**Hypothesis H2b:** *HC has a positive influence on IQ.*

**Hypothesis H2c:** *HC has positive impacts on SC.*

**Hypothesis H2d:** *HC has positive relations to relational capital (RC).*

## 2.5. *Relational capital*

Relational capital, also sometimes called external capital or social capital, refers to the value and knowledge in relationships with customers, suppliers, institutions, and other external agents (Bontis, 1998). It includes relationships with family members, customers, suppliers, and others. Kaplan *et al.* (2004) also state that relational capital is considered as the major drive for corporate growth. Relational capital can help SMEs by reducing cost of employees, customers, and suppliers, can help and aid in product and process innovation, and increasing firm performance. Thus, relational capital in SMEs affects their performance in the early stages. For this study, we want to investigate how relational capital influences innovation and how the interaction is between human capital and relational capital. Therefore, the following hypotheses are proposed:

**Hypothesis H3a:** *RC has positive impacts on IS.*

**Hypothesis H3b:** *RC has positive relations to IQ.*

## 2.6. *Innovation*

Innovativeness is considered as being able to create new products and/or processes and it is the critical element of business competitiveness. There is some prior research related to two dimensions

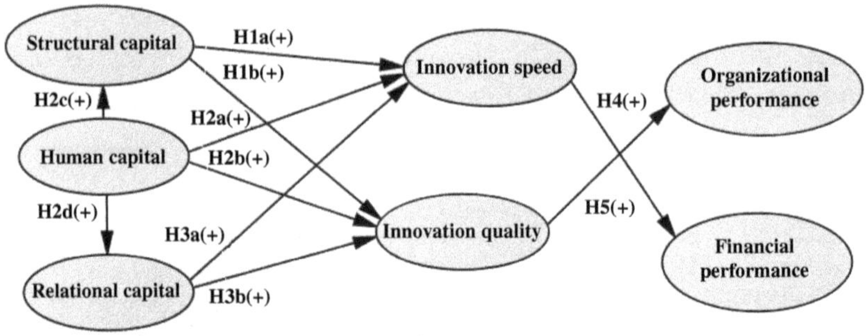


**Figure 1:** Model and some hypotheses of authors' study.

of innovation, including innovation speed and quality (Carbonell and Rodriguez Escudero, 2010; Wang and Wang, 2012). Innovation speed can be defined as the time interval between initial conception/definition of innovation and the ultimate commercialization of new products, services, and related activities (Kessler and Chakrabarti, 1996). Fast innovation speed can help establish early segments and customer loyalty leading to better firm performance (Tidd and Bessant, 2005). Innovation quality is defined as a firm's capability as well as its performance in other innovation, compared to its potential (Wang and Wang, 2012). Innovation quality is one of the most crucial factors to gain competitive advantage and improve quality of management and customer satisfaction (Haner, 2002; Tseng and Wu, 2006). Thus, firms with high innovation quality are more effective and tend to gain better firm performance (Tseng and Wu, 2006). In this study, it is seen that Tien Giang SMEs need to change their strategies to address external and internal environment changes in their business model, thus authors suggest that there is a relationship between business model innovation and SMEs' performance. Based on the analysis above, the authors put forward the following hypotheses (see Figure 1):

**Hypothesis H4a:** *IS has a positive effect on operational performance (OP).*

**Hypothesis H4b:** *IQ has positive relations to financial performance (FP).*

## 3. Research Method

### 3.1. *Study design and methodology*

The measurement of startup performance is most crucial. Venkatraman and Ramanujam (1986) emphasize using both financial and non-financial dimensions to measure firm performance. According to Wiklund (1999), to measure the performance of SMEs, both growth and financial aspects are needed to be considered. Non-financial aspect is also important to capture all the dimensions of firm performance. Based on the studies of Laukkanen *et al.* (2013) and Efrat and Shoham (2013), SMEs performance is measured by measuring the change in total sales revenues and profit (in last three years), number of employees, and change in customer base, by using Likert scale (in which "1" stands for least satisfactory and "5" stands for highly satisfactory). Gomes *et al.* (2004) suggest that both financial and non-financial measures can evaluate firm performance, non-financial measures are more important and useful for performance measurement of small organizations. Therefore, this study utilizes perceptual measures to evaluate SMEs' performance based on Wang *et al.* (2018). All items are measured with 5-point Likert-type scale. The questionnaire is validated through interviews to collect information about SMEs' performance measurement models and hypotheses (see Table 2).

According to Hair *et al.* (1998), in the Maximization Likelihood estimation method the minimum sample size is 100–150. In addition, the small sample size for the estimation method used in the linear structure (SEM) model is less than or equal to 100, a medium sample size is 100–200, and a large sample is $\geq$200. The sample size of this study is 395, suitable for the requirements of the analytical method. According to Henseler and Chin (2010), the research model is evaluated in two steps, including measurement model and structural model. First, indicator reliability, internal consistency reliability, convergent reliability, and discriminant validity are used to assess the validity of reflective measurement models (see Table 3).

Table 2: Measurement of construct, items, and coding.

| Construct | Items | Code |
|---|---|---|
| SC | 1. The overall operations procedure of our company is very efficient | SC1 |
| | 2. Our company responds to changes very quickly | SC2 |
| | 3. Our company has an easily accessible information system | SC3 |
| | 4. Systems and procedures of our company support innovation | SC4 |
| | 5. Our company's culture and atmosphere are flexible and comfortable | SC5 |
| | 6. There is support among different departments in our company | SC6 |
| | 7. Our company emphasizes new market development investment | SC7 |
| RC | 1. Our company discovers and solves problems through intimate communication and effective collaboration | RC1 |
| | 2. Our company has many excellent suppliers | RC2 |
| | 3. Our company maintains long-term relationships with customers | RC3 |
| | 4. Our company maintains appropriate interactions with its stakeholders | RC4 |
| | 5. Our company has stable and good relationships with the strategic partners | RC5 |
| HC | 1. Employees hold suitable work experience for accomplishing their job successfully in our company | HC1 |
| | 2. Employees of our company have excellent professional skills in their particular jobs and functions | HC2 |
| | 3. The company provides well-designed training programs | HC3 |
| | 4. The employees of our company often develop new ideas and knowledge | HC4 |
| | 5. Employees are creative in our company | HC5 |
| IS | 1. Our company is quicker in coming up with novel ideas than our key competitors | IS1 |
| | 2. Our company is quicker in new product launch than our key competitors | IS2 |
| | 3. Our company is quicker in new product development than our key competitors | IS3 |

*(Continued)*

**Table 2:** (*Continued*)

| Construct | Items | Code |
|---|---|---|
| | 4. Our company is quicker in new processes than our key competitors | IS4 |
| | 5. Our company is quicker in problem solving than our key competitors | IS5 |
| IQ | 1. Our company does better in coming up with novel ideas than our key competitors | IQ1 |
| | 2. Our company does better in new product launching than our key competitors | IQ2 |
| | 3. Our company does better in new product development than our key competitors | IQ3 |
| | 4. Our company does better in improving processes than our key competitors | IQ4 |
| | 5. Our company does better in improving management than our key competitors | IQ5 |
| OP | 1. Customer satisfaction with our company is better than that with our key competitors | OP1 |
| | 2. Quality development of our company is better than that of our key competitors | OP2 |
| | 3. Cost management of our company is better than that of key competitors | OP3 |
| | 4. Responsiveness of our company is better than that of key competitors | OP4 |
| | 5. Productivity of our company is better than that of key competitors | OP5 |
| FP | 1. Return on investment of our company is better than that of key competitors | FP1 |
| | 2. Return on assets of our company is better than that of key competitors | FP2 |
| | 3. Return on sales of our company is better than that of key competitors | FP3 |
| | 4. Average profitability of our company is better than that of key competitors | FP4 |
| | 5. Profit growth of our company is better than that of key competitors | FP5 |
| | 6. Sales growth of our company is better than that of key competitors | FP6 |

*Source*: Wang *et al.* (2018).

**Table 3:** Testing measurement model.

| Validity type | Criterion | Description | Literature |
|---|---|---|---|
| Internal consistency | Reliability Cronbach's Alpha | Should be greater than 0.70 to achieve the reliability of measurement model | Nunally (1978) |
| Internal consistency | Reliability Composite reliability | Alternative to Cronbach's Alpha that attempts to measure the sum of an LV's factor loadings relative to the sum of the factor loadings plus error variances | Nunally and Bernstein (1994) |
| Indicator reliability | Indicator loadings | Measures how much of the indicators variance is explained by the corresponding latent variables. | Chin (1998) |
| Convergent validity | Average variance extracted (AVE) | Proposed threshold value for AVE should be higher than 0.50 | Bagozzi and Yi (1988) |
| Discriminant validity | AVE numbers and latent variable correlations | Fornell and Larcker (1981) suggest that the "square root" of AVE of each latent variable should be greater than the correlations among the latent variables | Fornell and Larcker (1981) |

### 3.2. *Research process*

This study combines qualitative and quantitative research methods. Qualitative research is conducted by focus group discussions with 10 chief executive officers of SMEs in Tien Giang province at the meeting room of Statistics Offices to modify observational variables that are used to measure research concepts. All items are measured by using 5-point Likert scale, anchored by 1 (strongly disagree) and 5 (strongly agree). Quantitative research is conducted through direct interviews (face-to-face interviews) based on a random sampling of 400 SMEs in Tien Giang collected from January 2019 to May 2019 using a detailed questionnaire to test model and research hypotheses.

## 4. Analysis and Result

Data are analyzed by PLS-SEM software 3.0 with 395 valid respondents, about 98.75% of the questionnaires sent to the 400 respondents. According to the authors' study in Table 3, there are three main types of surveyed owners of SMEs selected, including the type of limited liability company with 69.7%, private company with 13.4%, and others with 16.9%. In addition, fields of commerce and service businesses have the majority of the total respondents, as shown in Table 4.

The next one to check is Indicator Reliability (see Table 5). It can be seen that all of the indicators have individual indicator reliability values that are much larger than the minimum acceptable level of 0.4 and close to the preferred level of 0.7. Table 5 represents the outer loadings and shows all scores are above 0.7, thereby meeting the standards as well.

Reliability is tested by measuring the composite reliability and Cronbach's Alpha, complemented with the indicator loadings. These tests are necessary to make sure there is internal consistency reliability. As Table 6 shows, all scores are above 0.8 and thereby meet the

**Table 4:** Types of surveyed companies.

| | Frequency | Percent |
|---|---|---|
| Limited liability company | 243 | 61.5 |
| Private company | 68 | 17.2 |
| Other | 84 | 21.3 |
| Total | 395 | 100.0 |

**Table 5:** The results of outer loadings.

| | FP | HC | IQ | IS | OP | RC | SC |
|---|---|---|---|---|---|---|---|
| FP1 | 0.789 | | | | | | |
| FP2 | 0.866 | | | | | | |
| FP3 | 0.709 | | | | | | |
| FP4 | 0.829 | | | | | | |
| FP5 | 0.800 | | | | | | |
| HC1 | | 0.804 | | | | | |
| HC2 | | 0.774 | | | | | |
| HC3 | | 0.853 | | | | | |
| HC4 | | 0.782 | | | | | |
| HC5 | | 0.848 | | | | | |
| IQ1 | | | 0.759 | | | | |
| IQ2 | | | 0.789 | | | | |
| IQ3 | | | 0.776 | | | | |
| IQ4 | | | 0.746 | | | | |
| IQ5 | | | 0.795 | | | | |
| IS1 | | | | 0.858 | | | |
| IS2 | | | | 0.861 | | | |
| IS5 | | | | 0.830 | | | |
| OP1 | | | | | 0.847 | | |
| OP2 | | | | | 0.843 | | |
| OP3 | | | | | 0.854 | | |
| OP4 | | | | | 0.851 | | |
| RC1 | | | | | | 0.816 | |
| RC2 | | | | | | 0.794 | |
| RC3 | | | | | | 0.796 | |
| RC5 | | | | | | 0.811 | |
| SC1 | | | | | | | 0.805 |
| SC3 | | | | | | | 0.825 |
| SC4 | | | | | | | 0.818 |
| SC5 | | | | | | | 0.808 |
| SC6 | | | | | | | 0.768 |

standard of internal consistency reliability. Construct reliability measures the extent of internal consistency of measures used, the results presented in Table 6 show that the observed variables and independent variables used to measure startup performance concepts satisfy the Cronbach's Alpha coefficient because they are greater than 0.70, thus achieving the reliability of measurement model (Nunally, 1978).

**Table 6:** Results of construct reliability and validity.

| | Cronbach's Alpha | rho_A | Composite reliability | Average variance extracted (AVE) |
|---|---|---|---|---|
| FP | 0.862 | 0.905 | 0.899 | 0.641 |
| HC | 0.872 | 0.876 | 0.907 | 0.661 |
| IQ | 0.832 | 0.833 | 0.881 | 0.598 |
| IS | 0.808 | 0.812 | 0.886 | 0.723 |
| OP | 0.871 | 0.872 | 0.912 | 0.720 |
| RC | 0.818 | 0.819 | 0.880 | 0.647 |
| SC | 0.864 | 0.865 | 0.902 | 0.648 |

Fornell–Larcker, cross-loadings, and the heterotrait-monotrait ratio (HTMT) are assessment factors to test discriminant validity (Fornell and Larcker, 1981). It is assessed through convergent validity and discriminant validity. The criterion of Fornell and Larcker (1981) is commonly used to assess the degree of shared variance between the latent variables of the model. According to this criterion, the convergent validity of the measurement model can be assessed by average variance extracted (AVE) and composite reliability (CR). According to Fornell–Larcker criterion and the cross-loadings (Table 7), the constructs' discriminant validity is established as follows: (1) the square root of each construct's AVE is higher than its correlation with another construct, and (2) each item loads highest on its associated construct.

Convergent validity can be assessed through construct factor (item) loadings (or cross-loadings in PLS), AVEs that should have minimum loading of 0.5, and CR with an acceptable minimum of 0.70 (Fornell and Larcker, 1981). From Table 6, the factor loadings of items to their respective constructs are stronger than they load on other constructs providing evidence to support the convergent validity of the derived measures. Discriminant validity is considered adequate since AVEs are greater than their respective inter-construct correlations as in Table 7. Given that the construct reliability and

**Table 7:** Discriminant validity (Fornell–Larcker criterion).

| | FP | HC | IQ | IS | OP | RC | SC |
|---|---|---|---|---|---|---|---|
| **FP** | 0.801 | | | | | | |
| **HC** | 0.059 | 0.813 | | | | | |
| **IQ** | 0.066 | 0.468 | 0.773 | | | | |
| **IS** | 0.061 | 0.532 | 0.519 | 0.850 | | | |
| **OP** | 0.054 | 0.611 | 0.613 | 0.647 | 0.849 | | |
| **RC** | 0.052 | 0.450 | 0.447 | 0.477 | 0.582 | 0.804 | |
| **SC** | 0.046 | 0.483 | 0.557 | 0.498 | 0.637 | 0.382 | 0.805 |

**Table 8:** Discriminant validity (heterotrait-monotrait ratio, HTMT).

| | BI | FP | GU | HC | IC | OC |
|---|---|---|---|---|---|---|
| BI | | | | | | |
| FP | 0.780 | | | | | |
| GU | 0.596 | 0.676 | | | | |
| HC | 0.654 | 0.699 | 0.532 | | | |
| IC | 0.637 | 0.717 | 0.535 | 0.549 | | |
| OC | 0.606 | 0.735 | 0.452 | 0.552 | 0.658 | |

validity conditions of the measurement model are acceptable, we proceed to assess the structural model.

HTMT values close to 1 indicate a lack of discriminant validity and values close to 0.85 indicate threshold values. To assess discriminant validity, heterotrait-monotrait ratio of correlations (HTMT) is tested. To secure discriminant validity all values must be lower than 0.85. Therefore, the results of Table 8 satisfy the discriminant validity in the measurement model.

### 4.1. *The results of the structural (inner) model*

Size and significance of path coefficients: The significance of the path coefficients are measured by executing Bootstrap method using 5.000 single performances. The results show a significant relationship between ($p$-values $< 0.05$).

**Table 9:** The results of path coefficients.

| | Original Sample (O) | Sample Mean (M) | Std. Dev. | *T* Statistics (\|O/STDEV\| | *p* Values |
|---|---|---|---|---|---|
| HC → IQ | 0.184 | 0.185 | 0.046 | 4.023 | 0.000 |
| HC → IS | 0.296 | 0.295 | 0.049 | 6.026 | 0.000 |
| HC → RC | 0.450 | 0.452 | 0.038 | 11.751 | 0.000 |
| HC → SC | 0.483 | 0.487 | 0.037 | 12.896 | 0.000 |
| IQ → OP | 0.613 | 0.617 | 0.030 | 20.228 | 0.000 |
| IS → FP | 0.061 | 0.071 | 0.075 | 0.817 | 0.414 |
| RC → IQ | 0.217 | 0.215 | 0.044 | 4.885 | 0.000 |
| RC → IS | 0.244 | 0.244 | 0.044 | 5.503 | 0.000 |
| SC → IQ | 0.386 | 0.389 | 0.042 | 9.172 | 0.000 |
| SC → IS | 0.262 | 0.265 | 0.044 | 5.984 | 0.000 |

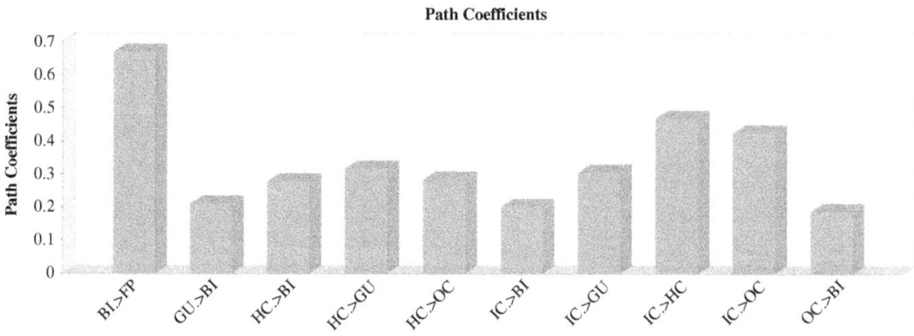


**Figure 2:** The results of path coefficients.

The conceptual model and its path coefficients (including $p$-values) are presented in Table 9 and Figure 2.

## 5. Discussion and Conclusions

That the results mentioned above indicate the suitability of the research model with data's research as well as the acceptance of the hypotheses in this research model shows the practical meaning of firm performance (see Table 10). The research results propose solutions

**Table 10:** The results of $R^2$.

| | $R^2$ | $R^2$ Adjusted |
|---|---|---|
| BI | 0.592 | 0.588 |
| FP | 0.679 | 0.677 |
| GU | 0.370 | 0.367 |
| HC | 0.300 | 0.299 |
| OC | 0.485 | 0.483 |

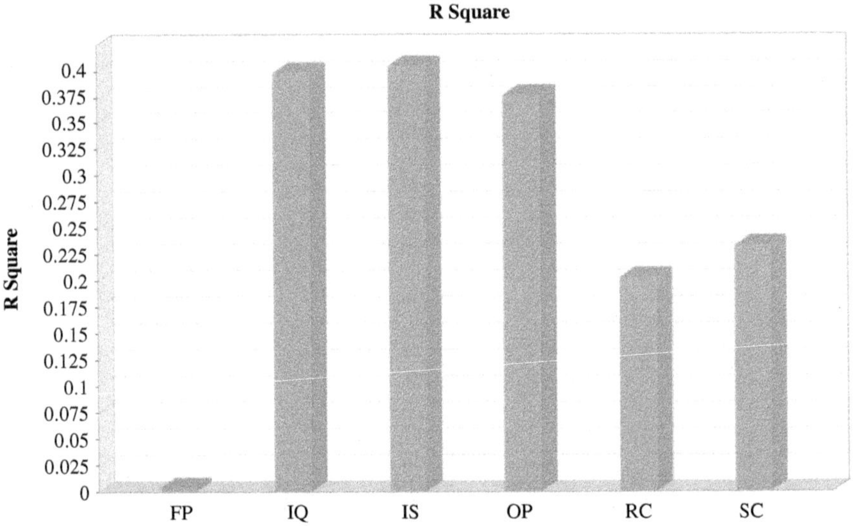


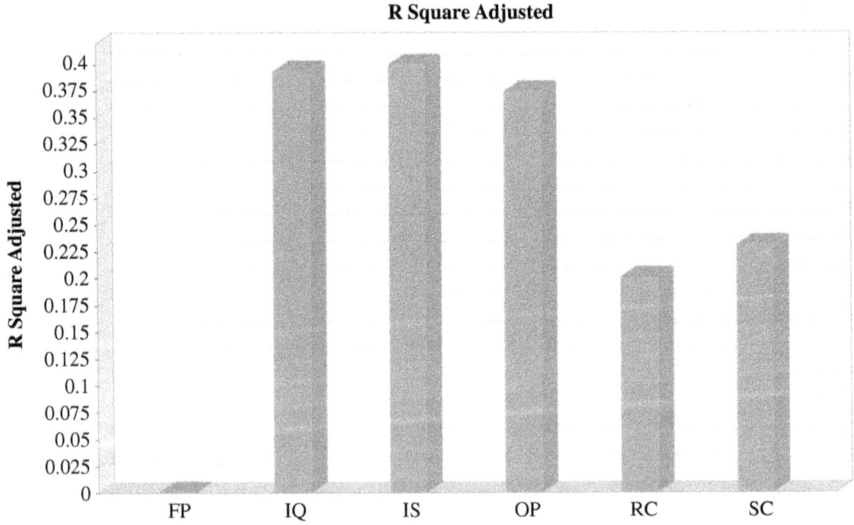

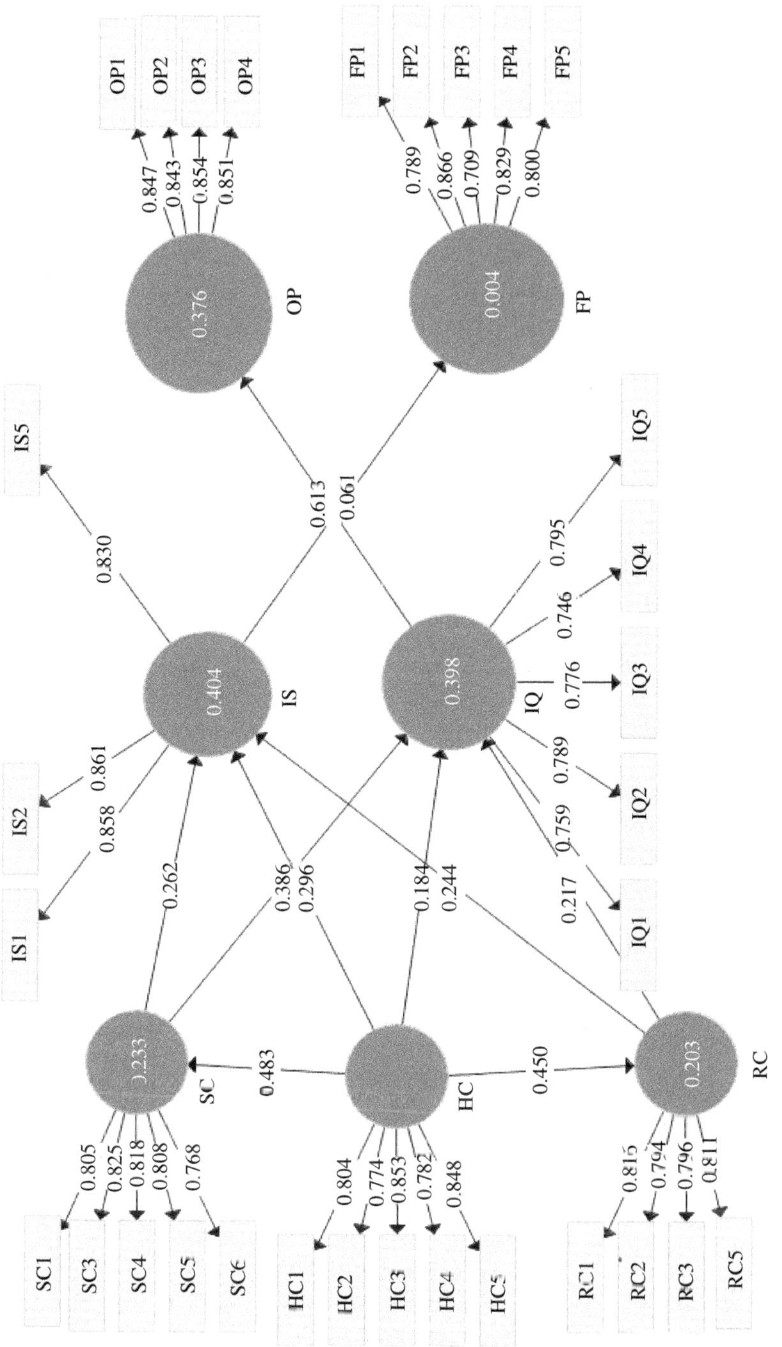


**Figure 3:** The results of the PLS-SEM model.

gaps when there is a combination between the firm performance and other factors of SMEs in Tien Giang province in the early stages.

The results of the study (see Figure 3) show that the operational and financial performance of Tien Giang SMEs is affected by innovation speed and quality, both of which are affected by other factors including *SC*, *human capital*, and *relational capital*. Besides, innovation is an indispensable trend that businesses need to consider, especially SMEs which are more flexible than large companies but have limited resources. Therefore, innovation is an opportunity for SMEs in the process of integration into the recent competitive environment.

## References

Ahmad, N., and Hoffmann, A. (2008). A framework for addressing and measuring entrepreneurship. *OECD Statistics*, STD/DOC(2008)2, 36 pages.

Appuhami, B.R. (2007). The impact of intellectual capital on investors' capital gains on shares: an empirical investigation of Thai banking, finance and insurance sector. *International Management Review*, 3(2), 14–25.

Barney, J., Wright, M., and Ketchen Jr, D.J. (2001). The resource-based view of the firm: Ten years after 1991. *Journal of Management*, 27(6), 625–641.

Bisharat, H., Obeidat, B.Y., Tarhini, A., and Mukattash, I. (2016). The effect of human resource management practices on organizational commitment in chain pharmacies in Jordan. *International Journal of Business and Management*, 12(1), 50.

Bontis, N. (1998). Intellectual capital: An exploratory study that develops measures and models. *Management Decision*, 36(2), 63–76.

Bontis, N. (2001). Assessing knowledge assets: A review of the models used to measure intellectual capital. *International Journal of Management Reviews*, 3(1), 41–60.

Cabello-Medina, C., López-Cabrales, À., and Valle-Cabrera, R. (2011). Leveraging the innovative performance of human capital through HRM and social capital in Spanish firms. *The International Journal of Human Resource Management*, 22(04), 807–828.

Cabrita, M.d.R., and Bontis, N. (2008). Intellectual capital and business performance in the Portuguese banking industry. *International Journal of Technology Management*, 43(1–3), 212–237.

Campbell, B.A., Coff, R., and Kryscynski, D. (2012). Rethinking sustained competitive advantage from human capital. *Academy of Management Review*, 37(3), 376–395.

Carbonell, P., and Rodriguez Escudero, A.I. (2010). The effect of market orientation on innovation speed and new product performance. *Journal of Business & Industrial Marketing*, 25(7), 501–513.

Chatterjee, S.R., and Lim, C.H. (2000). Regionalization strategies of SME sector: An empirical study of Singapore managers. *Journal of International Business and Entrepreneurship*, 8(2), 15–31.

Chelliah, S., Sulaiman, M., and Yusoff, Y.M. (2010). Internationalization and performance: Small and medium enterprises (SMEs) in Malaysia. *International Journal of Business and Management*, 5(6), 27.

Chen, C.-J., Liu, T.-C., Chu, M.-A., and Hsiao, Y.-C. (2014). Intellectual capital and new product development. *Journal of Engineering and Technology Management*, 33, 154–173.

Costa, R.V., Fernández-JardonFernández, C., and Figueroa Dorrego, P. (2014). Critical elements for product innovation at Portuguese innovative SMEs: An intellectual capital perspective. *Knowledge Management Research & Practice*, 12(3), 322–338.

Curado, C., and Bontis, N. (2007). Managing intellectual capital: the MIC matrix. *International Journal of Knowledge and Learning*, 3(2–3), 316–328.

Danneels, E. (2002). The dynamics of product innovation and firm competences. *Strategic Management Journal*, 23(12), 1095–1121.

Donate, M.J., and Guadamillas, F. (2015). An empirical study on the relationships between knowledge management, knowledge-oriented human resource practices and innovation. *Knowledge Management Research & Practice*, 13(2), 134–148.

Edvinsson, L., and Malone, M.S. (1997). Intellectual capital: The proven way to establish your company's real value by finding its hidden brainpower: *Piatkus Publisher*, ISBN: 0749918500, 9780749918507.

Eisenhardt, K.M., and Martin, J.A. (2000). Dynamic capabilities: What are they? *Strategic Management Journal*, 21(10–11), 1105–1121.

Elfring, T., and Hulsink, W. (2007). Networking by entrepreneurs: Patterns of tie — Formation in emerging organizations. *Organization Studies*, 28(12), 1849–1872.

Gilbert, B.A., McDougall, P.P., and Audretsch, D.B. (2006). New venture growth: A review and extension. *Journal of management*, 32(6), 926–950.

Gomes, C.F., Yasin, M.M., and Lisboa, J.V. (2004). A literature review of manufacturing performance measures and measurement in an organizational context: a framework and direction for future research. *Journal of Manufacturing technology management*, 15(6), 511–530.

Gomes, C.F., Yasin, M.M., and Lisboa, J.V. (2006). Performance measurement practices in manufacturing firms: An empirical investigation. *Journal of Manufacturing Technology Management*, 17(2), 144–167.

Grant, R.M. (1991). The resource-based theory of competitive advantage: Implications for strategy formulation. *California Management Review*, 33(3), 114–135.

Grant, R.M. (1996). Toward a knowledge' based theory of the firm. *Strategic Management Journal*, 17(S2), 109–122.

Haner, U.-E. (2002). Innovation quality — A conceptual framework. *International Journal of Production Economics*, 80(1), 31–37.

Hisrich, R.D., and Drnovsek, M. (2002). Entrepreneurship and small business research — A European perspective. *Journal of Small Business and Enterprise Development*, 9(2), 172–222.

Kaplan, R.S., Kaplan, R.E., Norton, D.P., and Davenport, T.H. (2004). *Strategy Maps: Converting Intangible Assets into Tangible Outcomes.* Harvard Business Press.

Kessler, E.H., and Chakrabarti, A.K. (1996). Innovation speed: A conceptual model of context, antecedents, and outcomes. *Academy of Management Review*, 21(4), 1143–1191.

Kianto, A., Sáenz, J., and Aramburu, N. (2017). Knowledge-based human resource management practices, intellectual capital and innovation. *Journal of Business Research*, 81, 11–20.

Kyereboah-Coleman, A. (2007). The impact of capital structure on the performance of microfinance institutions. *The Journal of Risk Finance*, 8(1), 56–71.

Marr, B., and Chatzkel, J. (2004). Intellectual capital at the crossroads: managing, measuring, and reporting of IC. *Journal of Intellectual Capital*, 5(2), 224–229.

Monteiro, L.F., Arvidsson, N., and Birkinshaw, J. (2008). Knowledge flows within multinational corporations: Explaining subsidiary isolation and its performance implications. *Organization Science*, 19(1), 90–107.

Newman, A., Schwarz, S., and Ahlstrom, D. (2017). Microfinance and entrepreneurship: An introduction. *International Small Business Journal*, 35(7), 787–792.

Nguyen, T.-L. (2019). STEAM-ME: A novel model for successful Kaizen implementation and sustainable performance of SMEs in Vietnam. *Complexity*, 2019.

Nunally, J.C. (1978). *Psychometric Theory*, 2nd edition. NY: McGraw-Hill.

Obeidat, B.Y., Al-Suradi, M.M., Masa'deh, R.e., and Tarhini, A. (2016). The impact of knowledge management on innovation: An empirical study on Jordanian consultancy firms. *Management Research Review*, 39(10), 1214–1238.

Parnell, J.A. (2002). Competitive strategy research: Current challenges and new directions. *Journal of Management Research*, 2(1), 1.

Peres, W., and Stumpo, G. (2000). Small and medium-sized manufacturing enterprises in Latin America and the Caribbean under the new economic model. *World Development*, 28(9), 1643–1655.

Phusavat, K., Comepa, N., Sitko-Lutek, A., and Ooi, K.-B. (2011). Interrelationships between intellectual capital and performance: Empirical examination. *Industrial Management & Data Systems*, 111(6), 810–829.

Roos, G., and Roos, J. (1997). Measuring your company's intellectual performance. *Long Range Planning*, 30(3), 413–426.

Samad, S. (2013). Assessing the contribution of human capital on business performance. *International Journal of Trade, Economics and Finance*, 4(6), 393.

Sebhatu, S.P. (2008). The challenges and opportunities of creating sustainable shared value at the base of the pyramid: Cases from sub-Saharan Africa. Greenleaf Publishing Ltd, pp. 146–162.

Seleim, A., Ashour, A., and Bontis, N. (2007). Human capital and organizational performance: A study of Egyptian software companies. *Management Decision*, 45(4), 789–801.

Sharabati, A.-A.A., NajiJawad, S., and Bontis, N. (2010). Intellectual capital and business performance in the pharmaceutical sector of Jordan. *Management Decision*, 48(1), 105–131.

Soo, C., Tian, A.W., Teo, S.T., and Cordery, J. (2017). Intellectual capital — Enhancing HR, absorptive capacity, and innovation. *Human Resource Management*, 56(3), 431–454.

Stewart, T., and Capital, I. (1997). The new wealth of organizations. *Nicholas Brealey, London.*

Subramaniam, M., and Youndt, M.A. (2005). The influence of intellectual capital on the types of innovative capabilities. *Academy of Management Journal*, 48(3), 450–463.

Tho, N.D. (2018). A configurational role of human capital resources in the quality of work life of marketers: FsQCA and SEM findings from Vietnam. *Applied Research in Quality of Life*, 13(2), 461–478. doi:10.1007/s11482-017-9535-6

Tidd, J., and Bessant, J. (2005). *Managing Innovation, Integrating Technological, Market and Organizational Change*, pp. 10–12.

Tseng, C.-Y., and Wu, L.-Y. (2006). Innovation quality in the automobile industry: Measurement indicators and performance implications. *International Journal of Technology Management*, 37(1–2), 162–177.

Ucbasaran, D., Westhead, P., and Wright, M. (2002). *Human capital based determinants of opportunity identification.* Paper presented at the Babson College, Babson Kauffman Entrepreneurship Research Conference (BKERC), Vol. 2006.

Venkatraman, N., and Ramanujam, V. (1986). Measurement of business performance in strategy research: A comparison of approaches. *Academy of Management Review*, 11(4), 801–814.

Wang, Z., Cai, S., Liang, H., Wang, N., and Xiang, E. (2018). Intellectual capital and firm performance: The mediating role of innovation speed and quality. *The International Journal of Human Resource Management*, 90, 1–29.

Wang, Z., and Wang, N. (2012). Knowledge sharing, innovation and firm performance. *Expert Systems with Applications*, 39(10), 8899–8908.

Zambon, S. (2002). Accounting, intangibles and intellectual capital: An overview of the issues and some considerations. PRISM Project, University of Ferrara.

# Part V

# Marketing

https://doi.org/10.1142/9789811227158_0017

# Chapter 17

# How does CSR Influence Customer Loyalty in the Banking Sector? Evidence from Vietnam

**Dang Khoa Tran**

## Abstract

This study is conducted to identify how corporate social responsibility (CSR) influences consumer loyalty in the banking sector in Vietnam — an emerging economy. The social identity theory, stakeholder theory, and signaling theory are used to answer the question "Does CSR directly or indirectly influence customer loyalty in the banking sector in Vietnam?" To accomplish the research objectives, qualitative and quantitative mixed research methods are used. Qualitative research aims to adjust the scale of constructs to suit the Vietnamese market through face-to-face discussions with 10 Vietnamese customers. A survey is then carried out with 299 Vietnamese customers who have experience dealing with banks in Vietnam. Data collected are processed by Smart Partial Least Square (PLS) software with Partial Least Squares Structural Equation Modeling (PLS-SEM). Research results showed that CSR has no direct impact on customer loyalty. However, CSR has an indirect effect on customer loyalty through an intermediate variable of service quality. Service quality has a strong influence on customer loyalty. The administrative implications of this research are that Vietnamese banks should consider CSR as a way to help improve service quality, thereby increasing customer loyalty. CSR factors to consider are legal, ethical, and philanthropic responsibilities. To improve service quality to increase customer loyalty, Vietnamese banks need to pay attention to the factors of reliability, responsiveness, assurance, and empathy. Future research directions that can be implemented include: use stakeholder dimensions for CSR; use other mediators such as brand image, customer satisfaction, and customer trust; and research in other countries with emerging economies similar to Vietnam to increase generalization.

**Keywords:** CSR; Customer loyalty; Service quality; Vietnamese banking.

## 1. Introduction

In recent years, corporate social responsibility (CSR) has become an interestingly important research field in various industries (Mercadé-Melé *et al.*, 2018). There is ample evidence that customers care about the ethics of business (Diallo and Lambey-Checchin, 2017). Therefore, when the business environment is increasingly competitive, the implementation of CSR activities becomes one of the strategies businesses aim at to achieve business success (Aguilera *et al.*, 2007). More and more companies are seeking a competitive advantage through CSR (Servera-Francés and Fuentes-Blasco, 2016). In addition, global pressure on sustainable development also compels businesses not to damage the resources in the course of their business operations. Consequently, research on CSR is conducted in many countries around the world in many fields, including research on causes and consequences of consumer perceived CSR (Stanaaland *et al.*, 2011).

CSR activities in the banking sector are essential (Al-bdour *et al.*, 2010) as this is a particularly important industry, playing a key role in the development of society through cash flow management, valuable financial assets, financial risk management, and payment system organization. The banking sector acts as a "circulatory system" of the economy, which dominates and leads other sectors. Numerous opinions state that the world financial crisis of 2008–2009 originated from the lack of ethics and social responsibility in banks. Banks are responsible for unsustainable loans in the real estate sector, resulting in a real estate bubble burst; the real estate market collapsed and led to the finance and banking crisis (Chandler, 2017). CSR in the banking sector is a matter of great concern.

Studies show that CSR contributes to the sustainable development of businesses. This is even more necessary for businesses operating in high-risk areas such as banks. The slogans of banks also emphasize honesty, integrity, transparency, professional ethics, respect, protection, brand development, sustainable development, and responsibility to the community. Therefore, it is indispensable to see CSR as a long-term strategy that helps create a bank's value, as it helps build customer trust, respect, and loyalty. In the context of fierce competition in the Vietnamese banking market, creating customer loyalty is considered the most effective defensive strategy.

Numerous studies affirm that CSR affects customer loyalty indirectly through customer satisfaction, perceived value, company reputation, and customer trust (Diallo and Lambey-Checchin, 2017; Mercadé-Melé *et al.*, 2018; Servera-Francés and Fuentes-Blasco, 2015, 2016). In addition, CSR is also considered to directly affect customer loyalty (Mercadé-Melé *et al.*, 2018). Research in the banking sector shows that CSR has both a direct impact (Al-Ghamdi and Badawi, 2019; Moisescu, 2017) and an indirect impact (Al-Ghamdi and Badawi, 2019; Chun and Bang, 2016) on customer loyalty. As a result, this study is conducted to determine whether there is a direct, indirect, or both direct and indirect impact of CSR on customer loyalty in the banking sector in Vietnam.

## 2. Theoretical Background

### 2.1. *Social identity theory*

According to the Social Identity Theory (SIT) (Tajfel, 1982), each individual tries to create and enhance his/her image and self-esteem through a social classification process — classifying himself/herself with those others into groups: in-group and out-groups (Tajfel and Turner, 1979). Individuals tend to make comparisons between their group (internal group) and external groups, and at the same time expand their characteristics and show interest (favoritism) for their groups or discrimination against other groups (Tajfel and Turner,

1979). SIT identifies three mental processes that each individual goes through to perform classification with the same or different groups:

*Social classification*, which is the process of organizing individuals into different social groups. This process allows each person to identify everyone, including the individual himself/herself, on the basis of the groups to which he or she belongs. People tend to identify others based on their social categories more than their characteristics. Social classification in general is an emphasis on the similarity between people in the same group and the differences from people in other groups. One person can belong to many social categories, but each different category is more or less important depending on the social situation.

*Social identification*, is the process to identify group members. Social identification is a process that makes individuals behave in the way they believe that members of the group should. For example, if a person claims to be an environmentalist, he/she can try to save water, recycle appliances if possible, and take part in parades in demonstrations to call for awareness of climate change. Also in the process, people become emotionally attached to their team members. Therefore, their self-esteem is affected by the status of the groups in which they participate.

*Social comparison* process, which is the process in which people compare the groups they engage in with other groups in terms of prestige and social status. To maintain self-esteem, members must be aware that the groups they are bidding to have a higher social status than other groups. Any comparisons must be approximate and appropriate for each particular context.

According to SIT, an organization's CSR activates provide information about its value (Turban and Greening, 1997) and contribute to increasing the customers' trust (Diallo and Lambey-Checchin, 2017; Servera-Francés and Fuentes-Blasco, 2015, 2016; Chun and Bang 2016), which positively influences consumer reactions, such as loyalty.

### 2.2. *Stakeholder theory*

According to Freeman (1984), a company can exist only if it can meet the needs of its stakeholders who have a significant impact on the company's welfare. From the traditional point of view, only the owners or shareholders of a company are important and the company is obliged to add value to them. Stakeholder theory instead states that there are others involved in the role that are important to the company, namely, employees, shareholders or investors, customers, suppliers, governments, and the community in which the company operates; they are included in the group of key stakeholders. The stakeholder theory also states that it is not companies that are responsible for society in general, but they should take care of individuals or groups that can be affected directly or indirectly by their activities (Freeman, 1984). Therefore, it can be said that a company with a good CSR image provides good quality goods and services to its customers.

### 2.3. *Signaling theory*

According to Boulding and Kirmani (1993), signaling theory provides a basis for describing and understanding behavior when entities participating in market interaction have access to or possess different information. Information asymmetry can occur between companies and their consumers. Information asymmetry poses a problem for testing products because sellers know the quality of their offer before trading, while customers can only evaluate it later when buying and using the product. Therefore, signals are considered to be effective in the product market for consumers who are sensitive to quality and lack important information about the company's goods or services (Kirmani and Rao, 2000). Companies want to reduce the information asymmetry between them and consumers. Consequently, companies taking on the role of the signaler convey unobservable quality by sending observable signals to emphasize the positive attributes of the organization and its services (Kirmani and Rao, 2000).

Banking service possesses empirical attributes that can only be assessed after the customer experiences the service. Therefore, it is assumed that banking institutions hold different types of information about their services than consumers. Based on this reason, most researchers believe that financial service providers need to provide observable signals to consumers to convey the unseen quality of the service. Signal theory is useful in exploring the relationship between consumer reviews of the company and loyalty. When buyers are uncertain about the quality of the goods or services of a company, they can look for information that allows them to distinguish companies. Therefore, a positive CSR assessment of customers about a bank can make them think well of its services.

### 2.4. *Corporate social responsibility*

CSR is first mentioned by Bowen (1953). Entrepreneurs conducting business activities, besides seeking profits, must not harm social benefits and must compensate for the losses caused by their business activities to society (Bowen, 1953). Bowen's point of view is opposed by Friedman (1970). According to Friedman (1970), the sole responsibility of businesses is to seek profits in addition to complying with the legal regulations accomplished by tax payment. Therefore, the government has the responsibility to take care of society. Handy (2002) argues that businesses benefit from society so businesses must be responsible for society. According to Carroll (1991), in a competitive context, businesses can create sustainable competitive advantage through the proactive implementation of CSR. Carroll (1991) argues that CSR has four dimensions: *economic, legal, ethical*, and *philanthropic responsibility.*

An organization fulfills economic responsibility when making a profit by providing goods and services that customers want. While it seems unusual to focus only on economic outcomes, this is the basis of all other types of responsibilities. If a business does not succeed financially, it is not able to serve its owners or employees, or engage in any other aspect of CSR. Legal responsibility is fulfilled when an organization operates within the framework of the law and complies with the requirements of different regulations from the outside. An organization fulfills its ethical responsibilities when its actions not only comply with legal expectations but also conform to the universal values and moral expectations of society. The highest level of social outcomes stems from the satisfaction of philanthropic responsibility — at this level, the organization grows above the basic economic, legal, and ethical expectations that lead to the increased welfare of individuals, communities, and the whole society.

### 2.5. *Customer loyalty*

The concept of customer loyalty comes from two perspectives, namely, *behaviors* and *attitudes*. Behavioral loyalty is expressed by the number of repurchasing behaviors displayed by consumers over a period of time. However, repurchasing behavior can be due to satisfaction or just because of the lack of alternatives. For this reason, it is believed that this scenario can lead to fake loyalty, or even no loyalty, which occurs when the repurchasing behavior takes place even if the organization has a bad image in its markets (Dick and Basu, 1994). A broader and more complete vision of loyalty refers to consumer loyalty as a step further in the emotional state assumed in satisfaction. An attitude of loyalty means that a positive assessment of the company is made and an emotional connection that is formed between consumers and the company creates true loyalty or, at least, loyalty potential. Positive loyalty (Ganesh *et al.*, 2000) does not only mean repurchasing behaviors but is also a positive word (Selnes, 1993). Delgado and Munuera (2001) define customer loyalty as the belief, self esteem, or desire of consumers to maintain relationships or to obtain products and services of the same brand. Finally, loyalty is also contributed by the cognitive component, which includes tolerance to pay a higher price for the product (Anderson, 1996). According to Oliver (1999), loyalty is defined as a deep commitment to buy-back or revisit a favorite product or service in the future, thereby causing repetitive action of purchasing the same brand or placing another order on the same order, although the contextual effects and marketing efforts can lead to a change in behavior.

### 2.6. *Service quality*

According to stakeholder theory, service quality can be seen as a mediator of the relationship between CSR and customer loyalty.

The customers are the evaluators of service quality. They appreciate the service when it meets or exceeds their expectations (Parasuraman *et al.*, 1985). Five aspects of service quality (*tangibles, reliability, responsiveness, assurance*, and *empathy*) are proposed by Parasuraman *et al.* (1988) in the SERQUAL model to shape part of the quality of service. These five components are measured by a set of scales with 22 questions (Parasuraman *et al.*, 1988). Although these aspects have different levels of importance for different markets, in general, these five components can all be applied in many different areas. Later, SERVPERF model of Cronin and Taylor (1992) suggested that service quality is the actual perception of customers, which makes it easier to survey service quality. The results of research on baking service quality in the world and Vietnam show that most studies use the five-component scale of SERQUAL service quality of Parasuraman *et al.* (1988) to measure banking service quality. Therefore, this study uses the service quality scale of Parasuraman *et al.* (1988) combined with the concept of service quality as the perception of customers (Cronin and Taylor, 1992).

- **Tangibles:** According to Parasuraman *et al.* (1988), an organization's physical environment is part of its physical media (premises, equipment, furniture, and other facilities). Besides, the employee's image is also a component of tangibles.
- **Reliability:** According to Parasuraman *et al.* (1988), reliability is a key factor promoting overall service quality in relation to an organization's ability to deliver the service as promised correctly and reliably.
- **Responsiveness:** Responsiveness indicates the company's willingness to support customers. Customers expect the company

to provide them with fast, featured, and high-quality service (Parasuraman *et al.*, 1988).

- **Assurance:** The employees working in the company form assurance. This is part of the quality of banking services. These employees are considered skilled employees that customers trust in the service delivery process (Parasuraman *et al.*, 1988).
- **Empathy:** The employees of the company spend time and effort to make customers feel special and valuable, which affects the quality of service. This refers to the way the company's transactions bring personalized attention to their customers (Parasuraman *et al.*, 1988).

## 3. Hypotheses and Conceptual Model

### 3.1. *CSR and customer loyalty*

According to the social identity theory (Tajfel, 1982), customers want to belong to groups that have a good image. Companies that do well with CSR activities will have a good public image, as a result, customers will want to engage with them by maintaining a connection with those companies. Customers can maintain relationships with companies by supporting their products and services. CSR is considered as a factor that directly affects customer loyalty (Mercadé-Melé *et al.*, 2018). And it has a direct impact on customer loyalty in the banking sector (Al-Ghamdi and Badawi, 2019; Moisescu, 2017). Thus, the following hypothesis is established:

**Hypothesis H1:** *Perceived CSR can positively influence customer loyalty.*

### 3.2. *CSR and service quality*

According to the stakeholder theory (Freeman, 1984), a company can exist only if it meets the desires and needs of its stakeholders. A company with good CSR activities indicates that it fully meets the needs of its stakeholders. Customers are one of the main stakeholders of the company and the most important need of any customer is low price and high quality of products and services. Therefore, a company with good perceived CSR will provide high-quality products and services. Many studies suggest that social responsibility has a positive impact on customer perceptions of service quality. Servera-Francés and Piqueras-Tomás (2019) suggest that CSR has a positive influence on the customer perceived value of service quality. Similarly, Servera-Francés and Fuentes-Blasco (2016) also say that good perceived CSR increases the perceived value of customers for the quality of service. Therefore, the following hypothesis is established:

**Hypothesis H2:** *Perceived CSR can positively influence customer perceived service quality.*

### 3.3. *Service quality customer loyalty*

One of the key determinants of a company's success is the way its customers perceive service quality because service quality is considered an important element of perceived value. Among the factors determining customer loyalty that have been studied, service quality is considered an important component (Cronin and Taylor, 1992). Providing high-quality service brings higher customer satisfaction and improves customer loyalty (Servera-Francés and Piqueras-Tomás, 2019; Servera-Francés and Fuentes-Blasco, 2015, 2016). Al-Ghamdi and Badawi (2019), in a Saudi banking sector study, confirm that the high quality of banking services increases customer loyalty through increased satisfaction. In addition, Moisescu (2017) also affirms that the bank's responsibility to customers also positively influences customers' loyalty. Thus, the following hypothesis is established:

**Hypothesis H3:** *Perceived service quality can positively influence customer loyalty.*

According to the aforementioned hypotheses (H1–H3), the conceptual model is as shown in Figure 1.

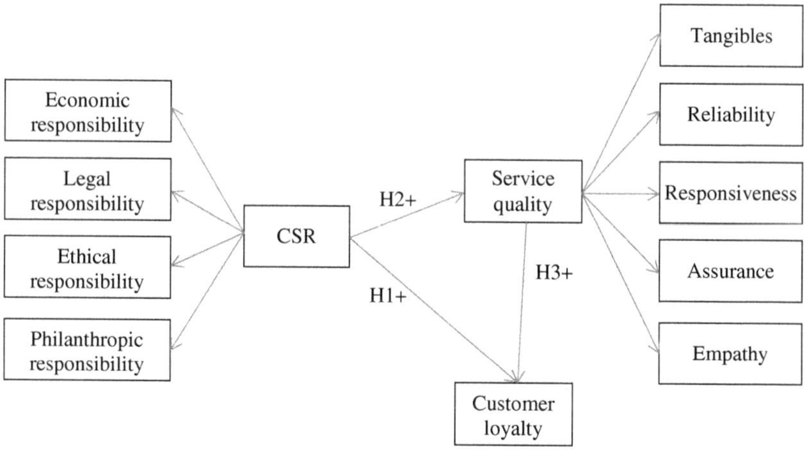


**Figure 1:** Conceptual model.

## 4. Methodology

Quantitative and qualitative mixed research methods are used.

There are two phases of qualitative research:

(1) **Phase 1:** This qualitative research aims to adjust the scale of constructs to suit the Vietnamese market through face-to-face discussions with 10 customers who have experience using banking services in Vietnam.
(2) **Phase 2:** In this phase, qualitative research aims to discuss the meaning of this study's results. There are six face-to-face discussions with customers who have experience using banking services in Vietnam and have taken part in the quantitative survey.

In the quantitative research, convenient sampling method is used to survey customers who have experience using banking services in Vietnam. A total of 299 customers participated in the survey. Data collected are processed by using the Partial Least Squares Structural Equation Modeling (PLS-SEM) with Smart PLS software version 3.0. The measurement model is evaluated through internal consistent reliability indicators (Cronbach's Alpha is higher than 0.7; composite reliability factor is higher than 0.5); evaluation of convergent validity (outer reliability is higher than 0.7; AVE is higher than 0.5); evaluation of discriminant validity (the Fornell–Larcker criterion and cross-loadings). Next, structural model is evaluated for collinearity; the path coefficients in the structural model are then assessed; coefficients of determination ($R^2$ values) are evaluated as well as the $f^2$ effect size; and the blindfolding procedure is used to assess the predictive relevance ($Q^2$ value) of the path model (Hair Jr *et al.*, 2016).

## 5. Results

### 5.1. *The demography analysis of the respondents*

The demography of 299 respondents (Table 1) can be described as follows:

There is a balance of gender (male 49.8%, female 50.2%). Most of the people are in the age group of above 22 (92%). About the

**Table 1:** Demographic variables of respondents.

| No. | Name and categories of variables | | Frequency | Percentage (%) |
|---|---|---|---|---|
| 1 | Gender | Male | 147 | 49.2 |
| | | Female | 152 | 50.8 |
| 2 | Age group | 18–22 ages | 24 | 8.0 |
| | | 23–30 ages | 112 | 37.5 |
| | | 31–40 ages | 103 | 34.4 |
| | | Above 40 ages | 60 | 20.1 |
| 3 | Education level | High school | 19 | 6.4 |
| | | Intermediate degree | 39 | 13.0 |
| | | College degree | 95 | 31.8 |
| | | B.A./B.S. degree | 101 | 33.8 |
| | | Postgraduate degree | 45 | 15.1 |
| 4 | Job | Students | 24 | 8.0 |
| | | Office employees | 229 | 76.6 |
| | | Entrepreneurs | 17 | 5.7 |
| | | Workers | 19 | 6.4 |
| | | Retired people | 10 | 3.3 |

education level, 65.6% of respondents have a college degree or a B.A./B.S. degree. Office employees constitute the highest rate in the sample (76.6%). The demography shows that this sample is suitable to conduct the data analysis for the study.

### 5.2. *Testing of reliability and validity of the measurement model*

The outer loading of all variables is greater than 0.7, so they are valid (Hair Jr *et al.*, 2016). The $p$-values of observed variables of tangibles are greater than 0.05, therefore tangibles cannot be a component of service quality. All $p$-values of other observed variables are also valid because they are smaller than 0.05 (Table 2).

- *Assessment of internal consistency reliability*: All variables show Cronbach's Alpha greater than 0.7 and composite reliability greater than 0.7 (Table 2). Thus, it can be concluded that latent variables all achieve consistent internal reliability (Hair Jr *et al.*, 2016).
- *Evaluation of convergent validity*: All variables have outer loading greater than 0.7. All AVEs are greater than 0.5 (Table 2). So, it can be concluded that all latent variables have convergent validity (Hair Jr *et al.*, 2016).
- *Evaluation of discriminant validity*: The first criterion is the Fornell–Larcker criterion, which demands that the root square of AVE (Table 3 in bold) for each latent variable be greater than the correlation with any other latent variable (Fornell and Larcker, 1981). In Table 3, we see that these criteria are achieved. In the second criterion, the loading of each indicator is expected to be greater than all of its cross-loadings. This is also analyzed and each construct has loadings with higher values than their cross-loadings; this result is available from the author upon request. The Hetrotrait-Monotrait (HTMT) ratio table (Table 4) is available upon request, and all values are below the threshold of 0.9 (Hair Jr *et al.*, 2016).

**Table 2:** Reliability and validity of the constructs.

| Latent constructs and questions | Source | Item | Outer loading | $p$-value |
|---|---|---|---|---|
| Economic responsibility ($\alpha = 0.932$; CR $= 0.957$; AVE $= 0.880$) | | | | |
| I believe X is trying to derive maximum profits from its operations. | Pérez and Del Bosque (2013) | ECO1 | 0.937 | 0.000 |
| I believe X is trying to achieve maximum long-term success. | | ECO2 | 0.936 | 0.000 |
| I believe that X always tries to improve economic efficiency. | | ECO3 | 0.942 | 0.000 |
| Legal responsibility ($\alpha = 0.933$; CR $= 0.957$; AVE $= 0.882$) | | | | |
| I trust X to ensure that its employees act according to the law. | Pérez and Del Bosque (2013) | LEG1 | 0.948 | 0.000 |
| I believe that X fulfills its obligations to its shareholders, suppliers, distributors, and agents. | | LEG2 | 0.926 | 0.000 |
| I believe that X always respects the standards prescribed by law when carrying out its activities. | | LEG3 | 0.943 | 0.000 |
| Ethic responsibility ($\alpha = 0.936$; CR $= 0.959$; AVE $= 0.887$) | | | | |
| I believe that X respects the ethical principles of its relationships and considers it a priority over achieving high economic efficiency. | Pérez and Del Bosque (2013) | ETH1 | 0.953 | 0.000 |
| I believe X has a well-defined ethical principle. | | ETH2 | 0.950 | 0.000 |
| I believe that X encourages creating equal opportunities when hiring new employees. | | ETH3 | 0.922 | 0.000 |

Table 2: (*Continued*)

| Latent constructs and questions | Source | Item | Outer loading | $p$-value |
|---|---|---|---|---|
| Philanthropic ($\alpha = 0.969$; CR $= 0.976$; AVE $= 0.891$) | | | | |
| I believe that X is interested in respecting and protecting the natural environment. | Pérez and Del Bosque (2013) | PHI1 | 0.918 | 0.000 |
| I believe that X actively sponsors social events (sports, music, etc.). | | PHI2 | 0.949 | 0.000 |
| I believe that X appropriates part of its budget for contributions and social work that benefits the disadvantaged. | | PHI3 | 0.947 | 0.000 |
| I believe that X is interested in improving the general condition of society. | | PHI4 | 0.959 | 0.000 |
| I believe that X places its responsibility on society beyond making pure profits. | | PHI5 | 0.945 | 0.000 |
| Tangibles ($\alpha = 0.954$; CR $= 0.965$; AVE $= 0.873$) | | | | |
| X has good equipment. | Parasuraman *et al.* (1988) | TAG1 | 0.943 | 0.185 |
| X's facilities are eye-catching | | TAG2 | 0.960 | 0.186 |
| X staff members have a neat appearance. | | TAG3 | 0.890 | 0.172 |
| Documents relating to services (such as leaflets or reports) of X are eye-catching. | | TAG4 | 0.943 | 0.183 |
| Reliability ($\alpha = 0.968$; CR $= 0.975$; AVE $= 0.886$) | | | | |
| When X promises to do something at a certain time, they will do it on time as promised. | Parasuraman *et al.* (1988) | REL1 | 0.937 | 0.000 |

(*Continued*)

Table 2: (*Continued*)

| Latent constructs and questions | Source | Item | Outer loading | $p$-value |
|---|---|---|---|---|
| When you encounter a problem, X shows a sincere interest in solving the problem. | | REL2 | 0.928 | 0.000 |
| X performs the exact service at the first time of transaction. | | REL3 | 0.945 | 0.000 |
| X offers its service at the time they promised. | | REL4 | 0.959 | 0.000 |
| X has the advantage of having error-free transaction records. | | REL5 | 0.938 | 0.000 |
| Responsiveness ($\alpha = 0.956$; CR = 0.968; AVE = 0.883) | | | | |
| X's staff tells you exactly when the services will be performed. | Parasuraman *et al.* (1988) | RES1 | 0.929 | 0.000 |
| X's staff provides you with quick service. | | RES2 | 0.949 | 0.000 |
| X's staff is always available to help. | | RES3 | 0.945 | 0.000 |
| X's staff is never too busy to respond to your request. | | RES4 | 0.936 | 0.000 |
| Assurance ($\alpha = 0.962$; CR = 0.972; AVE = 0.897) | | | | |
| Expression of X's employees creates trust in customers. | Parasuraman *et al.* (1988) | ASS1 | 0.946 | 0.000 |
| You feel safe in your transactions with X. | | ASS2 | 0.951 | 0.000 |
| X's staff is always polite to you. | | ASS3 | 0.931 | 0.000 |
| X's staffs knowledgeable to answer your questions. | | ASS4 | 0.960 | 0.000 |
| Empathy ($\alpha = 0.978$; CR = 0.983; AVE = 0.919) | | | | |
| X always gives you special attention, and inquires even on personal matters. | Parasuraman *et al.* (1988) | EMP1 | 0.951 | 0.000 |
| X has convenient operating hours for all its customers. | | EMP2 | 0.943 | 0.000 |

**Table 2:** (*Continued*)

| Latent constructs and questions | Source | Item | Outer loading | $p$-value |
|---|---|---|---|---|
| X's employees pay special attention to you. | | EMP3 | 0.962 | 0.000 |
| X' staff gives customers great attention. | | EMP4 | 0.965 | 0.000 |
| X's staff understands your specific needs. | | EMP5 | 0.971 | 0.000 |
| Customer loyalty ($\alpha = 0.982$; CR = 0.985; AVE = 0.917) | | | | |
| I will continue to use X as my main bank for the next few years. | Pérez and Del Bosque (2013) | LOY1 | 0.972 | 0.000 |
| When I need a new financial product or service, I always think of X as my first choice. | | LOY2 | 0.950 | 0.000 |
| I will continue to be a customer of X even if another bank offers a better price. | | LOY3 | 0.919 | 0.000 |
| I can say positive things about this X. | | LOY4 | 0.971 | 0.000 |
| I would recommend this X if someone asks for my advice. | | LOY5 | 0.967 | 0.000 |
| I would encourage my friends and relatives to use some products or services from this X. | | LOY6 | 0.965 | 0.000 |

Therefore, all the measures satisfy the discriminant validity of the constructs. The assessment of the construct reliability, convergent validity, and indicator reliability produce satisfactory results, indicating that the constructs can be used to test the conceptual model.

### 5.3. *Testing of the structural equation model*

The measurement model is satisfactory. So, it is possible to test the structural model. This study uses a bootstrapping of 500 resamples to estimate the statistical significance of path coefficients.

**Table 3:** Fornell–Larcker criterion.

| | **1** | **2** | **3** | **4** | **5** | **6** | **7** | **8** | **9** | **10** | **11** | **12** |
|---|---|---|---|---|---|---|---|---|---|---|---|---|
| 1. Assurance | **0.947** | | | | | | | | | | | |
| 2. CSR | 0.227 | **0.648** | | | | | | | | | | |
| 3. Customer Loyalty | 0.585 | 0.199 | **0.957** | | | | | | | | | |
| 4. Economics | 0.172 | 0.355 | 0.107 | **0.938** | | | | | | | | |
| 5. Empathy | 0.612 | 0.219 | 0.638 | 0.123 | **0.959** | | | | | | | |
| 6. Ethics | 0.068 | 0.738 | 0.077 | 0.095 | 0.005 | **0.942** | | | | | | |
| 7. Legal | 0.237 | 0.657 | 0.178 | 0.120 | 0.118 | 0.490 | **0.939** | | | | | |
| 8. Philanthropic | 0.166 | 0.814 | 0.167 | 0.187 | 0.281 | 0.372 | 0.242 | **0.944** | | | | |
| 9. Reliability | 0.461 | 0.140 | 0.610 | 0.190 | 0.466 | 0.050 | 0.183 | 0.052 | **0.941** | | | |
| 10. Responsiveness | 0.335 | 0.143 | 0.340 | 0.136 | 0.272 | 0.016 | 0.085 | 0.149 | 0.326 | **0.940** | | |
| 11. Service quality | 0.811 | 0.230 | 0.745 | 0.192 | 0.844 | 0.027 | 0.201 | 0.212 | 0.767 | 0.530 | **0.651** | |
| 12. Tangibles | 0.127 | 0.261 | 0.110 | 0.214 | 0.261 | 0.288 | 0.140 | 0.135 | 0.004 | 0.195 | 0.155 | **0.935** |

**Table 4:** Heterotrait-Monotrait Ratio (HTMT) ratio.

| | **Original sample** |
|---|---|
| CSR → Assurance | 0.262 |
| Customer Loyalty → Assurance | 0.602 |
| Customer Loyalty → CSR | 0.219 |
| Economics → Assurance | 0.182 |
| Economics → CSR | 0.534 |
| Economics → Customer Loyalty | 0.113 |
| Empathy → Assurance | 0.631 |
| Empathy → CSR | 0.250 |
| Empathy → Customer Loyalty | 0.651 |
| Empathy → Economics | 0.129 |
| Ethics → Assurance | 0.074 |
| Ethics → CSR | 0.771 |
| Ethics → Customer Loyalty | 0.081 |
| Ethics → Economics | 0.100 |
| Ethics → Empathy | 0.023 |
| Legal → Assurance | 0.251 |
| Legal → CSR | 0.704 |
| Legal → Customer Loyalty | 0.185 |
| Legal → Economics | 0.129 |
| Legal → Empathy | 0.123 |
| Legal → Ethics | 0.524 |
| Philanthropic → Assurance | 0.173 |
| Philanthropic → CSR | 0.850 |
| Philanthropic → Customer Loyalty | 0.170 |
| Philanthropic → Economics | 0.197 |
| Philanthropic → Empathy | 0.288 |
| Philanthropic → Ethics | 0.391 |
| Philanthropic → Legal | 0.253 |
| Reliability → Assurance | 0.477 |
| Reliability → CSR | 0.176 |
| Reliability → Customer Loyalty | 0.625 |
| Reliability → Economics | 0.201 |
| Reliability → Empathy | 0.478 |
| Reliability → Ethics | 0.053 |
| Reliability → Legal | 0.192 |
| Reliability → Philanthropic | 0.054 |
| Responsiveness → Assurance | 0.348 |
| Responsiveness → CSR | 0.175 |
| Responsiveness → Customer Loyalty | 0.351 |

(*Continued*)

**Table 4:** (*Continued*)

| | **Original sample** |
|---|---|
| Responsiveness → Economics | 0.146 |
| Responsiveness → Empathy | 0.281 |
| Responsiveness → Ethics | 0.036 |
| Responsiveness → Legal | 0.090 |
| Responsiveness → Philanthropic | 0.155 |
| Responsiveness → Reliability | 0.339 |
| Service quality → Assurance | 0.797 |
| Service quality → CSR | 0.349 |
| Service quality → Customer Loyalty | 0.731 |
| Service quality → Economics | 0.267 |
| Service quality → Empathy | 0.840 |
| Service quality → Ethics | 0.139 |
| Service quality → Legal | 0.244 |
| Service quality → Philanthropic | 0.245 |
| Service quality → Reliability | 0.753 |
| Service quality → Responsiveness | 0.649 |
| Tangibles → Assurance | 0.125 |
| Tangibles → CSR | 0.302 |
| Tangibles → Customer Loyalty | 0.107 |
| Tangibles → Economics | 0.236 |
| Tangibles → Empathy | 0.257 |
| Tangibles → Ethics | 0.305 |
| Tangibles → Legal | 0.153 |
| Tangibles → Philanthropic | 0.136 |
| Tangibles → Reliability | 0.036 |
| Tangibles → Responsiveness | 0.207 |
| Tangibles → Service quality | 0.476 |

All variance inflation factors (VIF) coefficients are below 2. It shows that there is no collinearity phenomenon (Hair Jr *et al.*, 2016). The adjusted $R^2$ value of service quality is 0.053, suggesting that the independent variable CSR only explains 5.3% of the variation in the service quality. The adjusted $R^2$ value of customer loyalty is 0.556, meaning that the independent variables explain 55.6% of the variation in customer loyalty (Hair Jr *et al.*, 2016).

The results of the hypotheses of the structural model are illustrated in Figure 2 and Table 5.

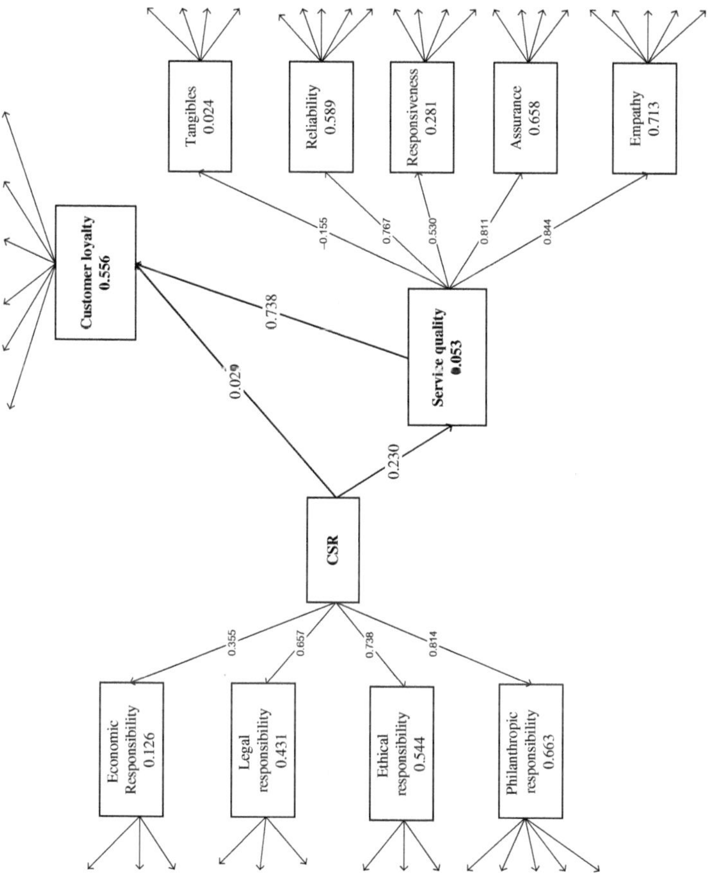


**Figure 2:** Structural equation model result.

**Table 5:** Path coefficients testing results.

| | $\beta$ | $p$-values | Hypotheses test |
|---|---|---|---|
| **CSR → Customer Loyalty** | **0.029** | **0.421** | **Not supported H1** |
| CSR → Economics | 0.355 | 0.000 | |
| CSR → Ethics | 0.738 | 0.000 | |
| CSR → Legal | 0.657 | 0.000 | |
| CSR → Philanthropic | 0.814 | 0.000 | |
| **CSR → Service quality** | **0.230** | **0.003** | **Supported H2** |
| Service quality → Assurance | 0.811 | 0.000 | |
| **Service quality → Customer Loyalty** | **0.738** | **0.000** | **Supported H3** |
| Service quality → Empathy | 0.844 | 0.000 | |
| Service quality → Reliability | 0.767 | 0.000 | |
| Service quality → Responsiveness | 0.530 | 0.000 | |
| Service quality → Tangibles | −0.155 | 0.331 | |

First, the research explains 5.3% of the variation in service quality in the conceptual model. The hypothesis of CSR ($\beta = 0.230$; $p < 0.01$) is statistically significant. Therefore, hypothesis H2 is supported to explain service quality.

Second, customer loyalty is explained as being 55.6% of the variation in the conceptual model. The hypothesis of service quality ($\beta = 0.738$; $p < 0.01$) is statistically significant. However, CSR ($\beta = 0.029$; $p > 0.10$) is not statistically significant. Therefore, hypothesis H3 is supported, but H1 is not supported to explain customer loyalty.

Third, CSR is explained by ethics, legality, and philanthropy. However, economics is not statistically significant because $\beta$ equals 0.335 and is smaller than 0.7. Thus, economics is not a component of CSR in this study.

Fourth, in this study, service quality components are reliability, responsibility, assurance, and empathy because their $\beta s$ are all greater than 0.7. But tangibles are not a component of service quality because their $\beta$ is smaller than 0.7 and their $p$ greater than 0.05.

**Table 6:** Impact factor $f^2$.

| | $f^2$ | Level of impact |
|---|---|---|
| CSR → Customer loyalty | 0.002 | Weak |
| CSR → Service quality | 0.056 | Weak |
| Service quality → Customer loyalty | 1.164 | Strong |

According to Table 6, it can be said that only service quality has a strong impact on customer loyalty, with impact factor $f^2$ of 1.164. CSR has a weak impact on service quality, with impact factor $f^2$ of 0.056 (Hair Jr *et al.*, 2016). The $Q^2$ value of customer loyalty is 0.0.507 (significantly larger than zero). This result shows a relevant forecast of the model of endogenous potential variables (Hair Jr *et al.*, 2016).

## 6. Discussion

### 6.1. *Theoretical implications*

This research has four theoretical implications. First, service quality is positively affected by CSR. This is consistent with previous findings (Al-Ghamdi and Badawi, 2019; Servera-Francés and Piqueras-Tomás, 2019; Servera-Francés and Fuentes-Blasco, 2016). Second, customer loyalty is positively affected by service quality. This is consistent with previous findings (Al-Ghamdi and Badawi, 2019; Moisescu, 2017). However, CSR ($\beta = 0.029$; $p > 0.10$) is not statistically significant, which is different from other studies (Al-Ghamdi and Badawi, 2019; Moisescu, 2017). Third, CSR is explained by legal responsibility, ethical responsibility, and philanthropic responsibility. Fourth, reliability, responsiveness, assurance, and empathy are components of service quality.

### 6.2. *Practical implications*

There are two implications from this study. Firstly, CSR has no direct effect on customer loyalty but has an indirect effect through service quality. Therefore, for the Vietnamese banking sector, CSR should be seen as a way to help banks deploy better business activities, thereby creating customer loyalty. Vietnamese customers think banks' CSR activities involve legal, ethical, and philanthropic responsibilities. Therefore, Vietnamese banks need to ensure their operations comply with the provisions of law, are ethical in nature, besides being focused on the welfare of their community. This is a vital requirement for banks to create a good image in the eyes of customers, contributing to customer loyalty.

Secondly, service quality has a strong influence on customer loyalty. The components of banking service quality that customers pay attention to are reliability, responsiveness, assurance, and sympathy. To improve customer loyalty, Vietnamese banks need: Firstly, to improve their reliability by maintaining their reputation with customers, fulfilling their promises to their customers, being always on time with their customers, and ensuring customers' peace of mind when there is any problem, such as in the service delivery process. Second, to improve responsiveness by training employees to understand banking services, employees must always be ready to meet customer requirements. Third, improve assurance through creating trust for customers, helping customers feel secure when dealing with the bank, and being always ready to answer customer questions. Fourth, improve empathy by always paying attention to the customers' needs. Bank staff should always give customers special attention.

### 6.3. *Limitations and future research*

There are several limitations. First, this study limits the intermediate variable between CSR and customer loyalty to service quality. Future studies can use other mediators such as brand image, customer trust, and customer satisfaction. Second, the CSR in this study is approached from the perspective of Carroll (1991), with four dimensions: *economic*, *legal*, *ethical*, and *philanthropic responsibility*.

Future studies can approach CSR in terms of stakeholder dimensions. Third, this research is only conducted in Vietnam. Future studies can be carried out in other emerging economies for more generalization.

## 7. Conclusion

To test the impact of CSR on customer loyalty, this study surveys 299 customers who have experience dealing with banks in Vietnam. The analysis results show that CSR has no direct impact on customer loyalty. However, CSR has an indirect effect on customer loyalty through an intermediate variable of service quality. Service quality has a strong influence on customer loyalty. The administrative implications of this research are as follows: Firstly, Vietnamese banks should consider CSR as a way to help improve service quality, thereby increasing customer loyalty. CSR factors to consider are legal, ethical, and philanthropic responsibilities. To improve service quality to increase customer loyalty, Vietnamese banks need to pay attention to the factors of *reliability*, *responsiveness*, *assurance*, and *empathy*. Future research directions that can be implemented include: an approach to CSR in terms of stakeholder dimensions; use other mediators such as brand image, customer satisfaction, and customer trust; and conduct research in other countries with emerging economies similar to Vietnam to increase generalization.

## References

Aguilera, R.V., Rupp, D.E., Williams, C.A., and Ganapathi, J. (2007). Putting the S back in corporate social responsibility: A multi-level theory of social change in organizations. *Academy of Management Review*, 32(3), 836–863.

Al-bdour, A.A., Nasruddin, E., and Lin, S.K. (2010). The relationship between internal corporate social responsibility and organizational commitment within the banking sector in Jordan. *International Journal of Human and Social Sciences*, 5(14), 932–951.

Al-Ghamdi, S.A.A., and Badawi, N.S. (2019). Do corporate social responsibility activities enhance customer satisfaction and customer loyalty? evidence from the Saudi banking sector. *Cogent Business and Management*, 6(1), 1662932.

Anderson, J.R. (1996). ACT: A simple theory of complex cognition. *American Psychologist*, 51(4), 355–365, https://doi.org/10.1037/0003-066X.51.4.355.

Boulding, W., and Kirmani, A. (1993). A consumer-side experimental examination of signaling theory: Do consumers perceive warranties as signals of quality? *Journal of Consumer Research*, 20(1), 111–123.

Bowen, H.R. (1953). *Social Responsibility of the Businessman*. New York: Harper and Row.

Carroll, A.B. (1991). The pyramid of corporate social responsibility: Toward the moral management of organizational stakeholders. *Business Horizons*, 34(4), 39–48.

Chandler, A. (2017). *Corporate Social Responsibility: Sustainable Value Creation*. Singapore: Sage.

Chun, K., and Bang, W. (2016). Effect of CSR on customer loyalty: Moderating effect of authenticity. *International Journal of u-and e-Service, Science and Technology*, 9(5), 135–142.

Cronin Jr, J.J., and Taylor, S.A. (1992). Measuring service quality: A reexamination and extension. *Journal of Marketing*, 56(3), 55–68.

Delgado-Ballester, E., and Munuera-Alemán, J.L. (2001). Brand trust in the context of consumer loyalty. *European Journal of Marketing*, 11(12), 1238–1258.

Diallo, M.F., and Lambey-Checchin, C. (2017). Consumers' perceptions of retail business ethics and loyalty to the retailer: the moderating role of social discount practices. *Journal of Business Ethics*, 141(3), 435–449.

Dick, A.S., and Basu, K. (1994). Customer loyalty: Toward an integrated conceptual framework. *Journal of the Academy of Marketing Science*, 22(2), 99–113.

Fornell, C., and Larcker, D. (1981). Structural equation models with unobservable variables and measurement error: Algebra and statistics. *Journal of Marketing Research*, 18(3), 382–388, http://dx.doi.org/10.2307/3150980.

Freeman, R.E. (1984). *Strategic Management: A Stakeholder Approach*. Boston: Pitman.

Friedman, M. (1970). A Friedman doctrine: The social responsibility of business is to increase its profits. *The New York Times Magazine*, 13, 32–33.

Ganesh, J., Arnold, M.J., and Reynolds, K.E. (2000). Understanding the customer base of service providers: An examination of the differences between switchers and stayers. *Journal of Marketing*, 64, 65–87.

Handy, C. (2002). What is a business for? *Harvard Business Review*, 80(12), 49–55, 132.

Hair Jr, J.F., Hult, G.T.M., Ringle, C., and Sarstedt, M. (2016). *A Primer on Partial Least Squares Structural Equation Modeling (PLS-SEM)*. Singapore: Sage Publications.

Kirmani, A., and Rao, A.R. (2000). No pain, no gain: A critical review of the literature on signaling unobservable product quality. *Journal of Marketing*, 64(2), 66–79.

Mercadé-Melé, P., Molinillo, S., Fernández-Morales, A., and Porcu, L. (2018). CSR activities and consumer loyalty: The effect of the type of publicizing medium. *Journal of Business Economics and Management*, 19(3), 431–455.

Moisescu, O.I. (2017). From CSR to customer loyalty: an empirical investigation in the retail banking industry of a developing country. *Scientific Annals of Economics and Business*, 64(3), 307–323.

Oliver, R.L. (1999). Whence consumer loyalty? *Journal of Marketing*, 63(4), 33–44.

Parasuraman, A., Zeithaml, V.A., and Berry, L.L. (1985). A conceptual model of service quality and its implications for future research. *Journal of Marketing*, 49(4), 41–50.

Parasuraman, A., Zeithaml, V.A., and Berry, L.L. (1988). Servqual: A multiple-item scale for measuring consumer perceptions of service quality. *Journal of Retailing*, 64, 12–40.

Pérez, A., and Del Bosque, I.R. (2013). Measuring CSR image: Three studies to develop and to validate a reliable measurement tool. *Journal of Business Ethics*, 118(2), 265–286.

Selnes, F. (1993). An examination of the effect of product performance on brand reputation, satisfaction and loyalty. *European Journal of Marketing*, 27(9), 19–35.

Servera-Francés, D., and Piqueras-Tomás, L. (2019). The effects of corporate social responsibility on consumer loyalty through consumer perceived value. *Economic Research-Ekonomska Istraživanja*, 32(1), 66–84.

Servera-Francés, D., and Arteaga-Moreno, F. (2015). The impact of corporate social responsibility on the customer commitment and trust in the retail sector. *Ramon Llull Journal of Applied Ethics*, 6, 161–178.

Servera-Francés, D., and Fuentes-Blasco, M. (2016). The relationship of corporate social responsibility, consumer value, satisfaction and loyalty: An empirical study. *Ramon Llull Journal of Applied Ethics*, 7, 167–190.

Stanaaland, A.J.S., Lwin, M.O., and Murphy, P.E. (2011). Consumer perceptions of the antecedents and consequences of corporate social responsibility. *Journal of Business Ethics*, 102, 47–55.

Tajfel, H. (1982). Social psychology of intergroup relations. *Annual Review of Psychology*, 33(1), 1–39.

Tajfel, H., and Turner, J.C. (1979). An integrative theory of inter-group conflict. In Austin, W.G., and Worchel, S. (eds.), *The Social Psychology of Inter-group Relations*. Monterey, CA: Brooks/Cole, pp. 33–47.

Turban, D.B., and Greening, D.W. (1997). Corporate social performance and organizational attractiveness to prospective employees. *Academy of Management Journal*, 40(3), 658–672.

https://doi.org/10.1142/9789811227158_0018

# Chapter 18

# A Critical Review of Factors Affecting Tourists' Loyalty

**Khanh Tung Nguyen and Dong Phong Nguyen**

## Abstract

Although there is common consensus that loyalty is an essential dynamic element in the competitive edge of certain enterprises, tourism destination loyalty has not been explored. This chapter concentrates on developing a greater understanding of the potential factors that have an impact on tourism destination loyalty. It is important to explore the importance of loyalty dimensions based on the previous theories to measure tourists' loyalty. The hypothesis shows destination loyalty is attributed to various factors such as destination image, destination quality, destination value, and attribute satisfaction.

**Keywords:** Image; Perceived quality; Attribute satisfaction; Overall satisfaction; Destination loyalty.

## 1. Introduction

This chapter introduces some relevant theories and an overview of the studied topic to clarify tourism contents and the relevance of factors in destination selection by tourists. From these, a model on the relevance of image, quality, value, and satisfaction is built.

## 1.1. *Overview of definitions of tourism*

### 1.1.1. *Definition of tourism*

Nowadays, tourism has become a popular socioeconomic phenomenon. World Tourism Organization recognizes tourism as the biggest economic sector in the world, exceeding automobile manufacture, electrical, steel, and agriculture. Therefore, tourism is the key economic sector in several countries around the globe. The popular term tourism originated from Greek, meaning going one round. It is attached to concepts of relaxation and leisure; however, due to different conditions, time, regions, and research viewpoints, its definition varies.

According to the Vietnamese Tourism Law, "Tourism can be defined as the activities relevant to the journeys of human beings (individual or organization) to places which are not their frequently residing areas to meet the demand of visiting, learning, entertainment, and rest for a specific period of time (excluding working purpose)".

International Union of Official Travel Organization (IUOTO) defines it as the travel to another place rather than the frequently residing area but not for the purpose of business, i.e., not working on a job or making a living.

Experts at United Nations' conference on tourism in Rome (Italy) (from August 21 to September 5, 1963) emphasized that tourism is the combination of relations and economic activities originated from the journeys and stay of an individual or organization at an external place rather than their frequently residing spot, even outside their nations, with a peaceful purpose; the place they come for residing is not their working place.

From the aspect of spatial change by tourists, tourism is one of the forms of temporarily moving from one area to another, from one country to another, without changing the residence or working place.

From the economic point of view, tourism is an economic and service sector, responsible for serving the need for leisure and relaxation, with or without the combination with medical, sport, research activities, and others.

From all the above definitions, tourism is considered a comprehensive economic service sector, with a cross-sectoral, cross-regional characteristic, highly privatized and with a profound cultural notion. It adds to the improvement in a country, by creating jobs, transferring economic structure and motivating other sectors to develop, bringing about benefits in economy, culture, society, politics, external relations, security, and national defense.

### 1.1.2. *Tourists*

According to Article 10 of Tourism Law (2017), tourists are persons who travel to a place, or combine traveling with other tasks, except for studying and working for a living at the destination. Tourists include domestic, inbound, and outbound visitors.

Domestic visitors are Vietnamese citizens or foreigners residing in Vietnam and traveling in the Vietnamese territory. Inbound visitors are foreigners or overseas Vietnamese traveling to Vietnam, while outbound visitors are Vietnamese nationals and foreigners residing in Vietnam who travel abroad.

In some other research, United Nations defines a tourist as "... an individual traveling in a series of 24 hours or more in different countries rather than his hometown". Shaw and William (1994) or Ogilvie (1933) state that "A tourist is a person traveling to a new place outside his or her frequent place for any purpose in the year (leisure or others besides making a living)". The definition of World Tourism Organization assumes that a tourist (inbound or outbound) is a traveler if his or her journey includes one overnight stay (UNWTO, 2014, p. 12).

### 1.1.3. *Tourism products*

Tourism products are a collection of services based on the exploitation of tourism resources to satisfy tourists' demands (Vietnamese Tourism Law, 2017). Invisible and visible factors are major components of a tourism product, in which invisible ones outnumber that of their counterparts.

A tourism product can also be defined as the comprehension of physical and spiritual satisfaction it provides tourists while traveling through the destination. A tourism product focuses on facilities and services designed to satisfy tourists' needs. It can be seen as a collective product, such as the total score for attracting tourism of a nation, transportation, accommodation, and leisure leading to the customer's satisfaction. Each component of a tourism product is provided by service providers such as restaurants, travel agencies, aviation (Shaw and William, 1994).

#### 1.1.4. *Tourism destination*

One tourism destination can be determined as a combination of tourism products and services used under one brand name, providing customers the integrated experience interpreted subjectively in accordance with the customer's travel itinerary, cultural foundation, and visit purpose (Yoon and Uysal, 2005). Besides, the visitors' satisfaction can influence destination choice and their decision of coming back (Buhalis, 2000; Fuchs and Weiermair, 2003).

According to Park and Gretzel (2007), a tourism destination is a package including natural, artistic, and cultural factors to satisfy visitors' demands from their vacation experience.

As Pike and Page (2014) put it, tourism destination is a combination of tourism resources and tourist spots, infrastructure, facilities, service providers, and other supporting industries to give customers the experience they expect from their chosen destinations.

## 2. Tourism Consumer Behavior

Tourism consumer behavior refers to the activities of tourists from the time they consider and make a decision to travel to the time they really experience and rate their trips and even after the journey. Post-journey intentions include the plan to come back or their readiness to recommend the place to others. Retaining a customer and making good impressions for their return or recommendation is more valuable than finding a new customer (Fratu, 2011).

### 2.1. *Destination image*

Destination image remains an important aspect of tourists' decision when choosing their destination. The better the image, the higher the tourists' satisfaction and loyalty (Bojanic, 1991). According to Lee (2009), destination image is the perception of tourists of a particular destination or a specific region. Most definitions of destination image cited from the research by Crompton (1979) and Barich and Kotler (1991) cover the expectations, thoughts, and feelings that tourists have towards the destination they experience (see Table 1).

The definitions of destination image, as given in Table 1, are disunited, multidimensional, and evaluated subjectively by an individual, as a tourism product is complicated and invisible. What is more, the destination image can be changed with time and space; therefore,

**Table 1:** Summary of definitions of tourism destination image.

| Author | Destination | Definition of destination image |
|---|---|---|
| Lawson and Bovy (1977) | London | Objective awareness, impressions, thoughts, imaginations of an individual or a group of individuals on a specific place |
| Um and Crompton (1990) | USA | Expectations from orienting attitudes towards perceived attributes of the destination image |
| Chon (1991) | South Korea | Result of a combination of beliefs, thoughts, emotions, and impressions of a person on a destination |
| Jenkins (1999) | Australia | Perceptions of a group of people |

*Source*: Synthesized and updated from the research by Rejesh (2013).

assessing tourists' awareness and perceptions during and after they experience each destination is necessary (Tasci *et al.*, 2007).

### 2.2. *Components of destination image*

According to Day and Crask (2000), an image structure covers cognitive and affective components. Echtner and Ritchie (1991) and Tasci *et al.* (2007) prove the comprehensive satisfaction of tourists from both cognitive and affective images, and they show that the intention of revisiting or word-of-mouth recommendation to others all positively impact the destination image.

Recent studies have proved that the intention of revisiting by tourists is a behavior influenced by several different factors such as destination image, perception quality, perceived value, and satisfaction (Chi and Qu, 2008), and of these it is the destination image that is the most influencing factor influencing tourists' intentions (see Table 2).

### 2.3. *Destination perceived quality*

The conceptual model of service quality is the evaluation between tourists' satisfaction and their expectations prior to using the service (Parasuraman *et al.*, 1988). Olssen (2002) points out that destination conceptual quality is the measure for customers' expectations to evaluate their satisfaction. In other words, destination conceptual quality is the measure for experienced service and expected service via tourists' satisfaction.

### 2.4. *Perceived value*

According to Zeithaml (1988), perceived value is a perception of what is received (Petrick and Backman, 2001). In conclusion, perceived value is the result or benefit the customer receives related to total expense (including the price paid plus other expenses related to the buying transaction) (Woodruff, 1997).

**Table 2:** Components of destination image.

| Author | Year | Components |
|---|---|---|
| Charlotte and Ritchie | 1991 | 1. Sights (natural spots)<br>2. Cost (service price)<br>3. Tourist spots (activities, nightlife)<br>4. Local infrastructure (historical heritages, museums, beaches, shopping facilities, accommodation, exhibition, festivals)<br>5. Economy (developed or prosperous)<br>6. Accessibility<br>7. Openness (different tradition, culture, different cuisine and food)<br>8. Atmosphere |
| Sonmez and Sriakaya | 2002 | 1. Architecture<br>2. Cultural heritage<br>3. Ethnic culture (lifestyle and tradition, living standard, dressing)<br>4. Safety (sanitation, food, security)<br>5. Price |
| Beerli and Martin | 2004 | 1. Natural resources<br>2. Recreation and tourism recreation (hotels, bars, clubs, restaurants and self-service, easy to access, tourism center, and tourism information network)<br>3. Natural environment (scenic beauty, attraction, cleanliness, overload)<br>4. Infrastructure (quality of road, airport and port, public and private transportation, medical service development, telecommunications, commercial infrastructure)<br>5. Culture, history, and arts (festivals, concerts, handicraft, cuisine, traditional culture, religion, museums, historical buildings, custom, and lifestyle)<br>6. Social environment (living quality, poverty and deprivation, language barrier, local hospitality, and friendliness)<br>7. Atmosphere |

*(Continued)*

**Table 2:** (*Continued*)

| Author | Year | Components |
|---|---|---|
| | | 8. Political and economic factors<br>9. Recreation and renewing (golf, fishing, hunting, skiing, sports and leisure, scuba diving, mountain climbing, adventures) |
| Chi and Qu | 2008 | 1. Tourism environment<br>2. Natural sightseeing spots (gorgeous mountains and valleys, natural scenery and spots, gardens, sightseeing drives, parks, lakes, rivers, wild animals, underground caves)<br>3. Recreation and events (exhibition, cultural events and festivals, quality, joy, music, nightlife, and leisure)<br>4. Historical spots (history, heritages, classic buildings)<br>5. Infrastructure (restaurants, cuisine, store system, and accommodation)<br>6. Accessibility (transportation flow and parking information, car parks, area accessibility right, trolleys)<br>7. Relaxation (spa, mind relief and body relaxation, spirit revitalization)<br>8. Outdoor activities (rowing, golf)<br>9. Price and value (food, accommodation, currency value, attractive shopping activities) |
| Kevin and Byon | 2009 | 1. Infrastructure<br>2. Tourist attractions<br>3. Currency value<br>4. Emotions (comfort, discovery) |
| Nguyen Thi Bich Thuy | 2013 | 1. Tourism services and price<br>2. Environment and society<br>3. Tourism infrastructure<br>4. Tourism atmosphere<br>5. General infrastructure<br>6. Cultural resource<br>7. Scenery |

**Table 2:** (*Continued*)

| Author | Year | Components |
|---|---|---|
| Artuger *et al.* | 2013 | 1. Scenery<br>2. Infrastructure<br>3. Atmosphere<br>4. Social environment<br>5. Service value |
| Phan Minh Duc | 2016 | 1. Natural characteristics<br>2. Tourism convenience<br>3. Tourism infrastructure<br>4. Local government's support |
| Le Thi Ha Quyen | 2017 | 1. Psychic<br>2. Safety (cleanliness, security)<br>3. Infrastructure (airports, restaurants, sightseeing spots)<br>4. Recreational activities (golf courses, casinos, cruises/yachts, festivals) |

*Source*: Synthesized from previous literature.

The structure of perceived value is recognized as one of the most essential factors to gain competitive advantage (Parasuraman, 1997) and it is the most essential index on repurchase intentions (Oh, 2000). The study identifies that perceived value can be a better forecasting factor on repurchase intentions than satisfaction or quality (Cronin *et al.*, 2000). Perceived value can be a good forecast for vacationers to reconsider one place (Petrick *et al.*, 2001). After making the decision of returning to a service provider, the customer can consider if they receive the equivalent monetary value or not (Zeithaml, 1988).

As Sheth *et al.* (1991) put it, perceived value is the comfort or discomfort when using a product or service, as well as the perception during the use of that product or service. For any tourism destination, perceived value is evaluated by whether that destination provides worthy service compared to the amount tourists pay, providing unforgettable impressions, and attractive experiences for tourists (Williams and Soutar, 2009).

### 2.5. *Attribute satisfaction*

Satisfaction is a measurement of efficiency and service quality (Gallarza and Saura, 2006). Attribute-level satisfaction is measured by the ability to explain the service quality scale (reliability, fulfillment, and guarantee). A tourist's satisfaction is measured by general attribute satisfaction as well as expectation satisfaction (Hwang *et al.*, 2005; Fidel *et al.*, 2007).

### 2.6. *Overall satisfaction*

Customer's satisfaction is decided by the overall emotion or attitude of a person toward a purchased product (Williams, 2009). It is often considered as a central issue of a company's marketing activities (del Bosque and San Martin, 2008) because it helps them achieve their strategic objectives. Higher customer satisfaction can increase customer loyalty.

In this research, customer's overall satisfaction is identified in accordance with service evaluation after purchase and comparison with customer's expectations as well as actual service experience (Forgas-Coll *et al.*, 2012). It is important to emphasize that in the era of social media, utilization period in the past can also be the experience to assess a product in the current time. Indeed, social media allows customers to post their comments on a service or product that they experienced during the utilization period as well as later. Overall satisfaction is a measure of attitude and it is not temporary nor a fixed destination, but it is a long-term process that customers can express (Oliver, 1997; Tse and Wilton, 1988).

### 2.7. *Destination loyalty*

Newman and Werbel (1973) define loyal customers as those who rebuy a brand, consider only that brand, and do not seek information for any related brands. Tellis (1988) states that loyalty can be defined in terms of customer behavior such as repeat purchasing frequency or relative volume of same-brand purchasing. The following definition of loyalty is taken from Jones and Taylor (2007): Customer's aim to maintain a relationship with a particular service provider and make his or her next purchase in the category from this service provider (Jones *et al.*, 2000).

In sum, it can be seen that the rebuy of a product or service which has been used before or recommending others to buy and use that product or service in a positive way is customer's loyalty. Therefore, likewise for tourists, their loyalty is shown via the fact that they return to the destination they experienced, at the same time positively introducing others to that destination.

## 3. Relations Among Studied Definitions

The suggested theoretical model in this research is based on a theoretical overview by Cerro *et al.* (2012) on factors creating destination loyalty, accommodation, and relevant tourism products. This research updates and focuses on theories related to the destination, major antecedents leading to destination loyalty, including image, quality, value, and satisfaction.

Building destination image is an important strategy not only for proposing appropriate marketing initiatives but also for understanding tourists' behavior (Echtner and Ritchie, 1991). Since the 1980s, researchers have proven that image is a valuable definition which helps to explain tourists' decisions on destinations (Baloglu and McCleary, 1999; del Bosque and San Martńn, 2008). In other words, the image has considerable impact on decision-making processes and future behavior intentions (Bigne *et al.*, 2001; Castro *et al.*, 2007, Chi and Qu, 2008). Destination image is often described as perceptions or awareness of the destination (Echtner and Ritchie, 1991). This is obviously a crucial variable in the building of tourists' loyalty, as many studies prove the importance of perceptions of destination image to quality and satisfaction, and afterward, leading to tourists' behavior (Hernádez-Lobato *et al.*, 2006; Castro *et al.*, 2007). In the context of tourism, Phillips *et al.* (2013) emphasize the importance of recommendation as a tool to attract new customers because positive word of mouth can create a positive image of destinations. The connection between image and recommendation is a way to create loyalty (Campón *et al.*, 2013).

The relations between image and overall satisfaction in the context of tourism destinations are greatly analyzed in previous studies (Bigne *et al.*, 2001; Alcañiz *et al.*, 2005; Hernández-Lobato *et al.*, 2006; Castro *et al.*, 2007; Chi and Qu, 2008; Assaker *et al.*, 2011; Prayag and Ryan, 2012; Sun *et al.*, 2013). Some other researchers have focused on the relations between image and loyalty or behavioral intentions (Hernández-Lobato *et al.*, 2006; Chen and Tsai, 2007; del Bosque and San Martín, 2008), using the two indexes of "returning intention" and "recommending to new visitors" as the main indexes for destination loyalty (Campón *et al.*, 2013). Based on this conceptual framework, we propose the following hypotheses:

**Hypothesis H1:** *Destination image has a positive impact on overall satisfaction.*

**Hypothesis H2:** *Destination image has a positive impact on loyalty level.*

Oliver (2014) confirms that in history, quality is considered to originate from technological advances and identified according to objective quality. However, the definition of quality from a customer's aspect is in accordance with subjectivity or perceptions. Parasuraman *et al.* (1985) are pioneers in introducing the latter definition in marketing, with the former notion for conceptualization and detailed service quality (Tian-Cole *et al.*, 2002). In the 1980s, studies on the quality of intangible goods were widely conducted. However, there are still discrepancies related to identifying and measuring service quality due to their distinctive characteristics, including intangibility, heterogeneity, and inseparability (Parasuraman *et al.*, 1985; Parasuraman *et al.*, 1988). These characteristics explain why it is harder to measure service quality than tangible goods quality, which is because service quality is related to the service distribution process (Parasuraman *et al.*, 1985). Chen and Tsai (2007) describe service quality as customer's evaluation on the service distribution process standard in connection with the journey experience. Murphy *et al.* (2000) also emphasize the importance of quality in tourism. In addition, another factor in quality assessment is "moments of truth"; accidental encounters bring about positive aspects to destinations, and infrastructure creates perceptions of service quality. The more positive the accidental encounters are, the higher the perceptions of quality. Besides, Lee *et al.* (2004) and Rivera and Croes (2010) state that quality is an important concept in marketing because it can be an indicator of profitability and success in business. Several theories show the relations between quality, overall satisfaction, and destination loyalty (Bigne *et al.*, 2001; Lee *et al.*, 2004; Alcañiz *et al.*, 2005; Castro *et al.*, 2007; Lee *et al.*, 2007; Rivera and Croes 2010; Žabkar *et al.*, 2010; Kim *et al.*, 2013; Reza Jalilvand *et al.*, 2014). Other researchers have also found evidence for relations between quality and loyalty intention/behavior (Castro *et al.*, 2007; Žabkar *et al.*, 2010; Kim *et al.*, 2013; Reza Jalilvand *et al.*, 2014). Based on these studies, the following hypotheses are established:

**Hypothesis H3:** *Destination perceived quality has a positive impact on overall satisfaction.*

**Hypothesis H4:** *Destination perceived quality has a positive impact on loyalty.*

A compilation of previous theories shows that studies on perceived quality by tourists towards destinations are still limited (Pandža Bajs, 2015). The definition of value developed by Zeithaml (1988) is most widely accepted, for both domestic and international tourism (Gallarza and Saura, 2006). According to Zeithaml (1988), perceived quality is an overall evaluation by the customer on level of usefulness of a product based on concepts from what is received and what has to be given. What is received can be perceived differently among customers; therefore, some can concentrate on quantity, others focus on quality, or other values. What has to be given can also be different depending on different viewpoints of customers. Some perceive based on the amount of money spent, others on time or effort. Hence, perceived quality describes the balance between what is received and what has to be given in customers' perceptions.

Murphy *et al.* (2000) state that quality can help renew and reposition tourism products; as a result, destination managers can exploit these factors to refresh their tourism. Agreeing with this viewpoint, Pandža Bajs (2015) says that tourists consider destination perceived value as the disparity between perceived profit and incurring cost from destination services. Ravald and Grönroos (1996) suggest two strategies to boost the value for products or services, which are enhancing profit and minimizing sacrifice. Nevertheless, the most popular approach to enhance value is adding technical features to major products in order to upgrade total value. By increasing value for these products, companies can find ways to improve customer satisfaction and loyalty.

The impacts of these two factors are studied by authors focusing on the relations between value and overall satisfaction (Gallarza and Saura, 2006; Castro *et al.*, 2007; Chen and Tsai, 2007; Williams and Soutar, 2009; Rivera and Croes, 2010; Forgas-Coll *et al.*, 2012; Kim *et al.*, 2013; Phillips *et al.*, 2013; Sun *et al.*, 2013; Reza Jalilvand *et al.*, 2014) and between value and loyalty/behavioral intentions (Hutchinson *et al.*, 2009; Rivera and Croes 2010; Kim *et al.*, 2013; Sun *et al.*, 2013; Reza Jalilvand *et al.*, 2014; Pandža Bajs, 2015). Based on these statements, two more hypotheses are suggested:

**Hypothesis H5:** *Destination perceived quality has a positive impact on overall satisfaction.*

**Hypothesis H6:** *Destination perceived quality has a positive impact on loyalty.*

Satisfaction is a central concept in marketing. However, it is often misperceived with perceived value (Sweeney and Soutar, 2001) or perceived quality (Bigne *et al.*, 2001). Oliver (2014) states that the definition of satisfaction most widely accepted can be "evaluation of the features of a product or service or the product or service itself is provided (or providing) with a pleasurable level of consumption-related fulfillment, including levels of under or over fulfillment".

Studies show that satisfaction needs to be clarified in the context in which it is incurred. Consequently, researchers should consider tourism features, such as intangibility, inseparability, heterogeneity, and perishability, strongly influencing satisfaction (Bowen and Clarke, 2002). Researchers apply this definition in several different tourism studies, including on travel agents, accommodation, and destination (del Bosque and San Martín, 2008; Kim *et al.*, 2013) and apply some viewpoints and theories (Yoon and Uysal, 2005). However, the main approach in these documents is the expectancy disconfirmation theory proposed by Oliver (1980), which is applied in many studied contexts (e.g., tourism product, destination, travel agents) (Petrick *et al.*, 2001; Jang and Feng, 2007; Lee *et al.*, 2012). According to this school of thought, researchers develop a frame of reference with which they carry out a comparative analysis. Any result that is lower than the reference point is ranked in negative disconfirmation, while the result that is higher than the reference point is categorized in positive disconfirmation (Oliver, 1980).

Satisfaction can be mentioned in a global way (Oliver, 1980) or in accordance with attributes (Oliver, 1993). According to Oliver (1993), different features of a polyhedral product or service allow customers to have different experiences; some positive and some negative. Therefore, attribute satisfaction can be formed from the subjective judgment of the consumers when they observe the attributes' expression. Although overall satisfaction also has features of attribute evaluation, overall satisfaction and attribute satisfaction have different structures, despite their interconnection. Therefore, Prayag and Ryan (2012) mention that destination satisfaction is the satisfaction accumulated on different aspects of the destination.

Attribute satisfaction has a positive and direct impact on overall satisfaction, and it greatly influences the change of overall satisfaction (Oliver, 1993). In addition, Kim and Brown (2012) suggest the cause and effect relations between these two definitions, and it is also widely discussed in numerous other studies (Chi and Qu, 2008; Ozdemir *et al.*, 2012; Eusébio and Vieira, 2013; Phillips *et al.*, 2013). Ozdemir *et al.* (2012) attest that tourists experience a series of attributes during their vacation, such as restaurants, hotels, shops, beach, cultural and historical sites, and evaluate the attributes separately. Therefore, logically, overall satisfaction is a function with specific attributes of a destination, as Oliver (1993) attested. These impacts should be considered in a detailed way; hence, it leads to the following hypothesis:

**Hypothesis H7:** *Attribute satisfaction has a positive impact on overall satisfaction.*

Marketing theories focus on the analysis of relations between customer satisfaction and loyalty (Chi and Qu, 2008). In tourism behavior, satisfaction also plays an important role (Kozak, 2001). Therefore, tourism destination managers must make great efforts to ensure customer satisfaction (del Bosque and San Martín, 2008). Dissatisfaction can reduce the chance of returning to a destination and chance of recommending the place to others (Riveerra and Croes, 2010). Most researchers accept that satisfaction leads to intention to return and recommendation to others; these are indexes of loyalty, as several studies find clear evidence of this relation (Chi and Qu, 2008). It is quite popular to find an analysis of satisfaction's impact on destination loyalty, especially in studies on satisfaction being the main premise for loyalty (Cerro *et al.*, 2012). Lee (2009) and Sun *et al.* (2011) show the evidence of the relationship between destination satisfaction and behavioral intention, including intention to return and recommend. With these judgments and cited studies, the following hypothesis is suggested:

**Hypothesis H8:** *Attribute satisfaction has a positive impact on loyalty.*

Besides, researchers attest that it is important to identify whether overall satisfaction is the mean of five variables (image, quality, value, attribute satisfaction, and loyalty). With the widely accepted fact that satisfaction and loyalty are interconnected, as discussed earlier, H8 focuses on the relationship between attribute satisfaction and loyalty. Therefore, it is necessary to understand more about the relationship between overall satisfaction and loyalty. The latter relationship is widely discussed in theory seminars (Yoon and Uysal, 2005; Gallarza and Saura, 2006; Hernández-Lobato *et al.*, 2006; Lee *et al.*, 2007; Chi and Qu, 2008; del Bosque and San Martín, 2008; Mechinda *et al.*, 2009; Kim and Brown, 2012; Liu *et al.*, 2012; Sun *et al.*, 2013; Reza Jalilvand *et al.*, 2014). However, Phillips *et al.* (2013), when studying tourism destinations, do not find the relationship between overall satisfaction and intentions to return. With this theory foundation, and based on research by Campón-Cerro *et al.* (2017), we propose the following hypothesis:

**Hypothesis H9:** *Overall satisfaction has a positive impact on loyalty.*

Figure 1 shows the relationship among the hypotheses and serves as the theoretical model suggested in current studies.

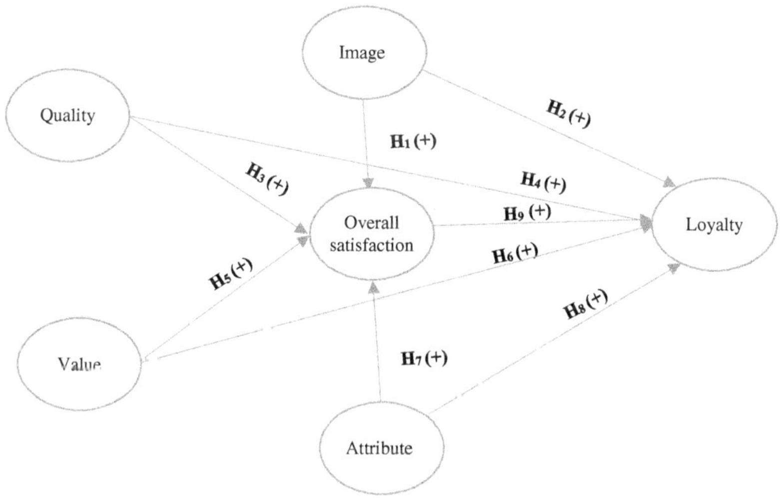


**Figure 1:** Conceptual framework.

## 4. Conclusion

The level of tourists' loyalty to a destination should be examined to explore the differences in tourists' purpose to revisit a certain destination and their suggestions to others. Therefore, information about tourists' loyalty is critical for destination marketers and managers in order to ensure destination attractiveness. It is essential to determine that overall satisfaction mediates between the five elements of image, quality, value, attribute satisfaction, and loyalty.

## References

Alcañiz, E.B., García, I.S., and Blas, S.S. (2005). Relationships among residents' image, evaluation of the stay and post-purchase behaviour. *Journal of Vacation Marketing*, 11(4), 291–302.

Alegre, J., and Juaneda, C. (2006). Destination loyalty: Consumers' economic behavior. *Annals of tourism research*, 33(3), 684–706.

Artuger, S.A., Cetinsoz, B.C., and Kilic, I. (2013). The effect of destination image on destination loyalty: An application in Alanya. *European Journal of Business and Management*, 5(13), 124–136.

Assaker, G., Vinzi, V.E., and O'Connor, P. (2011). Examining the effect of novelty seeking, satisfaction, and destination image on tourists' return pattern: A two factor, non-linear latent growth model. *Tourism Management*, 32(4), 890–901.

Baloglu, S., and McCleary, K.W. (1999). A model of destination image formation. *Annals of Tourism Research*, 26(4), 868–897.

Barich, H., and Kotler, P. (1991). A framework of marketing image management. *Sloan Management Review*, 32(2), 92–104.

Beerli, A., and Martin, J.D. (2004). Factors influencing destination image. *Annals of Tourism Research*, 31(3), 657–681.

Bigne, J.E., Sanchez, M.I., and Sanchez, J. (2001). Tourism image, evaluation variables and after purchase behaviour: Inter-relationship. *Tourism Management*, 22(6), 607–616.

Bojanic, D.C. (1991). The use of advertising in managing destination image. *Tourism Management*, December, 352–355.

Bowen, D., and Clarke, J. (2002). *Reflections on Tourist Satisfaction Research: Past, Present and Future*. Thousand Oaks, CA: Sage Publications Sage.

Buhalis, D. (2000). Marketing the competitive destination in the future. *Tourism Management*, 21(1), 97–116.

Campón-Cerro, A.M., Hernández-Mogollón, J.M., and Alves, H. (2017). Sustainable improvement of competitiveness in rural tourism destinations: The quest for tourist loyalty in Spain. *Journal of Destination Marketing and Management*, 6(3), 252–266.

Campón, A.M., Alves, H., and Hernández, J.M. (2013). Loyalty measurement in tourism: A theoretical reflection. *Quantitative Methods in Tourism Economics*. Springer, pp. 13–40.

Castro, C.B., Armario, E.M., and Ruiz, D.M. (2007). The influence of market heterogeneity on the relationship between a destination's image and tourists' future behaviour. *Tourism Management*, 28(1), 175–187.

Cerro, A.M.C., Mogollon, J.M.H., and Alves, H.M.B. (2012). Identifying the major determinants of loyalty in tourism. *Strategic Marketing in Tourism Services*, 163.

Charlotte, M.E., and Ritchie, J.R.B. (1991). The meaning and measurement of destination image. *The Journal of Tourism Studies*, 2(2), 1–11.

Chen, C.-F., and Tsai, D. (2007). How destination image and evaluative factors affect behavioral intentions?. *Tourism Management*, 28(4), 1115–1122.

Chen, J.S., and Gursoy, D. (2001). An investigation of tourists' destination loyalty and preferences, *International Journal of Contemporary Hospitality Management*, 13(2), 79–85.

Chi, C.G.-Q., and Qu, H. (2008). Examining the structural relationships of destination image, tourist satisfaction and destination loyalty: An integrated approach. *Tourism Management*, 29(4), 624–636.

Chon, K.S. (1991). Tourism destination image: Marketing implication. *Tourism Management*, 12(1), 68–72.

Crompton, J.L. (1979). Motivation for pleasure vacations. *Annals of Tourism Research*, 6(4), 408–424.

Cronin, J.J., and Taylor, S.A. (1994). SERVPERF versus SERVQUAL: Reconciling performance-based and perceptions-minus-expectations measurement of service quality, *Journal of Marketing*, 58(January), 125–139.

Day, E., and Crask, M.R. (2000). Value assessment: the antecedent of customer satisfaction. *Journal of Customer Satisfaction, Dissatisfaction and Complaining Behaviour*, 13, 42–50.

Del Bosque, I.R., and San Martín, H. (2008). Tourist satisfaction a cognitive-affective model. *Annals of Tourism Research*, 35(2), 551–573.

Echtner, C.M., and Ritchie, J.B. (1991). The meaning and measurement of destination image, *The Journal of Tourism Studies*, 2(2), 2–12.

Eusébio, C., and Vieira, A.L. (2013). Destination attributes' evaluation, satisfaction and behavioural intentions: A structural modelling approach. *International Journal of Tourism Research*, 15(1), 66–80.

Forgas-Coll, S., Palau-Saumell, R., Sánchez-García, J., and Callarisa-Fiol, L.J. (2012). Urban destination loyalty drivers and cross-national moderator effects: The case of Barcelona. *Tourism Management*, 33(6), 1309–1320.

Fratu, D. (2011). Factors of influence and changes in the tourism consumer behaviour. *Bulletin of the Transilvania University of Brasov*, 4(1), 119–126.

Gallarza, M.G., and Saura, I.G. (2006). Value dimensions, perceived value, satisfaction and loyalty: An investigation of university students' travel behaviour, *Tourism Management*, 27(3), 437–452.

Hwang, S.-N., Lee, C., and Chen, H.-J. (2005). The relationship among tourists' involvement, place attachment and interpretation satisfaction in Taiwan's national parks. *Tourism Management*, 26(2), 143–156.

Hernández-Lobato, L., Solis-Radilla, M.M., Moliner-Tena, M.A., and Sánchez-García, J. (2006). Tourism destination image, satisfaction and loyalty: A study in ixtapa-zihuatanejo, Mexico. *Tourism Geographies*, 8(4), 343–358.

Hutchinson, J., Lai, F., and Wang, Y. (2009). Understanding the relationships of quality, value, equity, satisfaction, and behavioral intentions among golf travelers. *Tourism Management*, 30(2), 298–308.

Jang, S.S., and Feng, R. (2007). Temporal destination revisit intention: The effects of novelty seeking and satisfaction. *Tourism Management*, 28(2), 580–590.

Jones, M.A., Mothersbaugh, D.L. and Beatty, S.E. (2000). Switching barriers and repurchasing intentions in services. *Journal of Retailing*, 76(2), 259–274.

Jones, T., and Taylor, S.F. (2007). The conceptual domain of service loyalty: How many dimensions? *Journal of Service Marketing*, 21(1), 36–51.

Kevin, K.B., Zhang, J.J. (2009). Development of a scale measuring destination image. *Marketing Intelligence and Planning*, 28(4), 508–532.

Kim, A.K., and Brown, G. (2012). Understanding the relationships between perceived travel experiences, overall satisfaction, and destination loyalty. *Anatolia*, 23(3), 328–347.

Kim, H., and Rechardson, S.L. (2003). Motion picture impacts on destination images. *Annals of Tourism Research*, 30(1), 216–237.

Kim, S.H., Holland, S., and Han, H.S. (2013). A structural model for examining how destination image, perceived value, and service quality affect destination loyalty: A case study of Orlando. *International Journal of Tourism Research*, 15(4), 313–328.

Kozak, M. (2001). Repeaters behavior at two distinct destinations. *Annals of Tourism Research*, 28(3), 784–807.

Lawson, F., and Baud-Bovy, M. (1977). *Tourism and Recreational Development.* London: Architectural Press.

Lee, J., Graefe, A.R., and Burns, R.C. (2004). Service quality, satisfaction, and behavioral intention among forest visitors. *Journal of Travel and Tourism Marketing*, 17(1), 73–82.

Lee, J., Graefe, A.R., and Burns, R.C. (2007). Examining the antecedents of destination loyalty in a forest setting. *Leisure Sciences*, 29(5), 463–481.

Lee, T.H. (2009). A structural model to examine how destination image, attitude, and motivation affect the future behavior of tourists. *Leisure Sciences*, 31(3), 215–236.

Lee, T.H. (2009). A structural model for examining how destination image and interpretation services affect future visitation behavior: A case study of Taiwan's Taomi eco-village. *Journal of Sustainable Tourism*, 17(6), 727–745.

Lee, J., Kyle, G., and Scott, D. (2012). The mediating effect of place attachment on the relationship between festival satisfaction and loyalty to the festival hosting destination. *Journal of Travel Research*, 51(6), 754–767.

Liu, C.-R., Lin, W.-R., and Wang, Y.-C. (2012). Relationship between self-congruity and destination loyalty: Differences between first-time and repeat visitors. *Journal of Destination Marketing & Management*, 1(1–2), 118–123.

Loureiro, S.M. (2010). Satisfying and delighting the rural tourists. *Journal of Travel and Tourism Marketing*, 27(4), 396–408.

Loureiro, S.M.C., and Kastenholz, E. (2011). Corporate reputation, satisfaction, delight, and loyalty towards rural lodging units in Portugal. *International Journal of Hospitality Management*, 30(3), 575–583.

Mechinda, P., Serirat, S., and Gulid, N. (2009). An examination of tourists' attitudinal and behavioral loyalty: Comparison between domestic and international tourists. *Journal of Vacation Marketing*, 15(2), 129–148.

Mike, F. (ed.) (2017). *The Travel and Tourism Competitiveness Report 2017.* Geneva, Switzerland: World Economic Forum.

Murphy, P., Pritchard, M.P., and Smith, B. (2000). The destination product and its impact on traveller perceptions. *Tourism Management*, 21(1), 43–52.

Newman, J.W., and Werbel, R.A. (1973). Multivariate analysis of brand loyalty for major household appliances. *Journal of Marketing Research*, 10(November), 404–409.

Ogilvie, F.W. (1933). *The Tourist Movement.* London: P.S. King.

Oliver, R.L. (1980). A cognitive model of the antecedents and consequences of satisfaction decisions. *Journal of Marketing Research*, 460–469.

Oliver, R.L. (1993). Cognitive, affective, and attribute bases of the satisfaction response. *Journal of Consumer Research*, 20(3), 418–430.

Oliver, R.L. (1997). *Satisfaction: A Behavioral Perspective on the Consumer*. New York: Irwin/McGraw-Hill.

Oliver, R.L. (1999). Whence consumer loyalty? *the Journal of Marketing*, 33–44.

Oliver, R.L. (2014). *Satisfaction: A Behavioral Perspective on the Consumer*. Routledge.

Ozdemir, B., Aksu, A., Ehtiyar, R., Çizel, B., Çizel, R.B., and İçigen, E.T. (2012). Relationships among tourist profile, satisfaction and destination loyalty: Examining empirical evidences in Antalya region of Turkey. *Journal of Hospitality Marketing & Management*, 21(5), 506–540.

Pandža Bajs, I. (2015). Tourist perceived value, relationship to satisfaction, and behavioral intentions: The example of the Croatian tourist destination Dubrovnik. *Journal of Travel Research*, 54(1), 122–134.

Parasuraman, A., Zeithaml, V.A., and Berry, L.L. (1985). A conceptual model of service quality and its implications for future research. *The Journal of Marketing*, 49(4), 41–50.

Parasuraman, A., Zeithaml, V.A., and Berry, L.L. (1988). Servqual: A multiple-item scale for measuring consumer perc. *Journal of Retailing*, 64(1), 12.

Parasuraman, A. (1997). Reflections on gaining competitive advantage through customer value. *Journal of the Academy of Marketing Science*, 25(2), 154–164.

Park, Y.A., and Gretzel, U. (2007). Success factors for destination marketing web sites: A qualitative mega- analysis. *Journal of Travel Research*, 46(1), 46–63.

Peña, A.I.P., Jamilena, D.M.F., and Molina, M.Á.R. (2012). Validation of cognitive image dimensions for rural tourist destinations: A contribution to the management of rural tourist destinations. *Journal of Vacation Marketing*, 18(4), 261–273.

Petrick, J.F., Morais, D.D., and Norman, W.C. (2001). An examination of the determinants of entertainment vacationers' intentions to revisit. *Journal of Travel Research*, 40(1), 41–48.

Petrick, J.F., and Backman, S.J. (2001). An examination of golf travelers' satisfaction, perceived value, loyalty, and intentions to revisit. *Journal of Tourism Analysis*, 6(3/4), 223–237.

Prayag, G., and Ryan, C. (2011). Antecedents of Tourists' loyalty to Mauritius: The role and influence of destination image, place attachment, personal involvement and satisfaction. *Journal of Travel Research*, 51(3), 342–356.

Phillips, W.J., Wolfe, K., Hodur, N., and Leistritz, F.L. (2013). Tourist word of mouth and revisit intentions to rural tourism destinations:

A case of North Dakota, USA. *International Journal of Tourism Research*, 15(1), 93–104.

Pike, S., and Page, S. (2014). Destination marketing organizations and destination marketing: A narrative analysis of the literature. *Tourism Management*, 41, 202–227.

Pike, S., Murdy, S., and Lings, I. (2011). Visitor relationship orientation of destination marketing organizations. *Journal of Travel Research*, 50(4), 443–453.

Prayag, G., and Ryan, C. (2012). Antecedents of tourists' loyalty to Mauritius: The role and influence of destination image, place attachment, personal involvement, and satisfaction. *Journal of Travel Research*, 51(3), 342–356.

Pritchard, M., and Howard, D.R. (1997). The loyal traveler: Examining a typology of service patronage. *Journal of Travel Research*, 35(4), 2–10.

Ravald, A., and Grönroos, C. (1996). The value concept and relationship marketing. *European Journal of Marketing*, 30(2), 19–30.

Reza, J., Khazaei Pool, M., Nasrolahi Vosta, J., and Shabani Nafchali, J.L. (2014). The effect of marketing constructs and tourists' satisfaction on loyalty to a sport destination: A structural equation model and analysis. *Education, Business and Society: Contemporary Middle Eastern Issues*, 7(4), 316–332.

Rivera, M.A., and Croes, R. (2010). Ecotourists' loyalty: Will they tell about the destination or will they return? *Journal of Ecotourism*, 9(2), 85–103.

Shaw, G., and William, A.M. (1994). *Critical Issues in Tourism: A Geographical Perspective*. Blackwell Publishers.

Sheth, J.N., Newman, B.I., and Gross, B.L. (1991). Why we buy what we buy: A theory of consumption values. *Journal of Business Research*, 22(2), 159–170.

Sonmez, S., and Sriakaya, E. (2002). A distorted destination image? The case of Turkey. *Journal of Travel Research*, 41(November), 185–196.

Sun, X., Chi, C.G.-Q., and Xu, H. (2013). Developing destination loyalty: The case of Hainan Island. *Annals of Tourism Research*, 43, 547–577.

Sweeney, J.C., and Soutar, G.N. (2001). Consumer perceived value: The development of a multiple item scale. *Journal of Retailing*, 77(2), 203–220.

Tasci, A.D.A., Gartner, W.C., and Cavusgil, S.T. (2007). Conceptualisation and operationalisation of destination image. *Journal of Hospitality and Tourism Research*, 31(2), 194–223.

Tellis, G.J. (1988). Advertising exposure, loyalty, and brand purchase: A two stage model of choice. *Journal of Marketing Research*, 25(May), 134–144.

Tian-Cole, S., Crompton, J.L., and Wilson, V.L. (2002). An empirical investigation of the relationships between service quality, satisfaction and behavioral intentions among visitors to a wildlife refuge. *Journal of Leisure Research*, 34(1), 1–24.

UNWTO (2014). *Glossary of Tourism.* Available at https://dugi-doc.udg.edu/bitstream/handle/10256/14825/GhanemJoey_Treball.pdf?sequence=1 [Accessed 31 October 2018].

Williams, P., and Soutar, G.N. (2009). Value, satisfaction and behavioral intentions in an adventure tourism context. *Annals of Tourism Research*, 36(3), 413–438.

Woodruff, R.B. (1997). Customer value: The next source for competitive advantage. *Journal of the Academy of Marketing Science*, 25(2, Spring), 139–153.

Yoon, Y., and Uysal, M. (2005.) An examination of the effects of motivation and satisfaction on destination loyalty: A structural model. *Tourism Management*, 26(1), 45–56.

Zeithaml, V.A. (1988). Consumer perceptions of price, quality, and value: A means-end model and synthesis of evidence. *The Journal of Marketing*, 52(3), 2–22.

https://doi.org/10.1142/9789811227158_0019

# Chapter 19

# Supply Chain Integration: A Case Study of Vietnamese Dairy Industry

**Thi Thu Suong Huynh**

## Abstract

The purpose of this research is to explore the factors affecting supply chain (SC) and SC integration (SCI). To achieve the purpose of this study, a literature survey related to SC and SCI is carried out, and an empirical analysis is conducted among 320 partners in this industry with the results analyzed using Cronbach's Alpha analysis, exploratory factor analysis (EFA), and regression analysis (RA), with primary data collected of 300 valid samples from 305 samples in Vietnam. This chapter explores and confirms that there are six basic factors affecting the integration in SC, including (i) *trust*, (ii) *price policy*, (iii) *culture of enterprise*, (iv) *leadership capacity*, (v) *maturity level*, and (vi) *product strategy*. The results of the research show strong evidence for policymakers and enterprises for management of the SC integration at each partner level in SC as well as its contribution to SCI of Vietnam's milk industry.

**Keywords:** Integration; supply chain; dairy industry; Vietnam.

## 1. Introduction

In today's competitive and fast-moving business environment, the viability of organizations depends on integrating with other supply chain (SC) actors. In other words, their complementary skills and compatible goals help them survive and prosper (Agata, 2017). Therefore, companies link their internal processes to external suppliers and customers, with different levels of integration, to reduce cost and improve responsiveness and service level. The aim of SC integration (SCI) is to become a main component of SC management discipline in achieving competitive advantage and performance improvements. Different types and levels of integration are defined, and a basic integrated SC model is described to help in understanding the meaning and aspects of this term in Vietnam's dairy industry. Finally, the partnership development process including partner selection, contracting, and maintenance, along with various aspects of each phase, is reviewed. In fact, milk competition gets fierce in Vietnam and dominant brands, in both domestic and foreign markets, have effective business strategies. The three top-ranked businesses in Vietnam's dairy market are Vinamilk, TH True Milk, and Moc Chau Milk (EVBN Report, 2018). Vinamilk is a dominant company in the liquid milk segment of Vietnam's dairy products and continues to lead the industry with about 55% market share as Vinamilk has a continuous advertising strategy and research effort, and always introduces new milk lines. TH True Milk, another dominant enterprise, accounts for 11%, while Moc Chau Milk occupies 6% of market share (EVBN Report, 2018). To survive and grow, companies related with Vietnam's dairy industry are constantly researching and applying methods in business, production, and administration to optimize resources, which helps to maximize efficiency in each stage of SC. With the current business environment, the dairy business needs to focus on researching the application of supply models in the current operating situation. Linking SC is a sharp weapon to help businesses cut costs but still ensure the timeliness of materials put into production as well as to meet market demands. The strength of the business depends on SC operation, from the purchase of raw materials, semi-finished products, production, inventory management, to distribution. Linkage in SC helps the dairy industry maintain and develop stably; it not only helps dairy businesses to fulfill their capacity but also helps many small and medium companies develop their SC. In Vietnam, such linkage is still weak and is in need of establishment and improvement.

## 2. Literature Review

### 2.1. *Overview of supply chain integration*

#### 2.1.1. *Supply chain integration*

SC is a network of production and distribution which performs the functions of purchasing raw materials, converting raw materials into finished products, and distributing them to customers (Suong, 2017). It means the SC consists of relevant, direct or indirect stages, to meet customer needs. SC not only includes manufacturers and suppliers but also carriers, warehouses, retailers, and customers themselves (Chopra and Meindl, 2001). In general, SC is considered as the connection between suppliers, customers, manufacturers, and service providers involved in the business process (Bask and Juga, 2001). In other words, SC is a process that starts from raw materials until the end product which is made and delivered to consumers to achieve two basic objectives: (i) establishing a relationship between suppliers of suppliers and customers of customers as they affect results and efficiency of SC, (ii) gaining effectiveness and efficiency throughout SC. Therefore, building an integrated relationship is necessary to improve the business efficiency in SC.

SCI involves information sharing, planning, coordinating, and controlling materials, parts, and finished goods at the strategic, tactical, and operational levels (Towill *et al.*, 2002). SCI lessens the transaction costs in addition to the searching, contracting, negotiating, and monitoring costs which are allied with outsourcing due to the fewer partners involved. Therefore, companies can employ SCI as a potent option to gain the advantages of both *make* and *buy* (Shen, 2007).

Today, competition enforces organizations to enhance their capabilities for delivery, reliability, and product flexibility in response to customer needs and many organizations take advantage of SCI to reach this goal (Charu and Jānis, 2016). SCI intends *the degree to which an organization strategically cooperates with its SC partners and manages intra- and inter-organization processes to achieve effective and efficient flows of products, services, information, money, and decisions, to provide maximum value to its customer* (Fabbe-Costes and Jahre, 2007). While outsourcing can result in fewer production costs, SCI lessens the transaction costs in addition to the searching, contracting, negotiating, and monitoring costs that are allied with outsourcing due to the fewer partners involved.

In spite of the opportunities offered by SCI, intense level of integration is associated with some inherent threats for the firms that engage in alliances (Charu and Jānis, 2016), including the threat of spreading the firm's knowledge out to the potential competitors, difficulties in aligning business strategies, information sharing due to the existence of frequent or overlapping suppliers, and the potential interdependence created among partners. SCI partners require investment in new assets to customize the technology and machinery, and expenditure for building and instructing new programs for work and consulting teams, which are too costly and raise the vulnerability of benefiting from the partnership by exchanging of partners (Fabbe-Costes and Jahre, 2007). Furthermore, the lack of trust and reliance among SC partners might lead to opportunistic behavior at the expense of overall SC performance and profitability (Handfield and Bechtel, 2001).

### 2.1.2. *Types of SCI*

The relations of SC are mostly active vertically or horizontally. Vertical relations cover all of the relationships within the enterprises, between components in different classes. While horizontal relations are within the same class. A vertical relation completely connects the first provider in many ways to final customers. These relations occur when central factors increase influence on other factors in many different classes. Vertical alignment is always directed at both the relationship between the manufacturer and the first supplier and between the manufacturers and the final customer (Christopher and Towill, 2001). There are three forms of building SC integration, including vertical, horizontal, and multidimensional integration (Benita, 1997; Suong, 2012).

Different types of SCI are discussed in the literature, which are classified as follows. Vertical integration is *the degree to which an organization owns the network of processes* (Simatupang and Sridharan, 2005). This type of integration involves the coordination between businesses located at different stages of SC. Customer integration and supplier integration are major instances of vertical integration (Bäckstrand, 2007). On the other hand, horizontal integration is the coordination between businesses located at the same stage of SC. Horizontal integration aims to identify some organizational and managerial synergies enhancing inter-functional integration in SC.

### 2.1.3. *Levels of SCI*

The integration in SC includes three main components or more, referred to as transaction activity, integration, and relationship (Suong, 2012). Each level of integration contains continuum type of relations as follows: (i) Transaction is generally understood as the exchange or transfer of goods, services, or finance with each other. A transaction relationship means the activity of exchanging discrete value, especially about price (Bästrand, 2007). A commercial transaction involves price negotiation when the relationship with suppliers is a rival relationship and the goal is to increase the personal profit of a member in SC; (ii) Cooperation is like working together or cooperating with a partner with whom one cannot connect immediately. In other words, cooperation can be beneficial for all actors among SC. The types of integration relationships are rival cooperation or non-rival cooperation, partners, and the cooperation between manufacturer and supplier (Harland, 1996); (iii) Linking form is often viewed as a union of the two entities into one entity for business progress between two actors, the affiliate relationship consists of vertical link, buyback and venture, and full-ownership or merged (Togar and Sridharan, 2002).

The integration of different business activities among units becomes vital as organizations pay much attention to their core activities. Thus, their fruitfulness constantly relies on the capacity to coordinate internal and external activities in the value chain outside their own boundaries. The need for integration is evident in SCs, as companies forming an SC are dependent on the performance of other organizations. SC coordination is achieved when a decision maker, acting rationally, makes decisions that are efficient for the SC as a whole. The term *arcs of integration* representing two dimensions of integration, direction, and degree has been proposed (Christopher and Towill, 2001). The first dimension refers to the direction of integration towards customers and/or towards suppliers, and the second dimension, degree, or level of integration defines to what extent organizations collaborate operationally and by sharing information.

## 2.2. *Framework of the factors affecting SC integration*

### 2.2.1. *Structure of Vietnamese dairy SC*

Depending on the industry it belongs to, there are different actors in an SC. In the dairy industry, there are three major actors within an SC, including *supplier, manufacturer*, and *distributor*, as shown in Figure 1.

Surveying characteristics of enterprises within the dairy industry, three major actors emerge, including *material suppliers, manufacturers, and distributors*. It is found that these companies do not have

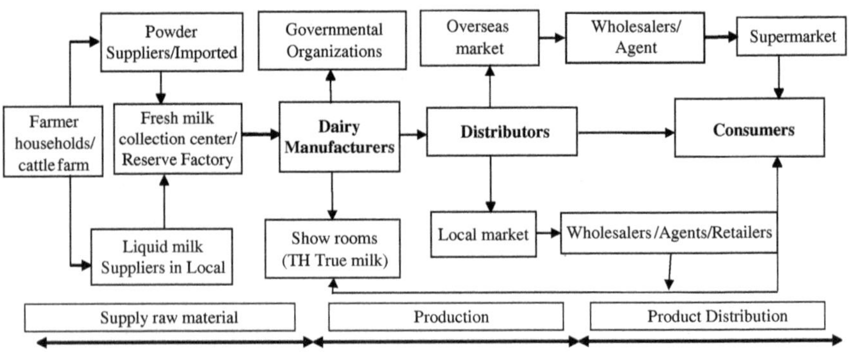


**Figure 1:** SC of Vietnam dairy industry.
*Source*: Based on survey and synthesis by Suong (2019).

sustainable integration (both vertical and horizontal) among them. For example, they are not aware of using the same technical production to maintain raw milk standards, in compliance with specifications and quality standards. This reveals that actors' activities in this SC are spontaneous and scattered. To understand the role and relations among actors in SCI better, this research focuses on analyzing the role of each actor, as follows:

- **Suppliers:** There are two main sources of milk input such as domestic producer and imported milk powder. About 37% of powder materials for processing rely on imported sources and the remaining 33% are collected from farms or households. In Vietnam, the dairy industry is one of the fast-growing and dynamic industries. According to the index from EVBN Report (2018), this business sector has enjoyed consistent and sustainable development over the recent decade. However, while Vietnam is an agricultural country originally, milk cow raising is not a strong career, neither a familiar business. Most of the milk cow farming happens in small and medium scale. As a result, the productivity of domestic dairy production is low compared to the high cost of final goods (Kaur *et al.*, 2015). Powder is imported mainly from New Zealand, Dairy Farmers in Australia, Arla from Denmark, and Dean Foods from America. Vietnam recently has had to import most of its dairy products and the trend moves from the US to Australia and New Zealand. In spite of the fact that Vietnamese authorities have introduced many rules and instructions on the development of dairy products, the effects are still limited (see Figure 2).
- **Manufacturers:** Typical dairy companies in Vietnam (Vinamilk, TH True Milk) not only have their own cow farms but also sign contracts with farmers, who increase their income of livestock by selling cow's milk. For example, Vinamilk successfully creates world-class dairy farming technology by having the right vision, orientation, specific objectives, investment, and applying innovative technologies to specific conditions in Vietnam. They develop a system of high-tech dairy cow farms from the North to

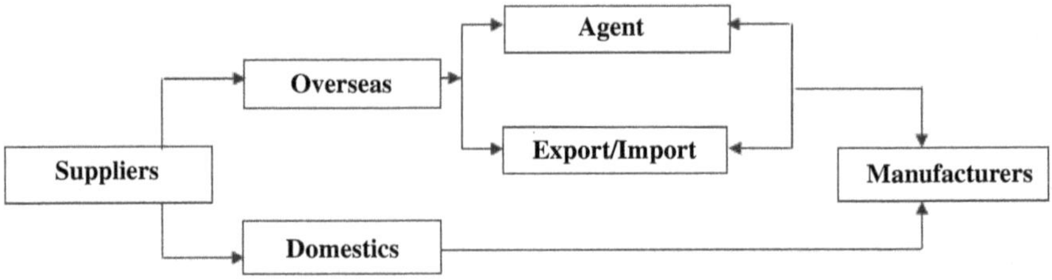


**Figure 2:** Suppliers and their relationships.
*Source*: Based on surveyed and synthesized by Suong (2019).

the South and provide active and effective support to dairy farmers nationwide while cooperating with companies in many areas from logistics, transportation, to distribution system. Dairy factories play a role in receiving imported milk materials and implementing production stages. They are responsible for milk materials that undergo a process of standardization, air conditioning, assimilation, and duplication and then packaging into finished products. Raw milk is delivered to the factory's stockpile and production plant, then finished milk is produced with lines for different subjects. Finished milk is stored and through partners, companies distribute and deliver milk to manufacturers or directly to consumers. The habit of manufacturers is to order raw materials when needed; they rely less on demand forecasts for efficient inventory management. To set up a standard dairy farming system, businesses need a big amount of investment capital. Moreover, to meet the market's demand, businesses in the dairy industry must import technology, materials, and equipment due to the limitations of domestic techniques, product prices, and business revenues. To date, every year Vietnam still imports nearly one billion USD of dairy products, mainly from New Zealand because domestic supply is in short supply, only meeting 40% of domestic demand (EBVN Report, 2018).

- **Distributors:** The distribution partner system of the dairy industry includes traditional channels, which are agents and wholesalers, and modern channel distribution businesses include supermarkets.

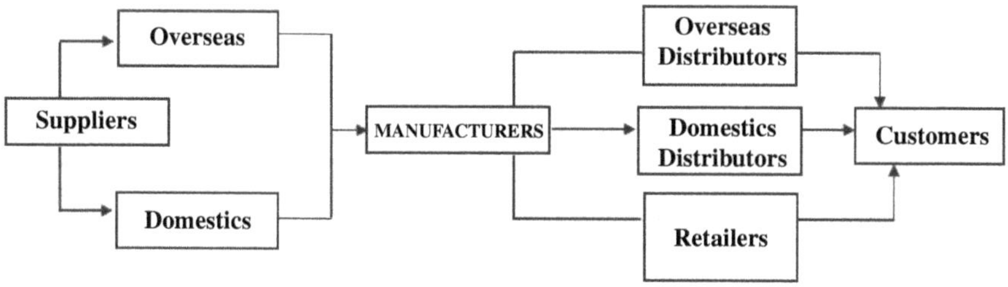


**Figure 3:** Manufacturers and their relationships.
*Source*: Based on surveyed and synthesized by Suong (2019).

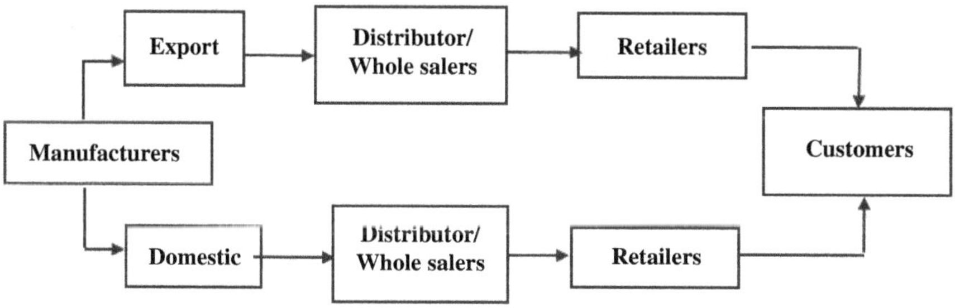


**Figure 4:** Distributors and their relationships.
*Source*: Based on surveyed and synthesized by Suong (2019).

Distribution partners are actors that help deliver dairy products to customers; dairy manufacturers have a discount policy for distribution companies (wholesalers and retailers as agents) and vice versa coordinating their products under an agreed and signed commitment (see Figure 3). In addition, distributors also have key-accounts which deliver to consumption units such as restaurants, hotels, schools, and offices/companies. To export, some typical distributors are chosen such as Acumatica from India (TH True Milk), supermarket and agent (Vinamilk), and nationwide store system like a showroom that is combined with a supermarket (Moc Chau Milk) (see Figure 4).

In brief, this study focuses on SCI in which there are three basic actors: *suppliers*, *manufacturers*, and *distributors*. Thus, it aims

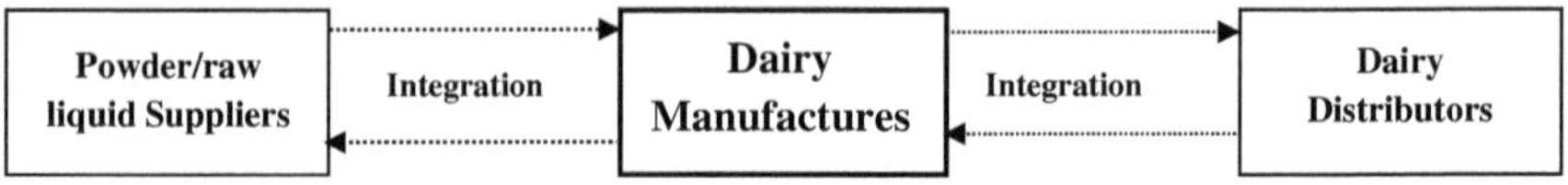


**Figure 5:** Relationship between the basic actors of the Vietnam dairy SC.
*Source*: Based on research approach by Suong (2019).

to look into the relationship between manufacturers–suppliers and manufacturers–distributors, which are displayed in Figure 5.

In fact, the domestic dairy industry still depends heavily on imported materials. This makes businesses unable to be proactive in quantity, quality, and unit price of products affecting production and business activities. To compete with foreign milk brands, large domestic enterprises such as Vinamilk, TH True Milk, and Moc Chau Milk invest in technology, expand scale, as well as built up material areas in place. However, current milk production only meets 30–33% of demand. Statistics from the General Statistics Office (2018) show that the production of dairy companies is favorable and the output increases in both the segment of fresh milk and powdered milk. To distribute products to the final consumers, there are three main channels for producers, including supermarkets, purchasing companies, and agents.

### 2.2.2. *Factors affecting integration of Dairy SC in Vietnam*

Focused on analyzing relationships among components within SC, the research shows eight basic factors affecting the SCI as follows:

(1) **Trust (TRU):** A positive belief, attitude, or expectation of one party concerning the likelihood of action or outcome of another is satisfactory. This factor affects positively on CSC (Handfield and Bechtel, 2001; Handfield, 2004; Bäckstrand, 2007; Suong, 2012).
(2) **Maturity (MAT):** Increasing SC interaction maturity leads to reduced uncertainty, which improves business performance and helps achieve competitive advantage. The characteristics of the maturity process are predictability, capability, control,

effectiveness, and efficiency (Towill and Childerhouse, 2002; Handfield, 2004; Bäckstrand, 2007; Suong, 2012).

(3) **Culture (CUL):** Defined as shared values and beliefs that can help enterprises of SC to understand organizational functioning process and provide behavioral norms. The collective programming of their mind distinguishes the members of one group or category of people from others. Differences in organizational or social level can create differences in opinion or conflicts of interest (Togar and Sridharan, 2004; Barrat, 2004; Suong, 2012).

(4) **Leadership (LEA):** To promote the level of cooperation forward, each company needs a leader who can influence the organization (Mentzer *et al.*, 2000). The leadership of any SC is a conceptual relationship between an SC leader and one or more organizations following that SC. Leadership implies an authority characterized by power, the influence of an organization in the SC to influence other member organizations with the aim of compliance in the chain, or combining the vision of leaders for the entire SC (Defee, 2007). All SC leaders have a vision, a commitment to that vision, and a group of followers.

(5) **Price Policy (PRI):** Kaur *et al.* (2015), through empirical research, discovered three variables that reduce prices: purchase in large quantities, fluctuations in prices, and dependence on organizations that affect factors of price coordination and research. They also point out that these factors can maximize SC cooperation, thereby improve efficiency. Pricing can also be a tool to measure SC performance. The value advantage and price advantage will create a strong linkage between partners when there is a mutual benefit or benefit sharing (Mentzer *et al.*, 2000). From a broader perspective, the price advantage can help businesses grow stronger through the market share.

(6) **Product Strategy (PRO)**: Implying development of new products, Kaur *et al.* (2015) argue that the decision to develop new products, trust, and cross-functional teams should be coordinated with SC management at the strategic level to reduce the competitiveness in SC. The degree of integration in SC is

also required to be considered at the earliest stage of cooperation when starting a new product, as innovation brings a competitive advantage to the product while enhancing the level of cooperation (Hilletofth and Eriksson, 2011). Technical progress and innovation are popular product features that bring product success. The innovation of products helps meet new criteria of market trends such as tastes and customer needs, increasing competitiveness of enterprises, reducing costs, thereby increasing revenue and profit, and helping businesses survive and grow in the future.

(7) **Technology Information (TEC):** Akhadian (2015) argues that IT is capable of coordinating and sharing information to minimize coordination costs. In addition, IT has integration and oversight of the ability to reduce transaction risks (Gunasekaran and Ngai, 2004). IT can connect buyers, suppliers, and provide information related to suppliers and customers that reduce transaction costs, allowing a company to integrate its SC with partners. IT can facilitate sharing information between a company and its suppliers effectively, sharing information in real-time to lower inventory costs due to improved forecasts (see Figure 6).

(8) **Information Sharing (INF):** Mentzer *et al.* (2000) find the possible financial benefits of the level of cooperation in SC such as reduced costs due to reduced inventory, improved customer services, efficient human resources, and better delivery through reduced cycle time. In addition, non-financial benefits include focus on core competencies, increased information sharing, ideas, and technology. Sharing information brings benefits to links in SC. Sharing good information can help reduce inventory by accurately forecasting the demand for raw materials, products, improving customer service, and product quality by responding to shortcomings in management or resource constraints (Haghighat, 2008). Simatupang and Sridharan (2002) also offer different forms of coordination in chains such as links. These collaborative methods are required to support SC members and enhance sustainable SC benefits.

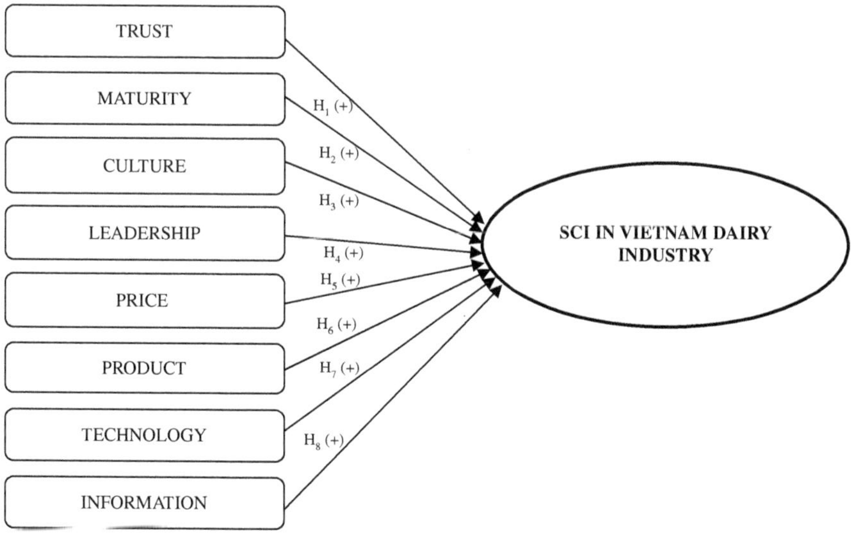


**Figure 6:** Initial research model for dairy SC in Vietnam.
*Source*: The results of qualitative research by Suong (2019).

### 2.3. *Proposed research model*

Previous research shows lots of factors affect SCI in different industries, however, in this study, combining literature review and experimental basis, eight factors have been determined to create a model for research. From the initial proposal model, the author uses survey data to process and input exploratory factors of analysis to identify factors that affect SCI before having the final research model.

## 3. Research Methodology

This research is conducted based on two methods: (1) Qualitative research aims to construct and calibrate the component scale: the trust rate among the partners, the maturity level of the relationship among partners, the cultural cooperation, the leadership of partners, the price policy of partners, the product strategy of partners, and technology and information sharing within partners in SC of Vietnam dairy industry; (2) Quantitative research aims to collect, analyze survey data, as well as test the component scale, and measure the research theory model and hypothesis. Preliminary research is built and calibrated by scale and the variables are added through observation for qualitative and quantitative methods. Preliminary qualitative research is done by experts with great consideration and group discussions with managers concerned with the dairy industry by the sampling method. The content of the discussion related to the factors that affect actors in SC are related to factors that influence integration of SC's actors; comment on, give out the research model for the discussion group to comment on the factors that affect SCI and the draft scale built up by the author group and corrected by the discussion group. After exchanging of ideas, the discussion group agrees with the proposed model. The discussion group calibrates some of the names in the scale components, proposes to amend the scale, and modify some observed variables. From that, the research group agrees that the factors affecting the dairy industry include: (1) *the degree of trust among partners*, (2) *the maturity level of the relationship among partners*, (3) *the cultural cooperation*, (4) *the leadership of partners*, (5) *the price policy of partners*, (6) *the product strategy of partners*, (7) *technology among partners*, (8) *information sharing within partners*. The scale of the research model includes 39 observation variables measured by 5-point Likert scale in which 1 point denotes completely disagree through to point 5, for completely agree.

## 4. Results and Discussion

The study concentrates on suppliers, local milk processing industries, and distributors (wholesalers and retailers). To conclude, for methodological reasons, and hence in line with the objectives, the general sample of this research includes all actors in the dairy industry along the chain of the market. Moreover, the target sample of the study includes milk producers, processors, and retail markets at various stages along the SC.

The data collection instrument uses a questionnaire which is administrated to a sample of 305 enterprises directly or indirectly related to the processing and distribution within the Vietnamese dairy industry. The number of valid questionnaires for the quantitative research is 300, with 242 small enterprises accounting for 80.6%, 41 medium enterprises accounting for 13.7%, and 17 large enterprises accounting for 5.7%. Statistics describe the sample according to its role in SC; from the results, we find that 69.7% of the surveyed subjects are distributors (managers at supermarkets, wholesalers, and retailers) and 30.3% are manufacturers (managers in various divisions related to production).

The list of scales used includes scale of trust and maturity of Suong (2017), scale of leadership of Defee *et al.* (2010), scale of price policy of Iyer (1998), scale of product strategy of Hilletofth and Eriksson (2011), scale of information technology of Haghighat (2008), scale of culture of Denisa (2014), and scale of information sharing of Hilletofth and Eriksson (2011).

### 4.1. *Reliability analysis (RA)*

#### 4.1.1. *Explore factor analysis and regression analysis*

The Cronbach's Alpha is conducted to assess the reliability of each scale (Table 1). Alpha values average to 0.8 for one dependent variable and the other eight independent variables. This indicates all scales can be considered reliable (Creswell, 2002). For each of the item scales, factor analysis is used to reduce the total number of items to manageable factors. Principal components analysis is used to extract factors with eigenvalue of 1.147. Varimax rotation is used to facilitate the interpretation of the factor matrix. Sampling adequacy measurement tests are also examined via the KMO statistics to validate the use of factor analysis. The composition of independent variable scales has Sig. equal to 0.000 and KMO equal to 0.708, the

**Table 1:** Summarizes the results tested by Cronbach's Alpha scale.

| | No. of items | | |
|---|---|---|---|
| **Scales** | **Before** | **After** | **Cronbach's Alpha** |
| TRU | 6 | 5 | 0.869 |
| MAT | 4 | 4 | 0.846 |
| CUL | 4 | 4 | 0.825 |
| LEA | 4 | 4 | 0.841 |
| PRI | 4 | 4 | 0.867 |
| PRO | 4 | 4 | 0.884 |
| TEC | 4 | 3 | 0.705 |
| INF | 4 | 3 | 0.722 |
| INT | 3 | 3 | 0.801 |

*Source*: Results from the data process of researcher (2019).

variables converge to eight differentiating factors such as the original hypothesis and the total deviation of 66.28% for the deduction of 66.28%. Measurement variables with weighting factors of variables are greater than 0.5. From the above results, the weighting factors of variables and the total deviation satisfy the theoretical condition, so it can be concluded that the appropriate EFA model and the variables will continue to be included in the RA (Table 2).

Using Pearson's correlation coefficient to analyze the correlation between independent variables, we find that the correlation between independent variables and dependent variables is positive. Next, conducting a RA we determined the results of the model confirming assessment as shown in Tables 3 and 4.

Using $F$ test for the fit of the model in variance analysis we find Sig. equal to 0.000 and less than 0.05, thus rejecting the hypothesis that all regression coefficients of 0 simultaneously show the overall suitability of the regression model. In addition, 1 is less than Durbin–Watson, which is less than 1.684, less than three shows no first-order self-correlation, and VIF coefficients less than 2 indicate that the independent variables are not closely related.

**Table 2:** Results of EFA with eight-factor model.

| Concept | Variables | Observers | Cronbach's Alpha | Cumulative Variance (%) | Conclusion |
|---|---|---|---|---|---|
| | Trust | 5 | 0.892 | | |
| | Maturity | 4 | 0.846 | | |
| | Culture | 4 | 0.825 | | |
| Integration (INT) | Leadership | 4 | 0.841 | 66.28 | Accepted |
| | Price | 4 | 0.867 | | |
| | Product | 4 | 0.884 | | |
| | Technology | 3 | 0.595 | | |
| | Information | 3 | 0.672 | | |
| | Dairy SC Integration (INT) | 3 | 0.876 | 79.234 | |

*Source*: Results from the data process of researcher (2019).

**Table 3:** Model summary.[a]

| Model | $R$ | $R^2$ | Adjusted $R^2$ | Std. error of the estimate | Durbin–Watson |
|---|---|---|---|---|---|
| 1 | 0.805[b] | 0.657 | | 0.686 | 01.674 |

*Notes*: [a]Dependent variable: INT; [b]independent variable: TRU, MAT, CUL, LEA, PRI, PRO, TEC, INF.

**Table 4:** ANOVA.[a]

| Model | Sum of squares | *df* | Mean square | *F* | Sig. |
|---|---|---|---|---|---|
| Regression | 41.242 | 8 | 27.380 | 154.709 | 0.000[b] |
| Residual | 106.318 | 265 | 0.478 | | |
| Total | 145.570 | 265 | | | |

*Notes*: [a]Independent variable: TRU, MAT, CUL, LEA, PRI, PRO, TEC, INF. [b]Dependent variable: INT.

**Table 5:** Result of RA by entering method.

| | Unstandardized coefficients | | Standardized coefficients | | | Collinearity statistics | |
|---|---|---|---|---|---|---|---|
| **Model** | **B** | **Std. error** | $\beta$ | $t$ | **Sig.** | **Tolerance** | **VIF** |
| Constant | −0.972 | 0.332 | | −0.3034 | 0.003 | | |
| Trust | 0.823 | 0.086 | 0.467 | 9.665 | 0.000 | 0.528 | 1.736 |
| Maturity | 0.141 | 0.065 | 0.104 | 2.123 | 0.034 | 0.597 | 1.573 |
| Culture | 0.239 | 0.083 | 0.138 | 2.881 | 0.004 | 0.532 | 1.782 |
| Leadership | 0.179 | 0.051 | 0.142 | 3.505 | 0.001 | 0.821 | 1.239 |
| Price | 0.198 | 0.052 | 0.147 | 3.748 | 0.000 | 0.874 | 1.108 |
| Product | 0.121 | 0.051 | 0.091 | 2.188 | 0.002 | 0.843 | 1.160 |
| Technology | −0.121 | 0.049 | −0.009 | −0.237 | 0.704 | 0.983 | 1.008 |
| Information | −0.028 | 0.046 | −0.024 | −0.650 | 0.602 | 0.975 | 1.066 |

VIF values of the observed variables are both less than 2, so it is possible that the model is not affected by the multicollinearity phenomenon. Factors of Information Technology (TEC) and Information Sharing (INF) are excluded from RA model due to Sig. values respectively of 0.704 and 0.602, which are more than 0.05. Indeed, these are two factors from the results of the research in combination with the research group's knowledge which were included in the initial proposal model, however, during the analysis process, these factors are not expressed or found suitable for the model. The model retains six (06) factors that fit the model with the significance levels from 0.000 to 0.034, which are less than 0.05. The standardized regression coefficients (*Beta*) of the remaining factors are positive (+), indicating the same directional impact as integration, which means that when the value of the factors is high, integration is also highly correlated. *Beta* also expresses the level of impact on sequential integration from high to low: *trust, price, leadership, culture, maturity, and product* (see Table 5). From the results of the above test, we obtain the non-standardized regression equation as follows:

$$\text{Int} = -0.972 + 0.467\text{Tru} + 0.197\text{Pri} + 0.142\text{Lea} + 0.138\text{Cul} + 0.104\text{Mat} + \text{x}0.091\text{Pro}. \quad (1)$$

## 5. Conclusions

In today's business, competition is among integrated SCs instead of individual organizations. Hence, SC shall be well-coordinated, which will play a huge role in making SC attainable to customer demands. In fact, the domestic dairy industry still depends heavily on imported materials. This makes businesses unable to be proactive in quantity, quality, and unit price of products, thus affecting production and business activities. To compete with foreign milk brands, big domestic enterprises such as Vinamilk, TH True Milk, and Nuti Milk actively invested in technology, expanded scale as well as built up material areas in place. Especially building a value chain to enhance the value of enterprises. Large dairy companies in Vietnam not only have their own cow farms but also sign contracts with farmers, collecting cow's milk, which helps increase the income of livestock farmers. At the same time, links with related companies in many areas from logistics, transportation, to distribution system have been established.

The cooperation of SC in the Vietnam dairy industry with partners of supply and distribution companies is long-lasting and rigorous based on the profit-sharing foundation, enhancing their position. With the supplying partner, dairy manufacturers offer international standards for raw milk and milk powder, thereby helping suppliers to constantly improve product quality, increasing competitiveness. For partners who are distribution companies, with the goal of dominating market share, manufacturers request partners to improve distribution capacity through increasing revenue criteria. It can be affirmed that those manufacturers with qualified supply and distribution partners are really effective. With supply partners who are raw milk producers, they need to match their requirements at a high level to become powerful distribution partners that can help manufacturers' products move to the same lane. This ensures that their SC is operated smoothly and able to respond quickly to customers' needs effectively with the lowest operating cost to increase the efficiency of the chain and the competitiveness for the customers and SC's members. At the same time, the exchange of information through the use of software and information systems is organized scientifically and updated regularly to help the departments coordinate with each other to respond quickly to the regular and continuous action of the current business environment. To improve SC performance, manufacturers should pay special attention to building trust among other actors in the dairy SC, and its partners, products, and cultural prices because these factors have a strong effect on cooperation and increase SC performance. Ultimately, it helps the relations of enterprises reach economic efficiency.

## References

Agata, R. (2017). Sustainable SC maturity model. *Research in Logistics and Production*, 7(3), 201–209.

Akhadian, S.H. (2015). Roles of information technology in SC management. *Electronic Theses & Dissertations*, pp. 95–97.

Bäckstrand, J. (2007). Levels of interaction in SC Relations. Thesis for Doctorate in Jönköping University, Jönköping Sweden.

Bask, A.H., and Juga, J. (2001). Semi-integrated SCs: Towards the new era of supply chain management. *International Journal of Logistics: Research and Applications*, 4(2), 137–152. doi:10.1080/13675560110059434

Benita, M.B. (1997). Supply Chain design and analysis: Models and Methods, *International Journal of Production Economics*, 55(3), 281–294.

Charu, C., and Jānis, G. (2016). Scope of SC configuration problem, pp. 17–45. Available at www.springer.com.

Childerhouse, P., and Towill, D.R. (2003). Simplified material flow holds the key to SC integration. *Omega — The International Journal of Management Science*, 31(1), 17–27.

Chopra, S., and Meindl, P. (2001). *SC Management: Strategy, Planning and Operation*, 2nd edition. Prentice Hall, pp. 3–10.

Christopher, M., and Towill, D. (2001). An integrated model for the design of agile SC. *International Journal of Physical Distribution and Logistics Management*, 31(4), 235–246.

Creswell, J. (2002). *Research Design: Qualitative, Quantitative and Mix Method Approach*, 2nd edition. Sage Publications Inc.

Defee, C. (2007). SC leadership. *Tennessee Research and Creative Exchange*, 40(10), 23–46.

Defee, C.C., Stank, T.P., and Esper, T. (2010). Performance implications of transformational supply chain leadership and followership. *International Journal of Physical Distribution & Logistics Management*, 40(10), 763–791.

Denisa, M. (2014). The effect of organization culture and uncertainty in SC management. *The Albanian Beer Industry, 'Club of Economics in Miskolc' TMP*, 10(2), 49–57.

EVBN Report (2018). Vietnam Dairy Report: SC and Operation in South East Asia. CEL Consulting (2017).

Fabbe-Costes, N., and Jahre, M. (2007). SC integration gives better performance — The emperor's new suit? *International Journal of Physical Distribution & Logistics Management*, 37(10), 835–855. doi:10.1108/09600030710848941

Gunasekaran, A., and Ngai, E.W.T. (2004). Information systems in SC integration and management. *European Journal of Operational Research*, 159, 269–295.

Handfield, R., and Bechtel, C. (2001). The role of trust and relationship structure in improving SC responsiveness. *Journal of Industrial Marketing Management*, 31(2002), 367–382. Retrieved from http://www2.nkfust.edu.tw/ percy%20/Report6/TheRoleOfTrrustAndRelationshipStructureInImprovingSupplyChainResponsiveness.pdf [Accessed November 10, 2001].

Handfield, R. (2004). How Mature Is your SC? The SCRD Capability Maturity Model. *Report on 89th Annual International Supply Management Conference*. Carolina, U.S.A. Retrieved from https://www.instituteforsupplymanagement.org/files/Pubs/Proceedings/FCHandfieldStraight.pdf [Accessed December 30, 2011].

Harland, M. (1996). SC management: Relationships, chains and networks. *British Journal of Management*, 7(1), 63–80.

Haghighat, F. (2008) The impact of information technology on coordination mechanisms of supply chain. *World Applied Sciences Journal*, 3(2), 74–81.

Hilletofth, P., and Eriksson, D. (2011), Coordinating new product development with SC management. *Industrial Management & Data Systems*, 111(2), 264–281.

Iyer, G. (1998). Coordinating channels under price and non price competition. *Marketing Science*, 17(4), 338–355.

Kaur, L., and Singh, H. R. (2015). Determinants of SC coordination of milk and dairy industries in Ethiopia: A case of Addis Ababa and its surroundings. *Springer Plus*, 4(1), 498.

Lambert, D., Knemeyer, A., and Gardner, J. (2004). SC Partnerships: Model Validation and Implementation. *Journal of Business Logistics*, 25(2), 21–42.

Mentzer, J.T., Foggin, J.H., and Golicic, C.L. (2000). Collaboration: The enablers, impediments, and benefits. *Supply Chain Management Review*, 10, 33–37.

Simatupang, T., and Sridharan, R. (2005). An integrative framework for SC collaboration. *International Journal of Logistics Management*, 16(2), 257–274.

Suong, H.T.T. (2011). Factors affecting the cooperation in SC of wooden furniture in Vietnam. *Journal of Economic Development*, 254, 46–53.

Suong, H.T.T. (2012). Research on factors affecting the cooperation in the SC of Wooden furniture, the case researching the East Southern Region. Thesis for Doctorate in University of Economics Hochiminh City, HCMC, Vietnam.

Suong, H.T.T. (2017). Factors impacting on the SC collaboration of the furniture industry in Vietnam. *Journal of Asian Finance, Economics and Business*, 4(4), 67–77. http://doi:10.13106/jafeb.2017.vol4.n04.67

Suong, H.T.T., and Tri, N.M. (2019). Factors Impacting on the SC Collaboration of the Frieslandcampina Việt Nam. *Journal of Science and Technology*, Industrial University of Ho Chi Minh city, 5/2019.

Shen, Z.J. (2007). Integrated SC design models: A survey and future research directions. *Journal of Industrial and Management Optimization*, 3(1), 1–27. http://doi:10.3934/jimo.2007.3.1

Togar, M.S., and Sridharan, R. (2002). The collaborative supply chain. *The International Journal of Logistics Management*, 13(1), 15–30.

Togar, M.S., and Sridharan, R. (2004). The Collaboration index: A measure for supply chain collaboration. *International Journal of Physical Distribution & Logistics Management*, 35(1), 44–62.

Towill, D., Childerhouse, P., and Disney, S. (2002). Integrating the automotive supply chain: Where are we now? *International Journal of Physical Distribution and Logistics Management*, 32(2), 79–95. https://doi.org/10.1108/09600030210421705

https://doi.org/10.1142/9789811227158_0020

## Chapter 20

# Research on Solutions to Improve Destination Competitiveness for Tourism Development in Can Tho City

**Khanh Tung Nguyen and Dong Phong Nguyen**

**Abstract**

Many studies on destination competitiveness indicate that natural resources, human resources, infrastructure, policies, and services in a certain destination could mainly attract tourists and help tourists determine their preferred destinations compared to other competitive destinations. In this study, the authors collect information on, analyze, and evaluate visitor-related factors determining the competitiveness of tourism destinations in Can Tho City based on three factors: *infrastructure for tourism or facilities for tourism, tourism resources*, and *tourism human resources*. The study also proposes some research orientations to examine the destination competitiveness assessment model in Can Tho.

**Keywords:** Destination competitiveness; Tourism; Can Tho City.

## 1. Introduction

Destination competitiveness of each locality is a topic attracting attention of many scientists, managers, as well as tourism businesses (Poon, 1993; Crouch and Ritchie, 1999; Hassan, 2000; Heath, 2002; Dwyer and Kim, 2003; Enright and Newton, 2005).

According to a report by World Tourism and Travel Council in 2018, the tourism sector creates 10.4% of the global GDP (equivalent to approximately US$8,300 billion) and the figure is estimated to reach more than US$12,400 billion by 2028. Tourism also created more than 322 million jobs in 2018, accounting for 11.8%. The number is forecasted to be 413 million jobs in tourism and travel, accounting for 11.6%, by 2028 (UNWTO, 2018).

As a city that is located in the hub of Mekong Delta Area with its maze of rivers, Can Tho City distinguishes the values of culture and ecology, attracting both domestic and international visitors. Dubbed as Tay Do (capital of the west), being the metropolis of the southwestern area hundreds of years ago and currently central city, Can Tho's key economic sector is tourism, contributing to the city's socioeconomic development.

In the context of profound international integration, it is estimated that tourism destinations in Can Tho have to compete with several destinations of neighboring provinces as well as regional countries. Therefore, it is crucial and urgent to have research evaluating the competitiveness and capacity-building model for tourism destinations in Can Tho, to help managers find breakthrough solutions.

## 2. Overview of Theories and Analytic Framework on Destination Competitiveness

There are many different definitions of tourism destination competitiveness. Researchers with Porter's approach (1985) on national competitiveness strategy propose certain definitions. For example, Crouch and Ritchie (2000) state that tourism destination competitiveness is the competitiveness of one tourism destination in comparison with other destinations based on natural resources, environment, diverse culture, historical heritage, etc., to attract tourists' loyalty, enhancing sustainable development for local people. Meanwhile, Bordas (1994) identifies global factors of destination competitiveness, including low cost, distinction, and specialization. Hassan (2000) says that there are 4 indexes for destination competitiveness, which are environmental commitment, comparative advantage, distributing network, and demand orientation in each area. Besides, Craiwell and More (2008) suggest seven factors influencing destination competitiveness, including (i) price competitiveness; (ii) tourism human resources; (iii) infrastructure; (iv) environment; (v) technology; (vi) openness; and (vii) social aspects.

Based on the collected documents, the authors recommend a model for studying destination competitiveness in Can Tho City through three factors — *infrastructure (including infrastructure and physical facilities for tourism), tourism resources (distinguished products), and tourism human resources.*

## 3. Research Methodology

The research mainly uses secondary data and documents and analyzes them. In particular, relevant researches officially released are used to learn about theoretical basis and destination competitiveness framework; from that, factors of the model for destination competitiveness in Can Tho City are recommended.

The authors also use secondary data from statistical yearbooks, specialized reports, previous researches, etc., in the economy and tourism industry (especially distinguished products, infrastructure, and human resources) of Can Tho City. Data are collected, synthesized, and analyzed to clarify the current situation of tourism, destination competitiveness. The authors also propose some recommendations for enhancing destination competitiveness for tourism development in Can Tho City.

## 4. Results and Discussion

### 4.1. *Current background of Can Tho City tourism*

The common evaluation of Can Tho City tourism is that it has a positive growth and signals (Can Tho City Department of Culture, Sports, and Tourism, 2018).

Visitors come to Can Tho City mainly during festivals, the dry season, and when Can Tho City organizes regional, national, and international events or conferences. Every year, Can Tho City organizes more than 10 domestic and international fairs. In 2018, the city collaborated with central ministries and agencies to organize major events such as Meet Japan — Mekong Delta area, Southern Traditional Cake Festival, international conference on development vision for Mekong Delta tourism, ASEM conference on climate change adaptation, international volleyball competition, and Vietnam–Japan cultural festival. International visitors visiting Can Tho City, accounting for 15% of total international visitors to Mekong Delta area, are mainly from France, Germany, the United Kingdom, the United States, Australia, and South Korea; while domestic visitors are mainly from Ho Chi Minh City, Da Nang, Ha Noi, and Hai Phong. Total visitors to the city reached 7.5 million people in 2017 and 8.48 million people in 2018, ranking first in comparison with other provinces in the Mekong Delta area.

Tourism turnover in 2018 increased 130.60% compared to the one in 2017, coming third in the Mekong Delta area, achieving 28,900 thousand billion VND and 37,900 billion VND in 2017 and 2018, respectively (Appendix A). In 2018, the accommodation establishments served 2.6 million visitors (21.7% increase in comparison with that number at the same time in 2017), among which overnight stay by inbound visitors reached 363.81 thousand, a 19.2% growth compared to the same period in 2017, while domestic visitors' stay reached 2.29 million, an increase of 22% compared to 2017.

The analysis shows that lodging accounts for 30% of the total turnover of the tourism sector and it is the biggest source of revenue from the whole sector. Food and beverage account for 15% due to diverse cuisine activities. Can Tho City is the place of gathering renowned specialties and it is diverse with a system of restaurants, family food stores, bistros, and street vendors. Some specialties of Can Tho are favorites of visitors, for example, duck cooked in fermented bean curd, Da Ly salted fish hot pot, Thanh Van grilled sausage vermicelli, traditional cakes, sweet soups, and dishes made from countryside ingredients. The remaining sources of turnover from shopping and leisure are still modest.

Regarding tourism expenditure, Can Tho City is considered as the hub of the economy, trade, and services of the whole region. There are 100 traditional markets, 12 major supermarkets, trade centers of domestic and international economic corporations with sufficient goods and services as well as domestic and international fashion brands. However, visitor spend in Can Tho is still low, contributing only 2.01% to the total turnover from tourists, even less than the turnover of other provinces such as Ben Tre, Bac Lieu, Vinh Long, Soc Trang. The reason is that the city lacks shopping places specialized for tourists with featured goods and products and the scale, quantity, and effectiveness of leisure spots are still limited. These are factors running down the efficiency and turnover of the tourism industry.

## 4.2. *Assessment of factors influencing destination competitiveness*

### 4.2.1. *Tourism infrastructure and physical facilities*

Can Tho City, an urban area around a maze of rivers with developed infrastructure, is considered the economic, political, educational, medical center, and a hub for land, water, and air transport, of the whole Mekong Delta area. Besides the land system being well connected with other provinces, information and telecommunications systems, and financial organizations satisfying the demands of trade and tourism, Can Tho City has two important infrastructure facilities, which are the international airport and seaport. Can Tho international airport is designed to have the capacity of receiving 3 million passengers per year, with domestic flight routes to Ha Noi, Da Nang, Phu Quoc, Con Dao, and international routes to Thailand, Taiwan, and Japan. In 2018, the airport welcomed more than 83,000 people, an increase of 25% in comparison with the same time the previous year (Can Tho International Airport, 2018). Regarding the seaport system (Cai Cui, Hoang Dieu, Tan Cang), Cai Cui is considered as

**Table 1:** Travel accommodation establishments in Can Tho, 2008–2018.

| | 2008 | 2009 | 2010 | 2011 | 2012 | 2013 | 2014 | 2015 | 2016 | 2017 | 2018 |
|---|---|---|---|---|---|---|---|---|---|---|---|
| Number of establishments | 154 | 165 | 174 | 177 | 190 | 197 | 226 | 226 | 244 | 270 | 275 |
| Number of rooms | 3.737 | 3.950 | 4.086 | 4.173 | 4.749 | 5.288 | 6.176 | 6.176 | 6.517 | 6.931 | 7.188 |

*Source*: Can Tho City Department of Culture, Sports, and Tourism (2018).

the central port of the Mekong Delta area and can receive 20,000 ton vessels for the demand for goods transport and trade with regional provinces.

Meanwhile, the internal transport system is upgraded with several transport routes connecting famous tourist spots, such as Cai Rang floating market, Son Islet, Tan Loc Islet, Binh Thuy ancient house, and tourism facilities such as restaurants, hotels, leisure centers.

The accommodation system for overnight stay includes 275 tourism lodging establishments with approximately 7,200 rooms. Among them, there are 140 hotels ranked 1–5 stars with more than 41,400 rooms; average use capacity is more than 70%. In 2018, 5 more hotels were added to the list and Azerai hotel at Au Islet was ranked the first 5-star resort in Can Tho (Table 1). In addition, there are 32 ecological tourist sites and 19 homestays in Phong Dien and Binh Thuy Districts besides 59 international travel and domestic business companies with 17 companies and branches working in international travel (Can Tho Department of Culture, Sports, and Tourism, 2018).

Moreover, in order to build a legal corridor for tourism and tourism development, besides legal documents issued by central ministries and agencies, Can Tho City has its own policies and documents, such as Program No. 21/Ctr/TU dated May 12, 2017 by City Party Committee in implementing Resolution No. 08/NQ/TW dated January 16, 2017 by Politburo on making tourism a key economic sector; Resolution 03-NQ/TU dated August 01, 2016 on tourism development, Plan 111/KH-UBND dated September 19, 2016 on implementing Resolution 03-NQ/TU dated August 1, 2016 by the City Party Committee. Furthermore, Can Tho City also prepares and

**Table 2:** Tourism labor force in Can Tho City.

| Indexes | 2008 | 2009 | 2010 | 2011 | 2012 | 2013 | 2014 | 2015 | 2016 |
|---|---|---|---|---|---|---|---|---|---|
| Undergraduates and post-graduates | 245 | 255 | 350 | 371 | 400 | 410 | 425 | 435 | 445 |
| Vocational and colleges | 603 | 637 | 735 | 825 | 900 | 925 | 955 | 985 | 1.015 |
| Other training | 567 | 690 | 750 | 975 | 1.100 | 1.169 | 1.251 | 1.364 | 1.477 |
| Untrained | 664 | 613 | 690 | 824 | 840 | 849 | 852 | 858 | 870 |
| **Total** | **2.336** | **2.695** | **2.795** | **2.995** | **3.240** | **3.353** | **3.485** | **3.642** | **3.807** |

*Source*: Can Tho City Department of Culture, Sports, and Tourism (2018).

issues tourism plans, executes projects for developing tourism destinations, and the tourism network combined with infrastructure for tourism, which provides specific ways to mobilize investment capital from public and private sectors as well as FDI.

In general, the current infrastructure and physical facilities are advantageous for Can Tho City to develop its tourism and enhance the value of its destinations, contributing to higher prestige and brand name for tourism service of the city.

### 4.2.2. *Tourism human resources*

Currently, there are five establishments training tourism human resources, including two universities, two colleges, and one vocational school. The city has more than 6,500 employees working in tourism sector, with more than 55% of them under training. As evaluated by tourism expertise, currently the rates of labor use and labor quality are not homogeneous, and employees' quality in tourism businesses has considerable disparity. This is a major challenge for the city's development of tourism human resources. To overcome such a challenge and grow the quality of tourism human resources, Can Tho City established an objective that by 2020 the rate of trained tourism workforce should reach 80% (an equivalence of about 78,600 laborers/year) (Table 2).

Tour guides are considered the fundamental force of tourism human resources. They play an important role in enhancing the

**Table 3:** Number of licensed tour guides in Mekong Delta area (unit: license).

| | Can Tho | Long An | Tien Giang | Tra Vinh | Vinh Long | An Giang | Bac Lieu | Ben Tre | Hau Giang | Soc Trang | Ca Mau | Đong Thap | Kien Giang |
|---|---|---|---|---|---|---|---|---|---|---|---|---|---|
| Domestic | **452** | 11 | 229 | 17 | 79 | 96 | — | 104 | 18 | 8 | 30 | 44 | 120 |
| International | **150** | — | 64 | 4 | 56 | 28 | — | 42 | 14 | 2 | — | 9 | 13 |

*Source*: Mekong Delta Tourism Association (2018).

attraction of tourist spots through their provision of historical knowledge, and they also act as the connecting bridge among regions and cultural, ethnic races. Therefore, besides professional knowledge, tour guides should also be trained and supplemented with knowledge of the above-mentioned issues. In terms of language practiced, tour guides for international visitors in Can Tho City and Mekong Delta areas mainly use English, with a rare exception of other languages (Table 3).

In general, although there are still limitations in quantity and quality, tourism human resources and tour guides of Can Tho City serve their important roles in enhancing the value of destinations in Can Tho.

### 4.2.3. *Tourism resources*

#### 4.2.3.1. Nature-based tourism resources

River culture is typical of the Can Tho and Mekong Delta area. Can Tho City is a rivery urban region with a surrounding system of canals and rivers, creating islands and islets, such as Au, Khuong, Son, and Tan Loc. Thanks to such a natural advantage, Can Tho citizens have developed many diverse orchards. In specific, the river advantage makes the destination value for Cai Rang floating market one of the most distinguished floating market cultures. Cai Rang floating market is advertised and nominated on several prestigious tourism magazines in the world. With its own characteristics, Cai Rang floating market is the typical destination for tourists visiting Can Tho for the first time (Tran Viet Phuong, 2017).

#### 4.2.3.2. Socioeconomic-based tourism resources

Can Tho City has a special location, that is as the hub for regional transport, gateway to Ho Chi Minh City, a center of education, science, and technology. Especially, the accommodation establishments and trade centers are quite developed, so the city has good conditions to grow different types of tourism connected with historical and cultural heritage, countryside-based community tourism, and major Meetings, Incentives, Conferences, and Exhibitions (MICE) tourism. These are the advantages adding to the competitive edge of Can Tho in comparison with other provinces in the region, making tourism a key sector for city development by 2020.

Public and private medical systems with more than 15 general and specialized hospitals are growing rapidly, meeting demands of treatment for neighboring provinces in Mekong Delta area. In addition, a system of universities and colleges is serving well the training and scientific research. Newly formed private universities are functioning besides central universities such as Can Tho University and the Medical and Pharmaceutical University. What is more, Mekong Delta Rice Institute located in Can Tho is the place for researching and providing several new rice species for Mekong Delta market (Hong Giang, 2018).

Many different supermarkets and trade centers help tourists shop, visit, and enjoy, which in turn boosts trade services.

4.2.3.3. Humanity-based tourism resources

According to Can Tho City Department of Culture, Sports, and Tourism (2018), currently there are more than 104 types of intangible cultural heritages. Among them, Cai Rang floating market and Ky Yen Thuong Dien festival (thanking a fruitful harvest) at Binh Thuy Temple are two heritages enlisted by Ministry of Culture, Sports, and Tourism to be the national intangible cultural heritages. Besides, some other cultural forms creating Can Tho's identity are Can Tho traditional Chanty, wind dismissal festival in Can Tho, and Can Tho salted fish hot pot — all contributing to the local cultural diversity. These heritages are attached to the spiritual and cultural life of local people as well as tourists (Ngo Nguyen Hiep Phuoc, 2018).

Besides intangible cultural heritages, tangible cultural heritages including the ones from the historical development of Can Tho – Tay Do such as Ninh Kieu Quay, Binh Thuy Temple, Binh Thuy ancient house, and Ong Pagoda are attractive destinations to visitors (Hong Giang, 2018).

### 4.3. *Evaluating destination competitiveness of Can Tho in comparison with other provinces in Mekong Delta area*

Based on geographical location, Long An and Tien Giang provinces are the two provinces which have more advantages in attracting tourists as they are near Ho Chi Minh City; tourists can start in Ho Chi Minh City and visit these provinces during the day. Besides, Phu Quoc is an emerging destination with attractive beaches and offers several flight routes domestically and internationally. Currently, there are connecting flights from Phu Quoc to Ha Noi, Ho Chi Minh City, and Can Tho, and international charter flights also help Phu Quoc to serve many different inbound visitor segments.

In such context, Can Tho City has advantages from infrastructure and natural resources, such as Can Tho International Airport with many connecting routes to Ha Noi, Da Nang, Phu Quoc, Con Dao, and some charter flights to Taiwan, Thailand, and Japan, which are important conditions for tour agencies to bring tourists to Can Tho. With the aviation standard of 4E-ICAO, Can Tho International Airport can receive Boeing 777 and 787 aircraft. In Mekong Delta area, there are four airports, in Can Tho, Kien Giang, Phu Quoc, and Ca Mau; among them, Can Tho International Airport is able to receive 830,000 visitors. Moreover, with a modern and advanced system of accommodation establishments, Can Tho City has the opportunity to compete with advantages in tourism infrastructure. In addition, the city has destination competitiveness from its ability to organize domestic and international exhibitions and events, and the numerous tour operators compared to other provinces in Mekong Delta area.

The most important competitive asset in river-based tourism resources of Can Tho City is Cai Rang floating market, the national intangible cultural heritage. Furthermore, satellite orchards for the floating market, such as Mekong Rustic, UtHien garden, six Hoai

**Table 4:** Statistics on accommodation establishments in Can Tho, Ben Tre, and Kien Giang provinces in 2018.

| | **Can Tho** | **Ben Tre** | **Kien Giang** |
|---|---|---|---|
| Travel accommodation establishments (from 1 star) | 275 | 91 | 710 |
| Number of rooms | 7.188 | 1.590 | 19.764 |

*Source*: Mekong Delta Tourism Association.

rice noodle pizza, and Nam Bo restaurant, are particularly serving European visitors, especially French. There are many pleasure boats serving onsite accommodation services which are operating on river routes of Can Tho–Cai Be, Tien Giang. This service is for the high-end visitor segment, including the tour of rice farming and gardening experience, as well as the visit to traditional handicraft villages along the rivers. All catering and accommodation services are on the boat. Besides, there are other businesses exploiting waterway tours from Ho Chi Minh City to Can Tho and vice versa, with the final destination of Cai Rang floating market. This Table 4 shows that the number of rooms in Cantho city are better than Bentre province. However, Kien Giang province has a lot of room for hotels. It can be stated that Kiengiang province can supply hotels and rooms for tourists in Mekong delta.

## 5. Solutions for Tourism Development of Can Tho City

Based on the potential advantages of Can Tho tourism, the authors have come up with the following recommendations for the city's tourism development.

### 5.1. *Diversifying and developing featured tourism products*

River-based and MICE tourism are two competitive products of Can Tho compared to neighboring provinces in Mekong Delta area.

Activities that offer experiences of river-based lifestyle, floating market, and orchards are based on the advantage of an interlacing network of rivers and canals, islets and orchards around Cai Rang floating market. Another plus factor is the local cuisine and attractive food along the rivers in Ninh Kieu, Cai Rang, Phong Dien, and Binh Thuy Districts. To promote this strength, it is important to raise awareness of the community and visitors in keeping the rivers clean (e.g., putting trash in regulated places), and have tax incentives for households living in boats and help their children to go to school near the floating market area, maintaining natural beauty of Cai Rang and Phong Dien floating markets while satisfying tourists' demands.

Can Tho City needs to make good use of all resources and promote private capital to develop high-end cruises and high-speed boats with Can Tho–Con Dao, Can Tho–Phu Quoc, Can Tho–Ho Chi Minh City routes to create a highlight for the city tourism, attracting more visitors to Can Tho, especially international tourists. Besides, the city should have incentives for investment in ecological tourism at Son and Tan Loc Islets; Son Islet for community ecological tourism and high-end resorts, and Tan Loc for river-based community ecological tourism.

Moreover, as most turnover of Can Tho tourism is from accommodation and cuisine, to increase tourism turnover, Can Tho City should promote its role as a high-quality place for lodging and cuisine for visitors coming to Mekong Delta, focusing on making good use of the potential of leisure and shopping services. The city should also invest more in high-quality leisure spots such as a golf course and a tourism tower to meet the demands of domestic and international visitors. Also, MICE tourism, educational tourism, and medical tourism are suitable with the city's infrastructure and promise to bring about huge income if invested in and developed properly.

### 5.2. *Attracting and training high-quality tourism human resources*

Can Tho City tourism should have incentive policies to encourage and attract privatization and tourism human resources. The city should also connect training with social needs as well as demands from tourism employers. A close collaboration with local universities, colleges, and vocational schools is also recommended. In addition, the city should regularly exchange and share experiences with external training institutions, focusing on training skills and foreign languages to upgrade tourism human resources, especially tour guides, waiting staff, and salespersons at tourist spots.

### 5.3. *Enhancing quality of tour operators*

To enhance the quality of tour operators, Can Tho City should call for investment from major and prestigious companies. At the same time, the city should encourage current operators to strengthen their activities, expand their markets, enhance the connection in making tour destinations, and pay attention to quality improvement and service instead of price competition. Moreover, diverse activities and services can help accelerate tourist spending and contribute to the turnover from tourism for the city.

## 6. Conclusion

The research analyzes the current state of Can Tho City's tourism development as well as factors creating destination competitiveness of the city (i.e, including infrastructure, tourism resources, and tourism human resources). The research also employs Porter's approach (1985) on national competitive strategy, several models investigating tourism destination competitiveness in the work of different authors, and analyzes secondary data of socioeconomic and tourism development of Can Tho City. In particular, the evaluation of Can Tho's destination competitiveness in different aspects in comparison with other provinces in Mekong Delta area identifies general strengths and weaknesses of Can Tho's destinations. The results provide a broad assessment and some recommendations for enhancing the destination competitiveness of the city. It also serves as an important foundation for future quantitative research related to Can Tho's destination competitiveness.

## Appendix A: Tourism Statistics of Western Cities/Provinces in Mekong Delta Area, 2017–2018.

| | 2017 | | | | 2018 | | | | | | | |
|---|---|---|---|---|---|---|---|---|---|---|---|---|
| Province | Total visitors (persons) | Inbound (persons) | Domestic (persons) | Turnover (Million Vietnam Dong) | Total visitors (persons) Compared to the same period (%) | | Inbound (persons) Compared to the same period (%) | | Domestic (persons) Compared to the same period (%) | | Turnover (thousand Vietnamese dong) Compared to the same period (%) | |
| Can Tho City | 7,539,221 | 677,171 | 6,862,050 | 2,897,943 | 8,480,968 | 112.5 | 742,659 | 109.7 | 7,738,309 | 112.8 | 3,785,158 | 130.6 |
| An Giang | 7,300,000 | 75,000 | 7,225,000 | 3,700,000 | 8,500,000 | 116.4 | 100,000 | 133.3 | 8,400,000 | 116.3 | 4,800,000 | 129.7 |
| Kien Giang | 6,079,179 | 368,207 | 5,710,972 | 4,582,375 | 7,620,000 | 125.3 | 580,000 | 157.5 | 7,040,000 | 123.3 | 6,195,000 | 135.2 |
| Ca Mau | 1,240,000 | 25,000 | 1,215,000 | 670,000 | 1,440,000 | 116.1 | 27,480 | 109.9 | 1,412,520 | 116.3 | 2,200,000 | 328.4 |
| Bac Lieu | 1,500,000 | 40,000 | 1,460,000 | 1,200,000 | 1,690,000 | 112.7 | 41,000 | 102.5 | 1,649,000 | 112.9 | 1,290,000 | 107.5 |
| Hau Giang | 332,000 | 10,938 | 321,062 | 121,287 | 420,000 | 126.5 | 16,800 | 153.6 | 403,200 | 125.6 | 147,840 | 121.9 |
| Soc Trang | 1,530,403 | 59,962 | 1,470,441 | 557,092 | 1,976,000 | 129.1 | 70,200 | 117.1 | 1,905,800 | 129.6 | 736,700 | 132.2 |
| **Total** | **25,520,803** | **1,256,278** | **24,264,525** | **13,728,697** | **30,126,968** | **118** | **1,578,139** | **126** | **28,548,829** | **118** | **19,154,698** | **140** |

*Source*: Can Tho City Department of Culture, Sports and Tourism.

# Appendix B: Tourism Statistics of Can Tho City, 2008–2018.

| Index | Unit | 2008 | 2009 | 2010 | 2011 | 2012 | 2013 | 2014 | 2015 | 2016 | 2017 | 2018 |
|---|---|---|---|---|---|---|---|---|---|---|---|---|
| **1/Total turnover** | Billion VND | **455** | **507** | **649** | **761** | **851** | **975** | **1,169** | **1,747** | **1,826** | **2,897** | **3,785** |
| *Based on service types | ” | | | | | | | | | | | |
| + Accommo-dation | ” | 137 | 152 | 194 | 228 | 255 | 292 | 351 | 524 | 547 | 869 | 1, 191 |
| + Catering | ” | 69 | 77 | 97 | 114 | 127 | 146 | 175 | 262 | 273 | 434 | 595 |
| + Goods | ” | 46 | 51 | 64 | 76 | 85 | 97 | 117 | 174 | 182 | 293 | 404 |
| + Travel | ” | 92 | 102 | 129 | 152 | 170 | 195 | 234 | 349 | 365 | 579 | 793 |
| + Transport | ” | 46 | 51 | 64 | 76 | 85 | 97 | 117 | 174 | 182 | 289 | 396 |
| + Leisure | ” | 32 | 36 | 45 | 53 | 59 | 68 | 82 | 122 | 127 | 202 | 277 |
| + Others | ” | 33 | 38 | 56 | 62 | 70 | 80 | 93 | 142 | 150 | 231 | 129 |
| **2/Total visitors (overnight stay)** | Times | **817,250** | **723,528** | **880,252** | **972,450** | **1,174,823** | **1,251,625** | **1,367,726** | **1,619,070** | **1,726,531** | **2,184,385** | **2,658,740** |
| Inbound visitors | ” | 175, 094 | 150, 300 | 163, 835 | 170, 325 | 190, 116 | 211, 357 | 220, 280 | 207, 060 | 258, 400 | 305, 167 | 361, 811 |
| Domestic visitors | ” | 642, 156 | 573, 228 | 716, 417 | 802, 125 | 984, 707 | 1, 040, 268 | 1, 147, 446 | 1, 412, 010 | 1, 468, 131 | 1, 879, 218 | 2, 293, 929 |
| **Tourists** | ” | **1,597,462** | **1,620,000** | **1,682,172** | **1,749,500** | **1,925,367** | **2,125,779** | **2,300,000** | **4,702,203** | **5,349,817** | **7,539,221** | **8,840,968** |
| Inbound visitors | ” | 171, 893 | 180, 224 | 197, 308 | 215, 216 | 250, 482 | 278, 769 | 287, 140 | 305, 492 | 331, 887 | 387, 847 | 742, 659 |
| Domestic visitors | ” | 1, 425, 569 | 1, 439, 776 | 1, 484, 864 | 1, 534, 284 | 1, 674, 885 | 1, 847, 010 | 2, 012, 860 | 4, 396, 711 | 5, 017, 930 | 7, 151, 374 | 7, 738, 309 |

(*Continued*)

(*Continued*)

| Index | Unit | 2008 | 2009 | 2010 | 2011 | 2012 | 2013 | 2014 | 2015 | 2016 | 2017 | 2018 |
|---|---|---|---|---|---|---|---|---|---|---|---|---|
| **3/Days** | **Days** | **1,073,085** | **934,054** | **1,171,138** | **1,335,936** | **1,527,270** | **1,779,777** | **1,914,816** | **2,266,698** | **2,589,797** | **3,276,578** | **3,960,359** |
| Inbound visitors' days | " | 224, 577 | 192, 405 | 217, 387 | 233, 805 | 259, 927 | 302, 944 | 311, 310 | 310, 590 | 387, 600 | 457, 751 | 527, 442 |
| Domestic visitors' days | " | 848, 508 | 741, 649 | 953, 751 | 1, 102, 131 | 1, 267, 343 | 1, 476, 833 | 1, 603, 506 | 2, 118, 015 | 2, 202, 197 | 2, 818, 827 | 3, 434, 917 |
| **4/Average stay** | Days | 1 | 1,2 | 1,3 | 1,4 | 1,68 | 1,42 | 1,40 | 1,50 | 1,60 | 1,7 | 1,8 |

*Source*: Can Tho City Department of Culture, Sports and Tourism.

## References

### Vietnamese

Can Tho City Department of Culture, Sports, and Tourism (2018). Report on tourism activities in 2018 and major tasks for 2019.

Can Tho International Airport (2018). Report on business activities in 2018 and major tasks for 2019.

Hoang Ha. (2017). Resolution 08-special milestone in tourism history. Online: http://toquoc.vn/nghi-quyet-08-dau-an-dac-biet-trong-lich-su-nganh-du-lich-99166715.htm. Accessed on August 1, 2018.

Hong Giang. (2018). Can Tho develops tourism in connection with preserving cultural heritages. Online: https://baotintuc.vn/du-lich/can-tho-phat-trien-du-lich-gan-voi-bao-ton-di-san-van-hoa-20180722074327983.htm. Accessed on December 15, 2018.

Mekong Delta Tourism Association. (2018). Report activities in 2018 and major tasks for 2019.

Ngo Nguyen Hiep Phuoc. (2018). Advantages and potentials for tourism development of Can Tho City. Online:file:///C:/Users/Surface%20Pro/Downloads/124-Article%20Text-376-2-10-20180816%20(4).pdf. Accessed on December 11, 2018.

Tran Viet Phuong. (2017). Can Tho tourism orienting sustainable development. Online: http://baodulich.net.vn/Du-lich-Can-Tho-huong-toi-su-phat-trien-ben-vung-03-10212.html. Accessed on January 7, 2019.

### English

Bordas, E. (1994). Competitiveness of tourist destinations in long distance markets. *Tourism Review*, 4(3), 3–9.

Craiwell and More (2008). Foreign direct investment and tourism in SIDS: Evidence from panel causality tests, *Tourism Analysis*, 13.

Crouch, G.I., and Ritchie, B.J.R. (1999). Destination competitiveness and the role of the tourism enterprise. In *Proceedings of the Fourth Annual Business Congress*, Istanbul, Turkey, 43–48.

Dwyer, L., and Kim, C.W. (2003). Destination competitiveness: Determinants and indicators. *Current Issues in Tourism*, 6(5), 369–414.

Enright, M., and Newton, E. (2005), Determinants of tourism destination competitiveness in Asia Pacific: Comprehensiveness and universality. *Journal of Travel Research*, 43, 339–350.

Hassan, S.S. (2000). Determinants of market competitiveness in an environmentally sustainable tourism Industry. *Journal of Travel Research*, 38, 239–245.

Heath, E. (2002). Towards a model to enhance destination competitiveness: A Southern African perspective. *Journal of Hospitality and Tourism Management*, 10(2), 55–57.

Poon, A. (1993). *Tourism, Technology and Competitive Strategies.* Trowbridge, UK: Redwood Book.

Porter, M.E. (1990). *The Competitive Advantage of Nations.* New York: The Free Press.

Ritchie, B.J.R., and Crouch, G.I. (2003). *The Competitive Destination — A Sustainable Tourism Perspectives.* CABI Publishing, CAB International.

UNWTO (2018). A Practical Guide to Tourism Destination Management, Madrid, Spain.

https://doi.org/10.1142/9789811227158_0021

# Chapter 21

# Buyer–Supplier Relationships, Sustainable Supplier Management, Green Design, and Firms' Performance in Vietnam

**Van Phuong Nguyen, Hoang Thi Tho Lam, and Tien Khoa Tran**


## Abstract

This chapter aims to explore the causal relationships between the four dimensions of *sustainable supplier management* (sustainable supplier selection (SSS), sustainable supplier collaboration (SSC), sustainable supplier development (SSD), and sustainable supplier monitoring (SSM)), and buyer–supplier linkage. Moreover, the study also aims to test the connections between *buyer–supplier relationships* (BSRs), *green design*, and *firms' performance* (FP). Based on data collected from 156 manufacturers in Vietnam, the study uses the partial least squares structural equation modeling (PLS-SEM) approach to test the causality in a research framework. The findings indicate that sustainable supplier collaboration and development both have positive and significant effects on the BSR, whereas the BSR has a positive influence on green design for sustainability (GDS) and FP. Additionally, green design is positively associated with FP. Finally, the results contribute to the current literature by exploring the multiple dimensions of sustainable supplier management and address practical implications by providing some feasible suggestions for company leaders.


**Keywords:** Buyer–supplier relationship; Green design for sustainability; Sustainable supplier management; Firms' performance.

## 1. Introduction

Nowadays, sustainability is a significant concern for most corporations (Mariadoss *et al.*, 2016). The buying companies that apply a sustainable approach must consider three dimensions: environmental, economic, and social impacts (Graafland and Zhang, 2014). The achievement of sustainability depends on engaging and motivating the whole company, especially regarding the core procurement activities (Liu *et al.*, 2012). Procurement operations manage the acquisition of components, materials, and services from upstream providers (Prajogo *et al.*, 2012); thus, sustainable and green procurement studies have experienced a significant increase in popularity (Dubey *et al.*, 2014; Hoejmose *et al.*, 2014; Schaltegger *et al.*, 2012). Previous scholars have also considered other interesting topics, such as green supplier selection and green supplier development (Awasthi and Kannan, 2016; Govindan *et al.*, 2015; Kuo *et al.*, 2010). An efficient supplier management system can help firms solve related sustainability challenges, and researchers have affirmed that enterprises recognize the crucial importance of sustainable supplier management; thus, they should approach the issue of sustainable development with their suppliers (Mathiyazhagan *et al.*, 2013; Walker and Phillips, 2008). Furthermore, the supply chain studies have explored suppliers that are pursuing green design and joint decision-making and planning for sustainability in cooperation with buying firms (Moon, 2017; Pettersen, 2015; Rahimifard *et al.*, 2009).

Yang and Zhang (2017) investigated how sustainable supplier management can build a strong relationship between buyers and suppliers. In addition, various studies have mentioned the role of buyer–supplier relationships (BSRs) in enhancing firms' performance (FP) (Ambrose *et al.*, 2010; Duffy and Fearne, 2004; Hsu *et al.*, 2008; Kannan and Choon Tan, 2007; Revilla *et al.*, 2013), since cooperative BSRs, based on joint actions, can improve FP (Dubey *et al.*, 2014). At an operational level, BSRs can improve the quality, lead time, and delivery of products and minimize costs from the buying firms' perspective. At a strategic level, BSRs can improve sustainability benefits in terms of innovating quality products, enhancing competitiveness, and increasing market share (Kannan and Choon Tan, 2007). Due to fluctuating demand and intense market competition, buying organizations must pay more attention to their key suppliers and promote BSRs. Bag *et al.* (2018) found that BSR is positively associated with green design for sustainability (GDS). Green design in the supply chain has a beneficial impact on business performance, particularly regarding environmental and financial results.

The BSR topic has been examined in various countries, in many respects, and from the perspectives of both buying companies and suppliers. However, little research has investigated this topic in Vietnam. To fill this research gap, this study developed a research model to test the causal relationships between three dimensions of sustainable supplier management, green design, and BSRs and investigate the impact of the determinants on FP.

## 2. Literature Review

### 2.1. *Sustainable supplier management*

Sustainability, according to Butlin (1989), concerns how to use resources today without compromising future generations' needs. It is a key value to be considered across the whole supply chain process (Closs *et al.*, 2011). A massive number of organizations have become concerned about sustainability since the remarkable increase in environmental degradation, natural resource depletion, and climate change (Sen *et al.*, 2018). A variety of studies have explained that sustainable supply chain management involves an integration of economic, social, and environmental sustainability into traditional supply chain management (Ahi and Searcy, 2013; Walker and Phillips, 2008). From that point of view, sustainable supplier management depends on integrating the various dimensions of social, economic, and environmental sustainability into supplier management in terms of selecting, evaluating, and managing the supply base (Giunipero *et al.*, 2012). In particular, sustainable supplier management plays a leading role in sustainable supply chain management by improving economic, environmental, and social performance (known as *triple bottom line performance*) (Verghese and Lewis, 2007).

Since the buying companies trust their supply partners to survive and achieve a competitive market advantage (Yu and Wong, 2015), sustainable supplier management helps them achieve their business goals in a profitable and sustainable manner, and prevents the potential risks and uncertainty faced by supply partners or caused by them. If sustainable supplier management is to be incorporated into the fabric of an organization, it must be prompted by certain organizational forces that we term *drivers*. Management of supplier relationships encompasses various company practices, including selecting, evaluating, and developing suppliers (Schiele, 2007). Hoyt and Huq (2000) mentioned that the cooperation of suppliers is part of the BSR research stream. In a recent study, Yang and Zhang (2017) proposed that supplier monitoring is a subdimension of sustainable supplier management, and previous studies have demonstrated the essential supplier management elements from various angles (Gimenez and Tachizawa, 2012; Yang and Zhang, 2017). This study has concentrated on the four aspects of sustainable supplier management practices: sustainable supplier selection (SSS), sustainable supplier development (SSD), sustainable supplier collaboration (SSC), and sustainable supplier monitoring (SSM).

#### 2.1.1. *Sustainable supplier selection*

Supplier selection has been defined as a complicated decision-making task that includes objective (quantitative) and subjective (qualitative) evaluation criteria (Sen *et al.*, 2018). According to Yang and Zhang (2017), it means identifying, checking, and choosing the supplier characteristics that best suit and satisfy the firm's demands. Ho *et al.* (2010) indicated that the first, key criteria for decision makers is quality, followed by delivery, price or cost, manufacturing capability, service, and management. In earlier times, the buying companies completely relied on economics-based value to evaluate and select suppliers; therefore, price and delivery times were their most important concerns (Ehrgott *et al.*, 2011; Sen *et al.*, 2018; Tracey and Tan, 2001). Supplier selection is the most significant of purchasing activities, because of its benefits for companies, such as cost reduction, survival, competitive advantage, long-term and close cooperation, and quality consciousness. The more effective the supplier selection is, the greater are the buying firm's operational capabilities in terms of cost reduction, quality improvement, delivery times, and flexibility enhancement (Famiyeh and Kwarteng, 2018).

According to Tracey and Tan (2001), SSS involves the addition of sustainability factors into a traditional selection process. Recent studies have illustrated that it is necessary in supplier selection to achieve maximum ecological and economic benefits (Kannan *et al.*, 2014; Shaw *et al.*, 2012), either by considering the importance of incorporating economic and social issues into the supplier selection criteria (Reuter *et al.*, 2012; Trapp and Sarkis, 2016) or by discussing how to enhance the capabilities of suppliers to improve their environmental efficiency, such as by requiring relevant certifications and introducing sustainability factors (Govindan *et al.*, 2013).

In another study, Akman and Pışkın (2013) proposed that SSS can be defined as a method for identifying and evaluating suppliers that demonstrate the best performance regarding economic, environmental, and social sustainability along the upstream supply chain. From the buying companies' perspective, they require suppliers to exercise sustainability in environmental protection, labor rights, and anti-corruption (Xu *et al.*, 2013). In addition, green attributes may be key criteria for selecting suppliers, such as the reuse, recycling, or absence of toxicants. Researchers have also argued that efficient SSS should encompass ethical standards and ISO 14001 certification (Yazdani *et al.*, 2016).

### 2.1.2. *Sustainable supplier development*

Supplier development is an attempt of buying companies to help supply partners improve their effectiveness and capabilities and meet buyer's' needs (Arroyo-López *et al.*, 2012; Qi *et al.*, 2011). Overall, supplier development is a long-term activity that, in the initial stage, requires a great deal of time, financial investment, and resources but gives excellent results. Various studies have shown that the activities of supplier development, from the buying companies' perspective, are to evaluate suppliers' performance (Li *et al.*, 2012); recognize suppliers' progress (Naghavi and Ottaviano, 2010); be directly involved in supplier activities (Carmeli *et al.*, 2017); implement training (Khan and Nicholson, 2014); provide equipment, support technology, and budgets for suppliers (Mohanty *et al.*, 2014); and create professional personnel networks (Wagner, 2006). Regarding SSD, they enhance activities related to environmental and social objectives, such as evaluating environmental and social performance and collaborating with suppliers regarding health and safety training and environmental practices (Gimenez *et al.*, 2012; Sancha *et al.*, 2015; Zhu and Sarkis, 2004). Consequently, SSD motivates companies to practice innovative corporate social responsibility (Gimenez *et al.*, 2012; Zhu and Sarkis, 2004) and/or avoid scandals and reputational losses stemming from adverse media publicity (Sancha *et al.*, 2015). However, SSD investment involves enormous costs, including the cost of specific capital equipment investment, training, knowledge sharing, and other unexpected items and risks (Akamp and Müller, 2013).

### 2.1.3. *Sustainable supplier collaboration*

Supplier collaboration has been defined as cooperation with regard to internal resources and capabilities between buying companies and suppliers to create value together (Kanter, 2014; Wagner, 2006). The main activities of supplier collaboration consist of sharing product designs and manufacturing data, collectively solving quality issues, and collectively developing plans for the future (Eltantawy *et al.*, 2009). Corsten and Felde (2005) indicated that trust and information sharing are the core factors in collaborative processes. The closer the supplier collaboration, the more the information symmetries and the mutual trust.

SSD forges and maintains long-term, win–win relationships, rather than adversarial relationships, between buyers and suppliers (Soosay and Hyland, 2015). A variety of studies have shown that collaboration significantly reduces purchasing costs by reducing the cost of contracts, improving the frequency of communication, improving coordination, and facilitating the joint solving of operational problems (Cannon and Homburg, 2001; Scannell *et al.*, 2000). Regarding SSC, environmental and social objectives should be integrated into collaborative activities (Rostamzadeh *et al.*, 2015; Zhu, Sarkis *et al.*, 2011; Lai, 2013). Information sharing and joint research are activities that buying firms can implement to support sustainability goals; for instance, the buyer may cooperate with suppliers to develop innovative product design based on green design and green packaging.

### 2.1.4. *Sustainable supplier monitoring*

An early study defined supplier monitoring as an independent, but interrelated, process following the supplier selection process (Ittner *et al.*, 1999). Specifically, supplier monitoring is not only a technique for evaluating and replacing suppliers, but also a trigger to activate supplier development activities by inspecting the progress and success of development efforts (Zimmer *et al.*, 2016). According to Zimmer *et al.* (2016), it is necessary to develop common indicators for specific industries in order to facilitate annual supplier evaluation and compare suppliers' performance. Supplier monitoring activities consist of digging deeply into the performance of suppliers and providing feedback to suppliers; this feedback clarifies the expectations of the purchaser and can efficiently direct vendors toward further improvement (Prajogo *et al.*, 2012), so buying businesses should constantly monitor their suppliers to verify their adherence to appropriate requirements and provide timely enhancement feedback. Previous studies have shown that SSM involves continuously analyzing and evaluating suppliers and their supply chain information in accordance with minimum standards and quality improvements in relation to the three sustainability elements (Ragazzi *et al.*, 2013).

Overall, regarding SSM, firms should add environmental and social factors to their supplier monitoring programs (Gimenez and Tachizawa, 2012); however, some suppliers consider the sustainability criteria of SSM to be an administrative burden and buying companies should, therefore, conduct regular sustainable supplier monitoring through surveys, inspections, and audits (Yang and Zhang, 2017).

### 2.2. *Buyer–supplier relationships*

Definitions of BSRs have been given in a variety of previous studies. According to O'Toole and Donaldson (2002), these relationships can be defined as bilateral (e.g., cooperation), recurrent (the repeated or cyclical relationship is not as close as in the bilateral relationship), discrete (unrelated interaction), or hierarchical (involving a dominant partner). Kannan and Choon (2007) claimed that the buyer–supplier connection involves a cognitive reflection on certain purchases between the buyer and supplier, and cooperation instead of competition, to obtain mutual benefits. Specifically, BSRs have been explained as economic relations, that is commercial transaction partnerships, that depend on the mutual trust of both parties (Gullett *et al.*, 2009).

In the early 1900s, there was a shift in BSRs from short-term contracts with various suppliers to long-term connections with fewer suppliers (Galt and Dale, 1991; Han *et al.*, 1993). When the buying firms are limited in their choice of substitute suppliers, buyer loyalty to a specific supplier increases (Sriram and Mummalaneni, 1990). The concentration of purchase volumes with fewer suppliers helps the purchasing companies obtain a certain degree of continuity and efficiency from suppliers (Hahn *et al.*, 1986); both parties can enhance their performance, reduce purchasing costs, and develop technical cooperation. BSR management has developed with the support of supply chain researchers (Han *et al.*, 1993), who have proven that two characteristics — mutual trust and satisfactory exchange — are essential for establishing a good relationship. The former decreases performance uncertainty through the exchange of constant and detailed information and commitment to nurturing and maintaining the exchange relationship. The latter makes both parties satisfied with each other's performance; for instance, while suppliers may be satisfied by customers' payment procedures, the buying firms may be delighted about quality products delivered on time.

A variety of studies have claimed that trust, communication, commitment, dependence, and information sharing are the key elements in the relationship between suppliers and buying firms (Prior, 2012; Sari *et al.*, 2017; Terpend *et al.*, 2011). Like a process, trust improvement leads to communication enhancement, communication enables information exchange effectively, and knowledge is created by the information sharing (Sapukotanage *et al.*, 2016); thus, increases in communication and information sharing are strongly linked to price, quality, flexibility, and efficiency in innovation (Sapukotanage *et al.*, 2016), and it has been proven that trust has a positive effect on buyers' performance (Knemeyer and Murphy, 2004).

O'Toole and Donaldson (2002) claimed that the performance of BSRs could be divided into financial factors (speed of response, quality of product, comparison of benefits, lead times, stability, and satisfaction) and non-financial dimensions (cost sharing, long-term profits, cost, return on investment, purchased volumes, and running costs). Furthermore, Revilla *et al.* (2013) suggested that buyer–supplier exchanges can affect organizational performance. In BSRs, the parties cooperate closely to achieve cost reductions, shorter lead times, productivity increases, and enhanced quality (Wu *et al.*, 2016).

Buyers should use the key criteria of reliability and quality to carefully evaluate and select suppliers before making a final decision (Perez-Arostegui *et al.*, 2012). If both parties have a mutually elevated level of satisfaction, the green projects that they pursue will be successful. A firm's environmental performance is influenced by its production; thus, buying firms must build and maintain close collaboration with their suppliers to ensure green criteria for improving sustainable performance (Gimenez and Tachizawa, 2012).

## 2.3. *Green design for sustainability*

The concept of GDS, which is also known as eco-design or sustainable design, can be applied to the internal practice of green supplier management. It is also the method linked to the development of new products that encompass environmental, health, and product safety; resource conservation; avoidance of pollution; and economic hazard and waste management (Amemba *et al.*, 2013). The purpose of green design is to design products that minimize environmental effects throughout their whole life cycle (Diab *et al.*, 2015; Sarkis, 2003; Zhu *et al.*, 2007b), including activities ranging from the first stage of acquiring raw materials, through manufacture and use, to the final disposal without compromising performance, cost, and other crucial product criteria (Johansson, 2002). Furthermore, green design facilitates the reuse, recycling, and recovery of materials, components, and energy (Amemba *et al.*, 2013; Bag *et al.*, 2018; Zhu *et al.*, 2008). Reuter (2011) argued that companies need sophisticated instruments and green design solutions to generate sustainability.

From an environmental perspective, scholars have indicated that one of the green design tools is life cycle assessment (LCA), which can improve the product design by evaluating all the related resources and emissions used in all of a product's life cycle stages (Arena *et al.*, 2013). This tool helps the buyers select and develop green suppliers who take part in producing recycled products by applying advanced technology (Bag *et al.*, 2018). The success of green design depends on internal cooperation (cross-functional across the entire company) and external cooperation with other partners (buying firms and suppliers) (Zhu and Sarkis, 2006). Most firms try to introduce eco-design initiatives to enhance commercial competition (Chung and Wee, 2008). Green design plays a crucial role in improving operational performance when it is connected with green purchasing (Zhu *et al.*, 2013), particularly in the sustainable development stage (Bag *et al.*, 2018); products that consume less material and energy can generate greater profits and enhance market share (Zhu and Sarkis, 2006; Zhu *et al.*, 2013).

### 2.4. *Firms' performance*

Performance has been defined as a measure of success in effectively making decisions regarding strategic empowerment, resources, and sustainable business efficiency (Sari *et al.*, 2017). Balasubramanian and Shukla (2017) explained that performance is the way to measure the success of corporations' objectives and decide their future. FP has also been explained as the successful execution or achievement of work in several ways (Golicic and Smith, 2013) that are associated with a firm's strategic planning. Voola and O'Cass (2010) posited that the performance of a company is the main consequence of responsive market orientation, and Wheelen and Hunger (2012) indicated that performance is the ultimate result of a firm's activities, claiming that the choice of measures for evaluating performance should be based on the organizational unit to be checked and the goals to be achieved. Meanwhile, Morgan (2012) illustrated that business performance is fundamentally controlled by the level of competition in the market where the company chooses to operate.

In this study, FP was divided into three types or dimensions: environmental, economic, and operational. Operational outcomes focus on factors relating to operational efficiencies, such as costs, quality, flexibility, speed, and delivery. Economic outcomes are financial benefits, including profitability, sales, productivity, and market share (Zhu and Sarkis, 2004). Environmental results diminish transaction costs and increase the recycling of materials; furthermore, waste, emissions, and toxic materials can be reduced. Chien and Shih (2007) classified environmental outcomes into operative performance indicators (e.g., materials consumption, waste products, and energy management) and management performance indicators (e.g., administration efforts and environmental management).

## 2.5. *Impact of buyer–supplier relationships from the buying firms' perspective*

### 2.5.1. *Sustainable supplier management and buyer–supplier relationships*

Wu *et al.* (2016) posited that buyers tend to promote BSRs in order to reduce costs, minimize lead times, improve productivity, and boost quality; therefore, several studies have explored the correlation between practices of sustainable supplier management and BSRs. SSS and monitoring practices reduce potential uncertainties and risks, thus improving mutual trust, while sustainable supplier collaboration and development consolidate the relationships with suppliers through information sharing and joint research (Yang and Zhang, 2017). SSM programs may catalyze efficient, long-term BSRs, so we proposed the following hypotheses:

**Hypothesis H1a:** *SSS has a significant impact on the BSR.*

**Hypothesis H1b:** *Sustainable supplier monitoring has a significant impact on the BSR.*

**Hypothesis H1c:** *SSD has a significant impact on the BSR.*

**Hypothesis H1d:** *Sustainable supplier collaboration has a significant impact on the BSR.*

### 2.5.2. *Buyer–supplier relationships and green design for sustainability*

As mentioned above, the success of green design depends on internal cooperation (cross-functional across the whole firm) and external cooperation with other parties (the buying firms and suppliers) (Zhu and Sarkis, 2006), and the BSR plays a vital role in the success of GDS (Yang and Zhang, 2017). In other words, firms must promote a relationship with suppliers to achieve green product development (Bag *et al.*, 2018). Some studies have mentioned the positive impact of BSRs on the environmental performance of companies (Dubey *et al.*, 2014). Strong partnerships bolster communication and transparency, enabling companies to develop trust in each other (Bag *et al.*, 2018). Previous researchers have claimed that buyers that connect with key suppliers in designing and developing products and planning activities accomplish their green outcomes sustainably (Carter and Rogers, 2008; Hollos *et al.*, 2012; Kannan *et al.*, 2007; Vachon and Klassen, 2006); hence, the following hypothesis was introduced:

**Hypothesis H2:** *The BSR has a significant correlation with GDS.*

### 2.5.3. *Buyer–supplier relationships and firms' performance*

Frazier *et al.* (1998) described transaction costs as the sum total of "the cost of running a relationship" and these costs relate to the exchange agreements of negotiation, implementation, coordination, monitoring, adjustment, enforcement, and termination. Organizations can minimize the cost of their transactions, which leads to improve the firm's financial performance. Walker and Poppo (1991) showed the connection between transaction costs and BSR management. According to Zhao *et al.* (2008), coordination between the supplier and the buyer can reduce the cost of the transactions associated with buying decisions. Useful inter-organizational processes for both parties are a way to lessen transaction costs, which include the costs of searching for suppliers; thus, buying firms that maintain fewer suppliers also lower their transaction costs. Partnerships between firms can damage the performance of a long-term relationship; however, the authors suggested that, when it tends to scale down, the firms will still collaborate to obtain mutual benefits. Consequently, a long-term connection with main suppliers leads to companies' positive financial efficiency (Han *et al.*, 1993).

Previously, researchers explained that there was a vital role for a BSR in controlling diversity, the utilization of knowledge, the mobilization of resources, and collaboration. According to Patterson *et al.* (1999), BSRs are important for reducing the uncertainty of the business exchange process; buyers can reduce their supplier base, provide demand forecasts and delivery performance, and finally, achieve optimal performance (Gomez-Mejia *et al.*, 2007). From the above discussion, a hypothesis could be clearly formed:

**Hypothesis H3:** *The BSR has a significant correlation with a firm's performance.*

### 2.5.4. *Green design for sustainability and firms' performance*

As mentioned above, green design is one of the practices included in the management of green supply chains. Numerous studies have

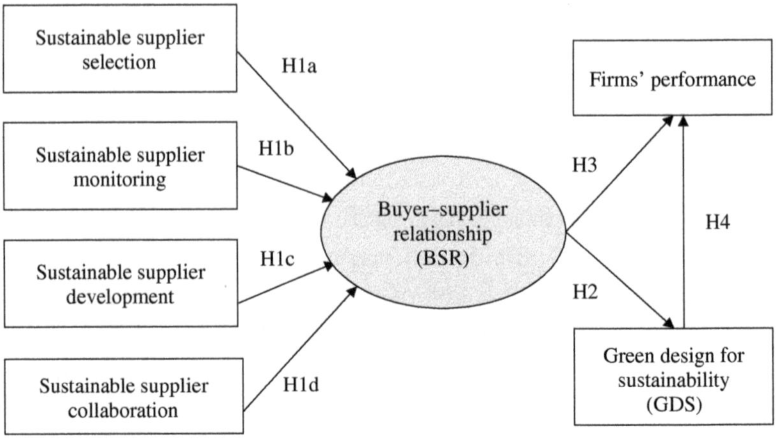


**Figure 1:** The research framework.

shown the positive influences of green supplier management practices on organizational effectiveness in terms of environmental, economic, and operational performance (Al-Ma'aitah, 2018; Choi and Hwang, 2015; Younis *et al.*, 2016; Zhu *et al.*, 2013). Additionally, Zhu *et al.* (2013) indicated that green design positively affects operational performance when green purchasing is in place. The results of previous research have also shown that eco-design is related, directly and indirectly, to FP (Choi and Hwang, 2015; Namagembe *et al.*, 2019). These studies provided evidence for the proposal of Hypothesis H4:

**Hypothesis H4:** *GDS has a significant correlation with FP.*

Figure 1 displays the research framework and hypothesis development.

## 3. Methodology

### 3.1. *Measures*

All measures for this chapter were adapted from previous studies, with minor adjustments to ensure suitable research for the context

**Table 1:** Structures, dimensions, and sources.

| Latent variables | Sources | Number of items |
|---|---|---|
| SSS | Kannan *et al.* (2007); Jabbour and Jabbour (2009); Xu *et al.* (2013) | 5 |
| SSM | Chan and Chin (2007); Talluri and Sarkis (2002) | 5 |
| SSD | Humphreys *et al.* (2004); Krause *et al.* (2007) | 5 |
| SSC | Flynn *et al.* (2010) | 5 |
| BSR | Chen and Paulraj (2004); Kannan *et al.* (2007) | 5 |
| GDS | Bag and Gupta (2017); Bakker *et al.* (2010); Carter (2005); Carter and Jennings (2004); de Pauw *et al.* (2015); Dubey *et al.* (2013); Habidin *et al.* (2018); Liu *et al.* (2011); Zhu and Sarkis (2004); Zhu *et al.* (2007a) | 6 |
| FP | Kannan and Choon Tan (2007) | 3 |

in Vietnam. Table 1 summarizes the structures, items, and sources of statements.

Specifically, this chapter used a 5-point Likert scale, with 1 for "not at all" and 5 for "extensively", on a questionnaire to assess the measurement indicators. The questionnaire was bilingual to enable the respondents to answer easily and ensure accurate responses. The English version of the questionnaire was first adapted and then translated into Vietnamese. To avoid cultural bias, the Vietnamese version was then translated back into English and compared to the original English version to ensure the precision of the translation and the clarity of the questions.

### 3.2. *Data collection and research method*

We conducted the survey over four months, from August 2018 to December 2018, and all the sample companies were doing business in manufacturing industries. We received invaluable support from the Vietnam Chamber of Commerce and Industry to attend a conference, in July 2018, on how to build sustainable collaboration with Japanese manufacturers. Through this conference, we connected with conference participants, then we used a convenience sampling method to invite the participants to complete the questionnaire survey by email. We also asked them to help by introducing their business partners to us.

We sent out 300 questionnaires to the target participants by email and, ultimately, collected 156 completed questionnaires, constituting a response rate of 52%. The sample provided adequate information, and met the sampling criterion that the minimum number of observations required was 70 (based on the calculation $10 \times$ paths $=$ $10 \times 7 = 70$ when using the PLS-SEM approach) (Hair *et al.*, 2014).

PLS-SEM is a very suitable method for analyzing a complex model with many simultaneous relationships. PLS-SEM has been widely used in business research, marketing, economic management, and many other social sciences. This study mainly focused on predicting the efficiency of the buying companies through the average values of the four dimensions of sustainable supplier management (SSS, SSC, SSD, and SSM) and the green design factor through BSRs. This was also an appropriate condition for using PLS-SEM as a prediction method for SEM (Rigdon, 2012).

## 4. Data Analysis and Results

### 4.1. *Data analysis*

The company information is presented in Table 2. The reasons we chose these industries was because they were experiencing intense market competition and their performance was primarily linked to their suppliers.

Small sample sizes can be controlled by PLS-SEM (Chin, 1998; Hair *et al.*, 2012). Based on previous studies (Hair *et al.*, 2012; Hair Jr. *et al.*, 2014), the minimum criteria of sample size for the PLS-SEM approach is to identify the distinct R-squared values at a significance of 5% while maintaining the simplicity of the PLS route system (i.e., the maximum number of arrows pointing to a construction). The maximum number of arrows for this research was seven, so 80

**Table 2:** Company information.

| | | Frequency | Percentage |
|---|---|---|---|
| Industry | Tools and equipment | 36 | 23 |
| | Electronic appliances | 30 | 19 |
| | Plastic and rubber | 28 | 18.3 |
| | Packing, packing material | 26 | 16.7 |
| | Other | 36 | 23 |

observations were needed to identify $R^2$ values of at least 0.25 at the significance level of 5%; therefore, our sample was large enough. The PLS-SEM technique, with the help of Smart-PLS, facilitated convenient manipulation and rapid calculation of CR and AVE indicators.

## 4.2. *Results*

### 4.2.1. *Measurement model*

Table 3 shows that most outer loadings were greater than 0.7, reinforcing the reliability of the scale, except for two observed variables with a load index less than 0.7. The common rule of thumb indicates that the values of outer item loadings should be equal to or greater than 0.7 (Hair Jr. *et al.*, 2014). However, Hulland (1999) mentioned that some items may have loadings lower than this threshold in circumstances of developing new scales or transferring existing scales to a new context. The values of the loadings range from 0.40 to 0.70; hence, they were considered for deletion only if their removal would increase the CR (composite reliability) or AVE (average variance extracted) (Hair Jr. *et al.*, 2014). To meet these criteria, we kept two items with accepted values after removing three items of GDS and two items of SSS due to their poor loadings. Cronbach's Alpha and CR were evaluated to assess reliability and convergent validity, which were all higher than 0.6, so this outcome confirmed that the scales had proper internal reliability.

The measures of convergent validity using the AVE are shown in Table 3. All AVEs greater than 0.53 were acceptable, meaning that the construct explained over 53% of the variance of all items.

Table 3: Reliability and convergent validity.

| Variables | Note | Mean | SD | Factor loading | Cronbach's Alpha | Rho_A | CR | AVE |
|---|---|---|---|---|---|---|---|---|
| Thresholds | | | | | ≥0.6 | ≥0.7 | ≥0.7 | ≥0.5 |
| Buyer–supplier relationship | | | | | 0.876 | 0.907 | 0.909 | 0.667 |
| Our company relies on our suppliers and views them as an extension of our company | BSR1 | 3.814 | 0.529 | 0.743 | | | | |
| Maintaining the relationships with our major supply partners to increase buyer–supplier cooperation and communication is very important to us | BSR2 | 3.859 | 0.645 | 0.793 | | | | |
| Our company is very committed to the relationships with our major suppliers, and it deserves our firm's maximum effort to maintain | BSR3 | 3.686 | 0.696 | 0.854 | | | | |
| Buyers involve key suppliers in innovative product development activities and reduce the time spent on development of new products | BSR4 | 3.731 | 0.603 | 0.797 | | | | |
| The relationship decreases product costs | BSR5 | 3.859 | 0.571 | 0.889 | | | | |
| *Firm Performance* | | | | | 0.848 | 0.851 | 0.908 | 0.767 |
| Reduced total cost | FP1 | 3.372 | 0.580 | 0.856 | | | | |
| Improved product quality | FP2 | 3.321 | 0.599 | 0.892 | | | | |
| Improved sales volume | FP3 | 3.551 | 0.623 | 0.879 | | | | |
| *Green design for sustainability* | | | | | 0.731 | 0.728 | 0.843 | 0.589 |

**Table 3:** (*Continued*)

| Variables | Note | Mean | SD | Factor loading | Cronbach's Alpha | Rho_A | CR | AVE |
|---|---|---|---|---|---|---|---|---|
| Our company designs new products to avoid or reduce the use of hazardous products with suppliers | GD3 | 3.481 | 0.796 | 0.415 | | | | |
| Our company designs new products to reduce the consumption of material/energy with suppliers | GD4 | 3.474 | 0.729 | 0.837 | | | | |
| Our company designs processes for minimization of waste with suppliers | GD5 | 3.763 | 0.833 | 0.848 | | | | |
| More costs are shared equally in the joint green design process when compared to others | GD6 | 3.718 | 0.766 | 0.874 | | | | |
| *Sustainable supplier collaboration* | | | | | 0.890 | 0.901 | 0.919 | 0.694 |
| The logistics activities take place in close coordination with us | SSC1 | 3.468 | 0.763 | 0.834 | | | | |
| Our company solves quality problems with supply partners | SSC2 | 3.455 | 0.683 | 0.779 | | | | |
| Our company cooperates with suppliers to achieve environmental objectives | SSC3 | 3.622 | 0.683 | 0.858 | | | | |
| Our company cooperates with suppliers to achieve social objectives | SSC4 | 3.590 | 0.724 | 0.846 | | | | |
| Our company coordinates closely with our supply partners | SSC5 | 3.647 | 0.749 | 0.847 | | | | |

(*Continued*)

**Table 3:** (*Continued*)

| Variables | Note | Mean | SD | Factor loading | Alpha | Rho_A | CR | AVE |
|---|---|---|---|---|---|---|---|---|
| *Sustainable supplier development* | | | | | 0.922 | 0.929 | 0.942 | 0.763 |
| Our company provides technical support to our supply partners | SSD1 | 3.333 | 0.754 | 0.854 | | | | |
| Our company provides training courses on sustainability issues to our suppliers | SSD2 | 3.436 | 0.690 | 0.829 | | | | |
| Our company provides feedback about sustainability performance evaluation to our supply partners | SSD3 | 3.481 | 0.804 | 0.907 | | | | |
| Our company suggests improvement targets to our suppliers | SSD4 | 3.474 | 0.828 | 0.881 | | | | |
| Our company supports our suppliers in improving their capabilities | SSD5 | 3.506 | 0.747 | 0.895 | | | | |
| *Sustainable supplier monitoring* | | | | | 0.925 | 1.062 | 0.934 | 0.740 |
| Our company hires trusted third-parties to supervise supply partners' factory conditions | SSM1 | 3.756 | 0.654 | 0.832 | | | | |
| Our company regularly reviews supply partners' social performance | SSM2 | 3.776 | 0.646 | 0.832 | | | | |
| Our company regularly reviews supply partners' environmental performance | SSM3 | 3.788 | 0.689 | 0.815 | | | | |

**Table 3:** (*Continued*)

| Variables | Note | Mean | SD | Factor loading | Alpha | Rho_A | CR | AVE |
|---|---|---|---|---|---|---|---|---|
| Our company regularly uses a supply partner's certification program to certify suppliers' quality | SSM4 | 3.763 | 0.661 | 0.937 | | | | |
| Our company regularly reviews supply partners to ensure they comply with the standards and specifications set by us | SSM5 | 3.744 | 0.688 | 0.878 | | | | |
| *Sustainable supplier selection* | | | | | 0.644 | 0.806 | 0.772 | 0.538 |
| Our company visits candidate supply partners' factories to assess their facilities and technology levels | SSS2 | 3.583 | 0.808 | 0.705 | | | | |
| Our company checks whether the candidate supply partners meet our predetermined environmental criteria | SSS3 | 3.564 | 0.810 | 0.578 | | | | |
| A formal supplier selection evaluation process is performed | SSS5 | 3.500 | 0.729 | 0.884 | | | | |

Additionally, rho_A indicators were greater than 0.7, which helped to consolidate the scale to ensure convergent and reliable values. Furthermore, Table 4 indicates that the values of discriminant validity were fine when the square root of the value of AVE surpassed the correlation between the latent variables in each couple (Fornell and Larcker, 1981). Table 5 clarifies that the Heterotrait–Monotrait (HTMT) ratios were all less than 0.85, following the threshold proposed by Clark and Watson (1995) and Kline (2005). Thus, the

**Table 4:** Discriminant validity (Fornell–Larcker criterion).

| | | Fornell–Larcker (FL) criterion | | | | | | |
|---|---|---|---|---|---|---|---|---|
| | | **1** | **2** | **3** | **4** | **5** | **6** | **7** |
| 1 | BSR | *0.817* | | | | | | |
| 2 | FP | 0.262 | *0.876* | | | | | |
| 3 | GDS | 0.261 | 0.367 | *0.768* | | | | |
| 4 | SSC | 0.339 | 0.230 | 0.323 | *0.833* | | | |
| 5 | SSD | 0.367 | 0.269 | 0.405 | 0.323 | *0.874* | | |
| 6 | SSM | 0.087 | 0.174 | 0.200 | 0.211 | 0.202 | *0.860* | |
| 7 | SSS | −0.068 | 0.013 | 0.003 | −0.134 | −0.061 | 0.090 | *0.733* |

*Notes*: Numbers on the diagonal (in italics) illustrate the AVE square root; numbers below the diagonal illustrate construct correlations.

**Table 5:** Discriminant validity (HTMT ratios of correlations).

| | | **1** | **2** | **3** | **4** | **5** | **6** |
|---|---|---|---|---|---|---|---|
| 1 | BSR | Criteria $\leq$ 0.85 | | | | | |
| 2 | FP | 0.298 | | | | | |
| 3 | GDS | 0.323 | 0.464 | | | | |
| 4 | SSC | 0.354 | 0.263 | 0.400 | | | |
| 5 | SSD | 0.389 | 0.299 | 0.497 | 0.358 | | |
| 6 | SSM | 0.100 | 0.190 | 0.219 | 0.217 | 0.185 | |
| 7 | SSS | 0.105 | 0.058 | 0.104 | 0.144 | 0.086 | 0.118 |

above-mentioned two different evaluation criteria affirmed that the scale of the model ensured discriminant validity.

### 4.2.2. *Structural model*

The analyzes of the structural model were conducted step by step according to the guidelines of Hair Jr. *et al.* (2014). The analytical outcomes showed that there was no additive phenomenon for any predictor variable (independent potential variable); in particular, all the variance inflation factors (VIFs) were less than 3.5 and, thus, less than the accepted value of 5 (Hair Jr. *et al.*, 2014). Furthermore, the $R^2$ value of the BSR factor was 0.190, the FP factor was 0.164, and the GDS factor was 0.068. Similarly, the results of blindfolding with a small omission distance of 7 gave the Q-squared value of BSR and FP, and GDS factors were greater than 0. These results supported the model's predictive power for forecasting outside the sample (Hair Jr. *et al.*, 2014; Hair *et al.*, 2012). Moreover, we continued to implement appropriate model testing through the standardized root mean square (SRMR) residual value. The synthesized result specifically provided by the Smart-PLS 3 software was as follows: SRMR = 0.070 < 0.08, so this result helped to confirm the overall PLS model as appropriate (Henseler *et al.*, 2014).

PLS-SEM's goal is to forecast, rather than evaluate, model fit and it tries to build corresponding statistics that have proven to be highly problematic (Henseler and Sarstedt, 2013). Alternative criteria for predicting endogenous constructs are the determination coefficients ($R^2$) and path coefficients. The variance explained for the endogenous constructs was 19% for BSR, 16.4% for FP, and 6.8% for green design. Table 6 illustrates the estimated results. Five out of seven hypotheses were supported by $p$-values below 0.05 after running a bootstrap with a sample of 5,000. The findings demonstrated that GDS had the strongest impact on FP, with an estimated coefficient of 0.320. The estimated results for the four dimensions of sustainable supplier management showed that SSD had the most substantial impact on BSR, with a standardized path coefficient of 0.291, followed by SSC as the second highest positive, with a standardized path coefficient

**Table 6:** Estimated results.

| Hypothesis | | Standardized-path-coefficient | $t$-Value | $p$-Value | Results |
|---|---|---|---|---|---|
| H1a | SSS → BSR | −0.015 | 0.164 | 0.870 | *Not supported* |
| H1b | SSM → BSR | −0.023 | 0.233 | 0.816 | *Not supported* |
| H1c | SSD → BSR | 0.291 | 3.785 | 0.000 | Supported |
| H1d | SSC → BSR | 0.248 | 3.325 | 0.001 | Supported |
| H2 | BSR → GDS | 0.261 | 3.067 | 0.002 | Supported |
| H3 | BSR → FP | 0.178 | 2.424 | 0.015 | Supported |
| H4 | GDS → FP | 0.320 | 4.639 | 0.000 | Supported |

of 0.248. Finally, BSR was positively associated with FP, with an estimated result of 0.178. However, SSS and SSM had no relationship with BSR.

## 5. Discussion

Based on the review of the empirical studies and the outcomes of the analysis of the PLS-SEM model based on the survey data, several following comments are given.

Unexpectedly, the outcomes emphasized that SSS had no significant effect on the BSR. This is not consistent with the finding of Yang and Zhang (2017). It means that large corporations in Vietnam may choose from various suppliers and may use their purchasing power to make suppliers comply with their green standards for environmental factors. In particular, they must measure inputs from high-quality suppliers regarding water and energy use to minimize contamination and overproduction. From the small and medium firms' perspective, most of them are limited in measuring their business' sustainability, so they cannot extend this review to their suppliers.

Strangely, sustainable supplier monitoring had no impact on the BSR. Chan and Chin (2007) claimed that the correlation between SSM and the BSR is significant when the monitoring procedure allows buying companies to obtain greater insights into suppliers. In this situation, suppliers in Vietnam may not allow buying firms to dig deeply into their monitoring procedures. It has been argued that the current research on sustainable supplier management ignores the social component of sustainability (Seuring and Müller, 2008). This may be the reason for the overlooking of social elements in supplier management. The above findings are compatible with the fundamental information of the study, indicating that a small proportion of companies perform periodic evaluation of environmental and social elements.

The results showed that the sustainable development of suppliers indicated a favorable connection with the BSR. Suppliers can obtain important resources and knowledge through supplier development programs (Fu *et al.*, 2012; Li *et al.*, 2012). Through the prominence of suppliers' power and expertise or professional training methods, the supplier can fulfill the demands of the manufacturers and enhance their collaboration.

The BSR was significantly correlated with sustainable supplier collaboration. The fundamental study data showed that a tiny proportion of sample companies were collaborating with their suppliers to attain both social and environmental goals. Collaboration with suppliers to meet environmental criteria gained more attention than the social objectives. Cooperation platforms for working closely with suppliers are emerging in response to the fear of losing commercial control and competitive advantage.

The relationship between buyers and suppliers had relatively little impact on eco-design. The empirical results indicated that high wastage and costs could be minimized through effective green design and the participation of main supply partners in the development phase, so that methods of dismantling, recycling, and reuse are not only effective but also cost-effective for companies. The resource dependence theory (RDT) supported the findings; it also implied that supply chain businesses should coordinate and work together to achieve superior efficiency (Sarkis *et al.*, 2011). Based on the RDT point of view, interactions between suppliers and buyers are significant avenues for companies to decrease uncertainty about their work setting (Carter and Rogers, 2008). It is crucial to note that green design is only successful when building trust and phenomenal relationships with major suppliers, which leads to improvement of FP (Bag *et al.*, 2018). The findings also showed that the BSR had a positive influence on company performance. The purpose of a relationship is to bring both buyers and suppliers a shared advantage. From the buying firm's perspective, this arises in the form of resource use enhancement, strategic concentration, and the capacity to leverage the knowledge and capacity of the provider. It manifests in improving the quality of products and competitiveness, which in turn drives market and financial efficiency. While this is an intrinsic logic behind the interaction of BSRs and FP, up to now few case studies have encouraged it; hence, this outcome is significant.

Finally, GDS has a relatively strong influence on FP. This can be explained by the fact that the indicators "reducing the environmental costs for firms" and "improving the quality of products without hazardous materials" had the highest weights. At the design stage, collaboration and cooperation with key suppliers was necessary to finalize the green design and further minimize waste and environmental impact. This result was reinforced by the previous study of Zhu and Sarkis (2004), which stated that green design has beneficial effects on environmental and economic performance, including energy consumption, cost savings, waste treatment, and disposal fees. Green design is a useful, evolving tool for improving the environmental performance of businesses by targeting item features while simultaneously minimizing the environmental effects of the product life cycle (Zhu and Sarkis, 2004). Currently, many foreign direct investment enterprises in Vietnam apply ISO 140001 certification as the basis for environmental management systems.

### 5.1. *Recommendations*

The results of this study show that both buying companies and supply partners gain a sense of sustainability and approach this by building long-term relationships. In Vietnam, it is certain that, in the next few years, sustainability will be applied more widely and effectively.

Such a strategy will provide many positive results by which to establish a sustainable certified supply based on widely recognized standards and this will bring benefits to companies. The current criteria include work environment norms, effects on the living environment, business ethics, and human rights. On the one hand, companies work with social organizations to establish sustainability standards and certification mechanisms relating to the environment, food, or agriculture; on the other hand, they carry out trial manufacturing programs and call for the accreditation of participating supply partners. McDonald's beef is an example of this effective approach in Vietnam.

Regarding green design for sustainability, Vietnam is a tropical monsoon country, which offers various opportunities to develop environment-friendly products. Owning raw materials such as bamboo fibers, natural wood pulp, mulberry silk, and natural cotton yarn can help businesses create products from these materials; for example, the product line of shirts made from Tencel™ material by the Vinatex Group is used by the fashion brand Mattana. Tencel™ is one of the new bio-fabric materials, made from wood pulp that is grown and exploited, completely non-invasively, in natural forests. The production process does not use chemicals, is harmless to humans, does not discharge waste into the environment, and does not cause chemical changes or side effects. Moreover, this material can be reused almost completely and many times. Similarly, the product line of high-quality Mollis cotton towels produced by the Phong Phu Group has accounted for a significant proportion of the Japanese market, following only domestic enterprises. These are opportunities that, if exploited successfully, create a strong brand and generate great economic value for businesses; hence, companies have the conditions to promote more environment and people-friendly products.

## 6. Conclusions

The identification of significant factors was used to underpin the development of the linkages. The findings showed that SSD and collaboration significantly improve the buyer–supplier relationship. Another key finding was that the connections between buyers and suppliers have strong links to GDS and buying FP. Similarly, green design has a significant positive correlation with FP. The design phase requires collaboration and cooperation with main suppliers to finalize the green design and further minimize waste and environmental effects. Overall, activities relating to sustainability tend to concentrate mainly on environmental factors, while social problems are widely ignored. The individual measures have relative importance and contribute to the research model.

Our study supports both researchers and practitioners. First, the chapter expands the theoretical understanding of supplier management by considering the concept of sustainability. It has provided a brief description of the literature relating to BSRs and green design.

Second, the path analysis model for Vietnam indicated that companies with limited resources or capacity to activate a wide range of sustainable supplier management initiatives may focus on pursuing main practices. Finally, the information used for the observational analysis was gathered from 156 Vietnamese manufacturing firms, adding to studies of supplier management in emerging countries.

Like any study, this one had a number of constraints. First, the findings may reflect only the buying companies' perspective; thus, future studies could involve upstream vendors and explore the ways in which they view sustainable supplier management practices and respond to them. Second, sustainable supplier management is a comparatively modern concept in Vietnam, so the measures in the literature review are still at a preliminary stage. Further research could, therefore, create and build measures from distinct angles to apply to sustainable supplier management constructs. Finally, in this research, the sample consisted of manufacturing enterprises in Vietnam, and the sample size was small. For a wider analysis, the study should be expanded to encompass a variety of sectors and different types of companies, in more countries across the world.

## References

Ahi, P., and Searcy, C. (2013). A comparative literature analysis of definitions for green and sustainable supply chain management. *Journal of Cleaner Production*, 52, 329–341. https://doi.org/10.1016/j.jclepro.2013.02.018

Akamp, M., and Müller, M. (2013). Supplier management in developing countries. *Journal of Cleaner Production*, 56(1 October), 54–62. https://doi.org/10.1016/j.jclepro.2011.11.069

Akman, G., and Pιşkιn, H. (2013). Evaluating Green Performance of Suppliers via Analytic Network Process and TOPSIS. *Journal of Industrial Engineering*, Article ID(915241), 1–13. https://doi.org/10.1155/2013/915241

Al-Ma'aitah, N. (2018). Green supply chain management (GSCM) practices and their impact on performance?: An insight from the Jordanian construction sector. *International Journal of Construction Supply Chain Management*, 8(2), 87–104. https://doi.org/10.14424/ijcscm802018-87-104

Ambrose, E., Marshall, D., and Lynch, D. (2010). Buyer supplier perspectives on supply chain relationships. *International Journal of Operations and Production Management*, 30(12), 1269–1290. https://doi.org/10.1108/01443571011094262

Amemba, C.S., Nyaboke, P.G., Osoro, A., and Mburu, N. (2013). Elements of Green Supply Chain Management. *European Journal of Business and Management*, 5(12), 51–61.

Arena, M., Azzone, G., and Conte, A. (2013). A streamlined LCA framework to support early decision making in vehicle development. *Journal of Cleaner Production*, 41(February), 105–113. https://doi.org/10.1016/j.jclepro.2012.09.031

Arroyo-López, P., Holmen, E., and de Boer, L. (2012). How do supplier development programs affect suppliers?: Insights for suppliers, buyers and governments from an empirical study in Mexico. *Business Process Management Journal*, 18(4), 680–707. https://doi.org/10.1108/14637151211253792

Awasthi, A., and Kannan, G. (2016). Green supplier development program selection using NGT and VIKOR under fuzzy environment. *Computers and Industrial Engineering*, 91(January), 100–108. https://doi.org/10.1016/j.cie.2015.11.011

Bag, S., and Gupta, S. (2017). Antecedents of Sustainable Innovation in Supplier Networks: A South African Experience. *Global Journal of Flexible Systems Management*, 18(3), 231–250. https://doi.org/10.1007/s40171-017-0158-4

Bag, S., Gupta, S., and Telukdarie, A. (2018). Exploring the relationship between unethical practices, buyer-supplier relationships and green design for sustainability. *International Journal of Sustainable Engineering*, 11(2), 97–109. https://doi.org/10.1080/19397038.2017.1376723

Bakker, C.A., Wever, R., Teoh, C., and de Clercq, S. (2010). Designing cradle-to-cradle products: A reality check. *International Journal of Sustainable Engineering*, 3(1), 2–8. https://doi.org/10.1080/19397030903395166

Balasubramanian, S., and Shukla, V. (2017). Green supply chain management: an empirical investigation on the construction sector. *Supply Chain Management*, 22(1), 58–81. https://doi.org/10.1108/SCM-07-2016-0227

Butlin, J. (1989). Our common future. By World commission on environment and development. *Journal of International Development*, 1(2), 284–287. https://doi.org/10.1002/jid.3380010208

Cannon, J.P., and Homburg, C. (2001). Buyer-supplier relationships and customer firm costs. *Journal of Marketing*, 65(1), 29–43. https://doi.org/10.1509/jmkg.65.1.29.18136

Carmeli, A., Zivan, I., Gomes, E., and Markman, G.D. (2017). Underlining micro socio-psychological mechanisms of buyer-supplier relationships: Implications for inter-organizational learning agility. *Human Resource Management Review*, Online(January), 100577. https://doi.org/10.1016/j.hrmr.2016.12.002

Carter, C.R. (2005). Purchasing social responsibility and firm performance: The key mediating roles of organizational learning and supplier performance. *International Journal of Physical Distribution and Logistics Management*, 35(3), 177–194. https://doi.org/10.1108/09600030510594567

Carter, C.R., and Jennings, M.M. (2004). The role of purchasing in corporate social responsibility: a structural equation analysis. *Journal of Business Logistics*, 25(1), 145–186. https://doi.org/10.1002/j.2158-1592.2004.tb00173.x

Carter, C.R., and Rogers, D.S. (2008). A framework of sustainable supply chain management: Moving toward new theory. *International Journal of Physical Distribution and Logistics Management*, 38(5), 360–387. https://doi.org/10.1108/09600030810882816

Chan, T.C.T., and Chin, K.S. (2007). Key success factors of strategic sourcing: An empirical study of the Hong Kong toy industry. *Industrial Management and Data Systems*, 107(9), 1391–1416. https://doi.org/10.1108/02635570710834027

Chen, I.J., and Paulraj, A. (2004). Towards a theory of supply chain management: The constructs and measurements. *Journal of Operations Management*, 22(2), 119–150. https://doi.org/10.1016/j.jom.2003.12.007

Chien, M.K., and Shih, L.H. (2007). An empirical study of the implementation of green supply chain management practices in the electrical and electronic industry and their relation to organizational performances performances. *International Journal of Environmental Science and Technology*, 4(3), 383–394.

Chin, W.W. (1998). The partial least squares approach for structural equation modeling. *Modern Methods for Business Research*, 295(2), 295–336. https://doi.org/10.1016/j.aap.2008.12.010

Choi, D., and Hwang, T. (2015). The impact of green supply chain management practices on firm performance: the role of collaborative capability. *Operations Management Research*, 8(3–4), 69–83. https://doi.org/10.1007/s12063-015-0100-x

Chung, C.J., and Wee, H.M. (2008). Green-component life-cycle value on design and reverse manufacturing in semi-closed supply chain. *International Journal of Production Economics*, 113(2), 528–545. https://doi.org/10.1016/j.ijpe.2007.10.020

Clark, L.A., and Watson, D. (1995). Constructing Validity?: Basic Issues in Objective Scale Development The Centrality of Psychological Measurement. *Psychological Assessment*, 7(3), 309–319. https://doi.org/10.1037/1040-3590.7.3.309

Closs, D.J., Speier, C., and Meacham, N. (2011). Sustainability to support end-to-end value chains: The role of supply chain management. *Journal of the Academy of Marketing Science*, 39(1), 101–116. https://doi.org/10.1007/s11747-010-0207-4

Corsten, D., and Felde, J. (2005). Exploring the performance effects of key-supplier collaboration. *International Journal of Physical Distribution and Logistics Management*, 35(6), 445–461. https://doi.org/10.1108/09600030510611666

De Pauw, I.C., Kandachar, P., and Karana, E. (2015). Assessing sustainability in nature-inspired design. *International Journal of Sustainable Engineering*, 8(1), 5–13. https://doi.org/10.1080/19397038.2014.977373

Diab, S.M., AL-Bourini, F.A., and Abu-Rumman, A.H. (2015). The Impact of Green Supply Chain Management Practices on Organizational Performance: A Study of Jordanian Food Industries. *Journal of Management and Sustainability*, 5(1), 149–157. https://doi.org/10.5539/jms.v5n1p149

Dubey, R., Bag, S., and Ali, S.S. (2014). Green supply chain practices and its impact on organisational performance: an insight from Indian rubber industry. *International Journal of Logistics Systems and Management*, 19(1), 20–42. https://doi.org/10.1504/IJLSM.2014.064029

Dubey, R., Bag, S., Ali, S.S., and Venkatesh, V.G. (2013). Green purchasing is key to superior performance: an empirical study. *International Journal of Procurement Management*, 6(2), 187–210. https://doi.org/10.1504/ijpm.2013.052469

Duffy, R., and Fearne, A. (2004). Buyer-supplier relationships: An investigation of moderating factors on the development of partnership characteristics and performance. *International Food and Agribusiness Management Review*, 7(2), 1–25.

Ehrgott, M., Reimann, F., Kaufmann, L., and Carter, C.R. (2011). Social Sustainability in Selecting Emerging Economy Suppliers. *Journal of Business Ethics*, 98(1), 99–119. https://doi.org/10.1007/s10551-010-0537-7

Eltantawy, R.A., Giunipero, L., and Fox, G.L. (2009). A strategic skill based model of supplier integration and its effect on supply management performance. *Industrial Marketing Management*, 38(8), 925–936. https://doi.org/10.1016/j.indmarman.2008.12.022

Famiyeh, S., and Kwarteng, A. (2018). Supplier selection and firm performance: Empirical evidence from a developing country's environment.

*International Journal of Quality and Reliability Management*, 35(3), 690–710.
Flynn, B.B., Huo, B., and Zhao, X. (2010). The impact of supply chain integration on performance: A contingency and configuration approach. *Journal of Operations Management*, 28(1), 58–71. https://doi.org/10.1016/j.jom.2009.06.001
Fornell, C., and Larcker, D.F. (1981). Evaluating Structural Equation Models with Unobservable Variables and Measurement Error. *Journal of Marketing Research*, 18(1), 39–50. https://doi.org/10.1177/002224378101800104
Frazier, G.L., Spekman, R.E., and O'Neal, C.R. (1998). Just-In-Time Exchange Relationships in Industrial Markets. *Journal of Marketing*, 52(4), 52–67. https://doi.org/10.2307/1251633
Fu, X., Zhu, Q., and Sarkis, J. (2012). Evaluating green supplier development programs at a telecommunications systems provider. *International Journal of Production Economics*, 140(1), 357–367. https://doi.org/10.1016/j.ijpe.2011.08.030
Galt, J.D.A., and Dale, B.G. (1991). Supplier Development: A British Case Study. *International Journal of Purchasing and Materials Management*, 27(1), 16–22. https://doi.org/10.1111/j.1745-493x.1991.tb00524.x
Gimenez, C., Sierra, V., and Rodon, J. (2012). Sustainable operations: Their impact on the triple bottom line. *International Journal of Production Economics*, 140(1), 149–159. https://doi.org/10.1016/j.ijpe.2012.01.035
Gimenez, C., and Tachizawa, E.M. (2012). Extending sustainability to suppliers: A systematic literature review. *Supply Chain Management*, 17(5), 531–543. https://doi.org/10.1108/13598541211258591
Giunipero, L.C., Hooker, R.E., and Denslow, D. (2012). Purchasing and supply management sustainability: Drivers and barriers. *Journal of Purchasing and Supply Management*, 18(4), 258–269. https://doi.org/10.1016/j.pursup.2012.06.003
Golicic, S.L., and Smith, C.D. (2013). A meta-analysis of environmentally sustainable supply chain management practices and firm performance. *Journal of Supply Chain Management*, 49(2), 78–95. https://doi.org/10.1111/jscm.12006
Gomez-Mejia, Luis and Balkin, D. (2007). Impact of supply chain management practices on firm performance Empirical evidence from a developing country. *Journal of Management Development*, 23(7), 635–648. https://doi.org/10.1108/MBE-09-2016-0047
Govindan, K., Khodaverdi, R., and Jafarian, A. (2013). A fuzzy multi criteria approach for measuring sustainability performance of a supplier

based on triple bottom line approach. *Journal of Cleaner Production*, 47(May), 345–354. https://doi.org/10.1016/j.jclepro.2012.04.014

Govindan, K., Rajendran, S., Sarkis, J., and Murugesan, P. (2015). Multi criteria decision making approaches for green supplier evaluation and selection: A literature review. *Journal of Cleaner Production*, 98(July), 66–83. https://doi.org/10.1016/j.jclepro.2013.06.046

Graafland, J., and Zhang, L. (2014). Corporate social responsibility in China: Implementation and challenges. *Business Ethics*, 23(1), 34–49. https://doi.org/10.1111/beer.12036

Gullett, J., Do, L., Canuto-Carranco, M., Brister, M., Turner, S., and Caldwell, C. (2009). The buyer-supplier relationship: An integrative model of ethics and trust. *Journal of Business Ethics*, 90(SUPPL 3), 329–341. https://doi.org/10.1007/s10551-010-0430-4

Habidin, N.F., Mohd Zubir, A.F., Mohd Fuzi, N., Md Latip, N.A., and Azman, M.N.A. (2018). Critical success factors of sustainable manufacturing practices in Malaysian automotive industry. *International Journal of Sustainable Engineering*, 11(3), 217–222. https://doi.org/10.1080/19397038.2017.1293185

Hahn, C.K., Kim, K.H., and Kim, J.S. (1986). Costs of Competition: Implications for Purchasing Strategy. *Journal of Purchasing and Materials Management*, 22(3), 2–7. https://doi.org/10.1111/j.1745-493x.1986.tb00161.x

Hair, J.F., Sarstedt, M., Hopkins, L., and Kuppelwieser, V.G. (2014). Partial least squares structural equation modeling (PLS-SEM) An emerging tool in business research. *European Business Review*, 26(2), 106–121. https://doi.org/10.1108/EBR-10-2013-0128

Hair, J.F., Ringle, C.M., and Sarstedt, M. (2012). Partial Least Squares: The Better Approach to Structural Equation Modeling? *Long Range Planning*, 45(5–6), 312–319. https://doi.org/10.1016/j.lrp.2012.09.011

Hair, J.F., Sarstedt, M., Pieper, T.M., and Ringle, C.M. (2012). The Use of Partial Least Squares Structural Equation Modeling in Strategic Management Research: A Review of Past Practices and Recommendations for Future Applications. *Long Range Planning*, 45(5–6), 320–340. https://doi.org/10.1016/j.lrp.2012.09.008

Han, S.L., Wilson, D.T., and Dant, S.P. (1993). Buyer-supplier relationships today. *Industrial Marketing Management*, 22(4), 331–338. https://doi.org/10.1016/0019-8501(93)90029-7

Henseler, J., and Sarstedt, M. (2013). Goodness-of-fit indices for partial least squares path modeling. *Computational Statistics*, 28(2), 565–580. https://doi.org/10.1007/s00180-012-0317-1

Ho, W., Xu, X., and Dey, P.K. (2010). Multi-criteria decision making approaches for supplier evaluation and selection: A literature review.

*European Journal of Operational Research*, 202(1), 16–24. https://doi.org/10.1016/j.ejor.2009.05.009

Hoejmose, S.U., Roehrich, J.K., and Grosvold, J. (2014). Is doing more doing better? The relationship between responsible supply chain management and corporate reputation. *Industrial Marketing Management*, 43(1), 77–90. https://doi.org/10.1016/j.indmarman.2013.10.002

Hollos, D., Blome, C., and Foerstl, K. (2012). Does sustainable supplier co-operation affect performance? Examining implications for the triple bottom line. *International Journal of Production Research*, 50(11), 2968–2986. https://doi.org/10.1080/00207543.2011.582184

Hoyt, J., and Huq, F. (2000). From arms-length to collaborative relationships in the supply chain: An evolutionary process. *International Journal of Physical Distribution and Logistics Management*, 30(9), 750–764. https://doi.org/10.1108/09600030010351453

Hsu, C.C., Kannan, V.R., Tan, K.C., and Leong, G.K. (2008). Information sharing, buyer-supplier relationships, and firm performance: A multi-region analysis. *International Journal of Physical Distribution and Logistics Management*, 38(4), 296–310. https://doi.org/10.1108/09600030810875391

Hulland, J. (1999). Use of partial least squares (PLS) in strategic management research: a review of four recent studies. *Strategic Management Journal*, 20(2), 195–204. https://doi.org/10.1002/(SICI)1097-0266(199902)20:2⟨195::AID-SMJ13⟩3.0.CO;2-7

Humphreys, P.K., Li, W.L., and Chan, L.Y. (2004). The impact of supplier development on buyer-supplier performance. *Omega*, 32(2), 191–143. https://doi.org/10.1016/j.omega.2003.09.016

Ittner, C.D., Larcker, D.F., Nagar, V., and Rajan, M.V. (1999). Supplier selection, monitoring practices, and firm performance. *Journal of Accounting and Public Policy*, 18(3), 253–281.

Jabbour, A.B.L.S., and Jabbour, C.J.C. (2009). Are supplier selection criteria going green? Case studies of companies in Brazil. *Industrial Management and Data Systems*, 109(4), 477–495. https://doi.org/10.1108/02635570910948623

Johansson, G. (2002). Success factors for integration of ecodesign in product development. *Environmental Management and Health*, 13(1), 98–107. https://doi.org/10.1108/09566160210417868

Kannan, D., De Sousa Jabbour, A.B.L., and Jabbour, C.J.C. (2014). Selecting green suppliers based on GSCM practices: Using Fuzzy TOPSIS applied to a Brazilian electronics company. *European Journal of Operational Research*, 233(2), 432–447. https://doi.org/10.1016/j.ejor.2013.07.023

Kannan, V.R., and Choon Tan, K. (2007). Buyer-supplier relationships. The impact of supplier selection and buyer-supplier engagement on relationship and firm performance Vijay. *International Journal of Physical Distribution and Logistics Management*, 36(10), 755–775. https://doi.org/10.1108/09600030610714580

Kannan, V.R., Choon Tan, K., and Tan, K.C. (2007). Buyer-supplier relationships. The impact of supplier selection and buyer-supplier engagement on relationship and firm performance Vijay. *International Journal of Physical Distribution and Logistics Management*, 36(10), 755–775. https://doi.org/10.1108/09600030610714580

Kanter, R. (2014). Collaborative advantage: the art of alliances. *Harvard Business Review*, 72(4), 96–108.

Khan, Z., and Nicholson, J.D. (2014). An investigation of the cross-border supplier development process: Problems and implications in an emerging economy. *International Business Review*, 23(6), 1212–1222. https://doi.org/10.1016/j.ibusrev.2014.05.001

Kline, R.B. (2005). Principles and practice of structural equation modeling. *Methodology in the social sciences*. (2nd Ed.). New York: Guiford.

Knemeyer, A.M., and Murphy, P.R. (2004). Evaluating the performance of third-party logistics arrangements: A relationship marketing perspective. *Journal of Supply Chain Management*, 40(4), 35–51. https://doi.org/10.1111/j.1745-493X.2004.tb00254.x

Krause, D.R., Handfield, R.B., and Tyler, B.B. (2007). The relationships between supplier development, commitment, social capital accumulation and performance improvement. *Journal of Operations Management*, 25(2), 528–545. https://doi.org/10.1016/j.jom.2006.05.007

Kuo, R.J., Wang, Y.C., and Tien, F.C. (2010). Integration of artificial neural network and MADA methods for green supplier selection. *Journal of Cleaner Production*, 18(12), 1161–1170. https://doi.org/10.1016/j.jclepro.2010.03.020

Li, S., Ragu-Nathan, B., Ragu-Nathan, T.S., and Subba Rao, S. (2006). The impact of supply chain management practices on competitive advantage and organizational performance. *Omega*, 34(2), 107–124. https://doi.org/10.1016/j.omega.2004.08.002

Li, S., Rao, S.S., Ragu-Nathan, T.S., and Ragu-Nathan, B. (2005). Development and validation of a measurement instrument for studying supply chain management practices. *Journal of Operations Management*, 23(6), 618–641. https://doi.org/10.1016/j.jom.2005.01.002

Li, W., Humphreys, P.K., Yeung, A.C.L., and Cheng, T.C.E. (2012). The impact of supplier development on buyer competitive advantage: A path analytic model. *International Journal of Production Economics*, 135(1), 353–366. https://doi.org/10.1016/j.ijpe.2011.06.019

Liu, S., Leat, M., and Smith, M.H. (2011). State-of-the-art sustainability analysis methodologies for efficient decision support in green production operations. *International Journal of Sustainable Engineering*, 4(3), 236–250. https://doi.org/10.1080/19397038.2011.574744

Liu, X., Yang, J., Qu, S., Wang, L., Shishime, T., and Bao, C. (2012). Sustainable production: Practices and determinant factors of green supply chain management of Chinese companies. *Business Strategy and the Environment*, 21(1), 1–16. https://doi.org/10.1002/bse.705

Mariadoss, B.J., Chi, T., Tansuhaj, P., and Pomirleanu, N. (2016). Influences of Firm Orientations on Sustainable Supply Chain Management. *Journal of Business Research*, 69(9), 3406–3414. https://doi.org/10.1016/j.jbusres.2016.02.003

Mathiyazhagan, K., Govindan, K., NoorulHaq, A., and Geng, Y. (2013). An ISM approach for the barrier analysis in implementing green supply chain management. *Journal of Cleaner Production*, 47(May), 283–297. https://doi.org/10.1016/j.jclepro.2012.10.042

Mohanty, M.K., Gahan, P., and Choudhury, S. (2014). Why most of the supplier development programs fail in discrete manufacturing-findings from selected Indian discrete manufacturing industries. *International Journal of Management Science and Engineering Management*, 9(3), 201–211. https://doi.org/10.1080/17509653.2014.884454

Moon, Y.B. (2017). Simulation modelling for sustainability: a review of the literature. *International Journal of Sustainable Engineering*, 10(1), 2–19. https://doi.org/10.1080/19397038.2016.1220990

Morgan, N.A. (2012). Marketing and business performance. *Journal of the Academy of Marketing Science*, 40(1), 102–119. https://doi.org/10.1007/s11747-011-0279-9

Naghavi, A., and Ottaviano, G.I.P. (2010). Outsourcing, complementary innovations, and growth. *Industrial and Corporate Change*, 19(4), 1009–1035. https://doi.org/10.1093/icc/dtp051

Namagembe, S., Ryan, S., and Sridharan, R. (2019). Green supply chain practice adoption and firm performance: manufacturing SMEs in Uganda. *Management of Environmental Quality: An International Journal*, 30(1), 5–35. https://doi.org/10.1108/MEQ-10-2017-0119

O'Toole, T., and Donaldson, B. (2002). Relationship performance dimensions of buyer-supplier exchanges. *European Journal of Purchasing and Supply Management*, 8(4), 197–207. https://doi.org/10.1016/S0969-7012(02)00008-4

Patterson, J.L., Forker, L.B., and Hanna, J.B. (1999). Supply chain consortia: The rise of transcendental buyer-supplier relationships. *European Journal of Purchasing and Supply Management*, 5(2), 85–93. https://doi.org/10.1016/S0969-7012(99)00013-1

Perez-Arostegui, M.N., Benitez-Amado, J., and Huertas-Perez, J.F. (2012). In search of loyalty: An analysis of the determinants of buyer-supplier relationship stability under a quality management approach. *Total Quality Management and Business Excellence*, 23(5–6), 703–717. https://doi.org/10.1080/14783363.2012.669999

Pettersen, I.N. (2015). Towards practice-oriented design for sustainability: The compatibility with selected design fields. *International Journal of Sustainable Engineering*, 8(3), 206–218. https://doi.org/10.1080/19397038.2014.1001468

Prajogo, D., Chowdhury, M., Yeung, A.C.L., and Cheng, T.C.E. (2012). The relationship between supplier management and firms operational performance: A multi-dimensional perspective. *International Journal of Production Economics*, 136(1), 123–130. https://doi.org/10.1016/j.ijpe.2011.09.022

Prior, D.D. (2012). The effects of buyer-supplier relationships on buyer competitiveness. *Journal of Business and Industrial Marketing*, 27(2), 100–114. https://doi.org/10.1108/08858621211196976

Qi, Y., Zhao, X., and Sheu, C. (2011). The Impact of Competitive Strategy and Supply Chain Strategy on Business Performance: The Role of Environmental Uncertainty. *Decision Sciences*, 42(2), 371–389.

Ragazzi, S., Crescentini, A., and Castelli, L. (2013). Evaluation and Monitoring of Innovation in school: A Case Study. *Procedia — Social and Behavioral Sciences*, 69, 414–421. https://doi.org/10.1016/j.sbspro.2012.11.428

Rahimifard, S., Coates, G., Staikos, T., Edwards, C., and Abu-Bakar, M. (2009). Barriers, drivers and challenges for sustainable product recovery and recycling. *International Journal of Sustainable Engineering*, 2(2), 80–90. https://doi.org/10.1080/19397030903019766

Reuter, C., Goebel, P., and Foerstl, K. (2012). The impact of stakeholder orientation on sustainability and cost prevalence in supplier selection decisions. *Journal of Purchasing and Supply Management*, 18(4), 270–281. https://doi.org/10.1016/j.pursup.2012.06.004

Reuter, M.A. (2011). Limits of design for recycling and "sustainability": A review. *Waste and Biomass Valorization*, 2(2), 183–208. https://doi.org/10.1007/s12649-010-9061-3

Revilla, E., Sáenz, M.J., and Knoppen, D. (2013). Towards an empirical typology of buyer-supplier relationships based on absorptive capacity. *International Journal of Production Research*, 51(10), 2935–2951. https://doi.org/10.1080/00207543.2012.748231

Ringle, C.M., Sarstedt, M., and Straub, D.W. (2012). A critical look at the use of PLS-SEM. *MIS Quarterly*.

Rostamzadeh, R., Govindan, K., Esmaeili, A., and Sabaghi, M. (2015). Application of fuzzy VIKOR for evaluation of green supply chain management practices. *Ecological Indicators*, 49, 188–203. https://doi.org/10.1016/j.ecolind.2014.09.045

Sancha, C., Longoni, A., and Giménez, C. (2015). Sustainable supplier development practices: Drivers and enablers in a global context. *Journal of Purchasing and Supply Management*, 21(2), 95–102. https://doi.org/10.1016/j.pursup.2014.12.004

Sapukotanage, S., Warnakulasuriya, B.N.F., and Yapa, S.T.W.S. (2016). A Conceptual Model for Understanding the Outcomes of Buyer-supplier Relationships in Supply Chains. *International Business Research*, 9(8), 72–83. https://doi.org/10.5539/ibr.v9n8p72

Sari, D., Kartini, D., Suryana, Y., and Najib, M.F. (2017). Market orientation, buyer-supplier relationship and firm performance with dynamic capabilities as an intervening variable: a research model. *International Journal of Business and Globalisation*, 19(4), 567–582. https://doi.org/10.1504/ijbg.2017.10007902

Sarkis, J. (2003). A strategic decision framework for green supply chain management. *Journal of Cleaner Production*, 11(4), 397–409. https://doi.org/10.1016/S0959-6526(02)00062-8

Sarkis, J., Zhu, Q., and Lai, K.H. (2011). An organizational theoretic review of green supply chain management literature. *International Journal of Production Economics*, 130(1), 1–15. https://doi.org/10.1016/j.ijpe.2010.11.010

Scannell, T.V., Vickery, S.K., and Droge, C.L. (2000). Upstream supply chain management and competitive performance in the automotive supply industry. *Journal of Business Logistics*, 21(1), 23–48.

Schaltegger, S., Burritt, R., Burritt, R.L., and Schaltegger, S. (2012). Measuring the (un-)sustainability of industrial biomass production and use. *Sustainability Accounting, Management and Policy Journal*. https://doi.org/10.1108/20408021211282377

Schiele, H. (2007). Supply-management maturity, cost savings and purchasing absorptive capacity: Testing the procurement-performance link. *Journal of Purchasing and Supply Management*, 13(4), 274–293. https://doi.org/10.1016/j.pursup.2007.10.002

Sen, D.K., Datta, S., and Mahapatra, S.S. (2018). Sustainable supplier selection in intuitionistic fuzzy environment: a decision-making perspective. *Benchmarking: An International Journal*, 25(2), 545–574.

Seuring, S., and Müller, M. (2008). From a literature review to a conceptual framework for sustainable supply chain management. *Journal of Cleaner Production*, 16(15), 1699–1710. https://doi.org/10.1016/j.jclepro.2008.04.020

Shaw, K., Shankar, R., Yadav, S.S., and Thakur, L.S. (2012). Supplier selection using fuzzy AHP and fuzzy multi-objective linear programming for developing low carbon supply chain. *Expert Systems with Applications*, 39(9), 8182–8192. https://doi.org/10.1016/j.eswa.2012.01.149

Soosay, C.A., and Hyland, P. (2015). A decade of supply chain collaboration and directions for future research. *Supply Chain Management*, 20(6), 613–630. https://doi.org/10.1108/SCM-06-2015-0217

Sriram, V., and Mummalaneni, V. (1990). Determinants of Source Loyalty in Buyer-Seller Relationships. *Journal of Purchasing and Materials Management*, 26(4), 21–26. https://doi.org/10.1111/j.1745-493x.1990.tb00517.x

Talluri, S., and Sarkis, J. (2002). A methodology for monitoring system performance. *International Journal of Production Research*, 40(7), 1567–1582. https://doi.org/10.1080/00207540110118659

Terpend, R., Krause, D.R., and Dooley, K.J. (2011). Managing buyer-supplier relationships: Empirical patterns of strategy formulation in industrial purchasing. *Journal of Supply Chain Management*, 47(1), 73–94. https://doi.org/10.1111/j.1745-493X.2010.03215.x

Tracey, M., and Tan, C.L. (2001). Empirical analysis of supplier selection and involvement, customer satisfaction, and firm performance. *Supply Chain Management*, 6(4), 174–188. https://doi.org/10.1108/EUM0000000005709

Trapp, A.C., and Sarkis, J. (2016). Identifying Robust portfolios of suppliers: A sustainability selection and development perspective. *Journal of Cleaner Production*, 112(3), 2088–2100. https://doi.org/10.1016/j.jclepro.2014.09.062

Vachon, S., and Klassen, R.D. (2006). Extending green practices across the supply chain. *International Journal of Operations and Production Management*, 26(7), 795–821. https://doi.org/10.1108/01443570610672248

Verghese, K., and Lewis, H. (2007). Environmental innovation in industrial packaging: A supply chain approach. *International Journal of Production Research*, 45(18–19), 4381–4401. https://doi.org/10.1080/00207540701450211

Voola, R., and O'Cass, A. (2010). Implementing competitive strategies: The role of responsive and proactive market orientations. *European Journal of Marketing*, 44(1), 245–266. https://doi.org/10.1108/03090561011008691

Wagner, S.M. (2006). Supplier development practices: An exploratory study. *European Journal of Marketing*, 40(5–6), 554–571. https://doi.org/10.1108/03090560610657831

Walker, G., and Poppo, L. (1991). Profit Centers, Single-Source Suppliers, and Transaction Costs. *Administrative Science Quarterly*, 36(1), 66–87. https://doi.org/10.2307/2393430

Walker, H., and Phillips, W. (2008). Sustainable procurement: emerging issues. *International Journal of Procurement Management*, 2(1), 41–61. https://doi.org/10.1504/ijpm.2009.021729

Wheelen, T.L., and David Hunger, J. (2012). Strategic Management and Business Policy Toward Global Sustainability. *Pearson/Prentice Hall.* (13 Ed).

Wu, J., Wu, Z., and Si, S. (2016). The influences of Internet-based collaboration and intimate interactions in buyer-supplier relationship on product innovation. *Journal of Business Research*, 69(9), 3780–3787. https://doi.org/10.1016/j.jbusres.2015.12.070

Xu, L., Kumar, D.T., Shankar, K.M., Kannan, D., and Chen, G. (2013). Analyzing criteria and sub-criteria for the corporate social responsibility-based supplier selection process using AHP. *International Journal of Advanced Manufacturing Technology*, 68(1–4), 907–916. https://doi.org/10.1007/s00170-013-4952-7

Yang, F., and Zhang, X. (2017). The impact of sustainable supplier management practices on buyer-supplier performance. *Review of International Business and Strategy*, 27(1), 112–132. https://doi.org/10.1108/ribs-08-2016-0043

Yazdani, M., Hashemkhani Zolfani, S., and Zavadskas, E.K. (2016). New integration of MCDM methods and QFD in the selection of green suppliers. *Journal of Business Economics and Management*, 17(6), 1097–1113. https://doi.org/10.3846/16111699.2016.1165282

Younis, H., Sundarakani, B., and Vel, P. (2016). The impact of implementing green supply chain management practices on corporate performance. *Competitiveness Review*, 26(3), 216–245. https://doi.org/10.1108/CR-04-2015-0024

Yu, C., and Wong, T.N. (2015). An agent-based negotiation model for supplier selection of multiple products with synergy effect. *Expert Systems with Applications*, 42(1), 223–237. https://doi.org/10.1016/j.eswa.2014.07.057

Zhao, X., Huo, B., Flynn, B.B., and Yeung, J.H.Y. (2008). The impact of power and relationship commitment on the integration between manufacturers and customers in a supply chain. *Journal of Operations Management*, 26(3), 368–388. https://doi.org/10.1016/j.jom.2007.08.002

Zhu, Q., and Sarkis, J. (2004). Relationships between operational practices and performance among early adopters of green supply chain management practices in Chinese manufacturing enterprises. *Journal of Operations Management*, 22(3), 265–289. https://doi.org/10.1016/j.jom.2004.01.005

Zhu, Q., and Sarkis, J. (2006). An inter-sectoral comparison of green supply chain management in China: Drivers and practices. *Journal of Cleaner Production*, 14(5), 472–486. https://doi.org/10.1016/j.jclepro.2005.01.003

Zhu, Q., Sarkis, J., and Lai, K. hung. (2007a). Green supply chain management: pressures, practices and performance within the Chinese automobile industry. *Journal of Cleaner Production*, 15(11–12), 1041–1052. https://doi.org/10.1016/j.jclepro.2006.05.021

Zhu, Q., Sarkis, J., and Lai, K. hung. (2007b). Initiatives and outcomes of green supply chain management implementation by Chinese manufacturers. *Journal of Environmental Management*, 85(1), 179–189. https://doi.org/10.1016/j.jenvman.2006.09.003

Zhu, Q., Sarkis, J., and Lai, K. hung. (2008). Confirmation of a measurement model for green supply chain management practices implementation. *International Journal of Production Economics*, 111(2), 261–273. https://doi.org/10.1016/j.ijpe.2006.11.029

Zhu, Q., Sarkis, J., and Lai, K. hung. (2013). Institutional-based antecedents and performance outcomes of internal and external green supply chain management practices. *Journal of Purchasing and Supply Management*, 19(2), 106–117. https://doi.org/10.1016/j.pursup.2012.12.001

Zimmer, K., Fröhling, M., and Schultmann, F. (2016). Sustainable supplier management — A review of models supporting sustainable supplier selection, monitoring and development. *International Journal of Production Research*, 54(5), 1412–1442. https://doi.org/10.1080/00207543.2015.1079340

https://doi.org/10.1142/9789811227158_0022

Chapter 22

# Exploring the Impact of Self-Construal on the Perceived Values of the Post-Purchase Product Customization: The Context of Motorcycle Customization in Vietnam

**Mai Dong Tran and Long Dang**

## Abstract

A few studies have partially analyzed the benefits of motorcycle modification activities in Western countries and Southeast Asian countries (Schouten and McAlexander, 1995; Lai and Aritejo, 2013). Since culture impacts consumers' value perceptions (Overby *et al.*, 2005), there are limitations to generalizing the findings from existing studies in foreign countries into Vietnam. To understand the effect of cultural difference in consumer behavior, Markus and Kitayama (1991) suggest the concept of "self-construal", which categorizes an individual's view of oneself into independent and interdependent. Other researchers (Atakan *et al.*, 2014; Kim and Drolet, 2003) argue that self-construal has a significant influence on how a consumer evaluates products. Vietnam is a collectivistic country; Vietnamese people share the interdependent self-construal view, which values harmonious relatedness of individuals. It is interesting to understand how such a view can affect the perceived values of vehicle modification activities, which emphasize an individual's uniqueness and preferences. This research aims to provide theoretical insights into the values of motorcycle customization for adults living in Ho Chi Minh City area. The primary data are collected from respondents in Ho Chi Minh City, who are aged between 23 and 39 years and have prior experience in customizing their motorcycle. The findings can be valuable information for motorcycle manufacturers, aftermarket manufacturers, and the custom shops, to have a better understanding of customers' needs and intentions.

**Keywords:** Self-construal; Perceived values; Post purchased product customization; Motorcycle customization; Vietnam.

## 1. Introduction

While the lotus represents Vietnamese culture, the motorcycle is seen as a specific "symbol" of transportation in Vietnam. Motorcycles are the most popular means of transportation in Vietnam, making up more than 90% of the registered motorized traffic (Hsu, 2003; Hsu *et al.*, 2003). After China, India, and Indonesia, Vietnam is the fourth largest market worldwide for motorcycles (EuroCham, 2018). Customization of private motorcycles, as a consequence, is a popular phenomenon easily encountered on every street in this developing country. It relates to adjustments to the original version of scooters from minor (addition of accessories) to extensive ones (changes in appearance and performance of vehicle) (Lai and Aritejo, 2013). Besides its daily purposes, the motorcycle is also considered as a personal device, through which the owner wants to express individualism and/or to add more value by customizing his/her bike.

Motorcycle customization brings many significant benefits in commercial and personal aspects. From a commercial standpoint, vehicle customization provides more business opportunities for aftermarket producers and custom shops. There is a well-known accessory market in District 5, called the Tan Thanh Market, which many locals refer to as the paradise of motorcycle accessories. Along narrow streets, there are hundreds of shops selling all kinds of accessories for any motorcycle brand. Besides traditional accessory shops, consumers can also find almost any custom parts on e-commerce websites such as doxemay.com.vn. From a personal standpoint, scooter customization is a way that people use to express their lifestyle. In an age where people are becoming more individualistic, especially the younger generation (Santos *et al.*, 2017), customization is one of the human behaviors supporting this trend. Hence, vehicle customization is not only seen as a hobby, but it can also be transformed into an industry which involves different parties. On the contrary, from a legal standpoint, vehicle modification requires a well-regulated policy framework to control the quality of spare parts and modification activities, as after-purchase vehicle modification can negatively affect vehicle functions and safety. Therefore, understanding the consumer's motivation and behaviors towards this activity provides necessary evidence for the authorities to address the issues in more constructive ways.

Product customization gains significant attention in the scholarly community, but surprisingly, it lacks literature on the sociological aspect towards this behavior. Most of the previous research focuses on various benefits of product customization at an individual level, including increasing preferences (Schreier, 2006), expressing personal characteristics (Merle *et al.*, 2010); improving consumers' enjoyment (Franke *et al.*, 2010); and enhancing consumers' sense of authorship (Franke *et al.*, 2010). A few studies partially analyze the benefits of motorcycle modification activities in Western countries and Southeast Asian countries (Schouten and McAlexander, 1995; Lai and Aritejo, 2013). Of these, Lai and Aritejo (2013) investigate the impacts of personal attitudes and social support from peers and parents on adolescents' intention to customize motorcycles in Indonesia. However, they only mention the relationship between opinions of customers' relatives and customization activity, not the role of society in vehicle customization behavior. On the other hand, consumers' value perceptions are impacted by culture (Overby *et al.*, 2005), so to understand the effect of cultural differences on consumers' behavior, Markus and Kitayama (1991) suggest the concept of "self-construal", which categorizes an individual's view of oneself into independent and interdependent. Other researchers (Atakan *et al.*, 2014; Kim and Drolet, 2003) argue that self-construal has significant influence on how consumers evaluate customized products. Vietnam is an extremely collectivist country (Parks and Vu, 1994) where people tend to share the interdependent self-construal view.

It is important to investigate how such a view can affect the perceived values of vehicle modification activities, which emphasize an individual's uniqueness and preferences.

Therefore, it is necessary to understand customers' behavior through post-purchase vehicle customization activity in Vietnam. This research aims to provide theoretical insights into social values that adults perceive when engaging in the customization activity of their motorcycles after purchase in Ho Chi Minh City. The purpose of this research is to develop a set of perceived values when an individual gets involved in post-purchase product customization, considering the effect of an interdependent view of self. The study only focuses on customizing activities that do not jeopardize the safety function of the vehicle, as well as that the modified motorcycles are not involved in any illegal activities such as street racing. The findings can be valuable information for motorcycle manufacturers, aftermarket manufacturers, and the custom shops to have a better understanding of customers' needs and intentions. The findings from this study can also support government authorities to re-consider the current laws and regulations to address both positive and negative effects of the behavior. Instead of forbidding the activities, the government can build a legal framework to monitor the quality of the accessories and to provide a regulatory environment for vehicle customization activities.

## 2. Literature Review

### 2.1. *Vehicle customization*

Product personalization, or customization, is a process that changes a product's appearance or functionality to increase its value to an individual. Before the mass production era, products were handmade and could be easily customized according to an individual's needs (Heskett, 1980). Since the First Industrial Revolution in the 18th century, products have been developed to suit the average needs of the general population; they are produced in large quantities with a standardized process to reduce production costs (Fralix, 2001).

Consequently, products become similar and lack the personal touch. This approach works as long as the market is large enough and consumers' preferences are relatively homogeneous (Schreier, 2006).

Consumers' needs have become increasingly diverse (Franke *et al.*, 2009). More often now it is required that products be customized to the needs of each individual. Cooper (1999) shows that poor customer fit can lead to failure in a new product launch. The customization process can be done prior to the product purchase or post-purchase. The automotive industry is one of the most successful examples of changing manufacturing from mass-production to custom-made (Pine *et al.*, 1993). Customers of major automotive manufacturers can personalize their products before making a purchasing decision. This strategy is referred to as mass-customization (Pine, 1993). In other situations, especially in the low-value market, people tend to purchase a standard product and customize it afterward. It is common for young adults in an emerging market, such as Indonesia, Thailand, and Vietnam, to buy standardized motorcycles and customize them after purchase (Lai and Aritejo, 2013; Cohen, 2009; Freire, 2009).

The benefits of product customization and consumer behaviors towards such activities have been well investigated. However, existing studies mainly focus on mass-customization in the automotive, consumer electronic devices, and apparel industries. Consumers' perception and behavior toward post-purchase motorcycle customization is not a well-studied topic. Among published English journals in Southeast Asia, there is only one study addressing adolescents' intentions to personalize their motorcycles with evidence from Indonesia (Lai and Aritejo, 2013). Vietnam and Indonesia share a specific point of view in terms of culture, which affects how consumers perceive and behave. Moreover, participants in Lai and Aritejo's research are selected among high school students in Yogyakarta city, Indonesia, while in Vietnam, high school students are not allowed to ride a motorcycle. Hence, the existing result cannot be applied to Vietnam.

Existing related studies are summarized in Table 1.

**Table 1:** Former works related to the topic.

| Year | Title | Author | Findings | Suggested further study |
|---|---|---|---|---|
| 2000 | "Personalization — A taxonomy" | Blom (2000) | • Provide definition of the term "personalization"<br>• Establish framework of personalization | • Field study of how to use existing technology for personalization<br>• Experiment new form of personalization |
| 2003 | "Theory of Personalization of Appearance: Why Users Personalize Their PCs and Mobile Phones" | Blom and Monk (2003) | User, system, and contextual dispositions lead to the appearance personalization desires. This behavior has cognitive, social, and emotional effects on consumers. | • Understand the relationship between consumers' personalization behavior and personalization dispositions.<br>• Study the consequences of personalization. |
| 2006 | "The Value Increment of Mass-Customized Products: An Empirical Assessment" | Schreier (2006) | Mass customized products create value for customers:<br>• Functional benefit (suitable between personal needs and product characteristics)<br>• Uniqueness (be different with the self-designed product)<br>• Process benefit (meet hedonic or experiential needs by "doing it oneself")<br>• Satisfaction of authorship (be proud of having self-designed the product) | • Collect empirical evident by employing structural equation modeling to explain WTP.<br>• Use different toolkits to empirically analyze the effects of toolkit characteristics in creating values. |

| | | | | |
|---|---|---|---|---|
| 2009 | "Testing the Value of Customization: When Do Customers Really Prefer Products Tailored to Their Preferences?" | Franke *et al.* (2009) | • Products customized based on measured customer preferences deliver clear benefits to the customer.<br>• The benefits of customization are dependent on consumer's characteristics: level of insight into own preferences, ability to express preferences, and degree of product involvement. | • Research with more realistic experimental setting.<br>• Study interaction effects between benefit components (preference fit, process of self-design).<br>• Integrate cost components.<br>• Study other perspectives (experience, economies of scale, manufacture and distribution cost) to understand when customization can be a promising marketing strategy. |
| 2009 | "Emotional Bonding with Personalized Products" | Mugge *et al.* (2009) | • Product personalization is a possible design strategy to encourage emotional bonding between consumers and products.<br>• The effect of emotional bonding can be partially explained by the product's self-expressiveness.<br>• Product's self-expressive values can be increased by personalizing its appearance. | • Perform a longitudinal study to derive the direction of causality in conceptual framework.<br>• Examine how product personalization could be implemented to get a suitable balance between the effort spent and the complexity of the personalization process.<br>• Study potential negative concerns of product personalization.<br>• Study the emotional bonding with products. |

(*Continued*)

**Table 1:** (*Continued*)

| Year | Title | Author | Findings | Suggested further study |
|---|---|---|---|---|
| 2010 | "Why Customers Value Self-Designed Products: The Importance of Process Effort and Enjoyment" | Franke and Schreier (2010) | The subjective value of a self-designed product, (measured as WTP) is affected by:<br>(1) preference fit<br>(2) process enjoyment<br>(3) interaction between process enjoyment and preference fit<br>(4) interaction between perceived process effort and preference fit | • Repeat the study in other subjects using various toolkits.<br>• Examine interaction between toolkits attributes and consumer values (i.e., process effort and enjoyment versus preference fit).<br>• Understand which sources of value can impact which types of customers. |
| 2010 | "The "I Designed it Myself" Effect in Mass Customization" | Franke *et al.* (2010) | Value consumers attribute to products is created by:<br>• The preference fit accomplished by self-designed process (e.g., benefits). It should be as high as possible.<br>• The required design effort (e.g., costs). It should be as low as possible. | • Analysis the correlation of "I designed it myself" effect versus the objective of making the self-design process convenient for the consumer.<br>• Analysis the balance of delivering high preference fit objective versus feeling of I am the product's originator and the factors moderating its optimum level.<br>• Analyze the extent to which the feelings of having contributed are desirable. |

| | | | | |
|---|---|---|---|---|
| | | | The accomplishment feelings from the self-designing process significantly affect the perceived value of the product, so-called "I designed it myself" effect. | • Find empirical evidence to quantify the degree to which feedback information actually improves the "I designed it myself" feelings.<br>• Determine if the effect can be generalized in other product category, and the moderate effect of situational and personal characteristics.<br>• Determine influence of customer groups and societies to the "I designed it myself" effect. |
| 2013 | "Personal and Social Factors Affecting Adolescent Motorcycle Riders' Intention to Customize their Vehicles: Evidence from Indonesia" | Lai and Aritejo (2013) | • Personal factors (need for uniqueness, attitudes, knowledge) and social factor (support from peers and parents) have significant impact to Indonesian adolescent's intention to customize a motorcycle.<br>• Budget and time constraints have insignificant influence. | • Employ longitudinal study.<br>• Examine different market segment, other type of vehicles (e.g. cars), other potential factors (e.g. marital status). |

(*Continued*)

**Table 1:** (*Continued*)

| Year | Title | Author | Findings | Suggested further study |
|---|---|---|---|---|
| 2018 | "An Exploratory Study of User Interaction with Smart Products for Customization in the Usage Stage" | Wang *et al.* (2018) | • Customized products can be fabricated based on the concept of "smart products": product customization in the usage stage (PCUS). | • Perform empirical study to validate the proposed design parameters for smart product and user interactions.<br>• Understand how consumers reacts when being shared control and collaborative alteration in different contexts. |

### 2.2. *Process enjoyment*

In general, consumers have a positive attitude towards product customization as it can enhance personal value and satisfaction (Schreier, 2006). It explains why consumers are willing to pay more to customize a product. Academic researchers address five benefits of customization: *Preference fit*, *Uniqueness*, *Self-expressiveness*, *Process enjoyment*, and *Creative achievement* (Dellaert and Stremersch, 2005; Schreier, 2006; Franke *et al.*, 2010; Merle *et al.*, 2010). Among these, process enjoyment can be considered as a social impact of motorcycle customization. This driving factor can directly affect the consumers' attitude toward customization.

Process enjoyment relates to the process of customizing a product that brought joy from its experience (Schreier, 2006; Merle *et al.*, 2010; Franke *et al.*, 2010). It is shown that people put effort into complex activities, such as open-source software development, simply because they enjoy it. Franke *et al.* (2010) conduct an experiment to test the existence of process enjoyment. After letting the participant design his/her own scarves, the researchers measure the users' willingness to pay (WTP) with the second-price sealed-bid auction — where the highest bidder wins but only needs to pay for the price of the second-highest bid, so-called Vickrey auction method (Vickrey, 1961). The result shows that subjects pay considerably more for their own designed scarves. The researchers prove that besides the improvement in preference fit, process enjoyment also has an impact on the increase in WTP. Furthermore, they identify the correlation between this effect and the perceived preference fit: the higher the preference fit the object can achieve, the more significant the increase in WTP through process enjoyment is, as illustrated in Figure 1. Franke *et al.* (2010) claim that the positive "mood" which is created during the process of using the toolkit for customizing is transferred into the process of products' value evaluation.

In mass customization, the "process" of customization usually happens before the product is produced. The consumer uses the tool kit to design his or her own preferred variant of a product and sends the information to the manufacturers. There is a certain barrier

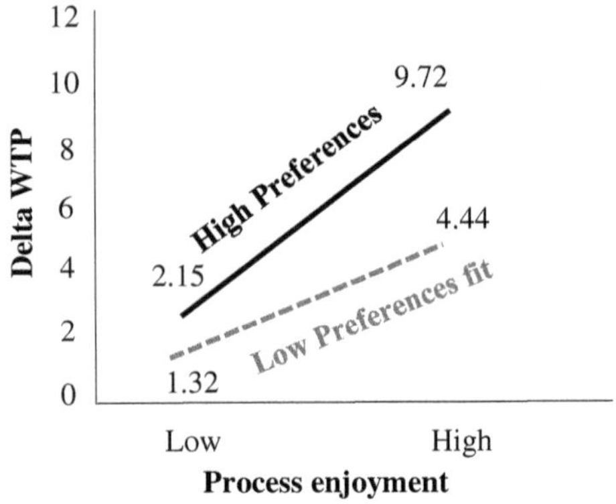


**Figure 1:** The effect of process enjoyment on WTP moderated by preference fit. Studied object: scarves.

*Source*: Franke *et al.* (2010).

between the future owner and the product itself during mass customization. The majority of activities take place through a virtual interface (e.g., toolkit software). There is a lack of physical interaction between consumers and the products. Patterson (1997) suggests that consumer value perceptions positively influence behavioral intentions and product/service evaluation. However, it is a challenge to determine what consumers actually valued, especially when considering the effect of cultural perspective (Wilson, 2003). Hence, it is necessary to understand how culture affects consumers' perceptions.

### 2.3. *Culture and self-construal*

According to Hofstede (1993), culture is defined as "collective programming of the mind that distinguishes the members of one human group from those of the others". Schwartz (2006) says that it is "the rich complex of meanings, beliefs, practices, symbols, norms, and values prevalent among people in a society". Despite differences in definitions, many researchers agree that culture has a broad influence on various aspects of consumers, including perception, information processing strategies, cognitive structures, and needs (Hofstede, 1984; Kim and Drolet, 2003). Hence, researchers propose to consider culture as a metaphorical lens that people use to perceive the world (Goldberger and Veroff, 1995). Further, Overby *et al.* (2005) suggest that culture has a direct impact on consumer value perceptions.

To characterize culture, many researchers have attempted to develop a framework with various psychological dimensions. The most internationally recognized model was originally developed in 1984 by psychologist Hofstede (1984) after more than 10 years' research on IBM employees' values. He suggests a four-factor model that can be used to distinguish cultures: *Power Distance*, *Individualism/ Collectivism*, *Masculinity/Femininity*, and *Uncertainty Avoidance*. The fifth dimension, *Long-term/Short-term Orientation*, was later added based on a co-study between Hofstede and Michael with evidence from students in 23 countries (Hofstede, 1993).

When examining the influences of different cultural aspects on consumer behaviors, it is commonly agreed that Individualism/ Collectivism is "the most worth-considering factor" (Usunier and Lee, 2013; Gouveia and Ros, 2000). According to Hofstede (1993), *Individualism* is the degree to which people prefer to behave individually rather than belong to a certain group. The opposite of this dimension is called *Collectivism*, in which the cohesiveness among individuals is emphasized, the group is prioritized over self. To further break down the construct of the Individualism/Collectivism concept, Singelis (1994) proposes four attributes to predict social behavior, which are *Self's definition*; *Personal goals versus ingroup's goals; Personal attitudes versus Perceived duties and obligations*; *Relationship's cost versus its benefit*. The most significant difference between Individualism and Collectivism is in the role that is assigned to the "other person" in the self's definition: independent view and interdependent view.

The independent view is a common belief in Western culture, where the norm for an individual is to become independent from others. In contrast, for many non-Western cultures, human beings are connected to each other. The social norm in these countries is individuals who are interdependent. This distinction of self's definition is referred to as *self-construal* by Markus and Kitayama (1991). They propose two categorizations in self-construal: *interdependent self-construal* and *independent self-construal* (Markus and Kitayama, 1991). These two definitions are well-connected, but it is important to distinguish between them. Cross *et al.* (2011) use the analogy of a football team to clarify this distinction. It is likely that a good defense team has members who are good in defense skills (corresponding to self-construal). But above the individual's ability, the team performance also requires good strategies and teamwork (corresponding to individualism/collectivism). In other words, self-construal can be used to describe individuals, whereas individualism/collectivism is a parameter to describe a culture. The self-construal can be considered as a component of individualism/collectivism (Cross *et al.*, 2011). Different cultural contexts provide different opportunities for an individual to experience the self, hence, self-construal varies across cultures (Markus and Kitayama, 1991; Triandis, 1989). Markus and Kitayama (1991) point out that Europeans and Americans define the self as a fundamental individual, separated from others. Meanwhile, the self in Asian culture is construed as fundamentally connected to others; it is defined by the relationship with others (Heine, 2001).

Product customization is a personal activity, tailored to an individual. To understand how culture affects consumers' perceived values from product customization, it is logical to consider self-construal, which is used to describe how an individual understands the relationship between him-/herself and others, to understand the impact of cultural differences in product customization activities.

## 2.4. *Self-construal and post-purchase customization*

Existing studies focus on determining the factors affecting consumer decision in buying motorcycles. Fatihudin and Mochklas (2017) conclude 10 factors having significant influences on consumer decisions in buying motorcycles which are *income*, *motivation*, *family*, *reference group*, *selling price*, *promotion*, *product attribute*, *service*, *experience*, and *location*. Another study specifically for automatic transmission motorcycle product in Ho Chi Minh area (Nguyen, 2012) points out that social value, functional value (price and quality dimensions), and emotional value could explain 52.1% of the variability of consumer's decisions. The basic utilitarian value of a motorcycle is its function of transportation. Interestingly, Freire (2009) argues that social value, not functional value, is the most significant factor that influences consumer's buying decisions of motorcycles in Vietnam. This leads to the argument that in Vietnam, motorcycles are purchased not only because of their utilitarian values.

Lai and Aritejo (2013) identify four factors having significant impacts on Indonesian adolescents' intention to customize a motorcycle, including *need for uniqueness*, *attitude*, *knowledge*, and *support from others* (peers and parents). This supports the argument that the expressiveness value of the motorcycle is sometimes more important than what it does (transporting). Some owners spend a lot of effort to customize the motorcycles to increase the vehicles' values perceived by themselves. Additionally, existing studies identify the effects of self-construal toward benefits of product customization. Atakan *et al.* (2014) argue that self-construal has a significant influence on the experience of product evaluation. Meanwhile, Kim and Drolet (2003) indicate that self-construal also affects how individuals favor uniqueness and self-expression.

In post-purchase personalization, it is likely that the owners have been physically interacting with the product for sometime before they modify it. Unlike mass customization, the involvement of the owner to post-purchase customization process is not limited only to the design phase but also expands to the physical modification process. Process enjoyment can still have a positive effect on the value of customization. Process enjoyment is also expected to affect the value of post-purchase customization. However, Atakan *et al.* (2014) argue that for consumers with independent self-construal, the self-made product is evaluated more favorably only if the process is positive. This is not usually true for consumers with interdependent self-construal, who prefer self-made products no matter whether the process is positive or negative. This suggests that self-construal characteristics can alter the perceived value of process enjoyment. Self-construal can be considered as a metaphorical lens through

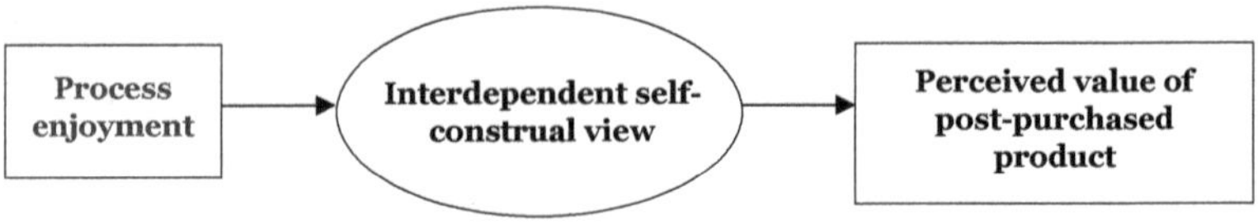


**Figure 2:** Preliminary theoretical framework.

which consumers perceive the process-related value of post-purchase customization (e.g., process enjoyment).

In conclusion, enjoyment is examined as a valuable driver of consumer's willingness to engage in post-purchase personalization. Since this research focuses on the Vietnamese market, these values are proposed to be perceived through the view of the interdependent self-construal lens. This sums up the preliminary theoretical framework of this research, as illustrated in Figure 2.

## 3. Method

### 3.1. *Procedure*

Due to the lack of literature research on consumer's perceived values of post-purchase customization topics, the exploratory approach from the qualitative method is a better fit in this research, for the attempt to study the complete situation and to evaluate the complexity of consumers' perceptions. Face-to-face interview is used to collect primary data for this research. The semi-structured interview is selected for this research for two reasons. First, it allows the researchers to investigate deeper into respondents' perceptions and the opinions towards research problems; new questions can be asked for clarification. Second, it can prevent the interview from wandering away from the main topic and also avoids making the interview too formal where in-depth answers can be cut off (Louise Barriball and While, 1994).

The interview questions cover characteristic, behavioral, and attitudinal aspects. The characteristic questions aim to find out what types of motorcycles the respondents purchase and modify, and what is the intended usages of the vehicles. This information helps to identify the roles of the vehicles in customers' daily lives. The behavioral questions help to understand why respondents decide to customize their motorcycles, what are the details of the modification, and how they perform the modification. The last set of attitudinal questions derives information that describes the participants' feelings and perceptions about the vehicles' customization. The purpose is to derive the values that participants perceive from the customization activities, and how those values can be affected by their self-construal. A cover letter is sent to potential participants together with a consent form. Since Vietnamese is the first language of both interviewer and respondents, all interviews are conducted in Vietnamese. Consent forms and participant information datasheet are also translated into Vietnamese. Participants sign the consent forms prior to each interview and agree that the interview can be recorded. Personal information of each respondent, including name, phone number, and email address, is maintained confidentially.

Considering the limitedness of resources, as well as the intention to learn from the under-studied topic, respondents for this research were purposively recruited using the snowball sampling method. To minimize the risk of violating interviewees' privacy, the researchers define a clear recruitment protocol. At the end of each interview, the interviewees are asked whether they are willing to pass the information about the study they just completed to other potential participants. When it is accepted, the researchers transfer the research information sheet or questionnaire to the originally selected interviewees and they can pass it on to others who are qualified and interested. Then, potential participants contact the researchers if they are willing to join the study.

### 3.2. *Participants*

The target population of the data collection is adults living in Ho Chi Minh City. The geometric location is selected purely based on the convenience for primary data collection since the authors are living in Ho Chi Minh City. Respondents' age is limited between 23 to 39 years. Since the study does not focus on the financial constraint of modification activities, the authors aim to select respondents who have a stable income and sufficient savings to invest in such activities. UNFPA (2016) study suggests that the population above 23 years of age in Vietnam have labor income higher than consumption, in other words, this population can create savings. The upper age limit of 39 years is selected based on a study (Fenech and Perkins, 2015) which suggests that people in the age group of 25–39 years have higher interest in personalized products and services than other age groups (16–24, 40–54 and 55+). The sample size is limited to eight respondents for the qualitative study. As suggested by Cormack (2010), a smaller selective sample is preferred for an in-depth study and data analysis. As the researchers intend to acquire a purposive sample, the interviewees need to meet certain criteria:

- The respondent must own a motorcycle.
- He or she must have modified his/her motorcycle or is doing so. This is to ensure that he/she has relevant exposure to modifications to provide meaningful and reliable information.

Table 2 provides an overview of participants' profiles. All participants have a motorcycle which has been modified from the original version. All participants are employed with a stable income. The selected participants, with secure income and status as middle-class workers, do not express any major concerns about budget constraints. Five out of eight participants are working in creative jobs. This commonality can either result from the snow-ball technique, or it suggests that people who want to customize their motorcycle are usually the creative type of people. Nevertheless, this study does not aim to develop linkages between the participants' occupation background and post-purchase product customization. The question

**Table 2:** Overview about participants' and their motorcycles' profiles.

| Code | Gender | Age | Occupation | Brand | Model Year | Duration of ownership (months) | Customized features |
|---|---|---|---|---|---|---|---|
| **R1** | Male | 30–29 | Video game producer | Suzuki | Grass-tracker Bigboy 250, 2001 | 48 | Tires, handle bar, head light, tail light, signals, mirrors, exhaust system |
| **R2** | Male | 30–39 | Office worker | Kawasaki | W800, 2012 | 24 | Everything except engine, fuel tank, frame, electrical system, braking system |
| **R3** | Male | 23–29 | Office worker | Kawasaki | Z800 ABS, 2016 | 4 | New color, wind shield, exhaust, LED headlight, phone holder with electricity charger, frame slider anti crash protector, bag-holder frame, passenger's back-rest |
| **R4** | Male | 30–39 | Engineer | Honda | CBR250R, 2012 | 60 | Brake lights kits, frame slider anti crash protector, exhaust |
| **R5** | Male | 23–29 | Marketing | Honda | Air Blade, 2015 | 36 | Carburetor, exhaust pipe, wheels and tires |
| **R6** | Male | 30–39 | Event organizer | Vespa | Piaggio PX150E, 1984 | 10 | Suspension system Upgrade kit for US market only |
| **R7** | Male | 23–29 | Interior designer | Honda | GB250, 1997 | 30 | New color, bigger tires, LED head light, smaller turn signal, classical fuel tank, aftermarket clutch lever, fuel filter, higher quality suspension. |
| **R8** | Female | 23–29 | Copywriter | Honda | MSX, 2017 | 18 | Body panel, Decal |

about occupations is mainly to confirm that participants have secure salary resources. The customization level is from slight changes, e.g., changing of color, to major modifications, including headlight, fuel tank, suspension, and crash protector. Only one participant is female, however, gender is not a concerning factor in this study. None of the respondents has performed engine modification; they have neither participated nor had the intention to join any illegal racing activities.

### 3.3. *Research evaluation*

One concern of the research is to ensure the quality and credibility of the qualitative method used in this study in which the following steps have been implemented to reduce systematic bias in the data, and improve the robustness and comprehensiveness of the study.

- **Sample consideration:** Initially, the authors carried out a set of interviews with another group of respondents. However, the results were not good for in-depth analysis. The first group of respondents was randomly selected at the motorcycle customization shops; most of them have limited experience with motorcycle modification. After that, the authors gathered the first set of data and repeated the interviews with the second set of respondents, who were carefully selected using the snowball technique.
- **Study reparation:** The main objectives and points of view of the authors are stated at the beginning of the study and also during the interview process. This is to reduce the effect of researchers' bias during analysis.
- **Multiple sources cross-checking:** The interviews are recorded and transcribed as thoroughly as possible. All notes and observations are put alongside each question or response for comparison. For some specific questions, the authors contacted the respondents after the interview to clarify. These exercises compared observation data and interview data, compared the responses from the interviewee in different conditions, and checked for the consistency in the response.

- **Peer debriefing:** The researchers' college acts as a peer examiner to review and challenges the researchers' rationale and objectives before a study takes place. The researchers frequently contacted the college during fieldwork to discuss issues and concerns during the data collection process.
- **Member checking:** The interview transcripts were sent to selected interviewees for validation. Summary of the findings (main themes and sub-themes) is also shared with interviewees for confirmation.

## 4. Results

The interview transcripts are coded into main themes based on the research objectives and the interview questions. The researchers use highlighters in different colors to mark different themes. Table 3 summarizes the main themes and sub-themes as an overview of the data analysis.

### 4.1. *Enjoyment from social connection enhancement*

A general benefit of being involved in post-purchase motorcycles customization is that the respondents can broaden their social network. Many respondents participate in online or offline social groups whose

**Table 3:** Overview of main-themes and sub-themes from participants' responses.

| Main-theme | Sub-theme | Explanation |
|---|---|---|
| Social interaction | Enjoyment from social connection enhancement | Individuals' social network is expanded when involving in customization activities |
| | Influence of interdependent self-construal | Interdependent view influences the selection of preferences but does not alter the need of being differences or ability to express oneself. |

members share similar interests in motorcycle customization. They acknowledge the benefits of having a forum to share ideas, passion, and experience. One particular group frequently organizes charity events to bring small gifts to less fortunate children in the area.

> "[···] just a small group of motorcycle riders only. [···] It's nice to be involved in the group, I can share my customization ideas, listen to others' opinions and check out their concepts" (R3).
>
> "I joined a club called [···]. It's a good place to share and discuss our bikes. Besides, we raise charity funds to buy things for poor children and use our bikes to bring the gifts to them" (R4).

### 4.2. *Influence of interdependent self-construal*

In an attempt to confirm the interdependent self-construal view of participants, respondents are asked to self-evaluate if they belong to independent self-construal or interdependent self-construal. Technical terms, such as independent, interdependent, self-construal, are not used directly to avoid confusion of participants. Applying Singelis self-construal Scale (Singelis, 1994), researchers are able to confirm all participants who normally have interdependent self-construal. Respondents are more comfortable in avoiding direct arguments, putting group benefits above self-interest, respecting group decisions, and maintaining harmony.

As an interdependent individual, participants are asked how such a view can impact the post-purchase-modification activities. There are several interesting observations. First, the respondents are likely to consider the opinions of those with whom they shared the closest relationships (e.g., girlfriend/boyfriend or husband/wife) about the functionality improvement of the motorcycles. Some respondents place additional modification features to meet their close ones' desires.

> "The back-rest was installed after my wife complained about the uncomfortable feeling when sitting on my bike for our road trip" (R3).

Second, the acceptance or approval from a social group for the modified motorcycles is not relevant. Participants acknowledge that they do not prefer to speak up at work or home in daily matters, which is typical behavior of an interdependent individual. However, they are not afraid to follow their opinions when involved in motorcycle customization.

> "I did it because I liked to, not because I wanted to [···] satisfy other people" (R6).
>
> "If [other people judge] about the appearance of the bike, I wouldn't consider it seriously" (R8).

This observation seems to contradict previous research on culture which concludes that individuals from East Asian cultural contexts prefer conformity instead of standing out or being unique (Kim and Markus, 1999). However, Kim and Drolet (2003) provide another interesting view of this interaction. They suggest that interdependent individuals seek conformity when they are forced to select one concept over another in certain situations. In such case, individuals show a "consistency-seeking tendency" between their choice and interdependent characteristic (Kim and Drolet, 2003). However, in personal activities such as motorcycle modification, the value for conformity and value for uniqueness are not against each other, the participant has the space to behave inconsistently.

Nevertheless, respondents respect inputs from experienced members toward the reliability and functionality of the modified motorcycles. They understand that safety and reliability are important. As long as the inputs do not impact their original concept of modifying the bike, they have no problem to follow.

> "Those guys [professional mechanics] have a lot of experience than me and therefore I am willing to listen to them and to change something if it is critical" (R2).
>
> "[···] as long as it [expert's inputs] does not alter the core style of the concept. [···] if the advice is from the experts [···] I would consider it carefully. [···] those will keep you safe on the road" (R3).

The last observation in this context is in general, participants positively evaluate their motorcycles after modifications. They feel proud and happy with the results, regardless if the modifying experience is positive (the modification is successful) or negative (it turned out not as good as expected).

> "After all, I felt happy [with my customized motorcycle]" (R4).
>
> "Although I had to remove the new exhaust, I'm happy that I've tried" (R8).

This observation is aligned with the conclusion from previous research about the effect of self-construal on the evaluation of self-made products (Atakan *et al.*, 2014). Atakan *et al.* (2014) empirically prove that for people with interdependent self-construal, the involvement in the production process leads to enhanced product evaluation no matter whether the process was positive or negative. This is, however, not true for an independent self-construal individual. If the process experience is negative, the involvement in the creation process will not improve product evaluation for people with independent self-construal (Atakan *et al.*, 2014). Similar behavior is also observed in cross-cultural studies. Markus and Kitayama (1991) suggest that negative self-related information is part of an interdependent individual's sense of self, while it is considered as a threat by those with an independent sense of self. For interdependent individuals, negative self-related information helps them to decide how to modify and construct a sense of self.

## 5. Discussion

This research aims to understand how consumers perceive social values from post-purchase motorcycle customization. The study focuses specifically on the motorcycle customization activities of adults who are between 23 and 39 years of age and living in Ho Chi Minh City. Three specific research questions are investigated in this qualitative research. First, what are the reasons individuals customize their motorcycles after purchase. Second, how the values from this activity

**Table 4:** Summary of findings and supporting literature.

| Findings | | Supporting literature |
|---|---|---|
| Social connection is enhanced | Individuals' social network is expanded when involving in customization activities | New observation |
| | Cooperating with social network groups involves unrelated activity like charity. It is one way to express creative results and encourage poor children in making dreams become true in the future | New observation |
| Interdependent self-construal has influences | Consumer acknowledges the influence of closed member into functional improvement. However, acceptance or approval from relevant social groups toward the modified product are not relevant. | Contradicts with (Kim and Markus, 1999) But aligns with (Kim and Drolet, 2003) |
| | Involvement in the customization process leads to enhanced product evaluation, despite of the process is positive or negative | Atakan *et al.* (2014); Markus and Kitayama (1991) |

are perceived by consumers. Finally, in the context of a collectivist culture, how the interdependent self-construal impacts the perceived values of motorcycle customization activities. The research questions construct the objective of this research, which is to develop a set of motivations and values from post-purchase product customization considering the effect of an interdependent view of self. All findings of this research are summarized in Table 4, including references to existing literature.

Putting the post-purchase product customization into the context of social interactions, it reveals some arguments. First, being involved in motorcycle modification activity helps to broaden an individual's social network. They become more active in engaging in social groups to learn about motorcycles, look for design ideas, and share experiences. Interestingly, participants tend to cooperate with social network groups not only for motorcycle customization but also for unrelated activities such as doing charity. Furthermore, they use their own modified motorcycles to send gifts to poor children. It is considered as one way to express their creative results as well as encourage poor children to work toward making dreams come true in the future.

Additionally, looking through the interdependent self-construal lens, participants acknowledge the influence of close partners on the functional improvement of the motorcycle (e.g., preference fit value). However, the level of acceptance or approval from social groups toward the modified vehicle is not relevant. Individuals prefer to stay with their perceptions of self-expressiveness and uniqueness when customizing their motorcycles. Post-purchase product modification is a personal activity; individuals are not under pressure to ensure their choices confirm their feelings toward other individuals or groups. Finally, the experience of being involved in modification activities leads to a positive feeling toward the modified product, regardless of whether the experience is desirable or undesirable. This is because, for interdependent individuals, negative self-related information is part of the sense of self.

The findings of this study provide a theoretical contribution to the understanding of consumers' value perceptions in post-purchase product customization, specifically in motorcycle products. The involvement of the consumers in the concept development and creation process is much deeper during post-purchase product customization as compared with mass-customization. Nowadays, many products and services give the consumers the choice to personalize them, especially for consumer electronics. Users can perform software modifications (add new applications in a smartphone, for example) or hardware improvements (lens kit upgrade in digital cameras, for example), or service personalizations (using artificial intelligence and machine learning to recognize usage patterns and suggest a new restaurant for dinner, for example). The flexibility and amount of options are infinite in post-purchase product customization. This contributes to the complexity of perceptions and behaviors toward product personalization.

The exploratory findings can also assist the Vietnamese Government, especially the Vietnamese Ministry of Transport, to recognize the valid needs of individuals to have opportunities to participate in vehicle modification. Government authorities can re-consider the current regulations and laws to conditionally support this demand. Besides, this research has a practical contribution for vehicle manufactures. A value-added feature that manufacturers can consider is the feasibility of the products' being further enhanced by post-purchase customization. A motorcycle that can be easily personalized at the end-user stage can appear to be more attractive to consumers. This feature can positively affect consumer purchase decisions. Accessory manufacturers and custom shops can also benefit from this study. For example, by understanding that process enjoyment is an important perceived value, a custom shop can consider modifying the tool shop to allow more involvement from the vehicles' owners during customizing process. The researchers believe these benefits are not only limited to motorcycles but can also be extended to other types of products and services.

There are many recommendations for future research to enhance the understanding of this interesting topic. First, the parameters from the authors' exploratory findings should be tested empirically to generalize the contribution of the result on broader samples or different types of products (e.g., cars and bicycles). Second, the consequences of the interactions of each parameter onto each other are also interesting subjects for study. For example, how consumers' perceived preference fit correlates with process enjoyment toward the likelihood of the decision to perform the modification. In another example, it can be interesting to understand if there is any negative correlation between uniqueness and functional preferences, a too unique product can lead to a reduction in its usage convenience. Third, it is beneficial to understand the impact of boundary conditions, such as budget or knowledge constraints, toward the perceived values of customization. Any customization feature requires a certain amount of time, effort, and financial resources. This can limit the consumer's desired features. Consumer knowledge on technical features of the product can also affect the customization process. They possibly have to rely more on mechanics or prefer to rely on their knowledge to decide to customize. Fourth, the process of consumers' decision-making throughout post-purchase customization needs to be further examined. It is interesting to understand when, why, and how consumers choose to start or to abort customization. It is beneficial to understand the negative outcomes to limit the undesirable overwhelming feeling when involved in the modification process. Consumers should feel "loyalty" toward the customization process, so they might repeat it with other products or services. This can help to further enhance consumers' experiences and providers' benefits. Lastly, the influence of self-construal on customization should be further explored. For example, it is interesting to understand whether there are differences between genders' perceptions and age groups' opinions toward perceived values of customization. This can help shed light on why product customization is more preferable in certain countries/groups than others.

## Acknowledgments

The authors are most grateful to two reviewers for very helpful comments and suggestions.

## References

Atakan, S.S., Bagozzi, R.P., and Yoon, C. (2014). Make it your own: How process valence and self-construal affect evaluation of self-made products. *Psychology and Marketing*, 31(6), 451–468. https://doi.org/10.1002/mar.20707

Blom, J. (2000). Personalization — A taxonomy. Extended abstracts of the CHI 2000 conference on human factors in computing systems, 1–6 April. The Hague, The Netherlands. NewYork: ACM.

Blom, J.O., and Monk, A.F., (2003). Theory of personalization of appearance: Why users personalize their PCs and mobile phones.

*Human–Computer Interaction*, 18(3), 193–228. https://doi.org/10.1207/S15327-051HCI1803_1

Cohen, A. (2009). Dek inter and the "other": Thai youth subcultures in urban Chiang Mai. Sojourn. https://doi.org/10.1355/SJ24-2A

Cooper, R. (1999). *Winning at New Products*, 2nd edition. Manchester: Perseus Books.

Cormack, D.F.S. (2010). *The Research Process in Nursing*, 4th edition. Oxford: Blackwell Sciences Ltd.

Cross, S.E., Hardin, E.E., and Gercek-Swing, B. (2011). The what, how, why, and where of self-construal. *Personality and Social Psychology Review*, 15(2), 142–179. https://doi.org/10.1177/1088868310373752

Dellaert, B.G.C., and Stremersch, S. (2005). Marketing mass-customized products: Striking a balance between utility and complexity. *Journal of Marketing Research*, 42(2), 219–227. https://doi.org/10.1509/jmkr.42.2.219.62293

EuroCham. (2018). EuroCham Whitebook 2018. Accessed April 18, 2018. https://www.eurochamvn.org/Whitebook

Fatihudin, D., and Mochklas, M. (2017). Analysis of factors affecting consumer decisions buy motorcycle (study on city of Surabaya Indonesia). *International Journal of Innovative Research and Development*, 6(6), 107–118. https://doi.org/10.24940/ijird/2017/v6/i6/jun17074

Fenech, C., and Perkins, B. (2015). The Deloitte consumer review made-to-order: The rise of mass personalisation. *Deloitte Development LLC*, 1–20. https://doi.org/035102\delimiter"026E30Fr10.1103/PhysRevB.75.035102

Fralix, M.T. (2001). From mass production to mass customization. *Journal of Textile and Apparel, Technology and Management*, 1(2), 1–7. https://doi.org/10.3850/9789628014194_0079

Franke, N., Keinz, P., and Steger. C.J. (2009). Testing the value of Customization: When do customers really prefer products tailored to their preferences? *Journal of Marketing*, 73(5), 103–121. https://doi.org/10.1509/jmkg.73.5.103

Franke, N., and Schreier, M. (2010). Why customers value self-designed products: The importance of process effort and enjoyment. *Journal of Product Innovation Management*, 27(7), 1020–1031. https://doi.org/10.1111/j.1540-5885.2010.00768.x

Franke, N., Schreier, M., and Kaiser. U. (2010). The "I designed it myself" effect in mass customization. *Management Science*, 56(1), 125–140. https://doi.org/10.1287/mnsc.1090.1077

Freire, A.D. (2009). Motorbikes against Ho Chi Minh? Or the consumption icons of a social transformation in Vietnam. Copenhagen *Journal of Asian Studies*, 27(1), 67–87. https://doi.org/10.22439/cjas.v27i1.1693

Goldberger, N., and Veroff, J. (1995). *The Culture and Psychology Reader.* New York: New York University Press.

Gouveia, V.V., and Ros, M. (2000). Hofstede and Schwartz's models for classifying individualism at the cultural level: Their relation to macro-social and macro-economic variables. *Psicothema.*

Heine, S.J. (2001). Self as cultural product: An Examination of East Asian and North American Selves. *Journal of Personality*, 69(6), 881–905. https://doi.org/10.1111/1467-6494.696168

Heskett, J. (1980). *Industrial Design.* London: Thames and Hudson.

Hofstede, G. (1993). Cultural constraints in management theories. *Academy of Management Perspectives.* https://doi.org/10.5465/ame.1993.9409142061

Hofstede, G. (1984). *Culture's Consequences: International Differences in Work-Related Values.* USA: Sage.

Hsu, T.-P., Mohd Sadullah, A.F., and Nguyen. X.D. (2003). A comparison study on motorcycle traffic development in some Asian countries — Case of Taiwan, Malaysia and Vietnam. In *The Eastern Asia Society for Transportation Studies (EASTS) International Cooperative Research Activity.*

Kim, H., and Markus, H.R. (1999). Deviance or uniqueness, harmony or conformity? A cultural analysis. *Journal of Personality and Social Psychology*, 77(4), 785. https://doi.org/10.1037/0022-3514.77.4.785

Kim, H.S., and Drolet, A. (2003). Choice and self-expression: A cultural analysis of variety-seeking. *Journal of Personality and Social Psychology*, 85(2), 373. https://doi.org/10.1037/0022-3514.85.2.373

Lai, M.K., and Aritejo, B.A. (2013). Personal and social factors affecting adolescent motorcycle riders' intention to customize their vehicles: Evidence from Indonesia. *Transportation Research Part F: Traffic Psychology and Behaviour*, 20, 6–16. https://doi.org/10.1016/j.trf.2013.04.001

Louise, B.K., and While, A. (1994). Collecting data using a semi-structured interview: A discussion paper. *Journal of Advanced Nursing*, 19(2), 328–335. https://doi.org/10.1111/j.1365-2648.1994.tb01088.x

Markus, H.R., and Kitayama, S. (1991). Culture and the self: Implications for cognition, emotion, and motivation. *Psychological Review*, 98(2), 224. https://doi.org/10.1037/0033-295X.98.2.224

Merle, A., Chandon, J.L., Roux, E., and Alizon, F. (2010). Perceived value of the mass-customized product and mass customization experience for individual consumers. *Production and Operations Management*, 19(5), 503–514. https://doi.org/10.1111/j.1937-5956.2010.01131.x

Mugge, R., Schoormans, J.P.L., and Schiffersteinb, H.N.J. (2009). Emotional Bonding with Personalised Products. *Journal of Engineering Design*, 20(5), 467–476. https://doi.org/10.1080/09544820802698550

Nguyen, L. (2012). Study about factors impact buying decisions of Ho Chi Minh citizen. Master Thesis. University of Economics Ho Chi Minh City.

Overby, J.W., Woodruff, R.B., and Gardial, S.F. (2005). The influence of culture upon consumers' desired value perceptions: A research agenda. *Marketing Theory*, 5(2), 139–163. https://doi.org/10.1177/1470593105052468

Parks, C.D., and Vu, A.D. (1994). Social dilemma behavior of individuals from highly individualist and collectivist cultures. *Journal of Conflict Resolution*, 38(4), 708–718. https://doi.org/10.1177/0022002794038004006

Patterson, P.G. (1997). Modeling the Determinants of Customer Satisfaction for Business-to-Business Professional Services. *Journal of the Academy of Marketing Science*, 25(1), 4–17. https://doi.org/10.1007/BF02894505

Pine, B. (1993). *Mass Customization: The New Frontiers in Business Competition*, 1st edition. Boston: Harvard Business School Press.

Pine, B., Victor, B., and Boynton, A. (1993). Making mass customization work. *Harvard Business Review*. Accessed April 2, 2018. https://hbr.org/1993/09/making-mass-customization-work

Santos, H.C., Varnum, M.E.W., and Grossmann, I. (2017). Global increases in individualism. *Psychological Science*, 28(9), 1228–1239. https://doi.org/10.1177/0956797617700622

Schouten, J.W., and McAlexander, J.H. (1995). Subcultures of consumption: An ethnography of the new bikers. *Journal of Consumer Research*, 22(1), 43–61. https://doi.org/10.1086/209434

Schreier, M. (2006). The value increment of mass-customized products: An empirical assessment. *Journal of Consumer Behaviour*, 5(4), 317–327. https://doi.org/10.1002/cb.183

Schwartz, S.H. (2006). A theory of cultural value orientations: Explication and applications. *Comparative Sociology*, 5(5–3), 137–182. https://doi.org/10.1163/156913306778667357

Singelis, T.M. 1994. The measurement of independent and interdependent self-construals. *Personality and Social Psychology Bulletin*, 20(5), 580–591. https://doi.org/10.1177/0146167294205014

Hsu, T.P., Dao, N.X., and Sadullah, A.F.M. (2003). A comparative study on motorcycle traffic development of Taiwan, Malaysia and Vietnam. *Journal of Eastern Asia Society for Transportation Studies*, 5, 179–193.

Triandis, H.C. (1989). The self and social behavior in differing cultural contexts. *Psychological Review*, 96(3), 506. https://doi.org/10.1037/0033-295X.96.3.506

Usunier, J., and Lee, J. (2013). *Marketing Across Cultures*. Harlow: Pearson.

UNFPA. (2016). Impact of changes in population age structure on Viet Nam's economic growth and policy recommendations. Hanoi: United Nations Population Fund.

Vickrey, W. (1961). Counterspeculation, auctions, and competitive sealed tenders. *The Journal of Finance*, 16(1), 8–37. https://doi.org/10.1111/j.1540-6261.1961.tb02789.x

Wang, N., Piller, F.T., and Wang, K. (2018). An exploratory study of user interaction with smart products for customization in the usage stage. In *Customization*, 4.0, 37–53. Springer, Cham. https://doi.org/10.1007/978-3-319-77556-2_3

Wilson, D.T. (2003). Value exchange as the foundation stone of relationship marketing. *Marketing Theory*, 3(3), 175–177. https://doi.org/10.1177/1470593103003001012

Part VI

# Economic Development

https://doi.org/10.1142/9789811227158_0023

Chapter 23

# How is Smartphone Advertising Important for Consumers' Purchase Intention in an Emerging Economy? Evidence from Vietnam

Dang Khoa Tran

## Abstract

This study is conducted to identify how smartphone advertising influences consumers' purchase intention in Vietnam — an emerging economy — compared with other studies' findings in developed economies. Ducoffe's model and flow experience theory are used to answer the following questions: What are the factors that impact advertising value and flow experience? How do advertising value and flow experience affect the customer's purchase intention? Qualitative and quantitative mixed research methods are used to accomplish the research objectives. Qualitative research aims to adjust the scale of constructs to suit the Vietnamese market and explain the research results through face-to-face discussions with 20 Vietnamese consumers (10 face-to-face discussions to adjust the scale of constructs and 10 face-to-face discussions to explain the research results). A survey is then carried out with 263 Vietnamese consumers. Data collected are processed by Smart PLS software with partial least squares structural equation modeling (PLS-SEM). Research results show that smartphone advertising in Vietnam — an emerging economy — has much weaker influence compared with those in developed economies. Incentives are the strongest positive factor, followed by entertainment and informativeness which influence advertising value to varying extents, while credibility influences advertising value very weakly and not significantly. Informativeness is the strongest positive influence factor, followed by incentives, credibility, entertainment, and advertising value, which influence flow experience, but irritation is not a statistically significant impact of flow experience.

Purchase intention is positively influenced by both advertising value and flow experience, however, advertising value has a stronger influence on purchase intention than flow experience does. The practical implication is that marketers and advertisers can refer to those results to plan suitable marketing strategies for the Vietnamese market and other emerging economies.

**Keywords:** Advertising value; Consumers' purchase intention; Flow experience; Smartphone advertising.

## 1. Introduction

The number of smartphone users increases significantly in Vietnam everyday. According to Nielsen Vietnam (2017), the proportion of smartphone users in Vietnam is about 72%. Vietnamese people have high online media consumption and mobile gaming habits. About 69% of Vietnamese people watch video clips and listen to music on their phones. Vietnamese people use the smartphone to access social networks (89% of daily behaviors) and watch videos (79% of weekly behaviors). The "golden hour" of a smartphone in Vietnam is between 9–11 am and 7–9 pm. This is the time during and after a Vietnamese meal and it is the time for them to talk with family/ friends on social media. Besides, 25% of Vietnamese smartphone owners use the Internet on mobile regularly to perform different tasks and services, which makes mobile phone not only a tool for communication but also for entertainment and work purposes. Mobile phones imply a list of the most intimate things for Vietnamese people because most Vietnamese people check their phones as soon as they wake up, and continue using it for an average of 2 h a day. Besides, 82% of Vietnamese people are willing to give away their personal information in exchange for free gifts. Brands reach users with ads, gifts, or items via the mobile application. About 75% of Vietnamese people spend 15 min on a phone after waking up, and only 7% of people do not use it until after 2 h since waking up. For e-commerce, 72% of all e-commerce site visits come from smartphones. 53% of online purchases are made by phones. Therefore, advertising on smartphone in Vietnam is important. The growth of the smartphone is a solid foundation for Digital Advertising campaigns in Southeast Asia (Nielsen Vietnam, 2018).

There are some studies around the world that investigate how antecedents of advertising value and flow experience on mobile advertising affect customers' decisions (Ducoffe, 1996; Brakett and Carr, 2001; Gao *et al.*, 2015; Hsu *et al.*, 2017; Kim and Han, 2014; Martins *et al.*, 2019). But in general, most of those are conducted in developed countries with different situations compared with Vietnam — an emerging economy. Therefore, the results of those are likely different from Vietnam because of culture, society, scientific, and technological levels.

This study aims to explore factors affecting Vietnamese customers' purchase intention after they watch advertisements on their smartphone. Ducoffe's model and flow experience theory are used to answer the following research questions:

What are the factors that impact the advertising value and flow experience?

How do advertising value and flow experience affect the customer's purchase intention?

This research's results are useful for marketers and advertisers to understand important issues when using smartphone advertising in Vietnam. First, this study provides knowledge and insights into how smartphone advertising affects customers' purchase intention. Second, advertisers learn factors they should pay attention to so as to make smartphone advertising more efficient. Third, marketers can form guidelines from this study to plan their smartphone advertising strategy in Vietnam.

## 2. Theoretical Background

### 2.1. *Mobile advertising and smartphone advertising*

According to The Mobile Marketing Association, mobile advertising is a series of activities that allow organizations to communicate and engage customers in an interactive way through mobile devices or networks (Chen and Hsieh, 2012). The development of information technology and telecommunication networks today increases mobile advertising via phones and other mobile devices, manifested in such forms as: mobile web advertising, SMS, multimedia messages, mobile movies, and mobile application software. Grewal *et al.* (2016) suggest that mobile advertising allows retailers, service providers, and manufacturers to provide consumers with increasingly relevant incentives. Such successful mobile advertising campaigns depend on a good understanding of the variables of the business environment, consumers, and technology contexts; high focus on advertising goals; bookkeeping for market elements that are intrinsically relevant to the interested parties and the economic environment; and appropriate mobile advertising formats to augment relevant results.

Smartphones are different from other traditional mobile phones because they have an operating system and can connect to the Internet. Smartphones are increasingly popular as a mobile computer because they are installed with application software, so the users can entertain, study, and work with a smartphone besides using it for communication. Normally, smartphone users access social networking, audio, video calling, messaging functions, check and reply emails, play games, watch movies, listen to music, and many other exploited functions which depend on the application software. Hsu and Lin (2015) notice an increasing number of smartphones being used, which can spur the use of mobile application programs. In addition, Kim and Han (2014) point out that smartphone advertising plays an increasingly important role in purchasing decisions.

### 2.2. *Advertising value*

Ducoffe (1995) argues that advertising value is the value of advertising that consumers perceive. In other words, the advertising value is the benefit or value that can be gained from an advertisement. The advertising value expressed by Ducoffe on its web advertising model is clearer. Ducoffe (1995) provides a model of advertising value that has informativeness, entertainment, and irritation as factors that influence advertising value. Ducoffe's web advertising model demonstrates a web advertising evaluation method that focuses on advertising value rather than the attitude towards an advertisement. An ad that makes consumers react negatively and backfires is a worthless ad. In contrast, a high value ad brings a positive response and a good attitude towards the ad. In other words, the value of advertising positively affects the attitude towards advertising by consumers.

Ducoffe (1996) emphasizes the value of advertising, which refers to a subjective assessment of the relative value or utility of advertising to consumers. Besides, the author also argues that the antecedent of advertising value are the factors such as informativeness, entertainment, and irritation. Ducoffe's web advertising model shows that advertising value is positively impacted by entertainment and informativeness. Advertising value is negatively affected by advertising irritation. From the perspective of consumers, Ducoffe and Curlo (2010) believe that advertising value is the value consumers receive through two-way information exchange between recipients and senders of advertisements. The advertiser wants interest in the ad and the recipient wants something positive from the ad. Advertising value is related to the question: "What do I expect to receive from advertising?" Ducoffe (1996) suggests that advertising value is evaluated by users through the perception of informativeness, entertainment, and irritation of advertising. Subsequently, a study by Brakett and Carr (2001) suggests that advertising value is assessed by consumers through informativeness, entertainment, irritation, and credibility values. Studies by Kim and Han (2014) and Martins *et al.* (2019) suggest that advertising value is influenced by informativeness, entertainment, irritation, credibility, and the incentives of advertising. So, advertising value can be considered as the value perceived by informativeness, entertainment, irritation, credibility, and incentives that advertising brings.

## 2.3. *Flow experience theory*

The flow theory is a theory of intrinsic motivation developed in the positive psychology model introduced by Csikszentmihalyi (1975).

The theory states that humans have certain basic motivations that affect their behavior. For example, a person can quickly learn that they are rewarded for doing one thing or punished for doing something else. According to Csikszentmihalyi (1975), flow is a psychological state in which an individual perceives himself to be effective, motivated, and happy.

A flow occurs in an individual's mentality when activities are challenging enough to encourage interest, discovery, and not be beyond the individual's ability (Csikszentmihalyi, 1975). If the challenges are beyond the reach of some individual ability, they can have an excessive anxiety response instead of a flow. Conversely, if the challenges are below the individual's ability, this creates boredom and no flow occurs. Csikszentmihalyi (1975) suggests that flow is measured by the following four factors: control, attention focus, curiosity, and intrinsic interest.

Flow experience, referred by Csikszentmihalyi (1975) in the flow theory, describes a person experiencing a complete immersion when they engage in a certain activity wholeheartedly. Individuals become engrossed in their activity in a state of flow and focus on the activity itself. Whatever the experience, it can be reflected in the mind as information. Individuals can feel in control of their environment and circumstances (Csikszentmihalyi, 1975). Flow experience is thought to encourage exploration behaviors (Csikszentmihalyi, 1975). When consumers receive ads on smartphones, the excitement and attractiveness of the ad content can make them feel excited and expect to experience it again (Kim and Han, 2014). Flow experience attracts consumers and significantly influences the attitude and subsequent usage behavior. Hsu *et al.* (2017) show that the flow experience has a positive impact on purchasing intent, or in other words, the buying decisions of consumers are positively affected by the flow experience.

Flow theory is widely used in many fields. Novak and Hoffman (2009) apply the flow theory to the study of web user behavior and online gaming; while Kim and Han (2014), Hsu *et al.* (2017), and Martins *et al.* (2019) apply flow theory to customer behaviors.

### 2.4. *Purchase intention*

Purchase intention is an expression of the likelihood that consumers may plan or be willing to purchase a product or service in the future (Wu *et al.*, 2011). When a consumer has a good attitude toward a product or service, it increases his buying intention (Ko *et al.*, 2005). As consumers' buying intention increases, the chances of selling products or services of the business also increase.

With increasingly fierce competition, consumers have more choices about products and services. Therefore, the impact on the consumers' purchase intention is one of the important concerns of businesses. Kim and Ko (2012) point out that the purchase intention is a combination of consumer interest and the ability to buy a product or service, which also shows attitudes and preferences for a brand or a product. Kim and Han (2014) study the relationship between perceived advertising value and purchase intention. Martins *et al.* (2019) also identify advertising values that positively impact purchasing intention. Advertising value and experience flow both influence consumers' purchasing intention (Martins *et al.*, 2019; Kim and Han, 2014).

## 3. Hypotheses and Conceptual Model

### 3.1. *Factors affecting advertising value*

Advertising value is an assessment of how customers perceive advertising (Ducoffe, 1995). When consumers evaluate advertising value positively, their attitude towards the product or service becomes positive. Ducoffe (1996) determines that advertising values are influenced by factors belonging to sensory perception and emotional attributes. In particular, the perception of rational thinking is informativeness and the emotional factors are entertainment and irritation. Customers enjoy watching an ad that contains fun and humor, and they also want to receive detailed information about the product or service. Besides, customers want to avoid boring and annoying advertisements. As such, the advertising value is evaluated by consumers through the following antecedents: informativeness, entertainment, and irritation that mobile advertising brings to customers (Ducoffe, 1996). According to Brakett and Carr (2001), besides factors affecting advertising value such as informativeness, entertainment, and irritation, advertising value is also affected by the credibility of advertising yield. Consumers will have more reliable reviews if they receive ads from reputable manufacturers or brands. According to Kim and Han (2014), the antecedents for evaluating advertising value include perceptions of informativeness and credibility; emotional factors are entertainment and irritation; economic factor is the incentives of advertising.

Based on the aforementioned studies, it can be assumed that advertising value is influenced by the informativeness, entertainment, irritation, credibility, and incentives of advertising (Ducoffe, 1995, 1996; Brakett and Carr, 2001; Liu *et al.*, 2012; Kim and Han, 2014; Martins *et al.*, 2019). The study of the factors affecting advertising value is shown in Table 1.

### 3.2. *Factors affecting flow experience*

Flow is referred to as a psychological state in which individuals have an effective awareness, motivation, and happiness (Csikszentmihalyi, 1975). Because the psychological flow occurs when an individual is facing a challenging activity, that person's awareness is aroused by curiosity, motivated to perform the challenging activity, to breakthrough to overcome this challenge, and achieve a sense of intrinsic interest. The four factors that occur when flow occurs are control, attention, curiosity, and intrinsic interest (Csikszentmihalyi, 1975). Besides, the activities of someone who experiences flow can constitute informativeness in his or her mind. Flow experience is described as a person in a state of complete immersion as they engage in a certain activity wholeheartedly (Csikszentmihalyi, 1975). Understanding this, marketers and advertisers seek to influence the flow of viewers' experiences to give viewers an effective awareness of advertising, thereby affecting their purchasing intention (Martins *et al.*, 2019). Hoffman and Novak (1996) suggest that when focusing on

**Table 1:** Factors affecting advertising value.

| No. | References | Factors affecting advertising value | | | | |
|---|---|---|---|---|---|---|
| | | **Informativeness** | **Entertainment** | **Irritation** | **Credibility** | **Incentives** |
| 1 | Ducoffe (1995) | x | x | x | | |
| 2 | Ducoffe (1996) | x | x | x | | |
| 3 | Ducoffe and Curlo (2010) | x | x | x | | |
| 4 | Brakett and Carr (2001) | x | x | x | x | |
| 5 | Liu *et al.* (2012) | x | | x | x | |
| 6 | Kim and Han (2014) | x | x | x | x | x |
| 7 | Martins *et al.* (2019) | x | x | x | x | x |

certain advertising content, people tend to forget that time and rational thoughts cannot be ignored. This proves that flow experience through advertising is influenced by entertainment content. Gao *et al.* (2015) explore the intention to continue buying on mobile devices in China, and find that informativeness affects flow experience. Rodriguez Ardura and Meseguer Artola (2018) in the study of mobile Facebook (m-Facebook) experience said that the "memorable presence" created by the credibility of something can imprint on Facebook users' minds, and impact their flow experience. Kim and Han (2014) in the study of why advertising via smartphones attract customers in Korea prove that flow experience is affected by entertainment, irritation, incentives, credibility, and advertising value. Martins *et al.* (2019) analyze smartphone advertising's influences on purchase intention in Portugal, determining that entertainment, irritation, incentives, credibility, and advertising value impact the flow experience.

In conclusion, it can be confirmed that factors that influence flow experience in a mobile advertising environment include informativeness, credibility, entertainment, irritation, incentives, and advertising value (Kim and Han, 2014; Gao *et al.*, 2015; Martins *et al.*, 2019). The study of the factors affecting the flow experience is shown in Table 2.

## 3.3. *Hypotheses*

### 3.3.1. *The relationship between informativeness and advertising value*

Ducoffe (1996) argues that informativeness — from a consumer perspective — is the ability of advertisements to inform consumers about product alternatives to ensure the greatest satisfaction for customers when they purchase goods or services. Martins *et al.* (2019) describe informativeness as the ability of an ad to inform consumers about the types of products and services. According to Gao *et al.* (2015), consumers want to use mobile websites to search for product information and buy products or services anytime, anywhere.

**Table 2:** Factors affecting flow experience.

| | Factors affecting flow experience | | | | | |
|---|---|---|---|---|---|---|
| **References** | **Informativeness** | **Entertainment** | **Irritation** | **Credibility** | **Incentives** | **Advertising value** |
| Gao *et al.* (2015) | x | | | | | |
| Rodríguez Ardura and Meseguer Artola (2018) | | | | x | | |
| Hsu *et al.* (2017) | x | | | | | |
| Hoffman and Novak (1996) | | x | | | | |
| Kim and Han (2014) | x | x | x | x | x | x |
| Martins *et al* (2019) | x | x | x | x | x | x |

With the help of technology, consumers increasingly access information about certain products or services quickly and conveniently. The information is updated and changed over time.

Ducoffe (1996) shows that information positively affects advertising value. In addition, according to Brakett and Carr (2001), web advertising will replace TV advertising as the most valuable source of informativeness in the future. At the same time, it is also confirmed that informativeness has a positive influence on advertising value. According to Kim and Han (2014), the informativeness in smartphone message content has a positive effect on advertising value.

**Hypothesis H1a:** *Perceived informativeness of smartphone advertisements can positively impact perceived advertising value.*

### 3.3.2. *The relationship between credibility and advertising value*

Advertising credibility is consumer's perception of advertising honesty and trustworthiness (MacKenzie and Lutz, 1989). According to Wang and Sun (2010), credibility is believed to influence attitudes to online advertising. When consumers believe that online advertising is trusted and trustworthy, they tend to be positive about online advertising. According to Aydogan *et al.* (2016), advertising credibility relates to consumers' perceptions of correctness and trust, so the credibility of advertising is directly related to advertising performance.

According to MacKenzie and Lutz (1989), an ad with high fidelity and trustworthiness increases the credibility of advertising. Credibility positively influences advertising value and increases consumer attitudes to advertising (Brakett and Carr, 2001). According to Wang and Sun (2010), the credibility of advertising increases a positive consumer attitude towards online advertising. According to Martins *et al.* (2019), credibility has a positive effect on advertising value in the mobile advertising environment.

**Hypothesis H2a:** *Perceived credibility of smartphone advertisements can positively impact perceived advertising value.*

### 3.3.3. *The relationship between entertainment and advertising value*

Entertainment brings relaxation to viewers. An attractive and popular ad has a positive impact on the attitude to a brand. The entertainment of advertising is expressed in attractiveness and inspires interesting feelings in the viewers as a result of which they pay attention to the advertising (Ducoffe, 1995). A highly entertaining ad has a positive impact on the advertising value and consumer attitude toward web advertising (Ducoffe, 1996). According to research by Kim and Han (2014), in the mobile advertising environment of smartphones, the entertainment factor of advertising has a positive impact on advertising value.

**Hypothesis H3a:** *Perceived entertainment of smartphone advertisements can positively impact perceived advertising value.*

### 3.3.4. *The relationship between irritation and advertising value*

Irritation is a reflection of the techniques used by advertisers that cause annoyance, discomfort, insult, and manipulation of ad viewers (Martins *et al.*, 2019). Receiving advertising messages is sometimes very annoying to consumers. When an advertisement is offensive or outrageous, the consumers are affected in an unpleasant and almost undesirable manner (Ducoffe, 1996). The more annoying an advertisement, the lower its value (Ducoffe, 1996; Brakett and Carr, 2001).

Customers are sometimes annoyed by advertising messages, therefore, almost no one wants to receive them (Martins *et al.*, 2019). According to Ducoffe (1996) and Liu *et al.* (2012), irritation has a negative impact on the advertising value, especially on the web. Based on these insights, the following hypothesis is offered.

**Hypothesis H4a:** *Perceived irritation of smartphone advertisements can negatively impact perceived advertising value.*

### 3.3.5. *The relationship between incentives and advertising value*

Incentives in advertising are interpreted as viewing a prize-winning ad for which the reward is the economic benefit received such as a coupon, prize, or gift (Varnali *et al.*, 2012). Customers focus on messages that have incentives or financial benefits (Hoffman and Novak, 1996). When customers receive a discount message via smartphone, they have the tendency to read and find ways to make the most of the offer (Kim and Han, 2014).

According to Tsang *et al.* (2004), benefits such as gifts and discount coupons offered to receive ads on mobile devices can affect consumers' intentions to receive ads on mobile devices or not, especially consumers who have agreed to receive ads before. According to Kim and Han (2014), the economic benefits of advertising that consumers receive have a positive impact on the advertising value in the mobile advertising environment. In addition, Martins *et al.* (2019) show that advertising values are influenced by the incentives of advertisements on smartphones.

**Hypothesis H5a:** *Perceived incentives of smartphone advertisements can positively impact perceived advertising value.*

### 3.3.6. *The relationship between informativeness and flow experience*

According to Kim and Han (2014), informativeness is a cognitive factor that impacts customer attention as soon as customers receive information that is appropriate to their needs. According to Hoffman and Novak (1996), consumers pay close attention to, and do not want to miss, product information. In a study explaining the intention to continue buying on mobile devices in China, Gao *et al.* (2015) indicate that there is a positive relationship between informativeness and user experience.

**Hypothesis H1b:** *Perceived informativeness of smartphone advertisements can positively impact flow experience.*

### 3.3.7. *The relationship between credibility and flow experience*

Mobile advertising is increasingly developed with technology so that users get more and more information when using mobile devices. Consumers may have certain doubts before they receive any information through the advertisements, so the credibility or reputation of the advertising source is one of the criteria for consumers to consider trusting mobile advertising. According to Kim and Han (2014), consumers have a positive perception of mobile advertising via a smartphone when it has a certain credibility. According to Martins *et al.* (2019), credibility has a positive impact on the flow experience in mobile advertising.

**Hypothesis H2b:** *Perceived credibility of smartphone advertisements can positively impact flow experience.*

### 3.3.8. *The relationship between entertainment and flow experience*

The entertainment of an advertisement can trigger emotional factors that affect consumers (Kim and Han, 2014). The more entertaining the ad is, the more attracted the consumer feels and the sense of time passes very quickly, too. Consumers' minds and rational perceptions are ignored (Hoffman and Novak, 1996). According to Martins *et al.* (2019), the advertising entertainment has a positive impact on flow experience in the mobile advertising environment via smartphones.

**Hypothesis H3b:** *Perceived entertainment of smartphone advertisements can positively impact flow experience.*

### 3.3.9. *The relationship between irritation and flow experience*

The irritation caused by advertisements triggers emotions, too, but contrary to the entertainment of the ad. An irritating ad causes discomfort and impatience in the viewer (Ducoffe, 1995). According to Kim and Han (2014), the higher the level of irritation of a mobile advertisement, the more negative the consumers become toward that advertisement. According to Martins *et al.*, (2019), the irritation of mobile advertising has a negative impact on the flow experience.

**Hypothesis H4b:** *Perceived irritation of smartphone advertisements can negatively impact flow experience.*

### 3.3.10. *The relationship between incentives and flow experience*

Taking into account economic benefits, consumers try to find ways to gain incentives and discounts when receiving promotional messages via smartphones (Kim and Han, 2014). From that, it can be said that consumers pay attention to the benefits through mobile advertising, with the ambition to find ways to achieve these incentives and economic benefits. According to Martins *et al.* (2019), the incentives of mobile advertising via smartphones have a positive effect on the flow experience.

**Hypothesis H5a:** *Perceived incentives of smartphone advertisements can positively impact flow experience.*

### 3.3.11. *The relationship between advertising value and flow experience*

Advertising value is a measure of the effectiveness of advertising (Ducoffe, 1995). Experiencing or focusing on advertising that includes informativeness, credibility, entertainment, irritation, and incentives of an advertisement is an indication of the influence of flow experience. According to Kim and Han (2014), consumers focus on valuable advertisements such as advertisements that have appropriate information for their needs, immerse in advertisements that are entertaining and make them forgetful of the passing of time, or focus on finding ways to achieve the preferential economic benefits of texting via smartphones. According to Martins *et al.* (2019), advertising value has a positive impact on the flow experience in the mobile advertising environment.

**Hypothesis H6:** *Perceived advertising value of smartphone advertisements can positively impact flow experience.*

### 3.3.12. *The relationship between advertising value and customers' purchase intention*

According to Kim and Han (2014), the higher the value of mobile advertising through smartphones, the more the increase in consumers' purchase intentions. As Martins *et al.* (2019) studied how smartphone advertising influences consumer purchasing intention, they also learned that the advertising value of smartphone advertisements has a positive impact on consumers' purchase intentions.

**Hypothesis H7:** *Perceived advertising value of smartphone advertisements can positively impact consumers' purchase intentions.*

### 3.3.13. *The relationship between flow experience and customers' purchase intentions*

According to the research of Hsu and Lu (2004) on why people like to play online games, the flow of experience is proved to affect the intention to play online games. According to Hsu *et al.* (2017), social network users who have a positive experience of personal computers and the Internet can form a flow experience, meaning that they have a positive psychological experience, which helps them sink more immersively in such user activities. Consequently, the flow experience leads them to a higher intention to buy online on social networks. According to Kim and Han (2014) and Martins *et al.* (2019), the flow experience has a positive impact on purchase intention in the mobile advertising environment.

**Hypothesis H8:** *Flow experience of smartphone advertisements can positively impact consumers' purchase intentions.*

According to the aforementioned hypotheses (H1 to H8), the conceptual model is as shown in Figure 1.

Quantitative and qualitative mixed research methods are used.

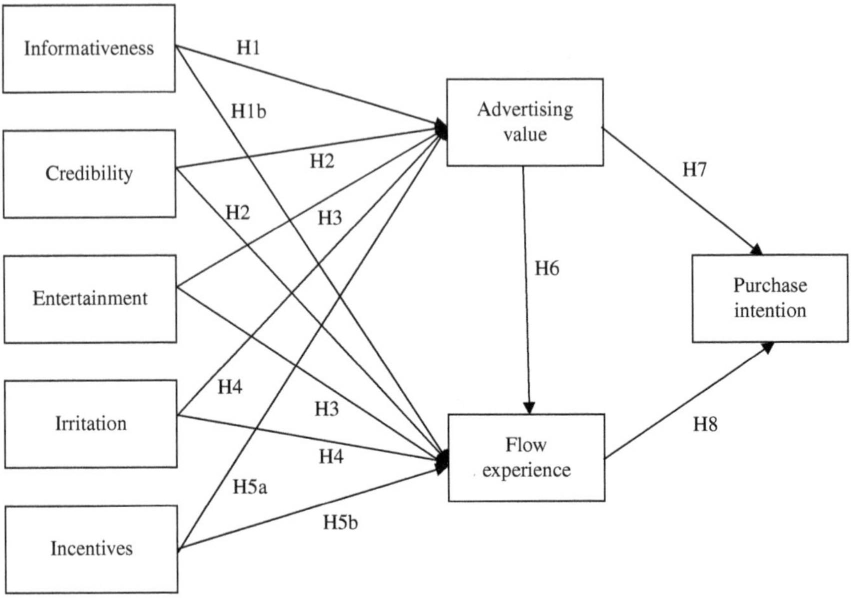


**Figure 1:** Conceptual model methodology.

There are two phases of qualitative research:

- **Phase 1:** This qualitative research aims to adjust the scale of constructs to suit the Vietnamese market through face-to-face discussions with 10 Vietnamese consumers who usually watch advertisements on their smartphones.
- **Phase 2:** In this phase, qualitative research aims to discuss the meaning of this study's results. There are 10 face-to-face discussions with Vietnamese consumers to explain the implications of structural equation model testing results.

In the quantitative research, convenient sampling method is used to survey Vietnamese consumers who watch advertisements on their smartphones. A total of 263 people participated in the survey. Data collected are processed by using the partial least squares structural equation modeling (PLS-SEM) with Smart PLS software version 3.0. The measurement model is evaluated through internal consistent reliability indicators (Cronbach's Alpha is higher than 0.7; composite reliability factor is higher than 0.5); evaluation of convergent validity (outer reliability is higher than 0.7; AVE is higher than 0.5); evaluation of discriminant validity (the Fornell–Larcker criterion and cross-loadings). Next, a structural model is evaluated: by examining for collinearity; assessing the path coefficients in the structural model; and evaluating the coefficients of determination ($R^2$ values) (Hair *et al.*, 2016).

## 4. Results

### 4.1. *The demography analysis of the respondents*

The demography of 263 respondents (Table 3) can be described as follows.

There is a balance of genders (male 50.2%, female 49.8%). Most of the people are in the age group from 20 to 39 years (93.2%). About the education level, 81% of respondents have a college degree or B.A./B.S. degree. Officers score the highest rate in the sample (61.6%) with businessmen in the second group (24%). People who earn an income between $250 and $1,000 per month are the majority in the sample (84.8%). Most of the respondents have been using smartphones for more than 1 year (92.4%). Only 12 respondents (4.6%) spend time online for lesser than 1 h per day. The demography shows that this sample is suitable to conduct the data analysis for the study.

### 4.2. *Testing of reliability and validity of the measurement model*

The outer loading of all variables is greater than 0.7 so they are valid (Hair *et al.*, 2016). All $t$-statistics of observed variables are also valid because they are greater than 1.96 (Table 4).

**Assessment of internal consistency reliability:** All variables have Cronbach's Alpha greater than 0.7 and composite reliability greater than 0.7 (Table 4). Thus, it can be concluded that latent variables all achieve consistent internal reliability (Hair *et al.*, 2016).

**Table 3:** The demography analysis of the respondents.

| | Items | Quantity | Ratio (%) |
|---|---|---|---|
| Gender | Male | 131 | 49.8 |
| | Female | 132 | 50.2 |
| Age group | Under 20 | 5 | 1.9 |
| | 20–29 | 147 | 55.9 |
| | 30–39 | 98 | 37.3 |
| | 40–49 | 8 | 3.0 |
| | 50–59 | 4 | 1.5 |
| | From 60 and above | 1 | 0.4 |
| Education level | High school qualification | 9 | 3.4 |
| | College degree | 58 | 22.1 |
| | B.A. or B.S. degree | 155 | 58.9 |
| | Post graduate degree | 26 | 9.9 |
| | Other | 15 | 5.7 |
| Job | Student | 9 | 3.4 |
| | Officer | 162 | 61.6 |
| | Housework | 5 | 1.9 |
| | Worker | 3 | 1.1 |
| | Businessman | 63 | 24.0 |
| | Other | 21 | 8.0 |
| Income per month | Under $250 | 12 | 4.6 |
| | $250–under $500 | 106 | 40.3 |
| | $500–under 1,000 | 117 | 44.5 |
| | $1,000 and above | 28 | 10.6 |
| Smartphone usage period | Under 6 months | 4 | 1.5 |
| | From 0.5–1 year | 16 | 6.1 |
| | More than 1 year | 243 | 92.4 |
| Time of online per day | Under 1 h | 12 | 4.6 |
| | 1–2 h | 93 | 35.4 |
| | 2–3 h | 58 | 22.1 |
| | More than 3 h | 100 | 38.0 |

- **Evaluation of convergent validity:** All variables have outer loading greater than 0.7. All AVEs are greater than 0.5 (Table 4). So, it can be concluded that all latent variables show convergent validity (Hair *et al.*, 2016).

**Table 4:** Reliability and validity of the constructs.

| Latent constructs and questions | Source | Item | Outer loading | $t$ Value |
|---|---|---|---|---|
| Informativeness ($\alpha = 0.932$; CR $= 0.951$; AVE $= 0.830$) (Kim and Han, 2014) | | | | |
| Smartphone advertising provides timely information on products or services. | | Inf1 | 0.881 | 52.412 |
| Smartphone advertising supplies relevant information on products or services. | | Inf2 | 0.931 | 95.011 |
| Smartphone advertising is a good source of information. | | Inf3 | 0.923 | 67.826 |
| Smartphone advertising is a good source of up-to-date products or services. | | Inf4 | 0.908 | 65.250 |
| Credibility ($\alpha = 0.872$; CR $= 0.921$; AVE $= 0.796$) (Martins *et al.*, 2019) | | | | |
| I feel that smartphone advertising is convincing. | | Cre1 | 0.904 | 53.715 |
| I feel that smartphone advertising is believable. | | Cre2 | 0.879 | 41.923 |
| I feel that smartphone advertising is a good reference for purchase. | | Cre3 | 0.893 | 42.546 |
| Entertainment ($\alpha = 0.889$; $CR = 0.923$; AVE $= 0.750$) (Martins *et al.*, 2019) | | | | |
| I feel that smartphone advertising is interesting. | | Ent1 | 0.866 | 32.689 |
| I feel that smartphone advertising is enjoyable. | | Ent2 | 0.891 | 41.734 |
| I feel that smartphone advertising is entertaining. | | Ent3 | 0.849 | 35.834 |
| I feel that smartphone advertising is pleasing. | | Ent4 | 0.858 | 32.169 |
| Irritation ($\alpha = 0.769$; CR $= 0.866$; AVE $= 0.683$) (Martins *et al.*, 2019) | | | | |
| I feel that smartphone advertising is irritating. | | Irr1 | 0.805 | 16.487 |
| I feel that smartphone advertising is annoying. | | Irr2 | 0.814 | 16.088 |
| I feel that smartphone advertising is intrusive | | Irr3 | 0.859 | 20.563 |

*(Continued)*

**Table 4:** (*Continued*)

| Latent constructs and questions | Source | Item | Outer loading | *t* Value |
|---|---|---|---|---|
| Incentives ($\alpha = 0.754$; CR = 0.853; AVE = 0.661) (Martins *et al.*, 2019) | | | | |
| I am satisfied to get smartphone advertisements that offer rewards. | | Use1 | 0.725 | 7.179 |
| I take action to get smartphone advertisements that offer rewards. | | Use2 | 0.849 | 32.218 |
| I respond to smartphone advertising to obtain incentives. | | Use3 | 0.858 | 34.051 |
| Advertising value ($\alpha = 0.767$; CR = 0.865; AVE = 0.682) (Martins *et al.*, 2019) | | | | |
| I feel that smartphone advertising is useful. | | Val1 | 0.854 | 34.566 |
| I feel that smartphone advertising is valuable. | | Val2 | 0.800 | 20.579 |
| I feel that smartphone advertising is important. | | Val3 | 0.822 | 13.092 |
| Flow experience ($\alpha = 0.914$; CR = 0.939; AVE = 0.795) (Martins *et al.*, 2019) | | | | |
| Smartphone advertising allows me to control my own purchase intention. | | Flo1 | 0.853 | 37.717 |
| I am not distracted by other online activities and stay focused on smartphone advertising. | | Flo2 | 0.894 | 54.629 |
| I find myself eager to press on advertising content or activity displayed on my smartphone. | | Flo3 | 0.899 | 49.134 |
| I like to pay attention to smartphone advertising. | | Flo4 | 0.919 | 79.543 |
| Purchase intention ($\alpha = 0.907$; CR = 0.941; AVE = 0.842) (Kim and Han, 2014) | | | | |
| I would consider purchasing goods or services with smartphone advertisement | | Pur1 | 0.938 | 90.900 |
| I intend to purchase goods or services with smartphone advertisement | | Pur2 | 0.901 | 38.824 |
| I would probably buy goods or services with smartphone advertisement | | Pur3 | 0.914 | 57.161 |

**Table 5:** Fornell–Larcker criterion.

| | 1 | 2 | 3 | 4 | 5 | 6 | 7 | 8 |
|---|---|---|---|---|---|---|---|---|
| 1. Advertising value | **0.826** | | | | | | | |
| 2. Credibility | 0.197 | **0.892** | | | | | | |
| 3. Entertainment | 0.348 | 0.172 | **0.866** | | | | | |
| 4. Flow experience | 0.381 | 0.306 | 0.302 | **0.891** | | | | |
| 5. Incentives | 0.480 | 0.192 | 0.370 | 0.409 | **0.813** | | | |
| 6. Informativeness | 0.198 | 0.191 | −0.018 | 0.366 | 0.131 | **0.911** | | |
| 7. Irritation | −0.218 | −0.196 | −0.103 | −0.209 | −0.150 | −0.263 | **0.826** | |
| 8. Purchase intention | 0.292 | 0.106 | 0.273 | 0.233 | 0.227 | 0.122 | −0.210 | **0.917** |

- **Evaluation of discriminant validity:** The first criterion is the Fornell–Larcker criterion, which demands that the root square of AVE (Table 5 in bold) for each latent variable be greater than the correlation with any other latent variable (Fornell and Larcker, 1981). In Table 5, we see that these criteria are achieved. The second criterion, the loading of each indicator, is expected to be greater than all of its cross-loadings. This is also analyzed and each construct has loadings with higher values than its cross-loadings; this result is available from the author upon request. The Hetrotrait-Monotrait (HTMT) ratio table (Table 6) is available upon request, and all values are below the threshold of 0.9 (Hair *et al.*, 2016).

Therefore, all the measures satisfy the discriminant validity of the constructs. The assessment of the construct reliability, convergent validity, and indicator reliability produce satisfactory results, indicating that the constructs can be used to test the conceptual model.

### 4.3. *Testing of the structural equation model*

The measurement model is satisfactory. So, it is possible to test the structural model. This chapter uses a bootstrapping of 500 resamples to estimate the statistical significance of path coefficients.

**Table 6:** Heterotrait–Monotrait (HTMT) ratio.

| | **Original sample** |
|---|---|
| Credibility → Advertising value | 0.235 |
| Entertainment → Advertising value | 0.420 |
| Entertainment → Credibility | 0.197 |
| Flow experience → Advertising value | 0.456 |
| Flow experience → Credibility | 0.344 |
| Flow experience → Entertainment | 0.334 |
| Incentives → Advertising value | 0.586 |
| Incentives → Credibility | 0.221 |
| Incentives → Entertainment | 0.441 |
| Incentives → Flow experience | 0.475 |
| Informativeness → Advertising value | 0.231 |
| Informativeness → Credibility | 0.210 |
| Informativeness → Entertainment | 0.043 |
| Informativeness → Flow experience | 0.395 |
| Informativeness → Incentives | 0.148 |
| Irritation → Advertising value | 0.272 |
| Irritation → Credibility | 0.241 |
| Irritation → Entertainment | 0.125 |
| Irritation → Flow experience | 0.252 |
| Irritation → Incentives | 0.185 |
| Irritation → Informativeness | 0.310 |
| Purchase intention → Advertising value | 0.344 |
| Purchase intention → Credibility | 0.116 |
| Purchase intention → Entertainment | 0.300 |
| Purchase intention → Flow experience | 0.251 |
| Purchase intention → Incentives | 0.247 |
| Purchase intention → Informativeness | 0.132 |
| Purchase intention → Irritation | 0.254 |

All VIF coefficients are below 2. It shows that there is no collinearity phenomenon (Hair *et al.*, 2016). The adjusted $R^2$ value of advertising value is 0.286, suggesting that the independent variables explain 28.6% of the variation in the advertising value. The adjusted $R^2$ value of flow experience is 0.325, meaning that the independent variables explain 32.5% of the variation in flow experience. The adjusted $R^2$ value of purchase intention is 0.095, meaning that the independent variables explain 9.5% of the variation in purchase intention. (Hair *et al.*, 2016).

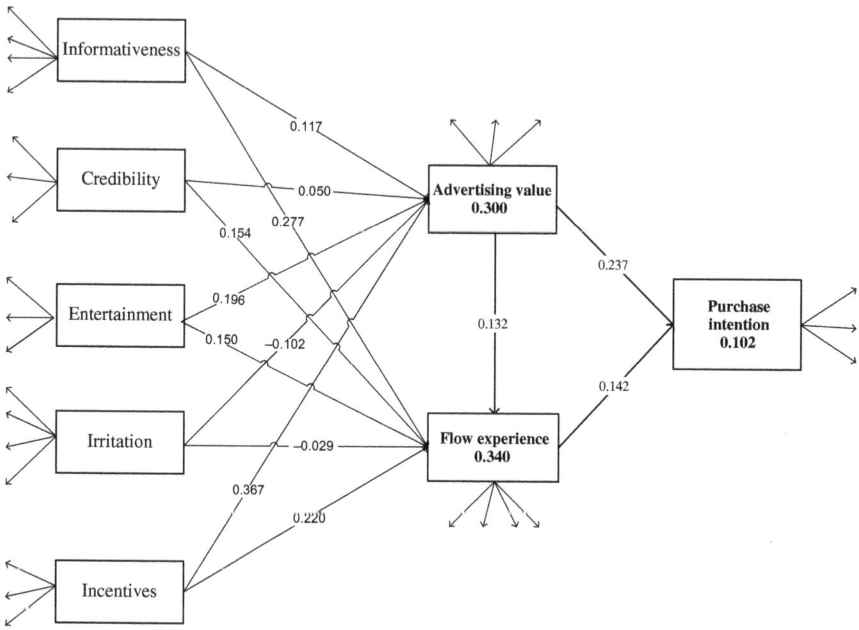


**Figure 2:** Structural equation model result.

The results of the hypotheses of the structural model are illustrated in Figure 2 and Table 7.

First, the research explains 28.6% of variation in advertising value in the conceptual model. The hypotheses of informativeness ($\beta = 0.117$; $p < 0.05$), entertainment ($\beta = 0.196$; $p < 0.01$), irritation ($\beta = -0.102$; $p < 0.10$), and incentives ($\beta = 0.367$; $p < 0.01$) are statistically significant. However, credibility value ($\beta = 0.050$; $p > 0.10$) is not statistically significant. Therefore, hypotheses H1a, H3a, H4a, and H5a, are supported, but H2a is not supported to explain advertising value.

Second, flow experience explains 32.5% of variation in the conceptual model. The hypotheses of informativeness ($\beta = 0.277$; $p < 0.01$), credibility ($\beta = 0.154$; $p < 0.05$), entertainment ($\beta = 0.150$; $p < 0.05$), incentives ($\beta = 0.220$; $p < 0.01$), and advertising value ($\beta = 0.132$; $p < 0.10$) are statistically significant. However, irritation ($\beta =$ 0.029; $p > 0.10$) is not statistically significant.

Table 7: Path coefficients testing results.

| | $\beta$ | $p$-Values | VIF | Hypotheses test |
|---|---|---|---|---|
| Informativeness → Advertising value | 0.117 | 0.036 | 1.116 | Supported H1a |
| Informativeness → Flow experience | 0.277 | 0.000 | 1.135 | Supported H1b |
| **Credibility → Advertising value** | **0.050** | **0.353** | **1.105** | **Not supported H2a** |
| Credibility → Flow experience | 0.154 | 0.018 | 1.108 | Supported H2b |
| Entertainment → Advertising value | 0.196 | 0.004 | 1.187 | Supported H3a |
| Entertainment → Flow experience | 0.150 | 0.019 | 1.241 | Supported H3b |
| Irritation → Advertising value | −0.102 | 0.066 | 1.114 | Supported H4a |
| **Irritation → Flow experience** | **−0.029** | **0.571** | **1.129** | **Not supported H4b** |
| Incentives → Advertising value | 0.367 | 0.000 | 1.207 | Supported H5a |
| Incentives → Flow experience | 0.220 | 0.002 | 1.400 | Supported H5b |
| Advertising value → Flow experience | 0.132 | 0.059 | 1.428 | Supported H6 |
| Advertising value → Purchase intention | 0.237 | 0.001 | 1.170 | Supported H7 |
| Flow experience → Purchase intention | 0.142 | 0.026 | 1.170 | Supported H8 |

Therefore, hypotheses H1b, H2b, H3b, H5b, and H6, are supported, but H4b is not supported to explain flow experience.

Third, purchase intention explains 9.5% of the variation in the conceptual model. The hypotheses of advertising value ($\beta = 0.237$; $p < 0.01$) and flow experience ($\beta = 0.142$; $p < 0.05$) are statistically significant. Therefore, hypotheses H7 and H8 are supported.

## 5. Discussions

### 5.1. *Theoretical implications*

This research has four theoretical implications. Firstly, the advertising value is positively affected by informativeness, entertainment, and incentives. Besides, irritation negatively impacts advertising value. Most of the results are consistent with previous findings (Ducoffe, 1996; Kim and Han, 2014; Martins *et al.*, 2019). Incentives are the strongest positive factor, followed by entertainment, and informativeness. There are only two differences. First, according to Kim and Han (2014) and Martins *et al.* (2019), credibility has the strongest positive impact on advertising value. But this study shows that credibility influences very weakly and not significantly to advertising value. In-depth interviews show that, in the Vietnamese market, when customers perceive that smartphone advertising has informativeness, they also think that it is reliable advertising. Therefore, the credibility factor is not necessary in this case. Second, in this study, irritation negatively impacts advertising value ($\beta = -0.102$; $p < 0.10$), which is consistent with Ducoffe (1996), but Kim and Han (2014) and Martins *et al.* (2019) show a weak influence or not statistically significant. It can be thus concluded that Vietnamese customers really do not like annoying smartphone advertisements.

Secondly, flow experience is positively affected by informativeness, credibility, entertainment, incentives, and advertising value. However, irritation ($\beta = -0.029$; $p > 0.10$) is not statistically significant. This is consistent with previous findings (Kim and Han, 2014; Martins *et al.*, 2019) except for the informativeness factor. Kim and Han (2014) and Martins *et al.* (2019) show that informativeness has no statistically significant impact on flow experience, but this study shows that informativeness positively influences flow experience, which is consistent with Ducoffe (1996). Informativeness is the strongest positively influencing factor, followed by incentives, credibility, entertainment, and advertising value.

Thirdly, purchase intention is positively influenced by advertising value and flow experience, which is consistent with Kim and Han

(2014) and Martins *et al.* (2019). Advertising value has a stronger influence on purchase intention than flow experience has.

Finally, the results of this study show that the adjusted $R^2$ values of the three dependent variables are quite low: advertising value (0.286), flow experience (0.325), and purchase intention (0.095). This is the biggest difference compared with the results of previous studies (Kim and Han, 2014; Martins *et al.*, 2019).

### 5.2. *Practical implications*

There are some practical implications of this study. First, through the smartphone advertising environment in the Vietnam market, factors such as informativeness, credibility, entertainment, irritation, and incentives only explain 28.6% of the variation of advertising value and 32.5% of the variation of flow experience. Then, advertising value and flow experience also explain 9.5% of the variation of purchase intention. This means that smartphone advertising has a limited influence on Vietnamese consumers' purchase intention. According to the face-to-face discussions with 10 Vietnamese smartphone users, they mainly use smartphones to read news, play games, and access social networks online. The percentage of time they use smartphones for shopping information is much lower. Therefore, smartphone advertising has a low influence on the purchasing intention of Vietnamese consumers, which is appropriate to the reality.

Second, the research results show that consumers are interested in smartphone advertising that is entertaining and attractive. An advertisement with high entertainment attracts the attention of consumers. On the contrary, consumers tend to avoid, do not want to see or receive boring and annoying smartphone advertisements that make consumers uncomfortable. Smartphone advertising must also contain sufficient details about the product or service offered to customers.

Third, from the research's results, administrators, advertisers, or marketers should create smartphone ads with high advertising value and high flow experience, thereby affecting consumers' purchase intention in the most effective way.

### 5.3. *Limitations and future research*

This research has some limitations. First, this study is just conducted in Vietnam. Therefore, future researches should conduct similar studies in other countries that have an emerging economy like Vietnam. This will give us a clearer understanding about how smartphone advertising influences consumers' purchase intention in emerging economies compared with developed economies. Second, only advertising value and flow experience are considered as positively influencing factors of customers' purchase intention. Thereby, future research should be conducted with more factors such as attitudes toward the smartphone advertising, emotions, and so on. Third, credibility is unsupported to explain advertising value. Thus, future studies should investigate the antecedents of credibility. Fourth, irritation is unsupported to explain flow experience and other studies should investigate mediating factors in the relationship between irritation and flow experience.

## 6. Conclusions

There are several contributions of this research. First, the study finds out that smartphone advertising in Vietnam — an emerging economy — has much weaker influence compared with the research results in developed economies. Second, incentives are the strongest positive factor, followed by entertainment, and informativeness to influence advertising value. Credibility influences advertising value very weakly and not significantly. Third, flow experience is positively affected by informativeness, credibility, entertainment, incentives, and advertising value. However, irritation is not statistically significant. Informativeness is the strongest positively influencing factor, followed by incentives, credibility, entertainment, and advertising value. Fourth, purchase intention is positively influenced by advertising value and flow experience. Advertising value has a stronger influence on purchase intention than flow experience does.

Marketers and advertisers can refer to the results of this study to plan suitable marketing strategies for the Vietnamese market and other emerging economies. Accordingly, they only need to pay attention to the smartphone advertising at a sufficient level and to pay more attention to other types of advertising such as TV advertising. To increase the effectiveness of smartphone advertising, advertisers need to focus on increasing attractiveness, entertainment value, and reducing irritation of advertisements.

## References

Aydogan, S., Aysuna, C., and Aktan, M. (2016). Web advertising value and students' attitude towards web advertising. *European Journal of Business and Management*, 8(9), 86–97.

Brakett, L.K., and Carr, B.N.J. (2001). Cyberspace advertising vs. other media. *Journal of Advertising Research*, 41(5), 23–32.

Chen, P., and Hsieh, H. (2012). Personalized mobile advertising: Its key attributes, trends, and social impact. *Technological Forecasting and Social Change*, 79(3), 543–557.

Csikszentmihalyi, M. (1975). Play and intrinsic rewards. *Journal of Humanistic Psychology*, 15(3), 41–63.

Ducoffe, R.H. (1995). How consumers assess the value of advertising. *Journal of Current Issues and Research in Advertising*, 17(1), 1–18.

Ducoffe, R.H. (1996). Advertising value and advertising on the web. *Journal of Advertising Research*, 36(5), 21–35. doi:10.1080/135272600750036364.

Ducoffe, R.H., and Curlo, E. (2000). Advertising value and advertising processing. *Journal of Marketing Communications*, 6(4), 247–262.

Fornell, C., and Larcker, D. (1981). Structural equation models with unobservable variables and measurement error: Algebra and statistics. *Journal of Marketing Research*, 18(3), 382–388. doi: 10.2307/3150980.

Gao, L., Waechter, K.A., and Bai, X. (2015). Understanding consumers' continuance intention towards mobile purchase: A theoretical framework and empirical study — A case of China. *Computers in Human Behavior*, 53, 249–262.

Grewal, D., Bart, Y., Spann, M., and Zubcsek, P. (2016). Mobile advertising: A framework and research agenda. *Journal of Interactive Marketing*, 34, 3–14.

Hair Jr, J.F., Hult, G.T.M., Ringle, C., and Sarstedt, M. (2016). *A Primer on Partial Least Squares Structural Equation Modeling (PLS-SEM)*. Singapore: Sage Publications.

Hoffman, D., and Novak, T. (1996). Marketing in hypermedia environment foundations: Conceptual foundations. *Journal of Marketing*, 60(3), 50–68. doi: 10.2307/1251841

Hsu, C.L., and Lu, H.P. (2004). Why do people play on-line games? An extended TAM with social influences and flow experience. *Information and Management*, 41(7), 853–868. doi: 10.1016/j.im.2003.08.014

Hsu, C., and Lin, J. (2015). What drives purchase intention for paid mobile apps?-An expectation confirmation model with perceived value. *Electronic Commerce Research and Applications*, 14(1), 46–57. doi: 10.1016/j.elerap.2014.11.003

Hsu, L.C., Chang, K.C., Kuo, N.T., and Cheng, Y.S. (2017). The mediating effect of flow experience on social shopping behavior. *Information Development*, 33(3), 243–256. doi: 10.1177/0266666916651918

Kim, A.J., and Ko, E. (2012). Do social media marketing activities enhance customer equity? An empirical study of luxury fashion brand. *Journal of Business Research*, 65(10), 1480–1486. doi: 10.1016/j.jbusres.2011.10.014

Kim, Y.J., and Han, J. (2014). Why smartphone advertising attracts customers: A model of Web advertising, flow, and personalization. *Computers in Human Behavior*, 33, 256–269. doi: 10.1016/j.chb.2014.01.015

Ko, H., Cho, C., and Roberts, M. (2005). Internet uses and gratifications: A structural equation model of interactive advertising. *Journal of Advertising*, 34(2), 57–70.

Liu, C., Sinkovics, R., Pezderka, N., and Haghirian, P. (2012). Determinants of consumer perceptions toward mobile advertising — A comparison between Japan and Austria. *Journal of Interactive Marketing*, 26(1), 21–32. doi: 10.1016/j.intmar.2011.07.002

Mackenzie, S., and Lutz, R. (1989). An empirical examination of the structural antecedents of attitude toward the ad in an advertising pretesting context. *Journal of Marketing*, 53(2), 48–65. doi: 10.2307/1251413

Martins, J., Costa, C., Oliveira, T., Goncalves, R., and Branco, F. (2019). How smartphone advertising influences consumers' purchase intention. *Journal of Business Research*, 94(December 2017), 378–387. doi: 10.1016/j.jbusres.2017.12.047

Nielsen Vietnam (2017). Smart phones continue to grow in both urban and rural areas. https://www.nielsen.com/vn/vi/insights/report/2017/nielsen-smartphone-insights-2017. Accessed on October 24, 2019.

Nielsen Vietnam (2018). The growth of mobile phones is a solid foundation for digital ad campaigns in Southeast Asia. https://www.nielsen.com/vn/vi/insights/report/2018/nielsen-digital-ad-report. Accessed on October 24, 2019.

Novak, T.P., and Hoffman, D.L. (2009). The fit of thinking style and situation: New Measures of situation-specific experiential and rational cognition. *Journal of Consumer Research*, 36(1), 56–72. doi: 10.1086/596026

Rodríguez-Ardura, I., and Meseguer-Artola, A. (2018). Imagine, feel "there", and flow! Immersive experiences on m-Facebook, and their affective and behavioural effects, *Information Technology & People*, 32(4), 921–947.

Tsang, M., Ho, S., and Liang, T. (2004). Consumer attitudes toward mobile advertising: An empirical study. *International Journal of Electronic Commerce*, 8(3), 65–78. doi: 10.1080/10864415.2004.11044301

Varnali, K., Yilmaz, C., and Toker, A. (2012). Predictors of attitudinal and behavioral outcomes in mobile advertising: A field experiment. *Electronic Commerce Research and Applications*, 11(6), 570–581. doi: 10.1016/j.elerap.2012.08.002

Wang, Y., and Sun, S. (2010). Examining the role of beliefs and attitudes in online advertising. *International Marketing Review*, 27(1), 87–107. doi: 10.1108/ 02651331011020410

Wu, P., Yeh, G., and Hsiao, C. (2011). The effect of store image and service quality on brand image and purchase intention for private label brands. *Australasian Marketing Journal*, 19(1), 30–39. doi: 10.1016/j.ausmj.2010.11.001

https://doi.org/10.1142/9789811227158_0024

## Chapter 24

# The Impact of Public Spending for Education on Sustainable Economic Growth in Asian Countries

Minh Tuan Truong

**Abstract**

This chapter focuses on the impact of public spending on education on sustainable economic growth. For this objective, the research analyzes the response function of the panel data analysis method with the Pool OLS model, FEM, and REM, gathering data from six Asian countries in the period from 2010 to 2016. The results show that public spending for education, labor, and globalization index has a positive impact on sustainable economic growth; private investment has an opposite effect; while health spending variables, inflation, and savings are not statistically significant.

**Keywords:** Public spending for education; Sustainable economic growth; POLS; FEM; REM.

## 1. Introduction

Economic growth depends on many factors important to its growth, namely *government policies, institutions, political and economic stability, geographical characteristics, natural resources, health, and education levels.*

According to the announcement of ASEAN Secretariat, ASEAN economies still maintain the momentum of growth of the global economy, which had many uncertainties in 2014. The actual gross domestic product (GDP) of all ASEAN countries increased to 4.6% (US$2.57 trillion). Therefore, GDP per capita increased to US$4,130 in 2014 from US$3,908 in 2013.

In recent years, there have been many studies on factors affecting economic growth. Although contrary conclusions exist, the most concentrated factor is how public spending (government spending) affects economic growth. Researchers are not only interested in the correlation between their pros or cons, but they are also wondering about the impact between the elements that constitute them such as the impact of budget spending on education.

Furthermore, faster economic growth contributes to environmental pollution, issues of social progress, and health. Ultimately, when the economy grows, it always comes with challenges. To sustainably grow an economy, there needs to be a balance between three factors: *Environment, Social Progress*, and *Economic Development.*

The research question is: What is the impact of education public spending on long-term economic growth? To answer this question, Section 2 presents the theoretical framework and literature review on sustainable growth and the impact of education expenditure on economic growth. The research model and methodology are presented in Section 3. Research results and policy recommendations are analyzed in Sections 4 and 5. Finally, Section 6 presents research limitations and research direction.

## 2. Theoretical Framework and Literature Review

### 2.1. *Sustainable factors in economic growth*

Development is always a necessity in every country and region. It demonstrates the economic, political, and cultural potential of that country and region. Economic development is a prerequisite for overcoming the economic lag in the advanced countries in the world, building an independent self-reliant economy, and expanding international relations. Therefore, for a country or region to assert its position in the world, it calls for the sustainable development of the economy (Aka and Dumont, 2008). For example, America is a world power with an economic capacity that affirms its leading position in the world. In Asia, China and Japan also confirm their positions through the sustainable economic growth they build.

To achieve sustainable and influential growth in the world, countries must strive to build and develop not only in the economic field but also in terms of the human and environmental factors.

Sustainable growth must balance the following three factors (UN environment and AIT, 2017):

1. **Environment:** Conserving natural resources, ecosystem quality (air, water, and soil) biodiversity, and reducing ecological footprints.
2. **Social progress:** Education, protection of human rights, hunger reduction, elimination of poverty and inequality, improvements in living and working conditions.
3. **Economic development:** Economic development, creating jobs, encouraging small and medium enterprises.

To balance these three factors, public spending needs to address the following existing situations:

- Eradicating poverty.
- Promoting sustainable agriculture, ensuring food issues, focusing on nutrition.
- Ensuring a healthy life and promoting happiness for all ages.
- Investing in the quality of education comprehensively and fairly, promoting the opportunity to study for all citizens anywhere.
- Ensuring gender equality and ensuring the rights of all girls and women.
- Investing in sustainable management, water supply, and sanitary conditions for everyone.
- Ensuring people use energy at a reasonable price, in ways that are reliable, sustainable, and modern for everyone.
- Promoting sustainable, comprehensive, continuous economic growth, creating full, effective, and sustainable jobs for everyone.

- Building a solid infrastructure system, promoting comprehensive and sustainable industrialization, and encouraging innovation.
- Managing equality in each region and between countries.
- Ensuring human cities and areas become comprehensive, safe, flexible, and sustainable.
- Ensuring climate change response and climate change impacts.
- Encouraging conservation and sustainable use of oceans, seas, and marine resources.
- Protection of ecosystems, sustainable forest management, desertification, prevention of land degradation, and loss of biodiversity.
- Strengthening global cooperation for sustainable development.

Therefore, *Sustainable economic growth* is not just an increase in income but also sustainable and stable development. This growth focuses on all three factors: *economic*, *social,* and *environmental* (Table 1). To maintain a high growth rate in the long term, the increase in income must be linked to the quality of life, including increased welfare and poverty reduction. Growth does not need to be too high; it needs to be reasonable and sustainable (Figure 1).

### 2.2. *Impact of education spending on economic growth*

Education is an important field for all countries and territories in all periods. In today's trend of development of knowledge, education–training is considered as the leading policy and measure to develop in many countries around the world. The human factor is both the goal and the motivation for social development. So, if we want to develop society, we must take care of the human factor physically and mentally, especially in education, with an awareness of the world around so they can contribute to building and improving society. Education contributes to improving intellectual standards in all countries (Figure 2).

High rates of education are seen as essential to help countries achieve high levels of economic growth (Eric, 2013). Along with that,

**Table 1:** Components in sustainable growth.

| Economic | Social | Environmental |
|---|---|---|
| • Best value for money (price, quality, availability, functionality, innovation) | • Human development | • Preservation of natural resources, ecosystems and biodiversity |
| • Life Cycle Costing | • Education | • Reduction of ecological footprint<br>• Reduction of GHG emissions |
| • Economic development<br>• Employment | • Human and labor rights<br>• Reduction of poverty and inequality | • Waste management |
| • Good governance<br>• Innovation | • Security<br>• Social inclusion<br>• Promotion of SMEs | |

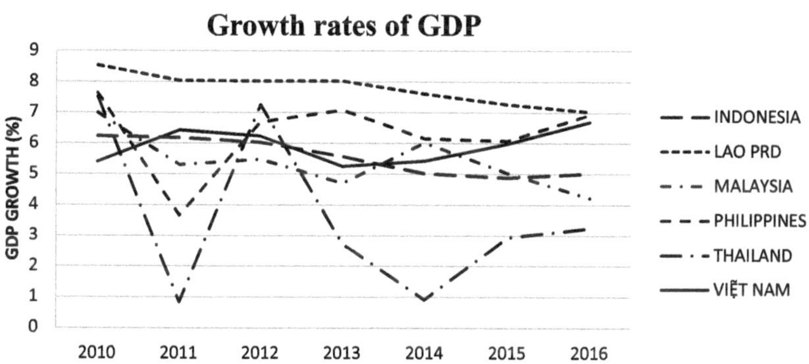


**Figure 1:** Growth rates of GDP from 2010 to 2016.
*Source*: World Bank (2017).

there exists the theory that poor countries can outgrow rich countries because poor countries can apply the leading technologies that rich countries have tried and tested, supported by experimental analyzes. However, without high skills and good professional knowledge, engineers and workers are not able to learn and operate the new

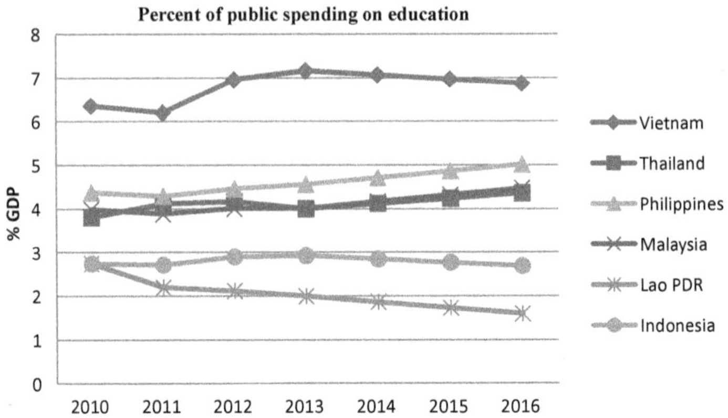


**Figure 2:** Percent of public spending on education (% of GDP).
*Source*: World Bank (2017).

technology transferred. Therefore, a nation's ability to learn from developed countries is a function of human capital.

Knowledge is the product of education and training and is the most valuable asset of people and society. Education–training fostering talents, building a high-skilled labor force, and high labor productivity, greatly contribute to socioeconomic development. All developed countries have an educational development strategy. UNESCO has also encouraged countries to spend at least 6% of GDP on education.

## 3. Models and Research Methodology

### 3.1. *Models and research data*

To explain the impact of educational public spending on sustained economic growth, the chapter uses a model developed upon three factors (UN environment and AIT, 2017), as follows:

$$pgd_{it} = \alpha_i + \beta_1\,(ECO) + \beta_2(ENV) + \beta_3(SOC) + \varepsilon, \qquad (1)$$

where $pgd_{it}$ is the growth rate of GDP per capita of country $i$ in year $t$; $ECO$ is a measure of the impact of economic factors on

**Table 2:** Measurement and data source.

| Variable | Measurement | Data source |
|---|---|---|
| Pdgd | Annual GDP growth per capita | World Bank (2017) |
| **ECO** | | |
| lnGDP | Logarit of GD (billion VND) | World Bank (2017) |
| LnGEXP | Logarit of total government spending (% GDP) | World Bank (2017) |
| INV | Private investment/GDP (%) | World Bank (2017) |
| SAV | Saving rate (%) | World Bank (2017) |
| INFL | Inflation rate (%) | World Bank (2017) |
| LAB | Labor scale (% GDP) | World Bank (2017) |
| TRA | Import-export ratio (% GDP) | World Bank (2017) |
| TAX | Tax revenue (% GDP) | World Bank (2017) |
| **SOC** | | |
| EDU | Public spending on education (% GDP) | World Bank (2017) |
| HEXP | Public spending on health (% GDP) | World Bank (2017) |
| GLB | Globalization index (%) | World Bank (2017) |
| **ENV** | | |
| LnCO2 | Logarit of CO2 into the environment (tons/person) | World Bank (2017) |

sustainable growth, *ENV* the variables to measure the impact of environmental factors on sustainable growth, *SOC* the variables to measure the impact of social factors on sustainable growth.

From the basic model, to measure the impact of education expenditure on economic growth, the econometric model is implemented as follows (Nijkamp and Poot, 2004; Eric, 2013) (Table 2):

$$\begin{aligned} pgd_{it} = \alpha_i &+ \beta_1 lnGDP_{i(t-1)} + \beta_2 lnGEXP_{it} + \beta_3 INV_{it} + \beta_4 EDU_{it} \\ &+ \beta_5 HEXP_{it} + \beta_6 SAV_{it} + \beta_7 INFL_{it} + \beta_8 LAB_{it} \\ &+ \beta_9 TRA_{it} + \beta_{10} TAX_{it} + \beta_{11} GLB_{it} + \beta_{12} CO2 + \varepsilon. \qquad (2) \end{aligned}$$

Research data are collected from the Worldbank database for six ASEAN countries: Vietnam, Laos, Thailand, Indonesia, Malaysia, and the Philippines in the period of 2010–2016.

### 3.2. *Research methodology*

The research process is carried out in the following order:

- **Step 1:** Estimating model by Pool OLS method, fixed effects model (FEM) and random effects model (REM).
- **Step 2:** Use the Hausman test to select results from FEM and REM.
- **Step 3:** Use Breush–Pagan test to select results from REM and POLS models.
- **Step 4:** Use regression coefficients from the selected model to give results.

## 4. Results of Inspection and Estimation

From the data collected, we present the results in Table 3.

The variable of economic growth rate, *Pdgd,* shows that the ASEAN countries in the study have an average growth rate of 5.76%, the highest reached 8.53%, and the lowest, 0.84%.

For public education expenditure variables, the smallest value is 1.71%, the highest is 6.06%, on average ASEAN countries spend

**Table 3:** Descriptive statistics.

| Variable | Mean | Std. Dev. | Min | Max | Obs |
|---|---|---|---|---|---|
| Pdgd | 5.764 | 1.776 | 0.840 | 8.527 | 42 |
| lnGDP | 30.298 | 4.857 | 22.514 | 36.984 | 42 |
| LnGEXP | 4.594 | 0.073 | 4.432 | 4.699 | 42 |
| INV | 20.335 | 5.299 | 12.331 | 31.201 | 42 |
| SAV | 30.802 | 8.017 | 16.221 | 48.080 | 42 |
| INFL | 4.403 | 4.242 | −0.587 | 24.261 | 42 |
| LAB | 1.956 | 1.527 | −1.506 | 5.186 | 42 |
| TRA | 0.893 | 7.060 | −9.814 | 15.916 | 42 |
| TAX | 14.665 | 2.980 | 10.332 | 22.324 | 42 |
| EDU | 3.858 | 1.295 | 1.709 | 6.058 | 42 |
| HEXP | 4.081 | 1.539 | 1.597 | 7.166 | 42 |
| GLB | 62.210 | 11.224 | 10.870 | 79.610 | 42 |
| LnCO2 | 0.573 | 1.076 | −1.416 | 2.101 | 42 |

3.86% of GDP on education. The standard deviation of 1.29% also shows that the level of spending on education among countries is relatively different.

The study is conducted to estimate the POOL OLS, FEM, REM models, the estimated results are as shown in Table 4.

The regression results table shows the extent to which economic, social, and environmental factors affect sustainable economic growth in some ASEAN countries.

Next, the study uses Hausman and Breush–Pagan tests to select the appropriate model. With Hausman test results ($p$-value = 0.9740), the REM model is more suitable than the FEM model to estimate the regression coefficient. In addition, the result of Breusch–Pagan test ($p$-value = 1.000 > alpha) shows that the Pool OLS model is suitable.

Finally, after implementing the tests and comparisons, we see that POOL OLS is the most suitable model for the study.

Based on the results of POLS regression model, overall labor growth has a positive impact on sustainable growth in ASEAN countries with a coefficient of 0.4349022 (1% significance level). With this

**Table 4:** Regression results.

| Variable | POLS (1) | FEM (2) | REM (3) |
|---|---|---|---|
| INV | −0.0534869* | −0.1309562* | −0.0534869* |
| LnCO2 | −1.030718 | 2.3133 | −1.030718 |
| SAV | −0.1416487 | −0.2598933 | −0.1416487 |
| HEXP | 0.7470206 | −0.666976 | 0.7470206 |
| LnGEXP | −115.1511 | −120.81 | −115.1511 |
| EDU | 0.1435473** | 0.0600889** | 0.1435473** |
| TAX | −0.4087366 | −0.565219 | −0.4086374 |
| INFL | 0.0486374 | 0.0155189 | 0.0486374 |
| LAB | 0.4349022*** | 0.3260894*** | 0.4349022*** |
| GLB | 0.0676673* | 0.251328* | 0.0676673* |
| TRA | −1.26162 | −1.343523 | −1.26162 |
| LnGDP | 0.0786731 | −2.445084 | 0.0786731 |
| Wald test ($p$-value) | 0.0058 | 0.6939 | 0.0002 |

*Notes*: *Significant at 10%; **significant at 5%; ***significant at 1%.

impact, the labor force is an important factor that not only promotes economic development in the short term but also helps the economy develop sustainably over the long term. Furthermore, the positive impact of labor-intensive growth on sustainable economic growth in ASEAN countries in the 2010–2016 period brings a new conclusion compared to previous studies of Nijkamp and Poot (2004).

In addition, public education expenditure is also a factor affecting sustainable growth. With a coefficient of 0.1435473 (5% significance level), over 14% of long-term economic growth is formed from public education expenditure. This is consistent with the modern development trend.

## 5. Recommendations

According to the model, within some ASEAN countries (Indonesia, Laos Malaysia, Philippines, Thailand, Vietnam) in the 2010–2016 period, the results are as follows: growth in public education expenditure, labor size, and globalization has a positive impact on sustainable economic growth, whereas private investment has an opposite effect. Besides that, health spending variables, inflation rates, and savings rates are not statistically significant.

The results of studies show that government public spending only addresses the economic problem; it cannot solve social and environmental problems at the same time. However, if the government has a policy of expanding the labor scale and increasing public spending on education, it can solve social problems such as unemployment and other evils.

To stabilize the economy in the long term, it must consider the following:

- Public spending on education is a factor affecting sustainable economic growth with over 14% of long-term economic growth formed from public education expenditure. So, government must not deny the role of education in economic development in an indirect way. It must manage labor quality, from unskilled labor, manual labor, to high-tech workers. Reasonable investments in human resource training must be made. To achieve a high quality of labor, education is a quality determinant. Therefore, investment in education is also an essential investment in any country. Building school infrastructure, investing in modern equipment, and facilitating access to learning practical programs and skill development activities are some of the various available forms of investment to help improve labor quality.

- According to the research results, the size of labor has a positive impact on sustainable economic development with over 43% of long-term economic growth formed from the labor force. However, the scale of expansion of labor also requires skilled and high-quality labor to compete with the international labor market in the strong technological revolution 4.0.

## 6. Limitations

- This chapter does not go into the analysis of the impact of education expenditure on economic growth through the impact on household income.
- Research does not distinguish the development of education derived from public investment or private investment in education.
- The chapter does not go into research on beneficiaries (by income) from public investment in education.

Further, the chapter does not fully explore the relationship between the quality of education and public education investment to analyze the impact of education's public spending on economic growth

## References

Aka, B.F., and Dumont, J.C. (2008). Health, education and economic growth: Testing for long-run relationship and casual links. *Applies Econometrics and International Development*, 8(2), 101–110.

Eric, A.H. (2013). *Economic Growth in Developing Countries: The Role of Human Capital.* Stanford University.

Nijkamp, P., and Poot, J. (2014). Meta-analysis of the Effect Of Fiscal Policies On Long-Run Growth. *European Journal of Political Economy,* 20(1), 91–124.

UN Environment and AIT (2017). Sustainable Public Procurement and Eco-lables.

https://doi.org/10.1142/9789811227158_0025

# Chapter 25

# The Role of Institutions in Economic Development: The Case of Vietnam During 2012–2015

**Nu Ngoc Han Ton and Prapon Sahapattana**


## Abstract

The panel regression tests the causal relationship between institutional factors and economic development of 63 Vietnamese provinces during the period 2012–2015, and to prove a new argument for New Institutional Economics that different developmental levels can intervene in this causal relationship. The secondary data are collected at the provincial level and the panel regression is used to test this causal relationship in the institutional models.

As a consequence, institutions creating conditions for human development, social capital development, and business development contribute to economic development. Meanwhile, the "payoff" mindset appears to be gaining economic priority in Vietnamese governance, as evidenced by, for example, low degree of participation, informal charges in public transactions, and low access to land and security.

When testing causal relationships between institutional factors and economic development in each developmental cluster, there are some new determinants (i.e., control of corruption, transparent business environment, and equitable business information) and some complex impacts with both negative and positive signs in different contexts (public administrative procedures, minimal informal charges).

The study contributes significant evidence from Vietnam to support New Institutional Economics and New Public Management (e.g., enabling government-oriented managerialism and good governance).

**Keywords:** Developmental clusters; Economic development; Institutional factors; New Institutional Economics.

## 1. Introduction

The world has witnessed a remarkable development in Vietnam after the Vietnam War and since the implementation of the Doi Moi policy in 1986. Chand *et al.* (2001) assert that "Vietnam has provided an excellent example of how getting the institutions right can deliver rapid rises in productivity". Indeed, Chand *et al.* (2001) provide proof for the proposition in the agricultural sector in Vietnam: "Institutional reforms can deliver significant gains in productivity and output" (Chand *et al.*, 2001). Subsequently, Vietnam evolved from being agriculturally dominant to industrially dominant from 1986 to the first decade of the 21st century. Currently, Vietnam pursues sustainable development on par with the rest of the world. Hence, the author wonders, "Do institutional reforms also play an essential role in economic development in Vietnam in the new era of an industrial economy with sustainable development?".

In New Institutional Economics, it is assumed that individuals deal with incomplete information and uncertainty as well as incur transaction costs in seeking information. Hence, institutions become essential to generating long-term economic growth through lowering transaction and transformation costs (Mennard and Shirley, 2008).

The study is to identify the role of the institutions in economic development in Vietnam. The concrete research questions of the study are:

1. Which are the institutional sub-indices leading to economic development across Vietnam's 63 provinces during 2012–2015?
2. How different developmental levels can intervene in the causal relationship between institutional factors and economic development?

## 2. Literature Review

### 2.1. *New institutional economics*

#### 2.1.1. *Definition of institutions*

Redek and Susjan (2005) rewrite the definition of institutions based on North (1990): "Institutions are the rules of the game in a society; more formally, they are the limitations to free behavior imposed on the individual by the society, shaping the relationships among individuals." Moreover, institutions can be represented as "collective action in control of individual action" with their political, social, and economic connections in the society (North, 1990; Redek and Susjan, 2005).

Aron (2000) introduces institutional frameworks based on North's definition with formal constraints (i.e., "constitutions and laws governing economics and politics") and informal constraints (i.e., "unwritten taboos, customs, and traditions"). Formal institutions impede the development of unwanted "customs, laws, trust, and normative rules" in the society. Informal institutions are impacted by various behaviors that likewise influence the role of said behavior within the local culture. Economic development along with labor specialization and complex societies requires *political, judicial, and economic rules and contracts* facilitating political and/or economic exchanges. In reality, States employ rules in the hierarchical form from constitutions "to state and common laws, to specific by-laws, to individual contracts" (Aron, 2000).

Shirley (2008) emphasizes an institutional framework taking form in a market economy with two basic mechanisms and two sets of institutions. For the first mechanism, some institutions create favorable conditions for exchanges with low transaction costs and reliable trust. For the second mechanism, other institutions create interventions to the State and/or any powerful actors for property protection. The first set of institutions encompasses enforcement contracts, norms, and rules (i.e., in commerce), common habits and beliefs for shared values, and human development. The second set of institutions encompasses constitutions, rules, and laws (i.e., in election, speech, and education), and common norms (i.e., "motivating people to abide by laws and cooperate in monitoring the government") (Shirley, 2008).

### 2.1.2. *New Institutional Economics: The causal relationship between institutions and economic development*

Mennard and Shirley (2008) express, "New Institutional Economics focuses on how such institutions emerge, operate, and evolve, how they shape the different arrangements that support production and exchange, as well as how these arrangements act to change the rules of the game." In neoclassical economics, the assumption is that "individuals have perfect information and unbounded rationality, and transactions are costless and instantaneous." In contrast, New Institutional Economics assumes that "individuals have incomplete information and limited mental capacity," thus, individuals experience "uncertainty about unforeseen events and outcomes", as well as "incur transaction costs to acquire information". Hence, human beings create both formal institutions and informal institutions to "reduce risk and transaction costs" (Mennard and Shirley, 2008).

Mennard and Shirley (2008) emphasize that "neoclassical economics was not created to explain the process of economic change, much less political or social change." In contrast, institutionalists understand change by "understanding human incentives and intentions and the beliefs, norms, and rules" that they create to pursue their goals (Mennard and Shirley, 2008).

Aron (2000) emphasizes the essential role of institutions in national economic growth. He writes a comprehensive literature review about measures of institutions and the relationship between "the quality of institutions and investment and growth". Aron (2000) further indicates five types of institutional measures, including quality of formal institutions, social capital, social characteristics, political institutions, and political instability (Aron, 2000). North (1990) and Aron (2000) indicate the reason for the lesser development of Third World countries. Institutional framework, with their formal

**Table 1:** List of organizations suffering from rules in institutional framework.

| Types of organizations | Examples |
|---|---|
| Political organizations | City councils, regulatory agencies, political parties, tribal councils |
| Economic organizations | Firms, trade unions, family farms, cooperatives, rotating credit groups |
| Educational bodies | Schools, universities, vocational training centers |
| Social organizations | Churches, clubs, civic association |

*Source*: Aron (2000, p. 104).

and informal rules, is defined as "the incentives and the wealth-maximizing opportunities of individuals and organizations". The poor countries get stuck in the devious situation because of different definitions of institutions between the Third World and the First World countries. Rather than spurring productivity as in the rich people's mindset, in the Third World countries institutions are seen as "a set of payoffs to political/economic activity". These rules impact individuals as well as organizations (i.e., political organizations, economic organizations, education bodies, and social organizations) (see Table 1) (Aron, 2000; North, 1990).

Aron (2000) points out the underpinning causal mechanism explaining the relationship between institutional framework and economic growth. Transaction costs and transformation costs are measurable outcomes reflecting the economic growth within the institutional environment. Transaction cost increases when property rights and/or the rule of law are unreliable. In this situation, private firms prefer small scale operations, even in an underground economy with illegal form, relying on bribery and corruption to facilitate operations. Moreover, transformation costs escalate with unenforceable contracts. Private firms prefer using inexpensive technology or low level of specialization leading to the consequence of less efficiency, less competition, and short-term horizon. Enterprises in weak institutional environments suffer from non-professional economic exchanges, such as being "restricted to interpersonal exchanges", low level of specialization, and involvement of social network and kinship ties in signing contracts. Indeed, in industrial economies with strong institutions, enterprises can engage in "complex, long-term, and multiple-contract exchanges with effective enforcement". Strong property rights alongside long-term contracting can create capital markets and spur economic growth (Aron, 2000). Agreeing with Aron (2000), Shirley (2008) describes how the low institutional environments curb economic growth. The general economy suffers from short-term growth in low institutional environments. With insecure property rights, and high transaction costs, the investors try to reap rapid returns/high returns by utilizing bribes/rent-seeking rather than investing in production, innovation, and human development (Shirley, 2008, p. 611).

Rodrik (2000) lists five main types of institutions, including *property rights, regulatory institutions, institutions for macroeconomic stabilization, institutions for social insurance, and institutions of conflict management.* He explains how these institutions contribute to economic growth, or in other words, "allow markets to perform adequately", or avoid market failure. Indeed, property rights and regulatory institutions impede the worst business forms (i.e., "fraud, anti-competitive behavior, and moral hazard"). Stable macroeconomic environments are necessary for growth with the crucial roles of central banks and the states. Social insurance and conflict management mitigate social cohesion with increased economic performance. Furthermore, Rodrik (2000) highlights local knowledge and the strategy for institutional building. Local knowledge is processed and aggregated under participatory political systems. Democracy is a buffer, or in other words, a meta-institution, to build good institutions. Hence, participatory democracies deliver quality growth (i.e., long-term growth, better resilience after economic shocks, better social distribution) (Redek and Susjan, 2005; Rodrik, 2000).

Kaldaru and Parts (2008) indicate the significant causal relationship between social-institutional factors and economic development.

This research is conducted at the macro-level across 34 European countries. Kaldaru *et al.* (2008) use Principal Component Analysis to find three latent variables as independent factors (i.e., "Human and Social Capital, Income Equality, and Redistribution") collected from related secondary data. Quality of governance is one of the determinants measured for social capital. They suggest Human and Social Capital has a positive impact on the GDP per capita and the Human Development Index (Kaldaru and Parts, 2008).

Gwenhamo (2011) indicates the positive relationship between Property Rights and Foreign Direct Investment (FDI) in the empirical research conducted in Zimbabwe from 1964 to 2005. Other significant explanatory variables involved in the model are *GDP, capital intensity, the ratio of external debt and GDP, political stability, and educational levels* (Gwenhamo, 2011).

Osman *et al.* (2012) affirm the positive driven institutional factors on economic performance in 27 Sub-Saharan African (SSA) countries from 1984 to 2003. By improving institutional quality (i.e., "enhancing rule of law and regulatory quality, improving contract enforcement, security of property rights, and reducing uncertainty") SSA countries can gain long-term economic development and social prosperity (Osman *et al.*, 2012).

Roy *et al.* (2014) conducted empirical research in different Indian states from 2004 to 2011 to prove the essential role of institutions on economic performance. They (Roy *et al.*, 2014) use Principal Component Analysis to find three latent institutional factors (i.e., Legal Institutions, State Interventions, and Political Institutions) collected from various indices. Firstly, they suggest that State Intervention impacts State's GDP Growth, especially fiscal governance as a positive determinant, and economic freedom as a negative determinant. Subsequently, Legal Institutions have significant impacts on Industrial Development, especially legal efficiency as a negative determinant, and the rule of law and property rights protection as positive determinants. Finally, Political Institution measured by political stability has a positive impact on Industrial Development (Roy *et al.*, 2014).

Vitola and Senfelde (2015) assert institutions are driven factors of socioeconomic development (i.e., GDP per capita and life satisfaction). This cross-national research uses the World Bank Worldwide Governance Indicators covering both economic institutions (i.e., *regulatory quality, rule of law, control of corruption*) and political institutions (i.e., *voice and accountability, government effectiveness, political stability, absence of violence*). Vitola's study (2015) contributes to the critical roles of formal and informal institutions in modern economies:

(1) **Formal institutions:** Well-established property rights and efficient markets are fundamental preconditions for socioeconomic development because they encourage investment in capital and human resources. Corruption control increases the efficiency of markets, as well as decreases costs for economic agents, whereas voice and accountability increase the participation of economic agents in decision-making, thus shaping legislation that supports and encourages socioeconomic development. Government effectiveness, post-materialism, collectivism, and initiative have a significant impact on socioeconomic performance at this stage of development.

(2) **Informal institutions:** Trust, initiative, voice, and accountability play essential roles in innovation-driven economies (Vitola and Senfelde, 2016, p. 277).

Yildirim and Gokalp (2016) analyze the causal relationship between institutions and macro-economic performance in 38 developing countries from 2000 to 2011. They state that some institutional structure indicators have positive effects on GDP per capita (i.e., *the integrity of the law system, regulations on trade barriers, restriction of foreign investments, the share of the private sector in the banking system, and employment-dismissal*). On the contrary, other institutional structure indicators have negative effects on GDP per capita (i.e., *judiciary independence, government expenditures, transfers and subsidies, civil freedoms, the black market exchange rate, collective bargaining, and political stability*) (Yildirim and Gokalp, 2016).

## 2.2. New Public Management

New Public Management is a new paradigm developed to displace Old Public Management. The emphasis in New Public Management is on incentives and competition; in contrast, Old Public Management emphasizes command and control, and compliance with rules of law. Indeed, New Public Management removes the obsolete considerations in Old Public Management, such as pure policy, traditional bureaucracies, development and investment, and classic command-and-control regulation. Alternatively, New Public Management looks toward measurable performance, "loosely coupled and quasi-autonomous units and competitively tendered services", effectiveness and cost-cutting, and self-regulation. Furthermore, New Public Management "allows public managers greater freedom to manage according to private sector corporate practice". New Public Management strikes to reduce the size of governments, shifts away "from the public bureaucracy in favor of para-government" with "subsidiarity principle in service delivery" and "reliance on the private for service delivery". New Public Management-oriented managerialism not only reduces the size but also reshapes the role of central governance, allocates resources, wealth, and provides collective goods differently (Lynn, 2006, pp. 1–18).

There are some common characteristics in New Public Management (Lynn, 2006, pp. 107–108):

> A business-oriented approach to government ⋯ a quality and performance-oriented approach to public management ⋯ an emphasis on improved public service delivery and functional responsiveness ⋯ an institutional separation of public demand functions (councils, citizens' characters), public provision (public management boards), and public service production function (back offices, outsourcing, agencification, privatization) ⋯ a linkage of public demand, provision, and supply units by transactional devices (performance management, internal contract management, corporatization, intergovernmental covenanting and contracting, contracting out) and quality management ⋯ wherever possible, the retreat of (bureaucratic) government institutions in favor of intelligent use of markets and commercial market enterprises (deregulation, privatization, commercialization, and marketization) or virtual markets (internal competition, benchmarking, competitive tendering).

### 2.3. *Developmental taxonomy*

The developmental taxonomy provides a picture of development in 63 Vietnamese provinces during 2012–2015 (see Table 2). There are four developmental clusters and many developmental transitions with their main characteristics:

- Cluster 1 comprises provinces with the largest industrial economies;
- Cluster 2 comprises provinces with traditional economies undergoing transfer to industrial economies with good governance;
- Cluster 3 comprises provinces with the largest traditional economies possessing low institutional environment;
- Cluster 4 comprises provinces with traditional economies, low human development, and good governance;
- Positive transitions, negative transitions, and messy transitions.

### 2.4. *Governance indices*

There are two governance indices used to capture the quality of governance in Vietnam, including The Vietnam Provincial Governance and Public Administration Performance Index (PAPI) and The Provincial Competitiveness Index (PCI) on Vietnam's business environment.

PAPI is known as "the country's largest annual time-series, citizen-centric, nationwide policy monitoring tool" (Centre for Community Support Development Studies, Centre for Research and Training of the Vietnam Fatherland Front, & United Nations Development Program, 2018). It captures the policy processes in general; such as policymaking, policy implementation, and policy monitoring of public service delivery (Centre for Community Support Development Studies *et al.*, 2018) (see details in Appendix A).

PCI is known as "an annual business survey, assessment, and ranking of the economic governance quality of provincial authorities in creating a favorable business environment for the development of

**Table 2:** Cluster membership.

| Province | Region | Developmental cluster | Developmental transition | Transitional trend |
|---|---|---|---|---|
| Binh Duong | South East | 1 | No | No |
| Bac Ninh | Red River Delta | 1 | No | No |
| Ba Ria — Vung Tau | South East | 1 | No | No |
| Dong Nai | South East | 1 | No | No |
| Ho Chi Minh* | South East | 1 | No | No |
| Binh Phuoc | South East | 2 | No | No |
| Ben Tre | Mekong River Delta | 2 | No | No |
| Can Tho | Mekong River Delta | 2 | No | No |
| Da Nang | North Central and Central coastal areas | 2 | No | No |
| Hai Duong | Red River Delta | 2 | No | No |
| Ha Nam | Red River Delta | 2 | No | No |
| Hai Phong | Red River Delta | 2 | No | No |
| Ha Tinh | North Central and Central coastal areas | 2 | No | No |
| Khanh Hoa | North Central and Central coastal areas | 2 | No | No |
| Long An | Mekong River Delta | 2 | No | No |
| Ninh Binh | Red River Delta | 2 | No | No |
| Nam Dinh | Red River Delta | 2 | No | No |
| Quang Binh | North Central and Central coastal areas | 2 | No | No |
| Quang Nam | North Central and Central coastal areas | 2 | No | No |
| Quang Ninh | Red River Delta | 2 | No | No |
| Thanh Hoa | North Central and Central coastal areas | 2 | No | No |

*(Continued)*

**Table 2:** *(Continued)*

| **Province** | **Region** | **Developmental cluster** | **Developmental transition** | **Transitional trend** |
|---|---|---|---|---|
| Thua Thien Hue | North Central and Central coastal areas | 2 | No | No |
| Vinh Long | Mekong River Delta | 2 | No | No |
| Vinh Phuc | Red River Delta | 2 | No | No |
| An Giang | Mekong River Delta | 3 | No | No |
| Bac Lieu | Mekong River Delta | 3 | No | No |
| Dak Lak | Central Highlands | 3 | No | No |
| Kien Giang | Mekong River Delta | 3 | No | No |
| Ninh Thuan | North Central and Central coastal areas | 3 | No | No |
| Soc Trang | Mekong River Delta | 3 | No | No |
| Tay Ninh | South East | 3 | No | No |
| Tra Vinh | Mekong River Delta | 3 | No | No |
| Bac Kan | Northern midlands and mountain areas | 4 | No | No |
| Cao Bang | Northern midlands and mountain areas | 4 | No | No |
| Dien Bien | Northern midlands and mountain areas | 4 | No | No |
| Dak Nong | Central Highlands | 4 | No | No |
| Gia Lai | Central Highlands | 4 | No | No |
| Ha Giang | Northern midlands and mountain areas | 4 | No | No |
| Hoa Binh | Northern midlands and mountain areas | 4 | No | No |
| Lao Cai | Northern midlands and mountain areas | 4 | No | No |
| Lai Chau | Northern midlands and mountain areas | 4 | No | No |
| Lam Dong | Central Highlands | 4 | No | No |
| Son La | Northern midlands and mountain areas | 4 | No | No |
| Tuyen Quang | Northern midlands and mountain areas | 4 | No | No |
| Yen Bai | Northern midlands and mountain areas | 4 | No | No |
| Quang Ngai | North Central and Central coastal areas | No | Messy | Cluster 4 to Cluster 2 to Cluster 3 |

| | | | | |
|---|---|---|---|---|
| Binh Dinh | North Central and Central coastal areas | No | Messy | Cluster 2 to Cluster 4 to Cluster 3 |
| Bac Giang | Northern midlands and mountain areas | No | Messy | Cluster 4 to Cluster 3 to Cluster 4 |
| Binh Thuan | North Central and Central coastal areas | No | Messy | Cluster 3 to Cluster 2 to Cluster 3 |
| Ca Mau | Mekong River Delta | No | Messy | Cluster 3 to Cluster 2 to Cluster 3 |
| Quang Tri | North Central and Central coastal areas | No | Messy | Cluster 4 to Cluster 2 to Cluster 4 |
| Hau Giang | Mekong River Delta | No | Negative | Cluster 2 to Cluster 3 |
| Nghe An | North Central and Central coastal areas | No | Negative | Cluster 2 to Cluster 4 |
| Thai Binh | Red River Delta | No | Negative | Cluster 2 to Cluster 4 |
| Tien Giang | Mekong River Delta | No | Negative | Cluster 2 to Cluster 3 |
| Dong Thap | Mekong River Delta | No | Positive | Cluster 3 to Cluster 2 |
| Ha Noi** | Red River Delta | No | Positive | Cluster 2 to Cluster 1 |
| Hung Yen | Red River Delta | No | Positive | Cluster 4 to Cluster 2 |
| Kon Tum | Central Highlands | No | Positive | Cluster 4 to Cluster 3 |
| Lang Son | Northern midlands and mountain areas | No | Positive | Cluster 4 to Cluster 3 |
| Phu Tho | Northern midlands and mountain areas | No | Positive | Cluster 4 to Cluster 2 |
| Phu Yen | North Central and Central coastal areas | No | Positive | Cluster 4 to Cluster 3 |
| Thai Nguyen*** | Northern midlands and mountain areas | No | Positive | Cluster 4 to Cluster 1 |

*Notes*: *Ho Chi Minh with the hugest contribution to national economic growth. **Ha Noi capital with developmental transition. ***Thai Nguyen with remarkable developmental transition towards industrial economy.

the private sector" (Vietnam Chamber of Commerce and Industry, 2017). It captures the institutional environment in Vietnam through 10 sub-indices reflecting various economic governance issues toward the development of the private sector (see details in Appendix B).

## 3. Methodology

The study uses panel data collected from 63 Vietnamese provinces from 2012 to 2015. For independent variables, Institutions are measured by all sub-indices of PAPI index and PCI index. For dependent variables, Economic Development is measured by GDP per capita (*GDPPC*), the value of exports (*EXPORTS*), and labor productivity (*PRODUCTIVITY*) (see Figure 1 and Table 3).

The raw database is manipulated to curb outliers and skewness by using algorithm transformation (i.e., cubic, square root, and logarithm) (see Table 3).

The multicollinearity is considered to detect potential significantly high correlation among independent variables/sub-PAPI variables (i.e., close to 0.9). Table 5 shows that there are some significantly acceptable correlations among sub-PAPI variables (i.e., less than 0.6); while, there are some significant correlations between each sub-PAPI variable and the dependent variables (i.e., *GDPPC*, *EXPORTS*, and *PRODUCTIVITY*) (see Table 5). Hence, these input variables are accepted to run several types of regression (i.e., multiple regression/pooled OLS, and panel regression).

The multicollinearity is considered to detect potential high correlations among independent variables/sub-PCI variables (i.e., close to 0.9). Table 6 shows there are some acceptable correlations among sub-PCI variables (i.e., less than 0.7), while there are some significant correlations between each sub-PCI variable and the dependent variables (i.e., *GDPPC*, *EXPORTS*, and *PRODUCTIVITY*) (see Table 6). Hence, these input variables are accepted to run several types of regression (i.e., multiple regression/pooled OLS and panel regression).

## 1. Conceptual Framework

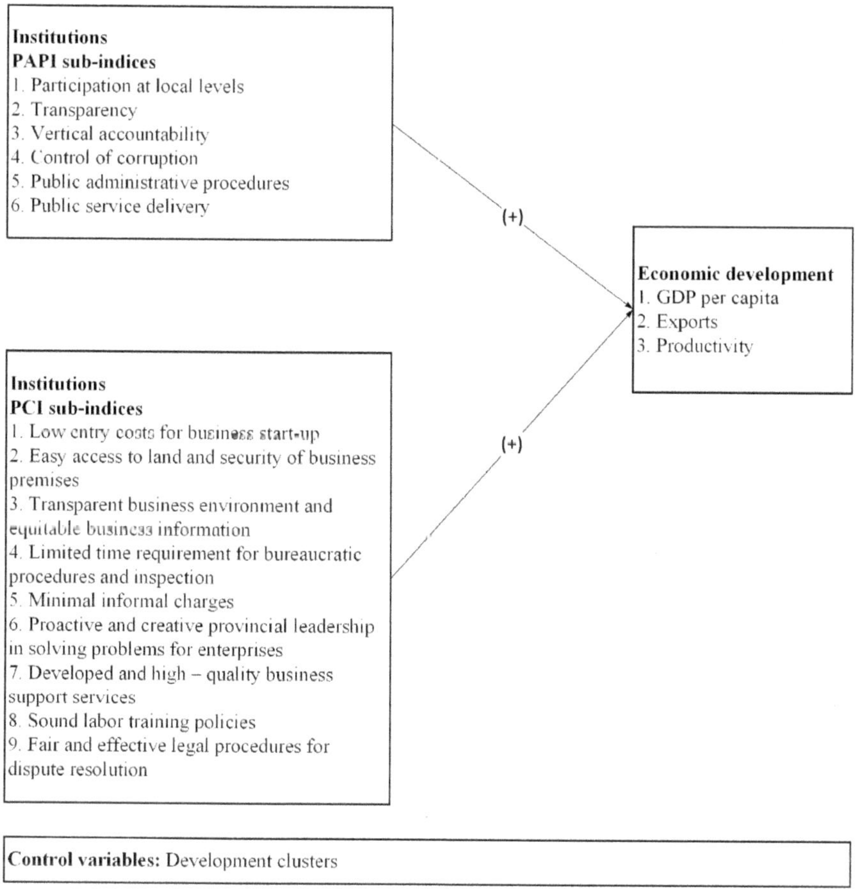


**Figure 1:** The proposed conceptual framework to identify the causal relationship between institutions and economic development.

There are some statistical tests to check the assumptions of the panel regression in each model, such as multicollinearity (i.e., detect potential high correlations between independent variables), the Breusch and Pagan Lagrangian test (i.e., choose random effect or pooled OLS), and the Hausman test (i.e., choose random effect or fixed effect) (Torres-Reyna, 2007).

Besides, developmental cluster (*DEVELOPMENT_CLUSTER*) (see Table 2) is added into the causal models to test whether it is possible that economic development is different among developmental clusters. Furthermore, the causal relationships between institutional factors and economic development are tested separately in each developmental cluster. These tests prove a new hypothesis that different levels of development can intervene in the causal relationship between institutions and economic development (see Table 4).

## 4. Data Analysis

### 4.1. *The prediction of economic development from PAPI indices*

Sub-PAPI variables have significant impacts on *GDPPC* in different sub-models. *PAPI1PARTI* has negative impacts on *GDPPC* completely ($p$-value $< 0.01$, Model 1a, Model 1c); meanwhile *PAPI6SERVICE* has a positive impact on *GDPPC* completely ($p$-value $< 0.01$, Model 1a, Model 1c). However, *PAPI5PROCEDURE* has negative impacts on *GDPPC* in the raw model ($p$-value $< 0.1$, Model 1a) (see Table 7).

Sub-PAPI variables have significant impacts on *EXPORT* in different models. *PAPI1PARTI* has negative impacts on *EXPORT* completely ($p$-value $< 0.05$, Model 2a, Model 2c). Meanwhile, *PAPI6SERVICE* has positive impacts on *EXPORT* completely ($p$-value $< 0.05$, Model 2a) ($p$-value $< 0.01$, Model 2c). Provincial *EXPORT* significantly gains more value in Cluster 1 compared to Cluster 2 as the baseline ($p$-value $< 0.01$, Model 2b and Model 2c) (see Table 7).

*Sub-PAPI* variables have significant impacts on *PRODUCTIVITY* in different models. *PAPI1PARTI* has significant negative impacts on *PRODUCTIVITY* completely ($p$-value $< 0.01$, Model 3a, Model 3c). *PAPI2TRANS* only has a significantly positive impact on *PRODUCTIVITY* in the raw model ($p$-value $< 0.1$, Model 3a). *PAPI5PROCEDURE* has significantly negative impacts

Table 3: Specification of variables.

| Dimension | Variable code | Variable description transformation process | Level of measurement |
|---|---|---|---|
| **Demographics** | PROVINCE | Name of province<br>None | String/Non-metric/Nominal |
| | YEAR | Year of data<br>None | String/Non-metric/Ordinal |
| | PRO_YEAR | Name of province + year of data<br>None | String/Non-metric/Ordinal |
| | DEVELOPMENT_CLUSTER | Developmental cluster of province<br>None | String/Non-metric/Ordinal |
| **Economic development** | GDPPC | GDP per capita (USD)<br>Logarithm (logX) | Metric |
| | EXPORTS | Value of exports (thousand USD)<br>Square root ($\sqrt{X}$) | Metric |
| | PRODUCTIVITY | Labor productivity (million VND/labor)<br>Negative reciprocal root ($-1/\sqrt{X}$) | Metric |
| **Good governance/ Institutions** | PAPI1PARTI | Participation at local levels<br>None | Metric |
| | PAPI2TRANS | Transparency<br>None | Metric |
| | PAPI3ACCOUNT | Vertical accountability<br>None | Metric |
| | PAPI4CORRUP | Control of corruption<br>None | Metric |
| | PAPI5PROCEDURE | Public administrative procedures<br>None | Metric |

| | | |
|---|---|---|
| PAPI6SERVICE | Public service delivery<br>None | Metric |
| PCI1ENVIR | Low entry costs for business start-up<br>None | Metric |
| PCI2LAND | Easy access to land and security of business premises<br>None | Metric |
| PCI3TRANS | Transparent business environment and equitable business information<br>None | Metric |
| PCI4TIME | Limited time requirement for bureaucratic procedures and inspection<br>None | Metric |
| PCI5UNOF | Minimal informal charges<br>None | Metric |
| PCI7ACTIVE | Proactive and creative provincial leadership in solving problems for enterprises<br>None | Metric |
| PCI8BUSSUP | Developed and high — quality business support services<br>None | Metric |
| PCI9LABOR | Sound labor training policies<br>None | Metric |
| PCI10LAW | Fair and effective legal procedures for dispute resolution<br>None | Metric |

**Table 4:** Models checking causal relationships between institutional factors and economic development.

| Models | | Equations |
|---|---|---|
| PAPI models | Model 1 | $\text{logGDPPC}_{it} = \alpha + \beta_1\ \text{PAPI1PARTI}_{it} + \beta_2\ \text{PAPI2TRANS}_{it} + \beta_3\ \text{PAPI3ACCOUNT}_{it} + \beta_4\ \text{PAPI4CORRUP}_{it} + \beta_5\ \text{PAPI5PROCEDURE}_{it} + \beta_6\ \text{PAPI6SERVICE}_{it} + v_{it} + \varepsilon_{it}$ |
| | Model 2 | $\text{sqrtEXPORTS}_{it} = \alpha + \beta_1\ \text{PAPI1PARTI}_{it} + \beta_2\ \text{PAPI2TRANS}_{it} + \beta_3\ \text{PAPI3ACCOUNT}_{it} + \beta_4\ \text{PAPI4CORRUP}_{it} + \beta_5\ \text{PAPI5PROCEDURE}_{it} + \beta_6\ \text{PAPI6SERVICE}_{it} + v_{it} + \varepsilon_{it}$ |
| | Model 3 | $\text{nsqrtPRODUCTIVITY}_{it} = \alpha + \beta_1\ \text{PAPI1PARTI}_{it} + \beta_2\ \text{PAPI2TRANS}_{it} + \beta_3\ \text{PAPI3ACCOUNT}_{it} + \beta_4\ \text{PAPI4CORRUP}_{it} + \beta_5\ \text{PAPI5PROCEDURE}_{it} + \beta_6\ \text{PAPI6SERVICE}_{it} + v_{it} + \varepsilon_{it}$ |
| PCI models | Model 4 | $\text{logGDPPC}_{it} = \alpha + \beta_1\ \text{PCI1ENVIR}_{it} + \beta_2\ \text{PCI2LAND}_{it} + \beta_3\ \text{PCI3TRANS}_{it} + \beta_4\ \text{PCI4TIME}_{it} + \beta_5\ \text{PCI5UNOF}_{it} + \beta_7\ \text{PCI7ACTIVE}_{it} + \beta_8\ \text{PCI8BUSSUP}_{it} + \beta_9\ \text{PCI9LABOR}_{it} + \beta_{10}\ \text{PCI10LAW}_{it} + v_{it} + \varepsilon_{it}$ |
| | Model 5 | $\text{sqrtEXPORTS}_{it} = \alpha + \beta_1\ \text{PCI1ENVIR}_{it} + \beta_2\ \text{PCI2LAND}_{it} + \beta_3\ \text{PCI3TRANS}_{it} + \beta_4\ \text{PCI4TIME}_{it} + \beta_5\ \text{PCI5UNOF}_{it} + \beta_7\ \text{PCI7ACTIVE}_{it} + \beta_8\ \text{PCI8BUSSUP}_{it} + \beta_9\ \text{PCI9LABOR}_{it} + \beta_{10}\ \text{PCI10LAW}_{it} + v_{it} + \varepsilon_{it}$ |
| | Model 6 | $\text{nsqrtPRODUCTIVITY}_{it} = \alpha + \beta_1\ \text{PCI1ENVIR}_{it} + \beta_2\ \text{PCI2LAND}_{it} + \beta_3\ \text{PCI3TRANS}_{it} + \beta_4\ \text{PCI4TIME}_{it} + \beta_5\ \text{PCI5UNOF}_{it} + \beta_7\ \text{PCI7ACTIVE}_{it} + \beta_8\ \text{PCI8BUSSUP}_{it} + \beta_9\ \text{PCI9LABOR}_{it} + \beta_{10}\ \text{PCI10LAW}_{it} + v_{it} + \varepsilon_{it}$ |

*Note*: Control variable: DEVELOPMENT_CLUSTER.

**Table 5:** Multicollinearity among sub-PAPI variables and economic development.

| | log GDPPC | sqrt EXPORT | nsqrt PRODUCTIVITY | PAPI1 PARTI | PAPI2 TRANS | PAPI3 ACCOUNT | PAPI4 CORRUP | PAPI5 PROCEDURE | PAPI6 SERVICE |
|---|---|---|---|---|---|---|---|---|---|
| logGDPPC | 1.0000 | | | | | | | | |
| sqrtEXPORT | 0.6596* | 1.0000 | | | | | | | |
| nsqrtPRODUCTIVITY | 0.9145* | 0.6900* | 1.0000 | | | | | | |
| PAPI1PARTI | | | | 1.0000 | | | | | |
| PAPI2TRANS | | | | 0.5822* | 1.0000 | | | | |
| PAPI3ACCOUNT | | | | 0.5520* | 0.5982* | 1.0000 | | | |
| PAPI4CORRUP | | | | 0.2298* | 0.3105* | 0.3684* | 1.0000 | | |
| PAPI5PROCEDURE | | | | 0.4073* | 0.4493* | 0.4364* | 0.1678* | 1.0000 | |
| PAPI6SERVICE | 0.2823* | 0.2948* | 0.3073* | | 0.1863* | 0.1306* | 0.1567* | 0.1529* | |

*Note*: $^{*}p < 0.05$.

on *PRODUCTIVITY* in different models ($p$-value $< 0.1$, Model 3a) ($p$-value $< 0.05$, Model 3c). *PAPI6SERVICE* has significantly positive impacts on *PRODUCTIVITY* completely ($p$-value $< 0.05$, Model 3a) ($p$-value $< 0.01$, Model 3c). Provincial *PRODUCTIVITY* significantly gains more value in Cluster 1 and gains less value in Cluster 4, compared to Cluster 2 as the baseline (different acceptable benchmarks of $p$-value, Model 3b and Model 3c) (see Table 7).

### 4.2. *The prediction of economic development from PCI indices*

Sub-PCI variables have significant impacts on *GDPPC* in different models. *PCI1ENVIR*, *PCI4TIME*, *PCI8BUSSUP*, and *PCI10LAW* have positive impacts on *GDPPC* completely (different acceptable benchmark of $p$-values, Model 4a, Model 4c). Meanwhile, *PCI5UNOF*

**Table 6:** Multicollinearity among sub-PCI variables and economic development.

| | log GDPPC | sqrt EXPORT | nsqrt PRODUCTIVITY | PCI1 ENVIR | PCI2 LAND | PCI3 TRANS |
|---|---|---|---|---|---|---|
| logGDPPC | 1.0000 | | | | | |
| sqrtEXPORT | 0.6596* | 1.0000 | | | | |
| nsqrt PRODUCTIVITY | 0.9145* | 0.6900* | 1.0000 | | | |
| PCI1ENVIR | | −0.1740* | | 1.0000 | | |
| PCI2LAND | −0.2056* | −0.1498* | −0.1438* | | 1.0000 | |
| PCI3TRANS | 0.1983* | 0.1917* | 0.2915* | 0.1743* | −0.1242* | 1.0000 |
| PCI4TIME | | | 0.1848* | 0.1265* | 0.3001* | 0.1774* |
| PCI5UNOF | | | | | 0.6565* | −0.1257* |
| PCI7ACTIVE | | | | | 0.5095* | 0.1576* |
| PCI8BUSSUP | 0.2947* | 0.2565* | 0.3634* | −0.2972* | −0.3009* | 0.1914* |
| PCI9LABOR | 0.4923* | 0.4635* | 0.4945* | −0.1378* | −0.3390* | 0.2881* |
| PCI10LAW | | | | −0.1949* | | 0.1889* |

| | PCI4 TIME | PCI5 UNOF | PCI7 ACTIVE | PCI8 BUSSUP | PCI9 LABOR | PCI10 LAW |
|---|---|---|---|---|---|---|
| logGDPPC | | | | | | |
| sqrtEXPORT | | | | | | |
| nsqrt PRODUCTIVITY | | | | | | |
| PCI1ENVIR | | | | | | |
| PCI2LAND | | | | | | |
| PCI3TRANS | | | | | | |
| PCI4TIME | 1.0000 | | | | | |
| PCI5UNOF | 0.2783* | 1.0000 | | | | |
| PCI7ACTIVE | 0.4297* | 0.5543* | 1.0000 | | | |
| PCI8BUSSUP | 0.2788* | −0.3622* | −0.1368* | 1.0000 | | |
| PCI9LABOR | | −0.2509* | | 0.5457* | 1.0000 | |
| PCI10LAW | 0.5396* | | 0.2055* | 0.5385* | 0.2491* | 1.0000 |

*Note*: $^*p < 0.05$.

has negative impacts on *GDPPC* completely ($p$-value $< 0.05$, Model 4a, Model 4c) (see Table 8).

In the causal models between sub-PCI variable and *EXPORT*, only *PCI9LABOR* has significant positive impact on developmental clusters (*p-value* $< 0.05$, Model 5c); and provincial *EXPORT* in Cluster 1 significantly gains more value compared to that in Cluster 2 as the base line (*p-value* $< 0.01$, Model 5b, and Model 5c) (see Table 8).

Sub-PCI variables have significant impacts on *PRODUCTIVITY* in different models. *PCI1ENVIR*, *PCI8BUSSUP*, and *PCI10LAW* have significant positive impacts on *PRODUCTIVITY* completely (different acceptable benchmarks of $p$-value, Model 6a, Model 6c). Meanwhile, *PCI2LAND* has significant negative impacts on

**Table 7:** Causal relationships between sub-PAPI variables and economic development.

| | log GDPPC | | | sqrt EXPORT | | | nrsqrt PRODUCTIVITY | | |
|---|---|---|---|---|---|---|---|---|---|
| | Random effect | Fixed effect | Fixed effect | Random effect | Fixed effect | Fixed effect | Random effect | Fixed effect | Fixed effect |
| | (Model 1a) | (Model 1b) | (Model 1c) | (Model 2a) | (Model 2b) | (Model 2c) | (Model 3a) | (Model 3b) | (Model 3c) |
| PAPI1PARTI | −0.0885474*** | | −0.0899514*** | −102.6413** | | −102.7152** | −0.0078642*** | | −0.0078714*** |
| PAPI2TRANS | — | — | — | — | | — | −0.003386* | | — |
| PAPI3ACCOUNT | — | — | — | — | | — | — | | — |
| PAPI4CORRUP | — | — | — | — | | — | — | | — |
| PAPI5 PROCEDURE | −0.0745536* | | — | — | | — | −0.0060021* | | −0.007499** |
| PAPI6SERVICE | 0.1928583*** | | 0.1776774*** | 313.7019** | | 192.0747*** | 0.0127948** | | 0.0111452*** |
| Developmental Clusters (Cluster 2 as baseline) | | | | | | | | | |
| Cluster 1 | | — | — | | 2323.992*** | 2296.237*** | | 0.0166787*** | 0.0256327*** |
| Cluster 3 | | — | — | | — | — | | — | — |
| Cluster 4 | | — | — | | — | — | | — | −0.0063921** |
| Prob > chi2 (Hausman test) Fixed effect vs. Random effect | 0.5649 | 0*** | 0*** | 0.2792 | 0*** | 0.0004*** | 0.1369 | 0*** | 0.0762 |

| | | | | | | | | | |
|---|---|---|---|---|---|---|---|---|---|
| Prob > chi (Breusch and Pagan Lagrangian multiplier test) Random effect vs. Pooled OLS | 0*** | 0*** | 0*** | 0*** | 0*** | 0*** | 0*** | 0*** | 0*** |
| $R^2$ within | 17.76% | 23.50% | 18.26% | 7.24% | 61.33% | 65.07% | 25.94% | 6.45% | 28.02% |
| rho | 94.75% | 94.04% | 94.67% | 92.55% | 88.92% | 89.40% | 93.01% | 90.22% | 88.79% |
| Prob > $F$ (Testparm) Fixed effect of dummy variable(s) | | | 0.735 | | 0*** | 0*** | | 0*** | |

*Notes*: $^{***}p < 0.01$; $^{**}p < 0.05$; $^{*}p < 0.1$.

*PRODUCTIVITY* ($p$-value $< 0.05$, Model 6a, Model 6c). Provincial *PRODUCTIVITY* in Cluster 1 significantly gains more value compared to that in Cluster 2 (different acceptable benchmarks of $p$-value, Model 6b, and Model 6c) (see Table 8).

### 4.3. *How different developmental levels can intervene in the causal relationship between institutions and economic development*

In Cluster 1, sub-PAPI variables have significant impacts on economic development. *PAPI1PARTI* and *PAPI6SERVICE* have significantly negative impacts on *GDPPC*, *EXPORT*, and *PRODUCTIVITY*. *PAPI2TRANS* only has a significantly positive impact on *EXPORT*; meanwhile, *PAPI4CORRUP* has significantly negative impacts on *GDPPC* and *PRODUCTIVITY* (different acceptable benchmarks of $p$-value, Model a, and Model e) (see Tables 9 and 10).

In Cluster 2, sub-PAPI variables (*PAPI1PARTI*, *PAPI2TRANS*, and *PAPI5PROCEDURE*) have significantly negative impacts on *GDPPC* and *PRODUCTIVITY* ($p$-value $< 0.05$; Model b, and Model j). However, sub-PCI variables have significant impacts on economic development. *PCI1ENVIR*, *PCI3TRANS*, *PCI4TIME*, and *PCI8BUSSUP* have significantly positive impacts on *GDPPC*, *EXPORT*, and *PRODUCTIVITY*. *PCI2LAND* has significantly negative impacts on *EXPORT* and *PRODUCTIVITY*; meanwhile, *PCI9LABOR* has significantly positive impacts on *GDPPC* and *EXPORT* (different acceptable benchmarks of $p$-value, Model ii, Model vi, and Model x) (see Tables 9 and 10).

In Cluster 3, sub-PAPI variables have significant impacts on economic development. *PAPI1PARTI* has significantly negative impacts on *GDPPC* and *PRODUCTIVITY*; meanwhile, *PAPI4CORRUP* has significantly positive impacts on *GDPPC* and *PRODUCTIVITY*. However, *PAPI5PROCEDURE* has significantly positive impact on *EXPORT* (different acceptable benchmarks of $p$-value, Model c, Model g, Model k). Furthermore, sub-PCI variables have significant impacts on economic development. *PCI1ENVIR* and *PCI5UNOF* have significantly positive impacts on *EXPORT*;

**Table 8:** Causal relationships between sub-PCI variables and economic development.

| | log GDPPC | | | sqrt EXPORT | | | nrsqrt PRODUCTIVITY | | |
|---|---|---|---|---|---|---|---|---|---|
| | Fixed effect | Fixed effect | Fixed effect | Fixed effect | Fixed effect | Fixed effect | Fixed effect | Fixed effect | Fixed effect |
| | (Model 4a) | (Model 4b) | (Model 4c) | (Model 5a) | (Model 5b) | (Model 5c) | (Model 6a) | (Model 6b) | (Model 6c) |
| PCI1ENVIR | 0.0293524** | | 0.0283894*** | — | | — | 0.001903*** | | 0.0018694*** |
| PCI2LAND | — | | — | — | | — | −0.0023694** | | −0.002579** |
| PCI3TRANS | — | | — | — | | — | — | | — |
| PCI4TIME | 0.0249216** | | 0.0242804* | — | | — | — | | — |
| PCI5UNOF | −0.0238183** | | −0.0250777** | — | | — | — | | — |
| PCI7ACTIVE | — | | — | — | | — | — | | — |
| PCI8BUSSUP | 0.0271331* | | 0.0266145* | — | | — | 0.0030457*** | | 0.0031793*** |
| PCI9LABOR | — | | — | — | | 59.21811** | — | | — |
| PCI10LAW | 0.0260773** | | 0.0260401*** | — | | — | 0.0022993*** | | 0.0021581*** |
| Developmental Clusters (Cluster 2 as baseline) | | | | | | | | | |
| Cluster 1 | | — | — | | 2323.992*** | 2227.161*** | | 0.0166787*** | 0.0088325** |
| Cluster 3 | | — | — | | — | — | | — | — |
| Cluster 4 | | — | — | | — | — | | — | — |
| Prob > chi2 (Hausman test) Fixed effect vs. Random effect | 0.0001*** | 0*** | 0*** | 0*** | 0*** | 0.0001*** | 0*** | 0*** | 0*** |

(*Continued*)

**Table 8:** (*Continued*)

| | log GDPPC | | | sqrt EXPORT | | | nrsqrt PRODUCTIVITY | | |
|---|---|---|---|---|---|---|---|---|---|
| | **Fixed effect** | **Fixed effect** | **Fixed effect** | **Fixed effect** | **Fixed effect** | **Fixed effect** | **Fixed effect** | **Fixed effect** | **Fixed effect** |
| | **(Model 4a)** | **(Model 4b)** | **(Model 4c)** | **(Model 5a)** | **(Model 5b)** | **(Model 5c)** | **(Model 6a)** | **(Model 6b)** | **(Model 6c)** |
| Prob > chi (Breusch and Pagan Lagrangian multiplier test) Random effect vs. Pooled OLS | | 0*** | 0*** | 0*** | 0*** | 0*** | 0*** | 0*** | 0*** |
| $R^2$ within | 48.49% | 23.50% | 49.49% | 16.04% | 61.63% | 67.63% | 60.97% | 6.45% | 62.68% |
| rho | 96.60% | 94.04% | 93.03% | 93.24% | 88.92% | 90.22% | 96.19% | 90.22% | 95.81% |
| Prob > $F$ (Testparm) Fixed effect of dummy variable(s) | | | 0.3254 | | 0*** | 0*** | | 0*** | 0.0057*** |

*Notes*: $^{***}p < 0.01$; $^{**}p < 0.05$; $^{*}p < 0.1$.

**Table 9:** Causal relationships between sub-PAPI variables and economic development in developmental clusters.

| | log GDPPC | | | | sqrt EXPORT | | | |
|---|---|---|---|---|---|---|---|---|
| | Fixed effect | Random effect | Random effect | Fixed effect | Fixed effect | | Fixed effect | Random effect |
| | In Cluster 1 | In Cluster 2 | In Cluster 3 | In Cluster 4 | In Cluster 1 | In Cluster 2 | In Cluster 3 | In Cluster 4 |
| | (Model a) | (Model b) | (Model c) | (Model d) | (Model e) | (Model f) | (Model g) | (Model h) |
| PAPI1PARTI | −0.2022321** | −0.0803768** | −0.1079876* | — | −948.304*** | | — | — |
| PAPI2TRANS | — | −0.094528** | — | — | 844.4187** | | — | — |
| PAPI3ACCOUNT | — | — | — | — | — | | — | — |
| PAPI4CORRUP | −0.1322504** | — | 0.0807559*** | — | — | | — | — |
| PAPI5PROCEDURE | — | −0.158627** | — | — | — | | 107.6594** | — |
| PAPI6SERVICE | 0.3008609** | — | — | — | 766.6454** | | — | 156.6559** |
| F-test (for Fixed effect) | 10.06*** | | | 3.71*** | 22.46*** | | 2.52* | |
| Wald test (for random effect) | | 61.71*** | 21.50*** | | | | | 19.95*** |
| $R^2$ within | 52.05% | 21.65% | 32.23% | 14.53% | 65.05% | | 23.67% | 12.85% |
| rho | 95.57% | 93.72% | 86.82% | 81.84% | 90.10% | | 95.09% | 90.10% |
| Prob > chi2 (Hausman test) Fixed effect vs. Random effect | 0.0085*** | 0.7162 | 0.8201 | 0.0465* | 0.0105** | | 0.003*** | 0.6046 |
| Prob > chi (Breusch and Pagan Lagrangian multiplier test) Random effect vs. Pooled OLS | 1 | 0*** | 0*** | 0*** | 1 | | 0*** | 0*** |

**Table 9:** (*Continued*)

| | nrsqrt PRODUCTIVITY | | | |
|---|---|---|---|---|
| | **Fixed effect** | **Random effect** | **Random effect** | **Fixed effect** |
| | **In Cluster 1** | **In Cluster 2** | **In Cluster 3** | **In Cluster 4** |
| | **(Model i)** | **(Model j)** | **(Model k)** | **(Model l)** |
| PAPI1PARTI | −0.0092654** | −0.0056527** | −0.0088388** | −0.0102891* |
| PAPI2TRANS | — | −0.0067489** | — | — |
| PAPI3ACCOUNT | — | — | — | — |
| PAPI4CORRUP | −0.0046786** | — | 0.0062415*** | — |
| PAPI5PROCEDURE | — | −0.0086822** | — | — |
| PAPI6SERVICE | 0.013528* | — | — | — |
| $F$-test (for Fixed effect) | 18.74*** | | | 4.70*** |
| Wald test (for random effect) | | 58.28*** | 25.90*** | |
| $R^2$ within | 45.76% | 21.12% | 38.46% | 29.13% |
| rho | 92.98% | 87.08% | 81.61% | 88.11% |
| Prob > chi2 (Hausman test) Fixed effect vs. Random effect | 0.0113* | 0.464 | 0.9879 | 0.0001*** |
| Prob > chi (Breusch and Pagan Lagrangian multiplier test) Random effect vs. Pooled OLS | 1 | 0*** | 0*** | 0*** |

*Notes*: $^{***}p < 0.01$; $^{**}p < 0.05$; $^{*}p < 0.1$. Model f has violation of assumptions.

**Table 10:** Causal relationships between sub-PCI variables and economic development in developmental clusters.

| | log GDPPC | | | | sqrt EXPORT | | | |
|---|---|---|---|---|---|---|---|---|
| | | Random effect | Random effect | Fixed effect | | Random effect | Random effect | Random effect |
| | In Cluster 1 | In Cluster 2 | In Cluster 3 | In Cluster 4 | In Cluster 1 | In Cluster 2 | In Cluster 3 | In Cluster 4 |
| | (Model i) | (Model ii) | (Model iii) | (Model iv) | (Model v) | (Model vi) | (Model vii) | (Model viii) |
| PCI1ENVIR | | 0.0287352** | — | 0.0458491** | | — | 32.1413* | — |
| PCI2LAND | | — | — | — | | −89.94731* | −57.96704** | — |
| PCI3TRANS | | 0.0523663** | — | −0.0399037** | | — | — | — |
| PCI4TIME | | 0.0437604*** | — | — | | — | 55.91773** | — |
| PCI5UNOF | | — | — | −0.0608275** | | — | 42.38065*** | — |
| PCI7ACTIVE | | — | — | — | | — | — | — |
| PCI8BUSSUP | | 0.0425421** | — | — | | — | — | 55.56321* |
| PCI9LABOR | | 0.0554625** | — | — | | 127.3615*** | — | — |
| PCI10LAW | | — | 0.0295157** | — | | — | 21.22131* | — |
| F-test (for Fixed effect) | | | | 31.66*** | | | | |
| Wald test (for Random effect) | | 500.12*** | 298.34*** | | | | 41.71*** | 19.66** |
| $R^2$ within | | 71.52% | 75.12% | 46.07% | | 42.85% | 54.47% | 24.27% |
| rho | | 96.75% | 94.41% | 87.85% | | 85.91% | 97.39% | 92.68% |
| Prob > chi2 (Hausman test) Fixed effect vs. Random effect | | 0.0932 | 0.9993 | 0.0004*** | | 0.5528 | 0.9994 | 0.1111 |
| Prob > chi (Breusch and Pagan Lagrangian multiplier test) Random effect vs. Pooled OLS | | 0*** | 0*** | 0*** | | 0*** | 0*** | 0*** |

**Table 10:** (*Continued*)

| | nrsqrt PRODUCTIVITY | | | |
|---|---|---|---|---|
| | | Random effect | Random effect | Fixed effect |
| | In Cluster 1 | In Cluster 2 | In Cluster 3 | In Cluster 4 |
| | (Model ix) | (Model x) | (Model xi) | (Model xii) |
| PCI1ENVIR | | 0.0020518** | — | 0.0028512** |
| PCI2LAND | | −0.0044185** | — | — |
| PCI3TRANS | | 0.0034801*** | — | −0.0047309*** |
| PCI4TIME | | 0.0023893*** | 0.0028205* | — |
| PCI5UNOF | | — | — | — |
| PCI7ACTIVE | | — | −0.0027782*** | — |
| PCI8BUSSUP | | 0.0032391*** | — | 0.0062666*** |
| PCI9LABOR | | — | — | — |
| PCI10LAW | | — | 0.002673*** | 0.0025604** |
| $F$-test (for Fixed effect) | | | | 9.31*** |
| Wald test (for Random effect) | | 457.58*** | 239.05*** | |
| $R^2$ within | | 72.99% | 75.76% | 66.12% |
| Rho | | 93.48% | 89.55% | 93.25% |
| Prob > chi2 (Hausman test) Fixed effect vs. Random effect | | 0.1135 | 0.9901 | 0.0455* |
| Prob > chi (Breuschand Pagan Lagrangian multiplier test) Random effect vs. Pooled OLS | | 0*** | 0*** | 0*** |

*Notes*: $^{***}p < 0.01$; $^{**}p < 0.05$; $^{*}p < 0.1$. Model i, Model v, and Model ix have violations of assumptions.

meanwhile, *PCI2LAND* has a significantly negative impact on *EXPORT*, and *PCI7ACTIVE* has a significantly negative impact on *PRODUCTIVITY*. *PCI4TIME* has significantly positive impacts on *EXPORT* and *PRODUCTIVITY*. *PCI10LAW* has significantly positive impacts on *GDPPC*, *EXPORT*, and *PRODUCTIVITY* (different acceptable benchmarks of $p$-value, Model iii, Model vii, and Model xi) (see Tables 9 and 10).

In Cluster 4, *PAPI1PARTI* has a significantly negative impact on *PRODUCTIVITY*; meanwhile, *PAPI6SERVICE* has a significantly positive impact on *EXPORT* (different acceptable benchmarks of $p$-value, Model h, and Model l). However, sub-PCI variables have significantly complex impacts on economic development. *PCI1ENVIR* has significantly positive impacts on *GDPPC* and *PRODUCTIVITY*. Meanwhile, *PCI3TRANS* has significantly negative impacts on *GDPPC* and *PRODUCTIVITY*. *PCI5UNOF* has a negative impact on *GDPPC*, meanwhile, *PCI10LAW* has a positive impact on *PRODUCTIVITY*. *PCI8SUPP* has significantly positive impacts on *EXPORT* and *PRODUCTIVITY* (different acceptable benchmarks of $p$-value, Model iv, Model viii, and Model xii) (see Tables 9 and 10).

## 5. Discussions

In general, institutions are driving factors of economic development in Vietnam from the perspectives of stakeholders (i.e., citizens and enterprises). A series of institutions create favorable conditions for human development, social capital development, and business development, leading to economic development (i.e., public service delivery, low entry costs for business start-ups, limited time requirement for bureaucratic procedures and inspection, developed and high-quality business support service, sound training policies, and fair and effective legal procedures or dispute resolution). Meanwhile, there are other institutions having negative relationships with economic development (i.e., participation at local levels, public administrative procedures, easy access to land and security of business premises, and minimal informal charges). On the one hand, this is consistent with New Institutional Economics in general; and Kaldaru and Parts (2008), Osma *et al.* (2012), Vitola and Senelde (2015) in particular. On the other hand, this is consistent with North (1990) and Aron (2000) explaining institutionalism in Third World countries with the payoff mindset (i.e., institutions are a set of payoffs to economic activity).

Adding Developmental Clusters into the causal models reveals that Cluster 1 significantly gains the most economic values than other clusters (i.e., GDP per capita, export, and labor productivity). It is consistent with the taxonomy of development in the previous study that Cluster 1 shoulders the national earnings, contributing enormously to the national economic growth. Cluster 2 with good governance has chased Cluster 1 to reach economic development with the huge gap between these two clusters. However, it indicates a positive development in Vietnam, reflecting an appreciated effort toward development orientation consistent with development theory and sustainable development.

When testing causal relationships between institutional factors and economic development in each developmental cluster, some new determinants (i.e., control of corruption, transparent business environment, and equitable business information) and some complex impacts with both negative and positive signs in different contexts (public administrative procedures, minimal informal charges) emerge. In Cluster 1 and Cluster 2 with higher developmental levels, it is revealed that provinces have created strong institutional environments for business development, human development, and social capital development; however, some payoffs exist to gain economic activity (i.e., participation at local levels, transparency of local decision-making, corruption, public administrative procedures, easy access to land and security of business premises). In Cluster 3, with a lower developmental level, a significant contrasting result is revealed, which is that provinces have gained significant positive points in control of corruption, the limited time requirement for bureaucratic procedures and inspection, minimal informal charges. Cluster 4, with the lowest developmental level, reveals that provinces are stuck trying to deal with the problem of transparent business environment and equitable business information, the limited time requirement for bureaucratic procedures and inspection, and minimal informal charges.

## 6. Theoretical Contribution

The study contributes significant evidence from Vietnam to support New Institutional Economics and New Public Management:

- Enabling government-oriented managerialism provides incentives and responsiveness, improves public service delivery, and creates a favorable environment for citizen satisfaction and business development. To do so, the government should be reformed toward smaller size, decentralization, cost-cutting, high quality performance, effectiveness, and a strong institutional environment.
- Good governance would enhance economic development by lowering transaction costs, lowering transformation cost, and increasing labor specialization/human development;
- Different levels of development would intervene in the causal relationship between Institutions and Economic Development.

## Appendix A: List of Dimensions, Sub-dimensions and Indicators of PAPI Index

| Dimensions | Sub-dimensions | Indicators |
|---|---|---|
| Dimension 1 Participation at Local Levels | Civic knowledge | Civic knowledge |
| | | Knows grassroots democracy decree (%) |
| | | Knows people know, people decide (%) |
| | | Correct term limit of 2.5 years (%) |
| | Opportunities for participation | Voted in last commune people's council election (%) |
| | | Voted in last national assembly election (%) |

(*Continued*)

*(Continued)*

| Dimensions | Sub-dimensions | Indicators |
|---|---|---|
| | Quality of Elections | Village chief elected (%)<br>Participated in election (%)<br>More than 1 candidate (%)<br>Invited to participate (%)<br>Paper ballot was used (%)<br>Votes were counted publicly (%)<br>Candidate was suggested (%)<br>Voted for winner |
| | Voluntary contributions | Voluntary contribution to project (%)<br>Community monitoring board monitors contribution (%)<br>Voluntary contribution recorded (%)<br>Participated in decision making to start project (%)<br>Provided input to project design (%) |
| Dimension 2 Transparency of local decision-making | Poverty lists | Poverty list published in last 12 months<br>Type 1 errors on poverty list (% agree)<br>Type 2 errors on poverty list (% agree) |
| | Communal budgets | Communal budget is made available (%)<br>Respondent read communal budget (%)<br>Believe in accuracy of budget (%) |
| | Land-use plan/pricing | Aware of communal land plans (%)<br>Comment on communal land plans (%)<br>Land plan acknowledges your concerns (%)<br>Impact of land plan on your families<br>Did not lose land as a result of land plan<br>Compensation close to market value (%)<br>Informed of land usage (%)<br>Land use for original purpose (%)<br>Know where to go to get land (%) |

(*Continued*)

| Dimensions | Sub-dimensions | Indicators |
|---|---|---|
| Dimension 3 Vertical accountability | Interactions with local authorities | Contacted village head (%) |
| | | Contacted commune PCOM (%) |
| | | Contact with village head successful (%) |
| | | Contact with commune successful (%) |
| | | Made a proposal to authorities (%) |
| | | Proposal successful (%) |
| | People's inspection boards | village has a PIB (%) |
| | | PIB selected by vote (%) |
| | | PIB effective (%) |
| | Community investment boards | Commune has a CISB (%) |
| | | CISB effective (%) |
| Dimension 4 Control of corruption | Limits on public sector corruption | No diverting of public fund (% agree) |
| | | No brides for land title (% agree) |
| | | No kickbacks on construction (% agree) |
| | Limits on corruption in service delivery | No bribes at hospital (% agree) |
| | | No bribes for teachers' favourism (% agree) |
| | Equity in employment | No bribes for state employment (% agree) |
| | | Total no relationship |
| | Willingness to fight corruption | Corruption had no effect on respondent (%) |
| | | Know anti-corruption law (%) |
| | | Provinces serious about combating corruption (%) |
| | | Denunciation price '000s VND (Imputed) |
| | | Victim did not denunciate bribe request (%) |
| Dimension 5 Public Administrative Procedures | Certification Procedures | Applied for certification service (%) |
| | | Total quality of certification procedures (8 criteria) |
| | Construction Permit | Applied for construction permit (%) |
| | | Did not use many windows for construction permit (%) |

(*Continued*)

(*Continued*)

| Dimensions | Sub-dimensions | Indicators |
|---|---|---|
| | | Received construction permit (%) |
| | | Total quality of construction procedures (8 criteria) |
| | Land procedures | Took part in land procedures (%) |
| | | Did not use many windows for land (%) |
| | | Received land title (%) |
| | | Total quality of land procedures (8 criteria) |
| | Personal procedures | Took part in personal administrative procedures (%) |
| | | Took quality of personal procedures (8 criteria) |
| | | Did not use many windows for personal procedures (%) |
| Dimension 6 Public service delivery | Public health | Share with health insurance (%) |
| | | Quality of health insurance (4 pt scale) |
| | | Quality of free medical care for kids (5 pt scale) |
| | | Poor households are subsidized (%) |
| | | Checks for children are free (%) |
| | | Total hospital quality (10 criteria) |
| | Primary education | Kilometer walk to school |
| | | Minutes to school |
| | | Rating of primary school (5 pt scale) |
| | | Total school quality (9 criteria) |
| | Infrastructure | Households with electricity (%) |
| | | Quality of road (1 = All dirt; 4 = All asphalt) |
| | | Frequency of garbage pick-up (0 = Never, 4 = Everyday) |
| | | Share drinking tap water (%) |
| | | Share drinking unclean water (%) |
| | Law and order | How safe is your locality (3 = Very safe) |
| | | Change in safety over time |
| | | Crime rate in locality (% Victim of crime) |

## Appendix B: List of Dimensions and Indicators of PCI Index

| Dimensions | Indicators |
|---|---|
| Dimension 1<br>Low entry costs for business start-up | Length for business registration in days (Median)<br>Length of business re-registration in days (Median)<br><br>Median number of days to wait for Land Use Right Certificate (LURC)<br>Percentage of firms waiting for more than one month to complete all steps necessary to start operations<br>Percentage of firms waiting for more than three months to complete all steps necessary to start operations<br>Percentage of firms registering or re-registering through one-stop-shop<br>Procedures at one-stop-shop are transparently listed (% Agree)<br>Guidance and instruction on procedures at one-stop-shop are clear and adequate (% Agree)<br>Staffs at one-stop-shop are professional and knowledge (% Agree)<br>Staffs at one-stop-shop are friendly (% Agree)<br>IT application at one-stop-shop is good (% Agree)<br>None of the criteria above are met (% Agree) |
| Dimension 2<br>Easy access to land and security of business premises | Percentage of firms that own land and are in possession of an LURC<br>Percentage of land that has been registered and provided with official LURCs<br>Percentage of firms that say nonstate enterprises do not have difficulties in accessing land or expanding premises<br>Firms' rating of expropriation risk (1: Very high to 5: Very low)<br>Percentage of firms that say compensation for land is always or highly likely fair<br>Percentage of firms that agree that changes in government land prices reflect changes in market prices |

*(Continued)*

(*Continued*)

| Dimensions | Indicators |
|---|---|
| | Percentage of firms that have completed land procedures in the last two years and have encountered no difficulties in land-related procedures |
| | Percentage of firms that want to have LURCs but don't have LURCs because of complicated procedures and troublesome staffs |
| Dimension 3<br>Transparent business environment and equitable business information | Access to planning documents (1 = easy to access; 5 = impossible to access) |
| | Access to legal documents (1 = easy to access; 5 = impossible to access) |
| | Relationship important or very important to get access to provincial documents (% Important or Very important) |
| | Negotiations with tax authority are an essential part of doing business (% Agree or Strongly agree) |
| | Predictability of implementation of central laws at the provincial level (% Usually or Always) |
| | Business Associations' role in advising and countering provincial policies (% Important or Very important) |
| | Openness and quality of provincial webpage |
| | Percentage of firms have accessed provincial websites (%) |
| | Budget documents have enough details for use in business activities (% Yes) |
| | Budget documents are published right after being approved (% Yes) |
| Dimension 4<br>Limited time requirement for bureaucratic procedures and inspection | Percentage of firm spending over 10 percentage of their time on understanding and complying with regulations |
| | Median number of inspections (all agencies) |
| | Median tax inspection hours |
| | Government officials are effective (% Strongly agree or Agree) |
| | Government officials are friendly (% Strongly agree or Agree) |

(*Continued*)

| Dimensions | Indicators |
|---|---|
| | Firms don't have to travel trips to obtain stamps and signatures (% Strongly agree or Agree) |
| | Paperwork is simple (% Strongly agree or Agree) |
| | Fees are listed publically (% Strongly agree or Agree) |
| | No noticeable improvements are made (% Strongly agree or Agree) |
| Dimension 5 Minimal informal charges | Enterprises in my line of business usually have to pay for informal charges (% agree or totally agree) |
| | Percentage of firms paying over 10% of their revenue for informal charges |
| | Rent-seeking phenomenon is popular in handling administrative procedures for business (% strongly agree or agree) |
| | Percentage of firms saying that informal charges usually or always deliver expected results |
| | Informal charges are at acceptable levels (% Strongly agree or Agree) |
| Dimension 7 Proactive and creative provincial leadership in solving problems for enterprises | Firms' assessment of the attitude of provincial government toward private sector (% Positive or Fairly positive) |
| | The PPC is flexible within the legal framework to create favorable business environment for nonstate firms (% Strongly agree or Agree) |
| | The PPC is very proactive and innovative in solving new problems (% Strongly agree or Agree) |
| | There are good initiatives at the provincial level but they are not well implemented by departments (% Strongly agree or Agree) |
| | Provincial leaders have good policies they are not well implemented at district level (% Strongly agree or Agree) |
| | Province's reaction to lack of clarity in central policies/documents: % delay and seek instructions and do nothing |

(*Continued*)

(*Continued*)

| Dimensions | Indicators |
|---|---|
| Dimension 8 Developed and high-quality business support service | Number of trade fairs held by province in previous year and registered for present year |
| | Ratio of the total number of service providers to the total number of firms (%) |
| | Ratio of the number of nonstate and FDI service providers to the total number of service providers (%) |
| | Firm has used business information search services (%) |
| | Firm used private provider for above business information search services (%) |
| | Firm intends to use above service provider again for business information search services (%) |
| | Firm used private provider for consulting on regulatory information (%) |
| | Firm intends to use above service provider again for consulting on regulatory information (%) |
| | Firm has used business matchmaking services (%) |
| | Firm used private provider for business match making services (%) |
| | Firm intends to use above service provider again for business matchmaking services (%) |
| | Firm has used trade promotion services (%) |
| | Firm used private provider for trade promotion services (%) |
| | Firm intends to use above service provider again for trade promotion services (%) |
| | Firm has used technology related services (%) |
| | Firm used private provider for technology related services (%) |
| | Firm intends to use above service provider again for technology related services (%) |
| | Firm has used accounting and financing training services (%) |
| | Firm used private provider for above accounting and financing training services (%) |
| | Firm intends to use above service provider again for accounting and financing training services (%) |

(*Continued*)

| **Dimensions** | **Indicators** |
|---|---|
| | Firm has used business administration training services (%) |
| | Firm used private provider for above business administration training services (%) |
| | Firm intends to use above service provider again for accounting and financing training services (%) |
| | Firm has used business administration training services (%) |
| | Firm intends to use above service provider again for business administration training services (%) |
| Dimension 9 Sound labor training policies | Services provided by provincial agencies: general education (% Very good or Good) |
| | Services provided by provincial agencies: vocational training (% Very good or Good) |
| | Firm has used labor exchange services (%) |
| | Firm used private provider for above labor exchange services (%) |
| | Firm intends to use above service provider again for labor exchange services (%) |
| | Percentage of total business costs spent on labor training |
| | Percentage of total business costs spent on labor recruitment |
| | Overall satisfaction with labor (% Agreeing labor meets firm needs) |
| | Ratio vocational training school graduates to untrained laborers |
| | Secondary school graduates as % of workforce |
| | Percentage of workers having completed training at vocational schools |
| Dimension 10 Fair and effective legal procedures for dispute resolution | Legal system provided mechanism for firms to appeal against officials' corrupt behavior (% Always or Usually) |
| | Firm confident that legal system will uphold property rights and contracts (% Strongly agree or Agree) |
| | Cases filed by non-state entities at Provincial Economic Court per 100 firms |
| | Non-state claimants as a percentage of claimants at Provincial Economic Court |

(*Continued*)

*(Continued)*

| Dimensions | Indicators |
|---|---|
| | Provincial court judge economic cases by the law (% Agree or Strongly agree) |
| | Provincial court resolve economic cases quickly (% Agree or Strongly agree) |
| | Court judgments are enforced quickly (% Agree or Strongly agree) |
| | Legal aid agencies support business in the use of law when disputes arise (% Agree) |
| | Formal and informal cost are acceptable (% Agree and Strongly agree) |
| | Judgment by the court is fair (% Agree or Strongly agree) |
| | Willingness to use court in case a dispute arises (% Yes) |

## References

Aron, J. (2000). Growth and institutions: A review of the evidence. *The World Bank Research Observer*, 15(1), 99–135.

Centre for Community Support Development Studies, Centre for Research and Training of the Vietnam Fatherland Front, & United Nations Development Program. (2018). PAPI. Retrieved August 9, 2018, from http://papi.org.vn/eng/index

Chand, S., Duncan, R., and Quang, D. (2001). The role of institutions in the development of Vietnam. *ASEAN Economic Bulletin*, 18(3), 276–288.

Gwenhamo, F. (2011). Foreign direct investment in Zimbabwe: The role of institutional and macroeconomic factors. *South African Journal of Economics*, 79(September), 211–223.

Kaldaru, H., and Parts, E. (2008). Social and institutional factors of economic development: Evidence from Europe. *Baltic Journal of Economics*, 8(1), 29–51. https://doi.org/10.1080/1406099X.2008.10840444Lynn

Lynn, L.E. (2006). *Public Management: Old and New*. New York: Routledge.

Mennard, C., and Shirley, M. (2008). Introduction. In *Handbook of New Institutional Economics*, edited by Claude Menard and Mary Shirley. Boston: Springer.

North, D. (1990). *Institutions, Institutional Change and Economic Performance*. New York: Cambridge University Press.

Osman, R.H., Alexiou, C., and Tsaliki, P. (2012). The role of institutions in economic development: Evidence from 27 Sub-Saharan African countries. *International Journal of Social Economics*, 39(1/2), 142–160. https://doi.org/10.1108/03068291211188910

Redek, T., and Susjan, A. (2005). The impact of institutions on economic growth: The case of transition economies. *Journal of Economic Issues*, 39(4), 995–1027. Retrieved from http://www.jstor.org/stable/4228204

Rodrik, D. (2000). Institutions for high-quality growth: What they are and how to acquire them.No. Working Paper 7540. Retrieved from https://www.nber.org/papers/w7540

Roy, B.C., Sarkar, S., Mandal, N.R., and Pandey, S.K. (2014). Role of institutions in economic performance: An empirical study on interstate differences in Indian States with reference to Jharkhand. *European Scientific Journal*, 10(10), 313–335.

Shirley, M. (2008). Institutions and development. In C. Menard & M. Shirley (eds.), *Handbook of New Institutional Economics*. Springer-Verlag Berlin Heidelberg, pp. 611–638.

Torres-Reyna, O. (2007). Panel data analysis fixed and random effects using Stata (v.4.2). Retrieved from https://www.princeton.edu/~otorres/Panel101.pdf

Vietnam Chamber of Commerce and Industry. (2017). About PCI. Retrieved from http://eng.pcivietnam.org/about/about-pci/. Accessed on October 11, 2018.

Vitola, A., and Senfelde, M. (2016). The role of institutions in economic development. *Business: Theory and Practice*, 16(3), 271–279. https://doi.org/10.1057/9781137480668_1

Yildirim, A., and Gokalp, M.F. (2016). Institutions and economic performance: A review on the developing countries. *Procedia Economics and Finance*, 38, 347–359. https://doi.org/10.1016/S2212-5671(16)30207-6

https://doi.org/10.1142/9789811227158_0026

## Chapter 26

# Science and Technology and their Applications in Enterprises in Ho Chi Minh City in the Context of the Fourth Industrial Revolution

**Thi Kim Hoa Luu**

## Abstract

Today, the ground-breaking technologies of the 4.0 Revolution are influencing the way companies operate, organize, and mobilize their resources, which forces enterprises to reflect, to review their business modes, and adopt new models. Having strategies for development, applications of new technologies, and the will to constantly innovate are crucial for enterprises to exist and thrive. This is the inevitable rule that businesses in Vietnam, particularly those in Ho Chi Minh City, should respect. Scientific and technological development and application of the revolutionary achievements of the 4.0 Revolution are the leading strategies to make a breakthrough in development. In this chapter, four issues have been focused on: (1) science and technology in the context of the Industrial Revolution 4.0, (2) the application of new technology in enterprises in the Industrial Revolution 4.0, (3) the science and technology and technology application in enterprises in Ho Chi Minh City, and (4) policy implications of the development of science and technology and the application of new technologies in enterprises in Ho Chi Minh City.

**Keywords:** Science and technology; Industrial Revolution 4.0; Ho Chi Minh City business.

## 1. Science and Technology in the Context of the Industrial Revolution 4.0

### 1.1. *Science and technology*

Science is a system of knowledge about the laws of motion of things, phenomena, as well as their relationships in the fields of nature, society, and thought. It helps people raise awareness and promote social development (Do Van Thang, 2016). Knowledge of science is formed and accumulated from the human research process on a practical basis.

People are not only aware of science but, more importantly, they also constantly use the scientific knowledge acquired to create tools and means, and find ways and methods of using them. It helps people to be more effective, especially in production work, which is becoming more and more convenient and efficient. Science and technology increase productivity and promote the development of society.

Technique is the total means of labor and methods of producing material values (Nguyen Lan, 1977). Along with the successive scientific and technological revolutions, the technical level of development jumps to new heights, changing the nature and the technical concept. The implication of the term "technology" (along with the socioeconomic context of development) has become cramped, not capable of containing new broader, deeper insights of humanity, and the term "technology" comes to be used in place of the term "technique" because it conveys and includes the term "technique".

Technology is a set of methods, processes, skills, tools, and means used to transform resources into products. Technology has four components, including *materials technology*, *people*, *information,* and *organization* (Do Van Thang, 2016). Other difference between technique and technology is that technology involves learning, training, and transfer, and technique involves only means and methods for people to work and produce. Technology is formed very early and continuously develops innovation. It has always played an important role in the development of production and social life, and it is the criteria to assess the level of development of social production.

Between science and technology lies a dialectical relationship; in terms of origin, technology comes first because of the needs of life; however, due to practical needs, it is necessary to be aware of all things, phenomena, needs of natural improvement, improvement of production efficiency, and living activities, which motivate people to study further and explore. Scientific knowledge is formed and developed. At the same time, technology for re-development has to be based on scientific knowledge, thanks to the application of science to the improvement, the production of new means of production with increasingly high features, the production process is increasingly perfect. Therefore, the more developed the science, the stronger the development of technology. As technology evolves, it requires more advanced science to meet the evolving needs of technology. The close integration of science and technology, which promotes mutual development and an increasingly modern society, brings science and technology "into the direct production" of goods. First, as the foundation, it is the main driving force for social development.

The requirements of life combined with scientific knowledge lead to the constant development of technology. The newer the technology, the higher the productivity, and the lesser the labor, raw materials, and fuel required per unit of the product. The quality, features, durability of the product, lower production costs, lesser environmental impact, and enhanced social life make the newer technology increasingly sophisticated, more modern, and promote the constant growth of society.

Thus, the fact that the higher the level of science and technology, the more modern the ability to create products of good serviceability, outstanding features, high value, and that are environmentally friendly plays an important role in modernizing the economy, promoting competition, and international cooperation, which are the important criteria in the development of the knowledge economy and international integration.

### 1.2. *Fourth Industrial Revolution (4.0)*

Industrial Revolution 4.0 is built on the foundation of the Third Industrial Revolution, centered on the inventions, innovations, and combinations of three "great trends": *physics*, *digitization,* and *biology*, the combination of the three worlds: the physical world, the virtual world (digital world), and the living world. The core elements of the digital revolution in 4.0 are *artificial intelligence*, *connectivity*, and *large data.* In the field of biotechnology, the revolutionary 4.0 focuses on research to create leaps and bounds in terms of developments in agriculture, fisheries, medicine, food processing, environmental protection, renewable energy, chemistry, and materials. In the field of physics, such focus is seen in the next-generation robot, 3D printers, self-driving vehicles, new materials, and nanotechnology.

The term "Industrial 4.0" was first introduced at Hannover Technology Fair in the Federal Republic of Germany in 2011. The concept of the Fourth Industrial Revolution was first mentioned in the "High-tech Strategy Action Plan" approved by the German government in 2012. This is a support program from the German Federal Government in cooperation with industry and industry-leading Germany to improve Process management and manufacturing in the manufacturing industry through "computerization". Since then, the term "Industry 4.0" has been used extensively in the world to describe the Fourth Industrial Revolution.

According to Prof. Klaus Schwab, Chairman of the World Economic Forum, Industrial Revolution 4.0 is defined as "a term for the technologies and concepts of an organization in the value chain" along with physical systems in cyberspace, the internet of things (IoT) and internet of services (IOS).

Characteristics of the Industrial Revolution 4.0: (1) The information processing capabilities are multiplied by technological breakthroughs in many areas, thanks to the ability to connect through mobile devices and capabilities. Access to large databases; (2) The previous industrial revolution took place at linear speed, while the growth rate of Industry 4.0 is exponential; (3) Radical change in the way people create products, thereby creating a "revolution" in the organization of production chain-value. The breadth and depth of these changes signal the dramatic transformation of the whole production system, management, and governance of human society.

### 1.3. *Technological trends in Industrial Revolution 4.0*

Every new development and technology has the same core characteristics: increasing the spillover effect of digital and information technology. For example, gene sequence decoding became a reality because of advances in technology, the suite of computing and data analysis capabilities; the existence of advanced robots is due to the development of artificial intelligence. Trends are responsible for the cost of reducing the widespread diffusion of technology; combining various types of digital technology and converging digital technology with other technologies, such as the combination of new sensor technology, large data analysis, cloud computing, and IoT, (all connected in the Internet environment) is driving the development of automation and intelligent manufacturing systems.

The technology platform includes (1) large data; (2) cloud computing; (3) connected robots; (4) IoT. Based on these four technologies, new application technologies are (1) 3D printing technology; (2) automation machinery; (3) artificial intelligence; (4) human–machine integration. The classification of the underlying technology, or application technology, is just relative because the fields of science and technology are interwoven with each other, integrating to assist one another in the same development.

### 1.4. *Major trends of science and technology till 2050*

More than 700 scientists from the IFTF and the International Electrotechnical Commission (IEEE) conducted a survey of science and technology expected to develop in 10 to 50 years, focusing on five trends in science and technology in the coming time (Thanh, 2007).

1. **The broad spectrum and computational spectrum:** Humanity undertakes sophisticated calculations of very high technological infrastructure to find patterns in huge amounts of data, to model and simulate increasingly complex phenomena.
2. **The trend of sensors is present in everything and everywhere:** In this trend, tiny sensors embedded in widgets form the sensor infrastructure.
3. **The new trend creates a small, neat, and light infrastructure:** In the coming time, new materials and information technology would create the ability to shift from the large infrastructure networks to the networks having modular structures and extending to higher levels.
4. **The trend of convergence of small appliances in the micro-world:** The real revolution in the micro-world is predicted as the convergence of small items; micro-robots made with microelectronics or with nanotechnology are important factors. IC manufacturing plays a pioneering role in nanotechnology.
5. **The trend of biology:** With today's technological advances, the success of reading and recording the genetic code of life gives humanity the ability to manipulate biology from the bottom-up.

### 1.5. *Impact of Industrial Revolution 4.0 on business*

In the era of Industrial Revolution 4.0, companies face increasingly fierce competition. In the field of information technology, companies like Google and Facebook are growing fast, while other well-known companies such as IBM, Microsoft, Cisco, Intel, or Japan's major electronic corporations are spreading all over the world through a difficult restructuring process.

In the manufacturing sector, traditional car manufacturers are under intense competition from emerging companies with an innovative approach, such as Tesla, which is boosting modern auto production and self-driving cars.

In the field of banking and finance, the large-scale restructuring process affects millions of employees due to the application of mobile banking and the drastic competition of startups. Silicon Valley offers cheaper financial services to customers through cloud computing. The insurance industry is also under pressure to restructure under the impact of artificial intelligence applications and the demand for auto insurance declines when the car itself is popular in the market.

The global competition has intensified with the advent of many micro-national companies. Startup companies which have only 3–5 employees have partners around the world thanks to the robust Internet information infrastructure.

The position of a company or a corporation does not completely depend on the company's size, number of employees, or initial investment capital.

It can be said that the Industrial Revolution 4.0 has four major impacts on businesses across different sectors:

(i) As consumer expectations are changing, individuals, businesses, and consumers are becoming the center of the digital economy; all around the way customers are served.
(ii) Data help improve products and asset utilization; new technologies are changing the way businesses view and manage their assets, as products and services are enhanced with features. Numbers help improve value.
(iii) New forms of partnerships emerge as companies realize the importance of new cooperative models; a world of customer experience, data-driven services, and asset performance analysis through analytics requires new forms of collaboration, especially in the context of new, groundbreaking innovation at current speed.
(iv) Operational models are transformed into new digital models; strategies and ways of working have to change; Revolution 4.0 requires companies to revise their operating models so that strategic planning faces the challenge of meeting the need for faster, more flexible and responsive operations. Companies that have the ability to combine digital, physical, and biological multipliers are often successful in creating breakthroughs for both industry and production, and distribution and consumption systems.

## 2. The New Technology Application of Enterprises in the Industrial Revolution 4.0

### 2.1. *On the world*

Artificial intelligence (AI) has made remarkable progress, many major technology companies in the world such as Google, Facebook, Microsoft, Amazon, IMB, and Samsung are actively investing in AI. In particular, Elon Musk built the Neuralink project to connect the human brain to the computer.

The fourth revolution in the world provides a number of significant gains, but especially in startups' development. The Wall Street Journal and Dow Jones Venture Source list the top 10 startups in the past few years, which are mainly in the US, China, and India markets. Taxi service providers such as Uber, Xiaomi Electronics, and Airbnb have a unique idea of a home-stay network of residents. Palantir specializes in providing software, technology, and services for analyzing confidential data from the input, which is a vast amount of data. The others are Snapchat, self-destruct video sharing application, Didi Kuaidi with Didi Dache taxi service application, and Flipkart the "Indian online retail giant"; the company that manufactures missile equipment and provides space shipment services, SpaceX; the website specializing in photo sharing, social networking video, Pinterest; online data storage service company, Dropbox (Phan Xuan Dung, 2018).

### 2.2. *Application of new technology of Vietnamese enterprises in the Industrial Revolution 4.0*

Vietnam makes the most of the achievements of the 4.0 Industrial Revolution and has initially had some results in a number of areas:

First, AI technology, Vietnam has a number of products from AI technology such as: (i) "Network data hunting system" is used by banks, VNAT and many enterprises to locate brands; for statistical results, analysis of text in large numbers up to several billion bytes, only artificial intelligence can do that. Some other projects have also been developed such as the Chatbot project replacing people answering phone calls, emails, and scheduling work. Vinamilk applies automation technology with artificial intelligence in manufacturing and operates quite effectively. At Vinamilk's modern dairy factory, almost all operations in the factory are automated; the RGV (Rail Guided Vehicle) robot automatically moves the finished pallet to the smart warehouse area, converting the rolls and packaging materials to fully automated plants that can charge the battery without monitoring or human intervention. (ii) The "Intelligent Software System" (KBOT) is a software development company of Hitelli. KBOT, the Virtual Assistant, is the product of the first AI technology in Vietnam for automated question and answer in many fields of life and society such as public administration, finance-banking, e-commerce, law, tourism, culture, agriculture, health, marriage, and socioeconomics. This unique intelligent product, effectively supporting the state management and enterprise management, has been applied by the City of Hanoi.

Second, there are applications in Cloud Computing technology. In September 2008 in Vietnam, IBM was the first foreign company to open a cloud computing center in co-operation with Vietnam Communication and Technology Corporation. Then, Microsoft followed up on the cloud computing market in Vietnam. In May 2010, FPT was the pioneer in cloud computing by signing a contract with Microsoft Asia — Trend Micro to collaborate on cloud development in Asia.

Third, application of Internet technology to connect with nature. New Internet connection (IoT) is at an early stage and there are opportunities for all countries, including Vietnam. There are three ways IoT helps businesses improve their business: reducing operating costs, increasing productivity, and expanding markets or developing new products. Some enterprises have applied IoT such as (i) Viettel is researching applications for transportation such as electronic ticketing, transportation supervision, and the field of health care related mainly to patients in Hai Phong City and Quang Ninh province. (ii) At Hoa Lac Hi-Tech Park, in July 2016, IoT Laboratories was established with the participation of Hoa Lac Hi-Tech Park, DTT,

Intel, and Dell Vietnam. (iii) MobiFone joins forces with communication programs, awareness-raising, providing business community experience on IoT, providing 4G MobiTV services, super-speed Internet, and 4K video. (iv) Bkav Technology Group has invested in the development of smart home solutions with devices and software that control houses via the Internet. (v) FPT provides intelligent hospital solutions in Singapore, launches Rogo Alfa through the use of smartphones to control devices in families; FPT Software has the first Predix project in the Japanese market with the mission of implementing IoT Platforms that can work well with Predix as well as existing cloud environments; FPT IS has a Smart Transport project being piloted in Ho Chi Minh City.

Fourth, large data technology has appeared in Vietnam. Robusta, for example, is an information technology training institute that has signed a cooperation agreement with EMC, the world's leading provider of cloud solutions, large data storage solutions to take big data training courses to Vietnam. There will be some Vietnamese enterprises that successfully exploit the data. Mobile trend and 4G, 5G Internet users will increase sharply. OTT (over-the-top) and social media services contribute more than 80% to online, online video, and mobile content (Phan Xuan Dung, 2018).

## 3. The States of Science and Technology and Application of New Technologies in Enterprises in Ho Chi Minh City

### 3.1. *The success of scientific and technological development of Ho Chi Minh City*

Developing software technology is an important means of implementing the Industrial Revolution 4.0. Quang Trung Software Park attracts 33 investors with the registered capital of VND5,735 billion after the establishment of Quang Trung Software City (QTSC) over a period of 18 years (2001). There are 135 software enterprises (84 domestic enterprises, 51 foreign enterprises) with registered capital of VND2,451 billion; total investment capital is VND 250 billion, total investment capital is over VND 8,186 billion. In the beginning of 2017, Quang Trung Software Park, with an area of 43ha, divided into 11 functional areas, had an occupancy rate of 88.2%. Of which, foreign-invested enterprises accounted for nearly 50%. In 2017, QTSC ranked third in terms of occupancy, telecom infrastructure, etc. According to KPMG, technology in Asia.[1] The brand name of Quang Trung Software Park is recognized internationally by international communities, contributing to the national branding of the information technology and software industries. It makes Vietnam a world leader in services and providers of outsourcing in the field of software and the world's most attractive destination for information technology investment.

The city invests tens of billions VND to build the infrastructure of the high-tech parks in District 9 (Saigon Hi-Tech Park, SHTP). By 2017, 107 projects were granted certificates with a total investment of \$6.09 billion (of which domestic investment: \$1.48368 billion/67 projects, FDI: \$4.61189 billion/40 projects) (Schwab, 2018).[2] High-tech projects contribute significantly to the development of science and technology.

In 2009, Ho Chi Minh City set up two laboratories of IC design worth US \$20 million: one is located in the Faculty of Electrical and Electronics Engineering of Ho Chi Minh City University of Technology. ICDREC signed "Memorandum of Understanding" with Mentor Graphics and AMCC from United States University of Ho Chi Minh City. Each lab consists of 20 laptops, a server, and IC design software. These are the foundations for the research and training of human resources in the field of IC design, which is one of the foundations for promoting the 4.0 Industrial Revolution in the city.

---

[1] http://tphcm.chinhphu.vn/qtsc-dung-thu-3-trong-so-cac-khu-cong-nghe-tai-chau-a

[2] http://www.shtp.hochiminhCity.gov.vn/TinTuc/thongcaobaochi/Lists/Post/Post

In the high-tech zone, the city set up Nanotechnology Laboratory under the Center for Research and Development which was established under Decision No. 19/QD-KCNC dated February 9, 2010 of the Management Board of the Technology Park High. Its functions and duties are to carry out scientific research and technological development in the field of nanotechnology, new materials, renewable energy, and scientific product testing. The department carries out a number of research projects and collaborations with enterprises in line with the objective of commercialization of research products according to their functions and tasks. The city also invests in the development of nanotech products such as solar cells, biomass, biodiesel, semiconductor chips, stem cells, pharmaceuticals such as split nano-extract from turmeric, and lycopene nanoparticles from gas. In the field of cosmetics, the R&D center also succeeds in making gold nanoparticles, silver nanoparticles with different properties, applied in skin whitening and bactericidal products and skin care, among other things.

Ho Chi Minh City has approved the "Chip Development Program for Ho Chi Minh City in the period 2013–2020" (IC industry is widely applied in life, computers, cars) in December 2012 with the common objectives, tasks associated with seven programs and projects. Specifically, the project is related to IC design training, IC microprocessor and embedded system development, microchip development. To date, Ho Chi Minh City has a number of products such as the 8-bit VN801 processor chip, the 32-bit VN1632 processor chip, the Analog LDO TH7105 chip, and the SG8V1 chip. Many chips are in the process of commercialization of products such as positioning equipment — black box GPS tracker for motorcycles, automobiles; electronic container lock and forthcoming electronic meter; many branded chips in Vietnam are commercialized, contributing to raising the position of microcircuits in Vietnam in the region and in the world. In addition, Ho Chi Minh City is also speeding up the construction of microelectronic plants with a capacity of 1.8 billion chips a year and an estimated turnover of $90 million a year.

The city supports the construction of a number of science and technology organizations to contribute to the city becoming a high technology center of Vietnam, including R&D Center of the Hi-Tech Park City, Biotechnology Center, New Equipment Design Center (Nep-tech), IC Design Research and Education Center, which serve the electronics industry, The Institute of Computational Science and Technology, Nanotechnology Laboratory — Ho Chi Minh City, National University, Ho Chi Minh, and Enterprise Technology Incubator.

Every year, about 220 inventions and useful solutions of scientists and workers are registered for protection in Ho Chi Minh City. From 2012, the Department of Science and Technology Ho Chi Minh City deployed and put Ho Chi Minh City — Techmart online into operation. At present, over 4000 technology and equipment institutes, schools, and scientists are introduced and offered on Techmart online, contributing to the technology products being brought to market at low cost.

The IoT has widely and extensively developed the citizens' socioeconomic life in public administrative services; e-commerce; financial and banking services such as payment, deposit; transport operations; tax administration; teaching and learning (online training); healthcare, newspapers, information, entertainment, shopping, architecture, and construction. The widespread deployment of 4G network infrastructure in the city accelerates the speed of Internet use in service production and the personal life of the city people. The city bravely builds up many breakthrough mechanisms and policies, such as policies to attract good science and technology experts at home and abroad, to work.

The Ho Chi Minh City Smart Project (the period of 2017–2020 with 2025-year vision) is a smart urban framework, with general issues including e-Government, Planning, Transportation, Health and Human Services, Public Utilities, Water and Wastewater, Construction, Environment (Waste and Air), Energy, Education and Training, Payments and Finance, Agriculture, and Communications. Although we are only at the first phase of the Smart City building process, it shows that the city promotes the idea to carry out the Industrial Revolution 4.0 extensively.

### 3.2. *Limitations in the development of science and technology in Ho Chi Minh City*

There are various limitations in the development of science and technology. First, the scientific and technological development of the city has not been strengthened yet, and the city has not become a center for science and technology development, which has an impact on the socioeconomic development of the South. It has no scientific and technological positions in Southeast Asia or the world. Second, the development of science and technology is also a movement, the quality of scientific and technological research is not high. Despite large investment (thousands of billion) for the development of the 4.0 Revolution, the achievements obtained have not yet been deemed commensurate. Third, the preferential policies in attracting high-quality human resources to Ho Chi Minh City are still limited in a number of cases. There is no summary and evaluation of the effectiveness of the human resources recruitment mechanism of this city. In addition, basic research in Ho Chi Minh City has not been paid much attention, or invested in, in the last 20–30 years. Fourth, investment for scientific and technological development is inadequate, and a large percentage is not used correctly or directly for its purpose. Fifth, the links in science and technology development centers between Ho Chi Minh City and those of other countries are not close. With other provinces, such links between the centers and enterprises of science and technology in the city are weak, so it has not created technological breakthrough products with wide influence. Technological universities in the city are not the nucleus for the development of new science and technology. Sixth, teams of technical experts, scientists serving the development and renewal of science and technology to meet the development requirements of the 4.0 Revolution lack in quantity and quality.

### 3.3. *Limitations for businesses*

The investment project for microelectronics plant, invested by the Saigon Industrial Corporation (CNS), is a core project of the city's microchip development program, but it is not yet established. Up to now, looking objectively, the microchip development program of Ho Chi Minh City has had initial successes and created "gravity", many delegations of experts in the field of international microchips came forward for research cooperation, order processing with the city's microchip research organization.

The number of producing and manufacturing enterprises having scientific and technological research units are still very low, including FDI. City businesses are not as strong in the science and technology market as the demand side of the market. Many businesses do not consider the development of science and technology as an important factor for enterprises to remain competitive in the context of increased economic integration. The city's scientists and technologists now work mainly at research institutes, with very few working in enterprises.

The number of enterprises operating in the field of science and technology is still low; according to the Ministry of Science and Technology, as of November 2015, there are 204 enterprises nationwide. According to the Department of Market Development and Science and Technology (Ministry of Science and Technology), there are very few enterprises having certificates of Science and Technology Enterprises in Vietnam, particularly in Ho Chi Minh City, where there are about 24 businesses. Meanwhile, Decision 1244/QD-TTg of the Prime Minister approved the orientation, objectives, and tasks of science and technology in the period 2011–2015, and orientation in 2015–2020 will develop 3,000 science and technology enterprises. This is because the demand for scientific technology services in the city in particular, and the country, in general, is very low.

The technology of Vietnamese enterprises, including Ho Chi Minh City, lags behind that of the world by about 30 years and several decades compared to the region, Information of the Minister of Science and Technology (Ministry of Science and Technology Science and Technology) Nguyen Quan said at a conference held in Ho Chi

Minh City on August 25, 2015. The application of information technology, robotics, real-time application technologies in production and life has a revolutionary impact, bringing the city to a development breakthrough.

### 3.4. *The reasons for limitations*

1. The interest in the scientific and technological development of the city is not satisfactory as there is no policy mechanism and investment breakthrough for science and technology development, implementing the Industrial Revolution 4.0. The economic development mechanism and the mechanism for scientific and technological development of the city are not closely linked. Socioeconomic development has not yet been ordered for science and technology, so science and technology is not well-researched to apply.
2. The main reason is that science and technology have not been seen as important factors in determining the speed and quality of economic growth in the city: though policy advocates have talked about science and technology. The implementation is limited, there is no breakthrough policy on science and technology development.
3. The Department of Science and Technology of the city does not do well in advising the city on selecting research directions, selecting products with advantages and potential for development, and proposing solutions, especially on the main mechanism. Especially on the policy to develop science and technology products to meet the requirements of the Industrial Revolution 4.0.
4. There are no salary policies and incentives to encourage students and workers to study science and technology. Meanwhile, this human resource plays the most important role in implementing the 4.0 technology revolution.
5. The city has no policy to encourage high-tech companies to come to it to set up research and development centers.
6. The effective protection of intellectual property rights has not been thoroughly and effectively managed, which it is a barrier to the development of science and technology.

7. There is no proper mechanism for policies of the State, cities, and enterprises to co-ordinate and support each other in the development of science and technology.

### 3.5. *The reason for limitations of businesses*

1. Enterprises have not paid much attention to technological innovation. Accordingly, most enterprises do not comply with State regulations on setting up the Science and Technology Development Fund, which deducts 3–10% of their pre-tax income. The Ministry of Science and Technology reports on the development of scientific and technological application in production and business to the Government Office (4-2014); technology transfer contracts in general and related to the 4.0 Revolution are inadequate.
2. The technology renovation process in enterprises in the city is still slow; the technology level of enterprises is mainly medium and low, leading to the quality and competitiveness of products in the market. At home and abroad, it is difficult to meet integration requirements.
3. The application of digital technology in production, trade, services, and market connection is limited.
4. The lack of capital and access to difficult capital sources affects the application of revolutionary achievements in production and business.
5. Entrepreneurs themselves are not interested in technological innovation and do not work with local scientists to find the most economical solutions for production, research new products, or replace the machines.

## 4. Policy Implications for Science and Technology Development and Application of New Technologies in Enterprises in Ho Chi Minh City

### 4.1. *Implications for businesses*

It is necessary to raise awareness of the 4.0 Revolution and its impact on the production and success of businesses in order to have suitable solutions for the development and application of the achievements of revolution 4.0 in its entirety. To promote creativity in enterprises, business owners must consider the development of science and technology, technical renewal, and application of technology 4.0, encouraging innovations and innovativeness of laborers, determining the competitiveness of enterprises. In addition, enterprises must develop strategies for scientific and technological development, technological renewal, application of the revolutionary achievements of the 4.0 Revolution, solutions, ways, and orders of implementation. Moreover, to formulate mechanisms and policies for rewarding and fostering scientific and technological researches and innovations for scientists and workers who contribute to enterprises. Further, to strengthen linkages in innovation, research cooperation between enterprises and between enterprises and research organizations, scientists, academics, and universities need to identify the business that is primarily responsible for implementing the achievements of the 4.0 Revolution. Businesses must also acknowledge that scientists, research institutes, and universities are the mainstay for the achievements of science and technology. Accordingly, large corporations should build rooms and proceed to build enterprises' research and development for science and technology.

### 4.2. *Implications for the city*

The city needs to create a favorable environment and adopt a breakthrough policy mechanism for the development of science and technology, including basic research and applied research to apply the achievements of Revolution 4.0; support policies for scientific and technological development, and application of technology 4.0 in enterprises; to create conditions for the science and technology market to develop; organization of technology assessment; accurate information, and timely development of technology for business.

The city invests capital and budgets for startups, supports startups contributing to science and technology development, and realizes the achievements of the revolution.

Developing a corporate, local, and national security strategy and strengthening intellectual property rights is key in attracting foreign

R&D, especially to attract large international corporations to set up R&D centers in the city.

Renovation of tax, credit policies and financial mechanisms can strongly encourage R&D, technological innovation, and the application of the results of the revolution. Encouragement of strong R&D centers' establishment in corporations and economic groups helps innovate the manufacturing technology of the sectors, and attract and cooperate with local and foreign scientists.

To increase human resources for innovation and renovate the wage mechanism to encourage the training of human resources for technical branches, cities should study mechanisms and policies to train and attract scientists and senior experts and promote links between universities, research institutes, and businesses to implement the 4.0 Revolution.

The Department of Science and Technology should coordinate with other departments and associations to disseminate the Industrial Revolution 4.0 to understand the opportunities and challenges for the sectors and areas to work out, to seize the opportunity, and proactively limit the challenges of this revolution.

## References

Do Van Thang, T.S. (2016). *Science and Technology with Industrialization and Modernization in Ho Chi Minh City.* Hanoi, Publishing House, National Politics.

Nguyen Lan, (1977). *Vietnamese dictionary.* Hanoi: Social Sciences Publishing House.

Phan Xuan Dung, T.S.K.H. (2018). *Revolutionary Fourth Revolution of Convergence and Savings*, Nxb. Science and Technology, Hanoi, pp. 174–212.

Schwab, K. (2018). *Fourth Industrial Revolution.* Hanoi: National Politics The Truth.

Thanh, L. (2007). The main trend of science and technology to 2020. *Sciencc and Development Newspaper*, September 20–26, No. 38.

University of Economics (2017). *Proceedings of the Scientific Conference on Economic Growth Model Based on Science, Technology and Innovation (STI).* Economy Ho Chi Minh City.

https://doi.org/10.1142/9789811227158_0027

Chapter 27

# Impact of the State-owned Investment and Other Factors on Economic Growth with SGMM and Bayesian Approach: The Case of Vietnam

Thi Thanh Huong Tran and Thu Hang Pham

## Abstract

This research focuses on the impact of the state-owned investment on economic growth in the case of Vietnam. System generalized method of moments (SGMMs) and minimum Bayes factor (MBF) are used with the dataset from 49 provinces of Vietnam. The results show that labor productivity of the state-owned sector (LP_S) has positively large impacts, while the number of working labors (LBs) and the rate of trained employees (RTEs) have no effect on economic growth. Additionally, implementing investment of the state-owned sector (II_S) and capital productivity (CP) negatively affected Vietnam's economic growth during the period from 2013 to 2017. Hence, Vietnam needs to use the state-owned investment more effectively and reduce its proportion while increasing the proportion of non-state investment and FDI. Moreover, the labor productivity of state-owned sector should be strongly improved to promote economic growth in the future.

**Keywords:** State-owned investment; Factors; GDP growth; SGMM; Minimum Bayes factor.

## 1. Introduction

Investment always plays an important role in promoting economic growth, especially for developing countries. Investment can be formed from different sources such as state-owned investment, private sector investment, and foreign investment. For developing countries, state-owned investment has been said to play a crucial role in pushing economic growth. However, this investment is always limited by ephemeral budget revenues in developing countries. But if the government effectively uses this source in socioeconomic objectives, it creates a direct and indirect impact on economic growth and development. Therefore, this issue becomes a topic of interest in research in many developing countries like Vietnam.

In the context of Vietnam, state-owned investment contributes significantly to the growth of total investment in the economy as well as economic growth. It accounts for a large part of the total investment. Because of the large proportion, any change in the pace of the state-owned investment profoundly affects the growth rate of total investment and economic growth. With the orientation in the economic policy of the Government of Vietnam, in recent years, there has been a trend of reducing the percentage of public investment to encourage and diversify investment sources in the economy. The proportion of private sector investment exceeds the share of state-owned investment (Table 1).

Through the data in Table 1, the proportion of investment carried out from 2013 to 2017 in Vietnam decreased rapidly (from 40.4% in 2013 to 35.7% in 2017). This downward trend is in line with the process of implementing the policy of restructuring the economy toward the market economy. The state-owned investment has gradually shifted the areas that were hardly implemented by the private sector to ensure the balance of the national economy. Another notable factor is that the size of state-owned investment depends heavily on the state budget revenues, although Vietnam's budget revenues are still unstable. In the structure of total state budget revenue, domestic revenue accounts for a low proportion, mainly from crude oil and

**Table 1:** Implemented investment of Vietnam in the period from 2013 to 2017 (at current prices).

| | | State-owned sector | | Private sector | | Foreign invested sector | |
|---|---|---|---|---|---|---|---|
| **Year** | **Total (billions dong)** | **Investment (billions dong)** | **(%)** | **Investment (billions dong)** | **(%)** | **Investment (billions dong)** | **(%)** |
| 2013 | 1094542 | 441924 | 40.4 | 412506 | 37.7 | 240112 | 21.9 |
| 2014 | 1220704 | 486804 | 39.9 | 468500 | 38.4 | 265400 | 21.7 |
| 2015 | 1366478 | 519878 | 38.0 | 528500 | 38.7 | 318100 | 23.3 |
| 2016 | 1487638 | 557633 | 37.5 | 578902 | 38.9 | 351103 | 23.6 |
| 2017 | 1668601 | 594885 | 35.7 | 677510 | 40.6 | 396206 | 23.7 |

*Source*: General Statistics Office of Vietnam.

from import taxes. These revenues do not directly reflect the efficiency of production and business. In the future, these sources can decrease because crude oil is increasingly being exhausted, while the road map to cut tariffs is emerging with the globalization process of Vietnam.

Before the downward trend, the amount of investment still increased and reached 441 924 billion Vietnamese dong in 2013, then 594 885 billion Vietnamese dong in 2017. In 2017, the investment of the state-owned sector still accounted for a high proportion of the total investment (accounting for 35.7% in 2017).

In Vietnam, the economic policy is in the process of shifting gradually from the growth in width to the growth in depth model. Over a long time, Vietnam's growth model has been evaluated in a wide range, heavily due to the size of labor and capital. Therefore, the investment policy of the Government in this period is focused on expanding and creating conditions to attract domestic and foreign investment. Policymakers expect to increase public investment in infrastructure and key economic sectors that help boost economic growth. But to avoid the "middle income trap", it is essential to quickly shift to a growth in depth model. That would lead to the situation where the role of investment contribution in economic growth decreases relative to the role of some other factors such as science and technology.

As seen through the actual data, investment of the state-owned sector tends to decrease in proportion. The average is relatively lower than other sources of investment, but the size of the state-owned investment is still quite larger than non-state investment. Thus, the state-owned sector investment still plays a very important role in Vietnam, although the efficiency as well as the sources of contributions to the state-owned sector are still limited. Researching and assessing the role and efficiency of investment in the state-owned sector still needs to be properly considered and evaluated to promote the effectiveness of the funds as well as to have solutions to overcome the limitations.

## 2. Literature Review

Investment from the state-owned sector has a profound effect on the economic pace of growth through direct and indirect impacts, which is expressed in terms of aggregate supply and aggregate demand. State-owned investment directly impacts aggregate demand as government spending and aggregate supply as a contributing factor in the production function. This investment affects indirectly and spreads to the aggregate demand by attracting private investment. Most of the studies focus on public investment because it accounts for a large percentage of the regional investment structure. These studies show that there are two conflicting trends in the contribution of state-owned investment and private investment in many countries.

First, any studies prove that both state-owned and private investment have a largely positive impact on GDP growth. Rabnawaz and Jafar (2015) point out that revenues from the state-owned sector boost economic growth. Increased revenue increases public investment, thereby it also boosts economic growth in a short period of time. However, in the long term, the increase in government revenues and public investment can slow down economic growth. For developed countries in the long term, Aaron (1990), based on endogenous theory, develops equilibrium equations with USA dataset from 1951 to 1985 in his research. This result shows that state-owned investment has a positive effect on output. For the approach from a production perspective, with the Cobb–Douglas function, many studies lead to the conclusion that investment has a major effect on economic growth (Munnell, 1990; Lynde, 1992; Lighthart, 2000; Ram and Ramsey, 1989). With a different approach from the translog profit function, some studies also conclude that the investment of state-owned sector brings many benefits to economic growth and labor productivity (Lynde and Richmond, 1993). For newly industrialized countries, the research study of Ramirez (1996), Ramirez and Nazmi (2003) indicate that both kinds of investments are substantial for growth.

The second trend, focusing on the public investment, states that state-owned investment may also slow down economic growth according to following explanations: (i) it is related or financed by debt; (ii) it competes with the private sector (Turnovsky, 1996; Phetsavong and Ichihashi, 2012), and (iii) it focuses on inefficient industries (Devarajan *et al.*, 1996). More clearly, when this amount of investment is financed by borrowing, it may limit growth (Khan and Kumar, 1997). Investigating the part of the state-owned investment in the economy, focusing on public investment, many other research papers also lead to the negative impacts as above (Evans and Karras, 1994; Tatom, 1991; Vijverberg *et al.*, 1997). Besides, some papers affirm the fact that private investment has a greater impact on the pace of economic growth than public investment (Coutinho and Gallo, 1991; Ghura, 1997; Beddies, 1999; Hague, 2013). For developed countries, it is acknowledged that, in a short period of time, the impact of public investment on economic growth is insignificant, while in the long term the impact is significantly seen (Aschauer, 1989). From the perspective of a research method, the applied methods are also very diverse. OLS (Ordinary Least Square) and 2SLS (two stages least square) are used to assess the impact of investment rate, public investment rate, and private investment rate on economic growth (Khan, 1996; Reinhart and Khan, 2009; Ghali, 1998). Research using the vector error correction model (VECM) with the Tunisia dataset from 1963 to 1993 shows that public investment slows down economic growth.

Apart from the studies on the role of investment independently on economic growth, some research show the relationship between state-owned and private sectors in the context of economic growth. Pereira (2001) with VAR with data of 11 countries in the period from 1960 to 1990 shows the role of public investment in boosting private sector output. With data from the developed countries of Japan, Canada, and US, the research of Afonso and Aubyn (2008) with VAR model proves the fact that both state-owned investment and private investment are very important for growth. Another study about the relationship between investment of state-owned sector and private sectors, by Lynde and Richmond (1991) with translog cost function and the USA dataset from 1958 to 1989, lead to the conclusion that state-owned investment is important, and it complements private investment. Studies of Merriman (1990) or Wang (2005) affirm the necessity of public investment expenditures in facilitating new private investment formation and thus promoting economic growth through its effects on activities.

In Vietnam, most studies also emphasize the impact of state-owned investment quite a lot, but mainly in qualitative or theoretical forms. In almost all studies, the goal of hypothesis testing revolves around the question of whether state-owned investment dominates or promotes private investment in Vietnam. To (2011) uses VECM to estimate the reaction functions for state-owned sector investment variables, private investment, and GDP from 1986 to 2010. Conclusion of this study is that the investment of both sectors has positive impacts on output, but the impact of the private sector is larger. The study of Tran and Le (2014) with ARDL model tests the effect of public investment on Vietnam's economic pace of growth from 1988 to 2012. Results show that the impact of public investment on short-term economic growth is not significant, but has a long-term growth impetus. According to Trinh and Nguyen (2014), investment and development activities of the state-owned economic sector make a substantial contribution to the socioeconomic development of the country. The investment allocation and implementation mechanism still focuses too much on infrastructure, not adequately investing in projects that are effective, directly create goods, or increase GDP.

Thus, through an overview of theoretical and experimental studies, the estimated results demonstrate that state-owned investment has both positive and negative impacts in the short and long term on the economic growth of countries. Previous studies mainly use ARDL, VECM. However, these studies do not solve the problem thoroughly, such as in terms of the heterogeneity and endogeneity of units in the research dataset. To overcome this phenomenon, in this study we use panel data and system generalized method of moments (SGMMs) and minimum Bayes factor (MBF) at the provincial level. In most of the studies conducted in Vietnam, the research objectives emphasize on public or private investment sector, so the results of these studies do not really reflect the role of investment resources in the state-owned sector in the economy. Hence, this research study focuses on assessing the impact of state-owned sector investment in general on Vietnam's economic growth. The results of the research contribute to the system of abundant research around the role of the state-owned sector in Vietnam's economic growth in recent years.

## 3. Data and Methodology

### 3.1. *Data*

Data for gross domestic product (GDP), labor force (LB), implemented investment (II), labor productivity in the state-owned sector (LP_S), and implemented investment in the state-owned sector (II_S) are collected from the Statistical Yearbook of 49 provinces in Vietnam. Variables representing the factors are summarized in Table 2.

### 3.2. *Methodology*

To investigate the effect of state-owned investment and other factors on economic growth in Vietnam, the following equation has been established:

$$\begin{aligned} \mathrm{GDRP}_{ij} &= \alpha_0 + \alpha_1 \lg \mathrm{LB}_{ij} + \alpha_2 \,\mathrm{RTE}_{ij} + \alpha_3 \lg \mathrm{CP}_{i(j-1)} \\ &\quad + \alpha_4 \lg \mathrm{II\_}S_{ij} + \alpha_5 \lg \mathrm{LP\_}S_{ij} + u_{ij}, \qquad (1) \end{aligned}$$

**Table 2:** Measurement of variables.

| Variables | Unit | Measurement |
|---|---|---|
| Growth rate of Gross domestic product (GDPR) | % | $(GDP_1 - GDP_0)/GDP_0$ GDP at constant 2010 prices |
| Labor force (LB) | People | Number of working labors |
| Rate of trained employees in the economy (RTE) | % | Number of trained employees/Total working labors |
| Implemented investment in state-owned sector (II_S) | Billions dong | Calculated at constant 2010 prices |
| Capital productivity (CP) | Times | GDP at constant 2010 prices/ capital at constant 2010 prices |
| Labor productivity in state-owned sector (LP_S) | Million VND/person | VA of state sector at constant 2010 prices/number of working labors of state sector |

where $i$, $j$ is province $i$ in year $j$; $\alpha$ are the estimated coefficients; $u_{ij}$ is error terms; $\mathrm{GDPR}_{ij}$ is the growth rate of gross domestic product of province $i$ in year $j$ at constant 2010 prices; $lgLB_{ij}$ is the logarithm of number of working labors in province $i$ year $j$; $\mathrm{RTE}_{ij}$ is the RTEs in province $i$ in year $j$; $lg\mathrm{CP}_{i(j-1)}$ is the logarithm of capital productivity of province $i$ in year $j$–1 at constant 2010 prices; $lg\mathrm{II\_}S_{ij}$ is the logarithm of implemented investment of the state-owned sector in province $i$ in year $j$ at constant price 2010; $lg\mathrm{LP\_}S_{ij}$ is the logarithm of labor productivity of the state-owned sector in province $i$ in year $j$ at constant 2010 prices.

In panel data regression, there are three common methods often used: pooled ordinary least squared (POLS), fixed effect model (FEM), or random effect model (REM). However, one disadvantage of panel data is heteroscedasticity and it is very difficult to overcome this problem. In addition, if there is an endogenous variable problem in the model, then REM and FEM estimations are no longer effective.

Therefore, in order to assess the impact of state-owned investment and other factors on Vietnam's economic growth, SGMM is chosen. The selection of SGMM model not only solves the endogenous problem in the research model but also has advantages over the instrument variable. SGMM is one of two main models of GMM method (including SGMM and DGMM) (Arellano and Bond, 1991). It introduces many instrument variables to achieve the condition of an overidentification of estimation easily. The SGMM approach generally produces "more efficient and precise estimates compared to DGMM by improving precision and reducing the finite sample bias" (Baltagi, 2008).

To check the validity of the model, the performance of the testing process is presented with $F$-test of joint significance: Arellano–Bond test for AR(1) and AR(2) in first differences and Hansen test of over identifying restrictions. Then, it is supposed that the results should be tested again because the Fisher $p$-value cannot lead to the accurate conclusion of the probability of the hypothesis without regard to the probability of the selected sample (Nguyen, 2019). According to Goodman's calculation method (Goodman, 1999), MBF should be calculated to compare with results with $p$-value from SGMM.

## 4. Results

### 4.1. *Impact of state-owned investment and factors on Vietnam's GDP growth in the period 2013–2017*

In order to assess the impact of state-owned investment and factors on Vietnam's GDP growth from 2013 to 2017, SGMM is used as presented in the previous section. Hence, the dataset of 49 provinces and cities of Vietnam are illustrated in Table 3.

SGMM is implemented in two steps with endogenous variable GDPR. Logarithm of labor productivity of the state-owned sector (lgLP_S), logarithm of implemented investment of the state-owned sector (lgII_S), the RTEs, and logarithm of capital productivity (lgCP) are independent variables. In order to check the validity (over identification) of SGMM model according to Arellano and Bond (1991), the authors perform two key tests, including: *Sargan*

**Table 3:** Impacts of state-owned sector investment and factors on Vietnam's GDP growth.

| The dependent variable is GDP | | | |
|---|---|---|---|
| **Variables** | **Coefficients** | ***Z*** | ***p* > \|*Z*\|** |
| GDPR_t–1 | −0.706569 | −12.80 | 0.000 |
| lgLB | 2.27446 | 1.70 | 0.090 |
| RTE | 0.879777 | 2.08 | 0.037 |
| lgCP | −8.99234 | −10.35 | 0.000 |
| lgII_S | −9.368492 | −7.02 | 0.000 |
| lgLP_S | 7.490337 | 3.34 | 0.001 |
| Number of observations | | 196 | |
| Number of instruments | | 39 | |

*or Hansen test and Arellano–Bond test.* The test results show that SGMM model is significant (Tables A.1 and A.2).

Using SGMM model, two steps are obtained to estimate results in Table 3. Estimated results show that the number of working labors (LB), the RTEs, and labor productivity of the state-owned sector (LP_S) have a positive impact on Vietnam's growth rate of GDP from 2013 to 2017. Capital productivity (CP) and the implemented investment of the state-owned sector (II_S) have a negative impact on Vietnam's growth rate of GDP from 2013 to 2017. Subsequently, for the purpose of evaluating the probability of the alternative hypothesis, MBF is used. The results are shown in Table 4.

Table 4 shows the MBF and the standard *p*-value for any given *Z* score. Thus, with the Bayesian test, the number of working labor (LB) is not statistically significant. Similarly, it can be seen that the RTEs is not statistically significant in evaluating the impact on economic growth. After the results of the Bayesian test, the real drivers of economic growth are capital productivity (CP), implemented investment of state-owned sector (II_S), and labor productivity of state-owned sector (LP_S).

More specifically, it can be seen that the opposite effect is quite clear between both capital productivity and implemented investment versus state-owned investment implementation on economic growth.

**Table 4:** Relation between $p$-value and MBFs.

| | $p$-Value (Z Score) | MBF | Decrease in probability of the null hypothesis, % | |
|---|---|---|---|---|
| | | | From | To no less than |
| GDPRt-1 | 0.000 | 0.0045 | 90 | 3.9 |
| | (3.29) | (1/224) | 50 | 0.4 |
| | | | 25 | 0.1 |
| lgLB | 0.090 | 0.407 | 90 | 78.56 |
| | (1.34) | 1/2.46 | 50 | 28.93 |
| | | | 25 | 11.84 |
| RTE | 0.037 | 0.203 | 90 | 64.59 |
| | (1.79) | 1/4.9 | 50 | 16.85 |
| | | | 25 | 6.27 |
| lgCP | 0.000 | 0.0045 | 90 | 3.9 |
| | (3.29) | (1/224) | 50 | 0.4 |
| | | | 25 | 0.1 |
| lgII_S | 0.000 | 0.0045 | 90 | 3.9 |
| | (3.29) | (1/224) | 50 | 0.4 |
| | | | 25 | 0.1 |
| lgLP_S | 0.001 | 0.008 | 90 | 7.06 |
| | (3.09) | 1/118 | 50 | 0.84 |
| | | | 25 | 0.28 |

The implemented investment of state-owned sector (II_S) has a negative impact on Vietnam's GDP growth from 2013 to 2017. The investment of the state-owned sector increased by one percentage point, the economic growth has an impact on the economy's GDP, which decreased by around 9.37 percentage points. Similarly, capital productivity increases one percentage point, which decreases GDP growth by approximately 9 percentage points. Only the labor productivity of state-owned sector has positive impact on GDP's growth. For each percentage point of labor productivity of the state sector, GDP's growth increases by about 7.5 percentage points, respectively.

Thus, using the SGMM method in combination with the Bayesian approach on the dataset of 49 provinces from 2013 to 2017, the results show that state-owned investment can slow down the pace of GDP growth. This result is also in the same trend as previous studies in other countries on the impact of state-owned investment (Tatom, 1991; Turnovsky, 1996; Ghali, 1998; Phetsavong and Ichihashi, 2012).

The results of this study also give the same direction as Tran and Le (2014). It is obvious that the impact of investment from state-owned sector on economic growth in the short term is not statistically significant. However, this research's outcomes contrast with a number of recent studies on the impact of public investment, such as To (2011).

### 4.2. *Discussion*

The results of empirical research in Vietnam from 2013 to 2017 lead to two main conclusions:

First, for state-owned investment, the increase in labor productivity of the state-owned sector has a very positive impact on economic growth. In contrast, increasing the size of this sector has a negative impact, causing negative economic growth.

Basically, the period from 2013 to 2017 shows that Vietnam's growth is still affected by a large change in the scale of investment implemented in the economy. Although the policy of shifting the growth model should be more effective, in fact, the role of the investment scale for general economic growth is still very large. With the current growth model of Vietnam, the factors of in-depth development are not really in focus. Particularly for the state-owned sector, policies to expand investment scale should be accompanied by improving labor productivity to promote the role of state-owned investment, which contributes to economic growth. In contrast, low labor productivity with low productivity growth associated with additional investment in this sector makes the process of using the investment less effective.

Second, the results show that the increase in implemented investment of the state-owned sector does not stimulate strong economic growth. Moreover, if the investment of this sector increases in scale in this period, it can reduce economic growth. This shows that the efficiency of the state-owned investment is generally low, the overall growth of the economy in terms of the contribution of capital factor is not rooted in this sector. Mainly, economic growth is due to the investment created by the non-state sector and the FDI sector.

The cause of this situation is that the investment efficiency of Vietnam's state-owned sector has been scanty and has not improved significantly compared to the expectations that the Government targets. Indicators for measuring the investment efficiency of this sector change in a positive direction, but there has been no big breakthrough compared to the previous period. There are still many issues about institutional management of state-owned investment such as planning, project selection, project implementation, construction management, project evaluation, and supervision, leading to the low efficiency of management of state investment. The investment efficiency of the state-owned sector is tenuous, so the increase in the investment in this sector is one of the factors hindering Vietnam's economic growth. From the state budget, the number of projects awaiting approval of budget funding has been increasing; in fact, it is no longer suitable with the ability to balance the annual investment.

Third, the research results show that the proportion of trained labor as well as size of the labor force in Vietnam have had no impacts on the economic growth of Vietnam in recent years. Therefore, improving labor quality is an important condition to improve labor productivity. Especially in the context of the industrial revolution 4.0, the more science and technology are developed, the more modern the machines and equipment are, and the more they require workers with corresponding professional qualifications. Employees with high education and technical qualifications are able to quickly absorb scientific and technical advances in production, thus creating the highest working efficiency. Therefore, in order to promote economic growth in the future, Vietnam needs to continue implementing good policies to encourage training institutions to improve training quality in order to provide high quality human resources for the economy.

## 5. Conclusion

The estimated results show that the number of working labors (LB) and the RTEs have no impact on economic growth in Vietnam. Implemented investment capital (II_S) and labor productivity in the state-owned sector (LP_S) have positive impacts on Vietnam's GDP growth from 2013 to 2017. However, implemented investment of the state-owned sector (II_S) and capital productivity (CP) have a negative effect on economic growth, while labor productivity of the state-owned sector is one important factor improving economic growth. In order to boost Vietnam's economic growth in the near future, Vietnam needs to take measures to effectively use the investment of the state-owned sector and reduce the proportion of state-owned investment.

First, Vietnam should overcome the situation of scattered investment and the slow progress in construction investment. Second, we need to strengthen the monitoring, evaluation, and inspection of investment from the state budget as well as conduct monitoring and evaluation based on results for investment projects with good implementation and supervision. Third, good control of corruption should be implemented as soon as possible. Fourth, we should improve the responsibilities of investment management agencies. Fifth, it would be more beneficial if we use the national budget in an economical way, with a focus on creating favorable conditions to attract private investment. Sixth, it is essential to reduce the proportion of investment in the state-owned sector. Finally, it seems to be urgent to focus on improving the quality of human resources; enhance training and retraining for workers; improve the quality of training in training institutions to provide the economy with high quality labor.

## Appendix

**Table A.1:** Summary of the variables in the model.

| Variables | Obs | Mean | Std. Dev | Min | Max |
|---|---|---|---|---|---|
| GDPR | 245 | 8.55467 | 10.933 | −3.49891 | 59.06257 |
| lgLB | 245 | 2.816085 | 0.3451878 | 1.151982 | 3.656883 |
| RTE | 245 | 19.41689 | 8.837131 | 8 | 47.9 |
| lgCP | 245 | 0.3554821 | 0.1824352 | −0.2965349 | 1.3734 |
| lgII_S | 245 | 3.659679 | 0.370035 | 3.008515 | 5.002822 |
| lgLP_S | 245 | 2.151915 | 0.5188916 | 0.8780676 | 5.436187 |

**Table A.2:** Test results for model (1) with SGMM.

| **The dependent variable is GDP** | |
|---|---|
| *F*-test | Wald $\chi^2$ (11) = 9157.44<br>Prob > $F$ = 0.000 |
| Arellano–Bond test for AR (1) in first differences | $z = -1.99$ |
| Arellano–Bond test for AR (2) in first differences | $z = 0.64$ |
| Hansen test | $\chi^2(27) = 23.92$<br>Prob > $\chi^2 = 0.635$ |
| Difference-in-Hansen tests of exogeneity of GMM instrument subsets | $\chi^2(12) = 8.98$ |
| Hansen test excluding SGMM instruments (i.e., the differenced instruments) | Prob > $\chi^2 = 0.704$ |
| Difference-in-Hansen tests of exogeneity of GMM instrument subsets | $\chi^2(2) = 0.3$ |

## References

Aaron, H. (1990). Discussion of "why is infrastructure important?" In Munnell, A. (ed.), *Is There a Shortfall in Public Investment*? Boston: Federal Reserve Bank of Boston, pp. 51–63.

Afonso, A., and Aubyn, M. (2008). Macroeconomic rates of return of public and private investment: Crowding-in and crowding-out effects. Working Papers, Department of Economics 2008/06, ISEG — Lisbon School of

Economics and Management, Department of Economics, Universidade de Lisboa.

Aschauer, D.A. (1989a). Is public expenditure productive? *Journal of Monetary Economics,* 23, 177–200.

Arellano, M., and Bond, S. (1991). Some tests of specification in panel data: Monte Carlo evidence and an application to employment equations. *Review of Economics and Statistics*, 58, 277–297.

Baltagi, B.H. (2008). *Econometric Analysis of Panel Data*, 4th edition. Chichester: John Wiley & Sons Ltd.

Beddies, C. (1999). Investment, capital accumulation, and growth some evidence from the Gambia 1964–98. IMF Working Paper No. 99/117.

Coutinho, R., and Gallo, G. (1991). Do public and private investment stand in each other's way. WDR Background Paper, World Bank, October.

Devarajan, S., Swaroop, V., and Heng-fu, Z. (1996). The composition of public expenditure and economic growth. *Journal of Monetary Economics*, 37, 313–344.

Evans, P., and Karras, G. (1994). Are government activities productive? Evidence from a panel of US. *The Review of Economics and Statistics*, 76(1), 1–11.

Ghali, K. (1998). Public investment and private capital formation in a vector error-correction model of growth. *Applied Economics*, 30(6), 837–844.

Goodman, S.N. (1999). Toward evidence-based medical statistics. 2: Bayes factor. *Annals of Internal Medicine*, 130(12), 1005–1013.

Ghura, D. (1997). Private investment and endogenous growth: Evidence from Cameroon. International Monetary Fund, IMF Working Paper, WP/97/165.

Hague, S.T. (2013). Effect of public and private investment on economic growth in Bangladesh: An econometric analysis. Research Study Series No FDRS05/2013, Finance Division, Ministry of Finance.

Khan, M.S., and Kumar, M.S. (1997). Public and private investment and the growth process in developing countries. *Oxford Bulletin of Economics and Statistics*, 59(1), 69–88.

Khan, M., and Reinhart, C. (1989). Private investment and economic growth in developing countries. IMF Working Paper, MPRA Paper No. 13655, posted 27. February 2009 19:05 UTC.

Khan, M. (1996). Government investment and economic growth in the developing world. *The Pakistan Development Review*, 35(4 Part I), 419–439.

Lynde, C., and Richmond, J. (1991). The role of public capital in production. *The Review of Economics and Statistics*, 74(1), 37–44.

Lighthart, J.E. (2000). Public capital and output growth in Portugal: An empirical analysis. IMF Working Paper, WP/00/11.

Lynde, C. (1992). Private profit and public capital. *Journal of Macroeconomics*, 14(1), 125–142.

Lynde, C., and Richmond, J. (1993). Public capital and long-run costs in U.K. manufacturing. *Economic Journal*, 103(419), 880–93.

Merriman, D. (1990). Public capital and regional output: Another look at some Japanese and American data. *Regional Science and Urban Economics*, 20(4), 437–458.

Munell, A. (1990). Why has productivity growth declined? Productivity and public investment. *New England Economic Review*, January/February, 3–22.

Nguyen, T.H. (2019). How to test without $p$-value. *Thailand Statistician*, 17(2), i–x.

Pereira, A. (2001). International evidence on public investment and private sector performance. *Public Finance Management*, 1(2), 261–277.

Phetsavong, K., and Ichihashi, M. (2012). The impact of public and private investment on economic growth: Evidence from developing Asian countries. International Development and Cooperation, IDEC Discussion Paper 2012, Hiroshima University.

Rabnawaz, A., and Jafar, R.M.S. (2015). Impact of public investment on economic growth. MPRA Paper 70377, University Library of Munich, Germany.

Ram, R., and Ramsey, D. (1989). Government capital and private output in the United States additional evidence. *Economic Letters*, 30, 223–226.

Ramirez, M.D. (1996). Public and private investment in Mexico and Chile: An empirical test of the complementarity hypothesis. *AEJ*, 24(4), 301–320.

Ramirez, M.D, and Nazmi, N. (2003). Public investment and economic growth in Latin America: An empirical test. *Review of Development Economics*, 7(1), 115–126.

Tatom, J. (1991). Public capital and private sector performance. *Review of the Federal Reserve Bank of St Louis*, 78(3), 3–15.

Turnovsky, S.J. (1996). Optimal tax, debt and expenditures policies in growing economy. *Journal of Public Economy*, 60, 21–44.

To, T.T. (2011). Public investment predominates private investment, from the VECM empirical model. In Workshop "Vietnam's Economy Issues Raised in the Medium and Long Term" Institute for Economic and Policy Research, National University.

Tran, N.N.A., and Le, H.P. (2014). Impact of public investment on economic growth in Vietnam: An experimental look of ARDL model, *Development and Integration*, 19, 3–10.

Trinh, V., and Nguyen, D. (2014). Situation of investment from state capital in Vietnam. *Review of Finance*, http://tapchitaichinh.vn/nghien-cuu-trao-doi/thuc-trang-dau-tu-tu-nguon-von-nha-nuoc-o-vietnam-72075.html

Vijverberg, W., Vijverberg, C., and Gable, J. (1997). Public capital and private productivity. *The Review of Economics and Statistics*, 79(2), 267–278.

Wang, B. (2005). Effects of government expenditure on private investment: Canada empirical evidence. *Empirical Economics*, 30(2), 493–504.

# Part VII

# Business and Law

https://doi.org/10.1142/9789811227158_0028

Chapter 28

# Factors Associated with Economic Growth: An Investigation into Government Spending on R&D

Nhat Thien Tran

**Abstract**

This chapter aims to study the impact of R&D programs on economic growth. The long-run growth rate is fueled by R&D investment, and the government levies taxes on labor income and capital returns to finance this investment. The research investigates the interplay between R&D activity and the effects of tax policies. In particular, this study shows that a rise in R&D investment enhances the efficiency of unskilled labor so that income inequality between unskilled and skilled workers can be reduced, consequently increasing economic growth.

**Keywords:** R&D investment; Economic growth.

## 1. Introduction

The contribution of total factor productivity (TFP) according to Solow (1956, 1957) is around 87% for economic growth. Solow explains long-run growth by considering the accumulation of capital, the growth of population, and increases in TFP, commonly referred to as technological progress. However, the restrictive assumptions of Solow's model are the constant growth rate of savings and exogenous technological progress. Furthermore, diminishing returns are the barrier to long-run growth in the Solow model. Even if technological improvements still occur exogenously over time, these assumptions are quite a restriction and their reexamination has given rise to a new approach, i.e., the notion of effective inputs (physical and human capital).

Indeed, the restrictive assumptions of the contribution of Solow and its reconsideration have opened the door in two different directions of endogenous growth theory. The first is to introduce new technology as a factor enhancing capital productivity (Romer, 1990). The second is to introduce education and training to improve labor productivity and human capital accumulation (see Romer, 1986; Lucas, 1988, 2015). This study calls for more attention to the latter approach where the rise of labor productivity is supported by R&D activity from government investment.

This chapter is in the spirit of Bosi and Nourry (2007) who examine the effect of public expenditure on economic growth. In contrast to their study, where education is financed by public investment, this study considers R&D activity fueled by government choice. In order to understand the impact of tax policies on economic growth apart from the decisions of households, this research assumes that households only invest in physical capital, while the government taxes both labor income and capital income on the whole population (both young and old generations). Thus, this study not only investigates the impact of taxation on long-run economic growth, but also sheds light on the role of R&D investment in reducing income inequality between unskilled and skilled workers.

The main idea runs as follows. The study considers an overlapping generation (OLG) model with heterogeneous economic agents. The newborn agents live in date $t$ when they are young and in date $t+1$ when they are old. They work when young, endowed with inelastic working time. They make decisions on consumption and investment in physical capital when young and consume what they get from savings when old. Furthermore, this research follows the study of Bosi and Pham (2016) in considering the R&D program (in line with Barro, 1990) financed by collecting taxes from labor income and capital returns. This study also assumes that the public R&D fund is divided into two parts for improving the quality of production technology for two different types of workers into efficient units of labor.

The main finding is that by increasing the fraction of the R&D investment in enhancing the efficiency of unskilled workers, policymakers can reduce income inequality between skilled and unskilled labor, consequently increasing growth. This fraction, however, cannot exceed a threshold value to sustain optimal economic growth.

Another finding is that two effects of taxation are noteworthy. Firstly, taxation reduces households' total income, lowering their investment in physical capital accumulation, which has a negative impact on output. Secondly, taxation raises the government's expenditure on R&D, thus enhancing the efficiency of unskilled labor, reducing income inequality, and increasing economic growth. Consequently, the net impact on growth is ambiguous.

## 2. Fundamentals

This study considers an OLG model where at each time $t$, the population of the newborn cohort is $N_t$. The demographic growth rate is assumed to be a constant $n = \frac{N_{t+1}}{N_t}$ and $n > 1$.

This model allows for physical capital accumulation. Young individuals work and spend their labor income on consumption and investment in physical capital accumulation. Old individuals do not work, but only consume. There are two types of labor, unskilled labor (denoted by $u$) with population density $\pi$ and skilled labor (denoted by $s$) with population density $1 - \pi$.

### 2.1. *Production*

In each period, a representative firm uses physical capital and labor. The economy's technology is represented by an augmented production function[1]:

$$Y = K^\alpha[(A_u L_u)^\psi + (A_s L_s)^\psi]^{\frac{1-\alpha}{\psi}},$$

[1]The production function is in line with Caselli and Coleman (2006) $y = k^\alpha(Ah)^{1-\alpha}$.

where $L_u$ denotes firms' demand for unskilled labor, and $L_s$ represents firms' demand for skilled labor. In this economy, labor input into production can be thought of as a constant-elasticity-of-substitution (CES) aggregate of unskilled and skilled labor. Furthermore, the elasticity of substitution between skilled and unskilled labor is defined as follows:

$$\frac{\partial(L_s/L_u)}{\partial(MPL_u/MPL_s)}\frac{MPL_u/MPL_s}{L_s/L_u}.$$

This elasticity of substitution is equal to $\frac{1}{1-\psi}$. The parameters, $A_u$, $A_s$ are the converted raw quantities of the two labor types into efficiency units. A representative firm chooses $L_u$ and $L_s$ to maximize its profit:

$$\begin{aligned}\max\{K_t^{\alpha}[(A_{u,t}L_{u,t})^{\psi} + (A_{s,t}L_{s,t})^{\psi}]^{\frac{1-\alpha}{\psi}} \\ - R_tK_t - w_{u,t}L_{u,t} - w_{s,t}L_{s,t}\}.\end{aligned} \tag{1}$$

At optimum, we obtain

$$R_t = \alpha K_t^{\alpha-1}[(A_{u,t}L_{u,t})^{\psi} + (A_{s,t}L_{s,t})^{\psi}]^{\frac{1-\alpha}{\psi}}, \tag{2}$$

$$\begin{aligned}w_{u,t} = (1-\alpha)K_t^{\alpha}[(A_{u,t}L_{u,t})^{\psi} + (A_{s,t}L_{s,t})^{\psi}]^{\frac{1-\alpha}{\psi}-1} \\ \times (A_{u,t}L_{u,t})^{\psi-1}A_{u,t},\end{aligned} \tag{3}$$

$$\begin{aligned}w_{s,t} = (1-\alpha)K_t^{\alpha}[(A_{u,t}L_{u,t})^{\psi} + (A_{s,t}L_{s,t})^{\psi}]^{\frac{1-\alpha}{\psi}-1} \\ \times (A_{s,t}L_{s,t})^{\psi-1}A_{s,t}\end{aligned} \tag{4}$$

Let $Y_t \equiv K_t^{\alpha}[(A_{u,t}L_{u,t})^{\psi} + (A_{s,t}L_{s,t})^{\psi}]^{\frac{1-\alpha}{\psi}}$, we now have:

$$\begin{aligned}R_tK_t &= \alpha Y_t, \\ w_{u,t}L_{u,t} &= (1-\alpha)Y_t\gamma_u, \\ w_{s,t}L_{s,t} &= (1-\alpha)Y_t\gamma_s.\end{aligned}$$

Here,

$$\gamma_u = \frac{(A_{u,t}L_{u,t})^{\psi}}{(A_{u,t}L_{u,t})^{\psi} + (A_{s,t}L_{s,t})^{\psi}} \quad \text{and } \gamma_s = 1-\gamma_u; \; w_{u,t} \text{ and } w_{s,t}$$

are the wage rates of unskilled and skilled labor, respectively.

## 2.2. *Consumers*

Suppose that at each date $t$, there are $\pi N_t$ unskilled agents $u$, and $(1 - \pi)N_t$ skilled agents $s$. An agent $i \in \{u, s\}$ maximizes her intertemporal utility: $\ln c_{i,t} + \beta \ln d_{i,t+1}$, under the following constraints:

$$c_{i,t} + s_{i,t} \leq (1 - \tau)w_{it},$$
$$d_{i,t+1} \leq (1 - \tau_k)R_{t+1}s_{i,t},$$

where $s_{i,t}$ denotes her savings in physical capital. $\tau$, $\tau_k$ are, respectively, the constant taxation rates on labor income and capital returns.

**Lemma 2.1.** *For each agent, we have*

$$c_{i,t} = \frac{1}{1+\beta}(1 - \tau)w_{it}, \quad (5)$$

$$s_{i,t} = \frac{\beta}{1+\beta}(1 - \tau)w_{it}, \quad (6)$$

$$d_{i,t+1} = (1 - \tau_k)R_{t+1}\, s_{i,t}. \quad (7)$$

**Proof.** See Appendix A.

Market clearing conditions:

- In the labor market:

$$L_{u,t} = \pi N_t, \quad (8)$$

$$L_{s,t} = (1 - \pi)N_t. \quad (9)$$

- In the physical capital market:

$$K_{t+1} = \pi N_t s_{u,t} + (1 - \pi)N_t s_{s,t},$$
$$nk_{t+1} = \pi s_{u,t} + (1 - \pi)s_{s,t}, \quad (10)$$

where $k_t \equiv \frac{K_t}{N_t}$ denotes the capital intensity.

The above market clearing conditions entail:

$$R_t k_t = \alpha y_t, \tag{11}$$

$$w_{u,t}\pi = (1-\alpha) y_t \gamma_u, \tag{12}$$

$$w_{s,t}(1-\pi) = (1-\alpha) y_t \gamma_s, \tag{13}$$

where $y_t \equiv Y_t/N_t$ denotes output per young individual. Consequently, we obtain the following relation between the different wage rates and output per young individual:

$$w_{u,t}\pi + w_{s,t}(1-\pi) = (1-\alpha) y_t. \tag{14}$$

## 2.3. *Public investment in R&D*

The total collected tax is expressed as follows:

$$\begin{aligned} \mathrm{G}_t = &\, \tau N_t(\pi w_{u,t} + (1-\pi) w_{s,t}) \\ &+ \tau_k N_{t-1} R_t(\pi s_{u,t-1} + (1-\pi) s_{s,t-1}). \end{aligned} \tag{15}$$

Denote $g_t \equiv \frac{G_t}{N_t}$, and by combining this equation with (10) and (14), we have:

$$g_t = [\alpha\tau_k + (1-\alpha)\tau] y_t. \tag{16}$$

In this economy, public investment in R&D is in line with Barro (1990): if a production function is of the form $Ak^{\alpha}h^{1-\alpha}$, then $A_t = \theta g_t^{1-\alpha}$. The public spending in R&D is $g_t$.

In addition, Bosi and Pham (2016) state "the government expenditure $G_t$ affects the TFP, the product and the revenues from labor, capital, and financial speculation. These revenues are supposed to affect in turn, within the same period, the tax receipt and the public spending $G_t$ at the end. This functional specification promotes endogenous growth dynamics." Accordingly, we have:

$$A_{u,t} = \theta_u z g_t, \tag{I}$$

$$A_{s,t} = \theta_s (1 - z) g_t, \tag{II}$$

where $z$ is the fraction of public spending in R&D for improving effective unskilled labor, and $1 - z$ of the collected tax is the other fraction of public spending in R&D for improving effective skilled labor. $\theta_u$ and $\theta_s$ are factors capturing government efficiency in each R&D program (efficiency of unskilled and skilled workers in R&D program).

**Definition 2.1.** An equilibrium is a positive sequence $(w_{i,t}, c_{i,t}, d_{i,t+1}, L_{i,t}, K_t, G_t)$ satisfying (2)–(10) and (15).

## 3. Equilibrium Properties

This section assumes the efficiency parameters in the R&D program for the two types of labor are the same. It turns out that $\theta_u = \theta_s \equiv \theta$.

**Proposition 3.1 (global dynamics).**

1. *There exists a unique equilibrium. In the equilibrium, the global dynamic system is given by* $\frac{k_{t+1}}{k_t} \equiv \rho$.
2. *The growth rate of the economy is given by*

$$\rho = \mathrm{C}\phi(\tau, \tau_k)[\varphi(z)]^{\frac{1-\alpha}{\alpha\psi}}, \tag{17}$$

*where*

$$\phi(\tau, \tau_k) \equiv (1 - \tau)[\alpha\tau_k + (1 - \alpha)\tau]^{\frac{1-\alpha}{\alpha}},$$

$$\varphi(z) \equiv (z\pi)^{\psi} + [(1 - z)(1 - \pi)]^{\psi},$$

$$\mathrm{C} \equiv \frac{1}{n}(1 - \alpha)\frac{\beta}{1 + \beta}\theta^{\frac{1-\alpha}{\alpha}}.$$

**Proof.** See Appendix A. □

## 4. Fiscal Policy

**Lemma 4.1.** 1. *If* $\tau_k > \left(\frac{1-\alpha}{\alpha}\right)^2$, *then* $\frac{\partial\phi}{\partial\tau} < 0$, $\forall\tau$: *when we tax too much on capital,* $\rho$ *is decreasing in* $\tau$.

$$2.\quad If\quad \tau_k < \left(\frac{1-\alpha}{\alpha}\right)^2, \quad \text{then} \quad \frac{\partial\phi}{\partial\tau} = 0 \quad \text{iff}$$

$$\tau = (1-\alpha) - \frac{\alpha^2}{1-\alpha}\tau_k \equiv \tau^*(\tau_k). \tag{18}$$

**Proposition 4.1.** *Given* $\tau_k$, *the optimal tax on labor income for the economy is given by* $\tau^*(\tau_k) = 1 - \alpha - \frac{\alpha^2}{1-\alpha}\tau_k$.

Furthermore, the rate of growth of the economy attains its maximum value at $\tau^*$.

**Proof.** See Appendix A.

**Assumption 4.1.** $\frac{1-\alpha}{\alpha} > 1$

**Proposition 4.2.** *If the ratio of taxes to GDP increases (decreases) 1%, then the rate of growth of the economy increases (decreases)* $\frac{1}{\alpha}$%.

**Proof.** See Appendix A. □

To depict Proposition 4.2, let us proceed with a numerical exercise with $\alpha = 1/3$, $\tau_k = 1/3$. We compute $\tau^*(\tau_k) = 0.61$ (these results come from the simulation of Equation (18)). Under this setup, we calculate the value of the ratio of taxes to GDP, $\xi = 0.52$. We next compute the elasticity of the ratio of taxes to GDP with respect to the tax on capital, $\frac{\Delta\rho/\rho}{\Delta\xi/\xi} = 3$. It turns out that if the ratio of taxes to GDP increases (decreases) 1%, then the rate of growth of the economy increases (decreases) 3%.

## 5. R&D Investment, Growth, and Inequality

In order to analyze the effect of R&D investment on economic growth and inequality, we now introduce the following definition:

**Definition 5.1.**

$$I_i \equiv \frac{w_{s,t}}{w_{u,t}} = \left(\frac{\pi}{1-\pi}\right)^{1-\psi} \left(\frac{\theta_s}{\theta_u}\frac{1-z}{z}\right)^{\sigma}, \tag{19}$$

where $I_i$ can be interpreted as an inequality index.[2]

Arguably, most empirical studies found that $\psi \in \left(0, \frac{1}{2}\right)$, and the population of highly skilled labor in many countries is less than the population of unskilled labor: $1 - \pi < \pi$.

**Assumption 5.1.** The inequality index, $I_i > 1$.

**Proposition 5.1.** *Let us introduce the parameter*

$$z^* \equiv \frac{\left(\frac{\pi}{1-\pi}\right)^{\frac{\psi}{1-\psi}}}{1 + \left(\frac{\pi}{1-\pi}\right)^{\frac{\psi}{1-\psi}}}. \tag{20}$$

*We next have the following findings:*

1. *If we fix all the parameters except $z$, then the growth rate of the economy $\rho$ attains its maximum value at $z = z^*$.*
2. *The inequality index $I_i$ is decreasing in $z$, for $z \in (0, z^*)$. It turns out that if a rise in R&D investment for unskilled workers occurs, then inequality is reduced, and consequently economic growth increases.*
3. *This proposition may not exceed the optimal level of the R&D investment program, $z^*$, in order to avoid slowing economic growth.*

**Proof.** See Appendix A. □

Comment. If the R&D investment program focuses more on improving the efficiency of unskilled workers, then obviously the wage rate of unskilled labor becomes higher. Consequently, inequality between the two types of labor income would be reduced. Nevertheless, the

[2] We may verify that the GINI coefficient is increasing in $I_i$.

government must maintain a reasonable level of investment in the R&D program that enhances the efficiency of skilled workers in order to sustain economic growth.

We next evaluate the inequality index $I_t$ at $z = z^*$.

Also, we have

$$I_i = \left(\frac{\theta_s}{\theta_u}\right)^{\frac{\psi}{1-\psi}} \left(\frac{\pi}{1\pi}\right)^{1-\frac{\psi}{1-\psi}}. \tag{21}$$

Note that, since the growth rate of the economy $\rho$ attains its maximum value at $z^*$, a change in the R&D investment policy (a change in the level of the R&D investment program, $z$) will diminish the growth rate of the economy $\rho$. Note also that $\frac{d_{s,t+1}}{d_{u,t+1}} = I_i$.

**Assumption 5.2.** The government always sets $z = z^*$ in order to ensure an optimal economic growth rate. Consequently, the only factors that affect inequality are, respectively, the ratios $\frac{\theta_s}{\theta_u}$ and $\frac{\pi}{1-\pi}$.

**Proposition 5.2.** *Inequality is worsened if the number of unskilled laborers increases, and/or skilled workers are used more efficiently than unskilled workers.*

**Comment.** The optimal level of R&D investment policy $z^*$ is decreasing in $\frac{\theta_s}{\theta_u}$. If skilled workers are used more efficiently than unskilled workers, then the optimal proportion of R&D funding devoted to improving unskilled labor is reduced.

## 6. Conclusion

This study considers an economy with capital accumulation where skilled and unskilled labors are not perfect substitutes in production, and the engine of endogenous growth is R&D investment policy from the government. The contribution shows that some tax policies are beneficial to economic growth. In particular, there is room for R&D strategies that reduce income inequality between unskilled labor and skilled labor by improving the efficiency of unskilled workers without harming economic growth.

## Appendix A

### A.1. *Proof of Lemma* 2.1

The Lagrange equation is given as follows:

$$\ln c_{i,t} + \beta \ln d_{i,t+1} - \lambda_t(c_{i,t} + s_{i,t} - (1-\tau)w_{i,t}) \\ - \mu_t(d_{i,t+1} - (1-\tau_k)R_{t+1}s_{i,t}).$$

From first-order conditions, we have

$$\frac{1}{c_{i,t}} = \lambda_t,$$

$$\frac{\beta}{d_{i,t+1}} = \mu_t,$$

$$\lambda_t = (1-\tau_k)R_{t+1}\mu_t,$$

which leads to

$$\frac{\lambda_t}{\mu_t} = \frac{d_{i,t+1}}{\beta c_{i,t}} = (1-\tau_k)R_{t+1}.$$

Moreover, the budget constraints are now binding, thus

$$d_{i,t+1} = (1-\tau_k)R_{t+1}s_{i,t},$$

$$\beta c_{i,t} = s_{i,t}.$$

Since $c_{i,t} + s_{i,t} = (1-\tau)w_{i,t}$, one has

$$\frac{1}{\beta}s_{i,t} + s_{i,t} = (1-\tau)w_{i,t},$$

which implies

$$s_{i,t} = \frac{\beta}{1+\beta}(1-\tau)w_{i,t},$$

$$c_{i,t} = \frac{1}{1+\beta}(1-\tau)w_{i,t},$$

and

$$d_{i,t+1} = (1-\tau_k)R_{t+1}s_{i,t}.$$

## A.2. *Proof of Proposition* 3.1

The equilibrium system is given by (6), (10), (14) (15), (I), and (II). Also, according to (6), (10), and (14), we have

$$nk_{t+1} = (1-\alpha)(1-\tau)\frac{\beta}{1+\beta}y_t. \tag{A.1}$$

Since

$$\begin{aligned} y_t &= \frac{1}{N_t}K_t^{\alpha}[(A_{u,t}L_{u,t})^{\psi} + (A_{s,t}L_{s,t})^{\psi}]^{\frac{1-\alpha}{\psi}} \\ &= k_t^{\alpha}[(A_{u,t}\pi)^{\psi} + (A_{s,t}(1-\pi))^{\psi}]^{\frac{1-\alpha}{\psi}}. \end{aligned}$$

Combining the later equation with (I) and (II), we get:

$$y_t = k_t^{\alpha}(\theta g_t)^{1-\alpha}\{(z\pi)^{\psi} + [(1-z)(1-\pi)]^{\psi}\}^{\frac{1-\alpha}{\psi}}. \tag{A.2}$$

According to (15) and (A.2), we have

$$\begin{aligned} y_t &= k_t^{\alpha}(\theta y_t)^{1-\alpha}[\alpha\tau_k + (1-\alpha)\tau]^{1-\alpha}\{(z\pi)^{\psi} \\ &\quad + [(1-z)(1-\pi)]^{\psi}\}^{\frac{1-\alpha}{\psi}} \\ y_t &= [\theta(\alpha\tau_k + (1-\alpha)\tau)]^{\frac{1-\alpha}{\alpha}}\{(z\pi)^{\psi} \\ &\quad + [(1-z)(1-\pi)]^{\psi}\}^{\frac{1-\alpha}{\alpha\psi}}k_t. \end{aligned} \tag{A.3}$$

The global dynamic is hence given by combining (A.1) and (A.3): $k_{t+1} = \rho k_t$ with

$$\begin{aligned} \rho &= \frac{1}{n}(1-\alpha)(1-\tau)\frac{\beta}{1+\beta}[\theta(\alpha\tau_k + (1-\alpha)\tau)]^{\frac{1-\alpha}{\alpha}}\{(z\pi)^{\psi} \\ &\quad + [(1-z)(1-\pi)]^{\psi}\}^{\frac{1-\alpha}{\alpha\psi}}. \end{aligned} \tag{A.4}$$

Let us denote $\phi(\tau, \tau_k) \equiv (1-\tau)[\alpha\tau_k + (1-\alpha)\tau]^{\frac{1-\alpha}{\alpha}}$,

$$\varphi(z) \equiv (z\pi)^{\psi} + (1-z)(1-\pi)]^{\psi},$$

and

$$\mathrm{C} \equiv \frac{1}{n}(1-\alpha)\frac{\beta}{1+\beta}\theta^{\frac{1-\alpha}{\alpha}}, \quad \text{we get}$$

$$\rho = \mathrm{C}\phi(\tau, \tau_k)[\varphi(z)]^{\frac{1-\alpha}{\alpha\psi}}. \tag{A.5}$$

### A.3. *Proof of Lemma* 4.1

$$\frac{\partial \phi}{\partial \tau_k} = (1\tau)(1\alpha)[\alpha\tau_k + (1\alpha)\tau]^{\frac{1-\alpha}{\alpha}-1} > 0. \tag{A.6}$$

and

$$\frac{\partial \phi}{\partial \tau} = [\alpha\tau_k + (1\alpha)\tau]^{\frac{1\alpha}{\alpha}1}\left[\left(\frac{(1-\alpha)^2}{\alpha}\alpha\tau_k\right)\frac{1\alpha}{\alpha}\tau\right]. \tag{A.7}$$

### A.4. *Proof of Proposition* 4.1

Obviously, $\frac{\partial \rho}{\partial \tau} = 0$ iff

$$\begin{aligned}
\frac{\alpha}{1-\tau} &= \frac{(1-\alpha)^2}{(1-\alpha)\tau + \alpha\tau_k} \\
\alpha(1-\alpha)\tau + \alpha^2\tau_k &= (1-\alpha)^2(1-\tau) \\
\alpha(1-\alpha) + \alpha^2\tau_k &= (1-\alpha)^2(1-\tau) + \alpha(1-\alpha) - \alpha(1\alpha)\tau \\
&= (1-\alpha)(1-\tau). \\
1-\tau &= \alpha + \frac{\alpha^2}{1-\alpha}\tau_k.
\end{aligned}$$

When $\tau_k$ is given, the optimal tax on labor income is

$$\tau^*(\tau_k) = 1 - \alpha - \frac{\alpha^2}{1-\alpha}\tau_k. \tag{A.8}$$

Since $(\tau^*)'(\tau_k) = -\frac{\alpha^2}{1-\alpha} < 0$, $\frac{\partial \rho}{\partial \tau} > 0$ iff $\tau < \tau^*(\tau_k)$. The rate of growth, $\rho$ hence attains its maximum value at $\tau^*$.

Moreover, the positivity of $\tau^*$ requires $1 - \alpha - \frac{\alpha^2}{1-\alpha}\tau_k > 0$, which is always ensured by the following assumption: $\frac{1-\alpha}{\alpha} > 1$.

## A.5. *Proof of Proposition 4.2*

We evaluate the elasticity of growth rate with respect to tax on capital: $\frac{\partial\rho/\rho}{\partial\tau_k/\tau_k}$ at $(\tau_k, \tau^*(\tau_k))$:

$$\begin{aligned}\frac{\partial\rho/\rho}{\partial\tau_k/\tau_k} &= \frac{\partial\phi/\phi}{\partial\tau_k/\tau_k}\\ &= \frac{(1-\alpha)\tau_k}{\alpha\tau_k + (1-\alpha)\tau^*(\tau_k)}\\ &= \left[\frac{\alpha}{1-\alpha} + \frac{\tau^*(\tau_k)}{\tau_k}\right]^{-1}.\end{aligned}$$

Since

$$\frac{\partial\rho/\rho}{\partial\tau_k/\tau_k} = \left(\frac{1-\alpha}{\tau_k} + \alpha\right)^{-1}. \tag{A.9}$$

We can see that

$$\frac{\partial\rho/\rho}{\partial\tau_k/\tau_k} < 1.$$

Furthermore, we get the elasticity of $\tau^*(\tau_k)$ with respect to $\tau_k$:

$$\frac{\partial\tau^*}{\tau^*}/\frac{\partial\tau_k}{\tau_k} = -\frac{\alpha^2\tau_k}{(1-\alpha)^2 - \alpha^2\tau_k}.$$

It would be interesting to study the ratio of taxes to GDP: $\xi \equiv g_t/y_t = \alpha\tau_k + (1-\alpha)\tau$. Evaluated at $\tau^*(\tau_k), \tau_k$, it is equal to $\xi = (1-\alpha)[(1-\alpha) + \alpha\tau_k]$. Thus,

$$\begin{aligned}\frac{\Delta\xi/\xi}{\Delta\tau_k/\tau_k} &= \frac{\alpha\tau_k}{1-\alpha+\alpha\tau_k}\\ &= \alpha\frac{\partial\rho/\rho}{\partial\tau_k/\tau_k}.\end{aligned}$$

Hence,

$$\frac{\Delta\rho/\rho}{\Delta\xi/\xi} = \frac{1}{\alpha}.$$

## A.6. *Proof of Proposition* 5.1

We have $\varphi'(z) = 0$ iff $z = z^*$ (which is equivalent to $\frac{z}{1-z} = \left(\frac{\pi}{1-\pi}\right)^{\frac{\psi}{1-\psi}}$), while we also get $\varphi'(z) > 0$ iff $z < z^*$, (or equivalently $\frac{z}{1-z} < \left(\frac{\pi}{1-\pi}\right)^{\frac{\psi}{1-\psi}}$). Thus, when we fix all the parameters except $z$, then the economic growth rate, $\rho$, reaches its maximum value, $z = z^*$.

## References


Barro, R.J. (1990). Government spending in a simple model of endogenous growth. *Journal of Political Economy*, 98(5, part 2), S103–S125.

Bosi, S., and Nourry, C. (2007). Growth and fluctuations: The role of public dividends and public spending. *Journal of Mathematical Economics*, 43(3–4), 420–445.

Bosi, S., and Pham, N. S. (2016). Taxation, bubbles and endogenous growth. *Economics Letters*, 143, 73–76.

Caselli, F., and Coleman II, J.W. (2006). The world technology frontier. *American Economic Review*, 96(3), 499–522.

Lucas Jr, R.E. (1988). On the mechanics of economic development. *Journal of Monetary Economics*, 22(1), 3–42.

Lucas Jr, R.E. (2015). Human capital and growth. *American Economic Review*, 105(5), 85–88.

Romer, P.M. (1986). Increasing returns and long-run growth. *Journal of Political Economy*, 94(5), 1002–1037.

Romer, P.M. (1990). Endogenous technological change. *Journal of Political Economy*, 98(5, Part 2), S71–S102.

Solow, R.M. (1956). A contribution to the theory of economic growth. *The Quarterly Journal of Economics*, 70(1), 65–94.

Solow, R.M. (1957). Technical change and the aggregate production function. *The Review of Economics and Statistics*, 39(3), 312–320.

https://doi.org/10.1142/9789811227158_0029

# Chapter 29

# Factors Affecting Youth Entrepreneurial Intention and Suggestions for Policymaking: The Case of Vinh Long Province

**Thu Hang Hoang and Quynh Hoa Le**

## Abstract

As a part of the Mekong Delta's development plan, Vinh Long province implements various policies and programs to promote entrepreneurial intentions, especially for young people to generate income for themselves and jobs for locals, thereby contributing to developing the provincial well-being. However, the number of startup enterprises in the province does not fulfill the expectation and economic growth target of Vinh Long, resulting in the province being ranked in the least developed group of all Vietnam's provinces (standing at 55/64 provinces and cities). The aim of this study is to identify the factors affecting the entrepreneurial intentions of young people, which are necessary to propose policymaking implications. Using an exploratory factor analysis (EFA) method with 359 samples, the results show that there are five factors affecting the entrepreneurial intentions of youth, including: *Perceived legitimacy of law and policy; Motivation to become an entrepreneur; Individual ability; Personality characteristics; and Family background*. In addition, the study also indicates one of the major constraints of starting a business in Vinh Long province is that the level of science, technology, and innovation applied in projects is underdeveloped, resulting in low quality business plans and low level of attention from supporting funds, investors, and businesses.

**Keywords:** Startup intention; Entrepreneurial intention; Youth; Vinh Long province; Policymaking.

## 1. Introduction

In recent years, entrepreneurship in Vietnam has received much attention from the Government and general businesses, in which the Government has set a target to have at least one million businesses operating in Vietnam by 2020 (MOIT, 2016). However, according to the report at the Vietnam Business Forum in the middle of 2019, the proportion of enterprises in the total population of Vietnam (96 million) is still low, with about 140 people having one enterprise (equal to nearly 700,000 businesses in the whole country). Meanwhile, in ASEAN, this rate is one enterprise per 80–100 citizens and in developed countries, including the US, Europe, and Japan, it is one enterprise per 10–12 citizens. Therefore, an increase in the number of entrepreneurs is necessary for a developing country like Vietnam for future economic development. First, for individuals pursuing startups, this activity helps them create jobs and income for themselves with a flexible schedule. They create a sense of career freedom, and if the business grows well, their income can be substantially greater than the income earned from working for others (Lüthje & Franke, 2003). Second, for society and the local economy, startup companies create more jobs, which helps the country resolve problems of unemployment, creating a stable source of income for workers to support themselves and their families (Zahra *et al.*, 1999).

Aiming to promote entrepreneurship, many vocational colleges and universities in Vietnam implement entrepreneurship education to equip the youth with functional knowledge and skills to build up their character, attitude, and vision for independent thinking. Since 2016, Vinh Long Provincial People's Committee has issued an official correspondence aimed toward the development of startup programs in the period 2016–2020, with the goal of motivating, encouraging, and promoting the creative spirit in business among individuals and groups that have a startup project and aim to establish an enterprise with the ability to grow quickly and effectively.

Despite being locally abundant with natural resources than many other localities in the Mekong Delta region, many business projects in Vinh Long province have not really made a strong impression on investors, and the intention of young talents to start up businesses seems to be much lower than expected. To attract investors and raise feasible startup projects, it is necessary to determine which factors affect the entrepreneurial intentions of students and young people. Based on these factors, the authors suggest some policy implications to promote young entrepreneurs in the province. Section 2 will provide a literature review on entrepreneurial intentions, followed by Section 3, presenting the methodology and research framework. Section 4 offers results and discussion. Lastly, Section 5 summarizes the findings of the study and suggests several policy implications.

## 2. Literature Review

Researches related to entrepreneurial intentions identify that intention is a predictive and significant element of one's behavior (Kautonen *et al.*, 2013). Therefore, grasping the source, the motivation of the intention, will help to predict the behavior (Ajzen, 1991). So far, there have been many studies by international authors and Vietnamese researchers that raise many theories explaining the intention to start a business, but one of the most effective models is the Theory of Planned Behaviour of Ajzen (1991). Many previous articles extend entrepreneurship research by applying Ajzen's (1991) Theory of Planned Behaviour, such as: Kolvereid (1996); Krueger *et al.* (2000); Turker and Selcuk (2009); Engle *et al.* (2010), Gurel *et al.* (2010); Castaño *et al.* (2015).

One of the leading studies that has applied Planned Behavior Theory of Ajzen (1991) in entrepreneurial intentions is the study of Kolvereid (1996) in Norway. In this research, the author predicts employment status choice intentions, and the result indicates that the role of family background, gender, and prior self-employment experience of respondents have a statistically significant impact on the intention of starting a business.

With a similar intention, the purpose of Engle's research (2010) is to test the ability of Ajzen's Theory of Planned Behavior to predict entrepreneurial intentions in 12 countries. The result concludes that the significant contributing model factors differ by country as the percent of the variance is explained by the model although social norms are a significant predictor of entrepreneurial intent in each nation. The study of Engle *et al.* (2010) provides insight into the role of cognition in the entrepreneurial process by examining a model of planned behavior in countries representing all global regional culture clusters. In addition, with the aim of finding out the relationship between entrepreneurial traits, sociocultural background, and intention to start a business, research in England and Turkey by Gurel *et al.* (2010) point out that there is a statistically significant relationship between innovation, risk-taking propensity, family background, and entrepreneurial intentions. Besides the behavioral theory of Ajzen (1991), researchers have recently considered a subjectivist theory of entrepreneurship that concentrates on individuals, their knowledge, resources and skills, and the processes of discovery and creativity (Kor *et al.*, 2007). In this view, the personal knowledge of entrepreneurship significantly influences the decision on starting up a business.

In Vietnam, the spirit of creative entrepreneurship is becoming strong and receiving more attention from the government, local authorities, and researchers. Specifically, 2016 was selected as the year of startups in Vietnam. Moreover, many studies are conducted to find effective factors and feasible solutions to promote innovation and entrepreneurship projects. However, each study is different in the scope of research, model, and research results. For instance, Lien (2016) proposes a model of 5 factors affecting entrepreneurial intentions of students at University of Labor and Social Affairs, including: *Education and Training at the University; Experience; Family and friends; Characteristics; and Financial capital.* Among which, training and education play the most important role for the students who intend to start a business. As a result, the school should implement entrepreneurship education for students to promote creativity and innovation; develop personal characteristics and skills; and raise students' awareness about self-employment and entrepreneurship before choosing careers.

In addition, with survey data of 354 samples, the research of Dinh and Thong (2016) concludes that attitude and creativity are the two factors that have the greatest impact on students' entrepreneurial intention in Ho Chi Minh City, followed by the factor of Subjective Standard. Context factors and Educational support, as expected, have a positive impact on attitude and creativity. From the results, some effective policy implications are suggested to promote entrepreneurship movement in Ho Chi Minh City and Vietnam.

In the study of "Analyzing factors impacting on intention to start a business of students from universities in Binh Duong province", Nhi *et al.* (2017) use the Model Factor Analysis (EFA), Assertive Factor Analysis (CFA), and Linear Structural Modeling (SEM) to determine factors that impact students' startup intentions, including: *Financial access; Non-financial access; Family and social support; Self-awareness; and Education and Training.* However, the role of Family and society support, Education and training, Self-awareness are more important than the others.

Based on the literature review, the authors found that most of the previous studies focused on the impact of subjective and personal attributes on the intention of starting a business. Therefore, the aim of this study is to contribute to the models by adding the role of objective factors such as *Perceived legitimacy of law and policy, Creativity and Innovation* in science and technology with the purpose to find a linkage between external factors in which public agencies are heavily involved with the intention of entrepreneurship of youngsters.

## 3. Research Methodology

### 3.1. *Research model*

In the light of previous studies, we propose a structural model to analyze the entrepreneurial intention of youth in Vinh Long Province, including: (1) Motivation to become an entrepreneur (M); (2) Personality characteristics (C); (3) Creativity and innovation in science and technology (S); Family background (B); (5) Education and training (E); (6) Financial capability (F); (7) Perceived legitimacy of law and policy (L) (see Figure 1 and Table 1).

### 3.2. *Data collection*

The quantitative empirical data in this study are collected via the survey method in terms of a questionnaire that is sent directly to students of universities and colleges in Vinh Long province, including Vinh Long University of Technology Education, Vinh Long Community College, and Vinh Long College of Economics and Finance. Besides that, we also survey young people about the intention to start their own business at the Center for Employment Services in the area. To meet the requirement of sample size in exploratory factor analysis (EFA), we follow the study of Hair *et al.* (2006). Specifically, we send

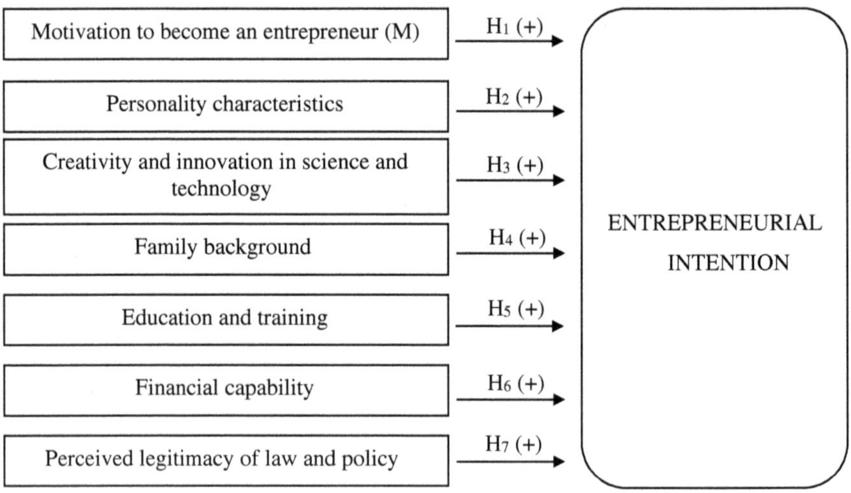


**Figure 1:** Research model.

**Table 1:** A summary of econometric studies on the factors affecting entrepreneurial intention.

| | Variables | Studies | Impact |
|---|---|---|---|
| M | Motivation to become an entrepreneur | Kautonen *et al.* (2013), Turker and Selcuk (2009) | + |
| C | Personality characteristics | Lien (2016), Liñán *et al.* (2010) | + |
| S | Creativity and innovation in science and technology | Gruel *et al.* (2010), Liñán *et al.* (2010) Lee *et al.* (2011) | + |
| B | Family Background | Lien (2016), Gruel *et al.* (2010), | + |
| E | Education and training | Gruel *et al.* (2010), Turker and Selcuk (2009), Lien (2016), | + |
| F | Financial capability | Lien (2016), Tu and Son (2015) | + |
| L | Perceived legitimacy of law and policy | Castaño *et al.* (2015), Turker and Selcuk (2009) | + |

**Table 2:** Sample characteristics.

| Group profile characteristics | | Frequency | Percentage |
|---|---|---|---|
| Gender | Male | 159 | 44.29 |
| | Female | 200 | 55.71 |
| Age | Under 20 | 86 | 23.96 |
| | From 20 to 25 years old | 258 | 71.87 |
| | From 25 to 35 years old | 15 | 4.18 |

360 questionnaires and receive 359 valid samples, with characteristics listed in Table 2.

### 3.3. *Data analysis*

After cleaning and coding data, we conduct descriptive statistical analysis which allows the researcher to explain and evaluate the variables numerically. Moreover, a reliability test and Cronbach's Alpha test are conducted to measure the internal consistency of the variables and their functioning in the research model. Then, EFA is used to identify the underlying relationships between measured variables that affect the entrepreneurial intention of youth. Next, these factors will be included in the multiple linear regression model to measure their impact.

## 4. Results and Discussion

### 4.1. *Entrepreneurial intention of youth in Vinh Long province*

When surveying the *entrepreneurial intention* for the future, 175 respondents answer that they want to start their own business, accounting for 48.75%. Whereas, the number of respondents who are reluctant about their plan is 125 students, accounting for 34.8% (see Table 3). Thereby, the proportion of students and youth with plans to be entrepreneurs in Vinh Long province is still low compared to the national average of 74% (Navigos Group, 2018). In contrast, in

**Table 3:** Statistics of Entrepreneurial intention of youth in Vinh Long province.

| Entrepreneurial intention | Percentage |
|---|---|
| + The number of young people who want to start their own business in the future. | 48.75 |
| + The number of young people who hesitate to start their own business in the future. | 34.82 |
| + The number of young people who never think about starting their own business in the future. | 16.43 |
| **Levels of entrepreneurship knowledge among young people** | |
| + Basic & advanced | 57.6 |
| + Unknown or mostly unknown | 42.3 |
| **Sources of assistance for entrepreneurs** | |
| + Build more subjects that equip students with entrepreneurial competencies in school | 74.9 |
| + Organize more entrepreneurship programs such as: competitions, clubs, conferences, ... | |
| + Build supporting funds and investment programs for startups | 76.9 |
| + Build science and technology consulting centers for startups | 73.8<br>78.3 |

Ho Chi Minh City, leading the startup movement in Vietnam, this rate is 81.7% (Quang and Cuong, 2017 survey of students of University of Economics and Law), and 85% for Can Tho (Tu and Son, 2015).

In addition, in terms of *knowledge* of entrepreneurship, only 57.6% of respondents answer that they have any knowledge of entrepreneurship. Over 70% of participants respond that it is important to build supporting tools for entrepreneurs, such as: training programs, entrepreneurial subjects, organizing startup programs: competitions, social clubs, conferences, or supporting funds and investment programs for startups. Specifically, nearly 80% of young people want schools and local authorities to have science and technology consulting centers for startups.

### 4.2. *Reliability test*

After testing Cronbach's Alpha reliability coefficient and implementing factor analysis with varimax rotation, 26 of 34 variables are retained (Corrected Item-Total Correlation value is higher than 0.3). Result of Cronbach's Alpha reliability coefficient is shown in Table 4.

### 4.3. *Exploratory factor analysis*

After conducting the EFA for the eighth time (last time) with 26 variables, the range of the KMO index is 0.942, which demonstrates that EFA analysis for grouping these variables together is

**Table 4:** Cronbach's Alpha reliability coefficient.

| **Factors** | **Cronbach's Alpha** |
|---|---|
| Motivation to become an entrepreneur (M) | 0.855 |
| Personality characteristics (C) | 0.884 |
| Creativity and innovation in science and technology (S) | 0.906 |
| Family background (B) | 0.832 |
| Education and training (E) | 0.911 |
| Financial capability (F) | 0.857 |
| Perceived legitimacy of law and policy (L) | 0.915 |

**Table 5:** KMO & Bartlett's test of sphericity.

| Kaiser–Meyer–Olkin measure of sampling adequacy | | 0.942 |
|---|---|---|
| Bartlett's Test of Sphericity | Approx. Chi-square | 6512.364 |
| | Df | 325 |
| | Sig. | 0.000 |

appropriate (see Table 5). Further, it indicates a high Bartlett's significant level (Sig. $= 0.000 < 0.05$) clearly showing that adequate correlation is found within the sample dataset to continue with factor analysis. Therefore, it is statistically confirmed that factor analysis can be performed on this dataset.

Table 6 presents all significant factors for entrepreneurial intention along with eigenvalues. Further, the percentage of variance attributable to each factor is also computed in this procedure. It can be seen from Table 6 that the total variance is 70.131%, satisfying the criterion of 60% or more for the total variance. This table also displays five factors with eigenvalues greater than 1, which will be extracted.

As depicted in Table 9, factor 1 is loaded with 9 variables having high factor loadings, factor 2 with 5 variables, factor 3 with 5, factor 4 with 4, and factor 5 with 3. After the factors are extracted by factor analysis, they can be labeled or placed in a meaningful category. Thus, variables with high factor loadings are combined and labeled as shown in Table 7.

From the above Cronbach's Alpha and EFA results, the research model is adjusted to include 5 factors affecting the entrepreneurial intention of youth, as follows in Figure 2.

### 4.4. *Regression analysis*

The regression analysis results in Table 8 show that all five factors in the final research model have a statistically significant impact on the intention of starting a business of students and youth in Vinh Long province ($p -$ value $< 0.05$).

**Table 6:** Total variance explained.

| | Initial Eigenvalues | | | Extraction sums of squared loadings | | | Rotation sums of squared loadings | | |
|---|---|---|---|---|---|---|---|---|---|
| Factor | Total | % of Variance | Cumulative % | Total | % of Variance | Cumulative % | Total | % of Variance | Cumulative % |
| 1 | 11.875 | 45.672 | 45.672 | 11.875 | 45.672 | 45.672 | 6.189 | 23.802 | 23.802 |
| 2 | 2.888 | 11.106 | 56.778 | 2.888 | 11.106 | 56.778 | 3.448 | 13.260 | 37.062 |
| 3 | 1.268 | 4.879 | 61.657 | 1.268 | 4.879 | 61.657 | 3.433 | 13.203 | 50.266 |
| 4 | 1.177 | 4.526 | 66.183 | 1.177 | 4.526 | 66.183 | 2.654 | 10.207 | 60.473 |
| 5 | 1.026 | 3.948 | 70.131 | 1.026 | 3.948 | 70.131 | 2.511 | 9.658 | 70.131 |
| 6 | .794 | 3.054 | 73.185 | | | | | | |

**Table 7:** Rotated components matrix.

| | Factors | | | | | |
|---|---|---|---|---|---|---|
| **Variables** | **1** | **2** | **3** | **4** | **5** | **Label name** |
| E5 — In my university, there are online training systems for students who want to start a business | 0.814 | | | | | **Individual ability** |
| E3 — Science incubators and clubs of the school support students to start a business | 0.808 | | | | | |
| E4 — Youth Union organized classes for students to build business projects | 0.798 | | | | | |
| F4 — There are many angel investors who are willing to invest capital for potential projects | 0.735 | | | | | |
| E2 — In my university, there are many entrepreneurship programs | 0.699 | | | | | |
| F3 — In Vinh Long province, there are supporting funds and investment programs for startups | 0.694 | | | | | |
| F2 — My close friends also want to contribute capital to start my business | 0.677 | | | | | |
| E1 — In my university, there are subjects that equip students with entrepreneurial competencies | 0.628 | | | | | |
| F1 — My family is willing to provide financial support | 0.581 | | | | | |

**Table 7:** (*Continued*)

| Variables | Factors 1 | 2 | 3 | 4 | 5 | Label name |
|---|---|---|---|---|---|---|
| C3 — I have optimism and confidence that failure is mother of success | | 0.803 | | | | **Personality characteristics** |
| C5 — I would like to make use of my creativity and realize my dreams | | 0.755 | | | | |
| C4 — I'm not easily discouraged despite losing money in investment | | 0.739 | | | | |
| C2 — I always make persistent efforts and work hard to achieve a goal | | 0.680 | | | | |
| C1 — I'm willing to take risks to earn profits | | 0.628 | | | | |
| M4 — Being an entrepreneur would give me a high level of income | | | 0.764 | | | **Motivation to become an entrepreneur** |
| M5 — Being an entrepreneur would contribute to the family and society | | | 0.750 | | | |
| M2 — I desire to have my own business | | | 0.749 | | | |
| M1 — I'm always attracted to subjects related to business administration | | | 0.687 | | | |
| M3 — I don't want to work as an employee | . | | 0.654 | | | |
| L3 — Policies related to entrepreneurship are public, transparent, and easily accessible | | | | 0.725 | | **Perceived legitimacy of law and policy** |
| L5 — Procedures related to entrepreneurship are easy and inexpensive (setting up companies, construction procedures, utilities, Internet, etc.). | | | | 0.685 | | |

(*Continued*)

**Table 7:** (*Continued*)

| Variables | Factors 1 | 2 | 3 | 4 | 5 | Label name |
|---|---|---|---|---|---|---|
| L2 — Many preferential policies at Central and local levels for startups | | | | 0.666 | | |
| L4 — Law enforcement affects entrepreneurship | | | | 0.643 | | |
| B1 — My family has run business | | | | | 0.753 | **Family background** |
| B4 — Family business brings many opportunities for me to startup | | | | | 0.753 | |
| B2 — My family is willing to support me with capital and inspiration to start a business | | | | | 0.666 | |

*Notes*: Extraction method: Principal component analysis. Rotation method: Varimax with Kaiser normalization. Rotation converged in eight iterations.

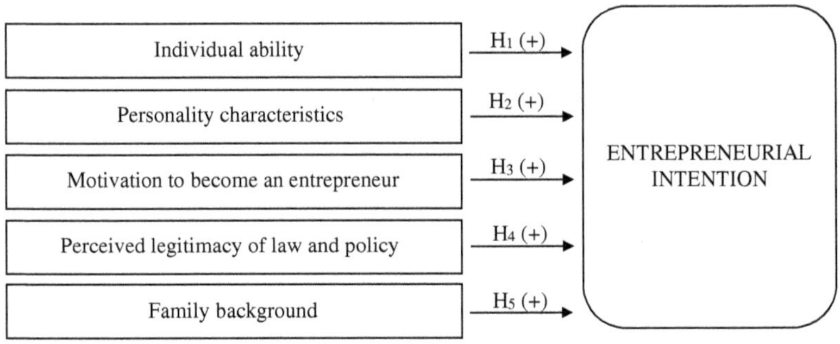


**Figure 2:** Official research model.

Specifically, *Perceived legitimacy of law and policy* has the greatest impact (beta value is 0.379), which indicates that young people are very concerned about the legal policies on startups. In particular, the statistical results of the knowledge of young people on entrepreneurship laws in the area are not effective as expected (mean value of this factor is about 3.13). Therefore, government and

**Table 8:** Coefficients.

| Model | *B* | Std.error | *t* | Sig. |
|---|---|---|---|---|
| Constant | 0.098 | 0.144 | 0.682 | 0.495 |
| X1: Individual ability | 0.137 | 0.060 | 2.274 | 0.024 |
| X2: Personality characteristics | 0.130 | 0.052 | 2.509 | 0.013 |
| X3: Motivation to become an entrepreneur | 0.237 | 0.050 | 4.718 | 0.000 |
| X4: Perceived legitimacy of law and policy | 0.379 | 0.050 | 7.639 | 0.000 |
| X5: Family background | 0.108 | 0.041 | 2.625 | 0.009 |

*Note*: Dependent variable: Y-Entrepreneurial Intentions.

local authorities should improve the policy and legal system on startups and have legal support centers for entrepreneurs with feasible projects. If there are any constraints on policies and legal regulations, projects will find it difficult to receive investment and commercialize products.

The second major impact is the *Motivation* factor of becoming an entrepreneur, with a coefficient of 0.237. This result is as expected and similar to previous studies. However, the majority of people in the Mekong Delta as well as in Vinh Long province earn a living by farming and feeding, which depend on the privileged natural resources the uncertainty of which induces in the people a fear of failure and expectation of external support. This is an invisible barrier but greatly affects the motivation of starting a business among students and youth in this region. The other three factors including individual ability, personal characteristics, and family background have the same effects with coefficients of 0.137, 0.130, and 0.108, respectively.

However, it is noticeable that in previous studies, the factor of *Creativity and Innovation* in science and technology is forecast to have a strong influence on students' entrepreneurial intentions. Because of the Industrial Revolution 4.0, science and technology innovation are always given top priority and have great potential for success, including the technology projects in Vietnam that receive huge investment such as: Foody, Momo, F88, Got It, Vntrip.vn, and Toong. However, with survey data in Vinh Long province, this factor is not appreciated and omitted from the regression model. A reasonable explanation for this could be that the Mekong Delta in general and Vinh Long, in particular, are considered to build up their competitiveness in the agricultural sector, which is deeply ingrained in the people. Therefore, most ideas and projects revolve around cultivating and processing manual and rudimentary agricultural products. As a result, ideas and startup projects in this land are not creative, with low technology application and infeasible products. That leads to simple business solutions which can be easily copied. This is the reason this sector does not attract the attention of many supporting funds, investors, and businesses.

## 5. Conclusion and Implication

Using EFA method with 359 samples in Vinh Long province, this study concludes that five factors are statistically significant to the entrepreneurial intentions of youth, including: *Perceived legitimacy of law and policy; Motivation to become an entrepreneur; Individual ability; Personality characteristics; and Family background.* Based on the regression model, the results show that the factor of laws and policies has the greatest impact on the intention. The second important role is played by the motivation of being an entrepreneur. Factors of Individual ability, Personality characteristics, and Family also have positive effects on youths' intention. However, though in the age of Industry 4.0 science and technology factor is expected to play an important role, the survey results show that this factor is not highly considered and is therefore omitted from the regression model. The underestimation of the science and technology factor is one of the reasons why startup projects are not highly effective and are not supported by funds, investors, and businesses. Therefore, some policy implications are proposed to promote the wave of startups in Vinh Long province, as follows:

- As one of the key players in the entrepreneurship ecosystem, policymakers enforce laws that make it difficult or possible for entrepreneurs to thrive. Therefore, government and local authorities should improve the business environment and support for feasible projects, such as by offering tax incentives, reducing the burden on business formation, and encouraging local banks to work with startups and small businesses by providing loans or investment.

- To promote students' motivation, the incorporation of entrepreneurship curricula within various levels of education is necessary. Promoting entrepreneurship at the educational level will help to create a culture of innovative, solution-orientated individuals who will grow to start their own businesses. Moreover, schools and universities should organize many entrepreneurship programs, competitions, science incubators, supporting centers, and conferences to enhance students' awareness of running their own business.
- Last but not least, there should be a startup community to link Vinh Long province and other localities in the Mekong Delta region, which provides the support and incubation that foster today's leading companies and drives the innovation for a brighter future.

### 5.1. *Limitations and future research*

This study is subject to certain limitations.

(1) Similar to the previous studies in the literature review, the research concentrates on the entrepreneurial intention, but it is a fact that intentions may not turn into actual behaviors in the future.
(2) Our sample consisted entirely of undergraduate business students or newly-graduates from three universities and employment services center located in Vinh Long province. Therefore, some may argue that the sample needs to be diversified to better predict the behavior of young managers or other non-student populations.
(3) A limitation of any survey research is the inability to ask follow-up questions and explore more fully the reasoning behind the answers of respondents.

Therefore, future research can consider qualitative interviews or focus group sessions to provide rich explanatory information that could add value to the survey data. Moreover, future research should classify and analyze different types of entrepreneurship, such as full-time and part-time entrepreneurship, private, state, and joint entrepreneurs, or for-profit and social enterprises. These distinctions are of considerable relevance to policy and lawmakers, for example, in terms of assessing the social and economic potential of latent entrepreneurship in different segments of the population, and in targeting and designing enterprise support initiatives.

In spite of the limitations, the findings of this study offer a number of opportunities for future research to advance our knowledge of the subjective and objective factors that predict intentions to start businesses.

## APPENDIX 1: Entrepreneurial intention measurements.

**Table A.1:** To what extent do you agree or disagree with the following statements?

| **Measurement** | |
|---|---|
| Motivation to become an entrepreneur (M) | |
| **M1** | I'm always attracted to subjects related to business administration |
| **M2** | I desire to have my own business |
| **M3** | I don't want to work as an employee |
| **M4** | Being an entrepreneur would give me a high level of income |
| **M5** | Being an entrepreneur would contribute to the family and society |
| Personality characteristics (C) | |
| **C1** | I'm willing to take risks to earn profits |
| **C2** | I always make persistent effort of working hard to achieve a goal |
| **C3** | I have optimism and confidence that failure is mother's success |
| **C4** | I'm not easily discouraged despite losing money in investment |
| **C5** | I would like to make use of my creativity and carry out my dreams |
| Creativity and innovation in science and technology (S) | |
| **S1** | I believe that new business ideas are necessary to start-up |
| **S2** | I believe that new technology improves business performance |
| **S3** | I believe that technology incubators encourage entrepreneurial intentions |
| **S4** | I believe that experts and supporting centers are important to promote entrepreneurial intentions |

Table A.1: (*Continued*)

| Measurement | |
|---|---|
| **S5** | I believe that the fourth industrial revolution encourages entrepreneurship |
| **S6** | I believe that programs for entrepreneurs are significant to support guidance and technology transfer |
| Family Background (B) | |
| **B1** | My family has run business |
| **B2** | My family is willing to support me with capital and inspiration to start a business |
| **B3** | My family always stand by me if my business goes down |
| **B4** | Family business brings many opportunities for me to start-up |
| Education and training (E) | |
| **E1** | In my university, there are subjects that equip students with entrepreneurial competencies |
| **E2** | In my university, there are many entrepreneurship programs |
| **E3** | Science incubators and clubs of the school support students to start a business |
| **E4** | Youth Union organized classes for students to build business projects |
| **E5** | In my university, there are online training systems for students who want to start-up |
| Financial capability (F) | |
| **F1** | My family willing to provide financial support |
| **F2** | My close friends also want to contribute capital to start my business |
| **F3** | In Vinh Long province, there are supporting funds and investment programs for startups |
| **F4** | There are many angel investors who are willing to invest capital for potential projects |
| Perceived legitimacy of law and policy (L) | |
| **L1** | Laws and policies related to entrepreneur are comprehensive |
| **L2** | Many preferential policies of Central and local for start-ups |
| **L3** | Policies related to entrepreneur are public, transparent, and easily accessible |
| **L4** | Law enforcement affects entrepreneurship |
| **L5** | Procedures related to entrepreneur are easy and inexpensive (setting up companies, construction procedures, utilities, Internet ...). |
| Entrepreneurial intention (I) | |
| **I1** | I want to start my own business in the future |
| **I2** | I have very seriously thought of starting a firm |
| **I3** | I have already prepared conditions to start a business |
| **I4** | I have already built my business plans or projects |
| **I5** | I will participate in entrepreneurship contests to consolidate, check plans, find funding and angel investors for my startups |

## References


Ajzen, I. (1991). The theory of planned behavior. *Organizational Behavior and Human Decision Processes*, 50(2), 179–211.

Castaño, M.-S., Méndez, M.-T., and Galindo, M.-Á. (2015). The effect of social, cultural, and economic factors on entrepreneurship. *Journal of Business Research*, 68(7), 1496–1500.

Dinh, T.G.T., and Thong, B.Q. (2016). Factors affecting on entrepreneurial intentions — The case of graduated students in Ho Chi Minh city. In *The 5th International Conference on Vietnam Studies (ICVNS2016)*, Vietnam National University, Hanoi.

Engle, R.L., Dimitriadi, N., Gavidia, J.V., Schlaegel, C., Delanoe, S., Alvarado, I., and Wolff, B. (2010). Entrepreneurial intent. *International Journal of Entrepreneurial Behavior & Research*, 16(1), 35–57.

Gurel, E., Altinay, L., and Daniele, R. (2010). Tourism students' entrepreneurial intentions. *Annals of Tourism Research*, 37(3), 646–669.

Hair, J.F., Black, W.C., Babin, B.J., Anderson, R.E., and Tatham, R.L. (2006). *Multivariate Data Analysis*, Vol. 6. Upper Saddle River: Pearson Prentice Hall.

Kautonen, T., van Gelderen, M., and Tornikoski, E.T. (2013). Predicting entrepreneurial behaviour: A test of the theory of planned behaviour. *Applied Economics*, 45(6), 697–707.

Kolvereid, L. (1996). Prediction of employment status choice intentions. *Entrepreneurship Theory and Practice*, 21(1), 47–58.

Kor, Y.Y., Mahoney, J.T., and Michael, S.C. (2007). Resources, capabilities and entrepreneurial perceptions. *Journal of Management Studies*, 44(7), 1187–1212.

Krueger, N.F., and Brazeal, D.V. (1994). Entrepreneurial potential and potential entrepreneurs. *Entrepreneurship Theory and Practice*, 18(3), 91–104.

Krueger, N.F., Reilly, M.D., and Carsrud, A.L. (2000). Competing models of entrepreneurial intentions. *Journal of Business Venturing*, 15(5-6), 411–432.

Lee, L., Wong, P.K., Foo, M.D., and Leung, A. (2011). Entrepreneurial intentions: The influence of organizational and individual factors. *Journal of Business Venturing*, 26(1), 124–136.

Lien, D.T.H. (2016). Factors affecting on entrepreneurial intentions of business administration students at University of Labour and Social affairs. *Journal of Yersin Science*, 1(11), 44–53.

Liñán, F., Rodríguez-Cohard, J.C., and Rueda-Cantuche, J.M. (2010). Factors affecting entrepreneurial intention levels: A role for education.

*International Entrepreneurship and Management Journal*, 7(2), 195–218.

Lüthje, C., and Franke, N. (2003). The "making" of an entrepreneur: Testing a model of entrepreneurial intent among engineering students at MIT. *R&D Management*, 33(2), 135–147.

MOIT (2016). Htrvà phát trien doanh nghi∩ẹp n năm 2020. Available at: https://moit.gov.vn/tin-chi-tiet/-/chi-tiet/ho-tro-va-phat-trien-doanh-nghiep-den-nam-2020-107057-16.html

Navigos Group (2018). New graduates with opportunities and challenges in the beginning of their careers. Navigos Report 2018. Available at: https://www.navigosgroup.com/vi/sinh-vien-moi-ra-truong-2018/

Nhi, D.T.Y., Chuong, H.N., Mai, N.T.T., Giang, V.T.L., and Thi, T.T. (2017). Analysing factors impacted on intention to start a business of students from universities in Binh Duong province. *Journal of Thu Dau Mot University*, 4(35), 107–114.

Quang, N.H., and Cuong, N.C.T. (2017). Determinants to student's entrepreneurial intentions of Faculty of Business Administration at University of Economics and Law. *Scientific Journal of Tra Vinh University*, 25, 10 19.

Tu, P.A., and Son, N.T. (2015). Determinants of economic graduates' business initiatives in Can Tho city. *Can Tho University Journal of Science*, 40, 39–49.

Turker, D., and Sonmez Selcuk, S. (2009). Which factors affect entrepreneurial intention of university students? *Journal of European Industrial Training*, 33(2), 142–159.

Zahra, S.A., Nielsen, A.P., and Bogner, W.C. (1999). Corporate entrepreneurship, knowledge, and competence development. *Entrepreneurship Theory and Practice*, 23(3), 169–189.

https://doi.org/10.1142/9789811227158_0030

# Chapter 30

# E-enterprise and the Law: Realizing the Potential Risks

**Van Long Tran and Quoc Tan Phan**

## Abstract

In the digital economy, the concept of e-enterprise is not new but keeps constantly developing, which results in a series of challenges for lawmakers: How to regulate this new model of business beneficially, on the one hand, and manage risks thereof effectively, on the other? This chapter aims to study the practice of establishment and development of e-enterprises and the current legal framework regulating e-business. Moreover, the authors point out the legal risks that can arise from this new model and suggest some legal solutions thereof. In doing so, the chapter starts with an in-depth discussion of the definition of e-enterprise in a literature review. Secondly, the chapter addresses the legal risks of e-enterprise in the case of Vietnam, where the model of e-enterprise can be abused to form a bogus company (or shell corporation). Finally, the chapter sketches out some recommendations relating to business law. Current Vietnamese laws need to be reconsidered to regulate this new type of business efficiently.

**Keywords:** E-enterprise; legal framework; business law; Vietnam.

## 1. Introduction

In the digital economy, the concept of e-enterprise is not new but keeps constantly developing, which results in a series of challenges for lawmakers: How to regulate this new model of business beneficially, on the one hand, and manage risks thereof effectively, on the other? This chapter aims to study the practice of establishment and development of e-enterprises and the current legal framework regulating e-business. Moreover, the authors point out the legal risks that can arise from this new model and suggest some legal solutions thereof.

In doing so, the chapter starts with an in-depth discussion of the definition of e-enterprise in a literature review. As Hoque (2000) states, e-business is the latest form of e-everything in the business environment. If the initial approach of e-commerce (brochure wave) has been known since the early 1990s, the forms of e-business have only been applied since the 2000s. E-enterprises can be understood as enterprises that apply electronic technology, right from the establishment, to the business organization, and human resource management. In this kind of business, all interactions between the management apparatus are entirely by data messages, communications with partners or customers mostly based on Information & Communication Technologies (ICTs), deemed as the result of the e-application development ladder in the business environment. This means that e-business is not new in business practice, but its concept is still very vague in the context of its legal framework. This chapter, in turn, refers to the direction of legalization of related issues.

Secondly, the chapter addresses the legal risks of e-enterprise in the case of Vietnam where the model of e-enterprise can be abused to form a bogus company (or shell corporation). Since the company itself is a complex structure adhering to legal responsibility thereof, the lawmakers need to realize the potential risks of an e-company including the existence of i-office ("intelligent office solutions"), or the practice of an initial coin offering (ICO), or the digitalization of business management activities. Can the partners, customers trust an e-company, without even seeing the director's face once? How is the attitude of the state and the society within the delicate boundary between the e-company and the bogus company? How can we access the legal responsibility of an e-business, of the managers of an e-enterprise?

From the aforementioned questionable assumptions, the chapter sketches out some recommendations relating to business law. Current

Vietnamese laws need to be reconsidered to regulate this new type of business efficiently.

## 2. The Concept of E-enterprise

This chapter discusses the organization and operation of businesses that are based partly or entirely on the development of digital and electronic environments (ICTs), namely e-enterprises. In other words, the digitalization of the organization and the operation of today's businesses have given rise to a new type of business whose interactions are built and developed largely on the basis of the digital industry in the era of digitizing everything (e-everything) currently. The e-enterprise discussed hereby is understood in such a way, not the electronics manufacturing business.

In fact, the concept of the e-enterprise aforementioned is not something new. Emerging from the advents and inventions in the field of digital technology, artificial intelligence, and the Internet of things,[1] the foundations of e-commerce have been established[2] not only in the business sector, the advent of ICTs has resulted in the system of e-everything, from e-government to e-democracy, from e-custom to e-banking, and it seems that all traditional interactive models in any field now also produce its electronic version (e-version). In this context, the concept of e-business has to be understood in a broader sense than the e-commerce concept. "Trade" or "commerce"

[1]See http://www.bbc.co.uk/history/scottishhistory/enlightenment/features_enlightenment_industry.shtml. This article only refers to the industrial revolution concerning the inventions and developments of the digital industry, marked by the birth of the first personal computers, in the 1970s. (Accessed on July 20, 2019).

[2]According to the UNCITRAL's Model Law on e-commerce, any type of information in the form of a data message used in any commercial activity is to be considered e-commerce. Meanwhile, Article 3, Clause 1 of Decree 53/2013 of the Vietnamese Government states: E-commerce activities are the conduct of part or the whole process of commercial activities by electronic means connected to Internet, mobile telecommunications network, or other open networks". Vietnamese law approach tends to narrow the concept of e-commerce.

refers to the supply side (output) of businesses including ways to consume goods and provide services to increase profits. Meanwhile, business is deemed as a process including investment activities, human resource management, corporate internal governance, and management (Reiley and Spulber, 2001). Therefore, e-commerce and e-business can be approached from different angles, and the concept of e-enterprise is an element of e-business, not e-commerce. König and Weitzel (2005) make this distinction clear, with the definition as follows:

> Electronic Business describes business transactions where participants interact electronically. In contrast to Electronic Commerce solely focusing on the relations with the eventual consumer (Business-to-Consumer, B2C), E-Business comprises the entire value creation; therefore, pinpoints digital and automated business processes within and between firms.

Hoque (2000) proves that e-enterprise is the latest form of e-everything in the business environment. If the initial form of e-commerce (brochure wave) has been around since the early 1990s, the forms of e-enterprises have only been found since the 2000s. In other words, e-enterprise means an enterprise applying electronic technology for its establishment, operational organization, human resource management, and all interactions between the internal entities of that enterprise or between the enterprise and external subjects are conducted online through data messages transmission, as the end result of the e-application development ladder (König and Weitzel, 2005, p. 8). This means that e-business is not something new in business practices, but its concept is still somehow vague in the context of its legal definition or legal framework which still has loopholes. This chapter, in turn, addresses the direction of legalization of related issues.

## 3. Outline of the Risks of E-enterprise in Vietnam

Let's begin with e-entrepreneurship, which is understood simply as starting a business entirely on the electronic environment, with the whole process of deploying business ideas to establishing a business based on digitalization. Sales or providing services are based on digital interactions. According to Kollmann (2006), electronic entrepreneurship is understood as follows: "E-entrepreneurship refers to establishing a new company with an innovative business idea within the Net Economy, which uses an electronic platform in data networks, offers its products and/or services based upon a purely electronic creation of value. Essential is the fact that this value offer is only made possible through the development of information technology."

Of course, the current ICTs platform, as well as the relevant legal framework, does not allow the founding of entirely virtual companies, completely virtual, meaning that nothing is real. The company itself is a complex structure associated with a system of legal personal responsibility imposed on its managers or owners. The question is to what extent can a company or enterprise be virtual, in order to avoid the risk of the formation of bogus companies[3] or shell corporations? Policymakers cannot ignore the appearance of digital companies, and in the future, many entrepreneurs may exploit the benefits of the advents of technology to optimize their profits. E-companies (smart companies) are a good choice for entrepreneurs to start up in the era of 4.0 technology. According to Mr. Vu Ngoc Anh, Executive Director of Association of Vietnamese Scientists and Experts (AVSE Global), an appropriate and comprehensive approach to the applications of digital technology for entrepreneurship is necessary, but first and foremost, the legal framework needs to be consolidated.[4]

---

[3] A bogus company with an address that doesn't even exist. Turns out it was a bogus company. It refers in particular to a new form of tax fraud, consisting in the creation of bogus companies for the purpose of committing tax offenses such as obtaining a double refund of tax or money laundering. According to https://glosbe.com/en/en/bogus%20company.

[4] Vnexpress (21/09/2018), https://kinhdoanh.vnexpress.net/tin-tuc/vi-mo/doanh-nghiep-nho-lo-hut-hoi-chay-theo-4-0-3812620.html.

### 3.1. *Risks from virtual office (i-office) and bogus company*

According to Article 43 Law on Enterprise in 2014: "The head office of an enterprise is the place for contacting the enterprise in the territory of Vietnam, has a definite address, including house number, alley, street name, names of hamlet or village, commune, ward or township, district, town or provincial city, province or centrally run city; telephone and facsimile numbers and email address (if any)."

There is no specific requirement for the minimum area or necessary equipment, there must be a business name tag attached to the head office. It must be a real address, although, in fact, many businesses use a non-existent address to register their head office and the business registration agency still cannot detect. For instance, the Department of Planning and Investment HCMC receives up to thousands of business registration applications per day, and is unable to examine or check the existence of each business head office registered. Even if a fake address is suspected, the dossier reception officer has no right to arrest the applicant to prove it is real.[5]

The head office of an enterprise address cannot be an e-mail, a post office box, nor the address of an apartment,[6] but a real, specific address. This is also in accordance with the laws of other countries, the address of the business is a place where the postal postmaster can come to deliver the parcel directly from the company authorized

[5]Life and Law (01/12/2016), https://vietnammoi.vn/tp-hcm-nhieu-doanh-nghiep-dung-dia-chi-ma-de-buon-lau-12107.html. (Accessed on July 28, 2019).

[6]Article 80:7, Decree 99/2015/Nd-CP dated 20/10/2015 on guidance of law on housing: "In case a business registration document issued by a competent authority indicates that an apartment is used as business location before the effective date of the Law on Housing, the organization, household, or individual granted with such business registration document must move the business to another location other than an apartment within 06 months from the effective date of this Decree. The competent authority that issued the business registration document must initiate procedures for changing the business location on the business registration document issued to the organization, household, or individual into another location by the deadline specified in this Clause. After this deadline, the organization, household, or individual must not do business at the apartment."

person.[7] Therefore, entrepreneurs, to save costs, can think of virtual office leasing (i-office) services that are flourishing today. With an i-office, the address of the business office appears spectacularly at an office building, and a team of i-office service companies does the jobs of businesses in the name of the enterprise, such as welcoming guests and customers, mail delivery, etc. The enterprise is thus virtual, because there are actually no business representatives who work permanently at the given address as they can delegate everyday, simple activities to the service company. Whenever any guest or customer wants to directly contact the representative of the enterprise, a sharing room is hired for conducting the meeting. Therefore, for just a few hundred thousand VND per month,[8] the entrepreneur can own a monumental business address, even symbolic, but most importantly, the law does not prohibit to do so.

The legal issue raised here is that the Enterprise Law 2014 absolutely does not reckon the existence of e-office (or i-office) mentioned previously. Customers, business partners, or creditors who want to communicate with the company at the head office assume that anyone who talks with them is an authorized person from the company (in fact, they are from the reception team of the service company), and if these persons make a transaction without the authorization of the e-enterprise that causes damage to customers (or any third party), are they responsible for compensation for customers? How can we define responsibilities between the two sides in the operation of the business: services company and e-enterprise? Is the service company accountable for providing services to ghost businesses, which are only used to legalize fraud, money laundering, or smuggling? We cannot find the answer through the current legal framework. Thus, e-enterprise would be beneficial for entrepreneurs, but it

[7]For instance, The Companies (Address of Registered Office) Regulations 2016 of the UK, available at https://www.legislation.gov.uk/ukdsi/2016/9780111143360

[8]See, for further information relating to i-office https://i-office.com.vn/goi-dich-vu-i-office/

may also be a challenge for state management and risky for customers and partners of e-enterprises.

### 3.2. *Lack of a legal framework regulating virtual capital mobilization*

Virtual capital (e-capital) (Brynjolfsson *et al.*, 2002) here is understood as the entrepreneur investing capital for his business as well as mobilizing capital from virtual assets, especially cryptocurrency (e-money, e.g., Bitcoin), from properties trading in online game genres, as well as countless other virtual assets in the online world, such as a Facebook account or a YouTube channel. Because they can all be priced in money, can be appraised by cash, and eventually can be objected to being transferred in civil contracts (Tran Le Hong, 2007).

E-property is virtual, but its value or price is real, and it has also been the object of many disputes recently. The laws of many countries have begun to look for legal models to govern transactions relating to e-money, for example, the European Union issued a Directive on management and supervision of E-money since 2009.[9] Unfortunately, regardless of many controversies, the Civil Code 2015 has been passed without any provisions regulating e-money or virtual property. More seriously, the State Bank also issued a series of documents to prohibit the use of virtual money in particular and virtual assets in general as a means of payment, and the violation of these regulations is likely to be criminally prosecuted.[10] However, by acknowledging the importance of having a legal framework for virtual asset-related transactions, the government is also aware of the importance of legalizing this kind of asset. Specifically, according to the Prime Minister's Directive 10 CT-TTG dated April 11, 2018 on

[9] https://ec.europa.eu/info/law/e-money-directive-2009-110-ec_en (Accessed on July 28, 2019).

[10] Decree No. 80/2016/ND-CP amend governments decree 101/2012/ND-CP on non-cash payments.

strengthening management of activities related to Bitcoin and other virtual currencies,[11] the government assigns the Ministry of Finance two tasks, including:

- Direct public companies, securities companies, fund management companies, and securities investment funds not to conduct transactions and brokerage transactions related to illegal virtual money, and to comply with legal regulations on money laundering prevention.
- Research international practices and experiences to propose measures to mobilize capital through issuing virtual currency (ICO).

We argue that the direction of the government seems contradictory; on the one hand, it strengthens management on e-currency, but logically, we cannot manage what we do not recognize. Considering the current situation of instability caused by this type of property to the social set-up, such as the case of the fraud of VND 15,000 billion through the multi-level virtual money business model,[12] the government finds it necessary to consolidate the state management regulations by "*directing credit institutions and payment intermediary service providers not to perform transactions related to illegal virtual money*", as well as "*detecting and punishing any usage of virtual money as means of illegal payment*".[13]

The bipolar attitude in state management is that e-currency usage is forbidden, but in reality, the state cannot deny the tremendous economic efficiency of virtual money and virtual assets, especially in the context of 4.0 startups, with capital mobilization through issuing virtual money (ICO). In Vietnam, many experts point out that startups calling capital through ICO creates opportunities to access international investment capital easily with the number of

[11] Full text is available at https://luatvietnam.vn/tai-chinh/chi-thi-10-ct-ttg-2018-quan-ly-hoat-dong-lien-quan-toi-bitcoin-va-cac-loai-tien-ao-161676-d1.html.

[12] Dantri online https://dantri.com.vn/suc-manh-so/vu-lua-dao-tien-ao-hon-15-nghin-ty-dong-vi-sao-lai-qua-de-dang-20180409080158734.htm.

[13] *Supra* note 10.

startup blockchains calling up to tens of millions of dollars in a short time.[14]

The question is: Why does the state limit the right of entrepreneurs to mobilize their capital by e-money just because of the absence of a suitable legal model to manage virtual capital and virtual assets? Recently, the government also agreed to assign the Ministry of Justice to propose an urgent draft for a legal framework for management and handling of virtual money and virtual assets earlier this year, signaling the optimistic view that we will have a relevant law in the near future. However, the Civil Code 2015, the basic law on property processing, still does not recognize this type of property, so the enactment of a legal mechanism for the contribution of capital in virtual currency still seems quite far out of reach.

### 3.3. *Digitizing corporate governance activities: is electronic evidence reliable enough?*

Corporate governance here is understood as a way to distribute and control the power and responsibility of elements in the organizational structure of a company, in accordance with the Company law and Company charter regulating the rights and obligations of the board of directors, shareholders' council, supervisory board, or director (OECD, 1999, 2004). The concept of corporate governance here does not include activities aimed at business administration, increasing profits, and reducing costs, which are aspects of e-commerce.

In the case of e-enterprises, how far can the activities of these entities be digitized? Does the law recognize a shareholder council meeting conducted through the conference function of Viber, or Hangout, or Skype? Is a resolution of a Member's council meeting concluded from an online conversation through Facebook messenger, confirmed by the electronic signatures of the members, legitimate?

[14]Investment Newspaper online: https://baodautu.vn/huy-dong-von-bang-tien-ao-de-khoi-nghiep-de-co-trieu-usd-nhung-kho-nuot-d78294.html (retrieved from 28/07/2019).

Are courts and judges willing to accept such pieces of electronic evidence in dispute settlement? Clearly, these practices pose a series of legal issues.

Imagine that the digitization of governance activities helps e-enterprises reduce many costs. There is no need for printer machines, corporate head offices with private work areas for managers who work 8 h per day. Rather, the owner can manage effectively his own e-enterprise online, managers and staff do their jobs at home and communicate with each other online, and the cyber environment is the main workspace. E-enterprise, an e-business operating in a network environment, is entirely possible, Uber or Grab are moving towards such virtual companies.

However, no matter how virtual an e-enterprise can be, legal responsibility is real, from the company's own responsibility as a commercial legal entity to the personal responsibility of the company's competent people. The director, or manager, despite carrying out purely electronic interactive activities, is still subject to legal responsibilities before the company, such as *duty of care.*[15] Obviously, the director or manager can electronically complete his or her operations, but a company cannot hire a robot to do the work of a director, no legal system in the world allows that.

If important documents of the company, such as the Resolution of the General Meeting of Shareholders or the Board of Directors, can be stored as electronic documents, such as Article 146, paragraph 1 of the Law on Enterprises provides: *The General Meeting of Shareholders shall be recorded in minutes and may be sound-recorded or stored in other electronic forms.* In principle, *Information in data message cannot be denied [its] validity for the sole reason that such information is shown in the form of data messages.*[16] The statement

[15]The term can be easily found in Corporate Laws of many countries, describing a company manager to be honest and diligent necessarily in all his activities, loyal to the company, and all management acts must be carried out for benefits of the company. This is also legalized in Article 71 of the Law on Enterprises 2014 (for limited companies), Article 160 (for joint stock companies).

[16]Article 11, Law on E-transactions 2006.

refers to the fact that the current Enterprise Law opens the way for digitizing administration activities as e-transactions recognized by the law. E-enterprises do not need to hire expensive places to organize their shareholders' general meetings when shareholders can fully attend and vote by video conferencing or another form of meeting; or send the vote to the meeting by mail, fax, or e-mail.[17] Similarly, members' council can conduct their meetings when each member is at a different location, through an online conference, and in doing so, the meeting place is defined as the chairman's location. Virtual meetings and minutes to the resolution of such meetings can be documented electronically, but the limited liability of the shareholders and e-enterprise itself, personal responsibility of the managers or directors, the company's legal responsibility to its shareholders as well as partners and customers in their commercial activities, are all real.

Do the contributors or shareholders of an e-enterprise feel confident about the safety of their investments? Do the partners and customers have enough trust in a company without even seeing the director's face once? How are the attitudes of the state and the society within the delicate boundary between the virtual company and the bogus company? The law recognizes that electronic transactions, electronic papers are as valuable as traditional transactions or hard copy documents, so the status and liability of e-enterprises should be treated fairly and equally. However, how to access the responsibility of an e-enterprise, a manager in an e-enterprise from electronic documents or electronic transactions? Are courts willing to consider a request to cancel or recognize a Resolution of the General Meeting of Shareholders under Article 147 of the Enterprise Law when that Resolution is the result of an online meeting and confirmed by a series of digital signatures? In reality, courts do not act in such a way.

[17] Article 140:1 Law on Enterprise.

## 4. Conclusion and Policy Suggestions

As mentioned above, the Vietnamese law actually creates the initial foundation for the development of e-enterprise model thanks to the provision of a flexible legal framework for the application of electronic interaction mode in an enterprise environment. Moreover, online business registration on the existence of virtual offices and the encouragement of using digital signatures to acknowledge the validity of online meetings or company documents in electronic form are also the factors that contribute to the foundation of e-enterprise. Overall, Vietnamese law appears to be not obsolete in comparison to advanced countries' legal framework relating to e-business. However, e-business, including e-commerce, actually generates many risks, so how should the law be governed to deal with e-risks from e-enterprises? We find that the following issues need to be addressed in legislative work in the near future:

First, the e-business model creates an ecology for entrepreneurship and controlling the risk of forming bogus companies.

As mentioned above, the boundary of bogus companies and virtual companies is very fragile, and then controlling this risk requires both pre-check and post-check procedures. Business registration procedures still have to be clear not to hinder business freedom; however, there needs to be a mechanism to control the legality of the virtual office (i-office), clarifying the responsibilities of the i-office service company.

Similarly, according to the provisions of the enterprise law, the enterprise only has to announce its information on the national portal. We assert that the law on enterprises needs to add regulations to force enterprises to publish their public information on their own website, information of legal representatives, or minutes of meetings (in case of public companies). Transparency, facilitating public oversight, still seems to be the most effective way to prevent the establishment of shell companies for fraud.

Secondly, the legal responsibility of the e-business needs to be carefully taken into account. E-commerce and e-business have specific risks, which may cause the psychology of suspicion for the model of e-enterprise. Although in principle, the legal responsibilities apply to all businesses regardless of whether they are electronic or not, the responsibility of the manager is real, that of the board of directors is also real. Unfortunately, the mechanism of dispute settlement relies on electronic evidence, which is not considered as a reliable source of evidence, because it is fragile and vulnerable to interference. Hence, we suggest that the law should aim to provide the role of third parties in the confirmation of electronic transactions, to share and reduce the legal risks. For example, the joint role of an agency or organization that certifies digital signatures in transactions of a business authorized person, the responsibility of an agency or business that provides virtual office services (i-office), and electronic invoices. These organizations and agencies with technological capabilities to assess electronic documents must be responsible and accountable for supporting the courts or investigation body in resolving disputes or investigating crimes, based on electronic evidence. In the current context, we still have to accept that the legal risk level of not only e-enterprise but also e-commerce is higher than the traditional mechanism.

## References


Brynjolfsson, E., Hitt, L.M., and Yang, S. (2002). Intangible assets: Computers and organizational capital. Brookings papers on economic activity, 2002(1), 137–181.

Hong L. Tran, T.S. (2007), Virtual assets — From awareness to protection. *Journal of Jurisprudence*, 7, 29–37.

Hoque, F. (2000). E-*Enterprise: Business Models, Architecture, and Components*, Vol. 2. Cambridge: Cambridge University Press, p. 8.

Kollmann, T. (2006). What is e-entrepreneurship? — Fundamentals of company founding in the net economy. *International Journal of Technology Management*, 33(4), 322–340.

König, W., and Weitzel, T. (2005). Towards the e-enterprise: Standards, networks and co-operation strategies. In *The Practical Real-Time Enterprise*. Berlin, Heidelberg: Springer, pp. 359–384.

OECD (1999, 2004). *Principles of Corporate Governance*, Paris: OECD.

Reiley, D., and Spulber, D.F. (2001). Business-to-business electronic commerce. *Journal of Economic Perspectives*, 15(1), 55–68.

https://doi.org/10.1142/9789811227158_bmatter

# Index

**A**

Aaron, H., 690
Abdullah, S.N., 288, 290
Aboody, D., 229
Abreu, M., 127
 accountant expertise (AC) (*see also* chief accountant expertise)
 definition of, 249, 251
accounting-based approach, 150, 154–155
acquisitions
 cross-border *versus* domestic, 8–9
 role of corporate governance in, 9–11
adaptive leadership, 306
Adhikari, A., 204
administrative leadership, 306
 advertising value, 582–583
 credibility and, 590
 customers' purchase intention and, 595
 entertainment and, 591
 factors affecting, 585–587
 flow experience and, 594
 incentives and, 592
 informativeness and, 588–590
 irritation and, 591
Afonso, A., 692
agency theory, 246
Ahmad, N., 390
Ahmed, S.N., 45
Ajit, D., 46
Ajzen, I., 725–726
Akman, G., 507
Alchami, M., 130
Al-Ghamdi, S.A.A., 420
Ali, K., 120, 132, 141, 143
Alimo-Metcalfe, B., 298
Al-Jafari, M.K., 130
Al-Mashari, M., 175
AL-Mutairi, A., 119
AL-Omar, H., 119
Ansari, M.I., 45
Anti-Corruption Law, 6
Anwar, S., 298
Ariss, R.T., 107
Aritejo, B.A., 547, 559
Aron, J., 625–628, 654
artificial intelligence, 670–675, 747
ASEAN-5 countries, 47
 development of stock market in, 51–52
 impact of stock market on economic growth in, 54–58
 market capitalization of, 51
 overview of, 49–51
ASEAN Economic Community (AEC), 28
 countries, 44
 stock markets in ASEAN countries, 44
Asrar-ul-Haq, M., 298

Asset (*see also* biological asset)
definition of, 226
features, 226
Association of Southeast Asian Nations Economic Communication, 3
Atakan, S.S., 559, 568
Athanasoglou, P.P., 119
Atje, R., 45
attitude of loyalty, 417
Aubert, F., 201
Aubyn, M., 692
Augusto, M., 366
authentic leadership
communication styles, 316
discussion, 330–331
employee–organization relationships and, 320–321
hypothesis testing results, 328–330
implications, 331–332
internal communication, 315–316
limitations and further research directions, 332–333
measurement scale, 322–323
reliability and validity test, 325–328
sampling and demographics, 323–324
and symmetrical internal communication, 318–320
average variance extracted (AVE), 77, 185, 358, 399, 519
Aydogan, S., 590
Azarmi, T., 46

**B**

Baber, W.R., 248
Badawi, N.S., 420
Bag, S., 505
Balago, G.S., 45
Balasubramanian, S., 513
bank consolidations, 150, 154, 158
Barich, H., 443
Barth, M.E., 229, 244
base erosion and profit shifting (BEPS), 27–29
aggregate tax rate differential, 30
country-specific data, 30
empirical analysis, 34–35
firm-specific data, 30
literature review, 29–32
measurement, 29–30
offshore investment matrix approach, 30, 32–34
results and discussion, 35–39
correlation matrix, 37
data sources and descriptive statistics, 37
tax haven spillover, 30
tax revenue losses and, 28–29
Batten, J., 140–141
behavioral leadership, 301–302
behavioral loyalty, 417
Beitel, P., 158
Bencivenga, V.R., 44
Bennis, W., 304
Bentler, P.M., 358
Berger, A.N., 97, 101, 131, 150, 152, 155
Bertrand, O., 21
Bhattacharya, S., 174
biological asset, 226–228
definition of, 227
features, 228
value relevance of, 232
Bkav Technology Group, 676
Blake, R.R., 301
Blanchard, K., 302
Board of directors, 272
Bolden, R., 305
Bolwijn, R., 29–32, 38
Bontis, N., 384, 388
Bordas, E., 486
Bosi, S., 708, 712
Boubakari, A., 45
Boulding, W., 415
Bowen, H.R., 416
Bradbury, D., 32
Brakett, L.K., 583, 586, 590
Brandstätter, H., 300

Breusch and Pagan Lagrangian test, 132, 134, 136, 637
Bris, A., 9
Brown, G., 453, 455
Bui, X.D., 118, 123–125, 133, 141–142
Burke, R., 276
Burns, J.M., 303
Butlin, J., 505
buyer–supplier relationships (BSRs), 504–505
  data analysis, 518–519
  definition of, 510
  discussion, 526–528
  firms' performance and, 515
  green design for sustainability and, 514
  literature review, 510–511
  methodology
    data collection and research method, 517–518
    measures, 516–517
  recommendations, 528–529
  results
    discriminant validity, 524
    measurement model, 519–524
    reliability and convergent validity, 520–523
    structural model, 524–526
  sustainable supplier management and, 513–514
Byrne, B.M., 360

**C**

Cabolis, C., 9
Callaway, E., 174
Can Tho City, 486–497
  accommodation establishments in, 495
  current background of, 487–489
  destination competitiveness of Can Tho in comparison with other provinces, 494–495
  humanity-based tourism resources, 493–494
  nature-based tourism resources, 492
  socioeconomic-based tourism resources, 492–493
  solutions for tourism development of, 495–497
  tour guides, 491–492
  tourism expenditure, 489
  tourism human resources, 491–492
  tourism infrastructure and physical facilities, 489–490
  tourism labor force in, 491
  tourism statistics of, 499–500
  tourism turnover, 488
  travel accommodation establishments in, 490
  visitors, 488
Capital, I., 384
capital adequacy indicators, 162–163, 165, 167
capital adequacy ratio (CAR), 120, 161
Câpraru, B., 121
Carroll, A.B., 416, 434
Carrón, G.C., 188
Câtâlina, F.P., 201
Çpğaltay, N., 300
Cerro, A.M.C., 449
Chamisa, E.E., 203–204
Chan, S.-G., 103
Chan, T.C.T., 526
Chand, S., 624
Charismatic leadership, 303
Charter value, 96–97
Chatterjee, S.R., 387
Chatzkel, J., 390
Chen, C., 10
Chen, C.-F., 450
chief accountant expertise, 249
Chien, M.K., 513
Chin, K.S., 526
Choon Tan, K., 510
Čihák, M., 97
Clark, C.M., 298
Clinch, G., 229

Coelho, F., 366
cognitive resource theory, 302–303
competition-fragility theory, 95–97, 107, 111
Competition Law, 6
competition-stability theory, 96–98, 110–111
competitive advantage, 384–385, 388, 390, 392
complexity theory of leadership, 306
 adaptive leadership, 306
 administrative leadership, 306
 enabling leadership, 306
 previous studies on, 307–309
 transformational leadership and, 307
composite reliability (CR), 77, 185, 358–359, 397, 399, 519
confirmatory factor analysis (CFA), 358–360
construct reliability, 185, 358, 398
consumer price index (CPI), 119–120, 124
contingency theory, 245, 302
control variables, 13
Cooper, R., 549
Corbett, M., 174
Corkindale, D., 174–175
Cornett, M.M., 150, 155–156, 162, 166
corporate governance, 754
 digitizing, 754–756
 role in acquisitions, 9–11
corporate social responsibility (CSR), 416–417
 competitive advantage through, 412, 416
 customer loyalty, 417–418
 economic responsibility, 416, 434
 ethical responsibility, 417, 434
 hypotheses and conceptual model
  CSR and customer loyalty, 419
  CSR and service quality, 419–420
  service quality customer loyalty, 420–421
 legal responsibility, 416–417, 434
 limitations and future research, 434–435
 methodology, 421–422
 philanthropic responsibility, 417, 434
 practical implications, 433–434
 results
  demographic analysis of respondents, 422–423
  Fornell–Larcker criterion, 428
  heterotrait-monotrait ratio, 429–430
  impact factor $f^2$, 433
  path coefficients, 432
  reliability and validity of measurement model, 423–427
  structural equation model, 427–433
 service quality and, 418–419
 signaling theory, 415–416
 social identity theory, 413–414
 stakeholder theory, 415
 sustainable development, 412–413
 theoretical implications, 433
correlation matrix, 37, 132, 134–135, 212–213
Corsten, D., 508
Crane, D., 156
Crask, M.R., 444
credit market share, 151, 158–159, 164, 166, 169
credit quality indicators, 162–163, 165, 167–168
credit risk, 98, 119–121
Croes, R., 451
Crompton, J.L., 443
Cronbach's Alpha, 357, 477
Cronin Jr, J.J., 418
Cross, S.E., 558

cross-border acquisitions, 8–9, 19, 23
*versus* domestic acquisitions, 8–9
cross-loadings, 399
Csikszentmihalyi, M., 583–584
culture, 556
four-factor model, 557
individualism/collectivism, 557
self-construal and, 556–558
Cummings, G., 321
cumulative abnormal return, 21
Curado, C., 384
Curlo, E., 583
customer loyalty, 417–418
attitude of loyalty, 417
behavioral loyalty, 417
CSR and, 419
service quality, 420–421

**D**

Danbolt, J., 21
Dang, M., 8, 10
David Hunger, J., 513
Day, E., 444
De Cabo, R.M., 276
Decree 16/2015/DecreeGovernment, 246, 252
Decree 71/2017/ND-CP, 288
Decree 99/2015/Nd-CP, 750
Decree No. 09/2018/ND-CP, 6
Decree No. 39/2018/ND-CP, 385–386
Decree No. 80/2016/ND-CP, 752
Decree No. 126/2017/ND-CP, 6
Defee, C., 477
de Jonge, A., 273, 288, 290
Delgado-Ballester, E., 417
DeLone, W.H., 178
Dong, X., 181
Denisa, M., 477
dependent variable, 12, 125–126
deposit market share, 151, 158, 164, 166, 169
Dess, G.G., 345
destination image, 443–444
components of, 444
definitions of, 443–444, 444
destination loyalty (*see also* loyalty), 448–449
Devezer, B., 348
DeYoung, R., 101, 131
Dima, B., 107
Dinh, J.E., 330
Dinh, T.G.T., 727
distributed leadership, 305
Doll, W.J., 181
Donaldson, B., 510–511
Doupnik, T.S., 204
Dozier, D.M., 323
Drnovsek, M., 390
Drolet, A., 559, 567
Ducoffe, R.H., 582–583, 585, 588, 590–591, 605
Ducoffe's model, 582–583

**E**

Easton, P.D., 229
Ebrahimi, P., 363, 365–366
e-business, 747–748
Echtner, C.M., 444
eco-design, 511
e-commerce, 748
economic development, 612–613
institutions in, 624–630
social-institutional factors and, 628–629
economic growth, 611–612
and environmental pollution, 612
factors affecting, 612
impact of education public spending on, 612
state-owned investment and, 688–690
economic growth, factors associated with, 707–709
consumers, 711–712
equilibrium properties, 713
fiscal policy, 714
production, 709–710
public investment in R&D, 712–713

R&D investment, growth, and inequality, 714–716
economic resource, 226
ecopreneurs, 341
ecopreneur-ship, 344
e-enterprise
concept of, 747–748
definition of, 745–746, 748
policy suggestions, 757–758
risks of, 748–749
digitizing corporate governance activities, 754–756
lack of legal framework regulating virtual capital mobilization, 752–754
virtual office (i-office) and bogus company, 750–752
e-entrepreneurship, 748–749
efficiency indicators, 162–163, 165, 168
Elsas, R., 131
employee–organization relationships (EOR), 321–322
authentic leadership and, 320–321
internal communication and, 317–318
leadership styles, 318
scale, 326
symmetrical communication and, 321–322
enabling leadership, 306
Engle, R.L., 726
Enterprise Law, 6
enterprise resource planning (ERP), 173–174
critical success factors in, 175
IS success, 179
success of, 178–179
TTF and, 175
entrepreneurial intentions
factors affecting, 726, 729, 732
limitations and future research, 739–740
literature review, 725–727
measurements, 740–741
perceived legitimacy of law and policy, 727–728, 736, 738
research methodology
data analysis, 729–730
data collection, 728–729
model, 727–728
results and discussion
exploratory factor analysis, 728, 731–732
regression analysis, 732–738
reliability test, 731
youth in Vinh Long province, 730–731
entrepreneurship (*see also* green entrepreneurship), 344–345, 724, 731, 738–740
at individual and organization levels, 344
knowledge of, 731
environment, 612–613
E-property, 752
Eriksson, D., 477
Estélyi, K.S., 291
ethical leadership, 298
European Union (EU), 10, 28
expenses management, 129
exploratory factor analysis (EFA), 355–356
external capital, 391

**F**

fair value (FV) accounting, 223–224, 229, 231
measurement of, 225
Farinelli, F., 344
Fatihudin, D., 558
Felde, J., 508
Fiedler's Contingency Theory, 302
Field, R.H.G., 298
FiinGroup, 11
financial autonomy (FA), 252
financial information, quality of, 244

financial information transparency, 242–243
accountability mechanism, 245–246
discussion, 260–262
literature review, 243–245
published information, 245, 247
quality of information, 245–247
research hypotheses
accountant expertise, 249–250
chief accountant expertise, 249
leaderships' support, 248
level of financial autonomy, 247–248, 252
research measurement, 250–252
research results and discussion
measurement of definitions, 255–257
mediation variables, 261
PLS evaluation, 258
research model evaluation, 259
testing measurement model, 253–254
testing structural model, 254–260
research sample, 252
role of human resources in, 245–246
financial performance, 388
Finney, S., 174
firm performance (*see also* financial performance; operational performance), 384–388
and buyer–supplier relationships, 515
and green design for sustainability, 515–516
literature review, 512–513
types or dimensions, 513
Fitrios, R., 262
Five-Factor Personality Model, 300–301
5-point Likert scale, 353–354, 517
fixed effect model (FEM), 47, 121–124, 132–138, 282, 288, 290, 292, 618–619, 694
flow, 586
flow experience, 584
credibility and, 593
customers' purchase intentions and, 595
entertainment and, 593
factors affecting, 586–589
informativeness and, 592
irritation and, 593–594
flow experience theory, 583–584
foreign direct investments (FDIs), 4–5, 28, 30–32, 338
Property Rights and, 629
Fornell, C., 185, 399
Fornell–Larcker criterion, 399, 428
Fourth Industrial Revolution (4.0), 670–671
FPT, 676
Franke, N., 555
Frazier, G.L., 515
Freeman, R.E., 415
free trade agreements, 4
Freire, A.D., 559
Friedman, M., 416
$F$-testing, 47, 478, 695
Fu, X.M., 103
Fuentes-Blasco, M., 420

## G

Gao, L., 588, 592
Gardner, W.L., 320, 331, 333
gender diversity, 272
analysis method, 281–282
data, 281
descriptive statistics, 285–287
hypotheses on determinants of
board size, 276–277
family firm, 275
firm size, 273–274
industry, 274
state ownership, 270

policy implications, 292–293
research model on, 280
results on determinants of, 288–290
variable descriptions, 283–284
generalized method of moments (GMM) method (*see also* system generalized method of moments (SGMMs)), 102, 119, 282, 288, 290, 292, 695
Global Industry Classification Standards (GICS), 281
GLS method, 133, 138–139
Goaied, M., 128, 131
Goetz, M.R., 98
Gokalp, M.F., 630
Gomes, C.F., 388, 393
Goodhue, D.L., 176
Grant, R.M., 385
green design for sustainability (GDS)
and buyer–supplier relationships, 514
discussion, 526–528
firms' performance and, 515–516
literature review, 511–512
recommendations, 528–529
research framework, 516
green economy/sustainable economy, 341
green entrepreneurs, 341
green entrepreneurship (GE)
autonomy, 369
conceptual model, 350
confirmatory factor analysis, 358–360
data collection, 354
descriptive statistics, 355
discussion, 364–366
effect of green innovation on, 343–345
empirical results
SEM of moderator analysis and hypothesis, 361–363
structural equation modeling, 360–361
exploratory factor analysis, 355–356
innovativeness, 345
limitations, 366–367
measures of constructs
mediator variables, 353
moderator variables, 354
pro-activeness, 345
proactive risk-taking, 368
qualitative research, 349–351
quantitative research, 351–352
reliability master, 357
risk-taking, 345–346
SME development and, 345–346
green innovation (GI), 338–340
adoption, 338
confirmatory factor analysis, 358–360
data collection, 354
descriptive statistics, 355
discussion, 364–366
effect on green entrepreneurship, 343–345
empirical results
SEM of moderator analysis and hypothesis, 361–363
structural equation modeling, 360–361
exploratory factor analysis, 355–356
independent variables, 352–353
limitations, 366–367
performance of management, 340
process innovation, 340, 343, 352–353, 368
product design, 340, 344
product innovation, 343–344
qualitative research, 349–351
quantitative research, 351–352
reliability master, 357
service innovation, 367–368
technological innovation, 340
Greve, P., 278, 291
Grewal, D., 582
Grönroos, C., 452
Grudnitski, G., 201

Grunig, J.E., 316–317, 322
Gul, S., 119
Gurel, E., 726
Gwenhamo, F., 629

**H**

Ha, V.D., 118, 122–123, 125, 129, 131, 133, 138, 140–142
Habibullah, M.S., 120
Haghighat, F., 477
Hair, J.F., 524
Hair Jr, J.F., 258
Han, J., 583–595, 605–606
Handy, C., 416
Hannan, T.H., 152
Hanoi Stock Exchange, 11
Ha Noi stock exchange (HNX), 281
Hardaker, G., 45
Harris, R., 46
Harris, R.S., 8
Harrison, C., 298
Harrison, T.M., 262
Hassab, E.H.R., 205
Hassan, S.S., 486
Hausman test, 37, 47, 132, 137, 288, 290, 618–619, 619, 637
Hernando, I., 10
Hersey, P., 302
Heterotrait-Monotrait (HTMT) ratio table, 187, 399–400, 423, 429–430
Hilletofth, P., 477
Hillman, A.J., 273–274, 288
Hisrich, R.D., 390
Ho, W., 506
Hoa Lac Hi-Tech Park, 675–676
Ho Chi Minh City, 548, 562, 568
  Chip Development Program for, 678
  limitations in development of science and technology in, 680
  Smart Project, 679
  success of scientific and technological development of, 676–680
Ho Chi Minh stock exchange (HOSE), 11, 281
Hoffman, D., 584, 586, 592
Hoffmann, A., 390
Hofstede, G., 556–557
Hoque, F., 746, 748
Hoque, M. E., 47
Horton, J., 201
Houston, J.F., 155, 157
Hoyt, J., 506
Hsieh, M.-F., 128
Hsu, L.C., 495, 584
Hu, L.t., 358
Hulland, J., 519
human capital, 390
Humphrey, D.B., 131, 155
Huq, F., 506

**I**

Ihnatov, I., 121
IMF's Balance of Payment and International Investment Positions Statistics (IMF BOP/IIP), 32
IMF's Coordinated Direct Investment Survey (IMF CDIS), 31–32, 35
impulse response functions (IRF), 102, 107–110
independent variables, 12–13, 127–132
indicator reliability, 185, 393, 396–397, 601
individualism/collectivism, 557
Industrial Revolution 4.0, 670
  impact on business, 672–673
  new technology application of enterprises in, 674–675
  technological trends in, 671
information asymmetry, 415
Information & Communication Technologies (ICTs), 746–747
information system (IS)
  accounting, 245–246, 248–249, 262
  success, 175
informativeness
  and advertising value, 588–590
  and flow experience, 592

initial coin offering, 746
innovation quality, 392
innovation speed, 392
innovation speed and quality in relationship, mediating role of
analysis and result, 397–400
discriminant validity, 400
PLS-SEM model, 403
results of construct reliability and validity, 399
results of path coefficients, 401
results of structural (inner) model, 400–401
discussion, 401–404
firm performance, 387–388
human capital, 389–391
innovation, 391–392
intellectual capital, 388–389
relational capital, 391
research method
measurement of construct, items, and coding, 394–395
research process, 396–397
study design and methodology, 393
testing measurement model, 396
structural capital, 389
institutional framework, 626–627
and economic growth, 627
mechanisms, 625
institutions
definition of, 625–626
formal, 626, 630
GDP per capita on, 630
informal, 626, 630
macro-economic performance and, 630
national economic growth in, 626
types of, 628
types of institutional measures, 626
institutions role in economic development
conceptual framework, 636
data analysis
developmental levels intervene in institutions and economic development, 646–653
economic development from PAPI indices, 640–642
economic development from PCI indices, 642–646
developmental taxonomy, 632–635
discussions, 653–655
economic development and, 641
governance indices, 632–636
methodology, 637–640
New Institutional Economics, 624–630
definition of institutions, 625–626
institutional factors, 629
institutional measures, 626
institutions and economic development, 626–630
neoclassical economics, 626
New Public Management, 631
theoretical contribution, 655
intangible resources, 384
intellectual capital (IC), 384, 388–389
defined, 384
firm performance and, 388
human capital, 388–391
relational capital, 388, 391
structural capital, 389–391
Intelligent Software System (KBOT), 675
International Accounting Standard Board (IASB), 225–228
International Accounting Standard (IAS)
IAS 16, 228
IAS 38, 228
IAS 40, 228
IAS 41, 224, 227–228, 230

International Accounting Standards (IAS/IFRS) adoption, 199–200
discussion, 215
factors affecting adoption of, 202–203
proposed model and research hypotheses, 203–205
recommendation for macro factors affecting adoption of IAS/IFRS, 216
economic growth factor, 217
educational system factor, 216
limitations of research, 217
political system factor, 217
research method, 205–208
data collection, 208
qualitative research, 206
quantitative research, 206–208
sample size, 208
research on benefits of adopting, 200–201
results of qualitative research, 208–209
results of quantitative research, 209–215
descriptive statistics of variables, 209–210
multivariate analysis, 212, 215
univariate analysis, 210–212
studies do not support, 201–202
International Electrotechnical Commission (IEEE), 671
international financial reporting standards (IFRSs), 223, 231
International Union of Official Travel Organization (IUOTO), 440
Investment Law, 6
i-office (intelligent office solutions), 746, 750–752, 757–758
IS success, 179
Iyer, C., 477
Iyer, K.N., 348
Izzeldin, M., 101–103

J

Jafar, R.M.S., 690
Jarupathirun, S., 181
Jensen, S.M., 321
Jermier, J.M., 302
Jin, D., 45
Jones, T., 449
Jovanovic, B., 45

K

Kabir, M.N., 97, 103, 107
Kajurová, V., 47
Kaldaru, H., 628–629
Kang, M., 322–323, 331
Kannan, V.R., 510
Kaoru, H., 153, 158
Kaplan, R.S., 391
Keeley, M.C., 96
Kemp, R., 340
Kerr, S., 302
Khan, H.H., 103
Kianto, A., 390
Kim, A.K., 453, 455
Kim, H.S., 559, 567
Kim, J.N., 321
Kim, W., 9
Kim, Y.J., 583–595, 605–606
Kirca, A.H., 366
Kirkwood, J., 341
Kirmani, A., 415
Kitayama, S., 547, 557–558, 568
Klassen, R.D., 340
Kling, G., 10
KMO and Barlett's, 370–373
knowledge-based resources, 384–385
knowledge-based view (KBV) theory, 384–385
Kollmann, T., 749
Kolmogorov–Smirnov test, 210–211
Kolvereid, L., 725
Komala, A.R., 251, 262
König, W., 748
Kotler, P., 443
Kurniawan, R., 226–227

## L


Lai, M.K., 547, 559
Laissez–Faire Leadership, 303
Land Law, 6
Larcker, D., 399
Larcker, D.F., 185
Lasmin, R., 201
Law on Real Estate Business, 6
Le, T.P., 118, 123–125, 133, 141–142
leader–member exchange leadership, 298
leaders
  relationship-oriented, 301
  task-oriented, 301
leadership, 297–299
  charismatic, 303
  complexity leadership and transformational leadership, 307
  complexity theory of, 306
  definition of, 299–300
  eras of, 298
  ethical, 298
  future research, 309–310
  leader-member exchange, 298
  relational, 305
  shared/distributed, 305
  transformational leadership, 303–304
Leadership: Theory and Practice (Northouse), 299
leadership–communication–relation framework, 318
Leadership in Organizations (Yukl), 299
leadership theories (*see also* Charismatic leadership; Fiedler's Contingency Theory; Path-Goal Theory; transactional leadership), 299, 306
  behavioral, 301–302
  competence, 300–301
  complexity, 306
  contingency, 302
  situational, 302–303
  trait, 300–301
Lee, C.-C., 128
Lee, G., 250
Lee, J., 443, 451, 454
Lerner index, 99–100
Levine, R., 44–45, 45
Lien, D.T.H., 726
life cycle assessment, 512
Lim, C.H., 387
Lin, Y., 363, 365
Linder, J., 156
Linear Structural Modeling, 727
liquidity risk, 98, 121
Liu, H., 98
loan loss provision ratio (LLPTA), 100–103
Lord, R., 304
Love, I., 101–102
loyalty, 417, 448
Lumpkin, G.T., 345, 348
Luthans, F., 321
Lutz, R., 590


## M


Maciver, G., 21
Mackenzie, S., 590
Malatesta, P.H., 155
management accounting system (MAS), 64–65
  hypothesis, 67–69
  moderating effects of leadership, 69–70
    dynamic capabilities, 71
    strategic capabilities, 70–71
  proposed methodology and experimental setup
    data collection, 72–73
    measurements of variables, 73–76
    procedure, 72
    statistical data analysis, 76
  research model, 71–72
  result
    descriptive characteristics of usable respondents, 76

moderating effects of leadership, 81–82
structural modeling analysis, 76–81
management accounting systems, 67–68
integration characteristics of, 68
timeliness, 68
managerial empire-building hypothesis, 153, 158
Mann–Whitney test, 211
Marcellino, P.A., 273, 288
Marion, R., 305, 307
market capitalization, 43–45, 51–54, 59
market power and risk, 95–96
capitalization perspective, 97–98
competition-fragility theory, 95–97, 107, 111
competition-stability theory, 96–98, 110–111
disruption of banks, 96–97
empirical results and discussion, 102–110
impulse response functions, 102, 107–110
market power and risk results, 102–103
panel VAR result, 103–107
variance decomposition, 102, 107–110
Lerner index, 99–100
literature and hypotheses, 96–98
loan loss provision ratio, 100–101
methodology
calculation-based risk, 100–101
calculating market power, 99–101
data, 98–99
panel VAR model, 101–102
stability of banks, 96–98, 101
theory of unstable competition, 96–97
$Z$-score index, 100–101
market power indicators, 162–165
market turbulence, 369
moderating impact of, 346–349
Markus, H.R., 547, 557–558, 568
Marr, B., 390
Martins, J., 583, 588, 590, 592–595, 605–606, 584–586
Martín-Ugedo, J.F., 274, 282
Masoud, N., 45
mass-customization, 549, 555–556, 570
Maximization Likelihood estimation method, 393
McCormick Hyland, M., 273, 288
McGee, R., 7
McLean, E.R., 178
McLeod, R., 244
Meetings, Incentives, Conferences, and Exhibitions (MICE) tourism, 493, 495–496
Mekong Delta Area, 486, 488–490, 492–494
evaluation of Can Tho's destination competitiveness in comparison with other provinces in, 494–495
total visitors, 488
tour guides, 492
tourism infrastructure, 489–490
tourism resources, 492
tourism statistics of Western cities/provinces in, 498
tourism turnover, 488
Men, L.R., 321–322, 331
Mendes, M., 308, 310
Mendes, V., 127
Menicucci, E., 139
Mennard, C., 626
merger and acquisitions (M&A), 4–10, 23–24, 149–155, 159–162, 169
micro, small, and medium enterprises (MSMEs) (*see also* small-medium enterprises (SMEs)), 337, 342
micro-enterprises, 385
Miller, D., 344
Mínguez-Vera, A., 274, 282

minimum Bayes factor (MBF), 693, 695–696
Mirbargkar, S.M., 363, 365–366
Mishra, V., 47
MobiFone, 676
mobile advertising, 581–582
Moc Chau Milk, 464
Mochklas, M., 558
Modified Wald test, 132, 137–138
Moisescu, O.I., 420
Molyneux, P., 130
Morgan, N.A., 513
motorcycle customization, 546–549, 555, 567–570
    factors affecting, 559
Mouton, J.S., 301
Mueller, G., 203
multinational enterprises (MNEs)
    tax planning of, 28, 31
    tax revenue losses from profit transfer of, 28–29, 39
Munuera-Alemán, J.L., 417
Murphy, P., 451–452
Murphy, S.E., 302
Musaji, Y., 177

**N**

Naceur, S.B., 128, 131
nationality diversity, 272
    analysis method, 281–282
    data, 281
    descriptive statistics, 285–287
    hypotheses on determinants of
        firm size, 277
        foreign ownership, 278
        proportion of foreign sales, 279–280
        state ownership, 277–278
        subsidiaries in foreign countries, 278–279
    policy implications, 292–293
    research model on, 280
    results on determinants of, 290–291
    variable descriptions, 283–284
National Strategy on Gender Equality, 276, 290
Nazmi, N., 691
Neider, L.L., 323
net interest margin (NIM), 118, 121, 124–126, 138–143
network data hunting system, 674
New Institutional Economics, 624–630
New Internet connection (IoT), 675–676
Newman, A., 390
Newman, J.W., 448
New Public Management, 631
Ngai, E.W., 174
Nguyen, D.H.A., 118, 122–123, 125, 129, 131, 133, 138, 140–142
Nguyen, P.N.T., 122–123, 138
Nguyen, P.T.T., 122–123, 138
Nguyen, T.V.T., 276, 288
Nhi, D.T.Y., 727
Nicolaou, A., 174
Nisar, T.M., 291
Nitzl, C., 188
Nobes, C., 203, 205
non-current assets, 228–229
non-OFCs, 32–36
non-value-maximizing hypothesis, 150–154
    government's influences, 154
    managerial influences, 153
Northouse, P.G., 299–300, 304
Nourry, C., 708
Novak, T., 584, 586, 592

**O**

Obamuyi, T.M., 127, 130
O'Cass, A., 513
Odhiambo, N.M., 46
offshore financial centers (OFCs), 32, 39
Offshore Investment Matrix (OIM) approach, 28–30, 32–34
    non-OFCs, 32–36
    share of investment stock, 33–34

special purpose entities (SPEs), 32–34, 36
tax havens, 32–34, 36
Ohlson model, 230, 232, 237
Oliveira, L., 229
Oliver, R.L., 417, 450, 452–454
operational performance, 388
Orbis database, 30, 32
ordinary least square (OLS), 119, 691
Organization for Economic Co-operation and Development (OECD), 28–30, 342
O'Toole, T., 510–511
Overby, J.W., 557
overlapping generation (OLG) model, 708–709
Owusu, E.L., 46
Oxelheim, L., 279, 282, 290–291
Ozdemir, B., 453

**P**

Pan, L., 47
Pandža Bajs, I., 452
panel VAR model, 101–107
eigenvalue stability condition, 105
equation, 101–102
Fisher-type unit-root test, 103–104
Granger causality analysis, 107
optimal lag length, 103–104
result of, 103–107
stability condition of, 106
Paolucci, G., 139
Parasuraman, A., 418, 450
Parnell, J.A., 387
Partial Least Squares Structural Equation Modeling (PLS-SEM), 252, 397, 403, 421, 518–519, 525–526, 579, 596
Parts, E., 628–629
Path–Goal Theory, 302
Patterson, J.L., 515
Patterson, P.G., 556
Pearson, P., 340
Pearson's correlation coefficient, 478
perceived ease of use (PEOU), 66–69
perceived financial cost, 67
perceived usefulness (PU), 66–67
perceived values, 444, 447, 548
Pereira, A., 692
Performance (*see also* financial performance; firms performance; operational performance), 512–513
Perry, P., 130
Pham, H.H.T., 122–123, 125, 129, 141
Pham, N. S, 708, 712
Phillips, W.J., 449, 455
Phusavat, K., 389
Pilloff, S.J., 150
Piqueras-Tomás, L., 420, 433
Pıskın, H., 507
PLS approach, 184
Podsakoff, P.M., 181–182
pooled OLS regression, 47, 281–282, 292
pooled ordinary least square (POLS) method, 119–120, 134, 619, 694
Poppo, L., 515
Porter hypothesis, 340
positive loyalty, 417
post-purchase product customization, 548–549, 558–560, 565, 568–570, 572
perceived values, 548, 558, 560
self-construal and, 558–560
social values from, 548, 558–559
Prayag, G., 453
principal components analysis, 477, 629
product customization, 547–549, 555, 558, 562, 569–572
and consumer behaviors, 549
literature review, 548–554
and mass-customization, 549, 555–556, 570
post-purchase, 548–549, 558–560, 565, 568–570, 572
process enjoyment, 555–556

profitability indicators, 162–163, 165–166, 166
- net margin on assets, 167
- return on assets (ROA), 166
- return on equity (ROE), 166

Provincial Competitiveness Index (PCI), 632, 659–664
Public Administration Performance Index (PAPI), 632, 655–658
public sector accounting, 252
public spending for education
- growth rates of GDP, 615
- impact of education spending on economic growth, 614–616
- limitations, 621
- models and research data, 616–617
- recommendations, 620–621
- research methodology, 618
- results of inspection and estimation, 618–620
- sustainable economic growth, 612–614

purchase intention, 585

**R**

Rabnawaz, A., 690
Raheja, C.G., 276
Ram, J., 174–175
Ramanujam, V., 387–388, 393
Ramirez, M.D, 691
Rammer, C., 340
random-effect model (REM), 47, 122–124, 132–137, 282, 288, 292, 618–619, 694
Randøy, T., 279, 282, 290–291
Ravald, A., 452
Ravenscraft, D., 8
R&D program, 708–709, 712–716
Reddin, W.J., 302
Reddin's theory, 302
Redek, T., 625
relational capital, 391
relational leadership, 305
relationship-oriented leaders, 301
Rennings, K., 340
resource-based theory (RBT), 384
resource dependence theory (RDT), 527
return on asset (ROA), 118–120, 122, 124–126, 142–143
return on average assets (ROAA), 121
return on average equity (ROAE), 121
return on equity (ROE), 118, 120, 122, 124–126, 142
Revilla, E., 511
Rhee, J., 348
Rhee, Y., 321
Rhoades, S.A., 155–156
Riber, C., 278
Rice, T., 131
Richard, O.C., 272
Ritchie, J.B., 444
Rivera, M.A., 451
Rodrik, D., 628
Rosing, K., 309
Rossi, S., 9
Roy, B.C., 629
Rozmahel, P., 47
Ruigrok, W., 275, 278–279, 291
Ruigrok, W., 278, 291
Ryan, C., 453
Ryngaert, M.D., 155, 157

**S**

Saeed, A., 275, 282
Saeed, M., 101–103
Saigon Industrial Corporation (CNS), 681
Salter, S.B., 204
Samad, S., 390
Santomero, A.M., 150
Sarkis, J., 528
Saurina Salas, J., 97
Sayogo, D.S., 262
Schaeck, K., 97
Schell, G.P., 244
Schipper, K., 244
Schneider, M., 307

Scholtens, B., 131
Schriesheim, C.A., 323
Schwartz, S.H., 556
science and technology, 668–669
application of new technology in enterprises in Ho Chi Minh City, 676–680
application of new technology in enterprises in Industrial Revolution 4.0, 674–676
context of Industrial Revolution 4.0 in, 670–671
impact of Industrial Revolution 4.0 on business, 672–673
limitations for businesses, 681–683
major trends of, 671–672
policy implications for businesses, 683–684
policy implications for city, 684–685
technological trends in Industrial Revolution 4.0, 671
SC integration (SCI), 464
Sebhatu, S.P., 387
Securities Law, 6
Seddon, P.B., 177, 181, 190
self-construal, 545, 547, 556–558, 557
and culture, 556–558
discussion, 568–572
independent, 558–559
individualism/collectivism, 558
interdependent, 547–548, 557–558, 566–568
method
participants, 562–563
procedure, 560–561
research evaluation, 564 565
post-purchase customization and, 558–560
preliminary theoretical framework, 560
product evaluation and, 559, 568
results
interdependent self-construal, 566–568
social connection enhancement, 565–566
self's definition, 557–558
Senfelde, M., 630, 654
separation of measurement strategy, 182
Serafeim, G., 201
Servera-Francés, D., 420, 433
service quality, 418–419
assurance, 419
customer loyalty, 420–421
empathy, 419
reliability, 418
responsiveness, 418–419
SERQUAL model, 418
SERVPERF model, 418
tangibles, 418
Shang, S., 177, 181, 190
Sharabati, A.-A.A., 390
shared/distributed leadership, 305
Sheth, J.N., 447
Shih, L.H., 513
Shirley, M., 625–626, 628
Shukla, V., 513
Sidik, I.G., 346
signaling theory, 415–416
Singelis, T.M., 557
Singh, A., 46
situational/contingency leadership, 302–303
small-medium enterprises (SMEs) development (*see also* ecopreneurs; green entrepreneurs; sustainable entrepreneurs), 369, 385
confirmatory factor analysis, 358–360
data collection, 354
definition of, 342–343
dependent variables, 353
descriptive statistics, 355
discussion, 364–366
empirical results
SEM of moderator analysis and hypothesis, 361–363
structural equation modelling, 360–361

exploratory factor analysis, 355–356
limitations, 366–367
literature review, 342–343
performance, 393
qualitative research, 349–351
quantitative research, 351–352
reliability master, 357
types of, 386

smartphone advertising, 581–582
advertising value, 582–583
conceptual model, 596
flow experience theory, 583–584
hypotheses
advertising value and customers' purchase intention, 595
advertising value and flow experience, 594
credibility and advertising value, 590
credibility and flow experience, 593
entertainment and advertising value, 591
entertainment and flow experience, 593
flow experience and customers' purchase intentions, 595
incentives and advertising value, 592
incentives and flow experience, 594
informativeness and advertising value, 588–590
informativeness and flow experience, 592
irritation and advertising value, 591
irritation and flow experience, 593–594
limitations and future research, 607
mobile advertising and, 581–582
practical implications, 606
purchase intention, 585
qualitative research, 596
quantitative research, 596
results
demography analysis of respondents, 597
discriminant validity, 601
HTMT ratio, 602
path coefficients, 604
reliability and validity of measurement model, 597–601
theoretical implications, 605–606

Smart PLS software, 254
Smart PLS software version 3.0, 254, 421, 519, 525, 596
social capital, 391
social classification, 414
social comparison, 414
Social Identity Theory (SIT), 413–414, 419
social classification, 414
social comparison, 414
social identification, 414
social progress, 612–613
Solow's model, 707
Somers, M., 307
Spearman correlation coefficients, 233–234
special purpose entities (SPEs), 29–30, 32
Stacks, D., 321–322, 331
stakeholder theory, 415
Starks, L.T., 9
STATA software, 132
state-owned enterprises, 6, 141, 276–278, 333
state-owned investment, 688–690
data, 693
discussion, 698–700
on economic growth, 688–693
impact of state-owned investment and factors
on Vietnam's GDP growth, 695–698

literature review, 690–693
methodology, 693–695
Stewart, T., 384
stock market for economic growth, 43–44
ASEAN countries in, 44
experiences for Vietnam, 59
literature review, 45–46
research methods, 47–48
research results
descriptive statistics, 55
effects of stock market on Vietnam's economic growth, 56–58
impact of stock market on economic growth in ASEAN-5 countries, 54–56
VIF variance, 55
results and discussion
development of stock market in ASEAN-5 in 2008–2018, 51–52
economic growth and stock market in Vietnam in 2008–2018, 52–54
GDP growth rates of ASEAN-5 in 2008–2018, 49–51
inflation rate of ASEAN-5 in 2008–2018, 50
market capitalization of ASEAN-5, 51
rate of FDI/GDP of ASEAN-5 in 2008–2018, 51
stock trade of ASEAN-5, 52
stock trade, 52–55
Stogdill, R.M., 298, 300
strategic market-entry hypothesis, 8–9
data, 11
deal- and firm-specific characteristics, 15
literature review and hypotheses, 8–9
methodology, 11–14
role of corporate governance in acquisitions, 9–11
sample descriptive statistics, 14–15
short-term stock performance of target firms, 21–22
target firms' corporate governance and bidders' location decisions, 15–20
structural capital, 389
Su, R., 10
Subramaniam, M., 390
Sufian, F., 120
Sun, S., 590
Sung, M., 322–323, 331
supplier collaboration, 508
supplier monitoring, 509
supplier selection, 506
supply chain integration (SCI), 465–466
factors affecting integration of Dairy SC, 472–475
culture of enterprise, 473
information sharing, 474
leadership capacity, 473
maturity level, 472–473
price policy, 473
product strategy, 473–474
technology information, 474
trust, 472
factors affecting structure of Vietnamese dairy SC, 468–472
distributors, 470–471
manufacturers, 469–470
suppliers, 469
horizontal integration, 467
levels of, 467–468
arcs of integration, 468
cooperation, 467
linking form, 467
transaction, 467
overview of, 465–466
proposed research model, 475
research methodology, 475–476
results and discussion, 476–477

factor analysis and regression analysis, 477–480
reliability analysis, 477–480
types of, 466–467
vertical integration, 467
supply chain (SC), 463, 465
Susjan, A., 625
sustainability, 504–505
sustainable design, 511
sustainable development, 412–413, 624
sustainable economic growth, 612–614
economic development, 613
environment, 613
social progress, 613
sustainable entrepreneurs, 342–343
sustainable supplier collaboration (SSC), 508–509
sustainable supplier development (SSD), 507–508
sustainable supplier management, 505–506
and buyer–supplier relationships, 513–514
data analysis, 518–519
discussion, 526–528
literature review, 505–506
methodology
data collection and research method, 517–518
measures, 516–517
recommendations, 528–529
results
measurement model, 519–524
structural model, 524–526
supplier collaboration, 508–509
supplier development, 507–508
supplier monitoring, 509–510
supplier selection, 506–507
sustainable supplier monitoring (SSM), 509–510
sustainable supplier selection, 506–507
symmetrical internal communication (SIC) and employee–organization relationships, 321–322
proposed model, 322
scale, 323, 326
system generalized method of moments (SGMMs), 693–697

**T**

Tan, C.L., 507
Tang, H.P., 46
tangible resources, 384
Tan Thanh Market, 546
Tasci, A.D.A., 444
task-oriented leaders, 301
task-technology fit (TTF), 176–177
data analysis, results and discussions, 184–185
effective use, 177–178, 180
implications for practice, 192–193
implications for research, 192
limitations, 193–194
measurement model assessment, 185–187
research methodology
data collection, 181–184
demographic characteristics, 183–184
measures, 181
sample frame, 180–181
structural model assessment, 187–192
alternative model, 189–190
hypotheses testing, 187–189
PLS multiple-group analysis, 190–192
success of ERP system, 175, 178–179
tax havens, 32–34, 36
tax rate differential, 30
tax revenue, 28
Taylor, S.A., 418
Taylor, S.F., 449

technological progress, 707
technology, 668
  components, 668
  science and, 668–669
  *versus* technique, 668
Tehranian, H., 155–156, 166
Tellis, G.J., 448
The Mobile Marketing Association, 581
theories
  of stable competition, 97
  of unstable competition, 96–97
Theory of Planned Behaviour, 725
Thompson, R.L., 176
Thong, B.Q., 727
Thornton, J., 130
TH True Milk, 464
Tondkar, R.H., 204
Torkzadeh, G., 181
total factor productivity (TFP), 707, 712
tourism
  definition of, 440–441
  destination, 442
  product, 442
tourism consumer behavior, 442–443
  attribute satisfaction, 448
  components of destination image, 444–447
  conceptual framework, 455
  destination image, 443–444
  destination loyalty, 448–449
  destination perceived quality, 444
  overall satisfaction, 448
  perceived value, 444, 447
  relations among definitions, 449–455
tourism destination competitiveness, 485–486
  Can Tho in comparison with other provinces, 494–495
  current background of Can Tho City tourism, 487–489
  factors influencing on, 487
    tourism human resources, 491–492
    tourism infrastructure and physical facilities, 489–491
    tourism resources, 492–494
  research methodology, 487
  solutions for tourism development of Can Tho City
    diversifying and developing featured tourism products, 495–496
    enhancing quality of tour operators, 497
    high-quality tourism human resources, 496–497
tourists' loyalty
Tracey, M., 507
trade or commerce, 747–748
trait theory of leadership, 300–301
Tran, T.M.D., 276, 288
Tran, V.D., 118, 122–128, 133, 140–142
transactional leadership, 303–304
transformational leadership, 298, 303–304
  and complexity leadership, 307
  full range model, 303
  limitation of, 304
transparency, 243–245
transparency in financial information measurement (TRANS), 250, 254
transparency of financial information, 243–245
triple bottom line performance, 506
Tsai, D., 450
Tsai, K.-H., 346
Tsang, M., 592
Tseng, M.-L., 363, 365
Tue, A., 118

## U

Ucbasaran, D., 390
Uhl-Bien, M., 305–310

Uslu, Y.D., 341
utilization, 177

**V**

value creation in Vietnamese bank mergers and acquisitions
    data description, 160–162
        deposits and loans, 161
        descriptive statistics, 161
        profitability, 161–162
        size, 161
    efficiency gains, 150, 157
    empirical results
        bank mergers of, 156–158
        increasing market power hypothesis, 164–166
        increasing operational efficiency hypothesis, 166–168
        Vietnamese consolidated banks' performance for, 165
    hypothesis testing, 158–159
        increasing market power hypothesis, 158–159
        increasing operational efficiency hypothesis, 159
    literature review, 151–154
        non-value-maximizing motivation, 153–154
        value-maximizing motivation, 152
    research methodologies, 154–156, 162–164
        accounting-based approach, 154–155
        indicators, 162
        market-based approach, 155–156
        measures definition, 163
value-maximizing hypothesis, 150, 158, 168
    increasing market power, 152
    increasing operational efficiency, 152
value relevance of biological assets under IFRS, 223–225
    asset's features, 226
    biological asset's features, 228
    IAS 41, 225, 227–228, 230
    literature review
        asset revaluations and value relevance of non-current assets, 228–229
        challenges of accounting of biological assets, 229–230
        concepts of asset and biological asset, 226–228
        development of hypotheses, 230–231
    methodology
        empirical model, 232–233
        sample, 231–232
    results
        correlations, 234
        descriptive analysis, 233–235
        model summary, 235
        regression results, 235
        research model, 235–236
    theoretical framework, 225
Van Ameijde, J.D.J., 305
Van Seters, D.A., 298
variance decomposition (VDC), 102, 107–110
varimax rotation, 477, 731
vector error correction model (VECM), 691–692
vehicle customization, 548–554
Venkatraman, N., 387–388, 393
Vietnam
    dairy market, 464
    integration into global economy, 3–4
    transportation in, 546
Vietnam Asset Management Company (VAMC), 143–144
Vietnam Business Forum, 724
Vietnamese commercial banks
    asset management, 132
    bank capitalization, 127

bank size, 130–131
bank-specific and macroeconomic factors on, 119–121
Breusch and Pagan Lagrangian test result, 136
correlation matrix, 135
cost to income ratio, 121, 126, 129
customer deposits, 128
descriptive statistics, 134
discussion, 142–144
equity to total assets ratio, 120, 124–125, 127, 140
estimation methods, 132–133
expenses management, 129
explanatory variables, 133
GDP growth rate, 130
GLS method, 133, 138–139
Hausman test result, 137
inflation rate, 130
literature review, 119–124
loan loss provisions, 128–129
loans, 127–128
loan to total assets ratio, 138
methodology, 124–133
    data collection procedure, 124–125
    dependent variable, 125–126
    independent variables, 127–132
    research model, 125
Modified Wald test result, 137
net interest margin, 118, 125–126
non-interest income over total operating income ratio, 118, 120–124, 130–133, 142–143
previous studies, 123
profitability of, 118–119
rationale, 118–119
results
    data description, 133–134
    regression results, 134–142
return on asset, 125–126
return on equity, 125–126
revenue diversification, 131–132
variables' description, 126
Woolridge test result, 137
Vietnamese Tourism Law, 440
Viet Nam Provincial Governance, 632
Vietnam War, 624
Viettel, 675
Vinamilk, 464
Vinh Long Provincial People's Committee, 724
virtual capital (e-capital), 752
Vitola, A., 630, 654
VNINDEX (Vietnamese stock index), 56–58
Vo, X.V., 140–141
Volpin, P.F., 9
Voola, R., 513
Vu, X.T.T., 321

**W**

Wald test, 212
Wales, W.J., 349
Walker, G., 515
Walton, S., 341
Walumbwa, F.O., 319–320, 331
Wang, B., 46
Wang, Y., 590
Wang, Z., 388, 393
Wei, K.D., 9
Weitzel, U., 10
Werbel, R.A., 448
Wheelen, T.L., 513
Whybark, D.C., 340
Wilson, J.O., 98
Wong, C., 320
Woolridge test, 133, 137
World Tourism Organization, 440–441
World Trade Organization, 3
Worthington, A.C., 97, 103, 107
Wu, J., 513

**X**

Xu, H., 243–244

**Y**

Yakob, N. A., 47
Yang, F., 506, 526
Yang, S.-Y., 346
Yildirim, A., 630
Youndt, M.A., 390
Yukl, G.A., 299–301, 304–306, 309

**Z**

Zambon, S., 390
Zeithaml, V.A., 451
Zervos, S., 45
Zhang, X., 506, 526
Zhao, A., 278
Zhao, X., 515
Zhu, P., 10
Zhu, Q., 528
Zicchino, L., 101–102
Zimmer, K., 509
Zitouna, H., 21
*Z*-score, 100–101

Lightning Source UK Ltd.
Milton Keynes UK
UKHW020653110221
378576UK00006B/321

9 789811 227141